Printed And Published, 1971
by
IRELAND COOKE PRINTING COMPANY
Maynardville, Tennessee 37807
(At Cooke Mortuary) Ph. 992-5456

Copyright

DEDICATION

To Elder Walter E. Lyons, Maryville, Tennessee, we dedicate this book; for it was he who, with loving intent, sought after and collected the Powell's Valley Primitive Baptist Associational Minutes with purpose to have them reproduced and bound into one volume, thereby making it available to all those who would treasure it.

PRICE $6.00

IN MEMORIAM

In Memoriam to Elder Theodore(G. Brantley, for
his painstaking care in preserving every single Associational Minute from 1906 (the first one printed) thru
the years he lived (after which his widow, Mrs. Virgie:
Brantley continued his files) we are printing a picture
of him with some history and record of his service to
this Association as well as to his Missionary Friends.
who loved him.

Elder Theodore Godfrey Brantley was born   Oct. 13, 1885.
He professed faith in Christ at the age of seventeen in the year

SECOND REPRODUCTION

of

The First 64 Original Printed Minutes

of

The Powell's Valley Association

of

Primitive Baptists

Years 1906 Thru 1970

Reproduced by Larry Bush

This book was given to me, Larry Bush, and I was happy to have it reproduced.

Knoxville, Tennessee
crippledbeaglepublishing.com

Paperback ISBN 978-1-958533-87-1, 978-1-958533-88-8

Hardcover ISBN 978-1-958533-89-5, 978-1-958533-90-1

Library of Congress Control Number: 2024908126

Reproduced in the United States of America

1903; one year later at the age of 18 years, he felt the call to the ministry. He joined the church at Mossy Springs April 10, 1909 and was baptized May 8, 1909. He was ordained to preach the Gospel, May 12, 1917 by the following Elders:

Elders: John F. Keck, J. T. McArthur, Alfred Boruff, M. B. Weaver, Leonard White, Moderator and Elza White, Clerk.

Elder Brantley Served in churches, Oak Grove, 1917-1948; Cave Springs, 1917-1922; Mossy Springs, 1918-1920; Black Fox Fox, 1919-1926; Red Hill, 1921-1938; Rocky Dale, 1922-1940; Hamilton Grove,1931-1936; Myers Grove, 1939-1944; Black Fox, 1939-1948; and Poplar Springs, 1944-1948.

Baptisms were recored as: Oak Grove-252, Cave Springs 29, Mossy Springs-82, Black Fox-76, Red Hill-50, Rocky Dale-59, Hamilton Grove-10, Myers Grove-18, Poplar Springs-0. Throughout the ministry of elder Brantley, 136 couples chose him to pronounce them man and wife, and he was called to conduct 884 funerals.

INTRODUCTION

The Powell's Valley Association of Primitive Baptists was constituted in Grainger County in 1816, with 17 churches, 603 members and 15 Elders.

(Hassell)

As the following statistics will support, this Association was not constituted in 1906, as some would have you believe.

The main body of the original association has stood all down thru the years on the Articles of Faith enclosed within this booklet.

A few doctrinal issues have arisen at different times and have caused divisions. But in 1905, a very unpleasant situation had developed. Not a doctrinal issue, but a practical one. The direct cause is little known but it bears a close relationship to the Civil War, war between the states: slavery caused secession and secession caused the war.

The issue now was secret orders, but since secret orders had been tolerated all down thru the years, why now? Secret orders were the indirect cause; preacher jealousy, the direct cause.

It is very much to be regretted that God's people will permit themselves to become engrossed in malice and hatred.

Each of these factions down through the years has claimed to be the original Powell's Valley Association. I love you both and late in the evening of life, I beseech both factions to heed the old prophet Jeremiah. Look for the old paths which were troden long before 1816.

Lovingly and Prayerfully Yours,

Elder Leonard White

Elder Leonard White

WORD OF THANKS

We wish to thank Elder Leonard White, Lafollette, Tennessee, for his fine response in answer to our request that he write the Introduction for this book. It was believed his experience, his love for his people, church and maker, his understanding and ability to write qualified him to write it; as he did so well.

FOREWORD

The 64 Powell's Valley Primitive Baptist Associational Minutes contained in this book were photographed and printed in their original page size. Nothing was deleted except --- repetition in pictures, Rules of Decorum and Articles of Faith, in order to reduce the size and cost of the book. Most all the original page numbers were left on along with the new numbering used for indexing.

Note: Each year book cover is treated as a page and numbered for easy reference in your Index pages.

...MINUTES...

OF THE

EIGHTY-SEVENTH ANNUAL SESSION

OF THE

Powell's Valley Association

...OF...

PRIMITIVE BAPTISTS,

HELD WITH THE CHURCH OF

Oak Grove, Union Co., Tenn.,

August 17, 18 and 19, 1906.

KNOXVILLE, TENN.

GAUT-OGDEN COMPANY, PRINTERS,

1906.

Printer's Fee, $13.00 for 800 copies.

MINUTES

...OF THE...

Eighty-Seventh Annual Session of the Powells' Valley Association of Primitive Baptists, held with the Church of Oak Grove, Union County, Tennessee, on August the 17th, 18th and 19th, 1906.

FRIDAY'S PROCEEDINGS.

1. Introductory sermon, by Elder S. M. Petree, from Revelation 1 : 8, "I am Alpha and Omega, the beginning and the ending, saith the Lord."

2. After intermission of fifteen minutes the Association was called to order by Elder M. B. Weaver.

3. By motion Elder S. M. Petree was chosen moderator pro tem, and James Ragan, clerk pro tem.

4. Called for letters, and received seven, which were read, and the messengers' names enrolled.

5. On motion, all the letters were received.

6. Election of officers being next in order, Elder S. M. Petree was elected moderator and James Ragan clerk, with Brother Leonard White, assistant clerk.

7. Called for petitionary letters, and received letter and messengers of Oak Grove church. Messengers came forward, and were welcomed to seats by moderator.

8. Invited ministers to seats with us.

9. Called for correspondence.

10.   Committees appointed to report Saturday morning, viz.:

(a)   *On Arrangements*—Elder M. B. Weaver, W. A. Drummonds, P. F. Keck, J. R. Evans, H. F. Hamilton.

(b)   *On Correspondence*—Elder S. M. Petree, Leonard White, Maston Dunn, Elder J. M. Drummonds, Elder J. D. Monroe.

(c)   *On Finance*—Brethren W. D. Warwick, J. L. Keck.

(d)   *On Preaching*—R. L. Dike, P. F. Keck, Hiram Shofner, W. A. Drummonds, James Ragan, W. A. Graves, together with Oak Grove church.

(e)   *On Requests*—P. F. Keck, James Evans, Mike Hensley, W. A. Drummonds, J. W. Alston.

11.   Request of Mossy Spring Church, for vindication of elders, called for and read.

12.   Following committee appointed to draft resolutions against Association exercising ecclesiastical powers over the churches, viz.: Elders M. B. Weaver, Alfred Boruff, Hiram Shofner.

13.   Adjourned to meet Saturday at 9 a. m.

SATURDAY MORNING.

1.   The Association met, pursuant to adjournment. Prayer and praise by Elder J. M. Drummonds.

2.   Committee on Arrangements submitted their report. On motion, said report was adopted, as follows:

We, your Committee on Arrangements, beg leave to submit the following order of business, viz.:
(a)   Call the roll.
(b)   Call for report of Committee on Preaching.
(c)   Call for reports of committees according to turn.
(d)   When and where shall our next Association be? Who shall preach the introductory sermon, and who shall be his alternate?

(e) How many copies of minutes, and who shall superintend printing of same?

Respectfully submitted,

ELDER M. B. WEAVER,
W. A. DRUMMONDS,
P. F. KECK,
W. A. GRAVES,
J. R. EVANS.

3. Called the roll and erased names of absentees.

4. The Committee on Preaching submitted their report, which was adopted as follows:

Friday Night at Arthur Boruffs—Elders M. B. Weaver, Jno. Hammack.

Friday Night at Big Sinks—Elders Jno. Capps, Alfred Boruff

Friday Night at Church—Elders J. M. Drummonds, J. D. Monroe.

For Saturday at the Stand—Elders J. M. Drummonds, J. D. Monroe, M. B. Weaver.

For Saturday Night at Church—Elders Alfred Boruff, J. M. Drummonds.

For Saturday Night at the Sinks—Elders Jno. Capps, Jno. Hammack.

For Sunday—Elders M. B. Weaver, J. D. Monroe, S. M. Petree.

Respectfully submitted,

W. A. DRUMMONDS,
H. A. SHOFNER,
P. F. KECK.

5. The Committee on Correspondence submitted their report, and on motion the following report was adopted, viz..

WHEREAS, There is so much wrangling among our people, and the Associations with whom we have formerly corresponded are in such a tangle (or some of them at least), we think it best to omit correspondence for the present; and while we are informed that our old mother association, viz.: the Chahooka, desires to raise correspondence with us, we think it expedient for us to await their solicitation, as we are involved in the present, or rather past, trouble, and they are not directly involved, that we have any knowledge of; and while we are at peace among ourselves and earnestly desire to con-

4

tend for the faith once delivered to the saints, and patiently wait in hope of reconciliation and restoration of peace and sweet fellowship among the Baptists.

We also invite all Baptists, who heed the great command of the eminent apostle, not to make a brother an offender for a word and who will not strive about words to no profit or minor points of the law which gender strife; and those who do not raise bars to fellowship for small offense which are not sufficient grounds for this, to visit us.

The foregoing signed by your committee.

S. M. PETREE, *Chairman,*
J. D. MONROE,
J. M. DRUMMONDS,
LEONARD WHITE,
M. C. DUNN, *Secretary.*

6. Committee on Finance reported, and report adopted as follows:

We, your Committee on Finance, beg leave to report total amount of contributions from churches and all sources amount to $13.10.

DAVID WARWICK,
J. L. KECK.

7. The committee, by request, submitted their report, and on motion the report was adopted as follows:

We, your Committee on Requests, respectfull submit the following, viz:

In regard to request from Mossy Spring Church, it is with profound sorrow that we find the elders have been so wrongfully published, and recommend that they earnestly pray for their enemies. 2d, We desire to cultivate friendship for all Christians, and that we hunt for the footprints of Jesus, and follow them closely, giving no heed to man-made rules which have been so hurtful to us.

The Association further recommends that the request from Mossy Spring Church be spread upon our minutes, which is as follows:

REQUEST OF MOSSY SPRING CHURCH.

WHEREAS, There are two parties claiming to be the Powells Valley Association, and one of them having published a false exclusion, stating the following named elders were excluded from the fellowship of the churches, to-wit: Elders S. M. Petree, M. B. Weaver, J. D. Monroe and Alfred Boruff. Said elders being in full fellowship with the original churches, and in good standing with said churches and the surrounding country, in fact their ministerial reputation is of the highest order and their Christian character of the highest grade, having never given any just grounds for any scandalous charges to be brought against them (in fact there are none). They are men of high standing in every respect, and if such exclusion does exist, it exists with factions who have been excluded from the original churches, to which said elders never did belong (some of said factions being very small). Therefore we ask the Association to publish in their minutes the standing of said elders or ministers, earnestly insisting on the brethren far and near to make a thorough investigation of this matter for their own satisfaction.

As we do solemnly regret that the real cause of said trouble is hid from so many of our good brethren, also we ask the Association to publish in said minutes that there is no issue between our people on doctrine, neither was the secret order question the original cause of said trouble, in fact we have had members belonging to secret orders in our fellowship for perhaps one hundred years or more, but said trouble growing out of the opposition to the churches making an earnest investigation of some reports of unbecoming conduct, of certain individuals who resorted to the secret order question, only for an excuse, under which (excuse) they hoped to get revenge, which resulted in a division.

The Association please copy.

This done by order of the Church, while in session.

ELD. M. B. WEAVER, *Moderator*,
ELVIN WEAVER, *Clerk*.

Respectfully submitted,

W. A. DRUMMONDS,
J. W. ALSTON,
M. C. HENSLEY,
P. F. KECK,
J. R. EVANS.

8. Report of Committee to draft resolutions against Association exercising ecclesiastical powers over the churches. On motion report adopted as follows:

We, your Committee, respectfully submit the following as our Rules of Decorum, and recommend their adoption and that same be spread upon the minutes; and furthermore, all rules and regulations conflicting with the same null and void.

RULES OF DECORUM.

1st. The churches composing the Powells Valley Association shall not be confined to any set rule as to the specified number of Messengers they shall have in the body, but shall have the right to name in their letters as many as they may choose, and in addition all orderly male members of any of the churches being present shall be entitled to seats in the body as Messengers of their respective churches, with all the rights and privileges of the same.

2d. The Messengers thus assembled shall be denominated the Powells Valley Primitive Baptist Association.

3d. For the purpose of historical information and statistical edification, the churches are requested to state in letters, the total number of members in fellowship, the number received by baptism, by letter, by confession of faith. The number dismissed, excluded and dead since last session; also the time of their meeting, their pastoral supply, and the amount of money contributed for ministers and other purposes, together with any other information they deem appropriate for the edification of the saints and the glory of God.

4th. This Association shall have no power to answer queries, give advice, or dictate to the churches in any case, or to lord it over God's heritage, nor any power by which she can directly or indirectly infringe on the internal rights of the churches, or censure and try any church or member in reference to faith and practice, or determine upon the validity of gospel ordinances. These things shall rest entirely with the churches; but henceforward our annual meeting shall be only for the purpose of hearing from each other, and for the worship of God and the mutual comfort and edification of the saints. To this we reserve the privileges annually on Friday before the third Saturday in August and the two following days, or at such other time as may be agreed upon with any church that may invite us, having due regard to priority of claims and the good of the cause; to protect our own stand while in session, from heresy and disorder; to recognize and invite any visiting Primitive Baptist minister or lay brother to worship with us, that we may deem proper; to request the brethren of our own body to visit other churches or bodies in our behalf, with whom we may desire to cultivate Christian fellowship; to publish a minute of our proceedings.

5th. Each session of the body shall have a Moderator and Clerk, who shall be duly chosen according to the rules hereinafter prescribed, and who shall hold office until re-election.

6th. Any orderly member of any church belonging to this body, when convened, being present, shall be eligible to election as Moderator and Clerk, or to sit on any committee appointed by the same.

7th. In all elections or questions that may be necessary to determine by vote, the vote shall be taken by churches, each church being entitled to three votes for any number of members less than one hundred, and one additional vote for every fifty or fraction thereof above the first hundred; but the Messengers of each church as a body may divide her vote as they see proper.

8th. All elections or questions coming to a vote shall be determined by a majority of the votes cast, and it shall be the duty of the minority to acquiesce in the decision thus reached.

9th. If new churches desire to be admitted into this union, they shall petition by letter and Messengers, and if vouched for or recommended by one or more sister churches, or the Presbytery constituting them, as orthodox and orderly, they shall be received by the voice of the body and manifested by the Moderator giving the Messengers the right hand of fellowship.

10th. Any motion or resolution introduced, clearly inconsistent with the above rules, shall be promptly ruled out of order unless withdrawn by the mover.

11th. Any Messenger being ruled out of order by the Moderator shall have the right to appeal to the body on the question of order, and if sustained shall be allowed to proceed; but if not, shall take his seat.

12th. Our meetings being held in the name of Christ, and the worship of God, each Messenger is expected to observe due and proper order therein.

13th. It will not be considered good order for any Messenger whose name has been enrolled as such, to abruptly break off or absent himself from the Association without leave.

14th. The Moderator shall be entitled to the same privileges of speech as other members, provided the chair be filled.

15th. The Minutes of the Association shall be read and approved by the body, and signed by the Moderator before adjourning.

16th. The Association shall be opened and closed by prayer.

17th. Amendments to these rules may be made at any time by a majority of the union voting by churches, when they deem it necessary, provided such amendments do not compromise the sovereignty of the churches, nor have a tendency to give this body undue power or jurisdiction over them.

ELDER M. B. WEAVER,
H. A. SHOFNER,
ELDER ALFRED BORUFF

9. On motion we appoint our next Association to be held with the church at Gibson's Station, Lee County, Va., commencing on Friday before the third Saturday in August, 1907.

10. On motion, Elder J. D. Monroe was appointed to preach the introductory sermon, and Elder M. B. Weaver to be his alternate.

11. On motion, agreed that the clerk superintend the printing and distribution of 800 copies of the minutes.

12. Minutes read, amended and adopted.

13. Resolved, That we tender our heartfelt thanks to Oak Grove church, and the surrounding community for kind hospitality during this Association.

14. On motion, adjourned to meet as above stated.

ELDER S. M. PETREE, *Moderator*,
Lost Creek, Tenn.

JAMES RAGAN,
Liberty Hill, Tenn.

SUNDAY.

On Sunday the congregation assembled at the stand. The sermons delivered by Elders M. B. Weaver, J. D. Monroe and S. M. Petree (in the order named), were characterized with much earnestness and power.

Ere the second sermon was fairly concluded, the Christians gave way to rejoicing and praising God's name, to such an extent that they took possession of the stand, many leaping for joy.

At the conclusion all Christians were invited to join in singing and extending the hand of love and fellowship. The blessing of God was invoked upon all the congregation, by Elder S. M. Petree.

MINISTERIAL ROLL

ELDERS	POST OFFICE	STATE
Alfred Boruff	R. D. No. 23, Liberty Hill	Tenn.
A. J. Boruff	R. D. No. 15, Washburn	Tenn.
J. A. Capps	R. D. No. 3, Maynardville	Tenn.
J. M. Drummonds	Manring	Tenn.
John Hammack	Washburn	Tenn.
J. D. Monroe	R. D. No. 1, Sharp's Chapel	Tenn.
S. M. Petree	R. D. No. 1, Lost Creek	Tenn.
M. B. Weaver	R. D. No. 1, Lost Creek	Tenn.

LICENTIATES

W. R. Petree	Goin	Tenn.
Leonard White	R. D. No. 2, Sharp's Chapel	Tenn.
C. B. Weaver	R. D. No. 2, Sharp's Chapel	Tenn.
J. A. Webb	Gibson Station	Va.

Churches.	Clerks.	Postoffice.	State.
Big Barren	W. R. Petree	Goin	Tenn.
Cedar Spring	W. A. Drummonds	New Tazewell	Tenn.
Dotson's Creek	James Ragan	Liberty Hill	Tenn.
Gibson's Station	S. S. Wilson	Gibson's Station	Va.
Hamilton Grove	H. F. Hamilton	Sharp's Chapel, R. D. 8	Tenn.
Mossey Spring	Elvin Weaver		
Oak Grove	P. H. Ousley	Sharp's Chapel, R. D. 1	Tenn.
Pleasant Point	P. F. Keck	Goin	Tenn.

TABLE OF STATISTICS.

CHURCHES.	NAMES OF MESSENGERS.	Rec'd by Expr'ce and Baptism	Rec'd by Letter	Dis'd by Letter	Received by Relationship	Excluded	Dead	Total	Sat'day Meetings
Big Barren	Can Goin, W. A. Graves, W. R. Petree	4	14	18	....	30	....	41	3
Cedar Spring	Elder J. M. Drummonds, W. A. Drummonds, J. W. Auston, H. L. Auston, J. J. Auston.	5	....	1	....	1	2	57	4
Dotson's Creek	Elders Alfred Boruff, Jno. Capps, Jno. Hammack, Jas. Ragan.	3	2	....	4	7	....	26	1
Gibson's Station	A. H. Shofner, Mc. Hensley, W. S. Collins, R. H. Ball.	5	....	....	....	5	1	28	1
Hamilton Grove	J. R. Evans, W. D. Warwick, H. F. Hamilton, J. A. Graves.	....	....	....	....	....	1	48	1
Mossy Spring	Leonard White, Maston Dunn, J. E. White, Daniel White, C. B. Weaver, Elders M. B. Weaver, S. M. Petree	25	2	....	11	....	....	163	2
Pleasant Point	J. L. Keck, Mc. Keck, T. C. Keck, P. F. Keck.	9	....	....	8	....	1	60	2
Oak Grove	Elder J. D. Monroe, W. M. Shofner, W. M. Shofner, P. H. Ousley, J. P. Russell, Allen Graves, Daniel Boruff, Jno. Boruff.	18	11	1	10	....	....	52	1
		69	29	20	33	43	5	475	

N. B.—Church Clerks will please be careful to give their postoffice address, together with address of all Ordained Ministers and Licentiates.

11

ARTICLES OF FAITH.

ARTICLE 1. We believe in only one true and living God, as He is revealed to us in the Holy Scriptures, Father, Son and Holy Ghost.

2. We believe that the Scriptures of the Old and New Testaments are the word of God and the only rule of all saving knowledge and obedience.

3. We believe in the doctrine of election according to the foreknowledge of God.

4. We believe in the doctrine of original sin.

5. We believe in man's impotency to recover himself from the fallen state he is in by his own free will or ability.

6. We believe that sinners are justified in the sight of God only by the imputed righteousness of Jesus Christ.

7. We believe the elect, according to the foreknowledge of God, will be called, converted, regenerated and sanctified by the Holy Spirit

8. We believe the saints will persevere and never fall finally away.

9. We believe that baptism and the Lord's Supper are ordinances of Jesus Christ, and that true believers are the only subjects of these ordinances, and that the true mode of baptism is by immersion.

10. We believe in the resurrection of the dead and the general judgment.

11. We believe that the punishment of the wicked will be everlasting, and that the joys of the righteous will be eternal.

12. We believe that no minister has the right to administer the ordinances except those who have been regularly baptised and called of God and come under the imposition of hands by the Presbytery.

MINUTES

OF THE

EIGHTY-EIGHTH ANNUAL SESSION

OF THE

Powell's Valley Association

OF

PRIMITIVE BAPTISTS

HELD WITH THE CHURCH AT

GIBSON'S STATION, VA.

AUGUST 16, 17 and 18, 1907.

BAIRD BROS. JOB PRINT, Fulton, Ky.

13

MINUTES

OF THE

Eighty-Eighth Annual Session. of the Powells' Valley Association of Primitive Baptists, held with the Church of Gibson's Station, Lee County, Va., on Aug. the 16, 17, and 18th. 1907.

FRIDAYS PROCEEDINGS.

Association met persuant to adjournment. Prayer and praise by Eld. J. M. Drummonds

Introductory sermon by Eld. J. D. Monre, Ephesians 1-3 "Blessed be the God and Father of our Lord Jesus Christ, who hath blessed us with all Spiritual blessings in heavenly Christ."

In the absence of Moderator, Eld. J. M. Drummonds was chosen moderator pro tem. On motion Eld. J. M. Drummonds was elected moderator and James Ragan re-elected clerk.

On motion E. D. Monroe was elected assistant clerk.

(1) Called for letters and received 8 which were read and messengers names enrolled.

(2) Petitionary letters called for, letter from the newly constituted church of Pleasant Hill presented, read and received, messengers welcomed to seats.

(3) Invited visiting ministers to seats with us. Eld. J. V. Kirkland of Fulton, Ky., came forward and was heartily welcomed.

(4) Transients invited. Eld. John Hammack came forward and was heartily welcomed.

14

(5)   On motion correspondence called for.   We had received minutes of the Hiwassee Association showing the appointment of messengers to convene with us but none were present.

(6)   Committes appointed.

(a)   On correspondence Eld. J. D. Monroe, E. D. Monroe, Wm. Drummonds.

(b)   On arraingments Bros. Geo. Bryant, Robert Ball, W. S. Collins, James Ragan.

(c)   On finance Bros. Wm. Drummonds and M. C. Hensley.

(d)   On preaching Bros. J. W. Alston, James Ragan, M. C. Edwards, Frank Hamilton, John Hopper, together with church.

(e)   On requests Eld. John Hammack, Hiram Shofner and J. A. Webb.

(7)   On motion above committees appointed.

(8)   Adjourned to meet Saturday at 9 a. m.

SATURDAY MORNING.

(1)   Association met pursuant to adjournment.

(2)   Invitation again extended to visitors, Bro. Silas W. Rammond came forward and was welcomed.

(3)   Called for report on finance.   We your committee on finance beg leave to submit the following; viz.

Received from the churches for printing and distributing minutes $11.50, total by brethren and friends $15.00.

W. A. DRUMMONDS.

M. C. HENSLEY.

On motion received and committee discharged.

(4)   Called the roll.

(5)   Committee on arrangements submitted their report on motion the report was adopted as follows; we your committee on arrangements beg leave to report the following order of business:

(1)   Call the roll.

(2)   Call for report of committees.

COMMITTEES AS FOLLOWS.

(a)   Report on Divine service.
(b)   Report on correspondance.
(c)   Report on finance.
(d)   Report on requests.

When and where shall our next association be?   Who shall preach the introductory sermon? And who shall be his alternate?   How many copies of minutes shall be printed? And who shall superintend the printing and distribution of same?   What shall he be allowed for his services.

Respectfully submitted,
R. H. BALL.
W. S. COLLINS.
JAMES RAGAN.
G. W. BRYANT.

(6)   Committee on preaching submitted their report, which was adopted as follows: Friday evening 4 p. m. Eld. J. D. Monroe with Eld. M. B. Weaver at Bro. G. S. Southers. Friday night at church Eld. J. V. Kirkland. Saturday at stand Elds. J. V. Kirkland, Jno. Capps and Jno. Hammack.   Sunday at the Stand Elds. J. D. Monroe, M. B. Weaver, J. V. Kirkland, Mod. to close.

FRANK HAMILTON.
JNO. HOPPER.
M. C. EDWARDS.
J. W. ALSTON.
JAMES RAGAN.
Together with the church.

(7) Committee on request submitted their report which was adopted as follows: We your committee on requests recommend that the next association be be held with Mossy Spring church.

Respectfully submitted,
ELD. JNO. HAMMACK.
H. A. SHOFNER.
JNO. WEBB.

(8) Committee on correspondence submitted their report, which was adopted as follows: Be it resolved that we correspond with Hiwassee association and appoint messengers to same.   That we send minutes of our last association to the Towalega, Tennessee, Sequatchie Valley and other associations.   That we solicit the correspondence of all Primitive Baptists, who are willing to live in peace and work together for the prosperity of our cause.   We recomend that this association send a messenger and letter to the General Conference meeting of Primitive Baptists, which meets at Halls, Tenn., August 21, 1907 and that this association help to defray his expense.

Respectfully submitted,

E. D. MONROE,

ELD. J. D. MONROE,

W. A. DRUMMOND.

(9) The committee appointed to draft resolutions of sympathy for the distressed family of Eld. S. M. Petree, report adopted as follows: That whereas, news has reached this association that our beloved brother, Eld. S. M. Petree is at the point of death and not expected live but a few hours. Be it resolved that the association extend to Eld. S. M. Petree and family its heart felt sympathy in their afflictions and that we all will remember them in our solemn petitions at a throne of Grace. Be it further resolved that this resolution be spread upon the minutes of this association.   Respectfully submitted,

ELD. J. V. KIRKLAND,

ELD. J. D. MONROE,

ELD. M. B. WEAVER.

On motion we appoint our next association to be held with the church at Mossey Spring Union Co. Tenn.

Commencing on Friday before the third Saturday in August 1908, and two succeeding days.

On motion Eld. J. M. Drummonds was appointed to preach the introductory sermon and Eld. Leonard White to be his alterenate.

On motion agreed that the Clerk superintend the printing and distribution of 500 copies of minutes and receive $3.00 for his service.

On motion Eld. M. B. Weaver was appointed as messenger to the general meeting of Primitive Baptist at Halls Tennessee.

On motion Elds. J. D. Monroe and M. B. Weaver with Brother James Ragan, were appointed as messengers to the Hiwassee Association.

Resolved that we tender our heart felt thanks to this church and community for kind hospitality during this association.

On motion adjourned to meet as above stated.

ELD. J. M. DRUMMOND, mod.
JAMES REGAN clerk.
E. D. MONROE asst. clerk.

SUNDAY

Sunday was turned to a funeral meeting in memory of the three children of a dear Brother and Sister Worley. The eldest, Luther, in his last moments said he saw his little sister and brother, who had gone on before, Said they had come to meet him and welcome him to that celestial home. It was declared by one of the ministers and was the general openion that the dear boy saw just what he said he saw. Another one of those precious children had foretold of his death, and asked his friends to meet him in glory, declaring his future home would be there.

At the conclusion much love was manifested with the brethren and sisiters, all united in singing to the praise of God with hand shaking and rejoicing.

It was touching to see Elds. J. V. Kirkland and J. D.

18

Monroe embrace each other, thereby manifesting that never failing love which animates every child of God.

SUPPLEMENT BY CLERK

In behalf of the association, will say that we appreciated the presence of the distinguished veteran, J. V. Kirkland. To become acquainted and know of the persecutions which have been heaped upon him, is to love him the more. Then his wholesome, scriptural doctrine the tenor of which is; that we as God's people should lay aside all unnecessary criticism, faultfinding, hatred and the like and worship God according as we received him to walk in him. Let us hope he may live to visit us again. I hereby acknowledge my gratitude to the former as well as the present assistant clerk for their very able and efficient help. We hereby tender our love to them and to all God's children.

J. M. DRUMMOND moderator.

JAMES RAGAN clerk.

E. D. MONROE asst. clerk-

MINISTERIAL ROLL

ELDERS	POST OFFICE	STATE
Alfred Boruff	R. F. D. No. 23, Liberty Hill	Tenn.
A. J. Buroff	R. F. D. No. 15, Washburn	Tenn.
Eli M. Branson	Zenda.	Kansas.
J. A. Capps	R. F. D. No. 3, Maynaryville	Tenn.
J. M. Drummonds	Manring	Tenn.
John Hammack		Tenn.
J. D. Monroe	R. F. D. No. 1 Sharps Chapel	Tenn.
S. M. Petree	R. F. D. No. 1. Lost Creek	Tenn.
M. B. Weaver	R. F. D. No. 1, Lost Creek	Tenn.
Leonard White	R. F. D. No. 2, Sharps Chapel	Tenn.

LICENTIATES

H. L. Alston	R. F. D. No 1. Tazwell	Tenn.
W. R. Petree	Goin	Tenn.
C. B. Weaver	R. F. D. No. 2. Sharps Chapel	Tenn.
J. Webb	Gibson Station	Va.

19

CHURCH	CLERKS	POSTOFFICES	STATE
Big Barren	W R Petree	Goin	Tenn
Cedar Springs	W A Drummond	New Tazewell, No. 3	Tenn
Dotson's Creek	James Ragan	Liberty Hill	Tenn
Gibson Station	G W Bryant	Gibson Station	Va
Hamilton Grove	H T Hamilton	Maynardsville	Tenn
Mossey Spring	Berry White	Sharps Chapel, No. 2	Tenn
Oak Grove	David White	" " No. 2	Tenn
Pleasant Point	P F Keck	Goin	Tenn
Pleasant Hill	J P Easterly	Speedwell R F D	Tenn

TABLE OF STATISTICS.

CHURCHES	NAMES OF MESSENGERS.	Contributions	Received by Baptism	Received by Letter	Rev'd by Relation'p	Restored	Dismissed by Letter	Excluded	Dead	Total	Sat. Meeting
Big Barren	W R Petree, M. C. Edwards									39	3
Cedar Spring	Eld. J M Drummond, W A Drummond, J W Alston, G B Drummond, H L Alston							2		60	4
Dotson's Creek	Eld. J A Capps, James Ragan	$1 00	3	2				1		30	4
Gibson Station	S S Wilson, J A Webb, Wm Collinss, R H Ball	$1 00	7	1						36	1
Hamilton Grove	H F Hamilton									53	
Mossey Spring	Eld. M B Weaver, E D Monroe, John Hopper	$2 00	10		6	1		1	2	69	1
Oak Grove	Eld. J D Monroe, Wm Shofner, Isaac Shofner	$2 00	11		5	1	8	3	176	64	2
Pleasant Point	T C Keck, J L Keck		4		1					12	4
Pleasant Hill	T J Miracle, J P Easterly										

20

MINUTES

OF THE

EIGHTY-NINTH ANNUAL SESSION

OF THE

Powell's Valley Association

OF

Primitive Baptists

Held with the Church at
Mossy Spring, Union County, Tenn.
August 14, 15 and 16, 1908

KNOXVILLE
PRINTING & PUBLISHING COMPANY
KNOXVILLE, TENN.

MINUTES

OF THE

Eighty-ninth Annual Session of the Powell's Valley
Association of Primitive Baptist, held with the
church at Mossy Spring, Union County,
Tennessee, on August 14th, 15th, and
16th, 1908.

FRIDAY'S PROCEEDINGS.

(1) The association met pursuant to adjournment.
Prayer and praise by Eld. J. M. Drummond.

(2) Introductory sermon, by Eld. J. M. Drummond, from Eph. 2:8,9. "For by grace are ye saved
through faith and that not of yourselves, it is the
gift of God: not of works lest any man should
boast."

(3) Called for letters from churches, and received
ten which were read and messengers names enrolled.

(4) On motion Eld. J. M. Drummond was elected
moderator, and E. D. Monroe, clerk, with James
Ragan, assistant clerk.

(5) Called for petitionary letters and none received.

(6) Invited ministers to seats with us.

(7) Called for correspondence and received letter from Hiwasee Association by their messenger,
Eld. J. M. Goodman, who was welcomed to a seat
with us.

(8) Appointed the following:

Committees.

(a) On arrangements—David Warwick, Joseph Smith, J. W. Alston.

(b) On Correspondence—James Ragan, Elvin Weaver, Alfred Boruff.

(c) On Preaching—Isaac Shoffner, Wm. Shoffner, James Drummond, Mannie Graves. Wm. Brantley, Wm. Graves, David Riding, Henry Hunter. Mannie Boruff, together with the church.

(d) On Requests—Eld. Leonard White, Elvin Weaver.

(e) On Finance—John Hopper, Wm. Brantley.

(9) On motion the following committee was appointed to draft resolution in memory of Eld. S. M. Petree and wife (Sister Sarah A. Petree, deceased).

(10) Adjourned to meet Saturday at 9 a. m.

SATURDAY MORNING.

(1) The association met pursuant to adjournment. Prayer and praise by Eld. J. M. Drummond.

(2) Committee on arrangements submitted their report. On motion the report was adopted as follows: We your committee on arrangement beg leave to submit the following order of business, viz:

(a) Call the roll.

(b) Call for report of committee on preaching.

(c) Call for reports of other committees in order of appointment.

(d) When and where shall our next association

be? Who shall preach the introductory sermon, and, who shall be his alternate?

(e) How many copies of minutes and, who shall superintend printing and distribution of same?

(3) Called the roll and names of absentees erased.

(4) The Committee on preaching submitted their report which was adopted as follows, viz:

Friday night at Blue Spring, Elds. Alfred Boruff, Leonard White.

Friday night at Cave Spring, Elds. John Hammock, John Capps.

Friday night at Church, Elds. M. B. Weaver, J. M. Goodman,

Saturday at the stand, Elds. J. M. Goodman, Alfred Boruff, J. D. Monroe.

Saturday night at Blue Spring, Elds. J. M. Drummond, J. M. Goodman.

Saturday night at Bro. Gordon Weaver's, Elds. J. D. Monroe, John Hammack, John Capps.

Saturday night at church Elds. M. B. Weaver, Leonard White.

Sunday at the stand, Elds. J. M. Goodman, Leonard White, J. D. Monroe, M. B. Weaver, Moderator to close.

(5) The Committee on Correspondence submitted their report, and on motion the following was adopted, viz:

We recommend that we continue our correspondence with the Hiwasee Association, and appoint messengers to the same. We further recommend that we correspond with the General meeting which begins August 26, 1908, at Mt. Moriah, Tenn., and that our clerk write letter and we appoint messengers to the same.

Respectfully submitted,
ELD. ALFRED BORUFF,
ELVIN WEAVER,
JAMES RAGAN.

(6) Committee on Finance reported and report adopted as follows, viz:

We your committee beg leave to report total amount of contribution from churches and all sources to amount of $15.15.

Respectfully submitted,
JOHN HOPPER,
WM. BRANTLEY.

(7) Committe on requests reported, which was adopted as follows, viz:

We your committee on requests beg leave to recommend that our next association be held with Hamilton Grove Church.

Respectfully submitted,
ELVIN WEAVER,
LEONARD WHITE.

(8) Committee on resolutions reported, which report was adopted as follows, viz:

We your committee appointed to draft resolutions in memory of Elder S. M. Petree, and wife, Sister Sarah Ann Petree, beg leave to submit the following, viz: Eld. S. M. Petree, born March 10, 1860, joined the church at Mossy Spring, January, 1876, died August 17, 1907, leaving his wife, Sister Sarah Ann, ten sons and two daughters, with many relatives and friends to mourn his loss. He was a faithful minister, serving his church as pastor until a few years before his death. He preached his last sermon, just one week before his death, at his home church. Sister Sarah Ann was sick at the time of her husband's death, from which she never recovered. She was born Dec. 28, 1861, died March 8, 1908, joined the Primitive Baptist, and lived a consistent member until death. Therefore, Be it resolved that we hereby express to the bereft sons and daughters, relatives and friends our heartfelt sympathies and urge upon them to press forward until they are called to meet their loved ones, beyond the Jordan of death.

Respectfully submitted,
ELD. M. B. WEAVER,
ELD. J. M. DRUMMOND,
JAMES RAGAN,
ELD. J. D. MONROE,
ELD. LEONARD WHITE,
JOHN HOPPER.

(9) On motion Elds. J. D. Monroe, M. B. Weaver, John Capps, John Hammack, were appointed messengers to the Hiwasee Association.

(10) On motion, Elds. J. D. Monroe, M. B. Weaver, were appointed messengers to the General Meeting which meets at Mt. Moriah, Tenn.

(11) On motion we appoint our next association to be held with the church at Hamilton Grove, Union County, Tenn., commencing on Friday before the 3rd Saturday in August, 1909 and two succeeding days.

(12) On motion Eld. Leonard White was appoint-

6

ed to preach the introductory sermon and Eld. J. D. Monroe to be his alternate.

(13) On motion agreed that the clerk superintend the printing and distribution of 500 copies of minutes and receive balance of contribution for his service.

(14) Resolved that we tender our heartfelt thanks to this church and community for their hospitality and kind treatment during this association.

(15) On motion adjourned to meet as above mentioned.

ELD. J. M. DRUMMOND,
Moderator.

E. D. MONROE, Clerk.
JAMES RAGAN, Asst. Clerk.

SUPPLEMENT BY CLERK.

On Saturday a very large congregation assembled at the stand and listened attentively to the preaching of Elds. J. M. Goodman, Alfred Boruff, J. D. Monroe. All joined in singing praises to God when a revival broke out, such as is seldom witnessed. 'Twas a touching scene to see the brethren embrace each other, while many were shouting and leaping for joy. On Sunday Elds. J. M. Goodman, Leonard White, J. D. Monroe, M. B. Weaver each delivered a short discourse which seemed to make a good impression upon the minds of the hearers. All joined in singing and extended the parting hand. The moderator invoked divine blessing. Dismissed in order.

CLERK.

Ministerial Roll.

ELDERS	POST OFFICE	STATE.
Alfred Boruff,	R. F. D. No. 23, Liberty Hill,	Tenn.
A. J. Boruff,	R. F. D. No. 15, Washburn,	Tenn.
Eli M. Branson,	Zenda,	Kan.
J. A. Capps,	R. F. D. 3, Maynardville,	Tenn.
J. M. Drummond,	Marning,	Tenn.
John Hammack,	Washburn,	Tenn.
J. D. Monroe,	R. F. D. 1, Sharp's Chapel,	Tenn.
M. B. Weaver,	R. F. D. 1, Lost Creek,	Tenn.
Leonard White,	R. F. D. 2, Sharp's Chapel,	Tenn.

Licentiates

H. L. Alston,	R. F. D. 1, Tazwell,	Tenn.
W. R. Petree,	Goin,	Tenn.
C. B. Weaver,	R. F. D. 2, Sharp's Chapel,	Tenn.
J. Webb,	Gibson Station,	Va.

CHURCHES	CLERKS	POST OFFICE	STATE
Big Barren	W. R. Petree	Sharp's Chapel	Tenn.
Cave Spring	S. A. Keller	Sharp's Chapel No. 2	Tenn.
Cedar Spring	W. A. Drummond	New Tazwell No. 3	Tenn.
Dotson's Creek	James Ragan	Liberty Hill	Tenn.
Gibson Station	George Bryant	Gibson Station	Va.
Hamilton Grove	H. F. Hamilton	Maynardville No. 3	Tenn.
Mossy Spring	Berry White	Sharp's Chapel No. 2	Tenn.
Oak Grove	David White	Sharp's Chapel	Tenn.
Pleasant Hill	J. P. Easterly	Speedwell	Tenn.
Pleasant Point	P. F. Keck	Goin	Tenn.

TABLE OF STATISTICS

Churches	Names of Messengers	Contributions	Received by Baptism	Received by letter	Rec'd by relationship	Restored	Dismissed by letter	Excluded	Dead	Total	Saturday meeting
Big Barren	W. R. Petree, W. A. Graves	$1.00					3			38	3
Cave Spring	Hes White, Joseph Smith, Joseph Keller, William Brantley	1.10	1				3		3	98	3
Cedar Spring	J. W. Alston, Elder J. M. Drummond, H. L. Alston, S. Myers, J. L. Drummond, J. A. G. Drummond									63	4
Dotson's Creek	Elder J. A. Capps, Elder A. Boruff, Elder J. Hammack, James Ragan, Mannie Boruff	1.50	3							32	4
Gibson Station	S. S. Wilson	1.55	2							39	1
Hamilton Grove	V. L. Raley, Wesley Raley, Mannie Graves, Lewis Raley, W. D. Warwick, Elvin Hunley, F. H. Warwick	1.00	3		1				1		
Mossy Spring	Elder M. B. Weaver, Elder Leonard White, Joseph White, D. White, E. D. Monroe, Gordon Weaver, C. B. Weaver, Elvin Weaver	1.50	11	2	2			8		52	1
Oak Grove	Elder J. D. Monroe, I. Shoffner, William Shoffner, J. P. Russell, Tays Carter, John Carter	2.00	13				1		3	193	2
Pleasant Hill	Henry Hunter	2.5			3					75	1
Pleasant Point	D. Riding, C. R. Cox, P. F. Keck, John Carey						1	1		16	4
								1	1	64	2
	Total								7	670	

MINUTES

OF THE

NINETIETH ANNUAL SESSION

OF THE

Powell's Valley Association

OF

Primitive Baptists

Held with the Church at
Hamilton Grove, Union County, Tenn.
August 20th, 21st and 22nd
1909

TENNESSEE PRINTING CO.
KNOXVILLE

MINUTES

Ninetieth Annual Session of the Powell's Valley Association of Primitive Baptists, Held with the Church at Hamilton Grove, Union County, Tennessee, on August, 20, 21, 22, 1909

FRIDAY'S PROCEEDINGS.

(1) The association met pursuant to adjournment. Praise and prayer by Eld. J. M. Drummond.

(2) Introductory sermon by Eld. Leonard White, from Heb. 10:16. "This is the covenant that I will make with them after those days saith the Lord, I will put my laws into their hearts and in their minds will I write them."

(3) Called for letters from churches and received nine, which were read and messengers' names enrolled.

(4) On motion Eld. J. M. Drummond was re-elected moderator and S. A. Keller clerk, with Eld. Leonard White assistant clerk.

(5) Called for petitionary letters and received one from Tackett Creek church, Claiborne County, Tennessee, and was received (on the recommendation of some of the messengers that know the church) and her messenger's name enrolled.

(6) Invited ministers to seats with us.

(7) Called for correspondence.

31

(8)   Appointed the following committees:

COMMITTEES.

(a)   On Arrangements—Eld. Leonard White, W. E. Myers and H. H. Shoffner.

(b)   On Correspondence—Elds.J. D. Monroe, A. Boruff, and Brethren Elvin Weaver and Mat. Keck.

(c)   On Preaching—Mat. Keck, W. H. Brantley, Mannie Graves, Thos. White, Wm. Shoffner, Ben Sowders, together with the church at Hamilton Grove.

(d)   On Request—Elds. J. D. Monroe, Leonard White and J. A. Capps.

(e)   On Finance—Matt. Dossett and Ben Sowders.

(9)   Adjourned to meet Saturday morning at 9 o'clock.

SATURDAY MORNING.

(1)   The association met pursuant to adjournment. Prayer and praise by the moderator.

(2)   Called for the reports of the committee on arrangements. We your committee on arrangements, submit the following:

(a)   Call the roll.

(b)   Call for report of committee on correspondence.

(c)   Call for report of committee on preaching.

(d)   Call for reports of other committees in order of appointment.

(e) When and where shall our next association be? Who shall preach the introductory sermon, and who shall be his alternate?

(f) How many copies of minutes, and who shall superintend the printing and distribution of the same?

Respectfully submitted,
ELD. LEONARD WHITE,
W. E. MOYERS,
H. H. SHOFFNER.

(3) Called the roll and erased the names of absentees.

(4) We your committee on correspondence, submit the following:

That we continue our correspondence with the Hiwassee association and with the general meeting, and that letters and messengers to the same.

Respectfully submitted,
ELD. J. D. MONROE,
ELD. A. BORUFF,
W. E. MOYERS,
M. C. KECK.

(5) We your committee on request, submit the following:

That we publish on our minutes the obituaries of Sisters Mary C. Collins, Orpha A. Boruff and Emily Cabbage.

Respectfully submitted,
ELD. J. D. MONROE,
ELD. LEONARD WHITE,
ELD. J. A. CAPPS.

(6)   We your committee on finance, submit the following:

Received from the church, $14.65.

Respectfully submitted,
MATT DOSSETT,
BEN SOWDERS.

(7)   On motion all the foregoing committees' reports were adopted and committees released.

(8)   A request was received from Noeton church inviting the churches of this association to visit them on the third Saturday and Sunday in September, 1909, on a communion occasion. On motion the request was granted.

(9)   On motion it was agreed for Eld. J. D. Monroe and Elvin Weaver to write a letter to the Hiawassee association, and Eld. M. B. Weaver and H. H. Shoffner to write a letter to the general meeting.

(10)   Elds. J. D. Monroe and M. B. Weaver as delegates to the general meeting, and Elds. J. D. Monroe and A. Boruff as delegates to the Hiawassee association.

(11)   On motion we appointed our next association to be held with the church at Tackett Creek, Claiborne County, Tenn., three miles west of Manring Depot, and four miles southeast of Clearfield Depot, commencing on Friday before the third Saturday in August, 1910, and the two succeeding days.

(12)   On motion Eld. J. D. Monroe was appointed to preach the introductory sermon, and Eld. M. Hensley to be his alternate.

(13)   On motion agreed that the clerk superintend the printing and distribution of 500 minutes and receive balance of contribution for his service.

(14)   Resolved, That we tender our heartfelt thanks to this church and community for their hospitality and kind treatment during this association.

(15)   On motion adjourned to meet as above mentioned.

ELD. J. M. DRUMMOND, Moderator,
Manring, Tenn.
S. A. KELLER, Clerk,
Sharp's Chapel, Tenn., No. 4.
ELD. LEONARD WHITE, Asst. Clerk,
Sharp's Chapel, Tenn., No. 2.

MINISTERIAL ROLL.

ELDERS	POSTOFFICE	STATE
Alfred Boruff	R. D. 23, Liberty Hill,	Tenn.
A. J. Boruff	R. D. 15, Washburn,	Tenn.
Eli M. Branson	Zenda	Kan.
J. A. Capps	R. D. 3 Maynardville,	Tenn.
J. M. Drummond	Manring	Tenn.
John Hammack	Washburn	Tenn.
J. D. Monroe	R. D. I, Sharp's Chapel,	Tenn.
M. B. Weaver	R. D. 2, Sharp's Chapel,	Tenn.
Leonard White	R. D. 2, Sharp's Chapel,	Tenn.
Mack Hensley	Gibson Station	Va.
J. Webb	Gibson Station	Va.

LICENTIATES.

H. L. Alston	R. D. No. 1, Tazewell,	Tenn.
W. R. Petree	Goin	Tenn.
C. B. Weaver	R. D. 2, Sharp's Chapel,	Tenn.

CHURCHES	CLERKS	P. O.	STATE
Big Barren	M. C. Edwards	Goin	Tenn.
Cave Spring	S. A. Keller	Sharp's Chapel, No. 4,	Tenn.
Cedar Spring	W. A. Drummond	New Tazwell	Tenn.
Dotson's Creek	James Ragan	Liberty Hill	Tenn.
Gibson Station	G. W. Bryant	Gibson Staton	Va.
Hamilton Grove	J. W. Raley	Maynardville	Tenn.
Mossy Spring	Elza Wilhite	Sharp's Chapel, No. 2,	Tenn.
Oak Grove	David White	Sharp's Chapel, No. 4,	Tenn.
Pleasant Hill	J. P. Easterly	Speedwell	Tenn.
Pleasant Point	P. F. Keck	Goin	Tenn.
Tackett Creek	W. H. Gibbs	Manring	Tenn.

OBITUARIES.

Sister Orpha A. Boruff was born March 28, 1844, deceased October 13. 1908. She joined the Missionary Baptist Church about 1859, then joined the Primitive Baptist Church in 1888. She has been a faithful and consistent member until her decease. Shortly before her death she frequently talked of the good home to which she was fast hastening. She patiently bore her afflictions 10 years. She leaves a loving hubsand three children, together with a host of friends to mourn her loss. Sure are we that our loss means her eternal gain in the beautiful home beyond.

Sister Emily Cabbage was born May 16, 1878, deceased September 10, 1908. She joined the Primitive Baptist Church, living a faithful member until death. She requested Elder J. D. Monroe to hold meeting at her home, for she saw she must soon die, but she said there was nothing in her way and that she could see her way clear and seemed to not fear death.

With deep sorrow we note the death of our dear Sister Mary Catharine Collins, wife of Brother William Collins. She had been a devoted member of Gibson street church for many years. She died about last Christmas, in the faith, telling her friends not to grieve after her, that she was going to a better world. Her earth life was that of a true Christian, and while we mourn her loss, yet we expect that by the grace of God to meet her in that rest prepared for all of God's people. We extend to Brother Collins and their six motherless children our love and sympathy, and admonish them to so strive to meet our dear sister in Heaven, where parting will be no more.

TABLE OF STATISTICS

Churches	Names of Messengers	Contributions	Rec'd by Baptism	Rec'd by Letter	Rec'd by Relat'nsh'p	Restored	Dismissed by Letter	Excluded	Dead	Total	Saturday Meeting
Big Barren	Mc Edwards and Lafayette Weaver	$ .75								36	3
Cave Spring	Matt Dossett, W. H. Brantly, Lafayette Ellison, Jas. Lynch and S. A. Keller	1.50	17	3			9	2	2	109	3
Cedar Spring	Elders J. M. Drummond and J. W. Alston	1.50	3						2	66	4
Dotson's Creek	Elders John Capps, A Boruff and John Hammack	1.00	8	1			1		2	39	4
Gibson Station	Elders J. Webb, Mc Hensley and H. H. Shoffner	1.00					1			40	1
Hamilton Grove	J. W. Raley, Mannie Graves, N. L. Raley, V. L. Raley, H. F. Hamilton and F. Warwick	1.50	6				1		2	62	1
Mossy Springs	Elders L. White, M. B. Weaver, Thos. White, J. H. Petree, Asroe Weaver and Elvin Weaver	2.25	13	4				28	21	176	2
Oak Grove	Elders J. D. Monroe, Wm Shoffner and J. P. Russell	2.10		2						81	1
Pleasant Point	M. C. Keck	1.30								68	2
Tackett Creek	W. E. Moyers and Ben Sowders	1.00								57	1
Total		$13.90	3	3		9	5	28	8	734	22

MINUTES

OF THE

NINETY-FIRST ANNUAL SESSION

OF THE

Powell's Valley Association

OF

PRIMATIVE BAPTISTS,

HELD WITH THE CHURCH AT

CAVE SPRING, UNION COUNTY, TENNESSEE,

OCTOBER 14, 15 AND 16, 1910.

MINUTES

OF THE

Ninety-first Annual Session of the Powell's Valley Association of Primitive Baptists, held with the Church at Cave Spring, Union County, Tenn., October 14th, 15th and 16th, 1910.

1. Praise and prayer by Elder J. M. Drummonds.
2. Introductory sermon by Elder J. D. Monroe, from St. John 5th chapter, 39th verse: "Search the Scriptures, for in them ye think ye have eternal life, and they are they which testify of me."
3. Fifteen minutes intermission. The Clerk being absent W. A. Drummonds was elected Clerk protem.
4. Called for letters from Churches. Ten received and read, and messengers names enrolled.
5. On motion Elder J. M Drummonds was re-elected Moderator, and W. A. Drummonds was elected Clerk, and J. H. Petree Assistant Clerk.
6. Called for petitionery letters.
7. Called for correspondence.
8. Ministers and Brethren were invited to seats with us.
9. Appointed the following Committees:
A. Committee on arrangements, J. L. Herrell, Elvin Weaver, H. L. Alston.
B. On correspondence: Elder J. D. Monroe, M. B. Weaver and Brother P. F. Keck.
C. On preaching: Mack Edwards, J. N. Fergerson, Green Bryant, Elzie White, Isaac Shaffner, Frank Hamilton, P. F. Keck, J. L. Herrell, together with the Church at Cave Spring.
D. On requests: Elder J. D. Monroe, H. A. Shaffner and LaFayette Ellison.

E, On finance: Isaac Shaffner and Mack Edwards.
10. Adjourned until tomorrow morning at 9:30.

SATURDAY'S PROCEEDINGS.

1. The Association met pursuant to adjournment.
2. Praise and Prayer by the Moderator.
3. On motion called for reports of Committees, which were read and approved as follows:

A. We, your committee on arrangements, beg leave to submit the following Order of Business:

1. Call the Roll.
2. On Preaching.
3. On Correspondence.
4. On Requests.
5. On Finance.
6. When and where shall our next Association be?
7. Who shall preach the Introductory Sermon, and who shall be his Alternote?
8. How many copies of the Minutes, and who shall superintend the printing and distribution of same.

Respectfully submitted,

J. L. HERRELL,
H. L. ALSTON,
ELVIN WEAVER.

9. Called the Roll and erased the names of absentees.

B. We, your committee on Preaching beg leave to submit the following report:

1. Friday night—Cave Spring, Elders Mike Hensley and Leonard White.

Mossy Spring—Elders J. M. Drummonds, M. B. Weaver and H. L. Alston.

Braden School House—H. A. Shaffner, W. R. Petree.

2. Saturday at Stand—Elder M. B. Weaver, Mike Hensley, Leonard White.

3. Saturday night—Mossy Spring, Elders M. B. Weaver, H. A. Shaffner.

Cave Spring, Mike Hensley, J. D. Monroe and J. M. Drummonds.

Braden School House—Elders Leonard White, W. R. Petree, H. L. Alston.

4. Sunday at Stand—Elders M. B. Weaver, J. D. Monroe and Moderator to close.

Respectfully submitted: Mack Edwards, J. N. Fergerson, Green Bryant, Elzie White, Isaac Shaffner P. F. Keck, Frank Hamilton, J. L. Herrell.

C. We, your committee on Correspoddence, beg leave to submit the following:

That, whereas, we have failed to send Letter or Messenger for the last two years to the Hiwassee Association, and haven't heard from them, that we send Letter and Messenger to their next Annual meeting, making a confession of our negligence, and revive correspondence, if there is no hindrance.

Also send Letter or Messenger, or both, to the next General Meeting of Primitive Baptists.

> Respectfully submitted: Elders M. B. Weaver, J. D. Monroe and Brother P. F. Keck.

D. We, your committee on Requests, beg leave to submit the following:

1. That we publish in our Minutes the obituaries of our well beloved sister, Sibby Drummonds and Elder John Capps.

2. That our next Association be held with the Church at Dotson's Creek, Union County, Tenn.

> Respectfully submitted: Elder J. D. Monroe and Brothers H. A. Shaffner, LaFayette Ellison.

E. We, your committee on Finance, beg to submit the following: Received from Churches, $13.00.

> Respectfully submitted: Isaac Shaffner, Mack Edwards.

3. By the Clerk for Noeton, 75 cents, making a total of $13.75.

4. All the Foreign reports received and committees discharged.

5. On moton Elders M. B. Weaver, J. D. Monroe and Brother Elvin Weaver were appointed as Messengers to visit the Hiwassee Association.

6. On motion our next Association will be held with the Church at Dotson's Creek, Union county, Tenn., which will convene on Friday before the 3rd Saturday in August 1911.

7. Elder M. B. Weaver to preach the Introductory Sermon and Elder Alfred Boriff to be his alternate.

8. That we have 400 copies of our Minutes printed and that the Clerk superintend the printing and distribution of same, and that he be allowed the remainder for his services.

9. Be it resolved that we tender our heart-felt thanks to this dear old Church and good community for their hospitality and kind treatment during our stay with them during this Association.

10. The Letter from Noeton received after Minutes were adopted.—Clerk.

11. By request of our beloved, aged and afflicted brother, J. W. Alston, be it Resolved, that we join together in prayer in his behalf, with Elder J. D. Monroe to lead the consecrated prayer, praying: "Thy will, oh Lord, not ours, be done." Amen!

12. Minutes adopted.

13. Then adjourned to meet as above stated.

> ELDER J. M. DRUMMONDS, Moderator.
> Manring, Tenn.

W. A. DRUMMONDS, Clerk,
Route 3, Box 46, New Tazewell, Tenn.

SUNDAY.

A large and at ntive audience assembled at the stand and listened so well at the good and well delivered sermons by Elders M. B. Weaver from Romans 5th chapter and 1st verse, therefore being justified by faith, we have peace with God through our Lord Jesus Christ; and J. D. Monroe from text: Romans the 11th chapter and 1st verse, I say unto them hath God cast away His people, God forbid for I am also an Israelite of the seed of. Abraham of the tribe of Benjamin. And closing remarks by the Moderator, all of which was so well and attentively listened to, and at the close of the services a most extraordinary interest was manifested by the sheding of tears, clapping of the hands and of invoking the blessings of God upon each other in such a reality surely the clerk exclaims he had never witnessed in an Association in forty-four years before.   CLERK.

OBITUARIES.

With sad haste we announce the death of our well beloved Sister Sibby Drummonds, wife of W. A. Drummonds, who was a mother in our church. She professed faith in Christ in 1867, joined the Primitive Baptist Church at Cedar Spring, October 2nd Saturday, 1871. Served the church as deaconess for eighteen years and departed this life August 31st, 1909; age, 61 years, 7 months and 26 days. She lived a consistent member and a faithful Christian. She was well beloved by all who knew her. She told her companion at 4 o'clock the morning before she died at ten that night, that she was going home, that she could not stay with him only until 10 o'clock that night, and bid him not to grieve after her that she was going home at ten. She fell asleep in the arms of Jesus. Died in full triumph of a living faith, leaving a dear companion, nine dear children and a host of friends and relatives to mourn the loss of a dear companion, a tender mother and a loving Christian. We extend to Brother Drummonds and his dear family our love and heart felt sympathy in his bereaved state.

With sad hearts we announce the death of our well beloved Elder John Capps, who was true in word and doctrine, who lived a faithful soldier until his death, while he has fallen asleep, he is very much missed among us, we can only say to the dear bereaved ones we hope our loss is his eternal gain.

43

CHURCHES.	NAMES OF DELEGATES.	Rec'd by Baptism.	Rec'd by Letter.	Rec'd by Relation.	Restored.	Dismissed by Letter.	Excluded.	Deceased.	Total.	Saturday Meeting.	Contribution.
Big Barren	Mack Edwards								41	3	
Cave Spring	Elder Mike Hensley, J. H. Dossett, W. H. Brantley, Joseph Smith, L. Ellison	12	1	3	1				1,22	3	$1.75
Cedar Spring	Elder J. M. Drummonds H. L. Alston, J. N. Fergerson, W. A. Drummonds	3						1	68	4	1.50
Dotson Creek	Green Bryant	5	2	2				1	43	3	1.00
Gibson Station	H. A. Shaffner							1	39	1	1.50
Hamilton Grove	Frank Hamilton, David Warwick, Mary Graves	2						1	63	4	1.50
Mossy Spring	T. V. Heath, F. Warwick, J. W. Raley, Elder M. B. Weaver, Leonard White, Daniel White, Elvin Weaver, Jno. H. Petree, Elza White.	3	1			1	14	5	161	2	2.25
Noeton	Letter but no delegates	3	1			1		1	35	3	75
Oak Grove	Elder J. D. Monroe, Isaac Shaffner, W. R. Petree, Jno. Shaffner, Jno. Carter, Tayce Carter								81	1	2.15
Pleasant Point	David Riden, P. F. Keck.								60	2	
Pleasant Hill	Pryor Lambert, Jas. Herrell								12	4	

MINISTER ROLL.

Elders.	Postoffice.	State.
Alfred Boruff	R. F. D. No. 23, Liberty Hill	Tenn.
A. J. Boruff	R. F. D. No. 15, Washburn	Tenn.
Eli Branson	Yenda	Kans.
M. B. Weaver	R. F. D. No. 1, Lost Creek	Tenn.
J. M. Drummonds	Manring	Tenn.
J. D. Monroe	Goin	Tenn.
Leonard White	R. F. D. No. 2, Sharp's Chapel,	Tenn.
Mike Hensley	Sharp's Chapel	Tenn.
John Hammock	Washburn	Tenn.
J. Webb	Gibson Station	Va.
Calvin Collins	R. F. D. No. 1, Noeton	Tenn.
LICENTIATES:		
H. L. Alston	R. F. D. No. 1, Tazewell	Tenn
W. R. Petree,	Goin	Tenn.
C. B. Weaver	R. F. D. No. 2, Sharp's Chapel,	Tenn.

CHURCHES.	CLERKS.	POSTOFFICE.	STATE.
Big Barren	Mack Edwards	Goin	Tenn.
Cave Spring	W. H. Brantley	Sharp's Chapel	Tenn.
Cedar Spring	W. A. Drummonds,	New Tazewell	Tenn.
Dotson's Creek	Jas. Ragan	Liberty Hill, R. F. D. No. 3	Tenn.
Gibson Station	G. W. Bryant	Gibson Station	Va.
Hamilton Grove	J. W. Raley	Maynards ville,	Tenn.
Mossy Spring	Eliza White	Sharp's Chapel, R. F. D. No. 2.	Tenn.
Nœton	J. L. Oliver	Nœton	Tenn.
Oak Grove	David White	Sharp's Chapel, R. F. D. No. 4.	Tenn.
Pleasant Hill	J P. Easterly	Speedwell	Tenn.
Pleasant Point	P. F. Keck	Goin	Tenn.

Minutes

= OF THE =

Ninety-Second Annual Session

= OF THE =

Powell's Valley Association

= OF =

Primitive Baptists

HELD WITH THE CHURCH AT

Black Fox, Grainger County, Tenn.

August 18, 19, and 20, 1911

Progress Print, Tazewell, Tenn.

MINUTES

Of the Ninety-Second Annual Session of Powell's Valley Association of Primitive Baptists, held with the Church at Black Fox, Grainger County, Tenn., August 18, 19, 20, 1911.

1. Praise and prayer by Elder J. M. Drummonds.

2. Introductory sermon by Elder M. B. Weaver, from text, 1st Samuel, 17th chapter, 45th verse: "Then said David to the Philistine, thou comest to me with a sword and with a spear, and with a shield, but I come to thee in the name of the Lord of Hosts, the God of the armies of Israel whom thou hast defied."

3. After 10 minutes intermission the Association was called to order.

4. Called for letters from churches; ten received and read and messengers names enrolled.

5. On motion, Elder M. B. Weaver was elected Moderator and W. A. Drummonds re-elected Clerk and Elder Leonard White Assistant Clerk.

6. Called for petitionery letters.

7. Called for correspondence.

8. Ministers and brethren were invited to seats with us.

9. Appointed the following committees: On Arrangements—Brothers Jas. Ragan, J. P. Easterly, Elvin Weaver. On Preaching—Brother Wm. Brantley, V. Meyers, R. H. Ball, V. L. Robey, Wm. Adkins, Jackson Boruff, Mc. Keck, J. P. Easterly, together with the church. On correspondence—Elders J. D. Monroe, Leonard White and Brother H. L. Alston. On Requests—Brothers La-Fayette Ellison, V. Meyers, David Warwick, J. P. Easterly, P. F. Keck. On Finances—Brothers A. H. Shaffner, R. H. Ball.

10. On motion, adjourned until tomorrow morning at 9 o'clock.

SATURDAY'S PROCEEDINGS

1. The Association met pursuant to adjournment.

2. Praise and prayer by Elders M. B. Weaver and Leonard White.

3. On motion, called for reports of committees, which were read and approved as follows:

We, your Committee on Arrangements, beg leave to submit the following order of business:

1st   Call the roll.

2nd On Preaching.

3rd On Correspondence.

4th On Requests.

5th On Finances.

6th When and where shall our next Association be?

7th Who shall preach the Introductory Sermon and who shall be his alternate?

8th How many copies of Minutes and who shall superinterd the printing and distribution of same.

Respectfully submitted,

JAS. RAGAN.
J. P. EASTERLY.
ELVIN WEAVER.

3. Called the roll and erased the names of absentees.

4. We, your Committee on Preaching beg leave to submit the following report:

1st FRIDAY NIGHT—At the church, 6 p. m.—Elders J. D. Monroe, Leonard White, J. M. Drummond.
2nd Mt. Eager—Elder John Webb and Brother A. H. Shaffner.
3rd Wood Dale—Elder M. B. Weaver, A. J. Boruff.
4th Long Bottom—Elder John Hammock, Brother H. L. Alston.
5th SATURDAY—At the Stand—Elders Jno. Webb, J. D. Monroe, Leonard White.
6th SATURDAY NIGHT—At the Church—Elders M. B. Weaver. J. M. Drummond and Brother H. L. Alston.
7th Wood Dale—Brother H.L. Alston and Elders Alfred Boruff, A. J. Boruff.
8th Mt. Eager—Elder Jno. Hammock.
9th Long Bottom—Elder Leonard White, Brother A.H.Shaffner.
10th Hickory Valley—Elder J. D. Monroe. Brother W. R. Petre.
11th Liberty Hill—Elder John Webb, Brother A. H. Shaffner.
12th SUNDAY—At the Stand—Elders J. M. Drummond, A. Boruff, J. D. Monroe, Moderator to close.

Respectfully submitted,

WM. BRANTLEY.
R. H. BALL.
V. MEYERS.
J. P. EASTERLY.
V. L. ROBEY.
WM. ADKINS.
JACKSON BORUFF.
MC. KECK.

5. Whereas, Elder Leonard White was chosen to go to the stand, Brother J. P. Easterly was chosen to fill his place as Assistant Clerk.

6. We, your Committee on Correspondence, beg leave to submit the following: That we send Minutes to the Hiwasse Association.

Respectfully submitted,

J. D. MONROE.
LEONARD WHITE.
H. L. ALSTON.

7. We, your Committee on Requests, beg leave to submit the following report:

1st   That we publish in our Minutes the obituaries of these, our well beloved brothers and sisters, whose names appear below: Willis White, Thomas White, Martha Petre, Elizabeth Weaver, Emma Allen, Della Bridges.

2nd   That our next Association be held with the church at Noeton, Grainger county, Tenn.

3rd   Elder Leonard White to preach the Introductory Sermon, and Elder J. M. Drummonds be his alternate.

Respectfully submitted,

J. P. EASTERLY.
V. MEYERS.
P. F. KECK.
LaFAYETTE ELLISON.
W. D. WARWICK.

8.   We, your Committee on Finances, beg leave to submit the following: Received from churches $14.50; being seventy-five cents left in the hands of the Clerk on Minutes last year, making a total of $15.25.   Respectfully submitted,

A. H. SHAFFNER.
R. H. BALL.

9. All the foregoing reports received and committees discharged.

10. On motion, our next Association will be held with the church at Noeton, Grainger county, Tenn., which will convene on Friday before the 3rd Saturday, in August, 1912, one and a half mile from Noeton station.

11. Elder Leonard White to preach the Introductory Sermon and Elder J. M. Drummonds be his alternate.

12. That we have five hundred copies of our Minutes printed, and that the Clerk superintend the printing and distribution of the same, and that he be allowed four dollars for his services.

13. Be it Resolved, That we tender our heart felt thanks to this dear old church and good community for their hospitality and kind treatment during our stay with them through this Association.

14. Minutes read and adopted.

15. Then adjouned to meet as above stated.

ELDER M. B. WEAVER, MODERATOR,

W. A. DRUMMONDS, CLERK,   R.F.D. 1, Lost Creek, Tenn.
R.F.D. 3, New Tazewell, Tenn

SUNDAY

A large and well attentive audience assembled at the Stand and listened so well and attentively to the good and well delivered sermons by Elders J. M. Drummonds, from James 1st chapter, 27th verse: "Pure religion and undefiled before God and the Father is this to visit the fatherless and widows in their affliction and to keep himself unspotted from the world," and Alfred Boruff and J. D. Monroe, and closing remarkes by the Moderator, all of which was well and attentively listened to. At the close of the services a most extraordinary interest was manifest by the sheding of tears, shaking of hands and invoking the blessings of God upon each other.

CLERK.

Obituaries

Of our beloved ones at Mossy Spring church, with sadness and sorrow we record the names and dates of births and deaths of these, our well beloved brothers and sisters:

1. Willis White, son of Elzie White and wife. He was a model young christian. Born Aug. 20, 1890. Joined the church in 1906, and died February 20, 1911.

2. Thomas White, husband of Eliza White, was born Nov. 19, 1876. Joined the church in 1906, and died October 22, 1910. Leaves a wife and six dear children to mourn the loss of a companion and dear father.

3. Martha Petre, wife of J. W. Petre, was born Jan. 7, 1865; professed a hope in Christ and joined the church in 1885. Died March 22, 1910. Leaves a husband and three children to mourn her loss.

4. Elizabeth Weaver, wife of Gordon Weaver, was born Nov. 2, 1846, died May 25, 1911. Leaves a husband and three children to mourn her loss.

6. Emma Allen, wife of Charley Allen, daughter of Daniel White and Tobitha White, was born Nov. 19, 1890, died June 3, 1911.

6. Della Bridges, daughter of Thomas Bridges and wife, was born Aug. 18, 1890, and died July 23, 1910. Della was a warm hearted young christian. She leaves a father, mother, one brother and two sisters to mourn her loss.

These all died in full confidence of God and Heaven. Their piety and cheerfulness will be missed among us—their places in the church can hardly be filled by others. They are our lovely brothers and sisters, but we must say good bye, we hope to greet you in Heaven. We extend to the bereaved ones our love and heart felt sympathy in their bereaved state in love.

ELDER M. B. WEAVER,
ELDER LEONARD WHITE,
Committee.

TABLE OF STATISTCS

CHURCHES	NAMES OF DELEGATES	Received by Baptism	Received by Letter	Received by Relation	Restored	Dismissed by Letter	Excluded	Deceased	Total	Saturday Meeting	Contributions
Big Barren	No letter, no delegates								4	3	$
Black Fox	Samuel Davis, Samuel Capps, C. M. Cabbage, Wm. Posy	11		1	2	1		1	56	3	1 00
Cave Spring	Mat Dosset, LaFayette Ellison, Jas. Lynch, W. H. Brantley					1	7		114	3	1 50
Cedar Spring	Elder J. M. Drummonds, J. W. and H. L. Alston, W. A. Drummonds, Vincent Meyers, S. W. and T. J. Drummonds, R. W. Poor, Charley Alston	3							69	4	1 50
Gibson Station	Elder Jno. Webb, A. H. Shaffner, R. H. Ball			1				2	39	1	1 25
Hamilton Grove	W. D. Warwick, V. L. Robey, J. W. Robey					2			63	4	1 30
Mossy Spring	Elders M. B. Weaver, Leonard White and G. J. Boruff, Theodore Brantley, Elvin Weaver, C. B. and Asoro Weaver, W. R. Cadle, Charley Cadle	9		2	1			4	169	2	2 60
Noeton	Wm. Adkins, John Hayes	1			1			1	33	3	75
Oak Grove	Elder J. D. Monroe, and W. R. Petre, Isaac Shaffner	8							89	1	2 00
Pleasant Point	David Biden, Gilbert Miracle, P. F. Keck Mc. Keck	8						2	60	2	1 75
Pleasant Hill	J. P. Easterly	5	1						26	4	75

MINISTER ROLL

ELDERS	POSTOFFICE	STATE
Alfred Boruff	R. F. D. No. 23, Liberty Hill	Tenn.
A. J. Boruff	R. F. D. No. 15. Washburn	Tenn.
Eli Branson	Yenda	Kan.
M. B. Weaver	R. F. D. No. 1, Lost Creek	Tenn.
J. M. Drummonds	Manring	Tenn.
J. D. Monroe	Goin	Tenn.
Leonard White	R. F. D. No. 2, Sharps Chapel	Tenn.
Mike Hensley	Gibson Station	Va.
John Hammock	Washburn	Tenn.
John Webb	Gibson Station	Va.
Calvin Collins	R. F. D No. 1, Noetou	Tenn.
A. Shelton	Tate	Tenn.
LICENTIATES		
H. L. Alston	R. F. D. No. 1, Tazewell	Tenn.
W. R. Petre	Goin	Tenn.
C. B. Weaver	R. F. D. No. 2, Sharps Chapel	Tenn.
Elvin Weaver	R. F. D. No 2, Sharps Chapel	Tenn.
William Adkins	Tate	Tenn.
A. H. Shaffner	Gibson Station	Va.

CHURCHES	CLERKS	POSTOFFICE	STATE
Big Barren	Mack Edwards	Goin	Tenn.
Black Fox	Jas. Ragan	Liberty Hill	Tenn.
Cave Spring	W. H. Brantley	Sharps Chapel	Tenn.
Cedar Spring	W. A. Drummonds	New Tazewell, R. F. D. No. 3	Tenn.
Gibson Station	G. W. Bryant	Gibson Station	Va.
Hamilton Grove	J. W. Robey	Maynardville	Tenn.
Mossy Spring	Elzie White	Sharps Chapel, R. F. D. No. 2	Tenn.
Noeton	J. L. Oliver	Noeton	Tenn.
Oak Grove	David White	Sharps Chapel, R. F. D. No. 4	Tenn.
Pleasent Point	P. F. Keck	Goin	Tenn.
Pleasant Hill	J. P. Easterly	Speedwell	Tenn.

MINUTES

—— OF THE ——

Ninety-third Annual Session

—— OF THE ——

Powell's Valley Association

—— OF ——

Primitive Baptists

HELD WITH THE CHURCH AT

Noeton, Grainger County, Tenn.

Aug. 16, 17, 18, 1912

MINUTES

Of the Ninety-Third Annual Session of the Powell's Valley Association of Primitive Baptists Held With the Church at Noeton, Grainger County, Tenn., August 16, 17, 18, 1912.

1. Praise and prayer by Elder M. B. Weaver.

2. Introductory sermon by Elder J. M. Drummonds from 1st Peter, 1st chapter, 1st and 2nd verses:

> 1 Peter, an apostle of Jesus Christ, to the strangers scattered throughout Pountus, Galatia, Cappidocia, Asia and Bithynia.
>
> 2 Elect according to the foreknowledge of God, the Father through sanctification of the spirit unto obedience and sprinkling of the blood of Jesus Christ, grace unto you and peace be multiplied.

3. The Association was called to order by the Moderator, Elder M. B. Weaver.

4. Called for letters from churches, ten received and read by the Clerk and Bro. James Ragan and messengers' names enrolled.

5. On motion Elder M. B. Weaver was re-elected moderator and W. A. Drummonds re-elected clerk.

6. Elder Alfred Boruff was elected assistant M. D. and Samuel Davis assistant clerk.

7. Called for petitionery letters and received Straight Branch letter which was read and received and delegates were invited to seats with us.

8. Called for correspondence.

9. Ministers and brethren invited to seats who were not delegates and Sister S. A. Bridges came forward and was welcomed to a seat with us.

10. Invited visitors to seats with us and Elder I. L. Ogle, Brother Jasper Webb and A. B. Morgan, Nolley Chuckey Association, came forward and were welcomed to seats among us.

11. Appointed the following committees:

A. On Arrangements: Elder Thomas Pierce, Bros. W. D. Warwick and Elvin Weaver.

B. On Preaching: Bros. Horace White, J. W. Alston, G. R. Southern, C. M. Cabbage, Gilbert Miracle, W. H. Brantly, James Taylor, together with the church.

C. On Correspondence: Elders J. D. Monroe and Alfred Boruff

and Bro. James Ragan.

D.   On Requests: Elders J. A. Webb, A. J. Boruff and Bro. J. L. Mincy.

E.   On Finances: Bros. J. F. Oliver, C. E. Bridges.

12.   On motion adjourned until to-morrow morning at 9 o'clock.

Saturday Proceedings

1.   The Association met pursuant to adjournment.

2.   Praise and prayer by Elder Thomas Pierce.

3.   On motion called for reports of committees, which were read and approved as follows:

A.   We, your Committee on Arrangements, beg leave to submit the following order of business, viz:

1.   Call the roll.

2.   On Preaching.

3.   On Correspondence.

4.   On Requests.

5.   On Finances.

6.   When and where shall our next Association be held?

7.   Who shall preach the introductory sermon and who shall be his alternate?

8.   How many copies of minutes and who shall superintend the printing and distribution of same?

Respectfully submitted

ELDER THOMAS PIERCE
ELVIN WEAVER
W. D. WARWICK

9.   Called the roll and erased the names of absentees.

B.   We, your Committee on preaching, beg leave to submit the following report:

1.   Saturday at the stand Elders J. D. Monroe, Thomas Pierce and I. L. Ogle, of Nolley Chuckey Association, moderator to close.

2.   Saturday night at the church—Elders J. A. Webb, A. J. Boruff, M. B. Weaver.

3.   Sunday at the stand—Elders I. L. Ogle, J. D. Monroe, Thomas Pierce, moderator to close.

Respectfully submitted,

HORACE WHITE   GILBERT MIRACLE
J. W. ALSTON   W. H. BRANTLY
G. R. SOUTHERN   JAMES TAYLOR
C. M. CABBAGE   Together with the church.

C. We, your Committee on Correspondence, beg leave to submit the following:

1. That we continue our correspondence with the Hiwasse Association by letter and the following named messengers, viz: Elders A. J. Boruff and Alfred Boruff. And that we send a letter with the following named messengers to the Nolley Chuckey Association, viz: Elders M. B. Weaver, J. D. Monroe, Thomas Pierce and Bros. C. M. Cabbage, Jas. Ragan. Whereas there has been a division in said Association we instruct our messengers to ascertain said causes and if said Association is found to be orthordox standing on the old original principles contending for bible principles, we solicit a continual correspondence with them.

Respectfully submitted,

ELDER J. D. MONROE
ELDER ALFRED BORUFF
BROTHER JAS. RAGAN

D. We, your Committee on Request, beg leave to submit the following report:

1. That we publish in our minutes the obituaries of these, our well beloved Brothers and Sisters, whose names appear below: Black Fox, Sister Clory Suffrage; Cedar Springs, Sister Elverenia Earl; Hamilton Grove, Brother John Keller, Sisters Oney Cheek and Mary E. Butcher; Mossy Springs, Sisters Summer E. Petree and Elvina Daniel.

2. That our next Association be held with the church at Cedar Springs, Claiborne county, Tennessee.

3. We recommend that the Association has no jurisdiction over the case of Elder M. C. Hensley.

Respectfully submitted,

ELDER A. J. BORUFF
ELDER J. A. WEBB
BROTHER J. L. MINCEY

E. We, your Committee on Finances, beg leave to submit the following: Received from churches $16.00. Being 92 cents left in the hands of the clerk last year, and received by the clerk $1.25 from Gibson Station church before minutes were printed, making a total of $18.17.

Respectfully submitted,

J. F. OLIVER
C. E. BRIDGES

10. All the foregoing reports received and committees discharged.

11. On motion Bro. Jas. Ragan writes a letter to the Hiwasse Association and Bro. Elvin Weaver writes to the Nolley Chuckey Association.

12. On motion Elder M. B. Weaver writes a circular letter to these Associations and have it prepared for print by the next meeting of the Association.

13. On motion our next Association will be held with the church at Cedar Spring, Claiborne county, Tennessee, two miles west of Cloud's Switch, beginning on Friday before the 3rd Saturday in August 1913.

14. Elder John A. Webb preaches the introductory sermon and Elder Thomas Pierce will be his alternate.

15. That we have five hundred copies of our minutes printed and that the clerk superintend the printing and distribution of the same and be allowed $5.00 for his services.

16. Be it resolved that we tender our heartfelt thanks and best wishes to this dear old church and good community for their hospitality and kind treatment during our stay among them through this Association.

17. Minutes read and adopted.

18. Adjourned to meet as above stated.

ELDER M. B. WEAVER, Moderator,

W. A. DRUMMONDS, Clerk,   R. F. D. 1, Lost Creek, Tenn.

R. F. D. 3, New Tazewell, Tenn.

OBITUARIES

With sadness and sorrow we record the names and dates of these, our well beloved brothers and sisters, of these, our sister churches, as shown below.

Black Fox.

Sister Clory Suffrage, born July 27, 1844, deceased October 18, 1911. She professed faith in Christ when a young woman and joined the primitive Baptist church at Salem. Age 67 years, 2 months and 20 days. She leaves 7 children to mourn after her.

Cedar Spring

Sister Elverenia Earl, daughter of Anderson and Susian

Drummonds. She professed a hope in Christ when but a youth and joined the church at Cedar Spring in 1876. Deceased April 6, 1912. She leaves a husband, one son and a dear mother, one brother and seven sisters to mourn her loss.

Hamilton Grove.

Brother John Keller was born April 4, 1827, deceased March 12, 1912. He professed faith in Christ and joined the church in his early days. He leaves a devoted wife and six children to mourn his absence.

Sister Oney Cheek joined the Primitive Baptist church at Hamilton Grove February the 1st Saturday, 1898 when quite young. Deceased September 4, 1911, age 17 years and 3 months. She leaves a husband, one child, a father and mother, 3 brothers and 4 sisters to mourn her departure.

Sister Mary E. Butcher was borned April 18, 1867. Died November 25, 1911. She joined the church at Hamilton Grove about 22 years ago. She leaves a dear husband and five lovely children to grieve after her.

Mossy Spring

Sister Summer E. Petree, wife of J. W. Petree. She was born May 24, 1877. Professed a hope in Christ and joined the church May 1894. Died November 5, 1911. She leaves a devoted husband and three children to mourn the loss of a dear companion and a tender mother.

Sister Elvina Daniel, wife of Frazier Daniel. She was born June 22, 1880. Professed a hope in Christ and joined the church in 1895. Deceased May 1912. She leaves a dear husband and eight children to mourn the loss of a dear companion and a kind tender mother.

They all died in full confidence of heaven. Their piety and cheerfulness will be missed among us. Their places can hardly be filled by others. They are our lovely brothers and sisters but we must say goodby loved ones, till we can greet you in the sweet by and by, where sorrows and trials never come. We extend to the bereaved ones our prayers and heart felt sympathy in their bereaved state.   CLERK.

SUNDAY.

A large and respectful audience assembled at the stand and

so well and attentively listened to the well delivered sermons by Elders I. L. Ogle from Genesis 49th chapter and 10th verse: "The sceptre shall not depart from Judah nor a law-giver from between his feet until Shiloh come; and unto him shall the gathering of the people be," Elder J. D. Monroe and closing remarks by our dear Moderator, all of which was well and attentively listened to and at the close of the services a most loving parting was expressed by the shaking of hands and the shedding of tears and invoking the blessings of God upon each other.

THE CLERK.

TABLE OF STATISTICS

CHURCHES	NAMES OF DELEGATES	Received by Baptism	Received by Letter	Received by Relation	Restored	Dismissed by Letter	Excluded	Deceased	Total	Saturday Meeting	Contributions
Big Barren	Not represented. Come on.								44	2	$ —
Black Fox	Elders A. J. Boruff, A. Boruff and Brothers C. M. Cabbage, Samuel Davis, Jas. Ragan, J. L. Mincey	9				2			63	4	1 20
Cave Spring	W. H. Brantly								114	3	1 60
Cedar Spring	Elder J. M. Drummonds, W. A. Drummonds, J. W. Alston	9	2	1		1		1	83	4	2 00
Gibson Station	Elder John Webb, G. R. Southern	3				2		2	44	1	1 25
Hamilton Grove	Brother W. D. Warwick					2		3	62	4	1 75
Mossy Spring	Elder M. B. Weaver and Bros. Elvin Weaver, C. E. Bridges, Horace White, Osra Weaver	5		1			1	3	165	2	2 55
Noeton	John Hayes, Reuben Collins	1	1				1		33	3	1 00
Oak Grove	Elder J. D. Monroe	12							98	1	2 25
Pleasant Point	Gilbert Miracle	1						2	65	2	1 50
Pleasant Hill	Priar Lambert	5		1				3	31	4	1 00
Straight Branch	Elder Thomas Pierce, Jas. Taylor, Jno. Ausmus	7				2		2	22	4	1 15

ELDERS	POST OFFICE	STATE
Alfred Boruff	Liberty Hill, R. F. D. 23	Tenn.
A. J. Boruff	Washburn R. F. D. 15	Tenn.
Eli M. Bronson	Yenda	Kans.
J. M. Drummonds	Manring	Tenn.
M. B. Weaver	Lost Creek, R. F. D. 1	Tenn.
J. D. Monroe	Goin	Tenn.
Leonard White	Sharps Chapel, R. F. D. 2	Tenn.
John A. Webb	Gibson Station	Va.
Calvin Collins	Noeton, R. F, D. 1	Tenn.
A. Shelton	Tate	Tenn.
Thomas Pierce	Speedwell, R. F. D. 3	Tenn.
James Ausmus	Speedwell, R. F. D. 3	Tenn.

LICENTIATES

H. L. Alston	R. F. D. No. 1, Tazewell	Tenn.
W. R. Petre	Goin	Tenn.
C. B. Weaver	R. F. D. No. 2, Sharps Chapel	Tenn.
Elvin Weaver	R. F. D. No. 2, Sharps Chapel	Tenn.
William Adkins	Tate	Tenn.
A. H. Shaffner	Gibson Station	Va.

CHURCHES	CLERKS	POSTOFFICE	STATE
Big Barren	Mack Edwards	Goin	Tenn.
Black Fox	James Ragan	Maynardsville	Tenn.
Cave Spring	W. H. Brantley	Sharps Chapel	Tenn.
Cedar Spring	W. A. Drummonds	New Tazewell, No. 3	Tenn.
Gibson Station	S. S. Wilson	Gibson Station	Va.
Hamilton Grove	J. W. Raley	Maynardsville	Tenn.
Mossy Spring	Elzia White	Sharps Chapel, R. 2	Tenn.
Noeton	J. L. Oliver	Noeton	Tenn.
Oak Grove	David White	Sharps Chapel, 4	Tenn.
Pleasant Point	P. F. Keck	Goin	Tenn.
Pleasant Hill	J. A. Hunter	Speedwell	Tenn.
Straight Branch	J. P. Taylor	Speedwell	Tenn.

MINUTES

——OF THE——

Ninety-fourth Annual Session

——OF THE——

Powell's Valley Association

Light of

The World

——OF——

Primitive Baptists

HELD WITH THE CHURCH AT

Cedar Springs, Claiborne County, Tenn.

Aug. 15, 16, 17, 1913

MINUTES

Of the Ninety-fourth Annual Session of the Powells Valley Association of Primitive Baptists, Held with the Church at Cedar Spring, Claiborne County, Tenn., August 15, 16 and 17, 1913.

1. Praise by Elder Thomas Pierce. Prayer by Elder J. M. Drummonds.

2. Introductory Sermon by Elder John Webb from St. John, 1st chapter, 1st and 2nd verses:

> 1 In the beginning was the Word, and the Word was with God, and the Word was God:
>
> 2 The same was in the beginning with God.

3. The Association was called to order by the Moderator, Elder M. B. Weaver.

4. Called for letters from churches; 11 received and read by the Clerk and Bro. Jas. Ragan and Messengers' names enrolled.

5. On motion Elder M. B. Weaver was re-elected Moderator and W. A. Drummonds re-elected Clerk.

6. On motion Elder Thomas Pierce was elected Assistant Moderator and Samuel Davis Assistant Clerk.

7. Called for petitionery letters and received a letter from Mossy Creek church by Elder M. B. Weaver, which was received.

8. Called for correspondence and received a letter and minutes from Nolley Chucky Association by the hands of her delegate, Elder I. L Ogle, who was welcomed to a seat among us.

9. Ministers and brethren invited to seats who were not delegates.

10. Invited visitors to seats.

11. Appointed the following committees:

    (a) On Arrangements—Brothers Jas. Ragan, Elvin Weaver.

    (b) On Preaching—Mack Edwards, C. M. Cabbage, W. S. Collins, Frank Hamilton, C. B. Weaver, P. F. Keck, J. L Harrel, J. H. Smith, Matthew

Oliver, together with the church.

 (c) On Correspondence—Elder J. D. Monroe, Bro. Jas. Ragan.

 (d) On Requests—Elder Leonard White, Bro. J. L. Harrel.

 (e) On Finances—Bros. J. R. Southern, Samuel Capps.

12. On motion called for circular letter written by Elder M. B. Weaver last year, which was read and by request of Elder M. B. Weaver, a committee was appointed to investigate the same— Elders Leonard White, I. L. Ogle J. D. Monroe.

13. On motion adjourned until tomorrow morning 9 o'clock.

Saturday's Proceedings.

1. The Association met pursuant to adjournment.

2. Praise by Elder Thomas Pierce. Prayer by Elder A. J. Boruff.

3. On motion called for reports of committees, which was read and approved as follows:

 (a) We, your Committee on Arrangements, beg leave to submit the following Order of Business:

  1. Call the roll.

  2. On Preaching.

  3. On Correspondence.

  4. On Requests.

  5. On Finances.

  6. When and where shall our next Association be?

  7. Who shall preach the Introductory Sermon and who shall be his alternate?

  8. How many copies of minutes and who shall superintend the printing and distribution of same?

   Respectfully submitted,

     BROTHERS JAS. RAGAN
     ELVIN WEAVER.

9. Call the roll and erase the names of absentees.

 (b) We your Committee on Preaching, beg lieve to submit the following report:

1. At the stand Friday Elders Thomas Pierce, James Aus-

mus; at night at the church Elders Leonard White, Thos. Pierce; at Lilly Grove Elders I. L. Ogle, J. A. Webb; at Pleasant Hill Elders M. B. Weaver, Dock Sutton, Bro. H. A. Shaffner; Cedar Spring Elders J. A. Boruff. James Ausmus. J. M. Drummonds; Saturday at the stand Elders Leonard White, I. L. Ogle; at night at the church Elders I. L. Ogle, J. M. Drummonds, A. J. Boruff; Cedar Spring Elders J. A. Webb, Dock Sutton; Lilly Grove Elders M. B. Weaver, James Ausmus, Thomas Pierce; Pleasant Hill Elders Leonard White, Matthew Oliver; Sunday at the stand Elders I. L. Ogle, Thomas Pierce, J. D. Monroe; Moderator to close.

Respectfully submitted.

MATTHEW OLIVER	C. M. CABBAGE
J. L. HARRELL	BRADFORD WEAVER
W. S. COLLINS	FRANK HAMILTON
P. F. KECK	Together with the
J. H. SMITH	Church.

(c)   We, your Committee on Correspondence, beg leave to submit the following:

1.   Inasmuch as we are in correspondence with Nolley Chuckey Association, which seems to be for the upbuiling and mutual benefit of each other, we fully appreciate the same and recommend that we continue our correspondence by sending messengers and minutes to the same.

2.   We further recommend a continuance of our correspondence with the Hiwassee Association by messengers and minutes.

Respectfully submitted,

BROTHER JAS. RAGAN

ELDER J. D. MONROE.

(d)   We, your Committee on Requests, beg leave to submit the following:

1.   We recommend that the Association send an investigation committee to the newly constituted church at Mossy Creek at once in order that they may have an opportunity to letter to our next Association.

2.   We also recommend that our next Association be held with the church at Pleasant Point, Claiborne county, Tenn.

Respectfully submitted.

ELDER LEONARD WHITE

BROTHER J. L. HARRELL.

(e) We, your Committee on Finances, report as follows: Received from churches $19.85; being $2.12 left in the hands of the Clerk last year, making a total of $21.97.

Respectfully submitted.

BROTHERS G. S. SOUTHERN

SAMUEL CAPPS.

We, your committee appointed to investigate the circular letter written by Elder M. B. Weaver, on examination of same, find it sound in the faith.   We therefore recommend that the Association adopt same.

Respectfully submitted.

ELDER LEONARD WHITE

ELDER I. L. OGLE

ELDER J. D. MONROE.

10.   On motion circular letter received.

11.   All the forgoing reports received and committees discharged.

12.   On motion that we send Elders J. D. Monroe, James Ausmus and Bro. Samuel Davis to the church at Mossy Creek   as committeemen.

13.   On motion that we appoint Elders M. B. Weaver, J. A. Webb and Bro. W. A. Drummonds as delegates to the Hiwassee Association.

14.   On motion we appoint Elders J. D Monroe, C. M. Cabbage, Jas. Ragan as delegates to the Nolley Chucky Association.

15.   On motion that our next Association be held with the church at Pleasant Point, Claiborne county, Tenn., five miles west of Clouds Switch, beginning on Friday before the third Saturday in August, 1914.

16.   Elder Thomas Pierce preach the introductory sermon and Elder Leonard White be his alternate.

17.   That we have 600 copies of our minutes printed and that the Clerk superintend the printing and distribution of the same and be allowed $7.00 for his services.

18.   Be it Resolved, That we tender our heartfelt thanks and best wishes to this dear old church and good community for their hospitali y and kind treatment during our stay among them through this Association.

19.   Minutes read and adopted.

20.   Adjourned to meet as above stated.

ELDER M. B. WEAVER, MODERATOR.

R. F. D. #1, Lost Creek, Tenn.

W. A. DRUMMONDS, CLERK.

R. F. D. #3, box 46, New Tazewell, Tenn.

Circular Letter.

By Elder M. B. Weaver.

According to previous appointment made nearly twelve months ago by this (the Powells Valley) Association, I now make the attempt to prepare a circular letter to be inserted in the minutes of 1913, God being my helper to do so.

Believing that the following Scripture would be a very appropriate one for a foundation, I will now make the quotation:

> 2nd Tim. 3:16—All Scripture is given by inspiration of God and is profitable for doctrine, for reproof, for correction, for instruction in righteousness, that the man of God may be perfect, thoroughly furnished unto all good works.

Will say to you, my dear precious brethren in the Lord and all who may be concerned, I take great pleasure in citing your minds to the Great Book, the Bible, the contents of which is the precious Word of God, given to us by divine inspiration and is true. It furnished us as the people of God with such instruction as, when heeded, makes us perfect disciples. The church of God needs no other Bible, for all others are false. It gives us all the spiritual instruction concerning the kingdom of God that is necessary from the cradle to the grave. Then, dear kindred, will you please read it that you may know and understand it, and thereby grow in grace and in the knowledge of the truth. It furnishes us with the great doctrine of Salvation by Grace—that is, it is taught in so many words, like this: Rom. 8:2—For the law of the spirit of life in Christ Jesus hath made me free from the law of sin and death. Now if Paul is true in this quotation, all other ways are wrong. He further says it is not of works, lest any man should boast. The text also says For Correction. So we see it is sufficient to try and to be tried by. Then let God be true and every man a liar. The church has gone astray when it has gotten so poor and has set up other rules and passed resolutions and declamations for the government of it, for that would be rather to ignore them or indicate that it is not sufficient, and upon this line the church is forbid to set up new landmarks, but be governed by the old, not what grandpa and Uncle John or others may have set up ten, twenty, fifty or even five hundred years ago, but the way the great Head of the Church has given a long time before. If the church appeals to men or institutions of men for a waybill it will only sever fellowship instead of binding it. But, beloved, let brotherly love continue. Mark them which cause divisions among you. Labor for peace and fellowship among the Zion of our God. Equip yourselves like men. Be strong. Stand upon Bible principles and let nothing move you therefrom. It is true that the disciples of Christ will be persecuted, but it is much better to suffer them and live for God and His great cause than to be backed down by the enemy and the cause suffer. So, little children, love one another is the prayer of

Your little servant in Gospel bonds,

ELDER M. B. WEAVER.

Sunday.

A large and respectful audience assembled at the stand and so well and attentively listened to the well delivered sermon by Elder I. L. Ogle from Matthew the 16th chapter and 18th verse: "And I say also unto thee, that thou art Peter, and upon this rock I will build my church, and the gates of hell shall not prevail against it." Proof text: Ephesians 2nd chapter, 20th verse: "And are built upon the foundation of the apostles and prophets, Jesus Christ himself being the chief corner stone." Elder Thomas Pierce, Elder J. D. Monroe and closing remarks by our dear Moderator, all of which were well and attentively listened to, and at the close of the services-a most loving parting was expressed by the shaking of hands and the shedding of tears and invoking the blessings of God upon each other, with a sad farewell. Live for God and His cause. THE CLERK.

TABLE OF STATISTICS.

CHURCHES	NAMES OF DELEGATES	Received by Baptism	Received by Letter	Received by Relation	Restored	Dismissed by Letter	Excluded	Deceased	Total	Saturday Meeting	Contributions
Big Barren	Not represented. Come on!								44	2	$
Black Fox	Jas. Ragan, C. M. Cabbage, Sam Nicely, Samuel Capps, S. Davis	12			1		1		75	3	1 50
Cave Spring	Charley Gils, Geo. Leach, Maney Brantley	4						2	116	3	2 10
Cedar Spring	Elder J. M. Drummonds, W. A. Drummonds, J. W. & H. L. Alston, T, J. & E. S. Drummonds, Vincent Meyers, D. P. & J. L. Drummonds, Willey Freece, G. B. Drummonds	5							88	4	2 00
Gibson Station	Elder J. A. Webb, H. A. Shaffner, G. R. Southern, W. S. Collins	2	2				1		46	4	1 50
Hamilton Grove	Frank Hamilton, Maney Graves	2	2						65	4	1 50
Mossy Spring	Elders M. B. Weaver, Leonard White, C. B. Weaver, Curtis Weaver, J. A. Boruff, Elvin Weaver, C. E. Bridges,	4		1		3	1		166	2	2 80
Noeton	Matthew Oliver	1			2	1			22	3	1 00
Oak Grove	Elder J. D. Monroe	7			1	4			105	1	2 10
Pleasant Point	Thomas Keck, M. C. Keck, C. R. Cox, S. G. Miracle, David Ridings, P. F. Keck								71	2	2 00
Pleasant Hill	J. L. Harrell	4		1					32	4	1 45
Straight Branch	Elders Thomas Pierce, James Ausmus, Harrison Smith	3		2					33	1	1 25

ELDERS	POST-OFFICE	STATE
Alfred Boruff	Liberty Hill, R. F. D. 23	Tenn.
A. J. Boruff	Washburn, R. F. D. 15	Tenn.
Eli M. Bronson	Zenia	Kans.
J. M. Drummonds	Manring	Tenn.
M. B. Weaver	Lost Creek, R. F. D. 1	Tenn.
J. D. Monroe	Goin	Tenn.
Leonard White	Sharps Chapel, R. F. D. 2	Tenn.
John A. Webb	Gibson Station	Va.
Calvin Collins	Noeton, R. F. D. 1	Tenn.
A. Shelton	Tate	Tenn.
Thomas Pierce	Speedwell, R. F. D. 3	Tenn.
James Ausmus	Speedwell, R. F. D. 3	Tenn.

LICENTIATES		
H. L. Alston	R. F. D. No. 1, Tazewell	Tenn.
W. R. Petre	Clear Fork	Tenn.
C. B. Weaver	R. F. D. No. 2, Sharps Chapel	Tenn.
Elvin Weaver	R. F. D. No. 2, Sharps Chapel	Tenn.
William Adkins	Tate	Tenn.
A. H. Shaffner	Gibson Station	Tenn.

CHURCHES	CLERKS	POSTOFFICE	STATE
Big Barren	Mack Edwards	Goin	Tenn.
Black Fox	Samuel Davis	Maynardsville	Tenn.
Cave Spring	W. H. Brantley	Sharps Chapel	Tenn.
Cedar Spring	W. A. Drummonds	New Tazewell, No. 3	Tenn.
Gibson Station	Lillie Cline	Middlesboro	Ky.
Hamilton Grove	J. W. Raley	Maynardsville	Tenn.
Mossy Spring	Elzia White	Sharps Chapel, R. 2	Tenn.
Noeton	J. L. Oliver	Noeton	Tenn.
Oak Grove	David White	Sharps Chapel, 4	Tenn.
Pleasant Point	P. F. Keck	Goin	Tenn.
Pleasant Hill	J. A. Hunter	Speedwell	Tenn.
Straight Branch	J. P. Taylor	Speedwell	Tenn.

MINUTES

—OF THE—

Ninety-fifth Annual Session

—OF THE—

Powells Valley Association

Light of

The World

—OF—

Primitive Baptists

HELD WITH THE CHURCH AT

Pleasant Point, Claiborne County, Tenn.

August 14, 15, 16, 1914.

THREE STATES PRINT, MIDDLESBORO, KY.

W. A. DRUMMONDS
CLERK

MINUTES

OF THE

Ninety-fifth Annual Session of the Powells Valley Association of Primitive Baptists, Held with the Church at Pleasant Point, Claiborne County, Tenn., Aug. 14th, 15th and 16th, 1914.

1. Praise and prayer by Elder M. B. Weaver.

2. Introductory Sermon by Elder Thomas Pierce from St. John 10th Chapter and 26th and 27th Verses—

> 26 But ye believe not because ye are not of my sheep, as I said unto you.
>
> 27 My sheep hear my voice and I know them and they follow me.

After ten minutes intermission, at the sound of singing the Association met. Praise and prayer by Elder Thomas Pierce.

3. The Association was called to order by the Moderator, Elder M. B. Weaver.

4. On motion, called for letters from churches; 11 received and read by the Clerk and Bro. Sam Davis.

5. On motion, letters received and messengers' names enrolled.

6. On motion, Elder M. B. Weaver was re-elected Moderator and W. A. Drummonds re-elected Clerk.

7. Called for report of committee which was to visit the newly constituted Church at New Hebron last year. Report received and committee discharged.

8. Called for petitionery letters and received a letter from New Hebron Church, Jefferson County, Tenn., by her delegates, Elder Calvin Collins and Bro. Jesse Smith, which was received and messengers were welcomed to seats amongst us.

9. Called for correspondence and received a letter and minutes from the Hiawassee Association by the hands of her delegate, Elder John Abbott, who was welcomed to a seat among us.

10. Ministers and Brethren invited to seats who were not delegates. Brothers Samuel Boruff, George Ragan and W. C. Sutherland came forward and were welcomed to seats among us.

11. Appointed the following Committees:

    (a) On Arrangement—Brothers Elvin Weaver, G. R. Southern, P. F. Keck.

    (b) On Preaching—Bros. Elvin Weaver, V. Meyers, A. D. Buckner, David White, W. C. Sutherland, Jesse Smith, J. H. Smith, Thomas Brantley, J. A. Hunter, W. S. Collins, P. F. Keck, together with the Church.

    (c) On Correspondence— Elders Leonard White, Thomas Pierce.

    (d) On Requests—Elder J. A. Webb, Bros. P. F. Keck, Sam Davis.

    (e) On Finances—Bros. J. F. Houston, Charley Gibbs.

12. On motion, committees received.

13 On motion, adjourned until tomorrow morning at 9 o'clock.

Saturday's Proceedings.

1. The Association met pursuant to adjournment.

2. Praise by Elder M. B. Weaver. Prayer by Elder A. J. Boruff.

3. The Association called to order by the Moderator.

4. On motion, called for reports of committees, which were read and approved as follows:

We, your Committee on Arrangement, beg leave to submit the following order of business, viz:

    1. Call the Roll.

    2. Cn Preaching.

    3. On Correspondence.

    4. On Requests.

    5. On Finances.

    6. When and where shall our next Association be?

    7. Who shall preach the introductory sermon, and who shall be his alternate?

8. How many copies of Minutes, and who shall superintend the printing and distribution of same?

Respectfully submitted,

ELVIN WEAVER
P. F. KECK
W. C. SUTHERLAND.

9. Called the roll and erased the names of absentees.

(b) We, your Committee on Preaching, beg leave to submit the following report: At the church Friday night—Elders John Abbott, J. M. Drummonds; Leatherwood—Elders J. A. Webb, M. B. Weaver; Big Barren—Elder Thomas Pierce, A. J. Boruff, Calvin Collins; Lilly Grove—Elder Leonard White, Bro. W. R. Petree. Saturday at the stand—Elders Calvin Collins, Thomas Pierce, J. H. Abbott; Saturday night at the church —Elders M. B. Weaver, Leonard White; Lilly Grove—Elders J. H. Abbott, Calvin Collins; Leatherwood—Elders J. A. Webb, A. J. Boruff; Barren—Elder Thomas Pierce, Bro. W. R. Petree; Sunday at the stand—Elders John Abbott, J. D. Monroe, the Moderator to close.

Respectfully submitted,

ELVIN WEAVER   VINCENT MEYERS
DAVID WHITE   A. D. BUCKNER
J. H. SMITH   THOMAS BRANTLEY
W. S. COLLINS   J. A. HUNTER
JESSE SMITH   Together with the Church

(c) We, your Committee on Correspondence, beg leave to submit the following: That we continue our correspondence with the following Associations, to-wit: The Hiawassee and the Nolley Chuckey Associations; and we further recommend that this Association send messengers and minutes to the same.

Respectfully submitted,

ELDER THOMAS PIERCE
ELDER LEONARD WHITE

(d) We, your Committee on Requests, beg leave to submit the following: We recommend that the Association print in her minutes all obituaries furnished by the churches.

Respectfully submitted,

J. A. WEBB
J. F. KECK
SAM DAVIS

(e) We, your Committee on Finances, beg leave to submit as follows: Received from churches $17.30
Having left in the hands of the Clerk last year .. 1.63

Making a total of..........................$18.93

Respectfully submitted,

J. F. HOUSTON
CHARLEY GIBBS

10. All the foregoing reports received and committees discharged.

11. On motion, we appoint Elders M. B. Weaver, J. D. Monroe and Bro. Elvin Weaver as Delegates to the Hiawassee Association.

12. On motion we appoint Elders A. J. Boruff, H. L. Alston, Calvin Collins and Bro. James Ragan as Delegates to the Nolley Chuckey Association.

13. That the Clerk write a letter to these Associations and insert it in our Minutes.

14. On motion, our next Association will be held with the Church at New Hebron, two miles west of Jefferson City, beginning on Friday before third Saturday in August, 1915.

15. Elder Leonard White preach the introductory sermon, and Elder J. D. Monroe be his alternate.

16. That we have 600 copies of our Minutes printed and that the Clerk superintend the printing and distribution of the same, and be allowed $7.00 for his services.

17. Be It Resolved, That we tender our heart-felt thanks and best wishes to this dear old Church and good community for their hospitality and kind treatment during our stay among them through this Association.

18. Minutes read and received.

19. Adjourned to meet as above stated.

ELDER M. B. WEAVER, Moderator,

R. F. D. 1, Lost Creek, Tenn.

W. A. DRUMMONDS, Clerk,

R. F. D. 3, Box 46, New Tazewell, Tenn.

Obituaries.

With sadness and sorrow we insert the names and dates of births and deaths of these our well beloved brothers and sisters.

J. W. Alston, an aged brother among us. Not being furnished with any dates, we cannot make this as full as we would like to, but Father Alston was up in 90 years of age at the time of his death. He served his country three years for freedom and Union, then came home and joined in to battle for the Lord and His cause. He joined the Primitive Baptist Church at Cedar Springs December, 1886; deceased in January, 1914, if not mistaken. He was a faithful member and always filled his seat unless providentially hindered.

Jemima McPhetridge was born December, 1832; professed faith in Christ in her 30th year; joined the Primitive Baptist Church at Dotsons Creek about five years later. She lived a consistent member till her death, which occurred June 24, 1914.

Lillie Harmon, wife of Charley Harmon, the only danghter of Sister Cora White was born June 5, 1894; joined the Primitive Baptist Church at Mossy Spring December, 1907; baptized the following June, and deceased January 1, 1914.

They all died with strong faith in God and in the hope of going home to Heaven. Their piety and cheerfullness will be missed among us and their places can hardly be filled. While they leave many dear ones and relatives to mourn after them, while they have gone to their long Soul Home, we can only say to the bereaved ones you have our prayers and best wishes.

THE CLERK.

Corresponding Letter.

August 14th, 15th and 16th, 1914.

We, the Powells Valley Association of Primitive Baptists, now in session with the Church at Pleasant Point, Claiborne County, Tennesssee, To our sister Associations, Greetings of Love, with whom we correspond, to-wit: The Hiawassee and Nolley Chuckey Associations:—

Dear Brethren: We are having a pleasant season. Love, peace and union seem to obtain among us. We desire to keep up our Christian correspondence with you, and hope to receive your letter and messengers at our next Association which will be held with the Church at New Hebron, Jefferson County, Tennessee, two miles west of Jefferson City, beginning Friday before the 3rd Saturday in August, 1915. We have chosen these our beloved brethren to bear this epistle of love to you: Elders M. B. Weaver, J. D. Monroe and Bro. Elvin Weaver to the Hiawassee and Elders J. A. Boruff, H. L. Alston, Calvin Collins and Bro. Jas. Ragan to the Nolley Chuckey. Our total membership is 878. Dear Brethren, pray for us, that love, peace and union may still abound among us. We remain,

Yours in Christ,

ELDER M. B. WEAVER, M. D.

P. O. Lost Creek, R. D. 1, Tenn.

W. A. DRUMMONDS, Clerk,

P. O. New Tazewell, R. D. 3, Box 46, Tenn.

Sunday.

A large and well-behaved and respectful audience assembled at the stand and so well and attentively listened to the well-delivered sermon by Elder John Abbot from St. John 18th Chapter and 36th verse—My kingdom is not of this world,—Elder J. D. Monroe and closing remarks by our dear Moderator, all of which were well and attentively listened to and at the close of the services, a most loving parting was expressed by the shaking of hands and the shedding of tears and invoking the blessings of God upon each other, and it was a touching scene to see the old ministers embracing each other in their loving arms. With a sad farewell—Live for God and His cause.

THE CLERK.

TABLE OF STATISTICS

CHURCHES	NAMES OF DELEGATES	Rec'd by baptism	Rec'd by Letter	Rec'd by Relation	Restored	Dismissed by Let.	Excluded	Deceased	Total	Saturday Meeting	Contributions
Big Barren	Not represented. Come on!										
Black Fox	Elder A. J. Boruff, Bros. Sam Davis, C. M. Cabbage, Jas. Ragan, Samuel Capps, E. C. Boruff	2							44	2	
Cave Spring	Charley Gibbs, Thomas Brantley							1	76	3	$1 60
Cedar Spring	Elders J. M. Drummonds, W. A. Drummonds, H. L. Alston, G. B. Drummonds, Vincent Meyers, Charley Stanifer, E. S. Drummonds, J. C. Drummonds								116	3	1 60
Gibson Station	Elder J. A. Webb, Bros. G. R. Southern, W. S. Collins	1						1	87	4	2 00
Hamilton Grove	H. F. Hamilton, A. D. Buckner, Troy Hamilton	4		1			1	1	45	1	1 00
Mossey Spring	Elders M. B. Weaver, Leonard White, Bros. Elvin Weaver, Berry White	1						2	64	4	1 50
New Hebron	Elder Calvin Collins, Bro. Jesse Smith	1					4	1	162	2	2 10
Noeton	Not represented. Come on!								15	1	50
Oak Grove	Elder J. D. Monroe, Bros. W. R. Petree, Wm. Shaffner, Taylor Carter, David White								22	3	
Pleasant Point	David Ridings, Thomas Keek, John F. Keek, John Caney, J. D. Keek, C. R. Cox, P. L. Keek	1				1		1	104	1	2 00
									78	2	2 00
Pleasant Hill	J. A. Hunter, Jas. Graves, J. L. Herrell	3						1	35	4	1 50
Straight Branch	Elder Thos. Pierce, Bros. Harrison Smith, Jno. Hunter	2					3	2	30	1	1 50

79

ELDERS	POST-OFFICE	STATE
H. L. Alston	Tazewell	Tenn.
James Ausmus	Speedwell, R. F. D. 3	Tenn.
Alfred Boruff	Liberty Hill, R. F. D. 23	Tenn.
A. J. Boruff	Washburn, R. F. D. 15	Tenn.
Eli M. Bronson	Zenia	Kas.
Calvin Collins	Morristown, R F. D. 4	Tenn.
W. A. Drummonds	New Tazewell, R. F. D. 3	Tenn.
J. M. Drummonds	Manring	Tenn.
J. D. Monroe	Goin	Tenn.
Thomas Pierce	Speedwell, R. F. D. 3	Tenn.
A. Shelton	Tate	Tenn.
M. B. Weaver	Lost Creek, R. F. D. 1	Tenn.
John A. Webb	Gibson Station	Va.
Leonard White	Sharps Chapel, R. F. D. 2	Tenn.

LICENTITIATES

Charley Stanifer	R. F. D. Speedwell	Tenn.
W. R. Petree	Clear Fork	Tenn.
C. B. Weaver	R. F. D. 2, Sharps Chapel	Tenn.
Elvin Weaver	R. F. D. 2, Sharps Chapel	Tenn.
William Adkins	Tate	Tenn.
A. H. Shaffner	Gibson Station	Va.

CHURCHES	CLERKS	POSTOFFICE	STATE
Big Barren	Mack Edwards	Goin	Tenn.
Black Fox	Samuel Davis	Maynardsville, R. 3	Tenn.
Cave Spring	W. H. Brantley	Sharps Chapel	Tenn.
Cedar Spring	W. A. Drummonds	New Tazewell, R. 3	Tenn.
Gibson Station	Lillie Cline	Middlesboro	Ky.
Hamilton Grove	J. W. Raley	Maynardsville, R. 3	Tenn.
Mossy Spring	Elzia White	Sharps Chapel, R. 2	Tenn.
Noeton	J. L. Oliver	Noeton	Tenn.
New Hebron	Jesse Smith	New Market, R 5.	Tenn.
Oak Grove	David White	Sharps Chapel, R. 4	Tenn.
Pleasant Point	P. F. Keck	Goin	Tenn.
Pleasant Hill	J. A. Hunter	Speedwell	Tenn.
Straight Branch	J. P. Taylor	Speedwell	Tenn.

MINUTES

—OF THE—

Ninety-sixth Annual Session

—OF THE—

Powells Valley Association

Light of

The World

—OF—

Primitive Baptists

HELD WITH THE CHURCH AT

New Hebron, Jefferson County, Tenn.

AUGUST 20th, 21st and 22nd, 1915

THREE STATES PRINT, MIDDLESBORO, KY.

MINUTES

OF THE

Ninety-sixth Annual Session of the Powells Valley Association of Primitive Baptists, Held with the Church at New Hebron, Jefferson County, Tenn., Aug. 20, 21, 22, 1915.

1. Praise by Elder Thomas Pierce. Prayer by Elder W. A. Drummonds.

2. Introductory Sermon by Elder John A. Abbott from St. Luke 14th Chapter and 22nd Verse:

> And the servant said, Lord, it is done
> as thou hast commanded.

After ten minutes intermission, at the sound of singing the Association met. Praise by Elder M. B. Weaver. Prayer by Elder Allen Gates.

3. The Association was called to order by the Moderator, Elder M. B. Weaver.

4. On motion, called for letters from churches; 8 received and read by the Clerk and Bros. J. F. Keck and Samuel Davis.

5. On motion, letters and messengers' names enrolled.

6. On motion, Elder Thomas Pierce was elected Moderator and Elder W. A. Drummonds re elected Clerk.

7. Called for petitionery letters. None received.

8. Called for correspondence, and received Minutes from Hiawassee Association by the hands of her delegates, Elder John A. Abbott and D. J. Abbott, who were welcomed to seats among us. And received Minutes from Nolley Chuckey Association by the hand of her delegate, Elder Allen Gates, who was welcomed to a seat among us.

9. Ministers and brethren invited to seats who were not delegates. Bros. Samuel Davis, John F. Keck, J. H. Smith, H. F. Hamilton, Troy Hamilton, came forward and were welcomed to seats among us.

10. Appointed the following committees:
   (a) On Arrangements—Bros. J. F. Keck, Samuel Davis, S. S. Wilson.
   (b) On Preaching—Bros. C. B. Weaver, Marshal Collins, H. F. Hamilton, together with the church.
   (c) On Correspondence—Bros. J. H. Smith, Therney Pierce, J. F. Keck.
   (d) On Requests—Elders Calvin Collins, M. B. Weaver, Bro. W. R. Poore.
   (e) On Finances—Bros. T. L. Hamilton, S. S. Wilson.
11. On motion, committees received.
12. On motion, adjourned until tomorrow morning at 9 o'clock.

Saturday's Proceedings.

---

1. The Association met pursuant to adjournment.
2. Praise by Elder Thomas Pierce; prayer by Bro. C. B. Weaver.
3. The Association called to order by the Moderator.
4. On motion, called for reports of committees, which were read and approved as follows:
   (a) We, your Committee on Arrangement, beg leave to submit the following order of business, viz:
      1. Call the Roll.
      2. On Preaching.
      3. On Correspondence.
      4. On Requests.
      5. On Finances.
      6. When and where shall our next Association be?
      7. Who shall preach the Introductory Sermon, and who shall be his Alternate?
      8. How many copies of Minutes, and who shall superintend the printing and distribution of the same?
         Respectfully submitted,
         J. F. KECK,
         S. S. WILSON,
         SAMUEL DAVIS.
9. Called the rolled and erased the names of absentees.

(b)   We, your Committee on Preaching, beg leave to submit the following report: At the church Friday night— Elders Thomas Pierce, M. B. Weaver; Saturday at the stand— Elders Matthew Oliver, Allen Gates, D. J. Abbott to close; **Saturday** night at the church—Elders Allen Gates, J. A. Abbott; Sunday—Elders M. B. Weaver, John Abbott, Moderator to close.

Respectfully submitted,

C. B. WEAVER,   MARSHALL COLLINS,

H. F. HAMILTON,   Together with the Church.

(c)   We, your Committee on Correspondence, beg leave to submit the following: That we still continue our correspondence with the following Associations, viz: The Hiawassee and the Nolley Chuckey Associations.   We fully appreciate such lovely correspondence, and we further recommend that this Association send messengers and Minutes to the same.

Respectfully submitted,

J. H. SMITH,

THIRNEY PIERCE,

JOHN F. KECK.

(d)   We, your Committee on Requests, beg leave to submit the following report, viz: (a) That we have all the obituaries published in our minutes that the churches furnish. (b) That we announce in our minutes a special meeting for all the Elders and Deacons of this Association to meet together at a place to be designated for the purpose of connecting together on such vital questions of importance for the churches and ministers.   Place selected for said meeting at Mossy Spring, Union county, Tenn., Friday before the second Saturday in November, 1915, and the two following days.

Respectfully submitted,

ELDER M. B. WEAVER,

ELDER CALVIN COLLINS,

BRO. R. W. POORE.

(e)   We, your Committee on Finance, beg leave to submit as follows: Received from churches $12.60.

Respectfully submitted,

S. S. WILSON,

TROY HAMILTON.

10. All the foregoing reports received and committees discharged.

11. On motion, appointed Elders M. B. Weaver, Thomas Pierce messengers to the Hiawassee Association.

12. On motion, appointed Elder W. A. Drummonds and Bro. John F. Keck messengers to the Nolley Chuckey Association.

13. That the Clerk write a letter to the Associations and insert it in our Minutes.

14. On motion, our next Association will be held with the church at Mossy Spring, Union county, Tenn., beginning on Friday before the third Saturday in August, 1916.

15. That Elder M. B. Weaver preach the Introductory Sermon and Elder W. A. Drummonds be his Alternate.

16. That we have 500 copies of our Minutes printed and that the Clerk superintend the printing and distribution of the same, and be allowed $5.00 for his services.

17. Be it resolved, That we tender our heartfelt thanks and best wishes to this beloved church and her good surroundance for their hospitality and kind treatment during our stay among them through this Association.

18. Minutes read and approved.

19. On motion, adjourned to meet as above stated.

ELDER THOMAS PIERCE, Moderator,
Speedwell, Tenn., R. F. D. No. 3.
ELDER W. A. DRUMMONDS, Clerk,
R. F. D. No. 3, Box 63.

Obituaries.

With sadness and sorrow we insert the names and dates of births and deaths of these our well beloved brothers and sisters.

Elder Jacob M. Drummonds, an aged minister of Cedar Spring, was born Aug. 27, 1845, professed faith in Christ and joined the Primitive Baptist church at Pleasant Point in the spring of 1867. He was licensed to exhort in February, 1869; ordained to the full work of the ministry June 3rd Saturday, 1875. He succeeded well and made an able defender of the doctrine of Christ. He was well beloved by all who knew him, but was a sufferer by affliction most of his life; hence the good

Lord said, Well done, thou faithful servant, enter into the joys of thy Lord. He departed this life Feb. 20, 1915. He leaves a dear companion, one son, two daughters, four brothers, one sister, with a host of relatives and friends to mourn his loss

Sister Sibby Abagill Poore was born May 29, 1848. She professed faith in Christ and joined the Primitive Baptist church at Cedar Spring July 2nd Saturday, 1870. She lived a Christian life until her death which occurred March 20, 1915. She leaves a companion, four sons, three daughters and four brothers to mourn the loss of a companion, a tender mother and loving sister.

Sister Emily Case, of Noeton church, was born in 1861; professed faith in Christ in 1876; lived a faithful member, always filling her seat in church; deceased Feb. 2, 1914. She leaves a husband and eight children to mourn her loss.

Sister Louise Adkins, wife of Arch Adkins, joined the Primitive Baptist church in 1870; deceased June 9, 1915. She lived a faithful member, contending for the faith. She leaves a husband and six children to mourn the loss of a loving companion and tender mother.

These all died in the hopes of Eternal Life and have gone home to heaven. Their piety and cheerfulness will be missed among us and their places can hardly be filled, while they leave many dear ones and relatives to mourn after them while they are gone. We can only say to those bereaved ones, You have our prayers and best wishes.   CLERK.

Corresponding Letter.

August 20-21-22, 1915.

We, the Powells Valley Association of Primitive Baptists, now in session with the church at New Hebron, Jefferson county, Tennessee, to our sister Associations, with greetings of love, to whom we correspond, to-wit: The Hiawassee and Nolley Chuckey Associations:

Dear Brethren:—We are having a pleasant season. Love, peace and union seem to abound among us. We desire to keep up our Christian correspondence with you and hope to receive your letters and messengers at our next Association which will be held with the church at Mossy Spring, Union county, Tenn.. beginning Friday before the 3rd Saturday in August, 1916. We have chosen these our well beloved brethren to bear this epistle of love to you, Elders M. B. Weaver and Thomas Pierce to the Hiawassee; Elder W. A. Drummonds and Bro. John F. Keck to the Nolley Chucky. Dear Brethren, pray for us that love, peace and union may still abound among us.

We remain yours in Christ,

ELDER THOMAS PIERCE, M. D.

Speedwell, Tenn., R. F. D. 3.

ELDER W. A. DRUMMONDS, Clerk,

New Tazewell, Tenn., R. F. D. 3, Box 63.

Sunday.

A well behaved and respectful audience assembled at the stand and well and attentively listened to the well delivered sermon by Elder M. B. Weaver from St. Matthew 28th Chapter, 19th and 20th Verses:

19 Go ye, therefore and teach all nations, baptizing them in the name of the Father, and of the Son, and of the Holy Ghost;

20 Teaching them to observe all things whatsoever I have commanded you, and lo! I am with you alway, even unto the end of the world. Amen.

Closing remarks by our dear Moderator, all of which were well and attentively listened to. At the close of the services a most loving parting was expressed. THE CLERK.

TABLE OF STATISTICS

CHURCHES	NAMES OF DELEGATES	Rec'd by baptism	Rec'd by Letter	Rec'd by Relation	Restored	Dismissed by Let.	Excluded	Deceased	Total	Saturday Meeting	Contributions
Big Barren	Not represented. Come on!								43	2	
Black Fox	Bro. Samuel Davis								58	3	$ 75
Cave Spring	Not represented. Come on next year!							2	116	3	1 00
Cedar Spring	Elder W. A. Drummonds, Bro. W. R. Poore	2						2	87	4	2 00
Gibson Station	Bro. S. S. Wilson								48	1	1 50
Hamilton Grove	Bros. Frank Hamilton, Troy Hamilton								64	4	1 50
Mossy Spring	Elder M. B. Weaver, Bro. C. B. Weaver	1					1		162	2	2 25
New Hebron	Bros. Lon Reno. Marshall Collins, Jesse Smith						3	1	12	1	1 00
Noeton	Eld. Matthew Oliver, Bros. Jno. Hayes, W. M. Adkins	3		11					21	3	75
Oak Grove	Not represented. Call next year								100	2	
Pleasant Point	Bro. John F. Keck	5		3					42	4	1 50
Pleasant Hill	Letter but no Delegates								54	1	1 50
Straight Branch	Eld. Thomas Pierce, Bro. J. F. Taylor, Therney Pierce	23								1	35

ELDERS	POST-OFFICE	STATE
H. L. Alston	Tazewell	Tenn.
James Ausmus	Speedwell, R. F. D. 3	Tenn.
Alfred Boruff	Liberty Hill, R. F. D. 23	Tenn.
A. J. Boruff	Washburn, R. F. D. 15	Tenn.
Eli M. Bronson	Zenia	Kas.
Calvin Collins	Morristown, R. F. D. 4	Tenn.
W. A. Drummonds	New Tazewell, R. F. D 3	Tenn.
J. D. Monroe	Goin	Tenn.
Matthew Oliver	Noeton	Tenn.
Thomas Pierce	Speedwell, R. F. D. 3	Tenn.
A. Shelton	Tate	Tenn.
M. B. Weaver	Lost Creek, R. F. D. 1	Tenn.
John A. Webb	Gibson Station	Va.
Leonard White	Sharps Chapel, R. F. D. 2	Tenn.

LICENTIATES

Charley Stanifer	R. F. D., Speedwell	Tenn.
W. R. Petree	Clear Fork	Tenn.
C. B. Weaver	R. F. D. 2, Sharps Chapel	Tenn.
Elvin Weaver	R. F. D. 2, Sharps Chapel	Tenn.
William Adkins	Tate	Tenn.
A. H. Shaffner	Gibson Station	Va.

CHURCHES	CLERKS	POSTOFFICE	STATE
Big Barren	Mack Edwards	Goin	Tenn.
Black Fox	Samuel Davis	Maynardsville, R. 3	Tenn.
Cave Spring	W. H. Brantley	Sharps Chapel	Tenn.
Cedar Spring	W. A. Drummonds	New Tazewell, R. 3	Tenn.
Gibson Station	Lillie Cline	Middlesboro	Ky.
Hamilton Grove	H. F. Hamilton	Maynardsville, R. 5	Tenn.
Mossy Spring	Elzia White	Sharps Chapel, R. 2	Tenn.
Noeton	Sherman Spirse	Noeton	Tenn.
New Hebron	Jesse Smith	New Market, R. 5	Tenn.
Oak Grove	David White	Sharps Chapel, R. 4	Tenn.
Pleasant Point	P. F. Keck	Goin	Tenn.
Pleasant Hill	J. A. Hunter	Speedwell	Tenn.
Straight Branch	J. P. Taylor	Speedwell	Tenn.

MINUTES

—OF THE—

Ninety-seventh Annual Session

—OF THE—

Powells Valley Association

Light
of

The
World

—OF—

Primitive Baptists

HELD WITH THE CHURCH AT

Mossy Spring, Union County, Tenn.

AUGUST 18, 19, 20, 1916.

THREE STATES PRINT, MIDDLESBORO, KY.

MINUTES

OF THE

Ninety-seventh Annual Session of the Powells Valley Association of Primitive Baptists Held With the Church at Mossy Spring, Union County, Tenn., August 18, 19 and 20, 1916.

1. Praise by Elder W. A. Drummonds.   Prayer by Elder J. J. Kirkland.

2. Introductory Sermon by Elder M. B. Weaver from Acts 2nd chapter, 24th verse—

> Whom God hath raised up, having loosed the pains of death, because it was not possible that he should be holden of it.

After ten minutes intermission, at the sound of singing, the Association met.   Praise by Elder Thomas Pierce.   Prayer by W. R. Petree.

3. The Association was called to order by the Moderator, Elder Thomas Pierce.

4. On motion, called for letters from churches.   There were nine received and read by the Clerk and Elder John F. Keck.

5. On motion, letters received and messengers' names enrolled.

6. On motion, Elder Thomas Pierce was re-elected Moderator and Elder W. A. Drummonds re-elected Clerk; John F. Keck Assistant Clerk.

7. Called for petitionery letters.

8. Called for Correspondence and received Elder G. W. Abbott from the Hiawassee Association, who was welcomed to a seat among us.   And received Minutes from the Nolly Chuckey Association.

9. Ministers and brethren invited to seats who were not delegates.   Elder J. J. Kirkland came forward as a visitor and was welcomed to a seat with us.   Brother Frank Hamilton came forward and was welcomed to a seat with us.

10. Appointed the following committees:
   (a) On Arrangement—Elder John F. Keck, Bros. E. S. Drummonds, E. D. Monroe.
   (b) On Preaching—Wm. Taylor, C. M. Cabbage, E. S. Drummonds, Wm. Brantley, Wm. Collins, J. F. Taylor, A. C. Goin, David White.
   (c) On Correspondence—Bros. John Taylor, John Hopper, David White.
   (d) On Requests—Elvin Weaver, Jackson Boruff, John F. Taylor.
   (e) On Finances—Bros. John Welch, J. L. Drummonds.
11. On motion, committees received.
12. On motion, adjourned until tomorrow morning at 9:00 o'clock.

Saturday's Proceedings.

1. The Association met pursuant to adjournment.
2. Praise and prayer by Bro. Wm. Shuffner.
3. The Association called to order by the Moderator.
4. On motion, called for reports of committees which were read and approved as follows:

   (a) We, your Committee on Arrangement, beg leave to submit the following order of business, viz:
   1. Call the roll,
   2. On Preaching.
   3. On Correspondence.
   4. On Requests.
   5. On Finances.
   6. When and where shall our next Association be.
   7. Who shall preach the Introductory Sermon and who shall be his alternate.
   8. How many copies of Minutes and who shall superintend the printing and distribution of the same?

   Respectfully submitted,

   ELDER JOHN F. KECK
   BRO. E. S. DRUMMONDS
   BRO. E. D. MONROE

9. Called the roll and erased the names of absentees.

(b) We, your Committee on Preaching, beg leave to submit the following report: At the church Friday night—Elders J. J. Kirkland, John F. Keck; at the Big Sinks—Elders ,H. A. Shoffner, Thomas Pierce; at Mossy School House—Elder J. D. Monroe and Bro. W. R. Petree; Saturday at the stand—Elders G. W. Abbott. H. A. Shoffner, J. D. Monroe; Saturday night at Braden School House—Elders A. J. Boruff, Thomas Pierce; at the church—Oscar Ausmus, Elder G. W. Abbott; at Big Sinks—Elder John F. Keck, Alford Boruff; Sunday at the stand—Elders J. J. Kirkland, J. D. Monroe, G. W. Abbott, Moderator to close.

Respectfully submitted,

JOHN F. TAYLOR   W. W. TAYLOR
W. S. COLLINS   C. M. CABBAGE
DAVID WHITE   A. C. GOIN
E. S. DRUMMONDS   Together with
WM. BRANTLEY   the Church.

(c) We, your Committee on Correspondence, beg leave to submit the following: That we still continue our long cherished correspondence with the following Associations, viz: the Hiawassee and the Nolley Chuckey Associations.

Respectfully submitted,

J. F. TAYLOR
JOHN HOPPER
DAVID WHITE.

(d) We, your Committee on Requests, beg leave to submit the following report: That we have all obituaries published in our Minutes that the churches furnish.

Respectfully submitted,

ELDER JACKSON BORUFF
ELVIN WEAVER
JOHN TAYLOR.

(e) We, your Committee on Finances, beg leave to submit as follows: Received from churches $16.25.
For Visiting Ministers (from Mossy   1.50.
                                    ——————
                    Total $17.75.
Respectfully submitted,

JOHN WELCH
J. L. DRUMMONDS.

10. All the foregoing reports received and committees discharged.

11. On motion, appointed Elders John F. Keck, J. D. Monroe as Messengers to the Hiawassee Association.

12. On motion, appointed Elders M. B. Weaver, Alford Boruff Messengers to the Nolley Chucky Association.

13. That the Clerk and Elder John F. Keck write a correspondence letter to these Associations.

14. On motion, our next Association will be held with the church at Hamilton Grove, Union county, Tenn., Friday before the third Saturday in August, 1917.

15. Elder W. A. Drummonds preach the Introductory Sermon and Elder John F. Keck be his Alternate.

16. That we have 400 copies of Minutes printed, that the Clerk superintend the printing and distribution of the same, and that he be allowed $7.00 for the same.

17. Be it resolved that we tender our heartfelt thanks and best wishes to this beloved old Church and her good surroundings for their hospitality and kind treatment through this Association.

18. On motion, Minutes approved.

19. On motion, adjourned to meet as above stated.

ELDER THOMAS PIERCE, Moderator,
P. O. Speedwell, Tenn., Rt. 3.

ELDER W. A. DRUMMONDS, Clerk,
P. O. New Tazewell, Tenn., Rt. 3. Box 63.

Obituaries.

With sadness and sorrow we insert the names and dates of the births and deaths of these our well beloved sisters:

Sister Cordelia Hopper, wife of Claud Hopper, was born March 4, 1869; professed faith and joined the Primitive Baptist church at Pleasant Point in early life, and lived a consistant Christian life in the church until her death July 3, 1916. She leaves an aged father, a loving husband and seven children, with a host of friends and loved ones to mourn the absence of a darling wife and a loving mother.

94

Sister Elizabeth Ausmus, aged 77 years, died April 12, 1916; professed faith in Christ and joined the Primitive Baptist church at about 16 years of age. She lived a faithful member until her death.

These are a few lines written by the lovely little daughter of Isaac and Lassie Shoffner Feb. 20, 1910:

"My Dear Friend Martha: If you please keep this letter forever and remember me till I die, and if I die first please come to my burying. I am just writing a speech. Please be baptized before I do die. Please put this in your book at home and say nothing about it. If you want me to tell you what song I want sung over me I will tell you, 'Jesus, Lover of My Soul' and 'God Be With You Till We Meet Again.' I guess that will be all. I will close. Write soon. Your loving one,

"Lillas B. E. Shoffner."

"When ever shall I see you again? Write me soon. What will I do when you go home? Martha, you know Home is where Jesus takes all to Heaven."

Lillas was born Jan. 2, 1901, and wrote this letter at the age of eight years, to her schoolmate, Martha Maples. She died May 9, 1912.

Carmon Farris, niece of T. G. Brantley, was born Sept. 1, 1911, died Nov. 13, 1915. During her sickness she often spoke of the Lord, and said from the beginning of her sickness that she could not get well. She said to her grandma, "I would like to stay with you and sister." While the doctor was waiting on her she said, "You can do nothing for me." While dying she called her mamma and said, "I am dying. I am going home to my God." She then said to her grandma, "I see them!" Her grandma asked, "What do you see?" "I see two of them! Glory! Glory! Glory!"

These are all gone from our midst; their places cannot be filled. With sorrow we pray for the bereaved ones and hope our loss is their eternal gain. CLERK.

Corresponding Letter.

August 18-19-20, 1916.

We, the Powells Valley Association of Primitive Baptists now in session with the church at Mossy Spring, Union county, Tenn., to our Sister Associations with whom we correspond, to-wit, the Hiawassee and Nolley Chuckey Associations:

Dear Brethren: We are having a pleasant season. Love, peace and union seem to abound among us. We desire to keep up our Christian correspondence with you, and hope to receive your letters and messengers at our next Association which will be held at Hamilton Grove, Union county, Tenn., and convene Friday before the third Saturday in August 1917. We have chosen these our brethren to bear this epistle of love to you, viz: Elders J. F. Keck and J. D. Monroe to the Hiawassee; Elders M. B. Weaver and Alford Boruff to the Nolley Chuckey. Dear Brethren, pray for us that love, peace and union may still abound throughout God's people. We remain,

Yours in Christ,

ELDER THOMAS PIERCE, M. D.

Speedwell, Tenn., Rt. 3.

ELDER W. A. DRUMMONDS, Clerk,

New Tazewell, Tenn., Rt. 3.

Sunday.

A well behaved audience assembled at the stand and well and attentively listened to the well delivered sermon by Elder J. J. Kirkland from Acts 8 chapter, verse 35—

Then Philip opened his mouth and began at the same Scripture and preached unto him Jesus.

and followed by Elder G. W. Abbott, which was delivered in a most lovely manner with the greatest interest to all, and were listened to with the closest attention and a loving parting was expressed. Pray for your poor old Clerk. Farewell, loved ones.

CLERK.

ELDERS	POST-OFFICE	STATE
H. A. Alston	Tazewell	Tenn.
James Ausmus	Speedwell, R. F. D. 3	Tenn.
Alfrod Boruff	Liberty Hill, R. F. D. 23	Tenn.
A. J. Boruff	Washburn, R. F. D. 15	Tenn.
Eli M. Bronson	Zenia	Kas.
Calvin Collins	Morristown, R. F. D. 4	Tenn.
W. A. Drummonds	New Tazewell, R. F. 3	Tenn.
John F. Keck	Goin	Tenn.
J. D. Monroe	Goin	Tenn.
Matthew Oliver	Noeton	Tenn.
Thomas Pierce	Speedwell, R. F. D. 3	Tenn.
H. A. Shoffner	Tate	Tenn.
A. Shelton	Harrogate	Tenn.
W. B. Weaver	Lost Creek, R. F. D. 1	Tenn.
John A. Webb	Gibson Station	Va.
Leonard White	Sharps Chapel, R. F. D. 2	Tenn.

LICENTIATES

Charlie Stanifer	R. F. D., Speedwell	Tenn.
W. R. Petree	Clear Fork	Tenn.
C. B. Weaver	R. F. D. 2, Sharps Chapel	Tenn.
Elvin Weaver	R. F. D. 2, Sharps Chapel	Tenn.
William Adkins	Tate	Tenn.
Oscar Ausmus	Speedwell	Tenn.

CHURCHES	CLERKS	POST-OFFICE	STATE
Big Barren	Mack Edwards	Goin	Tenn.
Black Fox	Samuel Davis	Maynardsville, R. 3	Tenn.
Cave Spring	W. H. Brantley	Sharps Chapel	Tenn.
Cedar Spring	W. A. Drummonds	New Tazewell, R. 3	Tenn.
Gibson Station	Lillie Cline	Middlesboro	Ky.
Hamilton Grove	H. F. Hamilton	Maynardsville, R. 5	Tenn.
Mossy Spring	Elza White	Sharps Chapel, R. 2	Tenn.
Noeton	Sherman Spirse	Noeton	Tenn.
New Hebron	Jesse Smith	New Market, R. 5	Tenn.
Oak Grove	David White	Sharps Chapel, R. 4	Tenn.
Pleasant Point	P. F. Keck	Goin	Tenn.
Pleasant Hill	J. A. Hunter	Speedwell	Tenn.
Straight Branch	J. P. Taylor	Speedwell	Tenn.

TABLE OF STATISTICS

CHURCHES	NAMES OF DELEGATES	Rec'd by Baptism	Rec'd by Letter	Rec'd by Relation	Restored	Dismissed by Let.	Excluded	Deceased	Total	Saturday Meeting	Contributions
Big Barren	Not represented. Hope to meet next year.								43	2	2 00
Black Fox	Elders Alford Boruff, A. J. Boruff, C. M. Cabbage, E. C. Boruff	6							64	3	$1 50
Cave Spring	Bros. Ben Lambert, W. H. Brantley, John White, Freeman Brantley								116	3	1 50
Cedar Spring	Elder W. A. Drummonds, E. S. Drummonds, J. A. G. Drummonds, S. W. Drummonds, J. J. Drummonds	2	2			2			88	4	2 00
Gibson Station	Elder H. A. Shoffner, W. R. Petree, Wm. Collins								50	1	1 50
Hamilton Grove	Frank Hamilton								64	4	
Mossy Spring	Elders Leonard White, M. B. Weaver, Bros. Sam Green, Elvin Weaver, J. J. Boruff, Theodor Brantley, John Hopper, C. M. Weaver	16						1	173	2	2 00
New Hebron	Not represented. Come next year								12	1	
Noeton	Not represented. Give us a call next year								21	3	
Oak Grove	Elder J. D. Monroe, Wm. Shoffner, J. P. Russell, David White		7					3	108	2	2 55
Pleasant Point	Elder John F. Keck, J. M. Cox, A. C. Goin, John Welch, Robert Welch	22		3		1			108	2	2 15
Pleasant Hill	Bro. Oscar Ausner								42	4	1 00
Straight Branch	Elder Thomas Pierce, J. F. Taylor, J. H. Smith, Wm. Taylor, Sterling Smith								50	1	2 05

For Visiting Ministers, $1.50

MINUTES

——OF THE——

Ninety-Eighth Annual Session

——OF THE——

Powell's Valley Association

Light
of

The
World

——OF——

Primitive Baptists

Held with the Church at

Hamilton Grove, Union County, Tenn.

August 17, 18, and 19, 1917

THREE STATES···PRINTERS···MIDDLESBORO, KY

MINUTES

—OF THE—

Ninety-eighth Annual Session of the Powell's Valley Association of Primitive Baptists held with the Church at Hamilton Grove, Union County, Tenn:, August 17, 18 and 19, 1917.

1. After Praise, Prayer by Wm. Shoffner.
2. Introductory Sermon by Elder McArthur of Georgia, from the 4th chapter and 1st verse of 2nd Timothy:

I charge ye therefore before God and the Lord Jesus Christ who shall judge the wicked and the dead at His appearing and His Kingdom.

After ten minutes intermission, at the sound of the bell, the Association met. Praise and Prayer by W. R. Petree.

3. The Association was called to order by the Moderator.
4. On motion, called for letters from churches. 10 received and read by the Clerk and John F. Keck.
5. On motion, letters received and messengers' names enrolled,

6. On motion, elected Elder M. B. Weaver, Moderator and re-elected Elder W. A. Drummonds Clerk,
7. Called for petitionary letters.
8. Called for Correspondence and received Elder William R. Gates and Minutes from the Nolachuckey Association who waa welcomed to a seat with us
9. Minsiters and Brethren invited to seats who were not delegates. Elder J. T. McArthur from Georgia, Elder J. J. Kirkland came forward and were welcomed to seats with us,

10. Appointed the following named committees:

(a) On Arrangemens—M. C. Keck T. G. Brantley, C. M. Cabbage.

(b) On Preaching—Bros. Sam Davis, E D. Monroe, Jas. Herrell and H. F. Hamilton together with the church.

(c) On Correspondence—Elders Jno. F. Keck, Thomas Pierce, Bro. W. R. Petree.

(d) On Requests—Elder Alfred Boruff, Bros. Mannie Graves and A. C. Goin.

(e) On Finances—E. D. Monroe, W. R. Petree.

(f) On Resolution of Draft of Respect for Elder J. D. Monroe.—Jno. F. Keck with the Moderator and Clerk.

11. On motion, committees received,

12. On motion, adjourned until tomorrow morning at 9:30 o'clock.

Saturday's Proceedings.

1. The Association met pursuant to adjournment.
2. Praise and Prayer by Elder M. B. Weaver.
3. The Association called to order by the Moderator.
4. On motion, called for reports of committees which were read and approved as follows:

(a) We, your Committee on Arrangements, beg leave to submit the following order of business:

1. Call the roll.
2. On Preaching.
3. On Correspondence.
4. On Requests.
5. On Finances.
6. On Resolutions.
7. When and where shall our next Association be.
8. Who shall preach the Introductory Sermon and who shall be his alternate.
9. How many copies of Minutes and who shall superintend the printing and distribution of same?

Respectfully submitted,

C. M. CABBAGE

T. G. BRANTLEY

M. C. KECK

10. Call the roll and erased the names of absentees.

(b) We, your Committee on Preaching, beg leave to submit the following report: Friday night at Buckners—Elders M. B. Weaver, Jno. F. Keck; at the Church—Elders J. J. Kirkland, W. A. Drummond; Oaklonia—Elders J. T. McArthur, T. Pierce; Saturday at the stand—J. T. McArthur, J. J. Kirkland, Wm. R. Gates; at night Buckners—Elders H. A. Shoffner, Jas. Ausmus; at the Church—Elders M. B. Weaver, T. Price, J. T. McArthur; Oaklonia—Elders Jno. F. Keck. Wm. R. Gats; Riverview—Elder T. G. Brantley; Sunday at the stand—Elders Wm. R. Gates, J. J. Kirkland, J. T. McArthur, Moderator to close.

Respectfully submitted,

SAMUEL DAVIS   H. F. HAMILTON

E. D. MONROE   Together with

JAMES HERRELL   the church

(c) We, your Committee on Correspondence, beg leave to submit the following: That we still continue our long cherished correspondence with the following Associations, viz: the Hiawasser and the Nolachuckey by letter and delegation, and solicit Correspondence from other Associations and Churches of our faith and order.

Respectfully submitted,

JOHN F. KECK

W. R. PETREE

THOMAS PIERCE

(d) We, your Committee on Requests, beg leave to submit the following report: That we have all obituaries published in our Minutes that the Churches furnish.

Respectfully submitted,

MAMIE GRAVES

A. BORUFF

A. C. GOIN

(e) We, your Committee on Finances, beg leave to submit the following report:

102

Received from churches for printing Minutes - $17.40
For Visiting Ministers Expense - - - 9.75
From other sources not turned in - - -
_____
Total - - $27.15

Your Committee wish to state that we believe the effort made to create a fund among our churches for the purpose of Ministerial Aid is a matter worthy of our most prayerful consideration. We further believe the same to be our Christian duty and privilege as well and will materially aid in building and strengthening the churches of this Association. Therefore, we recommend that each and every member of this association and of the churches, donate to this fund so much of their means as they may be able, that the same may ever be ready to meet the needs of our Ministers and Pastors of this Association and visiting Ministers from other Associations.

Respectfully submitted,

E. D. MONROE
W. R. PETREE

(f) We, your Committee on Resolutions, beg leave to submit the following: That we furthermore resolve that we tender our heart felt sympathy to the bereaved of our dear beloved Elder J. D. Monroe, also publish the obituary of said Elder Monroe.

11. All the foregoing reports received and Commitiees discharged.

12. On motion, appointed Elders M. B. Weaver, Alford Boruff Messengers to the Nolachuckey Association.

13. On motion, appointed Elders John F. Keck, M. B. Weaver, A. Boruff, Thomas Pierce, James Ausmus as Messengers to the Hiawassee Association.

14. That the Clerk write a corresponding letter to these Associations.

15. Appointed Elder Jno. F. Keck to write a circular letter to be printed in our minutes next year.

16. On motion, our next Association will be held with the Church at Pleasant Hill, Claiborne, County, Tenn , Friday before the third Saturday in August 1918.

103

17. Elder Alford Boruff preach the Introductory Sermon and Elder Thomas Pierce be his Alternate.

18. That we have 500 copies of Minutes printed, that the Clerk superintend the printing and distribution of the same and that he by allowed $7.00 for his service.

19. Be it resolved that we tender our heartfelt thanks to this beloved old church and her good surroundings for their hospitalites and kind treatment through this Association.

20. On motion minutes approved.

21. On motion adjourned to meet as above stated.

M. B. WEAVER, M. D.,

P. O. Lost Creek, Tenn. R. F. D. 2

ELDER W. A. DRUMMONDS, Clerk,

P. O. New Tazwell, Tenn., R.F.D. 3, Box 63.

Obituaries.

With sadness and sorrow we insert the names and dates of birth and deaths of these our well beloved brothers and sisters:

Blackfox: Sister Sarah Capp, wife of W. R. Capp, born April 16, 1877; was married July 29, 1893. She joined the Missioner Baptist when quite young, afterward she joined the Primitive Baptist Church at Blackfox and was baptized in fellowship with them October 7, 1905, with whom she lived a consistent member until her death which occured almost suddenly January 11, 1917.

Mossy Spring: Brother Ashbury Petree born November 22nd, 1881, deceased November the 5nd day, 1916. Professed faith in Christ in early life, joined the Primitive Baptist Church at Massie Springs and lived a faithful member until death.

Casley Bridges was born May the 29th day, 1896, deceased February the 5th day, 1917. His death was due to an operation for Appendicitis. He died in Lincoln Memorial Hospital, Knoxville, Tenn. He bore his suffering with great patience and while on his death bed he told his mother that he was glad that it was not her, for he had rather die than for her to die, with many other lovely expressions. He leaves a lovely mother, 8 brothers and sisters and 4 half brothers and sisters, but our loss is great.

Oak Grove: Elder J. D. Monroe, born June 4th 1860, and departed this life, March 1917, age 57 years, months and days. Elder Monroe was the son of Levi and Martha Monroe, born in Union County, Tenn.,was married to Nancy Sharp, May the 30th' 1879, and to their union were born 5 children, 2 sons and 3 daughters. The said wife died and J. D. Monroe was again married to Rachel L. Brogan, September 1888. Elder Monroe joined the Primitive Baptist Cuhrch at Union, Union County Tenn. in the year   and was ordained to the full work of the gospel ministry, October 1896 and made a faithful soldier in his work, and an able defender of the doctrine of the bible. Elder Monroe was one of our ablest Ministers and seemed to enjoy his work so well he almost gave the latter part of his life to the cross. At the time of his death he was the Pastor of 4 churches of the Powells Valley Association of Primitive Baptists and died when out on duty attending a revival service at Gibson Station, Va. His membership with the Oak Grove church which he Pastored from its organization until his death. Elder Monroe was a great man and will be missed much among us. He leaves a widowed wife, 2 sons and 1 daughter with a host of relations and friends to mourn his loss. He was strong in the Christian faith and gave strong evidence of going to his heavenly home. where we expect to meet him in the sweet bve and bye. Therefore, be it resolved, that we tender our heartfelt sympathy to his dear widowed wife in her sad bereaved affliction.

M. B. WEAVER
JOHN F. KECK
W. A. DRUMMONDS

Sister Rosa Shoffner, wife of William Shoffner. She was born January the 14th, 1860. Proffessed faith in Christ at the age of 28 years and joined the church of Primitive faith and lived a faithful member until her death. Sister Rosa was married to Wesley Sharp October 1876, and to their union were born 10 children, 3 sons and 7 daughters. After the death of Wesley Sharp she married Wm. Shoffner, January the 17th, 1895, and to their union were born 4 children, 3 sons and 1 daughter. She led a christian life until her death which occured March 19, 1917. She leaves a lonely husband and 8 children with a host of friends to mourn the absence of a darling wife and lovely mother.

Pleasant Point: Bro. Jasper Hopper, born Mar. 8, 1847, professed

105

faith in early life. He was married to Melvina Seal and to their union were born 7 children, 1 son and 6 daughters. Again he was married to Celia Lynch. Brother Hopper lived a consistant member with the Primitive Baptist Church at Pleasant Point until death. He departnd this life Feb. 17th, 1917, leaving a widowed wife and children with a host of friends to mourn his loss. but we hope that our loss is their eternal gain; these all died in full triumph of a living faith. The bereaved all have our prayers and best wishes in hopes of a heavenly home.

CLERK.

Corresponding Letter.

August 17-18-19, 1617.

We, the Powells Valley Association of Primitive Baptists now in session with the church at Hamilton Grove, Union County, Tenn., to our Sister Association with whom we correspond, to-wit: the Nolachuckey and Hiawassee Associations:

Dear Bretren in the Lord: We desire to continue our correspondence with you and for that purpose have chosen our dearly beloved brethren to bear this, our epistle of love to you whom we hope you will receive as sound in the faith, Elders M. B. Weaver, Alford Boruff to the Nolachuckey Association: Elders John F. Keck, M. B. Weaver, Alford Boruff, Thomas Pierce and Jas. Ausmus to the Hiawassee Association. Dear Beloved Brethren, pray for us that love, peace and union may still abound throughout God's people. May the great God of Heaven be with you and guide you in the way of all truth, is the prayers of your sister A sociation.

ELDER M. B. WEAVER, M. D.

W. A. DRUMMONDS, Clerk.

Sunday

A well behaved audience assembled at the stand and well and attentively listened to the well delivered sermon by Elder

William Gates from 2nd chapter,19-20 verses of Ephesians—
Now therefore ye are no more strangers and foreigners,
but fellow citizens with the Saints and of the household
of God. (20 vs.) and are built upon the foundation of
the Apostles and Prophets, Jesus Christ Himself being
the Corner Stone.
followed by Elder J. J. Kirkland. Closing remarks by Elder
J. T. McArthur, all of which was delivered in a most lovely manner with the greatest of interest to all and were listened to with
the closest attention and a lovely parting was expressed among
the people. It was a touching scene to see the dear Elders and
your poor old Clerk embracing each other in their lovely arms.
Farewell, pray for your dear old Clerk.

ELDERS	POSTOFFICE	CO. and STATE
T. G. Brantley	Lost Creek	Union County, Tenn.
Oscar Ausmus	Speedwell	Claiborne County, Tenn.
H. L. Alston	Tazewell	Claiborne County, Tenn.
James Ausmus	Speedwell	Claiborne County, Tenn.
Alford Boruff	Maynardsvillle	Union County, Tenn.
A. J. Boruff	Maynardsville	Union County, Tenn.
Calvin Collins	Morristown, R 4	Jefferson County, Tenn.
W. A. Drummonds	New Tazewell, R 3,	Claiborne Co., Tenn.
Jno. F. Keck	Goin	Claiborne County, Tenn.
Matthew Oliver	Tate Station	Grainger County, Tenn.
Thomas Pierce	Speedwell, R 3	Claiborne County, Tenn.
H. A. Shoffner	Harrogate	Claiborne County, Tenn.
A. Shelton	Tate Station	Claiborne County, Tenn.
M. B. Weaver	Lost Creek	Union County, Tenn.
Leonard White	Lost Creek	Union County, Tenn.
John A. Webb	Gibson Station	Lee County, Va.

LICENTIATES

Charlie Stanifer	Speedwell,	Claiborne County, Tenn.
W. R. Petree	Colmar,	Bell County. Ky.
C. B. Weaver	Lost Creek, Route 2,	Union County, Tenn.
Elvin Weaver	Lost Creek, Route 2,	Union County, Tenn.
W. M. Adkins	Tate Station,	Grainger County, Tenn.
Jno. Causby	Gibson Station,	Lee County, Va.
S. S. Wilson	Gibson Station,	Lee County, Va.
Arch Burchett	Gibson Station,	Lee County, Va.

TABLE OF STATISTICS

CHURCHES	NAMES OF DELEGATES	Rec'd by Baptism	Rec'd by Letter	Rec'd by Relation	Restored	Dismissed by Let.	Excluded	Deceased	Total	Saturday Meeting	Contributions for
Big Barren	Not represented. Come next year										
Black Fox	C. M. Cab'age, E. C. Boruff, Lum Sutherland, Wm. Perry, Samuel Davis	5				3			66	3	$1 50
Cave Spring	F. Brantley, Jas. Brantley, Wm. Brantley, represented by delegation, no letter	5							116	3	1 00
Cedar Spring	Elder W. A. Drummonds								88	4	2 00
Gibson Station	Elder H. A. Shoffner, Bros. W. S. Collins, W. R. Petree	5	2	2					46	1	2 09
Hamilton Grove	Elder Alford Boruff, J. A. Graves, A. L. Buckner, R. R. Malone, Troy Hamilton, H. F. Hamilton, L. N. Riley, M. Boruff	5	2						78	4	1 50
Mossy Spring	Elders M. B. Weavar, T. G. Brantley, Bros. J. J Boruff, Elvin Weaver, John Hopper, E. D. Monroe	18	1					2	190	2	2 00
New Hebron	No tidings. Come next year								12	1	1 00
Noeton	Represented by letter, no delegation								21	3	1 00
Oak Grove	Wm. Shoffner, Daniel Boruff, Wm. Graves, D. White, Wilcox	13					1	1	116	1	2 10
Pleasant Point	Elder Jno. F. Keck, M. C. Keck, A. C. Goin, M. J. Wilcox								108	2	2 05
Pleasant Hill	J. L. Herrell		5						47	4	1 00
Straight Branch	Elders Thomas Pierce, Jas. Ausmus, Bro. Harrison Smith	5							50	1	1 25

Received from other sources for visiting ministers never turned in.

CHURCHES	COUNTIES	PASTORS	CLERKS	CLERK'S P. O.
Big Barren	Claiborne	None	F. Edwards	Goin	Tenn.
Black Fox	Grainger	T. Pierce	Sam Davis	Liberty Hill	Tenn.
Cave Spring	Union	Leonard White	W. H. Brantley	Sharp's Chapel	Tenn.
Cedar Spring	Claiborne	M. B. Weaver	W. A. Drummonds	New Tazewell, R 3, Tenn.
Gibson Station	Lee	John F. Keck	Martha Sutherland	Gibson Station	Va.
Hamilton Grove	Union	A. Boruff	J. W. Raley	Maynardsville	Tenn.
Mossy Spring	Union	Leonard White	Elzia White	Sharp's Chapel	Tenn.
New Hebron	Jefferson		Jesse Smith	New Market	Tenn.
Noetown	Claiborne	Matthew Oliver	John Hayes	Tate Station	Tenn.
Oak Grove	Union	T. G. Brantley	David White	Sharp's Chapel	Tenn.
Pleasant Point	Claiborne	John F. Keck	P. F. Keck	Goin	Tenn.
Pleasant Hill	Claiborne	Leonard White	J. A. Hunter	Speedwell	Tenn.
Straight Branch	Claiborne	Thomas Pierce	J. P. Taylor	Speedwell	Tenn.

MINUTES

OF THE

NINTY-NINTH ANNUAL

SESSION

OF THE

Powell's Valley
ASSOCIATION

OF

PRIMITIVE BAPTISTS

HELD WITH THE CHURCH AT

MOSSY SPRINGS. UNION COUNTY. TENN.

AUGUST 16. 17 AND 18, 1918

Banner-Herald, Cordele, Ga.
1918

MINUTES

Of the Ninety-ninth Annual Session of the Powell's Valley Association of Primitive Baptists, Held With the Mossy Springs Church, Union County, Tenn., August 16, 17, and 18, 1918.

1. Praise and prayer by Elder G. J. Boruff.

2. Introductory by Elder Alfred Boruff; Text, Col. 3rd Chapter and 3rd Verse—"For ye are dead and your life is hid with Christ in God."

3. After ten minutes intermission the mesengers reassembled in the house and prayer by Elder Thomas J. Pierce.

4. The Association was called to order by the Moderator.

5. Called for leters from the churches and minuted the state of the churches.

6. On motion re-elected M. B. Weaver, Moderator, and Sam Davis, Clerk.

7. Called for petitionary letter.

8. Called for correspondence.

(a) From the Hiawassee—None.

(b) From the Nolachuckey—None.

9. Called for visitors—Elder J. T. McArthur from Cordele, Ga., and Elder J. J. Kirkland from Humboldt, Tenn., were received and welcomed to seats with us.

10. Appointed the following committee:

(a) ON ARRANGEMENTS—Sam Davis, E. C. Drummonds and C. B. Weaver.

(b) ON PREACHING—David White, M. C. Dunn, M. C. Keck.

(c) ON CORRESPONDENCE—Elder Alfred Boruff, W. H. Brantley, Elder Thomas J. Pierce.

(d) ON REQUEST—J. F. Houston, John Hopper, S. G. Miracle.

(e) ON FINANCE—Elder G. J. Boruff and J. H. Greene.

11. On motion, adourned until tomorrow morning 9.30.

Saturday Proceedings

1. The Association met pursuant to adjournment.
2. Praise and prayer.
3. The Association called to order by the Moderator.
4. On motion called for reports on committees, which were read and approved as follows:
   (a) ARRANGEMENTS—We your committee on arrangements beg to submit the following order of business.
   1. Call the roll.
   2. On preaching.
   3. On correspondence.
   4. On request.
   5. On finance.
   6. On resolutions.
   7. When and where shall our next association be?
   8. Who shall preach the next introductory sermon and who shall be his alternate?
   9. How many coppies of these minutes and who shall superintend the printing of the same?

COMMITTEE

Sam Davis   C. B. Weaver   E. S. Drummonds.
10. Call the roll and erase the names of absentees.
11. (b) Committee on preaching report as follows: Friday night at church Elder J. T. McArthur and J. J. Kirkland.
   At J. L. Bailey, Elder T. J. Pierce and G. J. Boruff.
   Saturday A. M.,Elder J. J. Kirkland and T. J. Pierce.
   Saturday night. J. T. McArthur.
   Sunday, Elder J. J. Kirkland, J. T. McArthur, closed by Moderator.
   (c) ON CORRESPONDENCE—Feport as follows: That we continue our correspondence with the Hiawassee and Nolachuckey Associations and send minutes and mesengers to the same.
   (d) ON REUEST—Committee recommends that we have all obituaries published in our minutes that the church furnish.
   (e) CN FINANCE—Committee reports as follows: From churches for minutes $16.20, for ministers

112

$8.60. From friends for minutes $1.70. Sunday collection $22.00.

12. All the foregoing reports received and adopted and committee discharged.

13. On motion Elder M. B. Beaver and Brother John Hopper and M. C. Dunn as delegates to the Hiawessee Association to be held with the church at Lenoir City, Tenn., fourth Friday and Saturday and Sunday in September, 1918.

13. On motion appointed Elder Theodore Brantley and Lafayette Ousley as delagates to the Nolachuckey Association.

14. That the clerk write the corresponding letter to the Asociation.

15. On motion appointed the next association to be held with Black Fox Church (near Liberty Hill) on Friday before third Saturday in August 1919.

16. On motion apointed Elder M. B. Weaver to preach the introductory sermon (Elder Theodore Brantley alternate.)

17. On motion agreed to have 500 copies of these minutes printed, and the clerk to superintend the printing and distribution of the same, and have balance of funds for his services.

18. Be it resolved that we tender our heartfelt thanks and best wishes to this church and community who so royally entertained us during our stay with them, and may God's richest blessings attend them.

19. Read and approved the minuptes.

20. On motion adjourned to the time and place abovementioned.

ELD .M. B. WEAVER. Moderator.
SAM DAVIS, Clerk.

CORRESPONDING LETTER

We, the Powell's Valley Association of Primitive Baptist. now in sesion with the church at Mossy Springs, Union County, Tenn., to our Sister Association with whom we correspond, sends greeting.

Dear Brethren in the Lord: We desire to continue our correspondence with you. We have delegated the brethren whose names you will find in the body of our minutes, to visit you at your stated time and place. Trusting and praying that you may have a good meeting,

ELDER M. B. WEAVER, Moderator.
SAM DAVIS, Clerk.

OBITUARIES

Mrs. Jane Pierce, wife of Elder Thomas Pierce, Pastor of Straight Branch Church. Sister Pierce was borned about the year 1860, professed a hope n Christ at the age of 15 years. She married Brother Pierce about 34 years ago, and by that union she bore and raised six children, she lived to see 21 grand children. Sister Pierce joined the Primitive Baptist Church at Straight Branch (Speedwell, Tenn.) and lived a consistent memberof same until the 19th day of last December. 1917. She departed this life to await the resurrection of the dead. Body and spirit shall be re-united then, to live forever with her blessed Redeemer.
Chi'dren and father weep not for she is gone from the evil to come to await the resurrerction from the dead. So Sister Pierce leaves a host of friends to mourn her loss, weep not for Sister Jane; children and friends our loss is her eternal gain. But let us all live in the good that Sister Jane lived, and lay down this life with a smile, and hear the welcome approbation "Come in ye blessed of the Father, inherit the kingdom prepared from the foundation of the world."

Clarence Crane was born June 18, 1891, died November 18, 1917, age 26 years and five months. He was a devoted christian and put his whole trust in God, and trusted in Him for His will to be odne. His last words were: "Good-bye father, mother, brothers and sisters, meet me in Heaven for I am going home."

HESTER ELNORA RALEY, wife of John W. Raley, daughter of Eugene and Josephine Monroe, was born July 19, 1891, she was married to John W. Raley on the 18th day of August, 1907, to this happy union were born four children, three of whom, Velma, age 9; Lucile, age 6 and Marie, age three, are now without a mother. Elnora professed faith in Christ, January 1905, being only 15 years old, she joined the Primitive Baptist Church soon after, and has lived a consistent and faithful member of the church until she was called away. Besides the father, mother, husband and children, she leaves four sisters, two brothers and many other relatives and friends to mourn her loss. She departed this life May 21, 1918.

ARTICLES OF FAITH

Article 1. We believe in one only true and living God, as He is revealed to us in the Holy Scriptures, Father, Son and Holy Ghost.

Art. 2. We believe that the Scriptures of the Old and New Testaments are the word of God and the only rule of all saving knowledge and obedience.

Art. 3. We believe in the doctrine of election according to the foreknowledge of God.

Art. 4. We believe in the doctrine of original sin.

Art. 5. We believe in man's impotency to recover himself from the fallen state he is in by his own free will or ability.

Art. 6. We believe that sinners are justified in the sight of God only by the imputed rightousness of Jesus Christ.

Art. 7. We believe in the elect, according to the foreknowledge of God, will be called, converted, regenearted and sanctified by the Holy Spirit.

Art. 8. We believe the saints will persevere and never fall finally away.

Art. 9. We believe that Baptism and the Lord's Supper are ordinances of Jesus Christ, and that true believers are the only subjects of these ordinances, and that the true mode of Baptism is by emersion.

Art. 10. We believe in the resurrection of the dead and the general judgement.

Art. 11. We believe that the punishment of the wicked will be everlasting, and that the joys of the righteous will be eternal.

Art. 12. We believe that no minister has the right to administer the ordinances except those who have been regularly baptized and salled of God and come under the imposition of hands by the Presbytery.

TABLE OF STATISTICS

NO.	CHURCHES	NAMES OF DELEGATES	Rec'd by Baptism	Rec'd by Letter	Rec'd by Relation	Restored	Dis. by Letter	Excluded	Deceased	Total	Saturday Meeting	Money for Minutes	Visiting Ministers
1.	Big Barren	Sam Davis, Rufus Boruff								66	3	$1.50	
2.	Black Fox	W. H. Brantley, James Brantley								126	3	2.00	
3.	Cave Springs									88	4	2.00	
4.	Cedar Springs	E. S. Drummonds	10							46			
5.	Gibson Station												
6.	Hamilton	Elder Alfred Boruff	4	2						70	4	1.60	1.60
7.	Mossy Springs	Elders M. B. Weaver, Theo. Brantley, G. J. Boruff	13	1						203	2	2.00	5.00
8.	New Hebron	Will Crum								20			
9.	Noeton	Represented by Letter	13							44	3	1.50	
10.	Oak Grove	David White, John Graves, Fate Ousley	14	2			1			127	1	1.50	2.00
11.	Pleasant Point	M. C. Keck, Eld. Jno. F. Keck, S. G. Miracle	1	2						104	2	2.00	
12.	Pleasant Hill									47			
13.	Straight Branch	Elder Thomas J. Pierce, J. F. Houston	6	2					1	56	1	1.70	
	TOTAL		61	7			1		1	997		16.20	8.60

116

ELDERS	POSTOFFICE	CO. AND STATE
T. G. Brantley	Lost Creek	Union County, Tenn.
Oscar Ausmus	Speedwell	Claiborne County, Tenn.
H. L. Alston	Tazewell	Claiborne County, Tenn.
James Ausmus	Speedwell	Claiborne County, Tenn.
Alford Boruff	Maynardsville	Union County, Tenn.
A. J. Boruff	Maynardsville	Union County, Tenn.
Calvin Collins	Morristown, Rte 4	Jefferson County, Tenn.
W. A. Drummonds	New Tazewell, R 3	Claiborne County, Tenn.
Jno. F. Keck	Goin	Claiborne County, Tenn.
Mathew Oliver	Tate Station	Grainger County, Tenn.
Thomas Pierce	Speedwell, R 3	Claiborne County, Tenn
H. A. Shoffner	Harrogate	Claiborne County, Tenn.
A. Shelton	Tate Station	Claiborne County, Tenn.
M. B. Weaver	Lost Creek	Union County, Tenn.
Leonard White	Lafollette	Union County, Tenn.
John A. Webb	Gibson Station	Lee County, Va.
G. J. Boruff	Lost Creek	Tenn.

LICENTIATES

Charlie Stanfier	Speedwell	Clai borne County, Tenn.
W. R. Petree	Colmar	Bell County, Kentucky.
C. B. Weaver	Lost Creek, Rte 2	Union County, Tenn.
Elvin Weaver	Lost Creek, Rte 2	Union County, Tenn.
W. M. Adkins	Tate Station	Grainger County, Tenn.
Jno. Causby	Gibson Station	Lee County, Va.
S. S. Wilson	Gibson Station	Lee County, Va.
Arch Burchett	Gibson Station	Lee County, Va.

ORGANIZED	CHURCHES	COUNTIES	PASTORS	CLERKS	CLERK'S P. O.
----	Big Barren	Claiborne	M. B. Weaver	F. Edwards	Goin ---------- Tenn.
----	Black Fox	Grainger	T. Pierce	Sam Davis	Liberty Hill ---Tenn.
1871	Cave Springs	Union	Theo. Brantley	W. H. Brantley	Sharp's Chapel ..Tenn.
1868	Cedar Spring	Claiborne	M. B. Weaver	W. A. Drummond..	New Tazwell, R3, Tenn.
----	Gibson Station	Lee, Va.	John F. Keck	S. S. Wilson	Gibson Station ----Va.
----	Hamilton Grove	Union	A. Boruff	J. W. Raley	Maynardsville --Tenn.
1868	Mossy Spring	Union	Leonard White	Elzia White	Sharp's Chapel --Tenn.
----	New Hebron	Jefferson		H. F. Cox	New Market ----Tenn.
----	Noetown	Grainger	Mathew Oliver	H. L. Pollock	Tate Station ----Tenn.
1905	Oak Grove	Union	T. G. Brantley	David White	Sharp's Chapel ..Tenn.
----	Pleasant Point	Claiborne	JohnF. Keck	P. F. Keck	Goin ----------Tenn.
----	Pleasant Hill	Claiborne	Leonard White	J. A. Hunter	Speedwell ------Tenn.
1912	Straigh Branch	Union	Thomas Pierce	J. P. Taylor	Speedwell -----Tenn.

MINUTES

-----OF THE-----

ONE HUNDREDTH ANNUAL SESSION

-----OF THE-----

POWELL'S VALLEY ASSOCIATION

-----OF-----

PRIMITIVE BAPTISTS

Held with the Chutch at

Black Fox, Grainger County, Tenn.,

August 15, 16, 17, 1919.

Progress Print, Tazewell, Tenn.

ASSOCIATION PROCEEDINGS.

* * *

Minutes of the one hundredth Annual session of the Powell's Valley Association of Primative Baptists, hed with the church at Blackfox, Grainger County, Tenn., August 15-16-17, 1919.

1st__Praise and prayer, by Elder M. B. Weaver.

2nd__Introductory sermon, by Elder M. B. Weaver, from 7th chapter St. John,16th and 17th verses.

"Jesus answard them and said: My doctrine is not mine, but His that sent me If any man will do His will he shall know of the doctrine, whether it be of God or whether I speak of my self.

3rd__After 10 minutes intermission the Association was called to order by Elder M. B. Weaver. Prayer by Elder Thomas Pierce.

4th__ By motion ,Elder T. G. Brantly was elected Moderator, and Sam Davis was re-elected clerk.

5th__On motion, called for letters from churches; 11 received and read by the clerk and E. D. Monroe.

6th__On motion, letters received and messengers' names enrolled.

7th__ Called for petitionary letters.

8th__Called for correspondence, and received Elder John Abbott, and Frank Norton, and Minutes from the Hiwassee Association, and Elder W. M. Gates, and Minutes from the Nolachuckey Association.

9th__Ministers and brethren invited to seats,who were not delegates. Elder S. S. Kent, from Georgia come forward and was welcomed to a seat with us.

10th__Appointed the following committies:

A. On arrangements, Elder John F. Keck, Brother C. M. Cabbage.

B. Onpreaching, Josh Drummonds, James Herrill and Robert Dike, together with the church.

C. On correspondence, Elder John F. Keck, H. L. Alston and M. B. Weaver.

D. On request, Elder John F. Keck, W. R. Petree and Brother W. M. Perry.

E. On finance, Brother Fate Owsley, George Southern.

11th__On motion, committee received.

12th On motion, adjourned until Saturday morning at 9:00 o'clock.

* * *

SATURDAY'S PROCEEDINGS.

* * *

1st__The Association met pursuant to adjournment.

2nd__Praise, by Elder T. G. Brantly, prayer by W. R. Petree.

3rd__The Association called to order by Moderator.

4th__On motion, called for reports of committies, which were read and approved.

A. We your committee on arrangements, beg leave to submit the following order of business:

1st__Call the Roll.

2nd__On Preaching.

3rd__On Correspondence

4th__On Requests.

5th__On Finances.

6th.__On Resolutions.

7th__When and where shall our next Association be.

8th Who shall preach the Introductory Sermon, and who shall be his alternate?

9th.__How many copies of Minutes, and who shall Superintend the printing and distribution of same?

Respectfully submitted, C. M. Cabbage, John F. Keck, Elvin Weaver.

10th__Called the roll and erased the name of absentees.

B. We your committee on preaching__beg leave to submit the following report:

Friday night, at the church at Blackfox, Elder Kent, John Abbott.

Woodale__Tom Pierce, M. C. Hensley.

Long Bottom__H. L. Alston John Webb.

Mt. Eager__T. G. Brantly, W. M. Gates.

Saturday at the Stand, Elder Kent, Gates, and Abbatt.

At church, at night__Elder Gates and Abbatt.

Long Bottom__Elder M. B. Weaver, Oscar Ausmus.

Wooddale__Elders Kent, A. J. Boruff.

Mt. Eager__Elder Hensley, and Pierce.

Sunday at Stand.__Elders Abbatt, and Gates.

Moderator to close. Respectfully submitted, John F. Keck, R. L. Dyke, Joshua Drummonds, J. L. Harrell, together with the church

C. We, your committee on correspondence, beg leave to sumit the following:

That we write letters and send Messengers to the Hiwassee and Nalachuckey Association, and have said Messengers report their success to our next Association.

Respectfully submitted, M. B. Weaver, H. L. Alston, John F. Keck.

D. We, your committee on Request—beg leave tosubmit the following report:

That we have all obituaries published in our Minutes that the church furnish.

Respectfully submitted, John F. Keck—W. R. Petree

E. We, your committee on Finance, beg leave to sumit the following:

Received from churches for printing Minutes, $21.00.

11th—All the foregoing reports received and committies discharged.

12—On motion appointed M. B., Weaver, John F. Keck, and delegates to the Hiwassee Association.

13th—On motion, appointed Elder T. G. Brantly and Brother W. A. L. Owsley, delegates to the Nalachuckey Association.

14th—That the clerk write corresponding letters to these Associations, and have it printed in our Minutes.

15—On motion, our next Association will be held with the church at Oak Grove, Union County, Tennessee, to commence on Friday before the 3rd Saturday in August, 1920.

16th—On motion, circular letter read and approved.

17th—Elder T. G. Brantly to preach the Introductory Surmon, and Elder John F. Keck be his alternate.

18th—That we have 600 copies of Minutes printed; that the clerk Superintend the printing and distribution of same, and be allowed $5.00 for his service.

19th—Be it Resolved: That we tender our heartfelt thanks to this beloved church and her surroundings for their hospitalities and kind treatment to us through this Association.

20th—On motion, Minutes approved.

21st—On motion, adjourned to meet as above stated.

M. B. WEAVER, Moderator.
Po—Lost Creek, Tenn.,R, 2.
SAM DAVIS, Clerk,
Po—Liberty Hill, Tenn., R, 1.

* * *

SUNDAY

A well behaved audaience assembled at the alter and attentively listened to the well delivered sermons by Elder Abbott from 2nd Timothy, bth Chapter, first verse: "I charge thee, therefore, before God and the Lord Jesus Christ, who shall judge the quick and the dead at His appearing and His

Kingdom." Followed by Elder Gates and White, and closing remarks by the Moderator, of all which was delivered in a most loving manner, with greatest interest to all, and were listened to with the closest attention, and a lovely parting was expressed among the people. It was a touching scene to see the dear Elders, Brothers and Sisters embracing each other in their loving arms, and invoking the blessings of God on each other. "Brothers and Sisters, pray for me and mine.'" The Clerk.

OBITUARIES.

With saddness and sorrow we insert the names and dates of births and deaths of these, our well beloved Brothers and Sisters:

Charlie Gibbs, husband of Sarah Gibbs, departed this life December 9, 1918. Born May 2.1894. Joined the Primative Baptist Church, December 1910.

Cedar Spring:---Sister Sarah L. Drummonds, wife of Elder J. M. Drummonds, professed faith in Christ and joined the Primative Baptist church at Cedar Spring, October 2, Sat. 1871 age about 76 years. Died December 25, 1919. She leaves one son. two daughters and one brother to mourn the loss of a loving mother and sister.

Sister Lillie Wilson, wife of Press Wilson, daughter of Clint and Lucinda Bunch, born April 23, 1894, joined the Primative Baptist church at Cedar Spring July 4th, Sat. 1912. Married Feburary 9, 1918, died December 28, 1918. She leaves father and mother, 4 brothers and one sister to mourn her loss. But we hope our loss is her eternal gain.

Sister Lucinda Simmonds, wife of Brother George Simmons; born December 18, 1858; joined the Primative Baptist church at Cedar Spring October 2 Sat. 1871.Died Feburary 24, 1919. She lived a faithful member until God saw fit to call her away She leaves a loving companion, 5 sons and 5 daughters, a host of friends and grand children to mourn the loss of a dear mother and friend. But our loss is her eternal gain.

These all died in full triumph of a living faith. The bereaved all have our prayers and best wishes, and hope to meet our loved ones in the sweet by and by. The Clerk.

CORRESPONDING LETTER.

We, the Powell's Valley Association of Primative Baptists, now in session with the church- at Blackfox, Grainger county, Tenn., to our sister Associations, with whom we correspond, to-wit: The Nalachuckey and Hiwassee Associations:

Dear Brethern, for the purpose of conttiun our corres-with us in the sitting of this meeting, Elder J. H. Abbott and Brother Frank Norton, from the. Hiwassee, and Elder Wm. Gates from the Nalachuckey.

Dear Brothern, for the purpose of containing our correspondence with you, we send you this, our epistle of Love and fellowship, bearing the same, by the hand of our messengers, whom we hope you will receive as sound in the faith, to sit with you in your annual meeting.

May the God of Heaven be with and guide you in the way of all thruth is the prayer of your sister Association.
of all truth is the prayer of your sister Association.

ELDER T. G. BRANTLY, Moderator,
SAM DAVIS, Clerk.

* * *

CIRCULAR LETTER.

By Elder Leonard White.
* * *

According to previous appointment of this, the Powell's Valley Association, I endevera to prepare a short circular letter to be inserted in the Minutes of 1919.

Believing the expresion of Paul to the Romans to be a very appropriate subject: "That ye may with one mind and one mouth glorify God, even the Father of our Lord Jesus Christ." Rom. 15: 6.

Although this statement was given about one-thousand eight-hundred and sixty one years ago, the truth it reveals stands out as prominent as when first spoken. We think it very important that we trust but one God, since there is but one living and true God. It has pleased this one God to give us but one book. This one book tells us there is but one body. It also tells us that this one body should have but one mind. The word mind, in a biblical sense, as expressed in our text, is from the Greek word meno, and signifies intention or inclining forward to an object. This object is Christ. If this explanation be true, it is absolutely impossible to prosper a cause when we have not the same mind. So dear readers, what is your mind? Or in other words, toward what object are you inclined?

We are also commanded in the text to have but one mouth. The word mouth in scripture, means words uttered.

"I called my servant, and he gave me no answer; I entreated him with my mouth." Job, 19. 16.

124

This is commanded of us to the one end: That God may be glorified. Then, inorder to attain to this end, wemust be of one mind, speak with one mouth, never hesitating to open our mouths in support of righteousness, even ready to condemn wrong.

In order to do this we must deny ourselves of many things which seem pleasing to us, but even remember the lines of the poetwhen he said:

"Pleasures are like the Popies spread.
You seize its flowers, the bloom is shed
Or like a snow flake in the r...
A moment white, then gone forever.
May God prosper these words to their intended use.
Your worthy servant.

Elder LEONARD WHITE.

ELDERS	POSTOFFICE	CO. and STATE
T. G. Brantley	Lost Creek	Union County, Tenn.
Oscar Ausmus	Speedwell	Claiborne County, Tenn.
H. L. Alston	Tazewell	Claiborne County, Tenn.
James Ausmus	Speedwell	Claiborne County, Tenn.
A. J. Boruff	Maynardsville	Union County, Tenn.
A. J. Bourff	Maynardsville	Union County, Tenn.
Calvin Collins	Morriston, R 4	Hamblin County, Tenn.
W. A. Drummonds	New Tazewell R 3	Claiborne Co., Tenn.
Jno. F. Keck	Goin	Claiborne County, Tenn.
Matthew Oliver	Tate Station	Grainger County, Tenn.
Thomas Pierce	Speedwell, R 3	Claiborne County Tenn
H. A. Shoffner	Harrogate	Claiborne County, Tenn.
A. Shelton	Tate Station	Grainger County, Tenn.
M. B. Weaver	Lost Creek	Union County, Tenn.
Leonard White	Lost Creek	Union County, Tenn.
John A. Webb	Gibson Station	Lee County, Va.

* * *

LICENTIATES

Charlie Standerfer	Speedwell,	Claiborne County Tenn.
W. R. Petree	Colmar	Bell County, Ky.
C. B. Weaver	Lost Creek, R 2,	Union County, Tenn.
Elvin Weaver	Lost Creek, R 2	Union County, Tenn.
W. A. Atkins	Tate Station	Grainger County, Tenn.
Jno. Causby	Gibson Station	Lee County, Va.
S. S. Wilson	Gibson Station	Lee County, Va.
Arch Burchett	Gibson Station	Lee County, Va.
Esaw Keck	Goin	Claiborne County, Tenn.

Churches.	Counties.	Pastors	Clerks.	Clerks Post Office
Big Barren	Claiborne	M. B. Weaver	Edwards	Goin, Tenn.
Blackfox	Grainger	T. G. Brantly	Sam Davis	Liberty Hill, Tenn
Cave Springs	Union	T. G. Brantly	W. T. Brantly	Sharps Chapel, Tenn.
Cedar Spring	Claiborne	M. C. Hensley	W. A. Drummond	New Tazewell, Tenn.
Gibson Station	Lee	John F. Keck	S. S. Wilson	Gibson Station, Va.
Hamilton Grove	Union	Alfred Boruff	J. W. Raly	Maynardville, Tenn.
Mossy Spring	Union	T. G. Brantly	I. E. White	Sharps Chapel, Tenn.
New Hebron	Jefferson	Mathew Oliver	H. F. Cox	New Market, Tenn.
Noeton	Grainger	T. G. Brantly	H. L. Patrick	Tate Station, Tenn.
Oak Grove	Union	M. B. Weaver	David White	Sharps Chapel, Tenn.
Pleasant Point	Claiborne	Leonard White	P. F. Keck	Goin, Tenn.
		Assistant G. J. Boruff		
Pleasant Hill	Claiborne	M. C. Hensley	J. A. Hunter	Speedwell, Tenn.
Strait Branch	Union		J. P. Taylor	Speedwell, Tenn.

126

TABLE OF STATISTICS.

Churches	Names of Delegates	Rec'd by Baptism	Rec'd by letter	Rec'd by Relation	Restored	Dismissed by letter	Excluded	Deceased	Total	Sat Meeting	Contributions
Big Barren	Not represented. Come on.										
Blackfox	C. M. Cabbage, W. M. Perry, Sam Davis. Rufus Boruff	10					1		76	4	$2.00
Cave Spring	No messenger	9						2	128	3	2.00
Cedar Springs	J. B. Drummonds, Elder H. L. Alston	9						3	61	4	1.50
Gibson Station	Elder J. A. Webb, G. S. Southers, W. R. Petree								46	1	1.50
Hamilton Grove	Elder Alford Boruff, H. F. Hamilton, Mamie Boruff								63	4	
Mossie Springs	Elder M. B. Weaver, Leonard White, T. G. Brantly. G. J. Boruff	4					2		205	2	3.25
New Hebron	No letter. Come on.										
Noeton	No letter. Come on.										
Oak Grove	W. M. Shofner, LaFayett Owsley	1					1	1	126	1	2.75
Pleasant Point	Elder John F. Keck					1			104	2	2.50
Pleasant Hill	J. L. Harrell, Lincoln Edwards							1	45	4	2.00
Straight Branch	Elder Thomas Pierce, M. C. Hensly, Thornie Pierce.	8	1						60	1	1.15

MINUTES

-----OF THE-----

ONE HUNDRED & FIRST ANNUAL SESSION

-----OF THE-----

POWELL'S VALLEY ASSOGIATION

-----OF-----

PRIMATIVE BAPTISTS

Held with the Church at

Oak Grove, Union County, Tenn.,

August 20, 21, 22, 1920.

PROGRESS PRINT TAZEWELL, TENN.

ASSOCIATION PROCEEDINGS.

Minutes of the One Hundred and First Annual session of the Powell's Valley Association of Primative Baptist, held with the church at Oak Grove, Union County, Tenn., August 20, 21, 22,, 1920.

1st. Praise by Elder T G. Brantly. Prayer by Elder G. J. Fo uff

2nd Introductory by Elder T. G. Brantly from Ephesians 2nd Chap. 20th verse. "And are built upon the foundation of the Apostles and Prophets, Jesus Christ himself being the chief corner stone." Followed by his alternate, Elder John F. Keck.

3rd. After 10 minutes the Association was called together by singing. Prayer by Elder James Ausmus.

4th. On motion called for letters from churches. Nine were received and read by the clerk, assisted by Elder John F. Keck.

5th. On motion letters received and the names of Messengers enrolled.

6th. On motion Elder T. G. Brantly was re-elected Moderator and Sam Davis was re-elected Clerk.

7th. Called for petitionary letters. Received none.

8th. Called for correspondence and received Elder W. R. Gates and minutes from the Nolachuckey Association, who was heartily welcomed to a seat among us.

9th. Ministers and brethren who were not delegates were invited to seats whereupon Brothers Elvin Weaver, Bradford Weaver, Thornic Pierce, and Elder James Ausmus came forward and were welcomed to seat with us.

10th. Appointed the following committies.

A. On arrangements, Elder James Ausmus and W. R. Petree.

B. On preaching, James Harrell, Elvin Weaver, Herman Munsey, together with the church.

C. On correspondence, Elder Thomas Pierce, Brothers Elvin Weaver, John Taylor.

D. On request. W. R. Petree, W. R. Capps, Harrison Shelby.

E. On finance, David White, James Brantly, Jr.

12th. On motion adjourned till 9:30 a. m., Saturday.

SATURDAY'S PROCEEDINGS.

1st. The Association met .pursuant to adjournment.

2nd. Praise and prayer by Elder M. B. Weaver.

3rd. The Association was called to order by Moderator.

4th. Called for reports of committies.

A. We, your committee on arrangements beg leave to submit the following order of business:

1st. Call the Roll.

2nd. On Preaching.

3rd. On Correspondence.

4th. On Requests.

5th. On Finances.

6th. On Resolutions.

7th. When and where shall our next Association meeting be held?

8th. Who shall preach the 'Introductory sermon, and who shall be his alternate.

9th. How many copies of Minutes, and who shall superintend the printing and distribution of same.

Respectfully submitted.

W. R. PETREE,

JAMES AUSMUS.

B. We, your Committee on Preaching beg to submit the following report:

Friday, at the stand, Elder Gates; Friday night at church, Elder M. B. Weaver, Thomas Pierce.

Saturday, at the Stand, James Ausmus, W. R. Gates; Saturday night at church, M. B. Weaver, G. J. Boruff.

At Big Sinks school house, W. R. Gates, John F. Keck, T. G. Brantly.

At Stiner Ridge, Thomas Pierce, James Ausmus.

Sunday, Leonard White, W. R. Gates, Moderator to close.

Respectfully submitted,

ELVIN WEAVER,

JAMES HARRELL,

HERMAN MUNSEY,

Together with the church.

C. We, your committee on Correspondence beg to report as follows:

That We write letters and send Messengers to the Nolachucky and Hiwassee Associations, and have said Mes-

sengers report their success to our next Association.
Respectfully submitted.

JOHN F. TAYLOR,
T. J. PIERCE,
ELVIN WEAVER.

D. We, your Committee on Request submit this report:
That we have all Obituaries furnished by the churches printed in our Minutes.

W. R. PETREE,
W. R. CAPPS.

E. We, your committee on Finance submit the following report:

Received from churches for printing Minutes $24.55.

DAVID WHITE,
JAMES BRANTLY.

11th. All of the foregoing reports ere received and the committies discharged.

12th. On motion appointed W. R. Petree, W. A. L. Ousley and Elder G. J. Boruff as Messengers to the Hiwassee and Nolachucky Associations.

13th. On motion, the Clerk to write corresponding letters to these Associations and print same in our Minutes.

14th. On motion, Elder M. B. Weaver write a circular letter, the same to be read at our next Association.

15th. On motion, our next Association will be held with the Church at Pleasant Hill, Claiborne County, Tenn., to commence on Friday before the third Saturday in August 1921.

16. On motion, Elder John F. Keck will preach the Introductory Sermon, and Elder G. J. Boruff be his alternate.

17. On motion, we have 600 copies of Minutes printed, and that the Clerk be allowed $10.00 for his services.

18. By motion, Be it Resolved, that we tender our heartfelt thanks to this beloved church and her surroundings for their hospitalities and kind treatment to us through this Association.

19. On motion, Minutes approved.

20. At this time Elder G. J. Boruff expressed a desire for prayer, when the Association bowed with him while he so ably invoked the blessings of God upon us, and a lovely parting was expressed.

Adjourned to meet as above stated.

ELDER T. G. BRANTLY, Moderator, Sharps Chapel, Tenn.
SAM DAVIS, Clerk, Liberty Hill, Tenn.

SUNDAY.

At the appointed hour Sunday a well behaved audience assembled at the alter and listened attentively to a well delivered sermon by Elder Gates from Rev. 7th chapter and 13th verse: "What are these arrayed in white robes, and whence came they?"

Closing remarks were made by the Moderator, all of which was delivered in a most loving manner. with greatest interest to all and was listened to with the closest attention and a lovely parting was expressed among the people by the sheding of tears and embracing each other while taking the parting hand.

THE CLERK.

CARRESPONDING LETTERS.

We, the Powell's Valley Associatoin of Primative Baptists, now in session with the church at Oak Grove, Union County, Tenn., to our sister Associations, with whom we correspond, to-wit: The Nollachucky and Hiwassee:

Dear Sisters: We desire to keep up our correspondence with you and have chosen these, our beloved brethren, to be with you in your next annual meeting, whom we hope you will reveive to sit with you in your Godly consultation, to-wit: Elder G. J. Boruff, W. R. Petree, W. A. L. Ousley.

May the God of all grace be with you and guide you in the way of all truth is the prayer of your little sister

ELDER T. G. BRANTLY, Moderator,
SAM DAVIS, Clerk.

OBITUARIES.

With sadness we insert the names, dates of birth and death ofthese, our beloved brothers and sisters:

Martha Smith was born May 18, 1855; professed faith in Christ in 1868, joined the Missionary Baptist and lived with them till the year 1871. then joined the Primative Baptist at Cave Spring where she lived a faithful member until death, August 4, 1920. She leaves her husband, 3 sons and 7 daughters and a host of friends to mourn her loss.

Alice Brantly was born July 31, 1885, professed faith in Christ and joined the church at Cave Spring and was baptised in 1913. Died Feburary 2, 1919.

Milfred, son of Elder Alfred and Barbara Boruff, was born Jan. 16, 1899, professed faith in Christ and joined the Primative Baptist church at Black Fox when quite young, of which he lived a consistent member until death, which occurred Jan. 31, 1920. He leaves a companion, father, mother, 2 brothers and 5 sisters, with a host of friends to mourn his loss.

Margaret Keck, wife of Sam Keck, professed faith in early life and joined the Primative Baptist church and lived a faithful Christain until Death set her free from her afflictions in the early spring of 1920. She leaves a number of children and a host of friends to mourn her loss.

Brother Charlie Cox, a member of Pleasant Point church. With sadness and sorrow we recall to memory our beloved brother Cox, who served in the church as Deacon for years, and his good Christain life has been missed in the church and community in which he lived. Bro. Cox leaves a number of children and a host of friends to mourn his loss. The bereaved ones have a hop ethat they will meet him again in the sweet bye and bye.

Sister Lanny Hill, wife of Samuel Hill, daughter of Wesley and Abigail Poore, leaves an aged father, a loving husband, 2 sons, 3 daughters and a host of friends to mourn her loss. Born Nov. 14, 186 . Joined the church at Meyers Grove Dec. 1884, of which she lived a consistent member until death, which occurred July 20, 1920. I ask the brothers and sisters to pray for her husband, sons and daughters.

With sad hearts we announce the death of our well beloved brother, W. A. Drummonds, who was a father in our church. He professed faith in Christ and joined the church at Pleasant Point, September 7, 1866; served the Church 29 years as Deacon and was ordained to the full work of the Ministry October 26, 1913. Departed this life June 6, 1920, aged 69 years, 5 months and 5 days. He lived a consistent Christain. He was well beloved by all who knew him. He fell asleep in the arms of Jesus; died in a full triumph of a living faith, leaving behind 3 brothers, 6 sons, 2 daughters and a host of grand children, friends and relatives to mourn the loss of a dear father and loving Christain. We extend to the children and grand-children our love and heart-felt sympathy in their bereaved state.

These all died in full triumph of the living faith. We could not wish them back again, but the memory of them has a resting place in our heart. The bereaved ones all have our prayers and best wishes, and we hope to meet our loved ones who have gone on before, in the sweet bye and bye.

THE CLERK.

ELDERS.	POSTOFFICE	CO. and STATE
T. G. Brantly,	Sharps Chapel,	Union County, Tenn.
Oscar Ausmus,	Speedwell,	Claiborne Co., Tenn
H. L. Alston,	Tazewell,	Claiborne Co., Tenn.
James Ausmus,	Speedwell,	Claiborne Co., Tenn
A. J. Boruff,	Lost Creek	Union County, Tenn.
Alfred Boruff,	Maynardville,	Union County Tenn
Calvin Collins,	R 4 Morristown,	Hamblin Co. Tenn.
Jno. F. Keck,	Goin,	Claiborne Co. Tenn.
Mathew Oliver,	Tate,	Grainger Co. Tenn.
Thomas Pierce,	Speedwell,	Claiborne Co. Tenn
H. A. Shofner,	Harrogate,	Claiborne Co. Tenn.
A. Shelton,	Tate,	Grainger Co. Tenn.
M. B. Weaver,	Lost Creek,	Union Co. Tenn.
Leonard White,	LaFollette,	Campbell Co. Tenn.
John A. Webb,	Gibson Station,	Lee Co Va.
Esau Keck,	Goin,	Claiborne Co. Tenn.

LICENTIATES.

Charlie Stanifer,	Speedwell	Claiborne County, Tenn.
W. R. Petree,	Gibson Station,	Lee County Va.
C. B. Weaver,	Lost Creek,	Union County, Tenn
Elvin Weaver,	Lost Creek,	Union County, Tenn.
W. A. Atkins,	Tate,	Grainger County, Tenn.
Jno. C. Owsley,	Gibson Station,	Lee County, Va.
S. S. Wilson,	Gibson Station,	Lee County, Va.

Table of Statistics.

Churches.	NAMES OF DELEGATES.	Rec'd by Baptism	Rec'd by letter	Rec'd by Relation	Restored	Dismissed by letter	Excluded	Deceased	Total	Sat. Meeting	Contributions
Big Barren	Not represented. Come on.										
Black Fox	W. M. Perry, Sam Capps, D. H. Shelby, Herman Munsey, W. M. Munsey, W. R. Capps.	3						1	78	4	$1.50
Cave Spring	James Brantly, Freeman Brantley, James Brantly, Jr., W. H. Brantly.	2	1	1				1	136	3	2.00
Cedar Spring	J. L. Drummonds.					2		1	63	4	4.80
Gibson Station	W. R. Petree.								65	1	2.00
Hamilton Grove	No letter. Come on.										
Mossie Spring	Elder G. J. Boruff, M. B Weaver, T. G. Brantly, Bros. Horace White, Curtis Weaver.	13				2	1	2	216	2	4.25
New Hebron	No letter. Come on.										
Norton	No letter. Come on.										
Oak Grove	W. A. L. Ousley, Jacob Jonson, R. L. Dyke, W M Lawson, W. M. Shoffner, David White, together with the Church.	25	7		1	1	1	2	157	1	5.25
Pleasant Point	Elder John F. Keck.					1	1	2	100	2	2.00
Pleasant Hill	J. L. Harrell, Verlin Edwards, J. M. Wilder.							1	43	4	2.25
Straight Branch	Elder Thomas Pierce, Brothers John Houston, J F. Taylor, T. A. Norton, John Norton, John Ausmus, G. N. Lamar.	1						1	69	1	2.00
	Left from last year's Minutes										5.00

135

OFFICIAL DIRECTORY

CHURCHES	County.	Pastors.	Clerks.	Clerk's Postoffices
Big Barren	Claiborne	M. B. Weaver	F. Edwards	Goin, Tenn.
Black Fox	Grainger	T. G. Brantly	Dan Davis	Liberty Hill, Tenn.
Cave Spring	Union	T. G. Brantly	W. H. Brantly	Speedwell, Tenn.
Cedar Spring	Claiborne	M. B. Weaver	J. L. Drummonds	New Tazewell, Tenn.
Gibson Station	Lee	J. F. Keck	Mary Ball	Gibson Station, Va.
Hamilton Grove	Union	Alfred Boruff	J. W. Raly	Maynardville, Tenn.
Mossie Springs	Union	T. G. Brantly	Eliza White	Lost Creek, Tenn.
New Hebron	Jefferson	MathewOliver	H. F. Cox	New Market, Tenn.
Noeton			H. L. Patrick	Tate, Tenn.
Oak Grove	Union	T. G. Brantly	David White	Sharp Chapel, Tenn.
Pleasant Point	Claiborne	M. B. Weaver	J. D. Keck	Goin, Tenn.
Pleasant Hill	Claiborne	Leonard White	Lincoln Edwards	Speedwell, Tenn.
Straight Branch	Union	Thomas Pierce	J. T. Taylor	Speedwell, Tenn.

136

MINUTES

OF THE

ONE HUNDRED AND SECOND ANNUALL SESSION

OF THE

POWELL'S VALLEY ASSOCIATION

OF

PRIMITIVE BAPTISTS

Field with the Church at

Pleasant Hill, Claiborne County, Tenn.,

August 19, 20, 21, 1921.

PROGRESS PRINT TAZEWELL. TENN.

137

ASSOCIATION PROCEEDINGS.

Minutes of the One Hundred and Second Annual session of Powell's Valley Association of Primitive Baptists, held with the church at Pleasant Hill, Claiborne County, Tennessee, August 19, 20, 21, 1921.

1st. Praise and prayer by Elder Thomas Pierce.

2nd. Introductory by Elder John F. Keck, from Revalation 1st. and 8th verses. God says: "I am Alpla and Omega; the beginning the end, followed by His alternate, G. J. Boruff.

3rd. After 15 minutes the Association was called to gather by singing. Prayer by Elder Thomas Pierce.

4th. On motion J. M. Wilder was elected Clerk Protem. Then called for letters from churches. Thirteen were received and read by the Clerk, assisted by John F. Keck.

5th. On motion letters received and the names of Messengers enrolled.

6th. On motion Elder T. G. Brantly was re-elected Moderator, and J. M. Wilder, Clerk.

7th. Called for petitionary letters. Received two, one from LaFollette, Campbell County, Tenn., and one from Red Hill, Claiborne County, Tenn.

8th. Called for correspondence and received Elder W. R. Gates from the Nolachucky Association, and Brother R. H. Petitt, from Hiwassee Association and minutes who were heartily welcomed to a seat among us.

9th. Ministers and brothers who were not deligates were invited to seats, whereupon Elder W. R. Gates, from the Nolachucky Association, and Elder J. C. Hayes, from the Wautanga Association, and Bro. R. H. Petett, from the Hifassee Association came forward and were welcomed to seats with us.

1th. Appointed the following committies.

(a) On arrangements, Bros. Elvin Weaver and Elder Leonard White.

(b) On preaching, Samuel Capps, J. L. Harrell, Joseph Smith, together with the church.

(c) On correspondence, Elder M. B. Weaver John F. Keck.

(d) On request, Elder W. R. Ferree and W. H. Brantly.

(e) On finance, Elder Hiram Shoffner, LaFayette Buckner.

12th. On motion adjourned till 9: a. m. Saturday.

SATURDAY'S PROCEEDING.

1st The Association met pursuant to adjournment.

2nd. Praise and prayer by Elder G. J. Boruff.

3rd. The Association was called to order by the Moderator.

4th. Called for reports of Committies.

(a) We, your Committee on arrangements beg leave to submit the following order of business:

1st. Call the roll.

2nd. On Preaching.

3rd. On Correspondence.

4th. On Requests.

5th. On Finance.

6th. On Resolutions.

7th. When and where shall our next Association meeting be held.

8th. Who shall preach the Introductory sermon, and who shall be his alternate.

9th. How many copies of the Minutes, and who shall superintend the printing and distribution of same.

Respectfully submitted,

ELDER LEONARD WHITE,

ELVIN WEAVER,

(b) We your Committee on preaching beg to submit the following report:

Friday at the stand, Elders, G. J. Boruff, Thomas Pierce.
Friday night at Pleasant Hill, Elders J. C. Hays, M. B. Weaver.
Davis Creek Elders W. R. Gates, Leonard White.
Strait Branch, Elders, G. J. Boruff, W. R. Petree.
Saturday at stand, Elders Leonard White, J. C. Hayes, Thomas Pierce.
Saturday night at Pleasant Hill, Elders, W. R. Gates, T. G. Brantly.
At Davis Creek, J. C. Hays, M. B. Weaver.
Sunday, Elders W. R. Gates, J. C. Hays, Leonard White.

Respectfully submitted,

SAMUEL CAPPS,

J. L. HARRELL,

JASPER SMITH.

Together with the church.

(c) We your Committee on Correspondence beg to report as follows: That we write letters and send Messengers to the Nolachucky and Hiwassee Associations, and have said Messengers report their success to our next Association.

Respetfully submitted,

M. B. WEAVER,

JOHN F. KECK.

(d) We your Committee on Requests submit this report: That we have all obituaries furnished by the churches printed in our Minutes.

Respectfully submitted,

W. R. PETREE,

W. H. BRANTLY.

(e) We your Committee on Finance submit the following report: Received from Churches for printing Minutes $32.85.

Respectfully submitted

HIRAM SHOFFNER,

LaFAYETTE BUCKNER.

11th. All of the foregoing reports are received and the Committies discharged.

12th. On motion appointed, T. G. Brantly, J. H. Smith, Elvin Weaver as Messengers to the Nolachucky Association, and write Correspondent letters to the Hiwassee Association.

13th. On motion the clerk to write Corresponding letters to these Associations and print same in our Minutes.

14th. On motion Elder John F. Keck, write a circular letter, the same to be read at our next Association.

15th. On motion our next Association will be held with the church at

New Hebron, Jefferson City, Jefferson County, Tennessee.

16th. On motion Elder Leonard White will preach the introductory sermon and Elder T. G. Brantly be his alternate.

17th. On motion we have 700 copies of Minutes printed and that the Clerk be allowed $6.00 for his service.

18th. On motion, be it resolved, that we tender our heartfelt thanks to this beloved Church and. her surroundings for their hospitalities and kind treatment to us through this Association.

19th. On motion Minutes approved.

Adjourned to meet as above stated.

Elder T. G. BRANTLY, Moderator, Sharps Chapel, Tenn.

J. M. WILDER, Clerk, Cumberland Gap, Tenn.

SUNDAY

At the appointed hour Sunday a well beloved audience assembled at the alter and listened attentively to the well delivered sermon by Elders W. R. GATES, J. C. HAYS, Leonard White, closing remarks were made by the Moderator all of which was delivered in a most loving manner, with greatest interest to all and was listened to with the closest attention. And a lovely parting was expressed among the people by the sheding of tears and embracing each other with shaking the parting hand.

THE CLERK.

CORRESPONDING LETTERS.

————****————

To the Nolachucky and Hiwassee Association, with whom we correspond, Dear Brethern as we have been blessed for many years to meet with you, by letter and Messengers we still hope to enjoy the same privelage we have had this meeting Elder W. B. Gates and R. H. Petitt, whose company and labor we greatly enjoy, we would love to meet with you at your next meeting whom we hope you will receive. in Godly council. May your meeting be a prosperous one, is the prayer of your little sister in greatest bounds of love.

ELDER T. G. BRANTLY, Moderator.

J. M. WILDER, Clerk.

CIRCULAR LETTER.

————****————

Near one year ago the Association choe me to prepare a circular letter for these Minutes, of 1921, and feeling unable for this great undertaking, I will ask the good Lord to guide my pen. I feel that there are many things that should be laid before our beloved people, for the benefit of our great cause I will refer the reading to Malachi 3rd chapter and 8th verse, will a man rob God, yet have robbed me, but ye say how we robbed thee in leather and offerings, we find the text refers to Sareal of old who should love him more loyal and obedient to our great Creator. Yet they seem to make strange that a man would rob God, yet they were guilty. Ye are cursed with a curse for ye have robed me, even this unholy nation. Verse nine.

If Isreal would have done such though would it look very strange for men in this last age where coveteousness is so prominent to down the same, there are various ways of robing God, but I can only mention a few in this letter, the Chief Priest answered him and said since the people began to bring the offering into the house of the Lord, we have had enough to eat, and have left plenty. 2nd, Chronicles 31st. 10th. We can easily see by the above that if each of us should bring offering proper to the alter there would not be so many bleating lambs and hungry children. The Parisees did not seem to understand how they was mistreating our Saviour, but he told them they was, by mistreating his children, his Deciples, were doing much because they were helping the poor. Many people are robbing God of his honor in telling the people salvation is by work, when it is by grace alone. God is not pleased with a robbery, one of the high way robbers is the fellow that says Jesus Christ has six or seven churches (Denominations) when the Bible tells us he has only one (Milintant.) The Lord tells us his table is prepared in his kingdom (church). The people say it may be anywhere. See Luke 22, 29, 30 and I appoint unto you a kingdom as my Father hath appointed unto me, that ye may eat and drink at my table in my kingdom. If you rob a man you have that which does not belong to you, the one robbed is damaged, now let each one during the next twelve months bring his gift, both spiritual and temporal, the house of the Lord, that all may have plenty to eat and enjoy life once more your humble servant in the Lord. M. B. WEAVER.

OBITUARIES.

With sadness we insert the names, date of birth and death of these beloved brothers and sisters.

Mary Capps was borned Jan. 16th, 1872, died May the 4th, 1921, aged 49 years 3 months and 18 days. Professed faith in Christ in her early days, and joined the Primative Baptist church, at Black Fox and lived a faithful member until her death. Was married to Sam Capps, and to their union was born ten children, six girls and four boys all of which are living to mourn the loss of a loving mother and companion.

Opal Beatris White daughter of J. E. and P. A. White. Born September 22, 1902, joined the church in December 1915, baptised the following May. Departed this life September 29, 1920, making her stay on earth 18 years and 7 days. She leaves a father and mother one sister with a host of relatives, friends and the church to which she belonged to mourn her loss. Opal was a good obedient daughter and one of the brightest of members of the Mossie Spring church, and writer feels that too much cannot be said of her life and virtue. She was our assistant clerk, and done her work well, we all miss her presence but father and mother miss her the most. But we would say dear Opal, sleep on until the great trump shall sound when we hope to see you again on that happy golden shore, we mourn not for her as one who has no hope. ELVIN WEAVER.

Leaty Weaver was born July 8, 1874 and was married to Louis Baily November 20, 1892, to this union was born ten children seven of this number still lives. She joined the church with her husband at Mossie Spring, January 2, 1894, they were both baptised in May following, and Leaty died June 26, 1921. She lived a writeous and consistent life was a loving and affectinate wife. A good Christian and was always honest, and loved her husband and children and also loved the church and was always ready to help the sick; was very patint and bore her own afflictions so well she told her husband that she could not get well. I am ready to go all I hate is leaving you and the children, you will be like the lonesome dove that mourns her absent mate. She talked of beautiful home in heaven during her last days, and was reconciled to the will of the Lord. Leaty will be missed by all who knew her, especialy her husband, children and church, but she has past into the great beyond. We mourn not for her as those whohave no hope.

Leonard Drummonds, son of E. S. and Margaret Drummonds. Born March 31, 1901, died July 8, 1921. Professed faith in Christ sometime ago and desired to join the Baptist church, and be baptised. And was married to Bertha Southerland, August 16, 1920. And to their union was born one son He leaves father, mother, five brothers and five sisters, a wife and baby and a host of friends to mourn his loss. But we believe our loss to be his eternal gain.

Bertha Robertson was born February 10, 1839, aged 84 years. She departed this life May 9, 1921. She professed faith in Christ about thirty years ago, and joined the Primitive Baptist at Moyers Grove, and lived a faithful member until death. She leaves three children two daughters and one son two sisters and a host of friends to mourn her loss. She told these who were present to meet her in heaven, and said for them to meet her and said it would be a happy change.

RULES OF DECORUM.

_____*♦♢*_____

1st. The churches composing the Powell's Valley Association shall not be confined to any set rule as to the specified number of Messengers. They shall have in the body, but shall have the right to name their letters as many as they choose and in addition all orderly maie members of any of the churches being present shall be entitled to seats in the body as Messengers of their respective churches, with all the rights and privileges of the same.

2nd. The Messengers thus assembled shall be denominated to be the Powell's Valley Primitive Baptist Association.

3rd. For the purpose of historical information and statsical edification the churches are requested to state in letters, the total number of members in fellowship, the received by baptism, by letter, by confession of faith. The number dismissed, excluded and died since last session. Also the time of their meeting, their pastoral supply and the amount of money contributed for Minutes and other purposes, together with any other information they deem appropriate for the edification of the saints and the glory of God.

4th. This Association shall have no power to answer queries, give advice or dictate to the churches in any case, or to lord it over God's heritage nor any power by which she candirectly ♠ e indirectly infringe on the etorneal rights of the churches, or censure and try any churches or member in reference to faith and practice or determine upon the validity of gospel ordinances. These things shall rest entirely with the churches, but henceforward our annual meeting shall be only for the purpose of hearing from each other and for the worship of God and the mutual confort and edification of the saints. To this we reserve the privileges annually on Friday before the third Saturday in August and two followings days, or at such other time as may be agreed upon with any church that may invite us, having due regard to priority of claims and the good of the cause to protect our own stand while in session from heresy and disorder, to recognize and invite any visiting Primitive Baptist Minister or lay brother to worship with us that we may deem proper to request the brethren of our own body to visit other churches or bodies in our behalf with whom we may desire to cultivate Christian fellowship; to publish a Minute of our proceedings.

5th. Each session of the body shall have a Moderator and Clerk, who shall be duly chosen according to the rules hereinafter prescribed and who shall hold office until re-elected.

6th. Any orderly member of any church belonging to this body, when convened, being present, shall be eligible to election as Moderator and Clerk, or to sit on committee appointed by the same.

7th. In all elections or questions that may be necessary to determine by vote, the vote shall be taken by churches, each church being entitled to three votes for any number of members less than one hundred, and one additional vote for every fifty or fraction thereof above the first hundred, but the Messengers of each church, as a body, may devide her vote as they see proper.

8th. All elections or questions coming to a vote shall be determined by a majority of the votes cast, and it shall be the duty of the minority to acquiese in the decision thus reached.

9th. If new churches desire to be admited into this Union they shall petition by letter and Messengers, and if vouched for or recommended by one or more sister churches or the presbyter constituting them as orthordox and orderly, they shall be received by the voice of the body and manifiested by the Moderator giving the Messenger the right hand of fellowship.

10th. Any motion or resolution introduced clearly inconsistent with the above rules shall be promptly ruled out of order unless withdrawn by the mover.

11th. Any Messenger being ruled out of order by the Moderator shall have the right to appeal to the body on the question of order and if sustained shall be allowed to proceed, but if not shall take his seat.

12th. Our meetings being held in the name of Christ and the worship of God, each Messenger is expected to observe due and proper order therein.

13th. It will not be considered good order for any Messenger, whose name has been enrolled as such, to abraptly break off or obsent himself from the Association without leave.

14th. The Moderator shall be entitled to the privileges of speech as other members, provide the chair be filled.

15th. The Minutes of the Association shall be read and approved by the body and signed by the Moderator before adjournment.

16th. The Association shall be opened and closed by prayer,

17th. Amendments to these rules may be made at any time by a majority of the union voting by churches when they deem it necessary, provided such amendments do not compromise the sovereignty of the churches, nor have a tendency to give this body undue power or jurisdiction over them.

ELDERS	POSTOFFICE	COUNTY & STATE
T. G. Brantly,	Sharps Chapel,	Union County Tenn.
Oscar Ausmus,	Speedwell,	Claiborne, County, Tenn.
H. L. Alston,	Tazewell,	Claiborne County, Tenn.
James Ausmus,	Speedwell,	Claiborne County, Tenn.
A. J. Boruff,	Lost Creek,	Union County, Tenn.
Alfred Boruff,	Maynardville,	Union County, Tenn.
Calvin Collins,	R 4 Morristown,	Hamblin County, Tenn
Jno. F. Keck,	Goin,	Claiborne County, Tenn.
Mathew Oliver,	Tate,	Grainger County, Tenn.
Thomas Pierce,	Speedwell,	Claiborne County ,Tenn.
H. A. Shofner,	Harrogate,	Claiborne County, Tenn.
A. Shelton,	Tate,	Grainger County, Tenn.
M. B. Weaver,	Lost Creek,	Union County, Tenn.
Leonard White,	LaFollette,	Cambpell County, Tenn.
John A. Webb,	Gibson Station,	Lee County, Va.
Esau Keck,	Goin,	Claiborne County, Tenn.
John Ausmus,	Speedwell,	Claiborne County, Tenn.

LICENTIATES.

Charlie Stanifer,	Speedwell,	Claiborne County, Tenn
W. R. Petree,	Gibson Station,	Lee County, Va.
C. B. Weaver,	Lost Creek,	Union County, Tenn.
Elvin Weaver,	Lost Creek,	Union County, Tenn.
W. A. Atkins,	Tate,	Grainger County, Tenn.
Jno. C. Owsley,	Gibson Station,	Lee County, Va.
S. S. Wilson,	Gibson Station,	Lee County, Va.

CLERKS AND THEIR POSTOFFICES.

Straight Branch, ... J. F. Taylor, ...Speedwell, Tenn

Plasant Hill, ... Lincoln Edwards, ... Speedwell, Tenn.

Pleasant Point, ...J. D. Keck, ... Goin, Tenn.

Mossie Spring, ...Curtis Weaver, ... Sharps Chapel, Tenn.

LaFollette,.................... ... Aaron Davis, ... LaFollettee, Tenn.

Hamilton Grove, ... H. F. Hamilton, ...Maynardville, Tenn.

Oak Grove, ... Lauret White, ... Sharps Chapel, Tenn.

Cave Spring, ...W. H. Brantly, ... Speedwell, Tenn.

Black Fox, ... Sam Davis, ... Liberty Hill, Tenn.

Cedar Spring, ... J. L. Drummonds, ... New Tazewell, Tenn.

New Hebron, ...,... Lon Revean, ...Jefferson City, Tenn.

Gibson Station, ...Mary Ball, ... Gibson Station, Va.

Red Hill, ...,.........Jeff Treece, ... Speedwell, Tenn.

CHURCHES	NAME OF DELEGATES	Received by Baptism	Received by relation	Dismissed by letter.	Deceased	Excluded	Sat Meeting.	Contributions	Total Member ship
Black Fox	J. L. Buckner, Sam Capps, C. M. Cabbage. T. G. Brantly, G. J. Boruff, M. B. Weaver,	12	2		2	1	3	$2.35	89
Mossie Spring	John Hopper, Leonard White, Eivin Weaver	6			2	2	6.75	120
Strait Branch	J. F. Taylor, J. N. Seymore, Thos Pierce, I.J. Norton, David Ausmus, Harrison Smith	2			2		1	2.15	
Ied Hill	W. F. Robinson, Jeff Treece			2				2.05	
Cave Spring	Joseph Smith, Jas. Brantly, Ben Brantly, W. H. Brantly.						3	1.55	136
New Hebron	By letter							50	
Gibson Station	H. A. Shoffner, John Webb, Geo. Shoffner, Job Ball, Geo. Southers, Sanders Wilson.	7	1				1	2.00	71
LaFollette	Aaron Davis, Thos. Davis, Geo. Heatherly						3	1.00	125
Pleasant Hill	J. L. Harrell, J. M. Wilder, Jeff Maddox, Vertin Edwards	8				1	4	2.00	50
Oak Grove	W. A. Owsley, R. L. Dike, W. R. Petree, LaFayette Ellison.	4	1			1	1	5.00	151
Cedar Spring	H. L. Alston, M. M. Welch	16				1	4	2.50	78

Table of Statistics

MINUTES

of the

ONE HUNDRED AND THIRD ANNUAL SESSION

of the

POWELL'S VALLEY ASSOCIATION

of

PRIMITIVE BAPTISTS

Held with the Church at

New Hebron, Jefferson County, Tenn.,

August 18, 19, 20, 1922

Next Association will be held with the Church at Red Hill, Claiborne County, Tenn., beginning on Friday before the third Saturday in August 1923

PROGRESS JOB PRINT, TAZEWELL, TENN.

OFFICIAL DIRECTORY

CHURCHES	COUNTY	PASTOR	CLERK	CLERK'S POSTOFFICE
Noeton	Grainger	Mathew Oliver	H. L. Patrick	Noeton, Tenn.
Black Fox	Grainger	T. G. Brantly	San Davis	Liberty Hill. Tenn.
Big Barren	Claiborne.	None		
Cave Spring	Union	None	W. H. Brantly	Speedwell, Tenn.
Cedar Spring	Claiborne.	M. B. Weaver		
		H. L. Alston, Assist.	G. L. Drummonds	New Tazewell, Tenn.
Gibson Station	Lee	Leonard White	Mary Ball	Gibson Station, Va.
Hamilton Grove	Union	John F. Keck	J. W. Benley	Maynardville, Ten.
Mossy Springs	Union	M. B. Weaver	Curtis Weaver	Lost Creek, Tenn.
New Hebron	Jefferson	C. C. Collins	Lon Finchum	R 5 New Market, Tenn.
Oak Grove	Union	T. G. Brantly	David White	Sharps Chapel, Tenn.
Pleasant Point	Claiborne.	John F. Keck	J. D. Keck	Goin, Tenn.
		Esau Keck, Asst.		
Pleasant Hill	Claiborne.	Leonard White	Lincoln Edwards	Speedwell, Tenn.
Straight Branch	Union	Thomas Pierce	J. T. Taylor	Speedwell, Tenn
Rocky Dale	Knox	T. G. Brantly	M. C. Dunn	Corryton, Tenn.
Red Hill	Claiborne.	T. G. Brantly	Jeff Treece	Speedwell, Tenn
Davis Chapel	Campbell	Leonard White	Aaron Davis	LaFollete, Tenn.

147

Association Proceedings.

Minutes of the One Hundred and Third Annual Session of the Powell's Valley Association of Primitive Baptists, held with the church at New Hebron, Jefferson County, Tenn., August 18-19-20-, 1922.

1st. After praise and prayer, Introductory Sermon by Elder Hembra, of the Nolachucky Association, from the 3rd chapter and 3rd verse of Philippians: "For we are the circumcission which worship God in the Spirit and rejoice in Christ Jesus, and have no confidence in the flesh."

2nd. The Association was called to order by the Moderator.

3rd. Called for letters from sister churches. Nine were received read by the Clerk and Elder John F. Keck.

4th. On motion letters received and Messengers names enrolled.

5th. On motion elected John F. Keck Moderator, and Sam Davis Clerk.

6th. Called for petitionary letters. Received one from Rocky Dale Church.

7th. On motion the letter from Rocky Dale Church was received, with her delegation. who was welcomed to a seat with us.

8th. Called for correspondence and received Elder Hembra and Minutes from the Nolachucky Association, who was welcomed to a seat with us.

9th. Ministers and brethren invited to seats who were not delegates. Elder W. R. Gates, of the Hiwassee Association came forward and was welcomed to a seat with us.

10th. Appointed the following committees:

A. On arrangements, Elder C. C. Collins, Bro. Elvin Weaver, W. T. Roberson, Marshall Collins.

B. On preaching, Elder W. R. Petree, W. M. Perry, M. C. Dunn, together with the Church.

C. On Correspondence, Bro. Elvin Weaver, Elder Mathew Oliver.

D. On request, Brother Earnest Hamilton, Edi Graves.

E. On Finance, Elder T. G. Brantley, Bro. W. A. L. Owsley, H. F. Cox.

11th. On motion circular letter called for and read by Elder John F. Keck.

12th. On motion an investigating committee was appointed to praise circular letter.

F. On investigation, B.os. M. C. Dunn, Eivin Weaver, Eli Graves.

13th. On motion committee received.

14th. On motion adjour.ied till Saturday morning at 9:30 o'clock.

SATURDAY'S PROCEEDINGS.

1st. The Association met pursuant to adjournment.

2nd. Praise and prayer by Elder M. B. Weaver.

3rd. The Association was called to order by the Moderator.

4th. On motion called for reports of committees, which were read a.id adopted as follows:

We your committee on arrangements beg leave to report the following order of business:

1st, Call the roll; 2nd, On preaching; 3rd, On correspondence; 4th, On request; 5th, On finances; 6th, On resolutions; 7th, When a.id where shall our next Association be held. 8th, Who shall preach the Introd.ctory Sermon, and who shall be his alternate; 9th, How many co ie.s of our Minutes, and who shall su eri.itend the printing and distribution of same?

Respectfully Submitted,   ELVIN WEAVER,
                 MATHEW OLIVER,
                 W. F. ROBERSON.

5th. Called the roll and erased the names of absentees.

6th. On motion the Clerk was instructed to write corresponding letters to the Hiwassee and Nolachucky Associations.

B. We, your committee on preaching beg leave to s..bmit the following arrangements

Friday night at the Church, Elder W. R. Gates, Mathew Oliver, the Moderator to close.

Sat rday at Stand, Elder T. G. Brantly, H. L. Alston, and Mathew Oliver to close.

Saturday evening at 5 o'cloc' the ordaination of Alfred Parks will be attended to, after which there will be a few mi.iutes intermission, then freaching by Brother W. R. Petree a.id Mathew Oliver.

Sunday at Stand, Elder W. R. Gate.i, M. B. Weaver and the Moderator to close.

Respectfully submitted,   M. C. DUNN,
                 W. R. PETREE,
                 W. M. PERRY,
                      To gether with the Church.

C. We, your committee on Correspondence beg leave to report as follows:

That we write letters and send Messengers to the Hiwassee and Nolachucky Associations, and as many other Associations as we can conveniently correspond with, and have said Messengers report their success to our next Association.

Respectfully submitted,   ELVIN WEAVER,
MATHEW OLIVER.

D. We, your committee on investigation of circular letter, after due examination recommend that it be inserted in o r Minutes.

Respectfully submitted,   M. C. DUNN,
ELVIN WEAVER,
ELI GRAVES.

E. We, your committee on requests make this report:

That we have all obituaries furnished by the Churches printed in our Minutes.

R espectfully submitted,   W. E. HAMILTON,
ELI GRAVES.

F. We, your committee on fiance make the following report:

Received for printing Minutes, ... $21.43
Visiting Mini ters traveling expenses .... $ 4.45
Res ectfully submitted,   T. G. BRANTLY,
W. A. L. OWSLEY,
H. F. COX.

7th. All the foregoing reports received and committees discharged.

8th. On motion, be it resolved that each Church is requested to contribute for the traveling expenses of visiting Ministers expected to visit our Associations.

9th. On motion appointed Elder M. B. Weaver, and T. G. Brantly as Messengers to the Hiwassee Association, and W. A. L. Owsley, Mathew Oliver and M. B. Weaver to the Nolachucky Association.

10th. That the Clerk write a corresponding letter to these Associations.

11th. Appointed Elder Leonard White to write a circular letter for the Association next year.

12th. On motion, we have 600 copies of our Minutes printed and that Clerk superintend the printing and distribution of same, that he be allowed $6.00 for his services.

13th. On motion, it was ordered that the printer's fee be inserted in our Minutes.

14th. On motion our next Association will be held with the Church at Red Hill. Claiborne County, Tenn., to commence on Friday before the third Saturday in August, 1923.

15th. On motion Elder Mathew Oliver will preach the Introductory Sermon and Elder. M. B. Weaver w ll be his alternate.

16th. Be it resolved, that we tender our heartfelt thanks to this beloved Church and her surroundings for their hospitalities and kind treatment through this Association.

17th. On motion Minutes were approved.

18th. On motion, adjourned to meet as above stated.

ELDER JOHN F. KECK, Moderator, Goin, Tenn.

SAM DAVIS, Clerk, Liberty H ll, Tenn.

NOTICE TO ALL.

That, whereas there appeared several mistakes in last year's Minutes, due to a misplacement of some of the papers, which rendered the Clerk unable to correct said mistakes, some of which appear in the statistical table; in Articles of Faith, in Obituaries and circular letter, we therefore ask that no offense be taken at said mistakes.

Sunday.

At the appointed hour on Sunday a well beloved audience assembled at the alter and attentively listened to the well delivered sermon by Elder W. R. Gates, from St. John, 3rd Chapter and 3rd verse: "Jesus answered and said unto him, verily, verily I say unto you, except a man be born again he can not see the kingdom of God," followed by Elder M. B. Weaver with closing remarks by the Moderator, John F. Keck, all of which was delivered in a most loving manner, with the gratest interest to all, and was listened to with the closest attention, and a loving parting was expressed among the people.

It was a touching scene to witness the dear Elders, brothers and sisters embracing each other and invoking the blessings of God upon each other.

While taking the parting hand, brothers and sisters, pray for unworthy me.

THE CLERK.

CORRESPONDING LETTER.

We, the Powell's Valley Association of Primitive Baptists, now in session with the Chuch at New Hebron Jefferson County, Tenn., to our sister Association with whom we desire to correspond, towit: The Nolachucky and Hiwassee Association, and for the purpose of continuing our correspondence with you, we send you this, our epistle of love, together with these, our beloved Elders and brothers, towit:

To the Hiwassee, Elder M. B. Weaver, T. G. Brantly.

To the Nolachucky, W. A. Owsley, Mathew Oliver, M. B. Weaver, whom we hope you will receive as such in the faith to sit with you in your Annual Meeting.

Now may the God of all grace be with and guide you in the way of all truth is the prayer of your sister Association.

ELDER T. G. BRANTLY, Moderator.

SAM DAVIS, Clerk.

Brother W. S. Collins.

This good old man passed to his reward October 6, 1921. He was born January 29, 1859, and was 62 years, 8 months and 7 days old. He is survived by his wife, 3 sons, 3 daughters, 21 grand children, 3 great-grand children and a host of friends to mourn his loss. He was married three times, the first time to Margaret Owens, the 2nd time to Mary Catherine Ingie, the 3rd time to Nancy Ayers. He professed faith in Christ about 1830, joined the Missionary Baptist Church in 1885. Joined the Primitive Baptist Church at Gibson Station, Va.. and lived a devoted and faithful member until death removed him to the great Church above. He never complained of his sufferings but often spoke of his happy home above.

SISTER POLLY ANN ENGLAND.

With sad hearts we announce the death of our dear sister, Polly Ann England. Sister England professed faith in Christ at an early age and joined the Primitive Baptist Church at Cedar Spring, December 1876. She lived a faithful member until her death, which occurred March 1, 1922. She leaves 2 daughters, 8 sons 1 brother, 6 sisters and a host of friends to mourn her loss. The bereaved ones have a hope that they will meet her again in the sweet bye and bye.

SISTER SUSAN DRUMMONDS.

Sister Drummonds was a member of Cedar Spring Church. With sadness and sorrow we recall to memory our beloved sister, who lived a Christian life. She joined the Primitive Baptist Church at Cedar Spring in July 1870. Died in 1922. She leaves 1 son. 6 daughters and a host of grand children and friends to mourn her loss. But we hope our loss is her eternal gain.

CIRCULAR LETTER.

Com lying with the order of last session of the Powell's Valley Association.

I endeaver to prepare a Circular Letter to be inserted in Minutes of 1922.

"But the Lord is the true God; He is the living God, an everlasting Kink. At His wrath the earth shall tremble and the natio.is shall not be able to abide His indignation." Jeremiah 10:10.

The 'pro het, speaking of the great disparity between God and Idols. Then amendiately after the Children of Isreal were brought out of Egypt.

And I brought you into a plentiful country to eat the fruits thereof and the goodness there of, but when ye entered ye defiled my land and made mine heritage an abomnation. Jeremiah 2:7.

Though troubles of distr. ctions, wars and famine that God sent on the people, this preacher of righteousness had the promise o. God being with him, and by persuation and asking that they worship a true and living God, instead of Idols, and it was contin..ed on throughout decades of time, until the restoration of Isreal.

God verfied His promise to the faithful. which was a covenant, that was made, which assured the people through the seed of their peo le the earth should be blest.

God verfied His promise to the faithful by sending Christ in for n, manner of life, purpose, which was to dedeem the peo le from under the curse of the law by preaching His own everlasting Gos el.

Evidently he taught three grand divisions in the Gos el (1) what God done fcr man. (2) what Gcd dcne in n an, (3) and what man must do to e.ijoy his Christian hope, that is to follow the spirit, a d give His body a ilving sacrifice, holy and acceptable to the Lord, which is his reasonable service.

Baptism being one in number of the req irements, prove your love to Him in this righteous act. Christ said: suffer it to be so. Now John, it becometh us to fullfil all rightiousness and by example showed how, a id commissioned His appostles to go into all the world and preach the Gos el to every creature, baptising them in His name.

Young converts, if you become in doubt of your ho ie, and feel by some cause you want to be ba tised, take it to the Lord in prayer, as the poet says;

> Am I a soldier of the Cross, a follower of t'ie lamb?
>> and shall I fear to own His cause
> or blush to speak His name.
> Must I be carried to the skies on flowery beds of ease,
>> While others fought to win the prize,
> and sail through bloody seas?

Then consider the spirit is willing but the flesh is weak, resolve to make a selfsacrifice in the house of God as you feel your many duties are Love

God supremly, love each other too, Live peaceably among all men as much as in you is, and so ful fil the love of Christ and live in hope of eternal life and the home where we will see Christ and be like him to shout his praises for ever more.

May God's Richest blesing rest on and prosper these words to their intended use.　　　　　　　　　　　ELDER JOHN F. KECK.

MINISTERIAL ROLL.

ELDERS.	POSTOFFICE.	STATE.
T. G. Brantly,	Sharps Chapel, Union County,	Tenn.
Oscar Ausmus,,	Speedwell, Claiborne County,	Tenn.
H. L. Alston,	R1 Tazewell, Claiborne County,	Tenn.
James Ausmus,	Speedwell, Claiborne County,	Tenn.
A. J. Boruff,	Corryton, Knox County,	Tenn.
Calvin Collins,	New Market, Jefferson County,	Tenn.
John F. Keck,	Goin, Claiborne County,	Tenn.
Mathew Oliver,	Noeton, Grainger County,	Tenn.
Thomas Pierce,	Speedwell, Claiborne County,	Tenn.
H. A. Shoffner,	Harrogate, Claiborne County,	Tenn.
... Shelton,	Tate, Grainger County,	Tenn.
M. B. Weaver,	Lost Creek, Union County,	Tenn.
Leonard White,	LaFollette, Campbell County,	Tenn.
John A. Webb,	Gibson Station, Lee County	Va.
Esaw Keck,	Goin, Claiborne County,	Tenn.
John Ausmus,	Speedwell, Claiborne County,	Tenn.
G. J. Coruff,	Maynardville, Union County,	Tenn.
Alfred Parks,	New Market, Jefferson County,	Tenn.

LICENTIATES.

Charlie Stanifer,	Speedwell, Claiborne County,	Tenn.
W. R. Petree,	Liberty Hill, Grainger County,	Tenn.
C. B. Weaver,	Lost Creek, Union County,	Tenn.
Flvin Weaver,	Lost Creek, Union County,	Tenn.
W. A. Atkins,	Tate, Grainger County,	Tenn.
John C. Owsley,	Gibson Station, Lee County,	Va.
S. S. Wilson,	Gibson Station, Lee County,	Va.
Geo. W. Moyers,	Goin, Claiborne County,	Tenn.

154

Table of Statistics.

CHURCHES.	NAME OF DELEGATES.	Rec'd by Baptism	Rec'd by letter	Rec'd by Relation	Restored	Dismissed by letter	Excluded	Deceased	Total Membership	Saturday Meetings	Contributions
Newton	Mathew Oliver, H. L. Patrick, W. M. Atkins	3							35	5	.75
Big Warren	Not represented. Come on next year								91	4	2.00
Black Fox	Sam Davis, W. M. Perry						1		63	4	2.00
Cave Spring	Not represented. Come on next year								63	4	2.00
Cedar Spring	H. L. Alston									1	
Gibson Station	Not represented. Come on next year					13		2			
Hamilton Grove	Earnest Hamilton, Troy Hamilton						2				
Mossy Spring	M. B. Weaver, T. G. Brantly, Elvin Weaver	1				17			203	2	2.50
New Hebron	Jessee L, Hisky, M. Collins, Lon Raneau	1							23		1.50
Oak Grove	W. O. L. Owsley, W. R. Pettee							2	149		3.80
Pleasant Point	John F. Keck	24						2	122	4	2.50
Pleasant Hill	Not represented. Come on next year										
Straight Branch	Not represented. Come on next year										
Rocky Dale	Eli Graves, M. C. Dunn, Elmer Graves, Cecil Pettee		4								
Red Hill	W. F. Roberson	1	11						21	3	2.18
Davis Chapel	No letter. Come on next year	13							25	2	2.00

Printing Minutes $20.00

MINUTES

of the

ONE HUNDRED AND FOURTH ANNUAL SESSION

of the

Powell's Valley Association

of

Primitive Baptists

Held with the Church at

Red Hill, Claiborne County, Tennessee

August 17, 18, 19, 1923

———**———

Next Association will be held with the Church at
Black Fox, Grainger County, Tenn., beginning on
Friday before the third Saturday in August 1924.

OFFICIAL DIRECTORY

CHURCH	COUNTY	PASTORS	CLERKS	CLERKS POSTOFFICE
Noeton	Grainger	Mathew Oliver	J. C. Oliver	Noeton, Tenn.
Straight Branch	Union	T. J. Pierce	John Taylor	Speedwell, Tenn.
Oak Grove		T. G. Brantly	David White	Sharps Chapel, Tenn.
Cave Spring	Union	T. J. Pierce	W. H. Brantly	Speedwell, Tenn.
Mossy Spring	Union	M. B. Weaver	Curtis Weaver	Lost Creek, Tenn.
Pleasant Hill	Claiborne	Leonard White	Lincoln Edwards	Speedwell, Tenn.
Rocky Dale	Knox	T. G. Brantly	M. C. Dunn	Corryton, Tenn.
Pleasant Point	Claiborne	Esaw Keck	J. D. Keck	Goin, Tenn.
Red Hill	Claiborne	H. A. Shoffner, Asst. John A. Wells	Jeff Treece	Speedwell, Tenn.
Davis Chapel	Campbell	Leonard White	Aron Davis	LaFollette, Tenn.
Moyer's Grove	Claiborne	H. L. Alston, Ast. H. A. Shoffner	J. L. Drummonds	Tazewell, Tenn.
Gibson Station	Lee, Va.	Leonard White, Ast. H. A. Shoffner	Mary Ball	Gibson Station, Va.
Black Fox	Grainger	T. G. Brantly	Sam Davis	Liberty Hill, Tenn.
Hamilton Grove	Union	John F. Keck	J. W. Bailey	Maynardville, Tenn.
New Hebron	Jefferson	C. C. Collins	Jessie L. Husky	New Market, Tenn.

157

Association Proceedings.

Minutes of the One Hundred and Fourth Annual Session of the Powell's Valley Association of Primative Baptist, held with the church at Red Hill, Claiborne County, Tenn., August 17, 18, 19, 1923.

Praise and prayer by Elder M. B. Weaver.

According to previous arrangements the Introductory Sermon was delivered by Elder Mathew Oliver, followed by Elder M. B. Weaver.

1st. After a few minutes intermission the Association was called to order by Moderator Elder John F. Keck.

2nd. Called for letters from Sister churches. Received 13, which were read by the Clerk and Bro. M. C. Dunn.

3rd. On motion all the letters were received and Messengers named enrolled.

4th. On motion Elder T. G. Brantly was elected Moderator and Sam Davis re-elected Clerk; M. C. Dunn assistant clerk.

5teh. Called for correspondence and received Minutes from Hiwassee Association by the hand of Elder W. R. Gates and Bro. L. L. Thomas.

6th. Minutes and brethren invited to seats, who were not delegates. Elder W. R. Gates and Bro. L. L. Thomas came forward and were heartily welcomed to seats with us.

7th. The following committees were appointed by Moderator:

A. On arrangements, Elder John F. Keck, Bro. M. C. Dunn, Elvin Weaver

B. On preaching, Josh Drummonds, Neal Lambert, William Brantly, together with the church.

C. On correspondence, Elder M. B. Weaver, Fli Graves, Elder T. J. Pierce.

D. On requests, Jeff Treece, Elvin Weaver, Esaw Keck.

E. On finance, Bro. M. C. Keck, Eli Graves, Elder Mathew Oliver.

8th. On motion committes received short talks of praise to this Association by Elder W. R. Gates, Bro. L. L. Thomas, Elders Mathew Oliver and John A. Webb.

9th. On motion, adjourned until Saturday morning at 9 o'clock.

Saturday Proceedings.

1st. The Association met pursuant to adjournment.

2nd. Praise and prayer by Elder Thomas Pierce.

3rd. The Association was called to order by Moderator.

4th. Called the roll and erased the names of absentees.

5th. On motion, call for the reports of committies.

A. We your committee on arrangements beg to report the following order of business:

That we take up the business of the Association, after the form of last year's Minutes.

Committee signed: Elvin Weaver, M. C. Dunn.

B. We your committee on preaching beg to submit the following: At the church Friday night, T. G. Brantly, W. R. Gates and H. L. Alston. Saturday, at the Stand, W. R. Gates, M. B. Weaver, Mathew Oliver.

Saturday night, M. B. Weaver, Thomas Pierce, L. L. Thomas at the church: At Thomas Hall, Saturday night, Elder T. G. Brantly, W. R. Gates.

Sunday at Stand, W. R. Gates, Leonard White and the Moderator to close. Committee signed, J. L. Drummonds, Neal Lambert, W. H. Brantly

to gether with the church.

Friday at the Stand, Elder G. J. Baruff, James Ausmus.

C. We your committee on correspondence beg to report the following That we continue our correspondance with the Hiwassee and Nolachucky Associations. That we write letters and send Messengers to the same.

Respectfully submitted, M. B. Weaver, T. J. Pierce, Eli Graves.

D. We your committee on Requests beg to submit the following: That we have all the obituarys published in our Minutes as we commonly do, and that our next annual session of the Powell's Valley Association be held with the church at Blackfox, Grainger County, Tennessee, to commence on Friday before the third Saturday in August 1924 Esaw Keck, Jeff Treece.

E. We your committee on finance beg to submit the following:

Received from churches for Printing Minutes $32.10. Fof ministers traving expesnes, $4.05. Respectfully submitted Bros. M. C. Keck, Eli Graves, Elder Mathew Oliver.

6th. On motion called for the circular letter which was presented and read by Elder Leonard White.

7th. On motion a committee was appointed to investigate circular letter, who reported the same to be correct.

Committee, Elder M. B. Weaver, James Lynch, Josh Drummonds.

8th. On motion Elder Leonard White, G. J. Boruff and Bro. Elvin Weaver were appointed Messengers to the Hiwassee Association, and Elder M. B. Weaver and T. J. Pierce Messengers to the Nolachucky Association.

9th. On motion the Clerk write Corresponding Letters to these Associations and have the same printed in our Minutes.

10th. On motion Elder Leonard White write a circular letter for the Association next year.

11th. On motion we have 800 Minutes printed; that the Clerk superintend the printing and distribution of same, and he be allowed remainder for his service.

12th. On motion our next Annual Session of the Powell's Valley Association will be held with the church at Black Fox, Grainger County, Tenn., to commence on Friday before the 3rd Saturday in August. 1924.

13th. On motion Elder Thomas Pierce preach the Introductory Sermon and Elder Leonard White be his Alternate.

14th. On motion be it resolved, That we tender our heartfelt thanks to this beloved church and her surroundings for their hospitalities and kind treatment during this, our stay with them through this Association.

15th. On motion Minutes approved.

16th. On motion adjourned to meet as above stated.

Signed: ELDER T. B. BRANTLY, Moderator. Sharps Chapel, Union County, Tennessee.

SAM DAVIS, Clerk, Liberty Hill, Tennessee.

SUMMARY OF PREACHING AT THE CHURCH DURING
THE ASSOCIATION:

1st. Friday at the Stand, Elder G. J. Boruff.

2nd. Friday night, Elder T. G. Brantly, W. R. Gates, H. L. Alston

3rd. Saturday, Elder M. B. Weaver from 13th and 14th verses Paul's letter to Timothy. "For if the blood of bulls and of goats, and the ashes of a heifer sprinkling the unclean, Sanctifiedth to the purifying of the flesh, how much more shall the blood of Christ, who through the eternal spirit, offered himself without spot to God, purge your conscience from dead works to serve the living God."

Followed by Elder W. R. Gates, Mathew Oliver.

4th. Saturday night, Elder M. B. Weaver, from Joshua 24 ch 15th verse · "If it seem evil unto you to serve the Lord, chose you this day whom you will serve, whether the Gods which your father served that were on the other side of the flood, or the Gods of the Amonites in whose land ye dwell, but as for me and my house, we will serve the Lord."

Followed by Elder Thomas Pierce and Bro. L. L. Thomas.

5th At the appointed hour Sunday a well behaved audiance assembled at the alter and attentively listened to the well delivered Sermons of Elders W. R. Gates, from 6th ch 37th verse St. John: "All that the father giveth me shall come to me, and him that cometh to me I will in no wise cast out." 44th verse: No man can come to me except the father which hath sent me draw him, and I will raise him up at the last day.

Followed by Leonard White and closing remarks by Moderator. All of which was delivered in a most loving manner, with greatest interest to all, and a loving parting was expressed among the people.

CORRESPONDING LETTERS TO OUR SISTER ASSOCIATIONS.

To-wit:
The Hiwassee and Nollachucky Association, with whom we correspond:

Very Dear Brethren in Christ: We desire to continue our correspondence with you and for that purpose have chosen the following named Elders and Brothers as corresponding delegates:

To the Hiwassee, Elder Leonard White, G. J. Boruff and Bro. Elvin Weaver.

To the Nolachucky, Elder M. B. Weaver, T. J. Pierce, whom we hope you will receive as sound in the faith and welcome them to sit with you in your Godly consultations.

May the God of all grace be with you and guide you in the way of all truth is the prayer of your little sister.
of your little sister.

ELDER T. G. BRANTLY, Moderator.

SAM DAVIS, Clerk.

OBITUARIES.

Mary Nicely, born October 6th, 1846. Joined the Primative Baptist Church at Dotson Creek in early life, of which she lived a faithful member until God saw fit to call her to Himself January 11th, 1923. Age 77 years, 8 months. 25 days. Sister Nicely will be missed by us, but we weep not for her as one for whom we have no hope.

In memory of our dear brother, Jacob Miller, who deceased this life April 7, 1923. Was born in the year 1857. He professed faith in Christ very early in youth. He joined the Primitive Baptist Church at Noeton in the year 1911. I believe Bro. Miller was a true hearted Christian and a faithful worker. He leaves to mourn his loss a wife, 4 children, 1 brother and a host of relatives and friends. But we believe he has gone where God's righteous people go, and when God calls His people, we believe he will be one among that number.

Noeton, Tenn., March, 1913.

I herein desire to give the travels of myself and wife. I professed faith in Christ in the year of our Lord, August, 1871, and joined the Primitive Baptist church and was baptized October, 1871. My wife also professed faith in Christ in the ear of our Lord, 1864, and joined the Primitive Baptist church in January and was baptized in July, 1871, and we were ordained Deacons by the Bean Creek church in the year of our Lord, 1878, and ever since that time we have strived to live to the glory of God. And I am made to express in the language of David: "I was young, but am now old, and have never seen the righteous forsaken nor his seed begging bread; and we have had our share of trouble, our conflicts and battles, but the God we serve has always given us the victory. And then we were made to cry out and say, "bless the Lord, O my soul," and we dedicated our home to the worship of God, and it has always been a great source of comfort to us, and we believe in our souls that the God we serve has multiplied the meal in the barrel and the oil in the cruse.

We never have failed to attend the communion meetings, and during this life I have finished my course and gone the way of all the earth. We have lived a life devoted all to the service of the Lord ever since the year 1871 and 1864. JOHN OLIVER died April 13, 1916.
MARY OLIVER, March 6, 1919.

Davis Chapel:—Brother Roy Goins was born July 4, 1885. Died July 22, 1923. He professed faith in Christ about 15 years ago and later became a member of this church and lived a consistant member until the day of his death. He being dead yet speaketh.

Sister Mattie Goins, wife of Roy Goins, was born March 29, 1895. Died March 26, 1923. Professed faith in Christ about 12 years ago and joined Davis Chapel Church and lived a consistent member until death. Died happy. Gone but not forgotten.

Circular Letter By Elder Leonard White

According to the previous appointment of this Association I endeavor to prepare a short circular letter to be inserted in the Minutes of 1923.

Dear brethren and sisters in Christ: While we are scattered in the various parts of the country, may we ever keep afresh in our minds the fact that we are one. One in purpose, one in design, one in love, worshiping one God, and serving Him through humanity. Witnessed by one spirit and served by one ministry. It should therefore be the height of our ambition to see our denomination grow and bloom as the fair rose of June. In order to a healthy body, and a rapid growth, we must take pure wholesome truth as the staff of life, and allow the minister to serve a balanced ration, handing forth both milk and meat, each individual, keeping daily in your mind the fact that there are other folks beside you. In order to keep in health as a body of Christians the following rules must be carried out.

1st. Pray continuous.

2nd. Pray for your enemies.

3rd. Love one another.

4th. Forsake not the assembling of yourselves to gether.

5th. Search the scriptures.

6th. Speak only the truth.

7th. Be careful what you say.

8th. Be careful what you do.

9th. Be good to your pastor.

10th. Obey the laws of your land.

Dear Brothers and sisters, please check daily on these ten rules and if carried out, I vouch for the greatest year of prosperity in the history of the Powell's Valley Association.

Oh! God, wake up thy good people to their real situation.

Oh! God in heaven, we do pray burden the minds and kindle anew the love in the hearts of your ministers. May the coming year be a year of great prosperity.

Lord, forgive and keep us humble at your feet, we ask it all in Jesus name.—AMEN

MINISTERIAL ROLL:

Elders	Postoffices.
T. G. Brantly,	Sharps Chapel, Union County, Tenn
H. L. Alston,	R 1 Tazewell, Claiborne County, Tenn.
James Ausmus,	Speedwell, Claiborne County, Tenn.
A. J. Boruff,	Corryton, Knox County, Tenn.,
Calvin Collins,	New Market, Jefferson County, Tenn.
John F. Keck,	, Goin, Claiborne County, Tenn.
Mathew Oliver,	Noeton, Grainger County, Tenn.
Thomas Pierce,	Speedwell, Claiborne County, Tenn.
A. Shelton,	Tate, Grainger County, Tenn.
H. A. Shoffner,	Harrogate, Claiborne County, Tenn.
M. B. Weaver,	Lost Creek, Union County, Tenn.
Leonard White,	LaFollette, Campbell County, Tenn.
John A. Webb,	Gibson Station, Lee County, Va.
Esaw Keck,	Goin, Claiborne County, Tenn.
John Ausmus	Speedwell Claiborne County, Tenn.
G. J. Boruff,	Maynardville, Union County, Tenn.
Alfred Parks,	New Market, Jefferson County, Tenn.

LICENTIATES:

Charlie Stanifer,	Speedwell, Claiborne County, Tenn.
W. R. Petree,	Liberty Hill, Grainger County, Tenn.
C. B. Weaver,	Lost Creek, Union County, Tenn.
Elvin Weaver,	Lost Creek, Union County, Tenn.
W. A. Atkins,	Tate, Grainger County, Tenn.
John C. Owsley,	Gibson Station, Lee County, Va.
S. S. Wilson,	Gibson Station, Lee County, Va.
George W. Mays,	Goin, Claiborne County, Tenn.

164

Table of Statistics.

CHURCHES:	NAMES OF DELEGATES.	Contribution	Sat. Meeting	Total Membership	Deceased	Excluded	Dis.-by-letter	Restored	Rec-by-relation	Rec-by-letter	Rec.by-ex-Bap
Black Fox	Sam Davis	$2.50	4	92	1			2	4		2
Gibson Station	Hiram Shoffner, John Webb, Herman Britton	2.50	4	92	1	1	1	2	4		8
Moyers Grove	Elder H. S. Alston, J. S. Drummonds, V. Moyers, E. S. Drummond, Will Drummonds, J. N. Furgerson										
Red Hill	Jeff Treece, Wily Treece, Bob Treece, Bee Treece Charlie Stanifer. W. T. Roberson.	2.65	4	67							4
Davis Chapel	Leonard White, Mossie White, G. E. Heatherly, Nancy Heatherly Cintha Heatherly, Murton Kitts.	2.80	2	36							1
Pleasant Point	M. J. Wilcok, M. C. Keck, Elder Esaw Keck, John F. Keck.	2.50	3	139	3	2				9	
Rock Dale	Elder G. J. Boruff, Eli Graves, M. C. Dunn	2.75	2	122							
Pleasant Hill	Vinlin Edwards, Lincoln Edwards, Neil Lambert, J. S. Mattocks.	4.00	3	33						3	9
Mossy Spring	Elder M. B. Weaver, W. M. White, Curtis Weaver, Rosen Meltebarger, Elven Weaver.	2.50	2	50							
Cave Spring	Freeman Brantely, W. H. Brantley.	4.05	2	197			5				2
Oak Grove	George Shoffner, John Graves.	1.20	3	100	2		6				1
Straight Branch	Elder T. J. Pierce, John Ausmus.	3.35	1	148		2					1
Noeton	Mathew Oliver	1.35	1	56	3						
Hamilton Grove	No Letter come on	2.00	3	35	1						
New Hebron	No Letter come on		4	63	3						
Big Barren	No Letter come on		1	23	1						

Printing Minutes, $20.00

165

MINUTES

of the

ONE HUNDRED AND FIFTH ANNUAL SESSION

of the

Powell's Valley Association

of

Primitive Baptists

Held With the Church at
Black Fox, Union County, Tennessee
August 15, 16, 17, 1924

———

Next Association will be held with the Church at
Gibson Station, Lee County, Va., beginning on
Friday before the Third Saturday in August 1925

Table of Statistics

CHURCHES	NAMES OF DELEGATES	Ministers Expenses	Contribution	Saturday Meeting	Total Membership	Deceased	Excluded	Dis. By Letter	Restored	Recd. By Letter	Recd. By Relation	Recd. By Ex. Bap.
Black Fox	Sam Capps, W. M. Munsey, Herman Munsey, Elder S. S. Pennington, C. L. Buckner, W. M. Perry		$3.00	3	90							
Gibson Station	S. S. Wilson, H. A. Shoffner		2.00	1	60			3				
Moyers Grove	H. L. Alston, E. S. Drummonds, J. L. Drummonds, G. B. Drummonds		2.65	4	70	3						6
Red Hill	Bee Treece, Wiley Treece, W. F. Roberson		2.00	2	37							1
Davis Chapel	No Letter—Come Next Year											
Pleasant Point	John F. Keck, M. C. Keck, George Mays, Curtis Keck		2.36	2	80					2		
Rocky Dale	Eli Graves, Elmer Graves, W. M. Lay, M. C. Dunn, J. C. Petree, L. F. Boruff, W. M. Loy		2.25	4	37							3
Pleasant Hill	Neal Lambert, J. L. Edwards, Verlin Edwards, G. H. Graves	$2.00	3.60	2	50							9
Mossy Spring	M. B. Weaver, T. G. Brantly, J. M. Kivett, Verlin Graves		2.00	2	206	1				1		
Cave Spring	W. H. Brantly	2.55	2.25	3	100							21
Oak Grove	W. R. Petree, W. A. L. Ousley		1.25	1	169							
Straight Branch	James Ausmus, John Ausmus, Thomas Pierce		3.50	1	50							
Noeton	Matthew Oliver		1.85	3	35							
Hamilton Grove	W. E. Hamilton, Cillus Hamilton, Emily Hamilton, Emma Hamilton, Henry Russell		3.00	4	65	1						2
New Hebron	Alfred Parks, Jim Collins		.75	1	23							
Big Barren	No Letter—Come On											

Association Proceedings

Minutes of the One Hundred and Fifth Annual Session of the Powell's Valley Association of Primitive Baptists, held with the Church at Black Fox, August 15, 16 and 17, 1924.

The Association met pursuant to .arrangements. Prayer by Elder John F. Keck.

Acccrding to previous arrangements the Introductory Sermon was delivered by Elder Thomas Price, from 1st Epistle of John, 3rd Chapter and 1st Verse: "Behold what manner of love the Father hath bestowed upon us, that we should be called the sons of God. Therefore the world knoweth us not, because it knew Him not." Followed by Elder T. G. Brantly.

1st. After 15 minutes intermission the Association was called to order by Moderator Elder T. G. Brantly.

2nd. Called for letters from sister churches; received 13, which were read by the Clerk and Bro. M. C. Dunn.

3rd. On motion all the letters were received and messengers names enrolled.

4th. On motion Elder H. L. Alston was elected Moderator.

5th. On motion Elder M. B. Weaver was elected Assistant Moderator.

6th. On motion Bro. Sam Davis was re elected Clerk.

7th. Called for Correspondence; received none.

8th. Called for Minutes, and Brethren who were not delegates. Elder Matthew Oliver came forward and was welcomed to a seat with us.

9th. Called for visiting ministers and Brethren and Sister Associations who were not delegates. Elder L. L. Thomas, of the Hiwassee Association came forward and was welcomed to a seat with us.

10th. The following committes were appointed by the Moderator:

A. On arrangements: M. C. Keck, W. H. Brantly, W. O. L. Ousley.

B. On Preaching: Will Roberson, E. S. Drummonds, M. J. Willcox, together with the church.

C. On Correspondence: S. S. Wilson, Elder Matthew Oliver, W. R. Petree.

D. On Request: James Kivett, C. L. Buckner, G. B. Drummonds.

E. On Finance: Eli Graves, Wiley Treece, J. L. Drummonds.

11th. On motion Committees received.

12th. On motion adjourned until Saturday morning at 9 o'clock.

Saturday Proceedings

1st. Met pursuant to adjournment.

2nd. Praise and prayer by Elder John Ausmus.

3rd. Called for report of committee on arrangements.

A. We your committee on arrangements beg leave to submit the following order of business:

1st. Call the Roll.

2nd. On Preaching.

3rd. On Correspondence.

4th. On Request.

5th. On Finance.

6th. On Resolutions.

7th. When and where shall our next Association be?

8th. Who shall preach the introductory sermon and who shall be his alternate?

9th. How many copies of Minutes, and who shall superintend the printing and distribution of same?

Respectfully submitted,

W H. BRANTLY, M. C KECK, W. A. L. OUSLEY.

10th. On motion report received and committee discharged.

11th. Call the roll and erase names of absentees.

12th. Call for report of the committee on Preaching.

B. We your Committee on Preaching beg leave to submit the following:

Saturday—At the stand, Elders M. B. Weaver, S. S. Wilson.

Saturda yNight—At the Church, Elders Matthew Oliver, H. A. Shoffner, Wooddale School House—Elders Thomas Price, James Ausmus.

Sunday—At the Stand—Elders Leonard White, Jake Ausmus, the Moderator to close.　　　　Respectfully submitted,

E. S. DRUMMONDS, M. J. WILLCOX, W. J. ROBERSON Together with the Church.

13th. On motion report received and committee discharged.

14th. Called for the report of the Committee on Correspondence.

C. We, your Committee on Correspondence beg leave to submit the following: That we continue our Correspondence with the Hiwassee and Nolachucky Associations, and that we write letters and send messengers to the same.　　　　Respectfully submitted,

MATTHEW OLIVER, W. R. PETREE, S. S. WILSON.

15th. On motion received the report and discharged committee.

16th. Called for the report of the Committee on Request.

D. We, your Committee on Request beg leave to submit the following. That we have all the obituaries published in our Minutes that the churches furnish, and that the next annual session of the Powel's Valley Association be held with the church at Gibson Station, Lee County, Va., to commence on Friday before the 3rd Saturday in August, 1925.

Respectfully submitted,

G. B. DRUMMONDS, J. M. KIVETT, C. L. BUCKNER.

17th. On motion report received and committee discharged.

18th. Called for the report of the Committee on Finance.

E. We, your Committee on Finance beg leave to submit the following: Received from churches for printing Minutes $30.15; for traveling Ministers expenses $5.50.   Respectfully submitted,

J. L. DRUMMONDS, WILEY TREECE, ELI GRAVES.

19th. On motion report received and committee discharged.

20th. On motion we have 800 copies of Minutes printed. That the Clerk superintend the printing and distribution of same and that he be allowed the remainder for his service.

21st. On motion the clerk write corresponding letter to the Hiwassee and Nolachucky Associations and have the same printed in our Minutes.

22nd. On motion we appoint Bro. W. A L. Ousley as delegate to the Hiwassee Association.

23rd. On motion we appoint Bro W. A. L. Ousley a delegate to the Nolachucky Association.

24th. On motion our next annual session of the Powell's Valley Association will be held with the Church at Gibson Station, Lee County, Va., to commence on Friday, before the third Saturday in August, 1925. That Elder T. G. Brantly preach the Introductroy Sermon, and Elder H. L. Alston be his alternate.

25th. On motion, Be it resolved that we tender our heartfelt thanks to this dear old church and the surrounding community for their hospitalities and kind treatment to us through this association.

26th. Adjourned to meet as above stated.

ELDER H. L. ALSTON, Moderator, Tazewell, eTnn.
SAM DAVIS, Clerk, Liberty Hill, Tenn.
M. C. DUNN, Asst. Clerk, Corryton, Tenn.

Sunday Proceedings

At the appointed hour Sunday a large and well behaved audience assembled at the stand and attentively listened to the well delivered sermon of Elder L. L. Thomas, from 2nd Chapter and 3rd Verse of 1st Corinthians: "For I determined to know anything among you, save Jesus Christ and Him crucified." followed by Johnie Ausmus and Elder T. G. Brantly from 1st Peter 2nd Chapter and 4th Verse: "Behold, I lay in Zion a chief corner stone. Elect Precious: and he that believeth on Him shall not be confounded," and closing remarks by Moderator, all of which was delivered in a most loving manner. With the greatest interest to all, and a loving parting was expressed by the shedding of tears, clapping of hands and invoking the blessings of God upon each other.

Corresponding letter to our sister Associations, to-wit:

The Hiwassee and Nolachucky Associations with whom we desire to correspond. Very dear brethren in Christ.—We desire to continue our long cherished correspondence with you and for that purpose have chosen the following named brother as corresponding delegate to the Hiwassee—Bro. W. A. L. Ousley, to the Nolachucky—Bro. W. A. L. Ousley, whom we hope you will esteem as sound in the faith and grant to sit with you in your annual meeting. May the God of all grace be with you and guide you in the way of all truth is the praper of this, your little sister Association.

ELDER H. L. ALSTON, Moderator.
SAM DAVIS, Clerk.

Obituaries

Brother R. W. Poore was born in the year 1847. Deceased August 13th, 1924. Professed faith in Christ and joined the Primitive Baptist Church at Cedar Spring October 1880, and lived a faithful member until death and leaves a companion, six children, four boys and two girls, two brothers, one sister and a host of grand children and great grandchildren and friends to mourn his loss.

———o———

In memory of our sister Franky Treece, who deceased this life January 22, 1924. She was born December 27, 1849. She professed faith in Christ very early in youth and joined the Primitive Church at Cedar Spring in the year, July 1874. We believe that sister Treece was a true christian. She leaves behind one son and two brothers and a host of friends to mourn her loss.

———o———

Rachel A. Meyers, was born July 2nd, 1858, and died after 23 years of suffering of paralysis at the home of her daughter, Mr. and Mrs. Joshua Drummonds, which occurred March 10th, 1924 at 8 o'clock, a. m., being 65 years. 8 months and 8 days old. She professed faith in christ and joined the Primitive Baptist Church at Cedar Spring December 1876, and lived a faithful member until death. Mrs. Meyers is survived by her husband, Vincent Meyers, near Clouds, Tenn., two sons, Alfred and Robert Meyers, of Middlesboro, Ky., and one daughter, Mrs. Della Drummonds, near Clouds. There are also surviving her eleven grandchildren and one gerat-grandchild, two brothers and a host of friends to mourn her loss, but our loss is her eternal gain. We highly appreciate the kindness and courtesy shown us during the sickness and death of our dear mother. Her remains were laid to rest in the Drummonds Cemetery, near Meyers Grove, which is the Cemetery she had selected for her resting place. Weep not, husband and children for me for I am waiting in Glory for you.

———o———

Sister Charity Brantly, wife of Augustus Brantly, was born May 19th, 1842. Deceased June 29, 1924. Age 82 years, 1 month and 10 days. Was married to Augustus Brantly August 7, 1862. To this union was born seven sons and six daughters. Four of the daughters deceased. She professed faith in God and joined the church at Mossy Spring in 1880, in which church she lived a consistent member until death

6

MINISTERIAL ROLL

Elder	Postoffice
H. L. Alston	Tazewell, Claiborne County, Tenn.
James Ausmus	Speedwell, Claiborne County, Tenn.
John Ausmus	Speedwell, Claiborne County, Tenn.
T. G. Brantly	Sharps Chapel, Union County, Tenn.
A. J. Boruff	Corryton, Knox County, Tenn.
G. J. Boruff	Corryton, Knox County, Tenn.
Calvin Collins	New Market, Jefferson County, Tenn.
John F. Keck	Goin, Claiborne County, Tenn.
Matthew Oliver	Noeton, Grainger County, Tenn.
Thomas iPerce	Speedwell, Claiborne County, Tenn.
Thornie Pierce	Speedwell, Claiborne County, Tenn.
A. Shelton	Tate, Grainger County, Tenn.
H. A. Shoffner	Harrogate, Claiborne County, Tenn.
Alfred Parks	New Market, Jefferson County, Tenn.
S. S. Wilson	Gibson Sation, Lee County, Va.
M. B. Weaver	Lost Creek, Union County, Tenn.
Leonard White	Lafollette, Campbell County, Tenn.
John A. Webb	Gibson Station, Lee County, Va.
Esaw Keck	Goin, Claiborne County, Tenn.

LICENTIATES

Charlie Stanifer	Speedwell, Claiborne County, Tenn.
W. R. Petree	Liberty Hill, Grainger County, Tenn.
C. B. Weaver	Lost Creek, Union County, Tenn.
Elvin Weaver	Lost Creek, Union County, Tenn.
W. A. Atkins	Tate, Grainger County, Tenn.
John C. Ousley	Gibson Station, Lee County, Va.
George W. Mays	Goin, Claiborne County, Tenn.
V. D. Graves	Sharps Chapel, Union County, Tenn.

OFFICIAL DIRECTORY

CHURCH	COUNTY	PASTORS	CLERKS	CLERKS POSTOFFICE
Noeton	Grainger	Matthew Oliver	J. C. Oliver	Noeton, Tenn.
Straight Branch	Union	James Ausmus	Thornie Price	Speedwell, Tenn.
Oak Grove	Union	T. G. Brantly	David White	Sharps Chapel, Tenn.
Cave Spring	Union	M. B. Weaver	W. H. Brantly	Sharps Chapel, Tenn.
Mossy Spring	Union	Leonard White	Curtis Weaver	Loyston, Tenn.
Pleasant Hill	Claiborne	Leonard White	Lincoln Edwards	Speedwell, Tenn.
Rocky Dale	Knox	T. G. Brantly	M. C. Dunn	Corryton, Tenn.
Pleasant Point	Claiborne	J. E. Keck	J. D. Keck	Goin, Tenn.
Red Hill	Claiborne	T. G. Brantly	Jeff Treece	Speedwell, Tenn.
Davis Chapel	Campbell	Leonard White	Jas. M. Kitts	LaFollette, Tenn.
Moyer's Grove	Claiborne	H. L. Alston	J. L. Drummonds	Tazewell, Tenn.
Gibson Station	Lee, Va.	Leonard White, Asst. H. A. Shoffner, Asst.	Mary Bell	Gibson Station, Va.
Black Fox	Grainger	T. G. Brantly	Sam Davis	Liberty Hill, Tenn.
Hamilton Grove	Union	John F. Keck	Frank Hamilton	Maynardvile, Tenn.
New Hebron	Jefferson	Calivn Collins	Jessie Husky	New Market, Tenn.

174

MINUTES

OF THE

106TH ANNUAL SESSION

OF THE

Powell's Valley Association

OF

PRIMITIVE BAPTISTS

HELD WITH THE CHURCH OF

GIBSON STATION, VA.

AUGUST 14, 15, 16, 1925

PROGRESS PRINT, TAZEWELL

ASSOCIATION PROCEEDNGS

Minutes of the One Hundred and Sixth Annual Session of the Powell's Valley Association of Primitive Baptists, Held With the Church at Gibson Station, Lee County, Virginia, on August 14, 15, 16. 1925.

1. Praise, by Elder M. B. Weaver and prayer by Elder Thornie Pierce.

2. The introductory sermon was delivered by Elder T. G. Brantly from 9th chapter, 13-14 verses of Paul's letter to the Hebrews: "For if the blood of bulls and of goats, and the ashes of a heifer sprinkling the unclean sanctifieth to the purifying of the flesh," followed by Elder M. B. Weaver.

After 15 minutes intermission, at the sound of singing, the Association reassembled, and was called to order by Moderator Elder M. B. Weaver.

3. Called for letters from sister churches. Received 14, which were read by the clerk and Elder John F. Keck.

4. All the letters were received. Messengers names enrolled.

5. On motion, Elder M. B. Weaver was elected Moderator and Elder Leonard White assistant Moderator.

6. On motion, Bro. Sam Davis was re-elected Clerk and Elder John F. Keck assistant Clerk.

7. Called for visiting brothers and sisters who were not delegates, when Bros. John Weaver, James Brantley and Will Brantley came forward and were welcomed to a seat with us.

8. Called for correspondence. Received Bro. L. L. Thomas and wife, sister F. M. Thomas, and minutes from the Hiwassee Association, who were welcomed to seats with us.

9. Called for visiting Brothers and Sisters who were not delegates, when Bros. C. E. and J. E. Thomas, and Sister Carlie Thomas came forward and were welcomed to seats among us.

10. Called for the report of the Clerk of 1924, which was read and received as follows, to wit:

I, Clerk of the Powell's Valley Association for the year 1924, beg leave to submit the folowing report:

Received for printing minutes $32.40. I had 800 copies printed at a cost of $20.00, postage $1.38, total $21.38, leaving the amount of $11.02, said amount being allowed me by section 20 of last year's minutes. Received $4.55 for traveling ministers' expenses and made the folowing distribution of same: T. J. Pierce, $1.00; H. A. Shoffner, $1.00; James Ausmus, $1.00; L. L. Thomas, $1.00; Johnie Ausmus, $1.00, making a total of $5.00.

Respectfully submitted,
SAM DAVIS, Clerk.

11. The following committees were appointed by Moderator:

(a) On Preaching—James Lynch, Eli Graves, J. L. Drummonds, together with the church.

(b) On Correspondence—W. A. L. Owsley, T. D. Brantly, M. C. Keck.

(c) On Request—Mathew Oliver, Thomas Pierce, James Kivet.

(d) On Finance—Elmer Graves, W. E. Hamilton.

12. On motion Committees received.

(13. On motion adjourned until Saturday morning 9 o'clock.

SATURDAY PROCEEDINGS

1. The Association met pursuant to adjournment.
2. Praise by Elder Leonard White by reading the 12th chapter of Paul's letter to the Romans.
3. Prayer by Elder Mathew Oliver.
4. Called the roll and erased the names of absentees.
5. Called for report of Committee on Preaching, which was read, received and on motion committee discharged.

(a) We, your committee on Preaching, beg leave to submit the following report:

Shawnee church Friday night, Elders Leonard White and John F. Keck.

Forge Ridge school house, Friday night, Elders T. G. Brantly and Thornie Pierce.

Greer's Chapel, Elders Verlin Graves and Elias Weaver at Church, M. B. Weaver, Mathew Oliver.

Saturday at stand, Elders Mathew Oliver and John F. Keck.

Saturday Night, Forge Ridge School House, Verlin Graves and E. G. Weaver.

Greer's Chapel, Elders John Ausmus and T. J. Pierce.

Shawanee, Elders Leonard White and Thornie Pierce.

At church, Elders M. B. Weaver and T. J. Brantly.

Sunday at Stand, Elders Mathew Oliver, T. G. Brantley, and Moderator to close.   Respectfully submitted,

> J. L. DRUMMONDS,
> ELI GRAVES,
> JAMES F. LYNCH,
> Together with the Church.

6. Called for letters from sister churches that failed to get in Friday. Received one from Pleasant Hill, which was read, received and messengers' names enrolled.
7. Called for members of sister churches who are not delegates, when Harry Patterson came forward and was welcomed to a seat with us.
8. Called for report of Committee on Correspondence.

(b) We, your committee on Correspondence, beg leave to submit the following: That we continue our correspondence with the Hiwassee and Nolachuckey Associations and that we write letters and send messengers to the same.

Respectfully submitted,

> M. C. KECK.
> T. G. BRANTLEY,
> W. A. L. OUSLEY.

9. Call for report of Committee on Arrangements.

(c) We, your Committee on Arrangements beg leave to submit the following order of business:

1st—Call the roll.
2nd—On Preaching.
3rd—On Correspondence.
4th—On Request.
5th—On Finance.
6th—When and where shall our next Association be?
7th—Who shall preach the introductory sermon and who shall be his alternate?

8th—How many copies of minutes and who shall superintend the printing and distribution of same?

Respectfully submitted,

LEONARD WHITE,
ELVIN WEAVER,
E. S. DRUMMONDS.

Report received and committee discharged.

10. Call for report of Committee on Request.

(d) We, your Committee on Request, beg leave to report the following: That we have all obituaries published in our minutes that the churches furnish, and that the next annual session of the Powell's Valley Association be held with the church at Cedar Springs, Claiborne County, Tenn., to commence on Friday before the third Saturday in August, 1926.

Respectfully submitted,

MATHEW OLIVER,
THORNIE PIERCE,
J. M. KIVETTE.

Report received and committee discharged.

11. Called for report of Committee on Finance.

(e) We, your Committee on Finance, beg leave to submit the following report: Received from churches for printing minutes, $35.25.

Respectfully submitted,

ELMER GRAVES,
W. E. HAMILTON.

On motion report received and committee discharged.

12. On motion, our next annual session of the Powell's Valley Association shall be held with the church at Cedar Springs, Claiborne county, Tennessee, to commence on Friday before the third Saturday in August, 1926.

13. On motion Elder Leonard White preach the introductory sermon and that Elder Mathew Oliver be his alternate.

14. On motion, we have the rules of decorum printed in our minutes.

15. By request of Bro. Elvin Weaver the rules of decorum were read by Elder Leonard White.

16. On motion, we have 800 copies of minutes printed; that the Clerk superintend the printing and distribution of same and that he be allowed $10.00 for his service.

17. On motion, the Clerk have the printer's fee printed in our minutes.

18. On motion, we erase the word "male" in section one, line five, of the rules of decorum.

19. On motion, the Clerk write corresponding letters to the Nolachucky and Hiwassee Associations and have same printed in our minutes.

20. On motion, we send Elders T. G. Brantly, M. B. Weaver, Leonard White, V. D. Graves, Bros. W. A. L. Ousley and W. R. Petree, messengers to the Hiwassee Association.

21. On motion we send Elders E. G. Weaver, Thornie Pierce, Bros. W. A. L. Ousley, messengers to the Nolachucky Association.

22. Motion in order that Elder W. B. Weaver write Elder L. L. Thomas in respect of his kind letter to this Association.

23. On motion, be it resolved, that we extend our heartfelt

thanks to this dear old church and the surrounding community for hospitality and kind treatment to us through this Association.

24. Adjourned to meet as above stated.

Elder M. B. Weaver, Moderator, Postoffice, Lost Creek, Union County, Tenn.

Elder Leonard White, Assistant Moderator, Postoffice, LaFollette, Campbell County, Tenn.

Sam Davis, Clerk, Postoffice, Liberty Hill, Grainger County, Tenn.

Elder John F. Keck, Assistant Clerk, Postoffice Goin, Claiborne County, Tenn.

Corresponding letter to our sister associations, to wit: The Hiwassee and Nolachucky Associations, with whom we desire to correspond.

Very dear Brethren in Christ: We desire to continue our long cherished correspondence with you and for that purpose have chosen the following named Elders and Brothers as correcponding delegates to the Hiwassee: Elders T. G. Brantly, M. B. Weaver, Leonard White, V. D. Graves, Brothers W. A. L. Ousley and W. R. Petree. And to the Nolachucky we send Elders E. G. Weaver, Thornie Pierce, Bro. W. A. L. Ousley, whom we hope you will esteem as sound in the faith and grant to sit with you in your annual meeting. May the God of all Grace be with you and guide you in the way of all truth, is the prayer of this, your little sister association.

ELDER M. B. WEAVER, Moderator,
SAM DAVIS, Clerk.

SUNDAY'S PROCEEDINGS

At the appointed hour Sunday a large and well behaved audience assembled at the stand and so attentively listened to the well delivered sermons of Elder Mathew Oliver from 10th chapter, first verse of Paul's letter to the Romans, "Brethren, my heart's desire and prayer to God is that Israel might be saved." Followed by Elder T. G. Brantly, from 27th chapter, 17th verse of St. Mathew, "Whom will ye that I release unto you," and closing remarks by the Moderator, all of which was delivered in a most loving manner, with the greatest interest to all, and a loving parting was expressed by the shedding of tears, clapping of hands and invoking the blessings of God upon each other, and after the close of the service when the whole assembly partook of the delicious hospitalities that this dear old church and the surrounding community had prepared. It seemed that joy was complete.

THE CLERK.

OBITUARY

of Brother Peter M. Miracle, son of P. A. W. and Nancie Miracle, was born November 27, 1898, departed this life April 18, 1925. Leaves father, mother, 7 brothers and 4 sisters and a host of friends to mourn his loss. Professed faith in Christ and joined the Primitive Baptist church at Myers Grove January the 4 Saturday in 1924 and lived a good and faithful member until death.

Bro. Maynard Muncy was born in the year 1863 and departed this life May 11th, 1924. He professed faith in Christ in early life and joined the Missionary Baptist church at Hickory Valley, with which he served a faithful member until December, 1910, he joined the Primitive Baptist church at Blackfox, where he lived a faithful member until death. Bro. Muncy is greatly missed among us, but we feel he has entered into his reward he so consistently lived during his stay among us. Gone but not forgotten.

Brother Jack Wilcox departed this life in the early Spring of 1925. Bro. Wilcox professed faith in Christ in early life and joined the Baptist church at Pleasant Point and lived a faithful member. We hope our loss is his eternal gain.

In remembrance of a dear sister, Josephine Watts, daughter of Bro. W. M. and Sister Cordie Collins, and wife of Eber Watts, who departed this life February 6. 1925. She professed faith in Christ and joined the Noeton church Sept. 21, 1924, and was baptized the same day. She leaves to mourn her loss a dear mother, husband one son, three sisters and two brothers, and a host of relatives and friends.

DECORUM

1. The churches composing the Powell's Valley Association shall not be confined to any set rules as to specific number of Messengers they shall have in the body, but shall have the right to name in their letters as many as they choose, and in addition all orderly members of and of the churches being present be entitled to seats in the body as Messengers of their respective churches, with all the rights and privileges of the same.

2. The Messengers thus assembled shall be denominated the Powell's Valley Primitive Baptist Association.

3. For the purpose of historial information and statistical edification, the Churches are required to state in letters, the number of members in fellowship the number received by Baptism, by letter, by confession of Faith, the number dismissed, excluded and dead since last session; also the time of their meeting, their pastoral supply, and the amount of money contributed for ministers and other purposes together with any other information they deem appropriate for the edification of the saints and glory of God.

4. This Association shall have no power to answer queries, give advice, or dictate to the Churches in any case, or to lord it over God's heritage nor any power by which she can directly or indirectly fringe on the internal rights of the church or censure and try any church or member in reference to faith and practice and determine upon validity of gospel ordinances. These things shall rest entirely with the churches; but henceforward our annual meetings shall be only for the purpose of hearing from each other, and for the worship of God and mutual comfort and edification of the Saints. To this end we reserve the privilege annually before the Third Saturday in August and the two following days or at such other time as may be agreed upon with any church that may invite us having to protect our own standard, while in session, from heresey and disorder to recognize and invite any primitive Baptist minister or any lay brother to worship with us that may deem proper; to request the brethern of our body to visit other churches or bodies in our belief with whom we may desire to culture Christian fellowship; to publish in a minute of our proceedings.

5. Each session of the body shall have a Moderator and Clerk who shall hold office until re-elected.

6. Any order member of any church belonging to this body, when convened, being present shall be eligible to elect on as Moderator and Clerk, or to sit on any committee appointed by the same.

7. In all election or questions that may be necessary to determine by vote, the vote shall be taken by churches, each church being entitled to three votes for and number less than one hundred, and one additional vote for every fifty or fraction thereof above the first hundred, but the Messengers of each church may divide their vote as they see proper.

8. All elections of questions coming to vote shall be determined by a majority vote cast, and it shall be the only duty of the minority to acquiesce in the decision thus reached.

9. If new churches desire to be admitted to this union they shall petition by letter and messengers and if voted for or recommended by one or more sister churches for her Presbytery constitution them, or orthox and orderly they shall be received by the voice of the body and manifested by the Moderator giving the Messengers the right hand of fellowship.

10. An motion or resolution clearly inconsistent with the above rules shall be promptly ruled out of order unless withdrawn by the mover.

11. Any Messenger being ruled out of order by the Moderator shall have the right to appeal to the body on the question or order, and if sustained shall be allowed to proceed, but if not take his seat.

12. Our meeting being held in the name of Christ and the worship of God; each Messenger is expected to observe due and proper therein.

13. It will not be considered good for any Messenger whose name has been enrolled as such to abruptly break off or absent himself from the Association without leave.

14. The Moderator shall be entitled to be same privilege of speech as other members provided the chair is filled.

15. The minutes of the Association shall be read and approved by the body and signed by the Moderator before adjourning.

16. The Association shall be opened and closed by prayer.

17. Amendments to these may be made at any time by a majority of the union voting by churches when they deem it necessary, provide such amendments do not compromise the sovereignty of the churches nor have tendency to give body undue power or jurisdiction over them.

MINISTERIAL ROLL

ELDERS	POSTOFFICE
H. L. Alston	Tazewell, Claiborne County, Tenn.
James Ausmus	Speedwell, Claiborne County, Tenn.
John Ausmus	Speedwell, Claiborne County, Tenn.
T. G. Brantly	Sharp's Chapel, Union County, Tenn.
A. J. Baruff	Corryton, Knox County, Tenn.
G. J. Baruff	Lost Creek, Union County, Tenn.
Calvin Collins	New Market, Jefferson County, Tenn.
John F. Keck	Goin, Claiborne County, Tenn.
Mathew Oliver	Noeton, Grainger County, Tenn.
Thomas Pierce	Speedwell, Claiborne County, Tenn.
Thornie Pierce	Speedwell, Claiborne County, Tenn.
A. Shelton	Tate, Grainger County, Tenn.
H. A. Shoffner	Harrogate, Claiborne County, Tenn.
Alfred Parks	New Market, Jefferson County, Tenn.
S. S. Wilson	Gibson Station, Lee County, Va.
M. B. Weaver	Lost Creek, Union County, Tenn.
Leonard White	LaFollette, Campbell County, Tenn.
John A. Webb	Gibson Station, Lee County, Va.
Esaw Keck	Goin, Claiborne County, Tenn.
E. G. Weaver	LaFollette, Campbell County, Tenn.
V. D. Graves	Sharp's Chapel, Union County, Tenn.

LICENTIATES

Charlie Stanifer	Speedwell, Claiborne County, Tenn.
W. R. Petree	Corryton, Knox County, Tenn.
C. B. Weaver	Lost Creek, Union County, Tenn.
Elvin Weaver	Lost Creek, Union County, Tenn.
W. A. Atkins	Tate, Grainger County, Tenn.
John C. Ousley	Gibson Station, Lee County, Va.
George W. Mays	Goin, Claiborne County, Tenn.
Steve Drummonds	Tazewell, Claiborne County, Tenn.

OFFICIAL DIRECTORY

CHURCHES	COUNTY	PASTORS	CLERKS	CLERKS P. O.
Gibson Station	Lee	Leonard White	Mary Ball	Gibson Station, Va.
New Hebron	Jefferson	Alfred Parks	H. F. Cox	New Market, Tenn.
Hamilton Grove	Union	John F. Keck	F. Hamilton	Maynardville, Tenn.
		V. D. Graves, Asst.		
Noeton	Grainger	Mathew Oliver	J. C. Oliver	Noeton, Tenn.
Straight Branch	Union	James Ausmus	Thornie Pierce	Speedwell, Tenn.
Oak Grove	Union	T. G. Brantly	David White	Sharp's Chapel, Tenn
Cave Spring	Union	V. D. Graves	Frank Berry	Speedwell, Tenn.
Mossy Spring	Union	M. B. Weaver	Curtis Weaver	Loyston, Tenn.
Pleasant Hill	Claiborne	Leanord White	Lincoln Edwards	Speedwell, Tenn.
Rocky Dale	Knox	T. G. Brantly	M. C. Dunn	Corryton, Tenn.
Pleasant Point	Claiborne	John F. Keck,	Fred Keck	Goin, Tenn.
		J. E. Keck, Asst.		
Davis Chapel	Campbell	Leonard White	Parie Heatherly	LaFollette, Tenn.
Red Hill	Claiborne	T. G. Brantly	Jeff Treece	Speedwell, Tenn.
Black Fox	Grainger	T. G. Brantly	Sam Davis	Liberty Hill, Tenn.
Cedar Spring	Claiborne	H. L. Alston	J. L. Drummonds	Tazewell, Tenn.
		H. A. Shoffner, Asst.		

TABLE OF STATISTICS

CHURCHES	NAMES OF DELEGATES	Rec'd by Expr'ce and Baptism	Rec'd by Relation	Rec'd by Letter	Restored	Dis'is by Letter	Excluded	Deceased	Total Membership	Sat'day Meetings	Contribution
Black Fox	Elder S. Pennington, John Burden, Herman Moncy, Sam Davis.	10	1						99	3	$3.20
Moyers Grove	J. L. Drummonds, E. S. Drummonds, V. Moyers.	1		1		1			70	4	3.00
Red Hill	Wiley Treece, Mose Treese, W. F. Roberson, Harry Patterson.	12		1					49	2	2.00
Davi's Chapel	B. Treece										
	Elder Leonard White, G. E. Heatherly, J. F. Lynch, Parie Heatherly, Nancy Heatherly	14		4	2	1			149	3	2.60
Pleasant Point	Elder John F. Keck, Fred Keck, M. C. Keck, Cecil Keck.	9		1		1			131	2	2.00
Rocky Dale	Eli Graves, Dewey Graves, Elmer Graves.	6	1	1		1			44	4	3.25
Pleasant Hill	Vester Ausmus, Mae Edwards, J. L. Edwards, G. H. Graves, Pollie Graves			1	1	1			48	2	1.50
Mossy Spring	Elder M. B. Weaver, T. G. Brantly, E. G. Weaver, W. D. Graves, Elvin Weaver, H. N. White, J. M. Kivet.	15	1	1	1	1			222	2	3.50
Cave Spring	Freeman Brantley, James Brantly	2				1	1		110	3	1.00
Oak Grove	W. R. Petree, George Shoffner, John Groves.	13							181	1	4.15
Straight Branch	T. J. Pierce, Thornie Pierce, Jno. Ausmus	5				1			63	1	1.70
Noeton	Mathew Oliver, J. C. Oliver	1				1			37	3	1.25
Hemilton Grove	Icy Hamilton, Sallie Hamilton, W. E. Hamilton, Silius Hamilton, W. A. L. Ousley		1	1					75	4	2.85
Gibson Station	George Southers, H. A. Shoffner, S. S. Wilson, Charlie Redmon		2						60	1	2.00
New Hebron	Letter. No messenger.								23	1	1.00
Big Barren	No letter. Come next year.										

Printers fee $20.00

MINUTES

OF THE

107TH ANNUAL SESSION

OF THE

Powell's Valley Association

OF

PRIMITIVE BAPTISTS

HELD WITH THE CHURCH AT

CEDAR SPRINGS, TENNESSEE

AUGUST 20, 21, 22, 1926

PROGRESS PRINT, TAZEWELL

ASSOCIATION PROCEEDINGS

Minutes of the One Hundred and Seventh Annual Session of the Powell's Valley Association of Primitive Baptists, Held With the Church at Cedar Spring, Claiborne County, Tennessee, on August 20, 21, 22, 1926.

1. Praise, by Elder M. B. Weaver.
2. Prayer, by Elder W. R. Gates.
3. According to previous arrangements, the introductory sermon was delivered by Elder Matthew Oliver, from 133rd Psalm, "Behold how good and how pleasant it is for brethren to dwell together in unity," etc., followed by Elder Gilbert Abbott.
4. After 15 minutes intermission, at the sound of the bell, the Association reassembled and was called to order by the Moderator, Elder M. B. Weaver.
5. Prayer, by Elder John F. Keck.
6. Called for letters from Sister churches. Received 9, which were read by the clerk and Elder John F. Keck.
7. On motion all the letters were received and messengers' names enrolled.
8. On motion, Elder M. B. Weaver was re-elected Moderator and Elder V. H. Graves was elected assistant Moderator.
9. On motion, Brother Sam Davis was re-elected Clerk and Elder John F. Keck Assistant Clerk.
10. Called for Brothers and Sisters who were not delegates, when Bro. W. M. Moncey, of Blackfox· H. V. White, of Mossy Spring; Jeff Treece, of Red Hill; H. E. Graves, of Rocky Dale, came forward and were welcomed to seats with us.
11. Called for corresponding letters from Sister Associations. Received one from the Hiwassee Association, which was read, and on motion was received with their delegation, to wit: Elder U. G. Abbott, Bro. L. L. Thomas and wife, Brother Roy and Sister Frankie Thomas.
12. Called for the report of the Clerk, when he reported $5.25 in his hand from last year.
13. On motion, the following committees were appointed by the Moderator:

a   On Preaching—M. C. Keck, Berry White, Steve Drummonds, together with the church.

b.   On arrangements—Wiley Treece, Elvin Weaver, C. W. Redmon.

c.   On Correspondence—V. H. Graves, H. L. Alson, W. R. Petree

d   On Request—Mathew Oliver, Elmer Bridges, Esau Keck.

e.   On Finance—J. L. Drummonds, Henry Simmonds.

14. On motion, all the committees were received.
15. On motion, the Association was dismissed until Saturday morning at 9 o'clock.

SATURDAY'S PROCEEDINGS

1. The Association met pursuant to adjournment.
2. Praise, by Elder M. B. Weaver.
3. Prayer, by Bro. L. L. Thomas.
4. Called for letters of Sister churches that failed to get in Friday. Received 3, which were read by the Clerk.
5. On motion, all the letters were received with their delegation.
6. Call for the report of the Committee on Arrangements.

a. We your, Committee on Arrangements, beg leave to submit the following order of business:

1. Call the Roll.
2. On preaching.
3. On Correspondence.
4. On Request.
5. On Finance.
6. When and wher shall our next Association be held?
7. Who shall preach the introductory sermon and who shall be his alternate?
8. How many copies of the minutes shall we have printed and who shall superintend the printing and distribution of same?

Respectfully submitted.

ELVIN WEAVER, WILEY TREECE, C. W. REDMOND.

7th. On motion report received and committee discharged.
8. Called the roll and eraced the names of absentees.
9. On motion, we accept Davis Chapel Church by request of Bro. Henry Simmonds, their letter not having reached us.
10. Called for the report of the Committee on Preaching.

b We, your Cimrittee on Preaching, beg leave to submit the following report: Friday night, Watson's Chapel, Elders S. S. Wilson, Thomas Pierce; Lily Grove, Elders W. R. Gates, W. R. Petree; Moyers Grove, Elder W. B. Weaver, W. G. Abbott; Cedar Spring school house, Chas Redmon, H. A. Shoffner. Saturday at the stand, Elders W. R. Gates and T. G. Brantley; Saturday night at the church, Elders Matthew Oliver, U. G. Graves; Cedar Spring School House, Elder H. L. Alston, H. A. Shoffner, Bro. W. R. Petree; Lily Grove, Elders W. G. Abbott and Oscar Keck; Watson's Chapel, Elders John F. Keck and S. S. Wilson; Sunday at the stand, Elders W. R. Gates, Matthew Oliver, and the Moderator to close. Respectfully submitted,

E. S. DRUMMONDS, BERRY WHITE, M. C. KECK.

11. On motion, report received and committee discharged.
12. Called for the report of the Committee on Correspondence.

c. We, your Committee on Correspondence beg leave to submit the following: That we continue our correspondence with the Hiwassee and Nolachuckey Associations. Respectfully submitted,

W. R. PETREE, V. H. GRAVES, H. L. ALSTON.

Report received and committee discharged.

13. Called for report of Committee on Request.

d We, your Committee on Request, beg leave to submit the following: That we have all obituaries published in our minutes that the churches furnish and that the next annual session of the Powell's Valley Association be held with the church at Pleasant Point. Respectfully submitted,

MATTHEW OLIVER, PALMER BRIDGES, J. E. KECK.

14. Report received and committee discharged.

15. Called for the report of the Committee on Finance.

e We, your Committee on Finance, beg leave to submit the following: Received from churches for printing minutes $29.35, and received from churches for traveling preachers' expense $4.10.

Respectfully submitted,

J. L. DRUMMONDS, HENRY SIMMONS.

16. On motion report received and committee discharged.

17. On motion, the next annual session of the Powell's Valley Association will be held with the church at Rocky Dale, Knox County, Tennessee, to commence on Friday before the third Saturday in August, 1927.

18. On motion; Elder H. A. Shoffner preach the introductory sermon and that Elder Thomas Pierce be his alternate.

19. On motion, we have one thousand copies of minutes printed. That the Clerk superintend the printing ad distribution of same, and that he be allowed $10.00 for his services.

20. On motion, the Clerk write corresponding letter to the Hiwassee and Nolachucky Associations and have the same inserted in our minutes.

21. On motion we send messengers and minutes to these, our Sister Associations, to wit: The Hiwassee , Elders V. H. Graves, M. B. Weaver, T. G. Brantley, Bro. Herbert Graves. To the Nolachucky, we appoint Elders V. H. Graves and S. S. Wilson.

22. On motion, be it Resolved, That we extend our heartfelt thanks to this dear old church and the surrounding community for their hospitality and kind treatment to us through this Association.

23. On motion, adjourned to meet as above stated.

Elder M. B. Weaver, Moderator, Postoffice, Lost Creek, Union County, Tenn.

Elder V. H. Graves Assistant Moderator, Postoffice, Speedwell, Union County, Tennessee.

Sam Davis, Clerk, Postoffice, Liberty Hill, Grainger County, Tenn.

Elder John F. Keck, Clerk, Postoffice, Goin, Claiborne County, Tenn.

To our Sister Associations, to wit: The Hiwassee and Nolachucky. Very dear Brothers and Sisters in Christ: We desire a continuance of our long cherished correspondence with you, and have chosen these our beloved Elders and Brothers to bear this, our epistle of love to you, the Hiwassee Association when convened with the church of Christ at Macedonia, Morgan County, Tennessee, beginning on Friday before the fourth Saturday in September, 1926, messengers, Elders V. H. Graves, M. B. Weaver, T. G. Brantley, Brother Herbert Graves. Messengers to the Nolachucky, Elders V. H. Graves and S. S Wilson, whom we pray that you esteem as sound in the faith and grant they sit with you in your Godly consultations. May the God of all Grace be with and guide you in the way of all truth, is the prayer of this your little Sister.

SUNDAY'S PROCEEDINGS

At the appointed hour Sunday a large and well behaved audience assembled at the stand and so attentively listened to the well delivered sermons of Elder W. R. Gates from Isaiah 42nd chapter and 4th verse, "He shall not fail nor be discouraged till he have set judgment in the earth and the Isles shall wait for his law." Followed by Elder Mathew Oliver, Gilbert Abbott and closing remarks of the Moderator, all of which was delivered in a most loving manner and with the greatest interest to all. A loving parting was expressed by the shedding of tears, clapping of hands and invoking the blessings of God upon each other, while the congregation sang that good old hymn, "How Firm a Foundation, Ye Saints of the Lord."   THE CLERK.

OBITUARIES

Pollyanne Hopper, wife of John Hopper, was born 1850, died May 11, 1926, age 76 years. Was married to Marion Dunn, 1865. To this union was born 5 children, three boys and two girls. The husband died 1880. She remained a widow until 1883, when she married John Hopper. To this union was born 4 children, 3 of whom are still living. She leaves a husband and six children, friends and relatives. She professed faith in Christ and joined the Primitive Baptist church in 1885 and lived a model life until death. Some of her last words was to give advice to her and that she now felt that she had a loving sympathetic heart and that she was anxious to go and get out of her suffering and be with the Lord.

Louisa Wilson, daughter of Caswell and Parley Wilson, born June 11, 1866, age 59 years, 11 months and 24 days. Married Marion Gentry. To this union was born 2 children, then he passed away. Then she married John Loy. To this union was born 11 children, 5 boys and 6 girls. Professed faith in Christ at an early age and joined the Primitive Baptist church at Rocky Dale and lived a faithful member until death. She leaves her children, grandchildren and mother, brothers and sisters, and a host e. friends to mourn her loss, but our loss is heaven's gain.

In remembrance of a dear darling, Glenn Eli Long, son of Mr. and Mrs. J. W. Long. Was born Dec. 16, 1924, and died August 19, 1925, age 8 months 2 days. We all loved him dearly, but the angels loved him more and took him to God's shining shore to live forever more on high. There was never a chain in their home broken until God sent the sad token and took their little darling away. His little body lies sleeping in the old churchyard cemetery to await the resurrection. He leaves a father and mother and a host of friends to mourn his loss. Grandson of Elder Matthew Oliver.   MARY ELLEN OLIVER.

David Ridings was born December 1, 1847, died July 30, 1926. Was married to Mary Tolmes, and to this union was born 8 children, six living, 4 boys and 2 girls. Bro. Ridings professed faith in Christ and joined the Primitive Baptist church at Pleasant Point and lived a faithful member. Mary Ridings, wife of David Ridings, aged 85 years, departed this life ————————————

Obituary of T. J. Hopper (son of John and Martha Hopper) who was born October 30, 1840, and died July 16, 1926, aged 85 years, 8 months and 17 days. He enlisted in the Civil War in 1862 and was honorably discharged at the close of the war. He was married to Harriet Francisco May 21, 1891, and to this union was born 6 children, 2 sons and 4 daughters, two of whom are dead. He joined the church at Davis' Creek in the year 1891 or '92, transferred his membership to Oak Grove, then to the Primitive Baptist church at Mossy Spring, where he remained until death. Uncle Thomas, as he was generally called, was a consistent christian, very much devoted to the church and his friends. Uncle Thomas was often referred to for his piety and harmless disposition. No doubt he is now numbered with the saints above waiting for his loving wife and dear children and three stepchildren, allof whom loved him so dearly, is looking on to that blessed immortality where they will see him again.—Written by Elders M. B. Weaver and T. G. Brantley.

G. W. Simmons was born July 29, 1855, died Nov. 24, 1925. Joined the Primitive Baptist church at Cedar Springs October, 1884 and lived a faithful member until death. He leaves 5 sons and 5 daughters and a host of grandchildren and friends to mourn his loss. Our loss is Heaven's eternal gain.

Sister Thula Perry, daughter of Bro. James and Melvina Capps, was bor Nov. 19, 1896. Professed a hope in Christ January, 1911, joined the church at Blackfox the same year and was baptized in June following. Was married to Bro. Newton Perry July 9, 1911. To this union was born four children, 1 boy and three girls. The two oldest, both girls, superceded her to the grave only a few days, leaving husband, the two remaining children, father, mother, relatives and a host of friends to mourn her absence. We believe that our loss is her eternal gain. We mourn not for her as those that have no hope. Funeral services were conducted in the home by Elder T. G. Brantley, after which the body was laid to rest in the Cabbage cemetery until the great resurrection morn.

Sister Dusky Bailey was born October 19, 1911, died January 13, 1926. Professed faith in Christ and joined the Primitive Baptist church at Blackfox Saturday, February 3, 1925. Sister Bailey will be greatly missed among us, as her seat is vacant in the church. But we should bow in humble submission to the will of Him that doeth all things well.

Adeline Berry, wife of Jihn Berry, was born January 22, 1830, died January 29, 1926, age 96 years and 7 days. Was married to John Berry Feb. 14, 1850, and to this union was born 13 children, 3 sons and 10 daughters, grandchildren 97, great grandchildren 252; great great grandchildren, 38. She is survived by 2 sons and 5 daughters, with many relatives and friends to mourn after her. We have lost a good friend, a Christian sister and loving mother —Written by Elder M. B. Weaver.

Brother J. C. Perry, son of P. L. and Sarah Perry, was born April 10, 1886, departed this life December 7, 1925. Leaves a wife, 4 children, father and mother, 3 brothers, 4 sisters. Professed a hope in his early days and joined the church at Cave Springs about 1919, lived a member of this church until death.

ARTICLES OF FAITH

ARTICLE 1.   We believe in only one true and living God, as he is revealed to us in the Holy Scriptures, Father, Son and Holy Ghost.

2.   We believe that the Scriptures of the Old and New Testaments are the word of God and the only rule of all saving knowledge and obedience.

3.   We believe in the doctrine of election according to the foreknowledge of God

4.   We believe in the doctrine of original sin.

5.   We believe in man's impotency to recover himself from the fallen state he is in by his own free will or ability.

6.   We believe that sinners are justified in the sight of God only by the imputed righteousness of Jesus Christ.

7.   We believe the elect, according to the foreknowledge of God, will be called, converted, regenerated and sanctified by the Holy Spirit.

8. We believe the saints will persevere and never fall finally away.

9. We believe that baptism and the Lord's Supper are ordinances of Jesus Christ, and that true believers are the only subjects of these ordinances, and that the true mode of baptism is by immersion.

10. We believe in the resurrection of the dead and the general **judgment**.

11. We believe that the punishment of the wicked will be everlasting, and that the joys of the righteous will be eternal.

12. We believe that no minister has the right to administer the ordinances except those who have been regularly baptized and called of God and come under the imposition of hands by the Presbytery.

MINISTERIAL ROLL

ELDERS	POSTOFFICES
H. L. Alston	Tazewell, Claiborne County, Tenn.
James Ausmus,	Speedwell, Claiborne County, Tenn.
John Ausmus	Speedwel, Claiborne County, Tenn.
T. G. Brantley	Sharp's Chapel, Union County, Tenn.
A. J. Boruff	Corryton, Knox County, Tenn.
G. J. Boruff	Lost Creek, Union County, Tenn.
Calvin Collins	New Market, Jefferson County, Tenn.
John F. Keck	Goin, Claiborne County, Tenn.
Mathew Oliver	Noeton, Grainger County, Tenn.
Thomas Pierce	Speedwell, Claiborne County, Tenn.
Thornie Pierce	Speedwell, Claiborne County, Tenn.
A. Shelton	Tate, Grainger County, Tenn.
H. A. Shoffner	Harrogate, Claiborne County, Tenn.
Alfred Parks	New Market, Jefferson County, Tenn.
S. S. Wilson	Gibson Station, Lee County, Va.
M. B. Weaver	Lost Creek, Union County, Tenn.
Leonard White	LaFollette, Campbell County, Tenn.
John A. Webb	Gibson Station, Lee County, Va.
Esaw Keck	Goin, Claiborne County, Tenn.
E. G. Weaver	LaFollette, Campbell County, Tenn.
V. H. Graves	Sharp's Chapel, Union County, Tenn.

LICENTIATES

Charlie Stanifer	Speedwell, Claiborne County, Tenn.
W. R. Petree	Corryton, Knox County, Tenn.
C. B. Weaver	Lost Creek, Union County, Tenn.
Elvin Weaver	Lost Creek, Union County, Tenn.
W. A. Atkins	Tate, Grainger County, Tenn.
John C. Owsley	Gibson Station, Lee County, Va.
George W. Mays	Goin, Claiborne County, Tenn.
Steve Drummonds	Tazewell, Claiborne County, Tenn.
Charlie Redmon	Harrogate, Claiborne County, Tenn.

OFFICAL DIRECTORY

CHURCHES	COUNTY	PASTORS	CLERKS	CLERKS P. O.
Gibson Station	Lee	V. H. Graves	Mary Ball	Gibson Station, Va.
New Hebron	Jefferson	Alfred Parks	H. F. Fox	New Market, Tenn
Hamilton Grove	Union	V. H. Graves	Frank Hamilton	Maynardville, Tenn.
		Asst: H. A. Shoffner		
Noeton	Grainger	Mathew Oliver	J. C. Oliver	Noeton, Tenn.
Straight Branch	Union	Thornie Pierce	Lussie Pierce	Speedwell, Tenn.
		Asst: M. B. Weaver		
Oak Grove	Union	T. G. Brantley	David White	Sharp's Chapel, Tenn.
Cave Spring	Union	V. H. Graves	Frank Berry	Speedwell, Tenn.
Mossy Spring	Union	V. H. Graves	Vicy Taylor	Sharp's Chapel, Tenn.
Pleasant Hill	Claiborne	Leonard White	Lincoln Edwards	Speedwell, Tenn.
Rocky Dale	Knox	T. G. Brantley	M. C. Dunn	Corryton, Tenn.
Pleasant Point	Claiborne	J. F. Keck	Fred Keck	Goin, Tenn.
Davis Chapel	Claiborne	Leonard White	Parie Heatherly	LaFollette, Tenn.
Red Hill	Claiborne	T. G. Brantley	Jeff Treece	Speedwell, Tenn.
Blackfox	Grainger	T. G. Brantley	Sam Davis	Liberty Hill, Tenn.
Cedar Spring	Claiborne	H. L. Alston	J. L. Drummonds	New Tazewell, Tenn.
		Asst: H. A. Shoffner		

TABLE OF STATISTICS

CHURCHES	NAMES OF DELEGATES	Rec'd by Ex. and Baptism	Rec'd by Rel.	Rec'd by Letter	Restored	Dis. by Letter	Excluded	Deceased	Total Mem'ship	Sat. Meetings	Contributions	Minister's Ex.
Black Fox	Elder S. S. Pennington, Bro. W. M. Perry, Sam Capps, R. Hamilton, H. I. Alston, Bro. V. Moyers, J. L. Drummonds, Henry Cupp	2						2	99	3	$2.00	
Cedar Spring	Isom Drummonds, E. S. Drummonds, D. P. Drummonds, B. Miracle.	6						1	75	4	2.50	
Red Hill	Wiley Treece, W. F. Roberson, Harry Peterson, B. Treece	7		1					56	3	2.10	
Davis Chapel	Henry Simmons. No letter, come on	3	2						143	3	3.10	
Pleasant Point	Elders John F. Keck, Esaw Keck, Bros. Milt Toliver, Austin Keck, J. R. keck, Troy Keck, M. C. Keck								134	2	3.10	
Rocky Dale	Bros. Eli Graves Elmer Graves, M. C. Dunn, Sister Emma Faris	4		1				1	49	4	3.35	
Pleasant Hill	No Letter. Come next year.								48	2		
Mossy Spring	Elders M. B. Weaver, V H Graves, T G Brantley, Bros. Elvin Weaver, Berry White	21		1	2				243	2	3.50	$4.10
Cave Spring	Bro. Chester Welch, Sisters Ola and Gladys Welch, Geo. Shoffner, J. P. Russell, W R Petree Palmer Bridges	10							111	3	2.00	
Oak Grove	John Graves, Clifford Russell					1			177	1	3.05	
Straight Branch	Elder T. J. Pierce	2							62	1	1.75	
Noeton	Elder Mathew Oliver								35	3	1.50	
Hamilton Grove	W. A. L. Owsley, Ernest and Lillius Hamilton, Forest and Mamie Hamilton, Emily Hamilton			1			1		60	4	2.00	
Gibson Station	Elders S. S. Wilson, H. A. Shoffner, Charlie Redmon								83	1	2.50	
New Hebron	Letter, but no messenger. Printer's Fee $30.00								23	1	1.00	

194

MINUTES

of the

ONE HUNDRED AND EIGHTH ANNUAL SESSION

of the

Powell's Valley
Association

of

Primitive Baptists

Held With the Church at
Rocky Dale, Knox County, Tennessee
August 19th, 20th, 21st, 1927.

Next Association will be held with the Church at
Pleasant Point, Claiborne County, Tenn., beginning
on Friday before the Third Saturday in August 1928

Table of Statistics

CHURCHES	NAMES OF DELEGATES	Rec'd. by Ex. Bap.	Rec'd. by Relation	Rec'd. by Letter	Restored	Dismissed by Letter	Excluded	Deceased	Total Membership	Saturday Meeting	Contribution	Ministers Expenses
Black Fox	Elder S. S. Pennington, Bro. C. M. Cabbage, W. R. Capps, Sam Davis, C. L. Buckner, Albert Capps.	1						3	95	2	$3.00	
Cedar Springs	J. L. Drummonds	1							76	4	2.75	
Straight Branch	Elder Thornie Pierce			2					68	4	3.00	
Oak Grove	W. R. Petree, J. P. Russell, George Shoffner	18					4	1	190	1	4.25	
Cave Spring	Freeman Brantley, James Brantly, Frank Berry								111	3	2.00	
Mossy Spring	Elders M. B. Weaver, T. G. Brantly, V. H. Graves, Bros. Berry White, J. M. Kivett, Bill Taylor, Lonnie Taylor, Louis Lamb	9	1			1		3	248	2	2.50	$2.90
Pleasant Hill	Elvin Weaver.				1		1	1	48	3	2.45	
Hamilton Grove	J. L. Edwards, Verlin Edwards, Earnest Hamilton, Tillius Hamilton, Forest Hamilton, W. A. L. Owsley, Elder Alfred Boruff				1				63	1	2.00	
New Hebron	Elder Alfred Parks, Jim Collins	8				1			22	1	1.00	
Gibson Station	Elders S. S. Wilson, H. A. Shoffner, Chas. Redmon	8				1	1		90	1	2.50	
Pleasant Point	Elder John F. Keck, Bros. Elvin Keck, Curtis Keck, Mell Rosson	7				1		2	138	2	3.85	
Davis Chapel	Elder Leonard White, Bros. James Lynch, Albert Davis						1	1	43	3	2.00	
Red Hill	Bros. Wily Treece, W. T. Roberson, Sisters Nora Treece, Mary Roberson		7				1		63	2	2.50	
Rocky Dale	Bros. Eli Graves, Elmer Graves, L. F. Boruff, M. C. Dunn		1	1			2	1	49	3	2.45	
Noeton	J. C. Oliver, No letter		1	1				1	35	3	2.00	
	Printers fee from—other sources										1.05	

Association Proceedings

Minutes of the One Hundred and Eighth Annual Session of the Powells Valley Association of Primitive Baptists, held with the Church at Rocky Dale, Knox County, Tennessee on August 19th, 20th and 21st, 1927.

1st. Praise by Elder M. B. Weaver. Prayer by Elder John F. Keck.

2nd. According to previous arrangements, the introductory sermon was delivered by Elder H. A. Shoffner, from St. John, tenth chapter, 11th verse. "I am the Good Sheepherd, the Good Shepherd giveth his life for sheep," followed by Elder M. B. Weaver.

3rd. After fifteen minutes intermission at the sound of singing the Association reassembled, and was called to order by the Moderator Elder M. B. Weaver.

4th. Prayer by Elder L. L. Thomas.

5th. Called for letters from sister churches, received twelve, which were read by the Clerk and Elder John F. Keck.

6th. On motion all the letters were received and messenger's names enrolled.

7th. By motion Elder T. D. Brantly was elected Moderator, and Elder Leonard White Assistant Moderator.

8th. By motion Brother Sam Davis was re-elected clerk and Elder John F. Keck was re-elected Assistant Clerk.

9th. Called for Brothers and Sisters who were not delegates, when Elder John F. Keck of Pleasant Point, Cilis White, G. J. Boruff and Harry Weaver of Mossy Spring, and James Rogan, R. D. Boruff of Blackfox came forward and were welcomed to seats with us.

10th. Called for corresponding letters. Received one from the Hiawassee Association, which was read by the Clerk.

11th. Called motion we received the letter and seated the delegation to-wit: Elders, W. R. Gates, L. L. Thomas, Brother L. L. Thomas and wife, Lathe and Lucile Thomas.

12th. Called for the report of the Clerk, who reported a balance of $4.07 due the Clerk for last years work.

13th. On motion, the following committees were appointed by the Moderator:

(a) On Preaching: Berry White, Press Russell, C. M. Cabbage, together with the Rocky Dale Church.

(b) On Arrangements: J. L. Drummonds, Leonard White, Lewis Boruff.

(c)   On Correspondence: Jim Lynch, Wiley Treece, Elvin Weaver.

(d)   On Request: Elders M. B. Weaver, Alfred Boruff, Verlin Graves.

(e)   On Finance: Elders Charlie Redmond, Thornie Pierce.

14th.   All the committees were received by the Moderator.

15th.   By motion the Association was dismissed until Saturday morning, 9:30 o'clock.

Saturday Proceedings

1st.   The Association met pursuant to adjournment.

2nd.   Praise by Elder Leonard White.   Prayer by Elder Alfred Boruff.

3rd.   Called for letter of sister churches, that failed to get in Friday.   Received two, and messenger from Noeton Church but no letter.

4th.   By motion the letters received and all the delegates were seated.

5th.   Called for the report of the Committee on Arrangements.

A.   We, your Committee on Arrangements beg leave to submit the following order of business:

1st.   Call the Roll.

2nd.   On Preaching.

3rd.   On Correspondence.

4th.   On Request.

5th.   On Finance.

6th.   When and where shall our next Association be held.

7th.   Who shall preach the introductory sermon, and who shall be his alternate.

8th.   How many copies of minutes shall we have printed.   Who shall superintend the printing and distribution of same.

Respectfully submitted,

LEONARD WHITE, J. W. DRUMMONDS, L. F. BORUFF.

6th.   By motion, report received and Committee discharged.

7th.   Called the roll and erased the names of absentees.

8th.   Called for report of committee on Preaching.

B.   We, your Committee on Preaching beg leave to submit the following report: Friday night at Church, Elders Alfred Boruff, V. H. Graves; at Graveston Church, Elders Leonard White, W. R. Gates; Saturday A. M. at Stand, Elders W. R. Gates, L. L. Thomas, Thornie Pierce; Saturday P. M. Elders M. B. Weaver, John F. Keck; Saturday night at Church, Elders G. J. Boruff, H. A. Shoffner; at Fairview Church Elder Leonard White; at Graveston Church Elder M. B. Weaver, W. R. Gates; Sunday at Stand. Elders Leonard White, W. R. Gates, and the Moderator to close.

Signed: C. M. CABBAGE, BERRY WHITE, PRESTON RUSSELL, together with the church.

8th. By motion report received and committee discharged.

9th. Called for the report of committee on Correspondence.

C. We, your Committee on Correspondence beg leave to submit the following report, and we continue our correspondence with the Hiawassee and Nolichucky Associations, and as many others as in our reach, or convenience of our faith and order.

ELVIN WEAVER, JAMES F. LYNCH, WILEY TREECE.

10th. On motion, report received and committee discharged.

11th. By motion we send letters and messengers to these sister Associations, to the Hiawassee Elders Verlin Graves, Alfred Boruff, Brother Elvin Weaver, to the Nolichucky, Elder M. B. Weaver, Brother W. A. L. Owsley.

12th. Called for the report of the Committee on Request.

D. We, your Committee on Request beg leave to submit the following: That we publish all the obituaries in our minutes that the churches furnish, and that the next annual session of the Powells Valley Association be held with the church at Pleasant Point, Claiborne County, Tenn. Respectfully submitted,

ELDERS M. B. WEAVER, ALFRED BOORUFF, W. H. GRAVES.

13th. By motion report received and committee discharged.

14th. Called for report of Committee on Finance.

E. We, your Committee on Finance beg leave to submit the following report:

Received from churches for printing minutes, $42.20.

Respectfully submitted,

ELDERS CHARLIE REDMOND, THORNIE PIERCE.

15th. On motion the report received and committee discharged.

(N B) I desire to make mention of a mistake in this report of the good Brothers of the Finance Committee. I find that $2.90 of this money was contributed by the Mossy Spring Church for visiting ministers expenses. This leaves a balance of $39.30 for printing minutes. Signed,

THE CLERK.

16th. On motion our next annual session of the Powells Valley Association will be held with the church at Pleasant Point, Claiborne County, Tennessee, to commence on Friday before the third Saturday in August, 1928.

17th. By motion Elder Verlin Graves preach the introductory sermon, and that Elder Alfred Boruff be his alternate.

18th. On motion we have 800 copies of minutes printed, that the Clerk superintend the printing and distribution of same and be allowed $10.00 for his service.

19th. On motion that the Clerk write corresponding letters to the Hiawassee and Nolichucky Associations and have them inserted in our minutes.

20th. By motion we allow the Clerk $4.07 out of the finance fund to pay him for last years work.

21st. By motion be it resolved that we extend our heartfelt thanks to the Rocky Dale Church and her surrounding community for their hospitality and kind treatment of us through this Association.

22nd. By motion we adjourned to meet as above stated.

ELDERS T. G. GRANTLY, Moderator, LEONARD WHITE, Asst'

P. O. SHARP, CHAPEL, Tennessee   P. O. LaFollette, Tennessee.

SAM DAVIS, Clerk, P. O. Liberty Hill, Tennessee.

JOHN F. KECK, Asst. Clerk, P. O. Goin, Tennessee.

Sunday Proceedings

At the appointed hour Sunday a large and well behaved audience assembled at the Stand and so attentively listened to the well delivered sermon of Elder Leonard White from the sixth chapter and ninth verse of St. John, "There is a lad here that hath five barley loaves, and two small fishes—," followed by Elder W. R. Gates, from fourth chapter, first verse of Isaiah, "And in that day seven women shall take hold of one man, saying, we will eat our own bread and wear our own apparel, only let us be called by thy name to take away our reproach," and closing remarks by the Moderator, all of which was delivered in a most pleasant manner and with great interest to all, and loving parting was expressed by the shedding of tears, clapping of hands, and invoking the blessings of God upon each other, while the congregation sang that good old song, "Children of the Heavenly King."

THE CLERK.

CORRESPONDING LETTER TO OUR SISTER ASSOCIATIONS WITH WHOM WE CORRESPOND, to-wit: The Hiawassee and Nolichucky Associations. Very dear brothers and sisters in Christ— We desire a continuance of our long cherished correspondence with you, and have chosen these, our beloved Elders and Brothers to bear this, our epistle of love to you, to-wit: Elders and Brothers to Alfred Boruff, Bro. Elvin Weaver, to the Hiawassee Association, when convened with the church at Newhope, Rockwood, Roane County, Tennessee, to commence on Friday before the fourth Saturday in September, 1927, and to the Nolichucky Association, we send Elder M. B. Weaver and Bro. W. A. L. Ousley, when convened with the church at Hopewell, Jefferson County, Tennessee to commence on Friday before the first Saturday in September 1927. Whom we pray your esteem as sound in the faith and grant they sit with you in your Godly consultations. Pray for this, your little sister,

ELDER T. G. BRANTLY, Moderator, P. O. SHARPS, Chapel, Tenn.

SAM DAVIS, Clerk, P.O. Liberty Hill, Tennessee.

Obituaries

Rachel Emaline Wilcox, daughter of M. J. Easter Wilcox was born Feb. 9, 1900. Professed faith in Christ and joined the Primitive Baptist Church at Pleasant Point, Feb. 1915. She was married to Lefter Jones aug. 1919. To this union were born four children, two sons and two daughters. Sister Jones departed this life April 13th, 1927. Sister Jones lived a beautiful life. We believe that our loss is her eternal gain.

---o---

William Shoffner born June 17th, 1853, died March 11th, 1926, age 72 years, six months and 22 days. Professed faith in Christ when quite young. Joined the Primitive Baptist church at Union, then moved to Oak Grove church, where he remained until death. Married to Martha Jane Brogan in early life. To this union were born nine children, two sons and seven daughters. His wife died, leaving him a widower. He then married Rosa Sharp, and to this union were born four children, three sons and one daughter, who are yet living. On June 4th, 1920 he was married to Nancy Hamic who is now left a widow.

Mr. Shoffner was a strong believer in the Christian religion and the Primitive faith. He was a strong believer in Christian prayers, which his practice proved. We believe Brother Shoffner has gone to his Heavenly home.

---o---

Brother Matthew Dossett, son of Brother James and Sister Pheba Dossett was born March 4, 1850, died Dec. 2, 1926, making him 76 years, 8 months, 29 days of age. He married Sarah Berry Dec. 18, 1873. To this union were born three children, two girls, one boy, twenty-seven grand children, twenty-two great grand children. Professed faith in Christ at an early age. Joined the Primitive Baptist Church at Cave Springs, Jan. 1907 and was baptized May the following and lived a faithful member until death. We feel that our loss is his eternal gain. We don't mourn for him as those that have no hope, but as a husband, father, grandfather, and noble Christian.

Sister Frankie Ivey departed this life Aug. 6, 1927, at about the age of 65 years leaving a heart-broken husband and children. Aunt Frankie will be much missed in her home, community and church. She leaves a host of friends to mourn for her, but their loss is her eternal gain.

---o---

Thomas Bart Lamb, who was born Jan. 19, 1910 age 17 years, 3 months, 17 days, came to his death by mine explosion at the Everettville mining district in W. Va., on April 30, 1927. Professed faith and joined the church two years hence. Has proven his loyalty to God by his orderly walks and Godly conversations. He leaves mother, brothers, and sisters to mourn after him. He was taken in the bloom of youth to his home above to wait his loved ones. Our dear good young Brother was so good and so promising. We lament his leaving so much.

---o---

Sister Eliza Ordona, daughter of I. M. and Minerva Davis, was born July 14, 1888. She was married to Charlie Capps, May 1911. To this union were born six children, four girls and two boys, all of which survive her. She joined the Primitive Baptist Church at Blackfox, Dec. 4, 1910. She lived a faithful member of this church until death called her to her reward Feb. 24, 1927. She leaves to mourn her loss a husband, six children, a mother, five brothers, four sisters and a host of friends. May our lives be such that when the battle is over we will see sister and mother again.

---o---

Brother Hiram Bryant was born about the year 1835. He joined the Primitive Baptist church at Blackfox, March 28, 1891, of which he lived a faithful member until death which occurred suddenly in the spring of 1927. Brother Bryant is greatly missed in the church, and our homes, but he is gone to his reward. So let us so live that we may meet him in the sweet by and by.

---o---

Brother Sam Nicely was born about the year 1850. He joined the Primitive Baptist church at Blackfox, May 4, Saturday, 1913, and was baptized Sunday following, by Elder J. D. Monroe, of which he lived an humble and faithful member until death, which occurred April 1927. In all of Brother Nicely's poverty, trials and hardships of life, I have never heard him complain. He is gone but not forgotten.

---o---

David Thomas Lamb was born May 3, 1871 and came to his death by mine explosion in W. Va., April 30th, 1927, age 55 years, 11 months and 27 days. He was married to Sarah Elizabeth Thacker in the year 1904, and to this union were born 11 children, 4 dead and 7 living, 3 sons and 4 daughters. He professed faith in Christ years ago, has been a member of Mossy Spring church about 16 years, in which time he made success in living a model Christian. He was a kind husband and loving father. Brother Lamb had great care for his wife and children, and often expressed thanks for the good way they lived. He will be missed at home, in the church, and the community, but we trust our loss is his gain.

Martha Garland was born, March 2, 1868, died June 29, 1927, age 55 years, 9 months, 26 days. She joined the church when she was 15 years old and she told her three daughters not to be uneasy about her, for she was not uneasy about dying. She s gone but not forgotten.

Sister Martha Williams, deceased about Nov. 16, 1926. She was a member of the church at Red Hill for years and was a faithful member until death. We hope that our loss is her eternal gain.

Sister Lizzie Sharp, daughter of Brother Andrew and Sister Alice Sharp, was born May 30, 1891. She professed a hope in Christ at the age of 12 years. Joined the Primitive Baptist Church at Oak Grove, August following, and lived a faithful member until death. She was married to Lawrence Bartley March 3, 1927. To this union were born three children, two girls and one boy. Deceased June 25, 1926, leaving children, father, brother and sisters, with the church to mourn their loss. We mourn not for her as those that have no hope. Funeral services were conducted by Elder Leonard White. Her body was laid to rest to await the Resurrection.

Harriet A. Hopper, wife of T. J. Hopper and daughter of James K. Polk and Elizabeth Mayes Polk was born August 9, 1867. She is survived by mother, 4 brothers, one sister, two sons, five daughters, thirty grand children and relatives and friends. She was a member of the Mossy Spring church. She died in the full triumph of a living faith, and in bidding her friends adieu, she requested her body be laid in the Hopper cemetery in Claiborne County, with her father and sister, relatives and friends. Weep not children, mother is waiting for you at Home Sweet Home.

MINISTERIAL ROLL

Elder	Postoffice
H. L. Alston,	Tazewell, Claiborne County, Tenn.
James Ausmus	Speedwell, Claiborne County, Tenn.
John Ausmus	Speedwell, Claiborne County, Tenn.
T. G. Brantley	Sharps Chapel, Union County, Tenn.
A. J. Boruff	Corryton, Knox County, Tenn.
G. J. Boruff	Lost Creek, Union County, Tenn.
Alfred Boruff	Maynardsville, Union County, Tenn.
Calvin Collins	New Market, Jefferson County, Tenn.
John F. Keck	Goin, Claiborne County, Tenn.
Matthew Oliver	Noetown, Grainger County, Tenn.
Thomas Pierce	Speedwell, Claiborne County, Tenn.
Thornie Pierce	Speedwell, Claiborne County, Tenn.
H. A. Shoffner	Harrogate, Claiborne County, Tenn.
Alfred Parks	New Market, Jefferson County, Tenn.
S. S. Wilson	Gibson Station, Lee County, Va.
M. B. Weaver	Lost Creek, Union County, Tenn.
Leonard White	LaFollette, Campbell County, Tenn.
John A. Webb	Gibson Station, Lee County, Va.
Esaw Keck	Goin, Claiborne County, Tenn.
E. G. Weaver	LaFollette, Campbell County, Tenn.
W. H. Graves	Sharps Chapel, Union County, Tenn.
S. S. Pennington	Liberty Hill, Grainger County, Tenn.
Gilbert Abbott	Knoxville, Knox County, Tenn.

LICENTIATES

Charlie Stanifer	Speedwell, Claiborne County, Tenn.
W. R. Petree	Corryton, Knox County, Tenn.
C. B. Weaver	Lost Creek, Union County, Tenn.
Elvin Weaver	Lost Creek, Union County, Tenn.
W. A. Atkins	Tate, Grainger County, Tenn.
John C. Ousley	Gibson Station, Lee County, Va.
George W. Mays	Goin, Claiborne County, Tenn.
Steve Drummonds	Tazewell, Claiborne County, Tenn.
Charlie Redmond	Harrogate, Claiborne County, Tenn.

OFFICIAL DIRECTORY

CHURCHES	COUNTY	PASTORS	CLERKS	CLERKS POSTOFFICE
Gibson Station	Lee	V. H. Graves	Mary Ball	Gibson Station, Va.
New Hebron	Jefferson	Matthew Oliver	Lucy Collins	New Market, Tenn.
Hamilton Grove	Union	B. H. Graves	Frank Hamilton	Maynardsville, Tenn.
		H. C. Shoffner, asst.		
Noeton	Grainger	Matthew Oliver	J. C. Oliver	Noeton, Tenn.
Straight Branch	Union	Thornie Pierce	Helen Masingo	Speedwell, Tenn.
		M. B. Wearer, asst.		
Oak Grove	Union	T. G. Brantly	David White	Sharps Chapel, Tenn.
Cave Spring	Union	W. H. Graves	Frank Berry	Speedwell, Tenn.
Mossy Spring	Union	Thornie Pierce	Lonnie Taylor	Sharps Chapel, Tenn.
Pleasant Hill	Claiborne	Leonard White	Lincoln Edwards	Speedwell, Tenn.
Rocky Dale	Knox	T. G. Brantly	M. C. Dunn	Corryton, Tenn.
Pleasant Point	Claiborne	V. H. Graves	Fed Keck	Goin, Tenn.
Davis Chapel	Campbell	Leonard White	Aaron Davis	LaFollette, Tenn.
Red Hill	Claiborne	T. G. Brantly	Jeff Treece	Speedwell, Tenn.
Blackfox	Grainger	Matthew Oliver	Sam Davis	Liberty Hill, Tenn.
Cedar Spring	Claiborne	Matthew Oliver	J. L. Drummonds	Tazewell, Tenn.

MINUTES

OF THE

ONE HUNDRED AND NINTH
ANNUAL SESSION

OF THE

Powell's Valley
Association

OF

Primitive Baptists

Held With the Church at
Pleasant Point, Claiborne County, Tennessee
August 17th, 18th, 19th 1928.

Next Association will be held with the Church at Mossy Springs, Union County, Tenn., beginning on Friday before the Third Saturday in August, 1929.

THREE STATES PRINT, MIDDLESBORO, KY.

Association Proceedings

Minutes of the One Hundred and Ninth Annual Session of the Powells Valley Association of the Primitive Baptists held with the church of Pleasant Point, Claiborne County, Tennessee, August 17-18-19, 1928.

1st. Praise by Elder T. G. Brantley. Prayer by Elder Thomas Pirce.

2nd. According to previous arrangements the introductory sermon was delivered by Elder Verlin Graves from Genesis 24 chap. 7-8. The Lord God of heaven, etc., followed by elder T. G. Brantley.

3rd. After 15 minutes intermission at the sound of singing the association reassembled and was called to order by Mod. Elder T. G. Brantley.

4th. Prayer by Elder Alfred Boruff.

5th. Called for letters from sister churches, received 12 which were read by the clerk and Elder John Keck, asst. clerk.

6th. On motion all the letters were received and messengers names enrolled.

7th. On motion Elder T. G. Brantley was re-elected Moderator. On motion Bro. Sam Davis was re-elected Clerk, and Elder John F. Keck Assistant Clerk.

9th. Called for Brothers and Sisters of Sister Churches, who were not delegates, when Bro. William Brantley of Cave Springs and Bro. Alfred Evans of Oak Grove came forward and were welcomed to seats with us.

10th. Called for newly constituted churches, received one from Capps Creek, which letter was read by the clerk.

11th. On motion said church was received, and the delegation was welcomed to seats with us.

12th. Called for corresponding letters from sister associations, received one from Hiwassee Association.

13th. On motion their letter was received and the delegation was welcomed to seats with us, to-wit: Bro. L. L. Thomas and Sister F. M. Thomas.

14th. Called for a report of the Clerk of last years contribution when he reported as follows: Received for printing minutes $39.80, cost of minutes from the press $24.50, allowed the Clerk $4.07 for service of 1926, and $10.00 for last years service. This leaves a balance in the clerks hand of 73 cents.

15th. Called for visitors from other associations, received one from South Union Association, to-wit: Elder Chas. Ponder, who was by motion welcomed to a seat with us.

Saturday Proceedings

SATURDAY PROCEEDINGS

1st. The Association met persuant to adjournment.

2nd. Prayer by Bro. L. L. Thomas.

3rd. Called for letters from sister churches that failed to get in Friday, received none.

4th. Called for the report of the Committee on Arrangements.

(a) We your Committee on Arrangements beg leave to report as follows:

1st. Call The Roll.

2nd. On Peaching.

3rd. On Correspondence.

4th On Request.

5th. On Finance.

6th. When and where shall our next Association be held?

7th. Who shall preach the introductory sermon, and who shall be his alternate?

8th. How many copies of minutes shall be printed?

9th. And who shall superintend the printing and distribution of same?

Respectfully submitted,
M. C. DUNN,
NEAL LAMBERT,
ELVIN WEAVER.

5th. On motion report received and Committee released.

6th. Called the roll and erased the names of absentees.

7th. Called for the report of the Committee on Preaching.

(b) We your Committee on Preaching beg leave to submit the following: Friday at Stand Verlin Graves, Alfred Boruff; Friday night at the church, M. B. Weaver, John Ausmus; at Edwards Church, Thornie Pierce, H. A. Shoffner; at Moyers Grove Church, Chas. Ponder, Verlin Graves; Saturday at Church, W. R. Gates, Thornie Pierce, Moderator to close; Saturday night at Church, Leonard White, M. B. Weaver; Edwards, W. R. Gates, Thomas Pierce; Sunday at Stand W. R. Gates, Leonard White, Moderator to close.

Respectfully submitted,
ELI GRAVES,
J. L. DRUMMONDS,
W. F. ROBERSON.

8th. On motion report received, and committee discharged.

9th. Called for the report of the Committee on Correspondence.

(c) We your Committee on Correspondence submit the following report: 1st. that we keep up our correspondence with the Hiwassee and Nolichucky Associations. 2nd, that we send delegates to visit them. 3rd, that we send them minutes of our association, and 4th that we appoint a committee of three to study the consistency of broader correspondance and report next year.

Respectfully submitted,
M. B. WEAVER,
T. G. PIERCE,
JOHN AUSMUS.

10th. On motion report received and committee discharged.

11th. Called for the report of the Committee on Requests.

(d) We your committee on requests beg leave to submit the following: That we print all the obituaries in our minutes that the churches furnish, and that the next annual session of The Powell's Valley Association be held with the church at Mossy Springs, Union County, Tennessee to commence on Friday before the third Saturday in August 1929.

Respectfully submitted,
WILY TREECE,
ELMER GRAVES,
G. W. SHOFFNER.

12th. On motion report received and discharge the Committee.

13th. Called for the report of the Committee on Finance.

209

(e)   We your Committee on Finance beg leave to report the following, received from churches for printing minutes $41.10.

Respectfully submitted,

E. S. DRUMMONDS,
H. A. SHOFFNER,
ELMER GRAVES.

14th.   On motion report received and committee discharged..

15th.   On motion the next annual session of the Powells Valley Association will be held with the Church at Mossy Springs, Union County, Tennessee to commence on Friday before the third Saturday in August 1929.

16th.   On motion Elder M. B. Weaver preach the introductory sermon and that Elder Alfred Boruff be his alternate.

17th.   On motion the Moderator appoint the following committees to the Hiwassee Association: Elders V. H. Graves, John F. Keck, T. G. Brantly, Bros. M. C. Dunn, Elvin Weaver to the Nalichucky Association, Elders Thornie Pierce, John Ausmus, M. B. Weaver, Bro. Edd McBee.

18th.   On motion the Clerk write corresponding letters to the Hiwassee and Nalichucky Associations and have them printed in our minutes.

19th.   On motion we have 800 copies of the minutes printed. That the Clerk superintend the printing of same and that he be allowed $15.00 for his service.

20th.   Motion in order that we have the rules of decorum printed in our minutes annually.

21st.   On motion we extend our heart felt thanks to this dear old church, and her surrounding community, for their hospitalities, and kind treatment to us through this Association.

22nd.   Motion to adjourn to meet as above stated.

ELDER T. G. BRANTLEY, Moderator.
Post Office, Sharps Chapel, Tenn.

SAM DAVIS, Clerk.
Post Office, Liberty Hill, Tenn.

ELDER JOHN F. KECK, Asst. Clerk.
Post Office, Goin, Tenn.

Sunday Proceedings

At the appointed hour Sunday a large and well behaved audience assembled at the stand and so attentively listened to the well delivered sermon of Elder W. R. Gates from 1st Chap. 16 verse of Romans. "For I am not ashamed of the Gospel of Christ, for it is the power of God unto salvation to every one that believeth, to the Jew first and also to the Greek." At the close of this sermon the congregation was so full with rejoicing. No more preaching was done, but of all the joyful seasons I have never seen this time excelled in singing, shouting and invoking the blessings of God upon each other. A lovely parting was sure expressed among the whole congregation. The service was closed with remarks from the Moderator.

Corresponding letters to our sister associations with whom we correspond to-wit: The Hiwassee and Nolichucky Associations, our very dear Bros. and Sisters and Christ, we desire a continuance of our long Cherished Correspondence with you and have chosen these our beloved Elders and Bros. to bear this our epistle of love to you to-wit: Elders W. H. Graves, John F. Keck, T. G. Brantley, Bro. M. C. Dunn to the Hiwassee Association when convened with the church at Poplar Spring, Roan County, Tennessee, on September 21-21-21, 1928 and to the Nolichucky Association; Elders Thornie Pierce, John Ausmus, M. B. Weaver, Bro. Edd McBee, whom we pray you grant to sit with you in all your Godly Constitutions.

Pray for this your little sister.

ELDER T. G. BRANTLEY, Moderator.
Post Office Sharps Chapel, Tenn.
SAM DAVIS, Clerk.
Post Office Liberty Hill, Tennessee.
ELDER JOHN F. KECK, Assistant Clerk.
Post Office Goin, Tennessee.

Obituaries

I. J. Norton

Bro. I. J. Norton, joined the Primitive Baptist Church at Straight Branch the first Saturday in August, 1918. Bro. Norton lived an honest Christian all the nine years. He was a man who loved to pay his debts, left owing no man anything but love and good will.

The Bro. leaves his aged parents to mourn his loss.

He married Adline Crutchfield, lived in union with her and in love and respect until death took him away. Poor wife left to grieve over her loss. So sleep on Brother, you have gone from the evil to come.

Bro. Norton was a great believer in the resurrection of the dead . Sleep on Brother, till God calls you. Lord hold up his weeping wife and parents, till you call them in. (This written by his father T. A. Norton, member of Straight Branch Church.)

I. J. Norton, Born April 1, 1882, died March 26, 1928. Age 46 years.

————o————

David Ausmus

David Ausmus, born July 28th, the year 1860, died September 9, 1927, age 67 years 1 month and 12 days. Professed faith in Christ when quite young. He joined the Primitive Baptist Church at Davis Creek, stayed there till January 23, 1909. Then moved his letter to Straight Branch where he remained until death.

Married to Amy Wright in early life. To this union were born six children, 4 sons and 2 daughters. His wife died leaving him a widower till death. Brother Ausmus is greatly missed in the church and our homes, but he is gone to his reward. So let us so live that we may meet him in the sweet by and by. Three orphan children left to morn his loss.

————o————

Brother Dolph Buckner

Brother Dolph Buckner, was born March 25 1873. Deceased August 28, 1927, age 54 years. Professed faith in Christ in youth and joined the Primitive Baptist church at Hamilton Grove in the year 1898 and lived a faithful member until death. He was a Deacon of the church for years. His illness was of long duration and borne with Christian fortitude. He leaves a companion and daughter to mourn his loss. The church has lost a faithful member. The wife an affectionate husband, the dear daughter a kind and loving father. Weep not for I am waiting in Glory for you.

————o————

Sarah Elizabeth Boruff

Sarah Elizabeth Boruff, was born October 20th 1853, died July 4, 1928, age 74 years, 8 months and 14 days. She was married to David White, February the 19, 1871. To this union were born 7 children, 4 girls and 3 boys which all survive her except a little girl which was taken away in infancy. She has 143 grand children, 22 great grand children. She professed faith in Christ about 58 years ago and joined the Primitive Baptist church at Cave Spring in 1872, where her membership remained until 1906 when it was removed to Oak Grove where it remained until death. The greater part of her last 4 years of life was spent in reading the Bible and religious literature. She often spoke of her hope of a blessed immortality beyond the grave. In her last 2 months of her sickness, she spoke of a song that rolled through her mind "O Happy Time Long Waited For," and said often that she was glad that she was born to die.

She leaves a loving husband and 6 children, grand children and great grand children and a host of friends to mourn her absence. But we believe that our loss is her eternal gain. The funeal service was conducted by Elder Leonard White, Elder J. G. Brantley. She was laid to rest in the Oak Grove Cemetery to rest till the resurrection morn.

PLEASANT POINT

Mary Ridings

Mrs. Mary Ridings, was born October 17 in the year of 1843 and died in the year of 1926 in the day of March 6.

David Ridings

Mr. David Ridings, was born in the year of 1847, died on the 28th day of July 1926.

————o————

Mary Toliver

Mary Toliver, was born in the year 1897, October 17.

————o————

Sister Pollie Webb, wife of John Webb was born June 22 1844. Died May 16, 1928, age 83 years, one month and 6 days old. Professed faith in Christ June 4, 1891, and joined the Primitive Baptist Church at Gibson Station, Virginia, September the first, Saturday 1905 and was baptized by Elder J. D. Monroe. She lived a member of the church until death. She leaves a husband, one son and a host of friends to mourn her lost. Our lost is her eternal gain.

————o————

Jessie Mae Cabbage Dyon

Jessie Mae, daughter of C. M. and Martha Cabbage was born July 5, 1896, was married to Chas Ryon, March 17, 1912, joined the church at Blackfox November 4th, Saturday, 1908, where she lived a member until death, which occurred in an auto wreck at Washington, D. C. March 25, 1928.

She leaves to mourn her loss, father, mother, husband, brothers and sister, the church and a host of friends.

Weep not for her as one that has no hope. Her remains were sent back to Tennessee and laid to rest in the old Cabbage cemetery.

Brother Luther Dale

Bro. Luther Dale was born in the year 1900, joined the Primitive Baptist church at Mossie Springs and was baptized June 9, 1918 by Elder T. G. Brantly and lived a constant member until death, which occurred October 31, 1927. Bro. Luther is greatly missed in the church and our homes, but he is gone to his reward, so let us live that we may meet him in that sweet bye and bye.

---o---

Joseph White

Joseph White, son of Mr. and Mrs. Elza White was born January 31, 1851, died January 21, 1928.

He joined the church at Mossy Springs in early life and lived a faithful member until death. He leaves a wife, 5 sons and one daughter and 3 brothers, 2 brothers and 6 sisters passing away before him. He leaves a host of friends and relatives to mourn his loss. Our loss is heavens eternal gain.

---o---

Ada Jones

Ada Jones, wife of Carl Jones and daughter of Mr. and Mrs. Annias Brantley was born October 19, 1904, died October 14, 1927, was a member of Mossy Springs church. She leaves a father, 1 sister and 3 brothers and a host of relatives to mourn her loss, but our loss is her eternal gain.

---o---

Elza Wilson

Elza Wilson, was born December 14, 1891 and died March 26, 1928. He was a member of Mossy Springs church. He married Miss Maryette Snoderly, to this union were born 4 children, 1 passing away in infancy, he leaves a wife, 1 son and 2 daughters, 1 brother and 1 sister and a host of friends and relatives to mourn his loss. Sleep on sweet sleep that knows no disturbances. Our loss is his eternal gain.

MINISTERIAL ROLL

Elders	Post Offices
H. L. Alston	Tazewell, Claiborne, County, Tenn.
James Ausmus	Speedwell, Claiborne, County, Tenn.
John Ausmus	Speedwell, Claiborne County, Tenn.
T. G. Brantley	Sharps Chapel, Unoin County, Tenn.
A. J. Boruff	Corryton, Knox County, Tenn.
G. J. Boruff	Layston, Union County, Tenn.
Alfred Boruff	Maynardville, Union County, Tenn.
Calvin Collins	New Market, Jefferson County, Tenn.
John F. Keck	Goin, Claiborne County, Tenn.
Mathew Oliver	Noeton, Grainger County, Tenn.
Thomas Pierce	Speedwell, Claiborne County, Tenn.
Thornie Pierce	Speedwell, Claiborne County, Tenn.
H. A. Shoffner	Harrogate, Claiborne County, Tenn.
Alfred Parks	New Market, Jefferson County, Tenn.
S. S. Wilson	Gibson Station, Lee County, Va.
M. B. Weaver	Loyston, Union County, Tenn.
Leonard White	LaFollette, Campbell County, Tenn.
John A. Webb	Gibson Station, Lee County, Va.
Esau Keck	Goin, Claiborne County, Tenn.
W. H. Graves	Sharps Chapel, Union County, Tenn.
S. S. Pennington	Liberty Hill, Grainger County, Tenn.
Gideon Abbott	Knoxville, Knox County, Tenn.

LICENTIATES

Charles Stanifer	Speedwell, Claiborne County, Tenn.
W. R. Petree	Corryton, Knox County, Tenn.
Elvin Weaver	Loyston, Union County, Tenn.
W. A. Atkins	Tate, Grainger County, Tenn.
John C. Ausley	Gibson Station, Lee County, Va.
George W. Mays	Goin, Claiborne County, Tenn.
Steve Drummonds	Tazewell, Claiborne County, Tenn.
Charlie Redmond	Harrogate, Claiborne County, Tenn.

TABLE OF STATISTICS

CHURCHES	NAMES OF DELEGATES	Declaration	Recd. by Ex-Bap.	Recd. by Relation	Recd. by Letter	Restored	Dismissed by letter	Excluded	Deceased	Total Membership	Saturday Meeting	Contribution
Blackfox	Sam Davis, C. M. Cabbage, Sallie Davis	5						1	1	98	2	$3.00
Cedar Spring	V. Moyers, E. S. Drummonds, J. L. Drummonds, Willie Drummonds, Martha Roberson, Delie Drummonds	1	4		2		2		1	77	4	2.75
Straight Branch	Thomas Pierce, Thornie Pierce, John Ausmus, Edd McBee	4	1		2				1	68	1	2.55
Oak Grove	W. R. Petree, J. P. Russell, George Shoffner, Verlin Hopper	1	24		1				1	225	1	5.50
Cave Spring	Letter but no messenger									111	3	2.00
Mossy Spring	M. B. Weaver, V. H. Graves, T. G. Brantly, Elvin Weaver, Berry White	2						1	4	240	2	5.00
Pleasant Hill	Neal Lambert, J. M. Wilder, J. L. Edwards, Verlin Edwards, Lucinda Moyers, Hassie Edwards, Mae Edwards, Jane Edwards	2					1	1		47	4	3.00
Hamilton Grove	Alfred Boruff, Ernest Hamilton, Sillius Hamilton, Forest Hamilton, Mamie Hamilton	3					1		1	70	3	2.00
New Hebron	No letter. Come no									22	2	---
Gibson Station	H. A. Shoffner, John Webb		6							86	1	2.25
Pleasant Point	John F. Keck, J. E. Keck, F. L. Keck				3				2	138	2	3.00
Davis Chapel	James Lynch, Albert Davis		4		3		1	1	2	147	2	3.00
Red Hill	Mose Treece, Will Roberson, Wily Treece		4				1	1		67	2	3.00
Rocky Dale	Eli Graves, Elmer Graves, M. C. Dunn			7	8				1	58	3	3.70
Noeton	No letter. Come on									35	8	---
Capps Creek	Linda Pail, Lizzie Weaver, Esther Braden, Mary Bowen									10	2	2.35

OFFICIAL DIRECTORY

CHURCHES	COUNTY	PASTORS	CLERKS	CLERKS POST OFFICE
Mossy Spring	Union	V. H. Graves	Louis Lamb	Sharps Chapel, Tenn.
Gibson Station	Lee	Leonard White	Mary Ball	Gibson Station, Va.
Hamilton Grove	Union	V. H. Graves	H. F. Hamilton	Maynardsville, Tenn.
		H. A. Shoffner, asst.		
Cave Spring	Union	V. H. Graves	B. F. Berry	Sharps Chapel, Tenn.
Oak Grove	Union	T. G. Brantly	David White	Sharps Chapel, Tenn.
Straight Branch	Union	Thornie Pierce	T. A. Norton	Speedwell, Tenn.
Red Hill	Claiborne	T. G. Brantly	Jeff Treece	Speedwell, Tenn.
Rocky Dale	Knox	T. G. Brantly	M. C. Dunn	Corryton, Tenn.
Cedar Spring	Claiborne	Mathew Oliver	J. L. Drummonds	Foute 3 New Tazewell, Tenn.
Blackfox	Grainger	Alfred Boruff	Sam Davis	Liberty Hill, Tenn.
Pleasant Point	Claiborne	V. H. Graves	Fred Keck	Goin, Tenn.
Davis Chapel	Campbell	Leonard White	Aaron Davis	LaFollette, Tenn.
Capps Creek	Union	H. A. Shoffner	Esther Braden	Goin, Tenn.
Pleasant Hill	Claiborne	Leonard White	J. L. Edwards	Speedwell, Tenn.
Noeton	Grainger	Mathew Oliver	J. C. Oliver	Noeton, Tenn.
New Hebron	Jefferson	Mathew Oliver	Lucy Collins	New Market, Tenn.

217

MINUTES

OF THE

ONE HUNDRED AND TENTH
ANNUAL SESSON

OF THE

Powell's Valley
Association

OF

Primitive Baptists

Held With the Church at
Mossy Spring, Union County, Tennessee
On August 16-17-18, 1929.

Our next Association will be held with the Church at Davis Chapel. Three miles east of LaFollette, Campbell County, Tennessee, beginning on Friday before the Third Saturday in August, 1930.

THREE STATES PRINT, MIDDLESBORO, KY.

Association Proceedings

Minutes of the One Hundred and Tenth Annual Session of the Powells Valley Association of the Primitive Baptists held with the church at Mossy Springs, Union County. Tenn., on August 16-17-18, 1929. Our next association will be held with the church at Davis Chapel, three miles east of LaFollette, Campbell County, Tennessee, beginning on Friday before the third Saturday in August 1930.

1st. Praise and prayer by Elder M. B. Weaver.

2nd. According to previous arrangements the introductory sermon was delivered by Elder M. B. Weaver from Deut. 19th chapter, 14th verse. Thou Shall Not Remove Thy Neighbors Land Mark. etc.

3rd. After 15 minutes intermission at the sound of singing the association reassembled and was called to order by Mod. Elder T. G. Brantley.

4th. Prayer by Elder Gilbert Abbott.

5th. Called for letters from sister churches, received 12 which was read by the clerk assisted by Elder Leonard White.

6th. By motion all the letters were received and messengers names enrolled.

7th. By motion Elder M. B. Weaver was elected Moderator.

8th. By motion Brother Sam Davis was re-elected Clerk.

9th. Called for Brothers and Sisters who were not delegates when five came forward. (The names of which the Clerk failed to get) and was welcomed to seats with us.

10th. Called for newly constituted churches, received none.

11th. Called for corresponding letters from sister associations received none.

12th. Called for the report of the Clerk on last years contribution, when he reported as follows: Received for printing minutes for the year 1927, $43.10. Balance in my hand of 73 cents making a total of 43.83. Cost of printing minutes of 1928 $32.00. This leaves a balance of $11.83. The clerk being allowed $15.00 for his service and mailing minutes. This leaves a balance of $3.17 due the clerk. Signed, Sam Davis, Clerk, P. V. A.

13th. By motion received the report.

14th. Called for visitors from sister associations, received none.

15th. By motion that the Moderator appoint the following committess:

(a)   On preaching, Brothers Mose Treece, Steve Drummonds and M. C. Dunn.

(b)   On arrangements, Brothers George Drummonds, George Heatherly, Walker Edmondson.

(c)   On correspondence, Fred Keck, Eli Graves, Alfred Evans.

(d)   On request, Brothers Press Russell, William Drummonds, Elmer Graves.

(e)   On finance, Herbert Graves, Johey Davis, Palmer Bridges.

16th.   By motion all the committees were received.

17th.   Motion in order to adjourn until 9:00 o'clock tomorrow.

18th.   Dismissed in order.

Saturday Proceedings

1st.   The Association met persuant to adjournment.

2nd.   Prayer by Elder A. L. Alston.

3rd.   Called for letters from sister churches that failed to get in Friday, received two which were read by the clerk.

4th.   By motion said letters was received and their delegation seated.

5th.   Called for the report of the Committee on Arrangements.

(a)   We your Committee on Arrangements beg leave to submit the following: That we follow the order of the last years minutes.

Respectfully Submitted,

GEORGE DRUMMONDS
M. W. EDMONDSON
GEORGE HEATHERLY.

6th.   On motion report received and discharged the committee.

7th.   Called the roll and erased names of absentees.

8th.   Called for the report of the Committee on Preaching.

(a)   We your Committee on Preaching beg leave to submit the following report: Friday night at the church, Elders Leonard White and Gilbert Abbott; at Blue Springs, Elders H. A. Shoffner and E. S. Drummonds; Saturday at Stand, Elders Thomas Pierce and Gilbert Abbott; Saturday n'ght, Blue Springs, Leonard White and H. L. Alston; Sunday at The Stand, Elders Leonard White, V. H. Graves and the Moderator to close.

Respectfully Submitted,

M. C. DUNN
MOSES TREECE,
E. S. DRUMMONDS.

9th. On motion report received and discharged the committee.

10th. Called for the report of the Committee on Correspondence:

(b) We your Committee on Correspondence beg leave to submit the following report: That we continue our correspondence with the Hiwassee and Nolichucky Associations and that we send minutes and messengers to the same. And that we appoint a comm'ttee of three to study the consistency of broader correspondence and report next year.

Respectfully submitted,

ALFRED EVANS
ELI GRAVES
FRED KECK.

11th. Called for the report of the Committee on Requests:

(c) We your Committee on Request beg leave to submit the following report: That we print in our minutes all the obituaries that the churches furnish and that the next annual session of the Powells Valley Association be held with the church at Davis Chapel, Campbell County, Tennessee, to commence on Friday before the third Saturday in August, 1930.

Respectfully submitted,

ELMER GRAVES
W. J. DRUMMONDS
PRESS RUSSELL.

12th. On motion report received and committee discharged.

13th. Called for the report of the Committee on Finance.

(d) We your Committee on Finance beg leave to submit the following report: Received for printing minutes $40.20.

Respectfully submitted,

JOHNEY DAVIS
HERBERT GRAVES
PALMER BRIDGES.

14th. On motion report received and discharged the committee.

15th. By motion the next annual session of the Powells Valley Association will be held with the church at Davis Chapel, Campbell County, Tennessee, to commence on Friday, before the third Saturday in August, 1930.

221

16th.   On motion Elder Gilbert Abbott preach the introductory sermon and that Elder V. H. Graves be his alternate.

17th.   On motion, we have 800 copies of minutes printed. That the Clerk superintend the printing and distribution of the same and that he be allowed $15.00 for his service.

18th.   On motion, we send Elders Leonard White, V. H. Graves and Brothers Elvin Weaver to the Hiwassee and Elders V H. Graves, M. B. Weaver, Thornie Pierce, Brothers M. C. Dunn, W. A. Lansley, to the Nolichucky Associations.

19th.   On motion the Clerk write corresponding letters to these associations and have them printed in our minutes.   We are sorry to insert that the well beloved and highly esteemed delegates from the Hiawassee Association, Brother L. L. Thomas and Sister Tim Thomas did not arrive until the business of our association had closed, however they were welcomed with glad hearts and we invite them back again.   The Clerk.

20th.   On motion we extend our heart felt thanks to this dear old church and her surrounding community for their hospitality and kind treatment to us through this association.

21st.   Motion in order that we adjourn to meet as above stated.

Elder M. B. WEAVER, moderator,
Layston, Tennessee.

SAM DAVIS, Clerk,
Liberty Hill, Tennessee.

Sunday Proceedings

At the appointed hour a large and well behaved audience assembled at the stand and so attentively listened to the well delivered sermons of Elders Leonard White from Isiah 53rd chapter, 11th verse, "He Shall See of the Travel of His Soul and Shall be Satisfied, etc." followed by V. H. Graves from —"If Any Man Come Unto You Having not this Doctrine, etc." and closing remarks by the Moderator.   All of which was delivered in the most loving spirit and a loving parting was expressed by all.

Corresponding Letter

To our sister associations, greetings with whom we correspond to-wit: The Hiwassee and Nalichucky, Associations, very dear Brothers and Sisters in Christ, we desire a continuance of our long cherished Correspondence with you and chosen these our beloved Brothers to hear this our epistle of love to you whom we hope you will esteem sound in the faith and grant them a seat with you in your godly consulations to-wit: Elders Leonard White, V. H. Graves, Brother Elvin Weaver, to the Hiwassee and Elders V. H. Graves, M. B. Weaver, Brothers, M. C. Dunn, W. A. Lansley and Elder Thomas Pierce, to the Nalichucky Associations. Come again.

Elder M. B. WEAVER, Moderator
SAM DAVIS, Clerk.

OBITUARIES

Mill Russan

Bro. Mill Russan was born October 21st, 1887, died September 30th, 1928. Brother Mill joined the church at Pleasant Point in January, 1927 and lived a beautiful christian life until God called him home. He leaves a loving wife, 7 children, his brothers and sisters and a host of friends to mourn his absence, but we hope our loss is heavens eternal gain.

————o————

J. W. Baley

Bro. J. W. Baley was born June 9, 1867, died October, 1928. Brother Baley professed faith in Christ and joined the Primitive Baptist Church at Hamilton Grove more than 20 years and lived a consecrated member until death. Survived by 10 children and a host of friends.

————o————

Nola Cabbage

Sister Nola Cabbage was born February 3, 1892, deceased May 25, 1929. Daughter of Sam and Mary J. Capps. Joined the Primitive Baptist Church at Black Fox in early life and lived till death. Our loss is heavens eternal gain. We hope to meet her in the sweet bye and bye.

————o————

Pauline McPhetridge-Moyers

Sister Pauline H. McPhetridge was born July 23, 1855. Professed faith in Christ 1871. Joined Primitive Baptist Church at Dotson Creek April 1, 1876, was baptized July 1, 1876.

223

Was married to Benjamin F. Moyers October 14, 1876 and to this union ten children were born. Six boys and 4 girls, of whom 6 are still living: J. L. Moyers, J. A. Moyers, A. R. Moyers, W. H. Moyers, and Mrs. Della M. Campbell.

The deceased had thirty-three grandch ldren all of whom were alive at her death.

Twelve Great Grandchildren living and one dead at her death.

The deceased was married to John Lay in 1918, and lived with him till her death May 1, 1929. Her request was that she be burried by her former husband B .F. Moyers, who died in 1914.

The deceased was a member of the Primitive Baptist Church at the time of her death at Black Fox.

————o————

Myrtle White-Harmon

Sister Myrtle White-Harmon, was born July 12, 1895 and died January 1, 1929. She professed a hope in Christ in her girlhood days and joined the church January 1909 and lived a faithful member until death. She leaves a husband and seven children to mourn for her, but our loss is her eternal gain.

————o————

Cora White

Sister Cora White wife of Daniel White was born June 9, 1864 died July 23, 1929, professed faith in Christ in her girlhood. Joined the Primitive Baptist Church at Mossy Springs, May 1906 and lived a faithful member until it pleased God to call her away. She leaves her husband and a host of friends to mourn her loss.

————o————

Maggie Sharp

Sister Maggie Sharp, daughter of William and Cinda Sharp, died July 2, 1929. She professed faith in Christ early in life and joined the church at Mossy Spring December 1913. She was about 36 years old and she lived a faithful member until death.

————o————

Sallie Robison

Sister Sallie Robison, wife of W. C. Robison, was born October 11, 1835 died January the 1st, 1929, age 93 years, two months and 20 days. Professed faith in Christ in her early days and joined the old Primitive Baptist Church and lived a faithful member until death. She leaves 7 children and 80 grand children and a host of friends to mourn her loss. She was a dear old mother in Israel. A loved one from us is gone, a voice we loved is still a place vacant in our home that never can be filled.

Thomas Davis

Brother Thomas Davis was born January 18, 1874. Died July 23, 1928. He professed faith in Christ at about the age of 21 years and joined the church and lived a faithful member until death. The night before his departure he shouted the praises to God and testified of his great love. We miss him so very much, but we believe our loss is his eternal gain.

MINISTERIAL ROLL

Elders	Post Offices
H. L. Alston	Tazewell, Claiborne County, Tenn.
James Ausmus	Speedwell, Claiborne County, Tenn.
John Au mus	Speedwell, Claiborne County, Tenn.
T. G. Brantley	Sharps Chapel, Union County, Tenn.
A. J. Boruff	Corryton, Knox County, Tenn.
G. J. Boruff	Layston, Union County, Tenn.
Alfred Boruff	Maynardville, Union County, Tenn.
Calvin Collins,	New Market, Jefferson County, Tenn.
John F. Keck	Goin, Claiborne County, Tenn.
Mathew Oliver	Noeton, Grainger County, Tenn.
Thomas Pierce	Speedwell, Claiborne County, Tenn.
Thornie Pierce	Speedwell, Claiborne County, Tenn.
H. A. Shoffner	Harrogate, Claiborne, County, Tenn.
Alfred Parks	New Market, Jefferson County, Tenn.
S. S. Wilson	Gibson Station, Lee County, Va.
M. B. Weaver	Loyston, Union County, Tenn.
Leonard White	LaFollette, Campbell County, Tenn.
John A. Webb	Gibson Station, Lee County, Va.
Esaw Keck	Goin, Claiborne County, Tenn.
W. H. Graves	Sharps Chapel, Union County, Tenn.
S. S. Pennington	Liberty Hill, Union County, Tenn.
Gilbert Abbott	Knoxville, Knox County, Tenn.

LICENTIATES

Charles Stanifer	Speedwell, Claiborne County, Tenn.
W. R. Petree	Corryton, Knox County, Tenn.
Elvin Weaver	Loyston, Union County, Tenn.
W. A. Atkins	Tate, Grainger County, Tenn.
John C. Owsley	Gibson Station, Lee County, Tenn.
George W. Mays	Goin, Claiborne County, Tenn.
Steve Drummonds	Tazewell, Claiborne County, Tenn.
Charlie Redmond	Harrogate, Claiborne County, Tenn.
Albert Davis	LaFollette, Campbell County, Tenn.

TABLE OF STATISTICS

CHURCHES	NAMES OF DELEGATES	Rec'd by Baptism	Rec'd by Relation	Rec'd by Letter	Restored	Dismissed by letter	Excluded	Deceased	Total Membership	Saturday Meeting	Contribution
Mossy Spring	Olis n Maize, Robert Graves, Arch e Lamb, Elvin Weaver, Berry White, E'ders M. B. Weaver, T. G. Brantley, V. H. Graves, Bros. Daniel White, J. M. Kivett	—	—	—	—	1	—	5	233	2	$5.00
Cedar Spring	Elders Steve Drummonds, H. L. Alston, Bros. J. V. Drummonds, John Drummonds, G. B. Drummonds, Sisters Maud, Bertha, Frankie and Dorie Drummonds	—	—	—	—	—	—	—	—	—	—
Blackfox	Sam Davis, Johnie Davis, Annie Davis, Adra Davis	6	—	—	—	—	—	—	77	4	2.50
Straight Branch	Elders Thomas Pierce, Thornie Pierce, Edd McBee	3	—	—	—	—	—	3	101	2	3.50
Oak Grove	George Shoffner, J. P. Ressell, John Graves	3	—	1	—	—	2	—	68	4	1.95
Cave Spring	James Brantley, Freeman Brantley, Nerve Brantly	—	—	—	—	—	—	1	216	1	5.05
Pleasant Hill	Lonzo Edwards, Verlin Edwards, Wily Duncan	4	—	—	—	—	—	—	111	3	2.00
Hamilton Grove	W. A. L. Owsley, M. W. Edmondson, S. R. Cook, Frank Hampton, Francis Hamilton	3	1	—	1	—	—	1	51	4	3.00
New Hebron	No letter. Come on	—	—	—	—	—	—	—	75	3	2.40
Gibson Station	Elder H. A. Shoffner	1	1	1	—	—	—	1	22	2	2.00
Pleasant Point	Elder Esaw Keck, Clarvel Keck	4	1	—	—	1	—	2	76	1	2.25
Davis Chapel	Elder Leonard White, Bros. Aaron Davis, George Heatherly, Albert Davis	12	2	1	—	2	—	2	140	1	2.75
Red Hill	Moses Treece, Harry Paterson, Howard Treece	3	—	1	—	—	5	—	153	3	1.65
Rocky Dale	Elder Gilbert, Abbott, Eli Graves, Elmer Graves, M. C. Dunn	—	—	—	—	—	—	—	70	2	4.40
Capps Creek	Elis Evans	5	—	—	—	—	—	—	58	—	1.75
Noeton	No letter. Come on	—	—	—	—	—	—	—	15 / 35	2	—

OFFICIAL DIRECTORY

CHURCHES	COUNTY	PASTORS	CLERKS	CLERKS POST OFFICE
Mossy Spring	Union	V. H. Graves	J. M. Kivette	Sharps Chapel, Tenn.
Gibson Station	Lee	Leonard White	Mary Ball	Gibson Station, Va.
Hamilton Grove	Union	H. A. Shoffner, asst.	H. F. Hamilton	Maynardville, Tenn.
Cave Spring	Union	V. H. Graves	B. F. Berry	Sharps Chapel, Tenn.
Oak Grove	Union	V. H. Graves	David White	Sharps Chapel, Tenn.
Straight Branch	Union	T. G. Brantly	T. A. Norton	Speedwell, Tenn.
Red Hill	Claiborne	John Ausmus, asst.	Jeff Treece	Speedwell, Tenn.
Rocky Dale	Knox	Thornie Pierce	M. C. Dunn	Corryton, Tenn.
Cedar Spring	Claiborne	T. G. Brantly	J. L. Drummonds	New Tazewell, Tenn.
Blackfox	Grainger	T. G. Brantly	Sam Davis	Liberty Hill, Tenn.
Pleasant Point	Claiborne	Mathew Oliver	Fred Keck	Goin, Tenn.
Davis Chapel	Campbell	T. G. Brantly	Aaron Davis	LaFollette, Tenn.
Capps Creek	Union	V. H. Graves	Esther Braden	Goin, Tenn.
Pleasant Hill	Claiborne	Leonard White	Lincoln Edwards, Verlin Edwards asst	Speedwell, Tenn.
Noeton	Grainger	H. A. Shoffner	J. C. Oliver	Noeton, Tenn.
New Hebron	Jefferson	Mathew Oliver	Lucy Collins	New Market, Tenn.

MINUTES

OF THE

ONE HUNDRED AND ELEVENTH
ANNUAL SESSION

OF THE

POWELL'S VALLEY
ASSOCIATION

OF

PRIMITIVE BAPTISTS

**Held With the Church at
Davis' Chapel, Campbell County. Tennessee
August 15, 16, 17, 1930.**

——:o:——

Next session of the Association will be held with the Church at Cave Spring, Union County, Tennessee, to commence on Friday before the third Saturday in August, 1931.

Elder E. S. Drummonds o preach the introductory sermon and Elder M. B. Weaver to be his alternate.

Association Proceedings.

1st. According to previous arrangements the Association met and the introductory sermon was preached by Elder Gilbert Abbott from 2nd Timothy, 4th ch., 7 verse, "I have fought a good fight," etc., followed by the alternate, Elder V. H. Graves.

2nd. After 10 minutes intermission, at the sound of singing the Association reassembled.

3rd. The Association was called to order by Moderator, Elder M. B. Weaver.

4th. Praise and prayer by Elder Mathew Oliver.

5th. Called for letters from sister churches of this Association, received 16 which was read by the clerk assisted by Sister Nannie B. Kitts.

6th. By motion all the letters were received and the delegates were seated.

7. By motion Elder V. H. Graves was elected Moderator

8th. By motion Bro. Sam Davis was re-elected clerk.

9th. Called for Brothers and Sisters who were not delegates when Sister Treece from Red Hill, Sister Duncan from Pleasant Hill, and Elder Thomas Pierce from St. Branch came forward and were welcomed to seats with us.

10th. Called for newly contsituted churches, received none.

11th. Called for corresponding letters, received two, one from the Nolachucky Association, and Messengers Elders U. J. Hembree, J. S. Hembree, John Edwards, from the Hiawassee Association Elder Milfred Hall.

12th. By motion the corresponding letters received, and all the delegates were welcomed to seats with us.

13th. By motion the Moderator appointed the following committees

(a) On preaching—Bros. George Heatherly, C. M. Cabbage, J. H. Lynch. Verlin Edwards together with the church.

(b) On arrangements—Bros. Elvin Weaver, Berry White, and Elmer Graves.

(c) On correspondence—Elders M. B. Weaver, Thomas Pierce, Bro. Thomas Brantley.

(d) On Request—Bros. Eli Graves, Jim Kivett, John Graves.

(e) On Finance—Bros. Josh Drummonds, Wily Treece, Dewey Graves.

14th. On motion all the foregoing committees were received.

15th. On motion we adjourned until Saturday morning, 9 o'clock.

16th. Dismissed in order.

Saturday's Proceedings.

1st. The Association met pursuant to adjournment.

2nd. Praise and prayer by Elder Gilbert Abbott.

3rd. Called for letters from sister churches that failed to get in Saturday. Received none.

4th. Called for the report of the committee on arrangements.

(a) We, your committee on arrangements, beg leave to submit the following order of business:

    1st. Call the Roll.

    2nd. On preaching.

    3rd. On correspondence.

    4th. On request.

    5th. On finance.

    6th. When and where shall our next Association be held.

    7th. Who shall preach the introductory sermon, and who shall be his alternate.

    8th. How many copies of Minutes shall be printed, who shall superintend the printing and distribution of same.

Respectfully submitted.

ELVIN WEAVER,

ELMER GRAVES,

BERRY WHITE

5th. By motion report received and discharged the committee.

6th. Call the roll and erase the names of absentees.

7th. Called for the report of the committee on preaching.

(b) We, your committee on preaching, beg leave to submit the following. Friday night at the church, Elders M. B. Weaver and Milfred Hall. At Coalidge School house Elders T. J. Pierce, Steve Rrummonds. Saturday at the Stand P. J. Hembree, Charlie Redmond, J. S. Hembree. Saturday night at church, Mathew Oiver, Gilbert Abbott. At Coalidge Saturday night, M. B. Weaver, G. M. Hall. At Pleasant Ridge, T. J. Pierce, Steve Drummonds. Sunday at the Stand. Mathew Oliver, Leonard White, Moderato rto close.

Respectfully submitted,

GEORGE E. HEATHERLY,

VERLIN EDWARDS,

C. M. CABBAGE.

JAMES F. LYNCH.

8th. By motion report received and discharged the committee.

9th. Called for the report of the committee on correspondence.

(c) We, your committee on correspondence, beg leave to submit the following. That we cheerfully keep up our correspondence with the Hiawassee and the Nolachucky Associations by letter and messenger.

Respectfully submitted,

M. B. WEAVER,

T. J. PIERCE,

THOMAS BRANTLY.

10th. Called for the report of the committee on request.

(d) We beg leave to submit the following: That we have printed in our minutes all the obituaries, that the churches furnish, and that the next annual session of the Powell's Valley Association be held with the church at Cave Spring, Union County, Tenn., to commence on Friday bfore the third Saturday in August, 1931.

Respectfully submitted,

J. M. KIVETT,

J. P. GRAVES,

ELI GRAVES.

11th. By motion report received and discharged the committee.

12th. Called for the report of the committee on finance.

(e) We, your committee on finance, beg leave to submit the following: Received from sister churches for printing minutes, $49.10.

Respectfully submitted,

J. L. DRUMMONDS,

DEWEY GRAVES,

WILY TREECE.

13th. By motion the report received and discharged the committee.

14th. By motion th next annual session of the Powell's Valley Association will be held with the church at Cave Spring, Union County, Tennessee, to commence on Friday before the third Saturday in August, 1931.

15th. By motion Elder E. S. Drummonds preach the introductory sermon, and that Elder M. B. Weaver be his alternate.

16th. By motion we have 800 copies of minutes printed, that the clerk superintend the printing of same and that he be allowed $10.00 for his services.

17th. By motion we send Elder M. B. Weaver and wife, Sister Easter Weaver, Gilbert Abbott, Thomas Pierce, Bros. Elvin Weaver, Sisters Emma Dunn, Freeda Weaver, Finnie Taylor, Ethel, Alice, Ida Sharp, Dela White and Va la Petree messengers to the Hiawassee Association, and Elders Gilbert Abbott, E. S. Drummonds M. B. Weaver messengers to the Nolachucky Association.

18th. By motion the clerk write corresponding letters to each of these associations and have them printed in the minutes.

19th. By motion we extend our heartfelt thanks to this dear old church and her surrounding community for their hospitalities and kind treatment to us through this Association.

20th. By motion we adjourn until 9 o'clock at the time and

place above stated.

ELDER V. H. GRAVES, Moderator,
Sharps Chapel, Tenn.

SAM DAVIS, Clerk,
Liberty Hill, Tenn.

Sunday's Proceedings

At the appointed hour a large and well behaved audience assembled at the altar and so attentively lisened to the well delivered sermons of Elders Mathew Oliver and Leonard White from 4 ch. 1st and 2nd verses of Paul's Letter to Timothy "I charge thee therefore before God and the Lord Jesus Christ," etc., and closing remarks by the Moderator all of which was delivered in the most loving spirit, and a loving parting was expressed by the shedding of tears, clapping of hands and invoking the blessings of God upon each other.

We are sorry to insert that the highly esteemed delgate from the Hiawassee Association, to wit: Brother L. L. Thomas, and three daughters, Lucile, Lydia and Hazel, did not arrive until the close of the service Sunday. However they were welcomed among us. And we invite them back again.

THE CLERK

Corresponding Letter

To our sister associations, greetings with whom we correspond, to wit: The Hiawassee and Nolachucky Associations. Very Dear Brothers— Sisters in Christ. We desire a continuance of our long cherished correspondence with you and have chosen these our Elders, Brothers, Sisters to bear this our epistle of love to you whom we hope you will esteem sound in the faith and grant them a seat with you in all your Godly consultations, to-wit: To the Hiawassee Elder M. B. Weaver and wife, Easter Weaver, Gilbert Abbott, V. H. Graves, T. J. Pierce. Brother Elvin Weaver, Sisters Emma Dunn, Freeda Weaver, Finnie Taylor Ethel, Elice and Ida Sharp, Dale White and Vada I Sree, to the Nolachucky Elders Gilbert Abbott, E. S. Drummonds, and M. B. Weaver, come again.

Elder V. H. Graves, Moderator.
Sam Davis, Clerk.

Obituaries
Elder S. Pennington

Elder S. Pennington was born June 13, 1838. Joined the church and was ordaintg to the Ministry in his youth in the fellowship of the United Baptist faith. Joined the church at Blackfox by letter about the year 1924, in which he lived a faithful member until death which occurred July 8, 1930. He was a pious father in Isreal, always filling his seat in the church as long as he could. Let us so live that we can meet him again.

Sister Lucinda Capps

Sister Lucinda, daughter of Elder J. A. and Nancy Capps, was born 1867, married to Lum Southerland when young. Joined the Primative Baptist Church at Rose Hill when quite young. Moved to Datson Creek by letter March 1, 1903, of which she lived a faithful member until death, which occurred December 25, 1929. She leaves husband several children, three brothers and a host of friends to mourn their loss. But our loss is heaven's gain. Weep not as for one that has no hope. We hope to meet her again in he sweet bye and bye.

P. L. Berry.

P. L. Berry was born August 22, 1854. Deceased January 8, 1930, age 75 years, 4 months, 16 days. He was married to Sarah Lynch 1885 To this union were born 9 children, 4 boys and 5 girls. Three boys and 4 girls still living. The widow and about 30 grandchildren. He joined the church at Cave Spring 1908. He has one brother, 4 sisters to mourn their loss. We hope to meet him in that Glory land some sweet day.

R. L. Dyke

R. L. Dyke born October 17, 1865, and married to Mary Turner July 1386. To this union was born 12 children, four of whom preceded him to the grave. Professed faith in Christ at an early age. Joined the Primitive Baptist Church at Cave Spring in 1894, later moved his membership to Mossie Spring Church, then to Oak Grove where he lived until death departed this life November 23, 1929. He leaves a wife, 8 children 34 grandchildren to mourn their loss. We feel that our loss is his eternal gain. He was a loving and kind father and a devoted husband. Funeral services conducted by his pastor, Rev. T. G. Brantley.

Bettie Monroe

Sister Bettie Monroe born June 8 1855, deceased February 23, 1929. Joined the Primitive Baptist Church at Oak Grove in early life and lived a faithful member until God called her away. Leaves three children, a host of grandchildren, a number of greatgrandchildren and a multitude of relatives and friends to mourn their loss but our loss is her eternal gain. She is in paradise waiting for the redemption of that precious body.

Anna Mae Ferguson-Treece

Sister Anna Mae Ferguson was born March 12th 1892, died August 22, 1929. Was married to Robert Treece, July 29, 1923. To this union were born four children. Two are living and two are dead. Sister Mae joined the Primitive Baptist Church at Moyers Grove April 4, 1907 and lived a faithful member until death. She leaves a husband, two children, father, one brother, three sisters to mourn their loss. But we hope our loss is heaven's gain.

Elder H. L. Olston

Elder H. L. Alston was born August 6, 1866. Married to Nancie M. Campbell June 7th, 1891. To this union was born 10 children, 7 boys and 3 girls. Joined the Phimitive Baptist church at Cedar Springs March 4th 1904. Was ordained deacon, August 4, 1906. In the year of our Lord 1913 was ordained to the full mark of the ministry. When departed this life leaves wife, two brothers, four boys, three girls, and several grandchildren, and a host of friends to mourn their loss. Our loss is his eternal gain.

MINISTERIAL ROLL

Elders	Post Offices
James Ausmus	Speedwell, Claiborne County, Tenn.
John Ausmus,	Speedwell, Claiborne County, Tenn.
T. J. Brantly,	Sharps Chapel, Union County, Tenn.
A. J. Boruff.	Corryton, Knox County, Tnn.
G. J. Boruff,	Loyston, Union County, Tenn.
Alfred Boruff,	Maynardville, Union County, Tenn.
Calvin Collins	New Market, Jefferson County, Tenn.
John F. Keck,	Goin, Claiborne County, Tenn.
Matthew Oliver	Noeton, Grainger County, Tenn.
Thornie Pierce	Speedwell, Claiborne County, Tenn.
Thomas Pierce,	Speedwell, Claiborne County, Tenn.
H. A. Stoffner	Harrogate, Claiborne County, Tenn.
Alfred Parks	New Market, Jefferson County, Tenn.
S. S. Wilson	Gibson Station, Lee County, Va
M. B. Weaver	Loyston, Union County, Tenn.
Leonard White	LaFollette, Campbell County, Tenn.
John A. Webb,	Gibson Station, Lee County, Va.
Esaw Keck,	Goin, Claiborne County, Tenn.
V. H. Graves,	Sharps Chapel, Union County, Tenn.
Gilbert Abbott,	Knoxville, Knox County, Tenn
E. S. Drummonds,	Tazewell, Claiborne County, Tenn.
Albert Davis	LaFollette, Campbell County, Tenn.

LICENTATES

Charlie Stanifer	Speedwell, Claiborne County, Tenn.
W. R. Petree,	Sharps Chapel, Union County, Tenn.
Elvin Weaver	Loyston Union County, Tenn.
W. A. Atkins	Tate, Grainger County, Tenn.
John C. Owsley	Gibson Station, Lee County, Va.
George W. Mays	Goin, Claiborne County, Tenn.
Charlie Redmond,	Harrogate, Claiborne County, Tenn.

Table of Statistics

CHURCHES	NAMES OF DELEGATES	Rec'd by Expr. Bapt.	Rec'd by letter	Restored	Dismissed by leter	Excluded	Deceased	Total Membership	Saturday Meetings	Contributions
Mossy Spring	Elders M. B. Weaver, T. G. Brantly, V. H. Graves, Bros. J. M. Kivett.	6					2	238	2	$4.00
Red Hill	Sallie Kivett, Elvin Weaver, Berry White	2					2	72	2	2.15
Hamilton Grove	Howard Treece, Harry Paterson, Wily Treece, Robert Treece	3						66		3.00
Oak Grove	Walker Edmondson			1			2	213	1	5.00
Pleasant Hill	Dewey Elison, John Graves					3		27	4	4.00
Rocky Dale	Neal Lambert, Wily Duncan, Verlin Edwards						3	58	3	3.50
New Hebron	W. G. Abbott, Eli Graves, Elmer Graves, Leona Petree, Belle Dunn	7				7		19	2	.75
Capp's Creek	Letterd, but no messenger	2						17	2	2.50
Pleasant Point	Ellis Evans	1					1	140	8	2.50
Gibson Statino	Esaw Keck	2					1	82	1	2.50
Noelon	Charlie Redmon, G. W. Bryant	7						39	3	2.00
Davis Chapel	Mathew Oliver				1	2		155		2.50
Cave Spring	Leonard White, Albert Davis, Henry Comer, George Heatherly, Nannie Kitts, Cintha Heatherly, Melda Davis	5	3					71	3	2.50
Black Fox	Jimmie Brantly, Elic Welch, Milton Brantly	10	3				1	109	2	3.00
Cedar Spring	C. M. Cabbage, Sam Davis	2					2	77	2	3.06
Straight Branch	E. S. Drummonds, J. L. Drummonds, Henry Cupp, John Drummonds. No letter. Come on						2	68	4	2.50

Official Directory

CHURCHES	COUNTY	PASTORS	CLERKS.	CLERK'S POSTOFFICES
Mossy Spring	Union	M. B. Weaver	J. M. Kivett	Sharps Chapel, Tenn.
Red Hill	Claiborne	T. G. Branly	Jeff Treece	Speedwell, Tenn.
Hamilton Grove	Union	V. H. Graves	H. F. Hamilton	Maynardville, Tenn.
Gibson Station	Lee	Mathew Oliver	Mary Ball	Gibson Station, Va.
Cave Spring	Union	V. H. Graves	S. F. Berry	Sharps Chapel, Tenn.
Oak Grove	Union	T. G. Brantly	David White	Sharps Chapel, Tenn.
Straight Branch	Union	Thornie Pierce	T. A. Norton	Speedwell, Tenn.
Rocky Dale	Knox	T. G. Brantly	M. C. Dunn	Corryton, Tenn.
Cedar Spring	Claiborne	Mathew Oliver	J. L. Drummonds	New Tazewell, Tenn.
		H. A. Shoffner, Ast		
Black Fox	Grainger	E. S. Drummonds	Sam Davis	Liberty Hill, Tenn.
Pleasant Point	Claiborne	V. H. Graves	Fred Keck	Goin, Tenn.
Davis Chapel	Campbell	Leonard White	Aaron Davis	LaFollette, Tenn.
Capps Creek	Union	H. A. Shoffner	Easter Braden	Goin, Tenn.
Pleasant Hill	Claiborne	Thorine Pierce	Lincoln Edwards	Speedwell, Tenn.
			Verlin Edwards, Asst.	
Noeton	Grainger	Mathew Oliver	J. C. Oliver	Noeton, Tenn.
New Hebron	Jefferson	E. S. Drummonds	Lucy Collins	New Market, Tenn.

237

MINUTES

OF THE

ONE HUNDRED AND TWELFTH
ANNUAL SESSION

OF THE

POWELL'S VALLEY
ASSOCIATION

OF

PRIMITIVE BAPTISTS

Held With the Church at
Cave Spring, Union County, Tennessee
August 14, 15, 16, 1931.

———————

Next session of the Association will be held with
the Church at Black Fox, Grainger County, Tennessee, to commence on Friday before the third Saturday in August, 1932.

Elder T. G. Brantly to Preach the introductory
sermon and Elder Leonard White to be his alternate.

S. B. NEWMAN & CO., KNOXVILLE, TENN.

ASSOCIATION PROCEEDINGS

1st. According to previous arrangements the Association met and the introductory sermon was preached by Elder E. S. Drummonds, followed by the alternate Elder M. B. Weaver from Mark, 26th chapter, 15-16 verses, Go ye therefore into all the world and preach the Gospel to every creature, etc.

2nd. After singing and prayer the Association was called to order by Moderator, Elder V. H. Graves.

3rd. Called for letters from sister churches, received thirteen which were read by the Clerk, assisted by Elder Leonard White.

4th. By motion all the letters were received and Messengers names enrolled.

5th. Called for Brothers and Sisters who were not delegates. When the followng came forward to wit: from Davis Chapel, Elder Leonard White, Bro. J. F. Lynch; Pleasant Hill, Lon Edwards, May Edwards; St. Branch, Bros. John Taylor; 'Cave Spring, Thomas Brantly, William Brantly; Black Fox, Odra Davis, John Bundon, Clayton Davis; Mossy Spring, C. B. Weaver; Rocky Dale, Vada Petree, Sister Eli Graves, who was welcomed to seats with us.

6th. Called for newly constituted churches, received none.

7th. Called for corresponding letters from Sister Associations, received one and Messenger from the Hiawassee to wit: Elders W. R. Gates, G. M. Hall, Brothers Elmer Hall Asburry Dyden, Floyd Andrews.

8th. On motion the letter was received and the delegates were welcomed to seats.

9th. By motion Elder V. H. Graves was re-elected Moderator and Brother Sam Davis was re-elected Clerk.

10th. By motion the Moderator appointed the following committees:

(a) On preaching—Brothers Will White, Walker Edmondson, M. C. Dunn, together with the church.

(b) On arrangements—Brothers Brad Weaver, Aaron Davis, James Brantly.

(c) On correspondence—Elders Leonard White, John Ausmus, Brother Josh Drummonds.

(d) On request—Brothers Neal Lambert, Elmer Graves, Elder M. B. Weaver.

(e) On finance—Elder Chas. Redmond, Brothers Harry Patterson, John Bundon.

11th. By motion all the foregoing committees were received.

12th. On motion we adjourned until Saturday morning, 9:00 o'clock, A. M.

13th. Dismissed in order.

3

SATURDAY PROCEEDINGS

1st. The Association met pursuant to adjournment.

2nd. Praise by Elder W. R. Gates.

3rd. Prayer by Elder T. J. Pierce.

4th. Called for letters from Sister Churches that failed to get in Friday, received one.

5th. On motion letter received and seated the delegation.

6th. Called for the report of the Committee on Arrangements.

(a) We your committee on arrangements beg leave to submit the following order of business.

1st. Call the roll.

2nd. Call for the reports of the committees on preaching.

3rd. On correspondence.

4th. On request.

5th. On finance.

6th. When an where shall our next association be held.

7th. Who shall preach the introductory sermon and who shall be his alternate.

8th. How many minutes shall we have printed and who shall superintend the same.

Respectfully Submitted,

BRAD WEAVER,

AARON DAVIS,

JAMES BRANTLY

9th. On motion report received and discharged the committee.

10th. Called the roll and eraced the names of absentees.

11th. Called for the report of the committee on preaching.

(b) We your committee on preaching beg leave to submit the following: Saturday at the Stand, Elders W. R. Gates, T. J. Pierce; Saturday night at Cave Spring Church, Elders E. S. Drummonds, Albert Davis; Saturday night at Blue Spring, Elders Leonard White, M. B. Weaver, at Mossy Spring, Elders W. R. Gates, G. M. Hall; Sunday at the Stand, Elders Leonard White, T. G. Brantly and the Moderator to close.

Respectfully submitted,

M. C. DUNN,

M. W. EDMONDSON,

W. M. WHITE,

With The Church.

12th. By motion received the report and discharged the committee.

13th. Called for the report of the committee on correspondence.

4

(c) We your committee on correspondence beg leave to submit the following report. That we keep up our correspondence with the Hiawassee and Nolachucky Associations by letter and messenger, and that the Clerk write corresponding letters to each of these and have them printed in our minutes.

Respectfully submitted,

ELDER LEONARD WHITE,
JOHN AUSMUS,
J. L. DRUMMONDS.

14th. By motion report received and discharged the committee.
15th. Called for the report of the committee on request.

(d) We your committee on request beg leave to submit the following report: That we have all the Obituaries printed in our minutes that the churches furnish, and that the next Annual Session of the Powells Valley Association be held with the church at Black Fox.

Respectfully submitted,

M. B. WEAVER,
NEAL LAMBERT,
ELMER GRAVES.

16th. On motion report received and discharged the committee.
17th. Called for the report of the committee on finance.

(e) We your committee on finance beg leave to submit the following report: Received from churches for printing minutes $38.75.

Respectfully submitted,

HARRY PATTERSON,
C. W. REDMOND,
JOHN BUNDON.

18th. On motion report received and discharged the committee.
19th. By motion the next Annual Session of the Powells Valley Association will be held with the church at Black Fox, Grainger County, Tennessee, to commence on Friiday before the third Saturday in August, 1932. Elder T. G. Brantly shall preach the introductory sermon and that Elder M. B. Weaver be his alternate.

20th. By motion we have 800 copies of minutes printed, that the Clerk superintend the printing and distribution of same, and that he be allowed $10.00 for his service.

21st. By motion the following named Elders and Brothers were appointed to our Sister Associations to wit: The Hiawassee, Elders V. H. Graves, T. J. Pierce, Leonard White.

To the Nolachucky, Elder Chas. Redmond and Brother W. A. L. Ousley.

5

22nd. By motion the Clerk write corresponding letters to each of these Associations and have them printed in our minutes.

23rd. By motion be it resolved that we tender our heartfelt thanks to this dear old church and her surrounding community for their hospitalities and kind treatment to us through this Association.

24th. Motion in order that we adjourn until 9:00 o'clock A. M. at the time and place above mentioned.

25th. Dismissed in order.

ELDER V. H. GRAVES, Moderator,
P. O. Sharps Chapel, Tenn.

SAM DAVIS, Clerk,
P. O. Liberty Hill, Tenn.

SUNDAY'S PROCEEDINGS

At the appointed hour Sunday, a large and well behaved audience assembled at the Stand and so attentively listened to the well delivered sermons of Elder Leonard White from the text, "What think ye of Christ and whose Son is He," followed by Elder T. G. Brantly and closing remarks by the Moderator, all of which was delivered in the most loving spirit and with great interest to all and a loving parting was expressed by the sheding of tears, clapping of hands and invoking the Blessing of God upon each other. While the Congregation sang that good old hymn, "Children of the Heavenly King."

CORRESPONDING LETTER

To our Sister Associations the Hiawassee and Nolachucky, we desire a continuance of our correspondence with you and for this purpose have chosen these our beloved Elders and Brothers to bear this our Epistle of love to you to wit: The Hiawassee Elders V. H. Graves, T. J. Pierce, Leonard White, to the Nolachucky Elder, Chas. Redmond and Brother W. A. L. Ousley.

ELDER V. H. GRAVES, Moderator.
SAM DAVIS, Clerk.

OBITUARIES

Sister Florence Lynch

Sister Florence Lynch age 57 years. Joined the Church at Cave Spring, January, 1895, was married to Jack White forty years ago. To this union was born two children, one boy and one girl. She leaves children and friends to mourn their loss, funeral conducted by Elder T. G. Brantly.

Brother Garret Lynch

Brother Garret Lynch was born, March 22, 1896. He joined the Primitive Baptist Church at Oak Grove, January, 1924. He lived a

8

faithful member until death. Deceased November 6, 1930. Gone but not forgotten.

Vincent Meyers

Vincent Meyers was born March 13th, 1851 and departed this life at the home of his daughter Mr. and Mrs. J. L. Drummonds which occurred March 20, 1931 at 2 A. M., being 80 years and seven days old. He was married to Rachel A. Treece, November 1st, 1883 to this union were born three children.

He professed faith in Christ in early life and joined the Primitive Baptist Church at Meyers Grove, January 4th, Saturday, 1911 and lived a faithful member until death.

Our father is survived by three children, two sons and one daughter, Alfred Meyers of Middlesboro, Ky., Robert Meyer and Delia Drummonds of Clouds, Tennessee. There are also surviving him ten grand children, three brothers and three sisters and a host of friends to mourn his loss but our loss is heavens eternal gain.

We highly appreciate the kindness and courtesy shown us during the sickness and death of our dear father. The remains were laid to rest in the Drummonds Cemetery. Funeral services conducted by Elders Mathew Oliver and Theodore Brantly.

Sister Jane Edwards

Sister Jane Edwards, wife of Jeff Edwards was born October 5th, 1866 and died October 13th, 1930. She joined the church at Davis Creek, January 1st, Saturday, 1887 and was baptized the following May. She left Davis Creek Church and was in the constitution of pleasant Hill Primitive Baptist Church in 1907, of which she lived a faithful member until God called her away. She lived a Christian life for forty-three years. While our home is sadder by her absence, Heaven is made brighter by her presence, but we hope to meet her in the sweet bye and bye.—The Children.

G. S. Southers

G. S. Southers, 86 years old. Was born April, 1845, joined the Church of Christ at Gibson Station, Primitive Baptist, December 1st, Saturday, 1901. Lived a consistent member until death and was faithful to bear his part of the burdens of the Church. Died February 12th, 1931. His death is mourned by the brethren and all who knew him but we feel his departure of this life was his eternal gain.

Elder John Webb

Elder John Webb, 75 years old. Joined the church, December 1st, Saturday, 1901. Deceased this life June 29, 1931. Ordained to the full work of the Ministry in the year of 1902 and was a faithful

9

supporter of the Faith that he loved until death and we believe is now reaping the happy reward that awaits all the faithful ones of eternal bliss.

Brother Hewey Webb

Brother Hewey Webb joined the Primitive Baptist Church at Gibson Station, Virginia, April 1st, Saturday, 1926 and lived a faithful member until death he departed this life July, 1930.

James Paterson Shoffner

James Paterson Shoffner was born May 20, 1908, age being twenty-two years seven months and two days. He professed faith in Christ in the year of 1927, joined the Primitive Baptist Church at Oak Grove where he lived a faithful member until death.

Survivors are his Parents, George and Lillie Shoffner and three Brothers and three Sisters and a host of friends to mourn their loss.

Myrtle Hill Cook

Myrtle Hill Cook, was born March 25, 1910, departed this life April 15, 1931.

She was married to Bill Cook, February 17, 1923. To this union one daughter was born.

Sister Cook professed faith in Christ and joined the Primitive Baptist Church at Red Hill the second Saturday in July 1925. Was baptized the second Saturday of August, 1925.

She leaves to mourn her loss, Father, Mother, four brothers and four Sisters. Her husband and daughter both died in less than a month after her death.

Elder Calvin Collins

Elder Calvin Collins joined the Primitive Baptist Church at New Hebron in the year 1913, departed this life April 19, 1931. He preached the Gospel about forty years and was a good faithful servant. He was loved by all who knew him.

Brother Frank Hamilton

Brother Frank Hamilton was born February 27, 1872, deceased January 19, 1931, age 58 years 10 months and 22 days. He married to Sarah Raly, December 25, 1891. To this union was born one daughter Ella. Second marriage to Emer Gilbert, December 15, 1907, to this union was born four children, one son and three daughters. The children all survive him and several grand children. He professed faith in Christ at an early age and joined the Primitive Baptist Church at Hamilton Grove and lived a faithful member until death. He was Church Clerk for many years. He was a loving

10

father, a devoted husband. We hope to meet him in the Glory land some sweet day.

Thornie Pierce

Thornie Pierce was born April 7, 1885, Son of Elder and Mrs. Thomas Pierce. Married Susan Clausan March 13, 1904. To this union were born eight children, four boys and four girls. Professed faith in Christ, Joined the Church and was Baptized at Straight Branch, May 1st, Sunday, 1919 and was ordained to the full work of the ministry January 9, 1924.

He has been greatly missed among the churches and all who knew him.

He was a lovely Preacher, a devoted Husband and a kind and affectionate father.

Departed this life December 30, 1930, funeral services were conducted at his home January 1, 1931.

MINISTERIAL ROLL

ELDERS	POST OFFICES
James Ausmus	Speedwell, Claiborne County, Tenn.
W. A. Moyers	Speedwell, Claiborne County, Tenn.
John Ausmus	Speedwell, Claiborne County, Tenn.
T. G. Brantly	Sharps Chapel, Union County, Tenn.
G. J. Boruff	Loyston, Union County, Tenn.
Alfred Boruff	Maynardville, Union County, Tenn.
John F. Keck	Goin, Claiborne County, Tenn.
Mathew Oliver	Noeton, Grainger County, Tenn.
Thomas Pierce	Speedwell, Claiborne County, Tenn.
H. A. Schoffner	Harrogate, Claiborne County, Tenn.
Alfred Parks	New Market, Jefferson County, Tenn.
S. S. Wilson	Gibson Station, Lee County, Va.
M. B. Weaver	Knoxville, Knox County, Tenn.
Leonard White	LaFollette, Campbell County, Tenn.
Esaw Keck	Goin, Claiborne County, Tenn.
V. H. Graves	Sharps Chapel; Union County, Tenn.
Gilbert Abbott	Knoxville, Knox County, Tenn.
E. S. Drummonds	New Tazewell, Claiborne County, Tenn.
Albert Davis	LaFollette, Campbell County, Tenn.
Charlie Redmond	Gibson Station, Lee County, Va.

LICENTATES

Charlie Stanifer	Speedwell, Claiborne County, Tenn.
W. R. Petree	Sharps Chapel, Union County, Tenn.
Elvin Weaver	Loyston, Union County, Tenn.
W. A. Atkins	Tate, Grainger County, Tenn.
John C. Ousley	Gibson Station, Lee County, Va.
George W. Mays	Goin, Claiborne County, Tenn.
Henry Comer	LaFollette, Campbell County, Tenn.
J. M. Wilder	Speedwell, Claiborne County, Tenn.

TABLE OF STATISTICS

CHURCHES	NAMES OF DELEGATES	Rec'd by Expr. Bapt.	Rec'd by letter	Restored	Dismissed by Letter	Excluded	Deceased	Total Membership	Saturday Meetings	Contributions
Mossy Spring	Elders V. H. Graves, M. B. Weaver, Bros. Wm., Allie, Berry and	Bal. in the hand of clerk								$6.50
	Ervin White, George and Tim Sweat, James and Sallie Kivett	4			2			240	2	$5.50
Red Hill	Bros. Harry Patterson, Albert Truce						1	71	2	1.80
Hamilton Grove	Bros. W. A. L. Ousley, Walker Edmondson, Earnest, Lillias,						1	65	4	3.00
	Hamilton and Mamie Forest	6	4				3	220	1	3.00
Oak Grove	Bros. Dewey Elison, Verly Hopper, George Schoffner	7		1			1	55	4	3.50
Pleasant Hill	Bros. Neal Lambert, W. M. McHenry, Verlin and J. L. Edwards	5						63	3	3.25
Rocky Dale	Bros. Herbert and Elmer Graves, M. C. Dunn	17		2				37	1	1.10
New Hebron	Letter, but no messenger	2				1		18	2	2.45
Capps Creek	Bro. Ellis Evans							140	1	3.25
Pleasant Point	Sister Etter Hopper						2	72	1	2.00
Gibson Station	Elder Charlie Redmond							39	3	
Noeton	No Letter	13						167	3	3.40
Davis Chapel	Elder Albert Davis, Bros. Aaron Davis, Henry Comer, Bud	3				1	1	73	3	3.00
	Berry, Carl McCarty				3			106	4	2.50
Cave Spring	Bros. James and Manda Brantly, Chester and Millard Welch,	2			1		2	76	4	2.00
	Tissie Creech	2	1		2		2	67	1	2.00
Black Fox	Bros. C. M. Cabbage, Sam Davis, John Davis									
Cedar Spring	Elder E. S. Drummonds, J. L. and Delia Drummonds, Henry Cupp									
Straight Branch	Elders John Ausmus, T. J. Pierce, Bros. I. N. Lamar, Dan Cain									

OFFICIAL DIRECTORY

CHURCHES	COUNTY	PASTORS	CLERKS	CLERK'S POSTOFFICES
Hamilton Grove	Union	T. G. Brantly	C. L. Hamilton	Maynardville, Tenn.
Mossy Spring	Union	V. H. Graves	James Kivett	Sharps Chapel, Tenn.
Red Hill	Claiborne	T. G. Brantly	Jeff Truce	Speedwell, Tenn.
Gibson Station	Lee	Mathew Oliver	Mary Ball	Gibson Station, Va.
Cave Spring	Union	V. H. Graves	B. F. Berry	Sharps Chapel, Tenn.
Oak Grove	Union	T. G. Brantly	Clifford Russell	Sharps Chapel, Tenn.
Straight Branch	Union	John Ausmus	I. N. Lamar	Speedwell, Tenn.
Rocky Dale	Knox	T. G. Brantly	M. C. Dunn	Corryton, Tenn.
Cedar Spring	Claiborne	Mathew Oliver	J. L. Drummond	New Tazewell, Tenn.
Black Fox	Grainger	V. H. Graves	Sam Davis	Liberty Hill, Tenn.
Pleasant Point	Claiborne	V. H. Graves	Fred Keck	Goin, Tenn.
Davis Chapel	Campbell	Albert Davis	Henry Comer	LaFollette, Tenn.
		H. A. Schoffner, Ast.		
Capps Creek	Union	Charlie Redmond.	Easter Braden	Goin, Tenn.
		Charlie Redmond	J. L. Edwards, Ast.	
Pleasant Hill	Claiborne	Ast. H. A. Schoffner	Verlin Edwards	Speedwell, Tenn.
Noeton	Grainger	Mathew Oliver	J. C. Oliver	Noeton, Tenn.
New Hebron	Jefferson	E. S. Drummond	Glenn Mitchel	New Market, Tenn.

247

MINUTES

OF THE

ONE HUNDREDTH AND THIRTEENTH

ANNUAL SESSION

OF THE

POWELL'S VALLEY ASSOCIATION

OF

PRIMITIVE BAPTISTS

Held With the Church at

Blackfox, Grainger County, Tennessee

August 19-20-21, 1932

Next Session will be held with the Church at Cedar Springs, Claiborne County, Tennessee, to commence on Friday before the third Saturday in August, 1933.

Elder Leonard White to preach the introductory sermon and Elder Mathew Oliver to be his alternate.

ASSOCIATION PROCEEDINGS

1st. According to previous arrangements the Association met and the introductory sermon was delivered by Elder T. G. Brantly from Hebrews, 10th chapter, 4th verse, For it is not Possible that the Blood of Bulls and of Goats should take away Sins.

2nd. After ten minutes intermission at the sound of Singing the people reassembled.

3rd. After Praise by Elder V. H. Graves and Prayer by Elder Mathew Oliver the Association was called to order by Moderator. Prayer by Elder E. S. Drummonds.

4th. Called for letters from Sister Churches, received 14 which were read by the Clerk assisted by Elder T. G. Brantly.

5th. By motion all the letters were received and messengers names enrolled.

6th. Called for Brothers and Sisters who were not delegates, received one from New Hebron, to wit, Brother Jim Collins and one from Davis Chapel, to wit, Brother Henry Comer who were welcomed to seats with us.

7th. Called for newly constituted churches, received none.

8th. Called for corresponding letters, received one from the Hiwassee Association with their Messenger, Elder W. R. Gates; received one from Nolachucky Association as a member to wit: Elder U. J. Hembree.

9th. By motion the letters were received and the Messengers were welcomed to Seats with us.

10th. By motion Elder V. H. Graves was re-elected Moderator.

11th. By motion Brother Sam Davis was re-elected Clerk.

12th. Motion in order that the Moderator appoint all the following Committees:

(a) On preaching—Brothers George Drummonds, C. L. Buckner. Sam Cook, Horace White, together with the Church.

(b) On arrangements—Brothers Elvin Weaver, Elmer Graves, Charlie Stanifer.

(c) On correspondence—Elders M. B. Weaver, Mathew Oliver, T. J. Pierce.

(d) On request—Brothers Eli Graves, C. B. Weaver, J. C. Oliver.

(e) On finance—Jim Drummonds, Geo. Shoffner, Sillis White.

13. By motion all the foregoing Committees was received.

14. Motion in order that we adjourn until 9:00 A. M. Saturday.

15. Dismissed in order.

2

SATURDAY PROCEEDINGS

1st. The Association met pursuant to adjournment.

2nd. Praise by Elder W. R. Gates.

3rd. Prayer by Elder T. G. Brantly.

4th. Called for letters from Sister Churches that failed to get in Friday, received one from Hamilton Grove which was read by Elder T. G. Brantly.

5th. By motion said letter was received and their delegation seated.

6th. Call for the report of the Committee on arrangements.

(a) We your committee on arrangements beg leave to submit the following order of business:

1st. Call the roll.

2nd. Call for the report of the Committee on Preaching.

3rd. On Correspondence.

4th. On request.

5th. On finance.

6th. When and where shall our next Association be held.

7th. Who shall preach the introductory sermon, and who shall be his alternate.

8th. How many copies of minutes shall we have printed, who shall superintend the printing of same and what shall he be allowed for his service.

Respectfully, submitted,

ELVIN WEAVER,

ELMER GRAVES.

CHARLIE STANIFORD.

7th. Received the report and discharged the committee.

8th. Called for the report of the committee on preaching.

(b) We your committe on preaching beg leave to report the following: Friday night at the church, Elders Mathew Oliver, U. J. Hembree; Saturday at the Stand, Elders Albert Davis, E. S. Drummonds, and W. R. Gates to close; Saturday, 3:00 P. M. at the Church, Elders W. A. Moyers, V. H. Graves; Saturday night at the Church, Elders Esaw Keck, M. B. Weaver, T. J. Pierce; Saturday night at Mt. Egar, Elders T. G. Brantly, Mathew Oliver; Sunday at the Stand, Elders Mathew Oliver, W. R. Gates and the Moderator to close.

Respectfully submitted,

G. B. DRUMMONDS,

SAM R. COOK,

HORACE WHITE.

3

250

9th. By motion report received and discharged the committee.

10th. Called for the report of the committee on correspondence.

(c) We your committee on correspondence beg leave to report the following: That we keep up our correspondence with the Hiwassee and Nolachucky Associations by letter and delegation and whereas we fail to hear from the Nolachucky that we appoint a committee to investigate the cause of such failure and report next year.

Respectfully submitted,

ELDER M. B. WEAVER,
ELDER T. J. PIERCE,
ELDER MATHEW OLIVER.

11th. By motion report received and discharged the committee.

12th. Called for the report of the committee on request.

(d) We your committee on request beg leave to make the following report: That we have all the Obituaries printed in our minutes that the churches furnish and that the next session of the Association be held with the Church at Cedar Springs.

Respectfully submitted,

C. B. WEAVER,
J. C. OLIVER,
ELI GRAVES.

13th. By motion report received and discharged the committee.

14th. Called for the report of the committee on finance.

(e) We your committee on finance beg leave to report the following: Received from Churches for printing minutes $34.43.

Respectfully submitted,

G. W. SHOFFNER,
J. A. DRUMMONDS,
SILLIS WHITE

15th. By motion received the report and discharged the committee.

16th. By motion the next Annual Session of the Powell's Valley Association will be held with the Cedar Springs Church, Claiborne County Tennessee to commence on Friday before the third Saturday in August, 1933. That Elder Leonard White Preach the introductory sermon and that Elder Mathew Oliver be his alternate.

17th. By motion we have 800 copies of minutes printed, that the Clerk superintend the printing and distribution of same and that he be allowed $10.00 for his service.

18th. By motion we appoint the following committees to our Sister Associations. To the Hiwassee, Elders M. B. Weaver, V. H.

4

Graves, Brothers Horace White, Elvin Weaver. To the Nolachucky, Elders Mathew Oliver, T. J. Pierce, Brother Sam Davis.

19th. By motion the Clerk write corresponding letters to the Hiwassee and the Nolachucky Associations and have the same printed in our minutes.

20th. By motion be it resolved that we tender our heartfelt thanks to this dear old church and her surrounding community for their hospitalities and kind treatment to us through this Association.

21st. Motion in order that we adjourn until 10:30 o'clock at the time and place above stated.

22nd. Dismissed in order by ELDER M. B. WEAVER.

ELDER V. H. GRAVES, Moderator,
P. O. Sharps Chapel, Tenn.
SAM DAVIS, Clerk,
P. O. Liberty Hill, Tenn.

SUNDAY'S PROCEEDINGS

At the appointed hour Sunday a large and well behaved audience assembled at the Stand and so attentively listened to the well delivered sermons of Elders Mathew Oliver from the 133rd Psalm, followed by W. R. Gates from the 24th verse of the 9th chapter of Hebrews and closing remarks by the Moderator, all of which was delivered in the most loving spirit and with the greatest interest to all, and a loving parting was expressed by the shedding of tears, clapping of hands and invoking the blessing of God upon each other.

CORRESPONDING LETTER

To our Sister Associations to wit: The Hiwassee and Nolachucky.

Dear Brothers and Sisters we desire a continuance of our long cherished correspondence with you and for this purpose have chosen these our beloved Elders and Brothers to bear this our epistle of love to you to wit: To the Hiwassee, Elders M. B. Weaver, V. H. Graves, Brothers Horace White, Elvin Weaver when convened with the Church at Poplar Springs, Roane County, Tennessee, to commence on Friday before the fourth Saturday in September, 1932, and we send to the Nolachucky, Elders Mathew Oliver, T. J. Pierce, Brother Sam Davis. May peace and love abound with you throughout your Associations is the prayer of this your little sister. The Clerk.

5

OBITUARIES

Sister Anna Davis

Sister Anna Davis, daughter of John and Lizzie Bundon was born December 4, 1905, departed this life November 11, 1931. She was married to John Davis, June, 1929 to this union was born one daughter, George Anna, who departed this life a week after her mother. Sister Davis professed faith in Christ at an early age and joined the Church at Blackfox and lived a faithful member until God saw fit to call her away. She lived a faithful Christian life to the end and bore her thorny cross of suffering with great patience. She welcomed the angel of death with a bright and shining countenance when she heard the rustle of their wings as they descended from the throne of God to carry her safely across the chilly water of the river of death. She is now at rest, safe in the arms of a loving Saviour, reaping a rich reward for faithful obedience to God during her stay here on earth. She has laid down this life and taken up a new one and is crowned with a lily white robe that will outshine the dazzling light of the sun and shall be likened unto a bright and morning star that shall shine throughout eternity. She was budded on earth to bloom in heaven, a precious one from us is gone, a voice we loved is stilled, a place is vacant in our homes that never can be filled, her songs and earnest prayer, our services are lonely, we miss her everywhere.

Her brother, HERBERT BUNDON.

Sister Ethel Hill

Sister Ethel Hill was born October 12, 1907, being 25 years, 5 months and 19 days old. She was married to Oscar Robertson, June 20, 1925, and departed this life March 31, 1932. She professed faith in Christ in early life joined the Primitive Baptist Church at Red Hill the second Saturday in July, 1925, was baptized the second Saturday of August, 1925. To this union were born four children, two boys and two girls, baby being one month old when mother died and it went home to its mother when four months and 10 days old.

She leaves Father, Mother, four Brothers, three Sisters, Husband and Children and a host of friends to mourn her loss. We believe our loss is heaven's eternal gain.

Mrs. Millie Harris

Mrs. Millie Harris born June 24, 1873, died, May 21, 1932. Professed faith in Christ in 1894, joined the church in 1930 and was baptized and has lived a faithful life unto death. She leaves to mourn her loss, her husband and mother and a host of friends.

We hope our loss is her eternal gain.

Brother J. R. Hamilton

J. R. Hamilton was born June 7, 1874, he was 57 years, 9 months and 7 days old. Died March 14, 1932. He professed faith in Christ January, 1894 about 38 years ago and joined the church and lived a faithful member until the Lord called him home.

He leaves to mourn their loss a widow, one daughter, three grand-children and seven sisters, a host of relatives and friends. He rejoiced through his sickness and praised the Lord.

Brother Robert Stapleton

Brother Robert Stapleton, age 38, joined the Primitive Baptist Church at Red Hill the second Saturday in April, 1927, and lived a faithful member until death. Departed this life December 7, 1931, leaving his loving wife and seven children to mourn their loss. We believe our loss is his eternal gain.

Philip F. Keck

Philip F. Keck was born 1851, departed this life October 17, 1931, was married to Sarah Sowder in 1872. To this union eleven children were born. Brother Keck professed faith in Christ about the year 1884, and joined the Primitive Baptist Church at Pleasant Point and served the church as Clerk for many years and he is missed by all who knew him, the bereaved ones hope to meet him in the sweet bye and bye.

George Ragan

George Ragan was born July 10, 1857, joined the Primitive Baptist Church of Blackfox when a young man in which he lived a faithful member until death, which occurred on the 24th day of January, 1932. Uncle George lived his religion, always filling his seat at Church as long as he could. He would rejoice in the field at work as same as he did at church and we are satisfied he fought the battle and won his reward, a home in heaven. He welcomed the grim monster death with a smile that remained on his face after he was dead. He leaves to mourn their loss two children, Martha and Fate Ragan of Texas, one brother James Ragan of Knoxville and one sister Martha Cabbage of Liberty Hill.

MINISTERIAL ROLL

ELDERS	POST OFFICES
James Ausmus	Speedwell, Claiborne County, Tenn.
W A. Moyers	Speedwell, Claiborne County, Tenn.
John Ausmus	Speedwell, Claiborne County, Tenn.
T. G. Brantly	Sharps Chapel, Union County, Tenn.
Alfred Boruff	Maynardville, Union County, Tenn.
John F. Keck	Goin, Claiborne County, Tenn.
Mathew Oliver	Noeton, Grainger County, Tenn.
Thomas Pierce	Speedwell, Claiborne County, Tenn.
H. A. Shoffner	Harrogate, Claiborne County, Tenn.
Alfred Parks	New Market, Jefferson County, Tenn.
S. S. Wilson	Gibson Station, Lee County, Va.
M. B. Weaver	128 Jordon St., Knoxville, Knox County, Tenn.
Leonard White	Lafollette, Campbell County, Tenn.
Esaw Keck	Goin, Claiborne County, Tenn.
V. H. Graves	Sharps Chapel, Union County, Tenn.
Gilbert Abbott	Knoxville, Knox County, Tenn.
E. S. Drummonds	New Tazewell, Claiborne County, Tenn.
Albert Davis	Lafollette, Campbell County, Tenn.
Charlie Redmond	Gibson Station, Lee County, Va.
George Mays	Goin, Claiborne County, Tenn.

LICENTATES

Charlie Stanifer	Speedwell, Claiborne County, Tenn.
W. R. Petree	Sharps Chapel, Union County, Tenn.
Elvin Weaver	Loyston, Union County, Tenn.
W. A. Atkins	Tate, Grainger County, Tenn.
John C. Ousley	Gibson Station, Lee County, Va.
Henry Comer	LaFollette, Campbell County, Tenn.
J. M. Wilder	Speedwell, Claiborne County, Tenn.
Jim Collins	New Market, Jefferson County, Tenn.
Milton Brantly	Sharps Chapel, Union County, Tenn.
Carl McCarty	Sharps Chapel, Union County, Tenn.

10

CHURCHS	NAMES OF DELEGATES	Rec'd by Expr. Bapt.	Rec'd by letter	Restored	Dismissed by Letter	Excluded	Deceased	Total Membership	Saturday Meetings	Contributions
Mossy Spring	Elders V. H. Graves, M. B. Weaver, Bros. Elvin Weaver, H. V. White, C. B. Weaver	3			2	4		237	2	$4.00
Red Hill	Charlie Stanifer, Moses Treece, Bee Treece, Isabell Stanifer	3			2		2	74	2	1.50
Hamilton Grove	Wm. Edmondson, Sam R. Cook, W. E. Hamilton, F. S. Hamilton, Lillius Hamilton, Fontella Hamilton, Asuella Hamilton							74	4	2.00
Oak Grove	Elders T. G. Brantly, Bros. George Shoffner, John Graves	6	2		2	1		223	1	3.10
Pleasant Hill	Elder W. A. Moyers	13		1		1	2	68	3	3.35
Rocky Dale	Bros. Eli Graves, Elmer Graves	3					2	66	1	3.50
New Hebron	Letter but no Messenger	4						41	2	.30
Capps Creek	Bro. Ellis Evans	5			2			23	2	2.00
Pleasant Point	Elder Esaw Keck, Bros. Estill Heath, Cecil Keck	6						140	1	2.00
Gibson Station	Letter but no Messenger							77	1	1.40
Noeton	Elder Mathew Oliver, Bros. J. C. Oliver, H. L. Patrick, Robert Atkins	5						44	3	1.50
Davis Chapel	Elder Albert Davis, Bro. Henry Comer	1		6		2		140	3	2.00
Cave Spring	Millard Welch, James Brantly, Charlie Pebley	11			2		1	87	3	2.15
Black Fox	Bros. Sam Davis, John Bundon, W. M. Muncy, C. L. Buckner, Sisters Hila Lafford, Roma Bailey, Lizzie Bundon, Carlie Capps, Sallie Davis	3	1					106	4	3.00
Cedar Spring	Elder E. S. Drummonds, Bros. Henry Cupp, G. B. and I. A. G. Drummond, Sisters Margaret and Cretie Drummond	3	2					79	4	1.75
Straight Branch	Elder Thomas Pierce	12	2				3	78	1	1.43

Printers Fee.

256

OFFICIAL DIRECTORY

CHURCHES	COUNTY	PASTORS	CLERKS	CLERK'S POSTOFFICE
Hamilton Grove	Union	T. G. Brantly	Fate Hamilton	Maynardville, Tenn.
Mossy Spring	Union	V. H. Graves	J. M. Kivett	Sharps Chapel, No. 3, Tenn.
Red Hill	Claiborne	T. G. Brantly	Jeff Treece	Speedwell, Tenn.
Gibson Station	Lee	Leonard White	Mary Ball	Gibson Station, Va.
Cave Spring	Union	V. H. Graves	B. F. Berry	Sharps Chapel, Tenn.
Oak Grove	Union	T. G. Brantly	Clifford Russell	Sharps Chapel, Tenn.
		John Ausmus	I. N. Lamar	
Straight Branch	Union	E. G. Weaver, Ast	M. A. Clauson, Ast	Speedwell, Tenn.
Rocky Dale	Knox	T. G. Brantly	M. C. Dunn	Corryton, Tenn.
Cedar Spring	Claiborne	Mathew Oliver	J. L. Drummonds	New Tazewell, Tenn.
Black Fox	Grainger	V. H. Graves	Sam Davis	Liberty Hill, Tenn.
Pleasant Point	Claiborne	George Mays	Fred L. Keck	Goin, Tenn.
Davis Chapel	Campbell	Albert Davis	Jas. M. Kitts	LaFollette, Tenn.
Capps Creek	Union	Albert Davis	Easter Braden	Goin, Tenn.
		Charlie Redmond	J. L. Edwards	
Pleasant Hill	Claiborne	H. A. Shoffner, Ast	Verlin Edwards, Ast	Speedwell, Tenn.
Noeton	Grainger	Mathew Oliver	J. C. Oliver	Noeton, Tenn.
New Hebron	Jefferson	Alfred Parks	Luella Mitchel	New Market, Tenn.

257

MINUTES

OF THE

ONE HUNDREDTH AND FOURTEENTH

ANNUAL SESSION

OF THE

POWELL'S VALLEY ASSOCIATION

OF

PRIMITIVE BAPTISTS

Held With the Church at

Cedar Springs, Claiborne County, Tennessee

August 18-19-20, 1933

———

Next Session will be held with the Church at Red Hill, Claiborne County, Tennessee, to commence on Friday before the third Saturday in August, 1934.

Elder Charley Redmond will preach the introductory sermon and Elder Henry Comer will be his alternate.

These are ministers of the Powell's Valley Primitive Baptist Association, No. 2, which was held at Cedar Springs or Meyers Grove, Claiborne County, Tennessee, August 18, 19, and 20 in its 114th annual session. The ministers are as follows: Seated, left to right, S. S. Wilson, Thomas Pierce, Henry Comer, H. A. Shoffner, U. J. Hembree, Steve Drummonds; standing, left to right, John F. Keck, V. H. Graves, C. W. Mayes, Albert Davis, Leonard White, (Moderator), M. B. Weaver, W. R. Gates, John Ausmus, Esau Keck, John Ausmus, Mathew Oliver.

FRIDAY'S PROCEEDINGS

1st. According to previous arrangements the Association met, and the body was called to order by reading the 1st chapter of 1st John, by Moderator-Elder V. H. Graves.

2nd. The introductory sermon was delivered by Elder Leonard White from the text Jesus. He was followed by his alternate, Elder Mathew Oliver.

3rd. After ten minutes intermission, at the sound of Singing the people reassembled.

4th. After praise by Elder V. H. Graves, prayer was given by Elder U. J. Hembree.

5th. The Association was called to order by the Moderator.

6th. Called for letters from Sister Churches, received 14 which were read by the Clerk and Elder John F. Keck.

7th. All the letters were received by motion, and the delegation was welcomed to seats by the Moderator.

8th. Called for members who were not delegates, and Brother John Bundon from Blackfox, and Jeff Treece from Red Hill, came forward and were welcomed to seats with us.

9th. Called for newly constituted churches, and received none.

10th. Called for corresponding delegates from Sister Associations; received minutes and delegates from the Hiwassee Association, to wit: Elder W. R. Gates and Brother R. H. Petitt who were welcomed to seats.

11th. Called for members who were not delegates, and Elder U. J. Hembree of the Nolachucky Association came forward and was welcomed to a seat.

12th. By motion Elder Leonard White was elected Moderator.

13th. By motion Brother Sam Davis was re-elected Clerk.

14th. By motion the Moderator appointed all the following committees:

(a) On preaching—Brothers Jeff Treece, Neal Lambert, Walker Edmondson, together with the Church.

(b) On arrangements—Brother J. C. Oliver, John Bundon, Abraham Shipley.

(c) On correspondence—Elders Mathew Oliver, T. J. Pierce, V. H. Graves.

(d) On request—Elders Albert Davis, M. B. Weaver, and Brother Verlin Edwards.

(e) On finance—Elder S. S. Wilson, and Brothers C. B. Weaver, and Estell Heath.

15th. Motion in order to adjourn until 9 o'clock Saturday morning.

16th. Dismissed in order.

2

SATURDAY'S PROCEEDINGS

1st. The Association met pursuant to adjournment.

2nd. Praise by Moderator-Elder Leonard White, and prayer by Elder John F. Keck.

3rd Called for letters from Sister Churches that failed to get in Friday; received two, Oak Grove and Rocky Dale which were read and on motion were received; the delegation was welcomed to seats.

4th. Called for the report of the Committee on arrangements.

(a) We, your committee on arrangements, beg leave to submit the following order of business:

1st. Call the roll.

2nd. Call for the report of the committee on preaching.

3rd. On correspondence.

4th. On request.

5th. On finance.

6th. When and where shall our Association be held.

7th. Who shall preach the introductory sermon, and who shall be his alternate.

8th. How many copies of minutes shall we have printed; who shall superintend the printing and distribution of same; and what shall he be allowed for his services.

Respectfully submitted.

J. C. OLIVER,

JOHN BUNDON,

ABRAHAM SHIPLEY.

5th. Called for the report of the committee on preaching.

(b) We, your committee on preaching, beg leave to submit the following report: At Clouds Church house Friday night, Elder W. R. Gates, Watsons School house, Elder Henry Comer, Pleasant Point Church, Elder Leonard White, at Cedar Spring Church, Elder Gilbert Abbott; Saturday at the Stand, Elders W. A. Moyers, H. A. Shoffner, U. J. Hembree; Saturday, 3 p. m., at Brother Branson's residence, Elders Mathew Oliver, John F. Keck; Saturday night at Cedar Spring Church, Elders Alfred Parks, M. E. Weaver; at Brother England's, Elders Henry Comer, John Ausmus; at Pleasant Point Church, Elders T. G. Brantly, T. J. Pierce; at Clouds Church house, Elders Leonard White, Albert Davis; at the Stand Sunday, Elders W. R. Gates, T. G. Brantly, and the Moderator to close.

Respectfully submitted,

NEAL LAMBERT,

JEFF TREECE,

M. W. EDMONDSON.

6th. Called for the report of the committee on correspondence.

(c) We, your committee on correspondence, beg leave to submit

3

the following report: That we keep up our correspondence with our Sister Associations and solicit correspondence with other Associations of our faith and practice.

Respectfully submitted,

ELDER MATHEW OLIVER,
ELDER T. J. PIERCE,
ELDER V. H. GRAVES.

7th. The foregoing reports received and discharged the committees.

8th. Called for the report of the committee on finance.

(d) We, your committee on finance, beg leave to submit the following report: Received from churches for printing minutes, $40.40.

Respectfully submitted,

S. S. WILSON,
C. B. WEAVER,
ESTELL HEATH.

9th. By motion the report was received and committee discharged.

10th. Called for the report of the committee on request.

(e) We, your committee on request, beg leave to make the following report: That we have all the obituaries printed in our minutes that the churches furnish; and that the next session of the Powell's Valley Association be held with the church at Red Hill, Claiborne County, Tennessee.

Respectfully submitted,

ALBERT DAVIS,
M. B. WEAVER,
VERLIN EDWARDS.

11th. By motion the report was received and committee discharged.

12th. By motion we send the following named delegates to the Hiwassee Association when convened on Friday before the 4th Saturday in September, 1933, to wit: Elders M. B. Weaver, John Ausmus, Leonard White, Henry Comer.

13th. Motion in order that the Clerk write corresponding letters to the Sister Associations and have the same inserted in our minutes.

14th. By motion the next Annual Session of the Powell's Valley Association will be held with the church at Red Hill, Claiborne County, Tennessee to commence on Friday before the third Saturday in August, 1934.

15th. By motion that Elder Charlie Redmnod preach the introductory sermon and that Elder Henry Comer be his alternate.

16th. By motion we have 800 copies of minutes printed; that the Clerk superintend the printing and distribution of same, and that he be allowed $10.00 for his service.

17th. Motion in order that we extend our heartfelt thanks to this

4

dear old Church and her surrounding community for their hospitalities and kind treatment to us throughout this Association.

18th. Motion in order to adjourn until 10:30 a. m. at the place above stated.

19th. Dismissed in order.

Respectfully submitted,

ELDER LEONARD WHITE, Mod.

P. O., Lafollette, Tennessee.

SAM DAVIS, Clerk

P. O., Liberty Hill, Tennessee

SUNDAY'S PROCEEDINGS

At the appointed hour Sunday a large and well behaved audience assembled at the Stand. Services were opened by Elder John F. Keck by reading the 13th chapter of Hebrew. Prayer was given by Elder Alfred Davis, after which the crowd so attentively listened to the well delivered sermons of Elder W. R. Gates, from the 7th verse of the 8th chapter of Hebrew; text, For if that First Covenant had been Faultless then Should No Place have been Sought for the Second; followed by Elder T. G. Brantly, and closing remarks by the Moderator. All of which were delivered in a most loving manner, and a loving parting was expressed by all the congregation by the shedding of tears, clapping of hands, and invoking the blessings of God upon each other.

CORRESPONDING LETTER

To our Sister Association, to wit: The Hiwassee.

Dear Brothers and Sisters, we desire a continuance of our long and cherished correspondence with you, and for this purpose have chosen these, our beloved Elders, to bear this, our Epistle of love, to you, whom we hope you will esteem sound in the faith and grant them a seat with you in all your Godly consultations when convened on Friday before the 4th Saturday in September, 1933, to wit: Elders M. B. Weaver, John Ausmus, Leonard White, and Henry Comer. May peace and love abound with you all throughout your Association is the prayer of this your Sister in Christ.

THE CLERK.

RULES OF DECORUM

1. The churches composing the Powell's Valley Association shall not be confined to any set rule as to the specified number of Messengers they shall have in the body, but shall have the right to name in their letters as many as they shall choose, and in addition all orderly members of any of the churches being present shall be entitled to seats in the body as Messengers of their respective churches, with all the rights and privileges of the same.

5

2. The Messengers thus assembled shall be denominated the Powell's Valley Primitive Baptist Association.

3. For the purpose of historical information and statistical edification, the churches are requested to state in letters, the total number of members in fellowship, the number received by baptism, by letter, by confession of faith; the number dismissed, excluded and dead since last session; also the time of their meeting, their pastoral supply, and the amount of money contributed for ministers and other purposes, together with any other information they deem appropriate for the edification of the saints and the glory of God.

4. This Association shall have no power to answer queries, give advice, or dictate to the churches in any case, or to lord it over God's heritage, nor any power by which she can directly or indirectly infringe on the internal rights of the churches, or censure and try any church or member in reference to faith and practice, or determine upon the validity of gospel ordinances. These things shall rest entirely with the churches; but henceforward our annual meeting shall be only for the purpose of hearing from each other, and for the worship of God and the mutual comfort and edification of the saints. To this end we reserve the privileges annually before the third Saturday in August and the two following days, or at such other time as may be agreed upon with any church that may invite us, having due regard to priority of claims and the good of the cause; to protect our own stand, while in session, from heresy and disorder; to recognize and invite any Primitive Baptist minister or any lay brother to worship with us, that we may deem proper; to request the brethern of our own body to visit other churches or bodies in our behalf with whom we may desire to cultivate Christian fellowship; to publish in a minute of our proceedings.

5. Each session of the body shall have a Moderator and a Clerk. who shall be duly chosen according to the rules hereinafter prescribed, and who shall hold office until re-election.

6. Any orderly member of any church belonging to this body, when convened, being present, shall be eligible to election as Moderator and Clerk, or to sit on any committee appointed by the same.

7. In all elections or questions that may be necessary to determine by vote, the vote shall be taken by churches, each church being entitled to three votes for any number of members less than one hundred, and one additional vote for every fifty or fraction thereof above the first hundred, but the Messengers of each church as a body may divide her vote as they see proper.

8. All elections or questions coming to a vote shall be determined by a majority of the votes cast, and it shall be the duty of the minority to acquiesce in the decision thus reached.

9. If new churches desire to be admitted into this union, they shall

6

petition by letters and Messengers, and if vouched for or recommended by one or more sister churches, for her Presbytery constituting them, or orthodox and orderly, they shall be received by the voice of the body and manifested by the Moderator giving the Messengers the right hand of fellowship.

10. Any motion or resolution introduced clearly inconsistent with the above rules, shall be promptly ruled out of order unless withdrawn by the mover.

11. Any Messenger being ruled out of order by the Moderator shall have the right to appeal to the body on question of order, and if sustained shall be allowed to proceed, but if not shall take his seat.

12. Our meetings being held in the name of Christ and the worship of God, each Messenger is expected to observe due and proper order therein.

13. It will not be considered good order for any Messenger whose name has been enrolled as such to abruptly break off or absent himself from the Association without leave.

14. The Moderator shall be entitled to the same privileges of speech as other members, provided the chair be filled.

15. The Minutes of the Association shall be read and approved by the body, and signed by the Moderator before adjourning.

16. The Association shall be opened and closed by prayer.

17. Amendments to these rules may be made at any time by a majority of the union voting by churches, when they deem it necessary, provided such amendments do not compromise the sovereignty of the churches, nor have tendency to give this body undue power or jurisdiction over them.

OBITUARIES

Brother-Elder James Ausmus

Brother-Elder James Ausmus was born in the year 1877, and was married to Rhoda Stiner in the year 1906. To this union were born three children, two of whom are still living. Brother Ausmus joined the Primitive Baptist Church at Davis Creek in early life, and was ordained to the full work of the ministry, and later moved his membership to Straight Branch Church of which he lived a faithful member until God saw fit to call him suddenly to his reward on November 20, 1932. Brother Ausmus was an able minister and a staunch supporter of the Primitive Baptist doctrine.

He leaves to mourn their loss a companion, two children, his Church, and a host of relatives and friends; so we weep not for him as one that had no hope.

7

Brother Eli Graves

Brother Eli Graves was born February 13, 1862, and professed faith in Christ when a young man. He joined the Primitive Baptist Church in 1890, and was a faithful member until death.

Brother Eli was married to Carolyn Keck in 1884.

He leaves a loving wife, 7 boys, 4 girls, 42 grandchildren, and one great grandchild.

He was 70 years, 10 months, and 24 days old, and died a member of the Rocky Dale Primitive Baptist Church.

We miss him so very much, but we believe that our loss is his eternal gain.

Brother John Elza White

Brother John Elza White was born February 16, 1871, deceased October 7, 1932, being 61 years, 7 months, and 21 days old at death. He was married to Polly Anne Wilson on November 66, 1889. To this union were born three children, two girls and one boy, one boy and one girl deceased, one child being Mrs. Stella Graves. He leaves a wife, one daughter, six grandchildren, a father, two brothers, one sister, and a host of friends to mourn their loss.

The deceased professed faith in Christ very early in life and united with the Primitive Baptist Church at Mossy Springs by experience and baptism. He was baptized by Elder M. B. Weaver nearly 30 years ago, and has been a loyal church member, and lived a devoted Christian life until death. Brother White lived up to the standard of Christianity in his daily walks of life, and all his business was conducted accordingly. He will be missed in his church and community. He has undergone much suffering in the last years of his life, but bore it all with patience and we believe that while his body sleeps in death, his soul has entered into the blessed rest that awaits God's children. May God's Holy Spirit comfort his companion and child, and other relatives, and help them to look forward to a glorious resurrection and a happy reunion on the other side of life.

Sister Nancy H. Abbott

Sister Nancy H. Abbott was born July 24, 1849, and died September 19, 1931. She was married to Elder G. B. Abbott on March 6, 1866. To this union were born twelve children, three of whom are living and nine deceased.

She professed faith in Christ and joined the Primitive Baptist Church at Bird's Creek in the year 1860. Her church membership at death was at the Rocky Dale Primitive Baptist Church, Corryton, Tennessee. Sister Abbott loved her church and family, and lived a devoted Christian life unto the end, and before death she expressed a willingness to depart this life and go to her home in Heaven. We know Sister Abbott's joy is complete in the presence of her Saviour, and with her prec-

8

266

ious children who had outstripped her in the lane of life.   We are sure that Sister Abbott died in the Lord and is sweetly resting from her labours, and her good works will follow on.

Her Pastor, ELDER T. G. BRANTLY.

Mary Bailey Wilson

Mary Bailey Wilson, wife of Shird Wilson, was born October, 1894. She joined the church in her girlhood days at Mossy Springs, some 20 or 25 years ago, and lived a constant member of the church until death on June 3, 1933.   She leaves a husband and two children to mourn their loss, two children having outstripped her in the narrow lane of life. We do not mourn their loss as one who does not have any hope.

Sister Mariah J. Mink

Sister Mariah J. Mink, wife of John H. Mink, was born February 9, 1850, and joined the Primitive Baptist Church at Cedar Spring on October, 1871, and lived a faithful member until death which occurred December 22, 1932.   She is survived by seven children, five daughters and two sons, five sisters, one brother, and a host of relatives and friends to mourn her passing, but our loss is her gain.

Sister Mary Wolf

Sister Mary, wife of Bob Wolf, was born about the year 1879, and joined the Primitive Baptist Church at Noeton, Grainger County, Tennessee, about 15 years ago, to which she lived a faithful member until it pleased God to call her home on July 7, 1933.

She leaves to mourn their loss a husband, one child, and a host of friends, but their loss is her eternal gain.

Sister Mary Jane Sturgill

Sister Mary Jane Sturgill was born January 26, 1865, and died February 12, 1933, age 68 years and 15 days.   She was married to W. H. Brantley on February 14, 1915 to which she lived a devoted life.   She professed a hope in Christ in her early life and joined the Primitive Baptist Church in Grainger County, Tennessee.   Later she moved her membership to Cave Spring Church, then to Straight Branch Church, and was a faithful member until death.   She left a host of friends and a husband to mourn their loss, but we trust our loss was her eternal gain.

Sister Minnie Harmon

Sister Minnie Harmon was born February 11, 1911, being 22 years and 25 days old at the time of her death.   She was married to William S Harmon on February 5, 1929, and departed this life on March 8, 1933. She professed faith in Christ in early life, and joined the Primitive Baptist Church at Capps Creek the second Saturday in November, 1930, and was baptized.   To this union were born two children, Alice Pauline and Bobby William.   She leaves father, mother, one brother, four sisters, husband, children, and a host of friends to mourn their loss.   She left

9

this world with a bright happy smile.   We believe our loss is Heaven's eternal gain.

John   A.   Hunter

John A. Hunter was born June 15, 1870, and departed this life April 13, 1933.   He professed a hope in Christ in early life and joined the Baptist Church at Davis Creek, and later on moved his membership to the Pleasant Hill Church.

He was married to Rachel Ausmus on January 19, 1892.   To this union were born six children, three of whom have preceded him to the glory land.

He leaves to mourn their loss his wife, three children, fourteen grandchildren, six brothers, and one sister.   The living children are Mrs. Jeff Madox, of Speedwell; Mrs. Fayett Berry, of Speedwell; and Jesse Hunter, of Goin.   The brothers are Fayett Hunter, of Pathfork, Ky.; Jeff, of Pineville, Ky.; Joe, of Goin Tenn.; Nathan, of Dunbar, Va.; Oscar Hunter, Bryson, and Harrison, of Monroe, Michigan.   The sister is Mrs. John Yoakum, of Bryson, Tenn.   He also leaves a host of other relatives and friends.

He was loved by all who knew him.   He said a few hours before he died that he was ready to go, that he had a better home than this.

Brother Johnson Hill

Brother Johnson Hill joined the Primitive Baptist Church in early life, and helped to constitute the church at Pleasant Hill in the month of August, 1907.   He died April 15, 1933.   He lived near Middlesboro, Kentucky when deceased.

Brother Jeff Edwards

Brother Jeff Edwards was born October 1, 1861, and died October 18, 1933.   He professed faith in Christ in early youth and joined the church at Davis Creek in June, first Saturday, 1895, of which he lived a faithful member until the division which occurred February, first Saturday, 1897.   He never attached himself to any other church, but always was ready to help in all good deeds.   He was blessed with a spiritual knowledge, and would always give good advice to his family and friends.   He was well loved and respected by all who knew him.

He leaves eleven children, forty grandchildren, and a host of friends to mourn their loss.   His wife departed this life two years and five days before him.

He was never known to complain, although he was helpless eight months and eight days.   We can say as the poet says,

Go home our friends
And dry your tears.
For they will arise
When Christ appears.

We hope to meet Daddy and Mother in the sweet bye and bye.

THE   CHILDREN.

10

MINISTERIAL ROLL

Elders	Post Offices
John Ausmus	Speedwell, Claiborne County, Tenn.
Gilbert Abbott	Knoxville, Knox County, Tenn.
T. G. Brantly	Sharps Chapel, Union County, Tenn.
Alfred Boruff	Maynardville, Union County, Tenn.
Henry Comer	LaFollette, Campbell County, Tenn.
E. S. Drummonds	New Tazewell, Claiborne County, Tenn.
Albert Davis	LaFollette, Campbell County, Tenn.
V. H. Graves	Sharps Chapel, Union County, Tenn.
Esau Keck	Goin, Claiborne County, Tenn.
John F. Keck	Goin, Claiborne County, Tenn.
W. A. Moyers	Speedwell, Claiborne County, Tenn.
George Mays	Goin, Claiborne County, Tenn.
Mathew Oliver	Noeton, Grainger County, Tenn.
Thomas Pierce	Speedwell, Claiborne County, Tenn.
Alfred Parks	New Market, Jefferson County, Tenn.
Charlie Redmond	Gibson Station, Lee County, Va.
H. A. Shoffner	Harrogate, Claiborne County, Tenn.
S. S. Wilson	Middlesboro, Star Route 1, Bell County, Ky.
M. B. Weaver	128 Jordan Street, Knoxville, Knox County, Tenn.
Leonard White	LaFollette, Campbell County, Tenn.
Carl McCarty	Speedwell, Claiborne County, Tenn.

LICENTIATES

W. A. Atkins	Tate, Grainger County, Tenn.
Milton Brantly	Sharps Chapel, Union County, Tenn.
Jim Collins	New Market, Jefferson County, Tenn.
John C. Ousley	Gibson Station, Lee County, Va.
W. R. Petree	Sharps Chapel, Union County, Tenn.
Charlie Stanifer	Speedwell, Claiborne County, Tenn.
Elvin Weaver	Loyston, Union County, Tenn.
J. M. Wilder	Speedwell, Claiborne County, Tenn.

TABLE OF STATISTICS

CHURCHES	NAMES OF DELEGATES	Rec'd by Expr. Bapt.	Rec'd by Letter	Restored	Dismissed by Letter	Excluded	Deceased	Total Membership	Saturday Meetings	Contributions
Mossy Spring	Elders V. H. Graves, M. B. Weaver, Brother C. B. Weaver.	8					2	226	4	$3.25
Red Hill	Charlie Stanifer, Bee Treece; Mose Treece, Will Roberson.							74	2	1.80
Hamilton Grove	Forest and Mamie Hamilton, W. A. L. Ousley, Sam Cook, Walker Edmondson.							60	4	2.10
Oak Grove	Elder T. G. Brantly, George Shoffner, John Graves.	13	1				1	237	1	3.20
Pleasant Hill	Neal Lambert, Verlin and J. L. Edwards, W. M. McHenry, Bill Cupp.	1	1				2	66	4	3.35
Rocky Dale	Elder G. W. Abbott, Brothers Aval Graves, M. C. Dunn, Elmer Graves.	3					1	69	3	3.50
New Hebron	Elder Alfred Parks, Brother Jim Collins, and others.	7				4	1	47	1	3.15
Capps Creek	Troy and Fannie Presley, Ellis and Lottie Evans.	9					1	31	2	1.25
Pleasant Point	Elders John F. Keck, Esau Keck, Brothers J. E. Heath, J. W. Keck, C. D. Keck, Jimmie Cox, A. H. Shipley.			1			2	137	1	4.50
Gibson Station	Elders H. A. Shoffner, S. S. Wilson, Charlie Redmond.						1	77	1	1.50
Noeton	Elder Mathew Oliver and wife, Brother J. C. Oliver and wife.	2	2			1	1	38	3	1.50
Davis Chapel	Elders Leonard White, Albert Davis, Henry Comer.	2	1					142	3	3.05
Cave Spring	James Brantly, Carl McCarty.							78	3	2.35
Blackfox	Sam Davis, J. M. Davis, Roy Bailey, W. M. Munsey, John Bundon, Hila Lifford.	1						107	2	2.50
Cedar Spring	Elder E. S. Drummonds, S. W., J. A., J. L., D. P., and T. J. Drummonds, Billie Miracle, Henry Cupp.	1					1	79	4	2.00
Straight Branch	Elders John Ausmus, T J Pierce, Brother Harrison Smith.	2		1			2	77	1	1.40

OFFICIAL DIRECTORY

CHURCHES	COUNTY	PASTORS	CLERKS	CLERK'S POST OFFICE
Hamilton Grove	Union	T. G. Brantly	C. L. Hamilton	Sharps Chapel, Tenn.
Mossy Spring	Union	Leonard White	J. M. Kivett	Sharps Chapel, Tenn.
Red Hill	Claiborne	T. G. Brantly	Jeff Treece	Speedwell, Tenn.
Gibson Station	Lee	Leonard White	Mary Ball	Gibson Station, Va.
Cave Spring	Union	V. H. Graves	B. F. Berry	Speedwell, Tenn.
Oak Grove	Union	T. G. Brantly	David White	Sharps Chapel, Tenn.
Straight Branch	Union	W. A. Moyers	I. N. Lamar	Speedwell, Tenn.
		John Ausmus, Asst.	M. A. Clawson, Ast.	
Rocky Dale	Knox	T. G. Brantly	M. C. Dunn	Corryton, Tenn.
Cedar Spring	Claiborne	Mathew Oliver	J. L. Drummonds	New Tazewell, Tenn.
Blackfox	Grainger	V. H. Graves	Sam Davis	Liberty Hill, Tenn.
Pleasant Point	Claiborne	V. H. Graves	Estell Heath	Goin, Tenn.
Davis Chapel	Campbell	Leonard White	J. M. Kitts	LaFollette, Tenn.
Capps Creek	Union	Albert Davis	Easter Braden	Goin, Tenn.
		T. J. Pierce, Asst.	J. L. Edwards	Speedwell, Tenn.
Pleasant Hill	Claiborne	Charlie Redmond	Verlin Edwards, Ast	
		H. A. Shoffner, Ast.		
New Hebron	Jefferson	Alfred Parks	Luella Mitchell	New Market, Tenn.
Noeton	Grainger	Mathew Oliver	J. C. Oliver	Noeton, Tenn.

271

MINUTES

OF THE

ONE HUNDREDTH AND FIFTEENTH

ANNUAL SESSION

OF THE

POWELL'S VALLEY ASSOCIATION

OF

PRIMITIVE BAPTISTS

Held With the Church at

Red Hill, Claiborne County, Tennessee

August 17, 18, 19, 1934

Next Session will be held with the Church at Gibson Station, Lee County, Virginia, to commence on Friday before the third Saturday in August, 1935.

Elder T. G. Brantly will preach the introductory sermon and Elder Leonard White will be his alternate.

FRIDAY'S PROCEEDINGS

1st.—According to the previous arrangements the Association met and was called to order by the Moderator, Elder Leonard White.

2nd—The introductory sermon was delivered by Elder Charlie Redmond from the text Romans 8th chapter, 28th verse. Quotation: "And we know that all things work together for good to them that love God." He was followed by Elder Leonard White.

3rd.—After ten minutes intermission, at the sound of singing the congregation reassembled at the altar. After prayer by Brother W. M. McHenry the Association was organized for business by electing Elder T. G. Brantly as Moderator and Brother Sam Davis as Clerk.

4th.—The Association was announced in order for business by the Moderator.

5th.—Called for letters from sister churches. Fourteen were received and read by the clerk, with Elder Leonard White assisting.

6th.—By motion all the letters were received and the delegation was welcomed to seats by the Moderator.

7th.—Called for members from sister churches who were not delegates. One from Pleasant Hill was received, to wit: Brother W. M. McHenry, who was welcomed to a seat.

8th.—Called for corresponding delegates from sister associations. Received letter and messenger from the Hiwassee, to wit: Elder W. R. Gates, and by motion he was welcomed to a seat with us.

9th.—Invited visiting brothers and sisters from sister associations. Brother J. E. Packet and wife from the Hiwassee Association were welcomed to seats with us.

10th.—Motion in order that the Moderator appoint all our committees.

(a)—On Preaching—Brothers Joshua Drummonds, John Bundon, J. M. Kivett, together with this church.

(b)—On Arrangements—Brothers Jimmie Cox, James Lynch, Ernest Hamilton.

(c)—On Correspondence—Elders Leonard White, Mathew Oliver, Verlin Graves.

(d)—On Request—Elders Thomas Pierce, Charlie Redmond, Henry Comer.

(e)—On Finance—Brothers J. C. Oliver, Wily Treece, Walker Edmondson.

11th.—Motion in order for adjournment until 9 o'clock Saturday morning.

3

1st.—The Association met pursuant to adjournment.

2nd.—After singing, praise by Moderator and prayer by Elder T. J. Pierce.

3rd.—Called for letter that failed to get in Friday. Received one which was read. By motion it was received and the messenger's name was enrolled.

4th.—Called for the report of the Committee on Arrangements.

(a)—We, your Committee on Arrangements, beg leave to make the ollowing order of business: That we follow the order of last year's minutes so far as it meets our present demands.

Respectfully submitted

BROTHER W. E. HAMILTON,
BROTHER JAMES LYNCH,
BROTHER JIMMIE COX.

5th.—By motion the report was received and the committee was discharged.

6th.—Called for the report of the Committee on Preaching

(b)—We, your Committee on Preaching, beg leave to make the following report: Friday night at the church Elders H. A. Shoffner, Mathew Oliver. Saturday at the stand Elder V. H. Graves, Albert Davis. Saturday night at the church Elders Henry Comer, Leonard White. Sunday at the school house Elders Thomas Pierce, Leonard White. At the stand Elders W. R. Gates, Mathew Oliver. The Moderator to close.

Respectfully submitted,

BROTHER J. L. DRUMMONDS,
BROTHER JOHN BUNDON,
BROTHER J. M. KIVETT.

7th.—By motion the report was received and the committe was discharged.

8th.—Called for the report of the Committee on Correspondence.

(c)—We, your Committee on Correspondence, beg leave to make the following report: That we keep up our correspondence with other associations of our faith and practice.

Respectfully submitted ,

ELDER LEONARD WHITE,
ELDER MATHEW OLIVER,
ELDER VERLIN GRAVES.

4

9th.—By motion the report was received and the committee was discharged.

10th.—Called for the report of the Committee on Request.

(d)—We, your Committee on Request, beg leave to make the following report: That we have all the obituaries printed in our minutes that the churches furnish, and that the next annual session of the Powell's Valley Association be held with the church at Gibson Station, Lee County, Virginia, to commence on Friday before the third Saturday in August, 1935.

Respectfully submitted,

ELDER HENRY COMER,
ELDER THOMAS PIERCE,
ELDER CHARLIE REDMOND.

11th.—By motion the report was received and the committee was discharged.

12th.—Called for the report of the Committee on Finance.

(e)—We, your Committee on Finance, beg leave to make the following report: Receiving from churches for printing minutes, $40.00.

Respectfully submitted,

BROTHER WILY TREECE,
BROTHER M. W. EDMONDSON,
BROTHER J. C. OLIVER.

13th.—By motion the report was received and the committee was discharged.

14th.—By motion the next annual session of the Powell's Valley Association will be held with the church at Gibson Station, Lee County, Virginia, to commence on Friday before the third Saturday in August, 1935.

15th.—By motion Elder T. G. Brantly will preach the introductory sermon and Elder Leonard White will be alternate.

16th.—By motion that we have 800 copies of minutes printed and that the Clerk superintend the printing and distribution of same, and that he be allowed $10.00 for his services.

17th.—By motion that we add the ordinance of foot-washing to our articles of faith.

5

18th.—By motion Elders Leonard White and V. H. Graves were chosen messenger to the Hiwassee Association when convened with the Hope Church in Roan County, Tennessee, to commence on Friday before the fourth Saturday in September, 1934.

19th.—By motion that the Clerk write corresponding letter to the Hiwassee Association and have same printed in our minutes.

20th.—On motion be it resolved that we extend our heartfelt thanks to this dear old church and her surrounding community for their hospitalities and kind treatment to us throughout this Association.

21st.—By motion that we empower the Moderator and Clerk to accept any letters from sister churches that should come in after adjournment.

22nd.—Motion in order to adjourn until 10 o'clock at the place above stated.

ELDER T. G. BRANTLY, Moderator
Sharps Chapel, Tennessee

SAM DAVIS, Clerk
Liberty Hill, Tennessee

SUNDAY'S PROCEEDINGS

At the appointed hour Sunday a large and well-behaved audience assembled at the stand and attentively listened to the well-delivered sermon of Elder W. R. Gates from the third verse of Jude. Text; "Ye should earnestly contend for the faith which was delivered to the Saints." This sermon was followed by Elder Mathew Oliver. Closing remarks were made by the Moderator. All of these were delivered in the most loving spirit and with great interest to all. A loving parting was expressed by all by the shedding of tears, clapping of hands and invoking the blessings of God upon one another.

Corresponding Letter to the Hiwassee Association

Very Dear Brother-Sister:

We desire a continuance of our long and cherished correspondence with you, and for this purpose we have chosen these, our beloved elders, to bear this message of love to you, whom we hope you will esteem sound in the faith and grant them a seat with you in all your goodly consultations, to wit: Elders Leonard White and V. H. Graves. May the sweet peace and communion of the everlasting Spirit abide with you all is the prayer of this, your little sister Association.

THE CLERK

6

OBITUARIES

Sister Martha England Robertson

Sister Martha England Robertson was born in Claiborne County Tennessee on March 20, 1864, age 70 years, 2 months, and 3 weeks. She professed faith in Christ and joined the Primitive Baptist Church of Moyers Grove in her early youth and was a very faithful member until her death. Surviving are one sister, Minerva Fields of Powell Valley; one half brother of Goin, Tennessee; four children, Richard of Clouds, Tenn.; Hester Emmats of Middlesboro; Lewis Smith of Luttrell, Tenn.; Charles of Knoxville, Tennessee.

She was laid to rest in the Shumate cemetery on June 11, 1934.

Sister Melvina Atkins

Sister Melvina Atkins professed faith in Christ in early life and joined the church at Noeton in which she lived a faithful member until death on May 25, 1934.

Brother Sherman Spires

Brother Sherman Spires, age about 65 years, joined the church at Noeton in which he lived a faithful and consistent member until God saw fit to call him to his reward on November 17, 1933. He is gone but not forgotten.

Sallie Ann Parrot

Sallie Ann Parrot was born July 21, 1876 and died October 25, 1933, being 57 years, 3 months, and 4 days old. Mrs. Parrot was the daughter of Bryce and Matilda Braden.

On July 28, 1896 she was united in marriage to Joe Parrot. To this union were born six children, three of whom have gone before their mother to that Great Beyond. The other three sons, Bryce of this place, John of Monroe, Michigan, and Rufus of Miami, Florida survive her. Surviving her also are her husband, seven grandchildren, two sisters, five brothers, besides many other relatives and friends.

She professed a hope in Christ when she was 19 years old and joined the Baptist Church at Cave Springs and was baptized. She said before she died that she was going to a better home.

9

MINISTERIAL ROLL

Elders	Post Office
John Ausmus,	Speedwell, Claiborne County, Tennessee
Gilbert Abbott,	Knoxville, Knox County, Tennessee
T. G. Brantly,	Sharps Chapel, Union County, Tennessee
Alfred Boruff,	Maynardville, Union County, Tennessee
Henry Comer,	LaFollette, Campbell County, Tennessee
F. S. Drummonds,	New Tazewell, Claiborne County, Tennessee
Albert Davis,	LaFollette, Campbell County, Tennessee
V. H. Graves,	Sharps Chapel, Union County, Tennessee
John F. Keck,	Goin, Claiborne County, Tennessee
W. A. Moyers,	Speedwell, Claiborne County, Tennessee
George Mays,	Goin, Claiborne County, Tennessee
Mathew Oliver,	Noeton, Grainger County, Tennessee
Thomas Pierce,	Speedwell, Claiborne County, Tennessee
Alfred Parks,	New Market, Grainger County, Tennessee
Charlie Redmond,	Gibson Station, Lee County, Virginia
H. A. Shoffner,	Harrogate, Claiborne County, Tennessee
S. S. Wilson,	Middlesboro, Star Route 1, Bell County, Kentucky
M. B. Weaver,	128 Jordan St., Knoxville, Knox County, Tennessee
Leonard White,	LaFollette, Campbell County, Tennessee
Carl McCarty,	Speedwell, Claiborne County, Tennessee

LICENTIATES

Milton Brantly,	Sharps Chapel, Union County, Tennessee
Jim Collins,	New Market, Grainger County, Tennessee
J. C. Ousley,	Gibson Station, Lee County, Virginia
W. R. Petree,	Sharps Chapel, Union County, Tennessee
Charlie Stanifer,	New Tazewell, Claiborne County, Tennessee
Elvin Weaver,	Loyston, Union County, Tennessee
J. M. Wilder,	Speedwell, Claiborne County, Tennessee

10

TABLE OF STATISTICS

CHURCHES	NAMES OF DELEGATES	Rec'd by Expr. Bapt.	Rec'd by Letter	Restored	Dismissed by Letter	Excluded	Deceased	Total Membership	Saturday Meetings	Contributions
Mossy Spring	Elders V. H. Graves, M. B. Weaver, J. M. Kivett, Elvin Weaver.	6				6		235	4	$4.25
Red Hill	Mose Treece, W. F. Robertson, Narcissus Treece, Mary Robertson, Charlie Stanifer, Jeff Treece, Wily Treece.	4						78	2	2.00
Hamilton Grove	W. E. and C. L. Hamilton, M. W. Edmondson.	3						68	4	2.45
Oak Grove	Elders T. G. Branly, B. D. England, John Graves.	2					1	237	1	4.30
Pleasant Hill	J. M. Wilder, Neal Lambert, James, Verlin and Lincoln Edwards.		1			6	1	61	4	3.75
Rocky Dale	M. C. Dunn, Emma Dunn.	2						69	3	3.00
New Hebron	Letter but no Messenger.							51	1	
Capps Creek	Troy and Walter Presley, Elis Evans.	3	1			1		35	2	1.50
Pleasant Point	Estill Heath, J. M. and Hettie Cox, Etter Hopper, A. H. Shipley, J. W. Keck.						2	135	1	4.00
Gibson Station	Elders H. A. Shoffner, Charlie Redmond.							76	1	2.00
Noeton	Elders Mathew Oliver, J. C. Oliver.	5		2				45	3	1.50
Davis Chapel	Elders Leonard White, Albert Davis, Henry Comer, Brother James Lynch.	2		1	1	4	1	136	3	3.00
Cave Spring	James Branly.							80	3	2.00
Blackfox	Sam Davis, John Bundon, T. A. Yaden, John Liford, Roy Bailey, W. M. Thomas.	7			1	5		108	2	2.50
Cedar Spring	J. L. Drummonds, J. A. Minton.	7					1	85	4	2.25
Straight Branch	Elders T. J. Pierce, Susan Pierce, Lussie McBee.					2		74	1	1.50

CHURCHES	COUNTY	PASTORS	CLERKS	CLERK'S POST OFFICE
Hamilton Grove	Union	T. G. Brantly	C. L. Hamilton	Sharps Chapel, Tenn.
Mossy Spring	Union	V. H. Graves	J. M. Kivett	Sharps Chapel, Tenn.
Red Hill	Claiborne	T. G. Brantly	Jeff Treece	Speedwell, Tenn.
Gibson Station	Lee	Mathew Oliver	Mary Ball	Gibson Station, Va.
Cave Spring	Union	V. H. Graves	B. F. Berry	Speedwell, Tenn.
Oak Grove	Union	T. G. Brantly	David White	Sharps Chapel, Tenn.
Straight Branch	Union	Carl McCarty	Lussie McBee	Speedwell, Tenn.
		T. J. Pierce, Ast.	Susan Pierce, Ast.	
Rocky Dale	Knox	T. G. Brantly	M. C. Dunn	Coryton, Tenn.
Cedar Spring	Claiborne	Mathew Oliver	J. L. Drummonds	New Tazewell, Tenn.
		E.S.Drummonds A's		
Blackfox	Grainger	V. H. Graves	Sam Davis	Liberty Hill, Tenn.
Pleasant Point	Claiborne	V. H. Graves	Estel Heath	Goin, Tenn.
Davis Chapel	Campbell	Leonard White	Aaron Davis	LaFollette, Tenn.
Capps Creek	Union	Albert Davis	Easter Braden	Goin, Tenn.
		T. J. Pierce, Ast.		
Pleasant Hill	Claiborne	Charlie Redmond	Lincoln Edwards	Speedwell, Tenn.
		H. A. Shofner, Ast.	Verlin Edwards, A't	
New Hebron	Jefferson	M. B. Weaver	Cordie Mitchel	New Market, Tenn.
Noeton	Grainger	Mathew Oliver	J. C. Oliver	Noeton, Tenn.

MINUTES

OF THE

ONE HUNDREDTH AND SIXTEENTH

ANNUAL SESSION

OF THE

POWELLS VALLEY

ASSOCIATION

OF

PRIMITIVE BAPTISTS

Held With the Church at

GIBSON STATION, LEE COUNTY, VIRGINIA

AUGUST 15, 16, 17, 1935

Next Session will be held with the Church at Pleasant Point, Claiborne County, Tenn., to commence on Friday before the Third Saturday in August, 1936

Elder Mathew Oliver will preach the introductory sermon and Elder V. H. Graves will be his alternate

FRIDAY'S PROCEEDINGS

1st—According to the previous arrangements the Association met and was called to order by the Moderator, Elder T. G. Brantly.

2nd—The introductory sermon was delivered by Elder T. G. Brantly from the text Hebrews 10th chapter, 9th verse. Then said He, "Lo I come to do thy will O God." He taketh away the first that he may establish the second.

3rd—After ten minutes intermission, at the sound of singing the congregation reassembled at the altar and after prayer by Elder Mathew Oliver the Association was organized by reelecting Elder T. G. Brantly moderator and Bro. Sam Davis clerk.

4th—Called for letters from sister churches. Received fourteen which was read by the clerk, assisted by Elder V. H. Graves.

5th—By motion all the letters was received and the delegates were welcomed to seats by the moderator.

6th—Called for corresponding letters from sister associations. Received one from the Hiwassee with their delegates to-wit: Elder W. R. Gates and Elder Lewis Ray, and Bro. J. E. Packet and wife.

7th—By motion said letter was received and the delegation was welcomed to seats with us.

8th—Motion in order that the moderator appoint all the committees.

(a)—On preaching—Bros. C. M. Cabbage, James Lynch, J. C. Oliver, together with the church.

(b)—On arrangements—Bros. R. H. Ball, Milton Brantly, Neal Lambert.

(c)—On correspondence—Elders Mathew Oliver, T. J. Pierce and M. B. Weaver.

(d)—On request—Elder Albert Davis, Bro. Josh Drummonds and Elder S. S. Wilson.

(e)—On finance—Bros Ernest Hamilton, George Shoffner and Jim Kivett.

9th—Called for the report of the committee on preaching.

(a)—We your committee on preaching beg leave to submit the present report Friday night at the church. Elders M. B. Weaver and W. R. Gates.

10th—Motion in order to adjourn until 9 o'clock Saturday morning.

3

SATURDAY'S PROCEEDINGS

1st—The Association met pursuant to adjournment.

2nd—After singing, praise by Elder M. B. Weaver and prayer by Elder H. A. Shoffner. The Association was announced in order for business by the moderator.

3rd—Called for letters from sister churches that failed to get in Friday. Received one which was read. On motion it was received and the delegation welcomed to seats by the moderator.

4th—Called for the report of the committee on arrangements.

(a)—We, your committee on arrangements, beg leave to submit the following order of business.

1st—Call the Roll.

2nd—Call for the report of the Committee on Preaching.

3rd—On Correspondence.

4th—On Request.

5th—On Finance.

6th—When and where shall our next Association be held. Who shall preach the introductory sermon and who shall be his alternate.

7th—How many copies of minutes shall we have printed. Who shall superintend the printing and distribution of same, and what shall he be allowed for his services.

Respectfully submitted
BROTHERN MILTON BRANTLY,
BROTHER R. H. BALL,
BROTHER NEAL LAMBERT.

8th—On motion the report was received and the committee discharged.

9th—Called the Roll and erased the names of absentees.

10th—Called for the report of the committee on Preaching.

(b)—We, your Committee on preaching, beg leave to submit the following: Friday night at the church Elders M. B. Weaver and W. R. Gates. Saturday at the church T. J. Pierce and E. S. Drummonds. Saturday night at the church Elders V. H. Graves, and H. A. Shoffner. Sunday at the church Elders W. R. Gates, Mathew Oliver, and the moderator to close.

Respectfully submitted
BRO. C. M. CABBAGE,
BRO. JAMES F. LYNCH,
BRO. J. C. OLIVER.

4

11th—On motion the report was received and committee discharged.

12th—Called for report of the Committee on Correspondence.

(a)—We your Committee on Correspondence, beg leave to submit the following report: That we keep up our long Christian and Cooperative correspondence with the Hiwassee Association by letter and delegation.

Respectfully submitted
ELDER M. B. WEAVER,
ELDER T. J. PIERCE
ELDER MATHEW OLIVER.

13th—By motion the report received and the committee discharged.

14th—Called for the report of the Committee on Finance.

(d)—We your committee on finance, beg leave to submit the following. Received from sister churches for printing minutes $34.11.

Respectfully submitted
BRO. J. M. KIVETT,
BRO. G. W. SHOFFNER,
BRO. W. E. HAMILTON.

15th—Called for the report of the Committee on Request.

(e)—We your Committee on Request, beg leave to submit the following: That we have all the obituary's printed in our minutes that the churches furnish and that the next annual session of the Powells Valley Association be held with the Church at Pleasant Point, Claiborne County, Tenn., to commence on Friday before the Tihrd Saturday in August, 1936.

Respectfully submitted
ELDER ALBERT DAVIS,
BRO. J. L. DRUMMONDS,
ELDER S. S. WILSON.

16th—By motion the report was received and committee discharged.

17th—By motion the delayed and absent letter of Pleasant Point church was received and their delegation welcomed to seats with us.

18th—By motion Elder Mathew Oliver preach the introductory sermon and that Elder V. H. Graves be his alternate.

19th—By motion we have 200 copies of minutes printed, that the Clerk superintend the printing and distribution of same and that he be allowed the remainder for his services.

20th—By motion the Clerk write corresponding letter to the Hiwassee Association and have the same printed in our minutes.

21st—By motion we send as messengers to the Hiwassee Association Elders V. H. Graves and M. B. Weaver.

5

22nd—By motion we empower the Moderator and Clerk to receive any letters from sister churches that arrive after adjournment.

23rd—On motion be it resolved that we tender our heartfelt thanks to this dear old church and the surrounding community for their hospitalities and kind treatment to us throughout this Association.

25th—By motion we adjourn until 9 o'clock at the time and place above stated.

ELDER T. G. BRANTLY, Moderator,
Sharps Chapel, Tennessee.
SAM DAVIS, Clerk,
Luttrell, Tennessee.

SUNDAY'S PROCEEDINGS

At the appointed hour Sunday a large and well-behaved audiance assembled at the altar and so earnestly listened at the well delivered sermons delivered by Elders W. R. Gates from Hebrews, 10th chapter and 14th verse, "For by One Offering He hath perfected Forever Them that are Sanctified," followed by Elder Mathew Oliver, and closing remarks by the Moderator. All of these was delivered in the most loving spirit and with great interest to all, and a loving parting was expressed by the shedding of tears, rejoicing together and invoking the Blessings of God upon each other.

Corresponding Letter to the Hiwassee Association

Very Dear Brother-Sisters:

Very Dear Brothers-Sisters in Christ:

We desire a continuance of our cherished correspondence with you, and for this purpose have chosen these, our beloved Elders to bear this, our Epistle of love to you, whom we hope you will grant a seat with you in your annual meeting when convened with the church at Flat Rock, Cumberlin County, Tennessee, to commence on Friday before the 4th Saturday in August 1935: Messengers Elder V. H. Graves and Elder M. B. Weaver. May the sweet peace and fellowship of the ever blest spirit abide with you, is the prayer of this, your little sister.

THE CLERK.

6

OBITUARIES

Sister Iva Walton

Sister Iva Walton, was born September 21, 1904, was married to Clayton Davis, November 7, 1925. Professed faith in Christ and joined the church at Blackfox and was batized June 2, 1929, of which she lived a consistant member until God saw fit to call her to her reward March 23, 1935. She leaves to mourn their loss a husband, two darling children, one son, 8 years, one daughter, four months, father, mother, brothers and sisters, with a host of friends. But we hope our loss is her eternal gain.

From us a loved one is gone,
A voice we loved is stilled,
This leaves a vacant in our home,
That never can be filled.

Bro. Pryor C. Lambert

Bro. Pryor C. Lamber was born January 22, 1881, departed this life November 12, 1934. Professed a hope in Christ at an early age and joined the church at Pleasant Hill in June, 1910, was baptised in August following. He married Louvena Edwards on September 20, 1914, to this union was born seven children, two boys and five girls. His request was that Elder Leonard White preach his funeral and sing that song, "The Account Was Settled Long Ago." We fell that Bro. Pryor settled his accounts before leaving this world of sorrow and that he has a better home above. He often spoke of his hope of Heaven and said just awhile before he died that his only regret in leaving was he hated to leave his wife and children.

Brother Arch F. Redmond

With the greatest degree of sadness intermingled with love and admiration, we announce the untimely death of our much beloved and highly esteemed Brother, Arch F. Redmond. He was born December 5, 1890; professed faith in Christ in early life and joined the Primitive Baptist Church at Gibson Station, Va., about five years ago, where he lived a faithful member until July 18, 1935, when he lost his life in an attempt to enforce the laws of our country. Truly it may be said of him, "Greater love hath no man

9

than this, that a man would lay down his life for his friends."

Dear Brother Redmond:

True, your form from us has vanished
And your ears deaf to our call,
But your golden portrait is hanging
High on memory's polished wall.

In that Haven of bright sunshine,
We shall meet you by and by.
Live forever in a country,
Where we'll never say boodbye.

A Friend,
CARL MAX.

Brother Andy Brumitte

Brother Andy Brumitte was born December 17, 1865 and died September 22, 1934. He was married to Jane Berry in 1883. He leaves his wife, eight children, five sons, three daughters and forty grandchildren and a few great grandchildren and a host of relatives and friends to mourn their loss.

Brother Andy professed faith in Christ very early in life and joined the Primitive Baptist Church at Cane Spring and lived a faithful member in the church until God called him home. Bro. Brumitte lived up to the standard as a Christian in his daily walks of life, and all his business was conducted accordingly. He will be missed in his church and community. He underwent much suffering in the last ten months of his life, but bore it all with patience and we believe that while his body sleeps in death, his soul has entered into the blessed rest that awaits God's children.

May God's Holy Spirit comfort his companions, children and relatives and help them look forward to a glorious resurrection and a happy reunion on the other side of life. We can say, Go Home our friend and dry up your tears, for they will arise when Christ appears.

Live in hope of meeting your Father in the sweet by and by.

Joseph Jefferson Alston

Joseph Jefferson Alston was born April 29, 1877, departed this life April 12, 1935, age 57 years, 11 months and thirteen days. He professed a hope in Christ about November 1899 and joined the Primitive Baptist Church at Meyer's Grove and was baptized by

10

287

Rev. Manna Weaver. He lived a faithful member until God called him away. He leaves to mourn his loss a wife, Ida B. Alston of Middlesboro, Ky., one son, Lee Alston; four grandchildren, Joe Stvie, Kyle, Alfred, Jessee, Alva and Reva Alston of Tazewell, Tenn., also one boy he raised, Charlie Mathis, of Middlesboro, Ky. He leaves one brother, Charlie Alston of Middlesboro, and three uncles, Steward, Floyd and Bill Wilson and a number of other relatives and friends. His last and departing words were: "Not to worry about him, for he had a better place to go to." Dear father has gone to meet an infant babe and other dear relatives that proceeded him in this life. Funeral services were held at the Moody cemetery on Monday, April 15, near Tazewell, Tenn. Rev. Hiram Shoffner of Gibson Station, Va., and Rev. E. S. Drummond of Meyers Grove conducted the services. The pallbearers were: Arthur Flannery, John Flannery, Paris Whitmore, Hubert Sowders, Bill Mathis, John Ruphert and Robert Presnell. The flower girls were: Manda Sowders, Etta Whitmore, Lola Mathis, Elzara Ruphert and Manorvie Flanery.

The home is left in sadness and grief, but thank God we have a promise of meeting Dear Father again in the sweet by and by where parting will be no more. We wish to thank his many friends and neighbors for their kind help and assistance during his illness. Also we thank the friends, church and Sunday School for the flowers they gave and especially Hobert Cawood for his kindness and assistance during our great trouble and bereamement.

THE FAMILY.

Sister Rava Pevley

Sister Rava Pevley was born April 9, 1891 and died May 28, 1935. She professed faith in Christ in early life and joined the Primitive Baptist Church at Cave Spring and lived a faithful member until death. She leaves one sister and three brothers and a host of friends to mourn their loss. Sister Rava Pevley will be missed in her church and community. She had undergone much suffering in the last few years of of her life. She bore it all with patience into the blessed rest that awaits God's children. May God's Holy Spirit comfort her relatives and friends and help them to look forward to a glorious resurrection and a happy reunion on the other side of life. We know sister Rava Pevley's joy is complete in the presence of her Saviour and with her precious father and mother and sister who has gone on before her. We are sure sister Rava died in the Lord and is sweetly resting. Our loss is her eternal gain.

11

Tivis Lynch

Tivis Lynch, son of Frank and Minnie Lynch was born October 22, 1907 and departed this life October 23, 1934, being 27 years and one day old. He professed faith in Christ about eight years ago, but did not make it known until about six months ago. His desire was to join the Primitive Baptist Church at Meyers Grove. During his last few days on earth he often talked of being ready and willing to go. He was preceeded to the grave by a little sister, Orpha, who died 18 years ago. He leaves to mourn their loss a father and mother of Goin, four sisters, Mrs. Martha Neely and Mrs. Roxie Drummonds of New Tazewell, and Misses Mae and Leona Lynch of Goin; three brothers, Roosevelt Lynch of Cardinal, Ky., and Theo and Charlie Lynch ot Goin, and a host of other relatives and friends. But our loss is his eternal gain. While our home is made sadder, Heaven is made brighter.

He had been ill for about eight months, being confined to his bed for six months. He bore his sickness with patience and said that he could meet death with a smile. Just a few moments before he died he asked to be raised up. He said, "I am blind and can't see and am dying." But he didn't seem to mind going. There is a vacant place in our home which can never be filled, we cannot see his sweet face nor hear his sweet voice, nor hear his soft foot-steps, but the memory of him will be in our minds forever. He cannot come to us but thank God we can go to him. Sleep on, Dear Brother, and take your rest, we hope to meet you in the sweet bye and bye, where we will never part again, where there is no sickness, nor pain, but where all is joy and happiness.

Services were held by Rev. W. W. Killion and Rev. E. S. Drummonds. Burial was in the Lilly Grove cemetery. We wish to thank our relatives and friends for their kindness shown us during the sickness and death of our Dear Brother.   A SISTER.

Elvin L. Bridges

Elvin L. Bridges, son of Robert and Mary Bridges was born in Knox county July 16, 1883. He professed faith in Christ at the age of 15 and joined the Lost Creek Baptist Church and later moved his membership to Mossy Spring Baptist Church where he remained an influential member until his death April 12, 1935. He was married to Miss Rhoda Weaver December 25, 1904 To this union three sons were born. He leaves his wife, three sons, one daugther-in-law and one brother; two sisters and a host of relatives and friends to mourn his loss. But we sincerely believe our loss is his eternal gain.   MRS. RHODA BRIDGES.

12

Elvin Weaver

Elvin Weaver was born Sept. 4, 1861. He professed faith in Christ at an early age and joined the Primitive Baptist Church at Mossy Springs and lived a faithful member until his death, March 18, 1935. He was married to Elizabeth Anderson Feb. 12, 1882 and to this union were born nine children, five sons and four daughters. Two sons died in infancy. He leaves his wife and seven children; 24 grandchildren and one great grandchild; seven brothers and one sister, all to mourn the loss, but we believe our loss is Heavens gain. He will be missed by his family, church and friends for years to come. To know him was to love him. He often spoke of his hope and his home in heaven while on his bed of affiction.

Written by a daughter, VERGIE WELCH.

13

OBITUARIES AND MINISTERIAL ROLL

Elders	Post Office
John Ausmus	Speedwell, Claiborne County, Tennessee
Gilbert Abbott	Knoxville, Knox County, Tennessee
T. G. Brantly	Sharps Chapel, Union County, Tennessee
Alfred Boruff	Maynardsville, Union County, Tennessee
Henry Comer	LaFollette, Campbell County, Tennessee
E. S. Drummonds	New Tazewell, Claiborne County, Tennessee
Albert Davis	LaFollette, Campbell County, Tennessee
V. H. Graves	Sharps Chapel, Union County, Tennessee
John F. Keck	Goin, Claiborne County, Tennessee
W. A. Moyers	Speedwell, Claiborne County, Tennessee
George Mays	Goin, Claiborne County, Tennessee
Mathew Oliver	Noeton, Grainger County, Tennessee
T. J. Pierce	Speedwell, Claiborne County, Tennessee
Alfred Parks	New Market, Grainger County, Tennessee
Charie Redmond	Gibson Station, Lee County, Virginia
H. A. Shaffner	Harrogate, Claiborne County, Tennessee
S. S. Wilson	Middlesboro Star R. 1, Bell County, Ky.
M. B. Weaver	128 Jordan St., Knoxville, Knox County, Tennessee
Leonard White	LaFollette, Campbell County, Tennessee
Carl McCarty	Speedwell, Claiborne County, Tennessee

LICENTIATES

Milton Brantly	Sharps Chapel, Union County, Tennessee
Jim Collins	New Market, Grainger County, Tennessee
J. C. Cosby	Gibson Station, Lee County, Virginia
W. R. Petree	Sharps Chapel, Union County, Tennessee
Charlie Stanifer	New Tazewell, Claiborne County, Tennessee
J. M. Wilder	Speedwell, Claiborne County, Tennessee
J. C. Bolin	Tazewell, Claiborne County, Tennessee

14

291

CHURCHES	COUNTY	PASTORS	CLERKS	CLERK'S POSTOFFICE
Hamilton Gro	Union	T. G. Brantly	C. L. Hamilton	Sharps Chapel, Tenn
Mossy Spring	Union	V. H. Graves	J. M. Kivett	Sharps Chapel, Tenn
Red Hill	Claiborne	T. G. Brantly	Jeff Treece	Speedville, Tenn.
Gibson Station	Lee	Mathew Oliver	Mary Ball	Gibson Station, Tenn.
Cave Spring	Union	Carl McCarty	B. F. Berry	Speedville, Tenn.
Oak Grove	Union	T. G. Brantly	David White	Sharps Chapel, Tenn
Straight Brand	Union	John Ausmus,	Lussie McBee	Speedville, Tenn.
		Ast. T. J. Pierce	Susan Pierce, asst.	
Rocky Dale	Knox	T. G. Brantly	M. C. Dunn	Coryton, Tenn.
Cedar Spring	Claiborne	Mathew Oliver	J. L. Drummonds	New Tazewell, Tenn.
		E. S. Drummonds, asst.		
Blackfox	Grainger	V. H. Graves	Sam Davis	Luttrell, Tenn.
Pleasant Point	Claiborne	V. H. Graves	Estell Heath	Goin, Tenn.
Davis Chapel	Campbell	Leonard White	O. R. Parrott	LaFollette, Tenn.
Capps Creek	Union	T. J. Pierce	Easter Braden	Goin, Tenn.
Pleasant Hill	Claiborne	Charlie Redmond	Lincoln Edwards	Speedville, Tenn.
		H. A. Shoffner, asst.	Verlin Edwards, ast	
New Hebron	Jefferson	M. B. Weaver	Cardil Mitchel	New Market, Tenn.
Noeton	Jefferson	Mathew Oliver	J. C. Oliver	Noeton, Tenn.

292

CHURCHES	NAMES OF DELEGATES	Committee Meetings	Contributions	Saturday Meetings	Total Membership	Deceased	Excluded	Dismissed by Letter	Restored	Received by Letter	Rec'd by Expr. Baptism
Mossy Spring	Elders V. H. Graves, M. B. Weaver, Bro. Robert Graves, W. M. White, Sister Sallie Kivett, Stella Graves	June	$5.00	4	232	2	2			1	
Cedar Spring	Elder F. S. Drummonds, Bros. J. L. Drummonds, J. C. Bolin, J. A. Minton, Margaret Drummonds, Delia Drummonds.	May	2.10	4	83			1			
Capps Creek	Linda Braden	M-Oc	1.61	2	34	1					
Cave Spring	Carl McCarty, Milton Brantly	June	1.25	3	30						
Noeton	Elder Matthew Oliver, Bros. Robert Atkins, Nathan Atkins, J. C. Oliver, Annie Oliver, Maude Atkins, Ida Atkins										1
Oak Grove	Elder T. G. Brantly, Bro. George Shoffner	M-S	1.50	3	45	1	2				
Blackfox	Bros. John Bundon, Herbert Bundon, J. M. Davis, Sam Davis	May	4.25	1	231		3	2			
Hamilton Grove	Bros. W. E. Hamilton, Lillis Hamilton, F. S. Hamilton, Marnie Hamilton, Mary Ausmus	June	2.50	2	102	1		3			3
Pleasant Hill	Bros. Neal Lamber, Walter Brewer, sister Tilda Lambert	June	1.25	4	60	1	6			1	
Straight Branch	Elder T. J. Pierce, sister Lussie McBee	June	3.00	4	62	1					
Davis Chapel	Elders Leonard White, Albert Davis, Bro. James Lynch	June	1.50	1	37				4		
Gibson Station	Elders H. A. Shoffner, Chas. Redmond, Bros. R. K. Ball, Henry Haskins, Frank Edwards	June	1.50	3	140						5
Red Hill	Henry Patterson	June	2.00	1	76						
Pleasant Point	Letters but no Messengers	July	1.65	2	83						
New Hebron	No Letter, Come on	July	5.00	1	134	1					
Rock Dale	No Letter, Come on	May		1	51						
		June		3	69						

M I N U T E S

—OF THE—

ONE HUNDREDTH AND SEVENTEENTH
ANNUAL SESSION

OF THE

POWELLS VALLEY
ASSOCIATION

—OF—

PRIMITIVE BAPTISTS

Held With the Church at

PLEASANT POINT, CLAIBORNE COUNTY, TENN.

AUGUST 14, 15, 16, 1936

Next Session will be held with the Church at Oak Grove, Union County, Tennessee, To Commence on Friday, before the Third Saturday in August 1937.

Elder M. B. Weaver will preach the Introductory Sermon and Elder John F. Keck will be his alternate

FRIDAY'S PROCEEDINGS

1st—According to the previous arrangements the Association met and was called to order by the Moderator, Elder, T. G. Brantly.

2nd—The Introductory Sermon was delivered by Elder Mathew Oliver first reading the 87th Psalm text "His name shall be called Jesus for He shall save His people from their sins."

3rd—After 15 minutes intermission the Association reassembled while singing the old hymn, "Children of the Heavenly King." After praises by Elder M. B. Weaver, and Prayer by Elder John F. Keck the Association was organized by re-electing Elder T. G. Brantley Moderator and Bro. Sam Davis, Clerk, and Elder John F. Keck assistant-clerk.

4th—Called for letters from sister churches: Received twelve which were read by the clerks.

5th—By motion said letters were received and messengers names enrolled.

6th—Called for corresponding letters from Sister Associations and received none.

7th—Motion in order that the Moderator appoint all our committees.

(a)—On Preaching—Bros. John Bundon, Wily Treece, Sam Cook, together with the church.

8th—Called for members and received the following from St. Branch, Elder T. J. Peirce.

(b)—Committee on Arrangements—Bros. J. C. Oliver, Estil Heath, J. A. Minton.

(c)—Committee on Correspondence—Elder V. H. Graves, Albert Paris, Minton Brantly.

(d)—Committee on request—Bros. M. C. Dunn, George Shoffner, Elder John F. Keck.

(e)—Committee on Finance—Bros. Jim Kivett, Henry Haskins, Forest Hamilton.

(f)—Committee on explanation concerning the isolated churches by TVA—Elder John F. Keck, Bros. Sam Davis, M. C. Dunn.

9th—Called for the report of the Committee on preaching.

(a) We, your Committee on Preaching beg leave to submit the following: Saturday at the stand Elder T. J. Pierce, Mathew Oliver. Saturday night, Elder V. H. Graves, Bill Moyers, Cars Branch Elder, T. G. Brantly, Mathew Oliver, Moyers Graves, M. B. Weaver, Milton Brantly. Sunday at the stand, Elders V. H. Graves, Leonard White.

Respectfully submitted,

SAM R. COOK & WILY TREECE.

Together with the church.

10th—By motion the report was seconded and the committee discharged.

11th—Motion in order to adjourn until 9:30 p. m. Saturday.

—2—

SATURDAY'S PROCEEDINGS

1st—The Association met pursuant to adjournment.

2nd—After singing praise by Elder T. G. Brantly and reading the 2nd Chapter of 1st Peter and prayer by Elder Milton Brantly.

3rd—The Association was called to order by Moderator.

4th—Called for letters from sister churches that failed to get in Friday. Received two which were read by the clerk.

5th—By motion said letters were received and messengers welcomed to seats with us.

6th—Called for the report of the Committee on Arrangements.

(b)—We, your Committee on Arrangements beg leave to report the following order of business.

1st—Call the roll.

2nd—Call for the report of the Committee on Preaching.

3rd—On Correspondence.

4th—On Request.

5th—On Finance.

6th —When and where shall our next Association be held. Who shall preach the introductory sermon and who shall be his alternate.

7th—How many copies of minutes shall we have printed. Who shall superintend the printing of same, and what shall he be allowed for his services.

Respectfully submitted,
BROTHER J. A. MINTON
BROTHER J. C. OLIVER,
BROTHER ESTIL HEATH.

7th—By motion report received and Committee discharged.

8th—Called for the report of the Committee on Correspondence.

(c)—We, your Committee on Correspondence beg leave to submit the following: That we keep up our long cherished correspondence with the Hiwassee Association by letter and messenger.

Respectfully Submitted
ELDER V. H. GRAVS,
ELDER ALBERT DAVIS,
ELDER MILTON BRANTLY.

9th—By motion the report was received and the Committee discharged.

10th —Called for the report of the Committee on the Isolated Churches by the TVA.

—3—

11th—By motion the report was received and the committee was discharged.

(d)—We, your Committee on Isolated Churches beg leave to submit the following report: Be it known that the TVA has taken over four of our churches, namely: Mossy Spring, with about 235 membership, Hamilton Grove of about 68 Membership. Cave Spring, of about 80 membreship, and Straight Branch, with a membership of about 74, all of these churches being in Union County. We very much regret the loss of these churches and we earnestly hope their members will have church fellowship and Homes with the Powell Valley Association of Primitive Baptist.

Respectfully Submitted,

BROTHER M. C. DUNN,
ELDER JOHN F. KECK,
BROTHER SAM DAVIS.

12th—Called for the report of the Committee on Request.

(e) We, your Committee on Request big leave to submit the following report: We have all Obituaries printed in our minutes that are furnished by the churches and that the next annual session of Powell Valley Association be held with the church at Oak Grove, Union county, Tenn., to commence on Friday before the Third Saturday in August, 1937.

Respectfully submitted

BROTHER G. W. SHOFFNER,
BROTHER M. C. DUNN,
ELDER JOHN F. KECK.

13th—By motion the report was received and the Committee discharged.

14th—Called for the report of the Committee on Finance.

(d)—We, your Committee on Finance beg leave to submit the following report: Received from Churches for Printing Minutes $39.75.

BROTHER FOREST HAMILTON,
BROTHER HENRY HOSKINS,
BROTHER JIM KIVETT.

15th—By motion the report was received and the committee was discharged.

16th—By motion the next Annual Session of the Powells Valley Association will be held with the Church at Oak Grove, Union County, Tennessee, to commence on Friday before the third Saturday in August, 1937. That Elder M. E. Weaver preach the introductory sermon and that Elder John F. Keck be his alternate.

—4—

17th—Motion in order that we have 800 copies of our minutes printed, and that the clerk superintend the printing and distributing of the same and that he be allowed $10.00 for his services.

18th—Motion in order that the clerk carry over the remainder of the finance until next year.

19th —Motion we send letter and messengers to Hiwassee Association. Messengers—Elder M. B. Weaver and V. H. Graves.

20th—Motion in order that the Clerk write corresponding letters to the Hiwassee Association and have the same printed in our minutes.

21st—By motion be it resolved that we extend our heart felt thanks to this old church and the surrounding community for their generous hospitalities and kind treatment to us throughout this Association.

22th—By motion we adjourned until 10 o'clock at the time and place above stated.

Dismissed in order by Elder M. B. Weaver.

ELDER T. G. BRANTLEY, Moderator,
Sharps Chapel, Tennessee.
SAM DAVIS, Clerk,
Luttrell, Tennessee.

SUNDAY'S PROCEEDINGS

At the appointed hour Sunday a large and well beheaved audience assembled at the Alter and so earnestly listened to the well delievred sermons of Elder V. H. Graves, followed by Elder Leonard White, from the text: "Jesus of Nathareth, King of the Jews" and closing remarks by the moderator. All these were delivered in a most loving spirit and with great interest to all and a lovely parting was expressed by the clasping of hands, sheding tears of rejoicing and in asking the blessings of God upon each other.

Corresponding Letter to the Hiwassee Association

Very Dear Brothers and Sister in Christ:

We desire a continuance of our long cherished corespondence with you, and fo this purpose have chosen these, our beloved Elders, to bear this, our epistle of love to you, and truly hope you will grant them a seat with you in your annual meeting, to-wit: Elders M. B. Weaver and V. H. Graves. May peace and sweet fellowschip of the ever Blessed Spirit abide with you, are the prayers of this, your little sister, Pray for us.

THE CLERK.

—5—

OBITUARIES

Brother James Campbell

In memory of James Campbell, age 68, who was a member of the Noeton Church for about 16 years and has lived faithful until death. He departed this life July 17, 1936, and greeted the death angels with a smile. He leaves to mourn their loss a wife, seven children and one brother, one sister and a host of other relatives and friends. After much physical suffering Uncle Jim left the earth to live with Jesus where there's neither pain nor death..

> From us a brother has gone,
> A voice from us is stilled;
> And a vacant place is in our church,
> That never can be filled.

Sister Essie Collins

Sister Essie Collins, age 41, wife of W. M. Collins professed faith in Christ and joined the church at Noeton in which she lived a faithful member until God saw fit to call her to her reward, April 12, 1936. She leaves a loving husband, 7 children, and a host of friends to mourn their loss.

Sister Nancy Heatherly

Sister Nancy (Davis) Heatherly born August 5th, 1869, departed this life May 9th, 1936, age 66 years, 9 months and 4 days. She professed faith in Christ at an early age and joined the church at Davis' Chapel 1895 in which she lived a faithful member until God called her away to live with him above. She was married to John Heatherly very early in life and to this union was born six children, one dead, five living. She is missed by all who knew her. We feel our loss is her eternal gain.

Sister Leona Petree

Leona Petree was born October 3, 1885. Died July 20, 1935. Married to J. W. Petree, February 24, 1912 and to this union were born two children. She professed faith in Christ at the age of 14 years and joined the Church at Barne in 1901 and later moved her memmership to Mossy Springs, then in the year of 1922 moved her letter to Rocky Dale as a Charter member of that Church, and lived a faithful member until death. She was loved by her family, the church and all who knew he, she was always willing to lend a helping hand in every thing that was right. It pleased the Lord to call her home to live with Him forever. May God bless her family, the Church and her friends, that miss her so much. Our loss is Heaven's gain.

ELDER T. G. BRANTLY

Brother B. D. England

Benjamin David England, was born January 3, 1868. Died January 26, 1936. Age being 68 years, 23 days old. He was married to Martha Jane Collins, March 18, 1888. To this union was born eleven children, 5 boys and 6 girls; eight now living, 3 deceased; William Thomas, Mathew, Timothy, Amos, and Elsie England all of Goin, Tennessee, Rachel Johnson of Speedwell, Tennessee, Cora Marsee of Middlesboro, Kentucky, Vesta Ellison of Sharps Chapel, Tennessee. Married to Margret Walker, June 30, 1910 and to this union was born 3 children, Alice ,John and Dewey, all of Goin, Tennessee; 33 grand children, 28 living. He professed faith in Christ at an early age. Later joined the Primitive Baptist church at Oak Grove, July 1933 and was baptized July 30, 1933, and lived a faithful member until death. He was a loving husband and a kind and affectionate father.

He will be greatly missed by all who knew him. He leaves a host of friends and relatives to mourn their loss, but we sincerely hope our loss is his eternal gain. He was laid to rest in the Hopper cemetery. Rev. T. G. Brantly officating. Gibson and Cone in charge.

From his wife and family, W. T. ENGLAND.

Sister Ola (Edwards) Beason

Ola (Edwards) Beason, born November 18, 1913, died April 22, 1936. She was 22 years, 5 months and 4 days of age. She professed faith in Christ at an early age and joined the church at Pleasant Point and lived a faithful member until death.

She was married to John Beason August 16, 1932. To this union three children were born, all deceased. She leaves to mourn their loss a husband, John Beason; a father, Spenser Edwards, a Stepmother, Rosie Edwards, four sisters, Laurada Cox, Edith Cole, Love Woods, Gertrude O'Dell, of Goin, Willie Edwards of Monroe, Michigan. One-half brother, Kenneth Edwards of Goin and a host of friends and relatives. Funeral services were held by Eld. Proctor Edwards.

—9—

300

Sister Lelia Mae Russell Ridenonr

Mrs. Lelia Mae Russell Ridenonr was Born July 16, 1910, died December 5, 1935. She professed faith in Christ and joined the church at Oak Grove and was baptized February 6, 1927. She was married to Homer Ridenonr December 21, 1934. To this union was born one daughter Wilmae Mae which were burried together. She leaves a husband, father and mother, eight brothers and two sisters, one half sister and a host of friends to mourn their loss. But our loss is heavens gain.

Sister Bell Petree Dunn

Bell Petree Dunn, daughter of Elder S. M. Petree, was born July 31, 1881. She professed faith in Christ and joined the church at Mossy Spring December 24, 1895. She was married to M. C. Dunn July 15, 1900. To this union were born four children, one boy and three girls. In 1922 she moved her membership to Rocky Dale as a Charter Member of that Church, then May 19, 1923 was ordained as a Deaconests and filleed that place as such, always willing to help those who were in need. She is missed by her loving family, her relatives, the church and friends who knew her . To know her was to love her. She was a mother in Isreal and stood for everything that was right. On September 1, 1935, she fell asleep in the arms of Jesus to rest from her labors. We feel that our loss is Heaven's gain.

ELDER T. G. BRANTLY

Sister Ollie Moyers

Mrs. Mary Ollie (Hopper) Moyers, wife of Mr. I. N. Moyers, died at her home December 13th at the age of 74 years, 11 months, and 25 days. Mrs. Moyers was a member of the Pleasant Point Church.

Surviving her are her husband I. N. Moyers; three children, Hascal and Mona Moyers and Edith Stiner, all of Goin; one brother, Henry Hopper, of Goin, and two sisters, Mrs. T. C. Keck, of Goin, and Mrs. Sadie Sharp, of Knoxville.

Funeral services were conducted at the home at ten o'clock by Rev. T. C. Brantly, with interment near Goin. Pall-bearers: Archie Williams, Horace Williams, Oden Sharp, Dillo Sharp, Emory Sharp and Amos Sharp.

Sister Sarah Sowder Keck

Sister Sarah Sowder Keck was born in 1857 and departed this life February 17, 1936. She joined the Primitive Baptist Church, and was baptized and remained a member of Pleasant Point church until her death. Her husband and one son, preceded her to the grave. Ten children still live to mourn the loss of a dear mother.

Brother John Cook

Brother John Cook died in January 1936, 76 years old, joined the Primitive Baptist church at Brownies Creek; Elder Richard Wilson baptised him the fourth Saturday in November and he and his wife Sister Mary Cook joined the church at Meyers Grove and lived a faithful member until death.

He leaves a wife, Sister Mary Cook, one daughter Elizabeth Edds and 10 step children to mourn their loss. He often talked of his heavenly home and we believe while his body sleeps in death his soul has entered into the blessed rest that awaits God's children. May God's Holy Spirit comfort his companions and relatives. He was laid to rest in Clear Fork Cemetery. Funeral services were conducted by E. S. Drummonds. He wanted brother Mathew Oliver to help hold the funeral services but he had gone to an appointment and we failed to get him.

Brother W. A. L. Owsley

W. A. L. Owsley was born August 11, 1857 departed this life February 16, 1936, being 78 years, 7 months and five days old. He professed faith in Christ in early boyhood, joined the church at Oak Grove, but later moved his membership to Hamilton Grove, where he lived a faithful member until God called him to that great beyond. He was married to Lucy Baker, March 20, 1879. To this union were born eight children, four boys and four girls. His wife and three children who have gone on before are with him in Heaven. He leaves to mourn their loss, two sons, three daughters, two sisters, one brother thirteen grand children and three great grandchildren, a host of relatives and friends. But we believe our loss is Heaven's gain. While our home is made sadder, Heaven is brighter.

He was ill twenty five months, but he bore his sickness with patience and he often spoke of that great beyond, he didn't mind going.

> A precious one from us is gone,
> A voice we love is still;
> A vacant chair is in our home,
> That never can be filled.

Sleep on dear daddy and take your rest, we hope to meet you in the sweet by and by.

Services were held at Sharp's Chapel by Elder T. G. Brantly. Burial was in the Graves Cemetery.

Brother Freeman Brantley

Brother Freeman Brantley was born March 26, 1878, and departed this life April 29, 1936, being 58 years, one month and two days old, he was mearried to Nervine Harrell on May 29, 1898 and professed faith in Christ in early life and remained faithful until death. He joined the Primitive Baptist church at Cave Springs and was baptized. He leaves to mourn their loss, one son Jimmie and his wife, 3 grand children, six brothers and one sister. We believe our loss is Heaven's gain.

Sister Ollie Kivett Coffee

Ollie Kivett Coffee died at Omberonathy, Texas, November 28, 1935. She was born in Union county, Tennessee, September 14, 1869 and was married to J. B. Coffee April 20, 1889 at Maynardville, Tennessee. To this union were born eleven children, all living and all were present when their mother died. She joined the Primitive Baptist church at Mossy Spring January 1894 and lived a faithful member until a few months before her death. She called for her letter. She was loved by all who knew her. She had been ill for several weeks. She leaves a husband, five sons and six daughters, one brother and several grandchildren.

May God's Holy Spirit Comfort her husband and children and other relatives and help them to look forward to a glorious resurrection and a happy reunion on the other side of life.

> True your form from us has vanished.
> And your ears deaf to our call;
> But your golden patroit is hanging high
> On memory's polished walls.
> In Heaven of bright sunshine,
> We shall meet you by and by.
> Live forever in a country
> Where we'll never say goodby.

MYRTLE KIVETT

Brother Dan Atkins

Brother Dan Atkins age 76, joined the Primitive Baptist church at Noeton in the year of 1914, in which he lived a faithful member until death, April 6, 1936. He leaves to mourn their loss, a number of children, grandchildren and a host of friends. But we hope our loss is his eaernal gain.

Brother Neal Henry

In loving remembrances of a son, Neal Henry, son of Mr. and Mrs. W. M. Henry of Leas Springs. He was born Feburary 17, 1893 departed this life March 21, 1936. He leaves to mourn their loss his parents, one sister, two brothers, a host of relatives and friends. Through life's rugged gateway he made a host of cherished friends who will miss him on earth. May we meet him in Heaven again.

Over earth has fell a shadow
Sadness now has crossed our door.
Jesus has called our loved one
To that bright and happy shore.

Why need we weep and mourn,
For ones that has past away,
They are at home in glory
Where God's chosen ones shall stay.

Just a few more days of labor,
Then away from earth to fly,
To live with Jesus and our loved ones
In a home beyond the skies.

Progress Print, Tazewell, Tenn.

—13—

304

MINISTERIAL ROLL

Elders	Post Offices
John Ausmus	Speedwell, Claiborne County, Tennessee
Gilbert Abbott	Knoxville, Knox County, Tennessee
T. G. Brantly	Sharp's Chapel, Union County, Tennessee
Alfred Boruff	Maynardville, Union County, Tennessee
Henry Comer	LaFollette, Campbell County, Tennessee
E. S. Drummonds	New Tazewell, Claiborne County, Tennessee
Albert Davis	LaFollettee, Campbell County, Tennessee
V. H. Graves	Sharps Chapel, Union County, Tennessee
John F. Keck	Goin, Claiborne County, Tennessee
W. A. Moyers	Speedwell, Claiborne County, Tennessee
George Mays	Goin, Claiborne County, Tennessee
Mathew Oliver	Noeton, Grainger County, Tennessee
T. J. Pierce	Speedwell, Claiborne County, Tennessee
Alfred Parks	New Market, Grainger County, Tennessee
Charlie Redmond	Gibson Station, Lee County, Virginia
H. A. Shoffner	Harrogate, Claiborne County, Tennessee
S. S. Wilson	Middlesboro Star R. 1, Bell County, Ky.
M. B. Weaver	128 Jordan St., Knoxville, Knox County, Tennessee
Leonard White	LaFollette, Campbell, County, Tennessee
Carl McCarty	Speedwell, Claiborne County, Tennessee

LICENTIATES

Milton Brantly	Sharp's Chapel, Union County, Tennessee
Jim Collins	New Market, Grainger County, Tennessee
J. C. Cosby	Gibson Station, Lee County, Virginia
W. R. Petree	Sharp's Chapel, Union County, Tennessee
Charlie Stanifer	New Tazewell, Claiborne County, Tennessee
J. M. Wilder	Speedwell, Claiborne County, Tennessee
J. C. Bolin	Tazewell, Claiborne County, Tennessee

—14—

CHURCHES	COUNTY	PASTORS	CLERKS	CLERKS POST OFFICE
Hamilton Grove	Union	T. G. Brantly	C. L. Hamilton	Maryville, Tenn.
Mossy Spring	Union	V. H. Graves	J. M. Kivett	Wortburg, Tenn.
Red Hill	Claiborne	T. G. Brantly	Jeff Treece	Speedwell, Tenn.
Gibson Station	Lee	Mathew Oliver	Mary Ball	Gibson Station, Va.
Cave Spring	Union	Carl McCarty	B. F. Berry	New Market, Tenn.
Oak Grove	Union	T. G. Brantly	R. P. Bridges	Sharp's Chapel, Tenn.
Straight Branch	Union	John Ausmus / T. J. Pierce, Asst.	Lussie McBee / Susan Pierce, asst.	Speedwell, Tenn.
Rocky Dale	Knox	V. H. Graves	M. C. Dunn	Corryton, Tenn.
Cedar Spring	Claiborne	T. G. Brantly	J. L. Drummonds	New Tazewell, Tenn.
Black Fox	Grainger	Mathew Oliver	Sam Davis	Luttrell, Tenn.
Pleasant Point	Claiborne	V. H. Graves	Estill Heath	Goin, Tenn.
Davis Chapel	Campbell	Leonard White	O. R. Parrott	LaFollette, Tenn.
Capps Creek	Union	T. J. Pierce	Easter Braden	Goin, Tenn.
Pleasant Hill	Claiborne	W. A. Moyers	J. L. Edwards / Verlin Edwards ast	Speedwell, Tenn.
New Hebron	Jefferson	Mathew Oliver	Cordelia Mitchel	New Market, Tenn.
Noeton	Grainger	Mathew Oliver	J. C. Oliver	Leas Spring, Tenn.

306

CHURCHES	NAMES OF DELEGATES	Rec. By Expr. Baptist	Rec. By Letter	Restored	Dismissed by Letter	Excluded	Deceased	Total Membership	Sat. Meetings	Contribution	Committee Meetings
Mossy Spring	Elders M. B. Weaver, V. H. Graves, Bros. J. M. Kivett, Robert Graves, Sister Stella Graves, P. H. White, Edna Graves.		1			95		115	4	4.25	June
Cedar Spring	Elder E. S. Drummonds, Bros. S. W., G. B., J. L., D. P., T. J. Drummonds, Billie Miracle, J. A. Minton; sisters Maude and Dellia Drummonds			2			1	84	4	1.50	May
Capps Creek	Bro. Troy Presley, Sister Mary Bolin.	1	1					35	2	1.55	M.O.
Cave Spring	Bros. Jimmie Brantly, Milton Brantly.	1					1	62	3	2.00	June
Noeton	Elder Mathew Oliver, Bro. J. C. Oliver, Sister Ellen Oliver	1					3	43	3	1.50	M.S.
Oak Grove	Elder T. G. Brantly, Bros. George Shoffner, Tom England.	2				3	6	233	1	5.00	May
Black Fox	Bros. John Sibord, Will Thomas, Sam Davis, J. M. Davis, Roy Bailey							102	2	3.20	June
Hamilton Grove	Bros. Sam Cook, M. W. Edmondson, W. E. Hamilton, Sister Mamie Hamilton, Sillias Hamilton.							63	4	1.50	June
Pleasant Hill	Elder W. A. Moyers.	2						65	4	4.00	June
Straight Branch	No Letter										
Davis Chapel	Elders Leonard White, Albert Davis.						1	139	3	2.50	June
Gibson Station	Brother Henry Hoskins.							76	1	1.50	June
Red Hill	Bros. Wily Treece, Mase Treece.						2	83	2	2.00	July
Pleasant Point	Elders G. W. Mays, John F. Keck, Bros. Jimmie Cox, F. C. Keck, A. C. Goin, J. E. Heath, J. W. Keck, Sisters Katie Keck, Hattie Cox, Letha Heath, Laura Keck, Myrtle Keck, Barbara Hopper and Etta Hopper.						4	130	1	4.50	July
New Hebron	Bro. Jimmie Collins							35	2	.75	M.S.
Rocky Dale	Bros. M. C. Dunn, Arvil Graves.	4			1	3	2	67	3	4.00	June

MINUTES

—OF THE—

ONE HUNDRED AND EIGHTEENTH

ANNUAL SESSION

OF THE

POWELLS VALLEY

ASSOCIATION

—OF—

PRIMITIVE BAPTISTS

Held With the Church at

OAK GROVE, UNION COUNTY, TENN.

AUGUST 20, 21, 22, 1937

Next Session will be held with the Church at Pleasant Hill, Claiborne
County, Tennessee. To commence on Friday before the
Third Saturday in August, 1937

Elder V. H. Graves to preach the Introductory Sermon and
Elder T. G. Brantley will be his Alternate

1st—According to the previous arrangements the Association met persuant to adjournments.

2nd—After singing, praise by Elder T. G. Brantly and prayer by Elder Matthew Oliver.

3rd—The Association was called to order by Moderator, Elder T. G. Brantley.

4th—The Introductory Sermon was delivered by Elder M. B. Weaver, from the 17th verse of the 1st chapter of Paul's Letter to the Phillipians. Quotation: "And He is before all things, and by Him all things consist." Followed by Elder T. G. Brantly.

5th—After 15 minutes intermission at the sound of singing the Association re-assembled and was organized as follows:

6th—By motion and second Elder T. G. Brantley was re-elected Moderator and Bro. Sam Davis re-elected Clerk with Bro. Lincoln Edwards as Asst. Clerk.

7th—Called for letters from sister churches of this Association and received 10 which were read by the Clerks.

8th—On motion the letters were all received and the delegation welcomed to seats.

9th—Called for newly constituted churches and received none.

10th—Called for corresponding letters from sister Associations and received delegates from the Hiwassee Association as follows: to-wit: Elders U. J. Hembree, Dan Abbott.

11th—Called for visitors who were not delegates and receivee one, to-wit: Elder W. R. Gates.

12th—On motion all were welcomed to seats with us.

13th—Called for members of our churches who were not delegates and received Bro. George Shaffner of Oak Grove and Bro. Jim Brantley of Red Hill.

14th—Motion in order that we conduct the business of this Association by the order of last years minutes so long as it does not conflict with the business of this meeting.

15th—Motion in order that the Moderator appoint all the following committees:

(a)—Committee on Preaching—Bros. M. W. Edmondson, Jim Brantly, Dewey Graves, together with the Oak Grove Church.

(b)—Committee on Arrangements—Bros. M. C. Dunn, Josh Drummonds, Henry Stiner.

(c)—Committee on Correspondence—Elders M. B. Weaver, Matthew Oliver, Albert Davis.

(d)—Committee on Request—Elder V. H. Graves, Brother Tom England, Verlin Hopper.

(e)—Committee on Finance—Elder H. A. Shaffner, Bros. John

—2—

Graves, A. E. Goin.

16th—Called for a report of the Committee on Preaching.

(a)—We your Committee on Preaching beg leave to make the following report: Friday night at the Church, Elders V. H. Graves, W. R. Gates. Saturday at the Church, Elders Matthew Oliver, Dan Abbott. Saturday night Elders John F. Keck, Matthew Oliver. Little Barren Church, Elders W. R. Gates, Albert Davis. At Taylors Grove, Elders Leonard White, V. H. Graves. Sunday at the Stand, Elders Matthew Oliver, Leonard White, Moderator to close.

Respectfully submitted,

BROS. M. W. EDMONDSON
DEWEY GRAVES
JAMES BRANTLY.

16th—Motion in order that we receive the report and discharge the Committee.

17th—Motion in order that we adjourn until 9:30 Saturday morning.

SATURDAY'S PROCEEDINGS

Saturday morning at 9:30 the Association met persuant to adjournment. After singing, praise by Elder John F. Keck by reading the 10th chapter of Matthew, and prayer by Elder V. H. Graves, the Association was called to order by the Moderator.

1st—Called for letters from Sister Churches that failed to get in Friday and received 2 which were read by the Clerks.

2nd—By motion said letters were received and the delegation welcomed to seats with us.

3rd—Called for the report of the Committee on Arrangements.

(b)—We, your Committee on Arrangements, beg leave to make the following report:

1st—Call the Roll.

2nd—Call for the report on Preaching.

3rd—On Correspondence.

4th—On Request.

5th—On Finance.

6th—When and where shall our next Association be held? Who shall preach the Introductory Sermon and who shall be his Alternate?

7th—How many copies of Minutes shall we have printed? Who shall superintend the printing of same and what shall he be allowed for his services?

Respectfully submitted,

BROS. M. C. DUNN
J. L. DRUMMONDS
HENRY STINER

4th—On motion the report was received and discharged the Com-

—3—

mittee.

5th—Call the roll and erase the names of absentees.

6th—Call for the report of the Committee on Correspondence.

(c)—We, your Committee on Correspondence, beg leave to make the following report: That we keep up our long cherished correspondence with the Hiwassee Association by letter and messengers.

Respectfully submitted,

ELDERS ALBERT DAVIS
MATTHEW OLIVER
M. B. WEAVER

7th—By motion the report was received and the committee discharged.

8th—Call for the report of the Committee on Request.

(d)—We, your Committee on Requests, beg leave to make the following report. That we have all obituaries printed in our Minutes that the churches furnish and that the next annual session of the Powells Valley Association be held with the Church at Pleasant Hill, Claiborne County, Tenn., to commence on Friday before the Third Saturday in August, 1938.

Respectfully submitted,

ELDER V. H. GRAVES
BROS. H. V. HOPPER
T. M. ENGLAND

9th—By motion the report was received and the committee discharged.

10th—Call for the report of the Committee on Finance.

(e)—We, your Committee on Finance, beg leave to make the following report. Received from churches for printing Minutes $33.00.

Respectfully submitted,

BROTHERS A. C. GOIN
JOHN GRAVES
ELDER H. A. SHAFFNER

11th—Motion in order that we receive the report and discharge the Committee.

12th—Called for the report of the Clerk on last years finance. I, Sam Davis, Clerk of the Powells Valley Association of Primitive Biptists, beg leave to make the following report of the year 1936. Received for printing minutes, $39.75. Cost of printing minutes and postage, $25.60. Clerks fee and mailing minutes to the various churcres, $10.00. This leaves a balance in my hand of $4.15.

Respectfully submitted,

SAM DAVIS, Clerk

13th—By motion the report was received.

14th—Motion in order that our next annual session of the Powells

—4—

Valley Association of Primitive Baptist be held with the Church of Pleasant Hill, Claiborne County, Tennessee, to commence on Friday before the third Saturday in August, 1938. That Elder V. H. Graves preach the Introductory Sermon and that Elder T. G. Brantly be his Alternate.

15th—Motion in order that we have 800 copies of minutes printed. That the clerk superintend the printing and distribution of same, and that he be allowed $10.00 for his service.

16th—Motion in order that we send the following delegates to the Hiwassee Association, to-wit: Elders M. B. Weaver, John F. Keck, and T. G. Brantly.

17th—Motion in order that Elder M. B. Weaver write a corresponding letter to the Hiwassee Association and that the Clerk have the same inserted in our minutes.

18th—By motion and second, Be it resolved that we extend our heartfelt thanks to this dear old church and the surrounding community for their hospitalities and kind treatment to us throughout our stay with them in this Association.

19th—Motion in order to adjourn until 10 o'clock A. M. at the place above mentioned.

20th—Dismissed in order.

ELDER T. G. BRANTLY, Moderator,
Sharps Chapel, Tennessee.
SAM DAVIS, Clerk,
Luttrell, Tennessee.

SUNDAY'S PROCEEDINGS

At the appointed hour a large audience assembled at the altar and so attentively listened to the well delivered sermons by Elder Matthew Oliver from text of the 9th verse of the 32nd chapter of Deuteronomy. Quotation: "The Lord's portion is His people. Jacob is the lot of his inheritance." Followed by Elder Leonard White and closing remarks by the Moderator. Each discourse was delivered in a most loving spirit with the greatest interest to all and loving parting was expressed.

CORRESPONDING LETTER

To the Hiwassee Association with whom we correspond, to meet at Hendrick's Chapel, Sevier County, Tenn., Sept. 24th, 1937. Very dear brother and sisters in the Lord, we are sending these our beloved Elders M. B. Weaver, John F. Keck and T. G. Brantly to your meeting for the purpose of a closer Christian correspondence and cooperation in the work of the Lord for the good of our people and the glory of God. We pray your souls may be filled with joy and your meetings crowned with great success. We are looking for you to meet with us at Pleasant Hill Church, Claiborne County. Tenn. on Friday before the Third Saturday in August 1938. We close with love to all.

ELDER M. B. WEAVER.

OBITUARIES

Mrs. Effie Watts

Mrs. Effie Watts, born March 29th, 1888. Death came into our home July 13th, 1937 and took with it our beloved daughter, Mrs. Effie Watts. She was born to Mr. and Mrs. W. M. Henry. She was married Ance Watts and to this union was born six children. She professed faith in Christ and lived a Christian life. After a short period of illness died happy in the Lord, leaving to mourn her loss her husband, children, parents, two brothers and a host of relatives and friends. We live in hopes of seeing our daughter again.

Jesus knows when the days are dark
And when we're alone and sad
When He takes a loved one Home
The best friend we ever had,
He leaves us lonely and troubled in mind
Searching for someone whose gone
In Him a gleaming light we find
When we are left alone.

Brother John Hayes

One of our brothers, John Hayes, died January 29, 1937, leaving a vacancy in our church that can never be filled. He was one of our oldest members, 86 years. He was a member of the Church at Norton, lived a faithful Christian and attended every meeting until he was disabled to get there. He leaves his wife and children and friends to mourn our loss but we are comforted to know that he was a faithful server of Christ.

God shall take care of those who serve
And takes them home to rest
Leaving those who mourn for them
Feeling comforted and blest.

Shed not a tear for those who serve
They need not a single sigh
For Jesus knows and loves them all
And takes them home on high.

Brother Billie Bolden

Brother Billie Bolden, age 57 years, died December 16, 1936. He first joined the church at M. E. in his young days. Later he

—9—

313

joined the Primitive Baptist Church about 8 years ago where he lived a faithful member until God called him. Was married to Thuly Gross. To this union was born two children, Raymond and Myrtle Boldin. His second wife Julie Laymond, two children, Rosamae and Ivan Jean. He leaves to mourn their loss his wife, four children, grandchildren and a host of friends. We hope to meet him in heaven.

> We loved him, yes we loved him
> But our Saviour loved him best
> And after years of toil and trouble
> God called him home to rest
> He could' not stay here longer
> Now with friends and loved ones
> He is forever blessed.

THE CLERK AND FAMILY

Hattie Owens Edwards

Hattie Owens Edwards, wife of James Edwards, was born Aug. 26, 1907, she joined the Church at Pleasant Hill, Jan. 17th, 1932 and died Oct. 10, 1936. She and her husband were ordained deacons in February 1933. She was always willing to do all she could for her church and lived a faithful member until the end. She leaves to mourn her loss her husband, one son, and six daughters, her father, nine sisters, two brothers and a host of relatives and friends. While her death was a great shock to her family and friends we can only repeat for them.

> For all their trials and troubles
> To leave at Jesus feet,
> And all the small annoyances
> Which they must daily meet
> He is so wise and tender
> Their problems He'll decide
> He will not suffer them to fall
> For He is close beside.

MAE EDWARDS

Cas Relford

Cas Relford was born Aug. 21, 1894, age 42 years. He professed faith in Christ in early life and joined the Church at Mt. Olive. He was married to Luster Welch, Nov. 27, 1927, and to this union were born two children, Alfred and Clifton.

Brother Clifford Russell

Brother Clifford Russell was born July 26, 1903, died Jan. 7, 1937. He professed faith in Christ at an early age and joined the Church at Oak Grove and was baptised. Lived a faithful member until God called him away. He leaves his father and mother, Mr. and Mrs. J. P. Russell, 7 brother and 3 sisters, Willoughby, Russell, Charlie, Otis, Delsie, Denzie, Milburn, Loyd, Clemna, Clara, which are living and one half sister, Mrs. H. Lee Monroe and a host of friends to mourn their loss but our loss is Heavens gain.

A pecious one from us is gone
A voice we love is still
A vacant chair is in our home
That never can be filled.

SISTER CLARA RUSSELL

Della Stiner England

Della Stiner England was born Nov. 20th, 1892, died Jan. 6th, 1937, being 44 years, 1 month and 17 days old. Was married to W. T. England Oct. 5, 1918, to this union was born 7 children, 6 of whom survive, Harding, Lottie, Arlie, Ottis, Noble, Odrie all at home, also 2 step-children, Robert of Goin, Mrs. Dottie Holiway of Sharps Chapel. Other survivors are her husband, W. T. England, father and mother, Mr. and Mrs. Henry Stiner of Sharps Chapel, 2 brothers, Willie Stiner of Sharps Chapel, James Stiner of Goin, 3 sisters, Miss Rena Stiner of Sharps Chapel, Mrs. Jane Moyers of Goin, Mrs. Hattie Simmons of Sharps Chapel, a host of other relatives and friends. She professed faith in Christ about 5 years ago joined the Church at Oak Grove, July 30th, 1933, was baptised July 31st, 1933 and lived a faithful member until death. Interment in the Stiner Cemetery.

From us a sister has gone
A voice from us is stilled
And a vacant place is on our Church
That never can be filled.

She will be missed in her home and community. We hope our loss is heaven's gain and that we will be reunited in the sweet bye and bye. Funeral services by Elder T. G. Brantly.

Mrs. Mary E. Turner Dyke

Mrs. Mary E. Turner Dyke was born Feb. 9, 1868, died Feb. 10, 1937. Age 69 years. She professed hope in Christ at an early

—11—

age, joined the Primitive Baptist Church at Mossy Springs and later moved her membership to Oak Grove where she lived a faithful member until God called her home. She leaves to mourn her loss two daughters and six sons, Emmet, James, Mannia, Henry and Charles Dykes of Sharps Chapel, John Dyke of Mascot, Mrs. Leslie Graves of Maynardville, Mrs. Aaron Rouse of Monroe, Mich., 43 grandchildren, 8 great grandchildren, 2 sisters, Mrs. Sadie Ellison of Middlesboro, Mrs. Mattie Waggoner of Harlan, Kentucky, 7 brothers, John, Wess, Jess, Bige, Johnson, and Jake, Frank Turner. Our loss is heaven's gain. We hope to meet her in the sweet bye and bye.

Brother J. A. Minton

Brother J. A. Minton was born Nov., 12, 1847, died July 11, 1937, being 89 years old. He professed faith in Christ in his young days. He joined the Primitive Baptist Church at Meyers Grove, Saturday, March 4th, 1934. He was baptised by Elder Matthew Oliver, was married to Orlina Cupp. To that union was born 3 children, one alive, Sister Alice Webb. Later on he married Sister Duthie Lundy. To that union was born 4 children, 3 living. Then he married Gennie Shinvles. He is survived by one brother, Uncle Joe Minton, and lived a faithful member until death.

MINISTERIAL ROLL

Elders	Post Offices
John Ausmus	Speedwell, Claiborne County, Tennessee
T. G. Brantly	Sharps Chapel, Union County, Tennessee
Alfred Boruff	Maynardville, Union County, Tennessee
Henry Comer	LaFollette Campbell County, Tennessee
E. S. Drummonds ....,	New Tazewell, Claiborne County, Tennessee
Albert Davis	Speedwell, Claiborne County, Tennessee
V. H. Graves	Goin, Claiborne County, Tennessee
John F. Keck	Goin, Claiborne County, Tennessee
W. A. Moyers	Speedwell, Claiborne County, Tennessee
George Mays	Goin, Claiborne County, Tennessee
Matthew Oliver	Noeton, Grainger County, Tennessee
T. J. Pierce	Speedwell, Claiborne County, Tennessee
Alfred Parks	New Market, Grainger County, Tennessee
H. A. Shaffner	Harrogate, Claiborne County, Tennessee
Charlie Redmond	Gibson Station, Lee County, Virginia
S. S. Wilson	Middlesboro, Star Route 1, Bell County, Kentucky
Leonard White	LaFollette, Campbell County, Tennessee
Carl McCarty	Speedwell, Claiborne County, Tennessee
Milton Brantly	Sharps Chapel Union County, Tennessee
J. M. Wilder	Speedwell, Claiborne County, Tennessee

LICENTIATES

Jim Collins	New Market, Jefferson County, Tennessee
J. C. Cosby	Gibson Station, Lee County, Virginia
W. R. Petree	Sharps Chapel, Union County, Tennessee
Charlie Stanifer	New Tazewell, Claiborne County, Tennessee
J. C. Bolin	Tazewell, Claiborne County, Tennessee
Sam Miller	New Market, Jefferson County, Tennessee

—13—

317

CHURCHES	COUNTIES	PASTORS	CLERKS	CLERKS POST OFFICE
Red Hill	Claiborne	T. G. Brantly	Jeff Treece	..... Speedwell, Tennessee
Gibson Station .	Lee	Matthew Oliver	Mary Ball	. Gibson Station, Virginia
Oak Grove	Union	T. G. Brantly	R. P. Bridges	. Sharps Chapel, Tennessee
Rocky Dale	Knox	T. G. Brantly	M. C. Dunn	..... Corryton, Tennessee
Cedar Springs ..	Claiborne	Matthew Oliver	J. L. Drummonds .	. New Tazewell, Tennessee
Black Fox	Grainger	Matthew Oliver	Sam Davis	...... Luttrell, Tennessee
Pleasant Point .	Claiborne	V. H. Graves	Estell Heath	.... Goin, Tennessee
Davis Chapel ..	Campbell	Leonard White	O. R. Parrott	..... LaFollette, Tennessee
Capps Creek ...	Union	Henry Comer	Easter Braden ...	.... Goin, Tennessee
Pleasant Hill ..	Claiborne	V. H. Graves	Lincoln Edwards ..	...... Speedwell, Tennessee
New Hebron ...	Jefferson	Henry Comer	Cordelia Mitchell ..	... New Market, Tennessee
Noeton	Grainger	Matthew Oliver	J. C. Oliver	.. Leas Springs, Tennessee

318

CHURCHES	NAMES OF DELEGATES	Rec. by Expr. Baptism	Rec. by Letter	Restored	Dis. by Letter	Excluded	Deceased	Total Membership	Sat. Meetings	Contribution	Communion Meeting
Cedar Springs	Bro. J. L. Drummonds, Sis. Delia Drummonds, Adaska Moyers, Gertrude Simmons, Bro. S. W. Drummonds	2					1	85	4	1.50	May
Capps Creek	Bros. Troy Pressley, Charlie Collins, Sis. Linda Paul					1		35	2	1.10	M.O
Noeton	Elder Matthew Oliver, Sister Eller Oliver							45	3	1.50	M.S
Oak Grove	Elder T. G. Brantly, Bros. J. P. Russell, W. F. England, W. H. Stiner, David White, A. J. Sharp, Elder M. B. Weaver	19	25							15.65	May
Black Fox	Bro. John Silbord, Roy Bailey, John Bundon, J. M. Davis, Sam Davis, Sam Cook	1	1	1		1	6	285	2	3.30	Jun
Pleasant Hill	Elder J. M. Wilder, W. A. Moyers, Bros. Loncoln Edwards, James Edwards	1	1					104			Jun
Davis Chapel	Elders Leonard White, Albert Davis, J. F. Lynch, Bro. Thomas Brantly		1				1	65	4	4.00	Jun
Gibson Station	Elder H. A. Shaffner		4			3		140	3	3.00	Jun
Red Hill	Bros. Mose Treece, Harry Patterson, Sis. Arlie Treece	7					1	81	1	2.00	Jun
Pleasant Point	Elders V. H. Graves, John F. Keck, Bros. A. C. Goin, J. W. Keck, J. E. Heath, C. D. Keck, Sis. Etta Hopper, Etta Keck, Myrtle Keck, Letha Heath, Alice Heath		3					86	2	3.00	July
New Hebron	Letter, but no messenger		1				1	134	1	4.00	July
Rocky Dale	Bros. Orvil Graves, Dewey Graves, M. C. Dunn, Sis. Caroline Graves						1	34	2	1.00	M.S
			3					70	3	3.00	Jun

$22.50 for Printing Minutes

319

MINUTES

——OF THE——

ONE HUNDRED AND NINETEENTH
ANNUAL SESSION

OF THE

POWELLS VALLEY
ASSOCIATION

——OF——

PRIMITIVE BAPTISTS

Held with the Church at

PLEASANT HILL, CLAIBORNE COUNTY, TENN.

AUGUST 19, 20, 21, 1938

Next Session will be held with the Church at Black Fox, Grainger County, Tennessee. Situated 10 miles Northeast of Maynardville and 4 miles West of Liberty Hill, on the Norris Lake. To commence on Friday before the Third Saturday in August 1939

Elder Henry Comer to preach the Introductory Sermon and Elder John F. Keck to be his alternate.

FRIDAY'S PROCEEDINGS

1st—According to previous arrangements the Association met pursuant to adjournment.

2nd—Praise by Elder M. B. Weaver.

3rd—Prayer by Elder T. J. Pierce.

4th—The Introductory Sermon was delivered by Elder V. H. Graves from text, stand, etc.

5th—Followed by Elder T. G. Brantley.

6th—After 15 minutes intermission the Association then proceeded to organize for transaction of business by electing Elder Albert Davis, Moderator and re-electing Brother Sam Davis, Clerk and Brother Jim Edwards, Assistant Clerk.

7th—Prayer by Elder Jim Abbott.

8th—Called for letters from Sister Churches of this Association. Received 8 which were read and on motion were received and the delegates welcomed to seats.

9th—Called for newly constituted Churches and received one from Braden's Chapel which was read and on motion was approved and the delegates welcomed to seats by the Moderator, giving them the right hand of fellowship.

10th—Called for Corresponding Letters from Sister Associations and received one with Minutes and Messengers from the Hiwassee. Messengers to-wit: Elders J. J. Abbott, C. C. Oliver, D. J. Abbott, Frank Norton, James Shelton and wife Calorina Shelton, Elder W. R. Gates and J. J. Kirkland.

11th—By motion said messengers were received and welcomed to seats. The Moderator giving them the right hand of fellowship.

12th—Called for members of this Association who were not delegates and received none.

13th—On motion we take the run of last years minutes so long as it don't conflict with the business of this Association.

14th—Motion in order that the Moderator appoint the following committees:

(a)—On Preaching—Brothers J. L. Drummonds, Neal Lambert, M. W. Edmondson, together with this Church.

(b)—On Arrangements—Brothers M. C. Dunn. Sam R. Cook. Verlin Edwards.

(c)—On Correspondence—Elders Henry Comer, M. B. Weaver. John Ausmus.

(d)—On Request—Elders V .H. Graves, J. M. Wilder, Brother Wily Treece.

(e)—On Finance—Brothers Brice Braden, Jim Brantley, John Graves.

15th—Called for the report of the committee on Preaching:

—2—

(a)—We your committee on Preaching beg leave to make the following report:Friday night at Church, Elders M. B. Weaver, C. C. Oliver. Saturday 10 a. m. at Church, Elders Oscar Moyers, W. R. Gates. Saturday evening at Church, Elders T. G. Brantley, James Abbott. At Mrs. Harrells, Elder M. B. Weaver, Henry Comer, Carl McCarty. At Brother Graves, Elders Dan Abbott, Frank Norton. Saturday night at Church, Elders Dan Abbott, J. J. Kirkland. Sunday at the Church, Elders Frank Norton, Leonard White, Moderator to close. At Davis Creek Church House, Elders V. H. Graves, C. C. Oliver.

J. L. DRUMMONDS

NEAL LAMBERT

WALKER EDMONDSON

14th—By motion the report was received and the committee discharged.

15th—Motion in order to adjourn until 9:30 a. m. Saturday.

SATURDAY'S PROCEEDINGS

1st—Saturday morning at 9:30 the Association met persuant to adjournment. After singing by the congregation and prayer by Elder John F. Keck, the Association was announced in order for business by the Moderator.

2nd—Called for newly constituted Churches that failed to get in Friday and received one from Beach Fork which was read, approved and the delegation was welcomed in our body by the Moderator giving them the right hand of fellowship with us.

3rd—Called for letters of Sister Churches of this Association that failed to get in Friday and received two which were read and on motion were received with the delegates being welcomed to seats with us.

4th—Called for the report of the Committee on Arrangements:

(b)—We your committee on Arrangements beg leave to make the following report:

1st—Call the Roll

2nd—Call for the report on Preaching.

3rd—On Correspondence.

4th—On Request.

5th—On Finance.

6th—When and where shall our next Association be held? Who shall preach the Introductory Sermon and who shall be his alternate.

7th—How many copies of Minutes shall we have printed and who shall superintend the printing and distribution of same? And

—3—

what shall he be allowed for his service?

Respectfully submitted,

M. C. DUNN

SAM R. COOK

VERLIN EDWARDS

8th—On motion the report was received and the committee discharged.

9th—The Roll was called and erased the names of absentees.

(c)—Called for the report of the committee on Requests.

9th—We your committee on Request beg leave to report the following: That we have all the Obituaries printed in our Minutes that the Churches furnish. That the next Annual Session of the Powell's Valley Association be held with the Church at Black Fox, Grainger County, Tennessee, to commence on Friday before the Third Saturday in August, 1939.

Respectfully submitted

ELDER V. H. GRAVES

BROTHER WILY TREECE

ELDER J. M. WILDER

10th—By motion the said report was received and the committee discharged.

11th—Called for the report of the committee on Correspondence.

(d)—We your committee on Correspondence beg leave to make the following report: That we send Messengers and Minutes to the Hiwassee Association when convened with the Church at Mt. Zion, Morgan County, Tennessee, to commence on Friday before the Fourth Saturday in September, 1938.

Respectfully submitted,

ELDERS M. B. WEAVER

HENRY COMER

JOHN AUSMUS

12th—By motion the report was received and the committee discharged.

13th—Called for the report of the committee on Finance.

(e)—We your committee on Finance beg leave to report the following received from Sister Churches for printing Minutes $30.95.

Respectfully submitted,

BROTHERS BRICE BRADEN

JOHN GRAVES

JAMES BRANTLEY

14th—By motion said report was received and committee discharged.

15th—Called for the Financial report of the Clerk who reported the amount in his hands from last years total was $4.70.

—4—

323

16th—By motion said report was received.

17th—Motion in order that the next Annual Session of Powell's Valley Association be held with the Church at Black Fox, Grainger County, Tennessee to commence on Friday before the Third Saturday in August, 1939 That Elder Henry Comer preach the Introductory Sermon and that Elder John F. Keck be his alternate.

18th—Motion in order that we have 800 copies of Minutes printed and that the Clerk Superintend the printing and distribution of same and that he be allowed $10.00 for his services.

19th—Motion in order that we send the following named delegates to the Hiwassee Association to-wit: Elders Leonard White, M. B. Weaver, Henry Coomer.

20th—Motion in order that we send an Investigating Committee to the Laurel River Association to-wit: Elders V. H. Graves, Henry Comer, Leonard White.

21st—Motion in order that Elder M. B. Weaver write a Corresponding Letter to the Hiwassee Association and that the same be inserted in our Minutes.

22nd—By motion be it resolved that we tender our heart felt thanks to this dear old Church and the surrounding community for their hospitality and kind treatment to us throughout this Association.

23rd—Motion in order to adjourn until 10 o'clock at the time and place above stated.

24th—Dismissed in order.

ELDER ABLERT DAVIS, Moderator
Speedwell, Tenn.
SAM DAVIS, Clerk
Luttrell. Tenn.

SUNDAY'S PROCEEDINGS

At the appointed hour Sunday a large crowd assembled at the place appointed and listened attentively to the well delivered Sermons of Elder Leonard White and Elder Frank Norton at the Church House, from the text, "If you do these things you shall never fall." At Davis Creek Church House by Elder V. H. Graves from text "He has redeemed us unto God out of every nation, kindred, tongue and people, etc." Followed by Elder C. C. Oliver, all of which was delivered in the most loving spirit and with the greatest interest to all and a loving parting was expressed.

CORRESPONDING LETTER

We the Powell's Valley Association of Primitive Baptists to our Sister Association, to-wit: The Hiwassee, with whom we Correspond, Greetings: We are asking to still keep up our long Christian Correspondence with you, and send these Elders, to-wit: M. B. Weaver, Henry Comer, Leonard White, our Messengers to your next Annual

—5—

Meeting to be held with the Church at Mt. Zion, Morgan County, Tenn., to commence on Friday before the Fourth Saturday in September 1938. We received your Messengers with gladness and feel that we were greatly benefitted by their coming. Please come again to our next meeting to be held with the Church at Black Fox, Grainger County, Tennessee, on Friday before the Third Saturday in August 1939. From your little Sister in Gospel Bonds.

ELDER M. B. WEAVER

OBITUARIES

T. C. Keck

T. C. Keck was born August 29, 1862. Died Feb. 9, 1938. He was married to Malinda Francisco in 1882. To this union three children were born. His wife and one child preceeded him to the grave. He was again united in marriage, this time to Katy Hopper. And to this union seven children were born. One child preceeded him to the grave. He professed faith in Christ at an early age and joined the Primitive Baptist Church at Pleasant Point in December 1889. He was ordained as a Deacon of the Church in 1920 and was serving as Deacon at his death. He was so efficient in his Church duties that we believe the words spoken in a parable by the Master might well be applied to him, that is: "Well done, good and faithful servant; thou hast been faithful over a few things, I will make thee ruler over many things: enter thou into the joy of thy Lord." During his brief illness he suffered untold agonies but bore it patiently, and begged the family not to mourn his departure. Said it only meant rest for him. Funeral services were held at Pleasant Point Church by Elders V. H. Graves, J. F. and Esau Keck. Burial in the Pleasant Point Cemetery.

Brother T. J. Drummonds

Our beloved father, T. J. Drummonds, was born Sept. 14, 1862 and departed this life April 9, 1938 at 1:00 P. M., being 76 years, 6 months and 25 days old. He was united in marriage to Jane Treece. To this union was born seven children, four sons and three daughters. Three sons preceeded him to the Glory Land years ago. He is survived by his wife, Mrs. Jane Treece Drummonds, 4 children, Clarence Drummonds, Mrs. Burnice Welch, Mrs. Veltie Muncey, all of New Tazewell and Mrs. May Robertson of Middlesboro. Twenty-six grandchildren and 2 great-grandchildren and a large number of other relatives. He was preceeded to the Great Beyond by four brothers and two sisters. He professed faith in Christ several years ago and later joined the Primitive Baptist Church in October 1910 and was baptised September 13, 1932 at Meyers Grove and was baptised by Elder T. G. Brantley. The family has lost a loving father and husband and the Church a faithful member. He will be greatly missed by all who knew him.

There is no death the stars go down
To rise upon some fairer shore
And bright in Heaven's jeweled crown

—9—

They shine for ever more.

We can only say farewell father, but not forever.

P. S.—At the first of his sickness he said to his nephew, J. L. Drummonds, that he was going home, that he saw his father, mother, brothers and sisters and children, and asked his nephew J. L. Drummonds if he couldn't see them too and asked him if he didn't want to go home with him. Funeral service were conducted by T. G. Brantley and D. P. Denton. Burial in family cemetery.

Sister Mary Hurst

Obituary of my loving Mother, Sister Mary Hurst, daughter of Squire and Joe Anna Hurst. She was born Sept. 14, 1843, departed this life Jan. 18, 1938, being 94 years and 4 months old. She was married to Richard Wilson in the year about 1860. To this union was born thirteen children of which eight have preceeded her to the grave. Her husband died in the year 1900. She was later married to J. C. Cook in 1904, who died in the year 1936. She joined the Primitive Baptist Church at an early age and later moved her membership to Meyers Grove and lived a faithful member until death. She is survived by five children, three boys and two girls who are as follows: Martha Robins, John Wilson, and Richard Wilson all of Middlesboro, Ky., and Margarette Drummonds of New Tazewell and Garfield Wilson of Rose Hill, Va. She died at the home of her daughter, Mrs. E. S. Drummonds. Funeral services were conducted by Elder S. S. Wilson and Erastus Patterson. She was laid to rest in the Palmer Cemetery.

A loved one from us is gone
A voice from us is still
A chair in our home is vacant
Which never can be filled

We thank the many friends and loved ones for the kindness shown to us during the sickness and death of locing mother and grandmother.—A daughter, Margarette Drummonds.

Mrs. Mary Cain Braden

Mrs. Mary Cain Braden was born June 17, 1884 and departed this life March 12, 1938, being 53 years, 9 months, 5 days old. Professed a hope in Christ at an early age and joined the Primitive Baptist Church at Strait Branch. Lived a devoted life and a loving mother. She was married to John Braden Dec. 24, 1904. To this union was born 12 children, 7 girls and 5 boys, 1 deceased. She leaves to mourn her a husband, 11 children, 2 sisters, and 1 brother

—10—

and 12 grandchildren and a host of friends and relatives. Our loss is her gain. She will be greatly missed by her friends and family and the church.

Mother is gone from toil and sadness, to a land of joy and peace. She is safe in the arms of Jesus where her pleasure never ceases. She has joined the bright angels there to live in endless days. We will meet you precious mother, where the toils of life have passed away.—The Family.

Barttons Ellison

Barttons Ellison was born Sept. 3, 1857 and died May 23, 1938, age 81 years, 8 months and 20 days. She was married to Robert Ellison about 63 years ago and to this union was born 9 children, 4 girls and 5 boys. Six survive her, 42 grandchildren and 53 great-grandchildren. She professed faith in Christ about 40 years ago and joined the Church at Mossy Springs about 27 years ago and remained there until death. She said she did not dread death and was ready to go. She leaves a host of friends and relatives to mourn her loss. But our loss is Heaven's gain. The funeral service was conducted by Elder T. G. Brantley and she was laid to rest in Oak Grove Cemetery to await the Resurrection Morn.

David White

David White was born May 8, 1853, died December 17, 1937 age 84 years, 7 months and 14 days. Was married to Sarah Bourff Feb. 19, 1871. To this union was born 7 children, 4 girls and 3 boys, who all survive him except one little girl which was taken away in infancy. He had 43 grandchildren and 61 great-grandchildren and 2 great-great-grandchildren. He professed faith in Christ about 68 years ago, joined the Church at Cave Springs in 1872 where his membership remained until about 30 years ago then removed to Oak Grove where he remained until death. He served as Church Clerk for 29 years and always filled his seat just as long as he was able to attend. He is missed at Church and at home for he was a good man and loved by all who knew him and was a loving good father to his children. He leaves 6 children, grand children, and great-grandchildren and a host of friends to mourn his loss but we believe our loss is Heaven's gain. The funeral service was conducted by Elder T. G. Brantley and was laid to rest in Oak Grove Cemetery to rest till the Resurrection Morn.

—11—

Jefferson Treece

Jefferson Treece was born Jan. 16, 1856, departed this life March 23, 1938. He was a faithful member of the Church for many years. Was Church Clerk 45 years. He leaves to mourn his loss his wife Narcissis Treece, eleven children and a host of grandchildren.

> From us a loved one is gone,
> A voice we loved is stilled,
> This leaves a vacant chair in our home,
> That never can be filled.

Sister Sarah C. Hamilton Perry

Sister Sarah C. Hamilton Perry, wife of W. M. Perry was born July 10, 1871 and died May 19, 1938. She professed faith in Christ at an early age and joined the Primitive Baptist Church at Black Fox. Sister Sarah will be missed by relatives and friends. She lived a faithful member until death. We feel her departure of this life was her eternal gain.

Sister Nancy Shoffner

Sister Nancy Shoffner was born in the year 1860. She professed faith in Christ in early life and joined the Church at Oak Grove years ago from which she got a letter of dismissal and joined at Black Fox by letter March 4th Saturday, 1932 where she lived a faithful member until God called her to her reward, July 25, 1938, making her stay on earth 78 years. Sister Shoffner will be greatly missed by the Church and all who knew her. The Church feels they have lost a mother in Israel, but we hope our loss is her eternal gain.

MINISTERIAL ROLL

Elders		Post Offices
John Ausmus	....	Speedwell, Claiborne County, Tennessee
T. G. Brantley	....	Sharps Shapel, Union County, Tennessee
Alfred Boruff	....	Maynardville, Union County, Tennessee
Henry Comer	....	LaFollette, Campbell County, Tennessee
E. S. Drummonds	......	New Tazewell, Claiborne County, Tennessee
Albert Davis	....	Speedwell, Claiborne County, Tennessee
V. H. Graves	....	Jamestown, Fentress County, Tennessee
John F. Keek	....	Goin, Claiborne County, Tennessee
W. A. Moyers	....	Speedwell, Claiborne County, Tennessee
George Mays	....	Goin, Claiborne County, Tennessee
Matthew Oliver	....	Noeton, Grainger County, Tennessee
T. J. Pierce	....	Sweedwell, Claiborne County, Tennessee
Alfred Parks	....	New Market, Jefferson County, Tennessee
H. A. Shaffner	....	Harrogate, Claiborne County, Tennessee
Leonard White	....	LaFollette, Campbell County, Tennessee
Carl McCarty	....	Speedwell, Claiborne County, Tennessee
Milton Brantley	....	Sharps Chapel, Union County, Tennessee
J. M. Wilder	....	Speedwell, Claiborne County, Tennessee

LICENTIATES

Jim Collins	....	New Market, Jefferson County, Tennessee
J. C. Cosby	....	Gibson Station, Lee County, Virginia
W. R. Petree	....	Sharps Chapel, Union County, Tennessee
Charlie Stanifer	....	New Tazewell, Claiborne County, Tennessee
J. C. Bolin	....	Tazewell, Claiborne County, Tennessee
Sam Miller	....	New Market, Jefferson County, Tennessee

--13--

CHURCHES	COUNTIES	PASTORS	CLERKS	CLERK'S POST OFFICE
Red Hill	Claiborne	T. G. Brantley	Moses Treece	...... Speedwell, Tennessee
Gibson Station .	Claiborne	Matthew Oliver	Mary Ball	...... Gibson Station, Virginia
Oak Grove	Union	T. G. Brantley	R. P. Bridges	... Sharps Chapel, Tennessee
Rocky Dale	Knox	T. G. Brantley	M. C. Dunn	.... Corryton, Tennessee
Cedar Springs .	Claiborne	Matthew Oliver	J. L. Drummonds .	... New Tazewell, Tennessee
Black Fox	Grainger	Matthew Oliver	Sam Davis	.... Luttrell, Tennessee
Pleasant Point .	Claiborne	V. H. Graves	Estell Heath	.... Goin, Tennessee
Davis Chapel ..	Campbell	Leonard White	O. R. Parrott	.... LaFollette, Tennessee
Capps Creek ...	Union	John F. Keck	Froney Vaughn ...	.... Goin, Tennessee
Pleasant Hill ..	Claiborne	John Ausmus	Lincoln Edwards .	.... Speedwell, Tennessee
New Hebron ...	Jefferson	Henry Comer	Cordelia Mitchell .	...... New Market, Tennessee
Noeton	Grainger	Matthew Oliver	J. C. Oliver	... Leas Springs, Tennessee
Black Fork	Roane	W. R. Gates	Jessie Sweat	.... Wartburg, Tennessee
Bradens Chapel .	Union	Henry Comer	Lucy Sparks	.... Speedwell, Tennessee

CHURCHES	NAMES OF DELEGATES	Rec. by Expr. Baptism	Rec. by Letter	Restored	Dismissed by Letter	Excluded	Deceased	Total Membership	Saturday Meetings	Contribution	Communion Meetings
Beech Fork	Jessie Kivett, Will White, Jim Kivett, Sallie Kivett ..		2					11	3	1.00	
Cedar Springs	J. L. Drummonds, S. V. Drummonds, Horace White, Sister Della Drummonds, Velma Drummonds, Thelma Mayers	4					2	89	4	1.75	May
Capps Creek	Charlie Collins, Sister Malinda Paul	2						45	3	1.00	M. S
Norton	No Letter — Come On		15	2		3	3	280	1	7.40	May
Oak Grove	Elders T. G. Brantley, M. B. Weaver, Bro. John Graves	2			2		2	100	2	2.60	June
Plack Fox	Brothers Sam R. Cook, Sam Davis										
Pleasant Hill	Elders John Ausmus, J. M. Wilder, W. A. Moyers, T. J. Pierce, Brother Lincoln Edwards, Neal Lambert, James Edwards	2	2	2		2		67	4	4.00	June
Davis Chapel	Elders Leonard White, Albert Davis, Henry Comer, Brothers Tom Brantley, J. F. Lynch, Charlie Smith	10	3			3			3	3.15	June
Gibson Station	Brother Henry Hoskins	5			1	2		84	1	11.00	June
Red Hill	Brothers James Brantley, Mose Treece, Albert Treece,							154			
Pleasant Point	Harry Patterson	2					1	86	2	2.00	July
New Hebron	Elders V. H. Graves, J. F. Keck, Bro. Estell Heath ...						2	132	14	14.00	July
Rocky Dale	No Letter — Come On							34	2		M.S.
Bradens Chapel	Orvil Graves, Dewey Graves, M. C. Dunn, Oris Braden, Brice Braden	2						72	4	2.50	June
								16	1	1.25	

MINUTES

——OF THE——

ONE HUNDRED AND TWENTIETH
ANNUAL SESSION

OF THE

POWELLS VALLEY
ASSOCIATION

——OF——

PRIMITIVE BAPTISTS

Held with the Church at

BLACK FOX, GRAINGER COUNTY, TENN.

AUGUST 18, 19, 20, 1939

Next Session will be held with the Church at Pleasant Point, Claiborne County, Tenn. To commence on Friday before the Third Saturday in August, 1940.

Elder M. B. Weaver to Preach the Introductory Sermon and Elder Matthew Oliver to be his alternate.

FRIDAY'S PROCEEDINGS

1st—According to previous arrangements the Association met persuant to adjournment.

2nd—Praise by Elder Albert Davis.

3rd—Prayer by Elder Matthew Oliver.

4th—The Introductory Sermon was delivered by Elder Henry Comer, from 1st chapter and 9th verse of Romans. Text for God is my witness, etc.

5th—After fifteen minutes intermission at the sound of singing the Association reassembled and proceeded to organize for the transaction of business by reelecting Elder Albert Davis Moderator and reelecting Brother Sam Davis, Clerk and Brother J. L. Drummonds Assistant Clerk.

6th—Prayer by Elder V. H. Graves.

7th—Called for letters from Sister Churches of this Association. Received 9 which were read by the Clerks.

8th—Motion in order that all the letters be received with their delegates. Motion carried and the delegates were welcomed to seats by the Moderator.

9th—Motion in order that we take the run of last years minutes so long as it does not conflict with the Business of the Association. Motion carried.

10th—Called for Corresponding Letters from Sister Associations and received Minutes and Messengers from the Hiwassee Association. Messengers to-wit: Elders C. C. Oliver and D. J. Abbott.

11th—On Motion said Messengers were received and welcomed to seats with us. Received Messengers from the Nolachucky Association to-wit: Elder Lawson Philips.

12th—By Motion said Delegate was welcomed to a seat.

13th—Called for newly constituted Churches and received none.

14th—Called for members of Corresponding Associations who were not delegates and received two from Hiwassee, to-wit: Brothers M. C. Cole and C. C. Cooper.

15th—On Motion said members were welcomed to seats.

16th—Called for members of our Association who were not delegates and received none.

14th—On Motion the Moderator appointed all the Committees:

(a)—On Preaching—Brothers Brice Braden, Silas Drummonds, James Brantley, together with the Church.

(b)—On Arrangements—Brothers C. M. Cabbage, J. C. Oliver, S. R. Cook.

(c)—On Correspondence—Elders E. S. Drummonds, Alfred Boruff, Henry Comer.

(d)—On Request—Elders V. H. Graves, Matthew Oliver, Broth-

—2—

ei Harry Patterson.

(d)—On Finance—Brother Harry Stiner, Henry Hoskins, John Weaver.

18th—Called for the report of the committee on Preaching:

(a)—We your committee on Preaching beg leave to report the following: Friday night at Church. Elders M. B. Weaver and Dan Abbott. Saturday at the Stand, Elders V. H. Graves from 8th chapter and 1st verse of Hebrews. Elders Lawson Phillips from 13th chapter and 1st verse of Hebrews followed by Elder Elfred Boruff and Elder F. S. Drummonds. Saturday night at the Church Elder John F. Keck, Elder C. C. Oliver, Elder Oscar Moyers. Saturday night at Pennington's Chapel, Elders E. S. Drummonds, Elder Charley Redmond, Elder Henry Comer. At Bhotre Muncey's, Elder Albert Davis, Elder Henry Comer. Saturday at Stand, Elder U. J. Hembree, Elder Dan Abbott, Elder Matthew Oliver to close.

JAMES BRANTLEY
BRICE BRADEN
SILAS DRUMMONDS
Together with the Church.

19th—By Motion the report was received and the committee discharged.

20th—Motion in order to adjourn until 9:30 Saturday morning.

SATURDAY'S PROCEEDINGS

Saturday morning at 9:30 a. m. the Association met persuant to adjournment. After singing and the reading of the 1st chapter of Romans by the Moderator and prayer by Elder M. B. Weaver the Association was announced in order for Business by the Moderator.

1st—Called for letter that failed to get in Friday and received 2 which were read and on motion were received and the delegates welcomed to seats with us.

2nd—Called for the report of the committee on Arrangements:

(b)—We your committee on Arrangements beg leave to submit the following report:

1st—Call the Roll.
2nd—Call for the report on Preaching.
3rd—On Correspondence.
4th—On Request.
5th—On Finance.
6th—When and where shall our next Association be held. Who shall preach the Introductory Sermon and who shall be his alternate.

7th—How many copies of Minutes shall we have printed? Who shall superintend the printing and distribution of same and what

—3—

335

shall be he allowed for his services?

Respectfully submitted,

S. R. COOK

J. C. OLIVER

C. M. CABBAGE

3rd—On motion the report was received and committee dismissed.

4th—Called the Roll and erased the names of absentees.

5th—Called for members of Sister Churches who were not delegates that failed to get in Friday. Received one from Oak Grove Church, to-wit: Elder T. G. Brantley. Received one from Blackfox, to-wit: Bro. John Bundon. Received one from Cedar Springs, to-wit: S. W. Drummonds.

6th—Called for the report of the committee on Correspondence:

(c)—We your committee on Corrspondence beg leave to submit the following: That we send letters and Messengers to the Hiwassee Association and that we make an effort to revive our previous Correspondence with the Nolachucky Association by sending letters and messengers by the request of Elder Lawson Philipps of the Nolachucky Association.

Respectfully submitted,

ELDER M. B. WEAVER

ELDER HENRY COMER

ELDER E. S. DRUMMONDS.

7th—On motion report was received and discharged the committee.

8th—Called for the report of the committee on Request:

(d)—We your committee on Request beg leave to submit the following report: That we have all the Obituaries printed in our Minutes that the Churches furnish. That the next Annual Session of the Powells Valley Association be held with the Church at Pleasant Point, Claiborne County, Tennessee, to commence on Friday before the third Saturday in August, 1940.

Respectfully submitted,

ELDER V. H. GRAVES

ELDER MATTHEW OLIVER

BROTHER HARRY PATTERSON

9th—By motion the report received and the committee discharged.

10th—Called for the report of the committee on Finance.

(e)—We your committee on Finance beg leave to make the following report: Received for printing Minutes from Churches: Cedar Springs $2.95. Noeton $1.50. Oakgrove $5.20. Davis Chapel $3.00. Pleasant Point $5.00. Braden's Chapel $1.00. Black Fox $3.00. Red Hill $1.00. Pleasant Hill $5.00. Rocky Dale $2.25. Gibson's Station $1.50. In hand from last year $2.65. Total $33.60.

Respectfully submitted,

—4—

BROTHER JOHN R. WEAVER
BROTHER HENRY HOSKINS
BROTHER HENRY STINER

11th—On motion report received and the committee discharged.

12th—Called for the Financial report of the Clerk who reported $2.65 from last year.

13th—By motion said report was received.

14th—On motion that the Clerk carry balance over until next year.

15th—On motion the next Annual Session of the Powells Valley Association be held with the Church at Pleasant Point, Claiborne County, Tennessee, to commence on Friday before the third Saturday in August, 1940. That Elder M. B. Weaver preach the Introductory Sermon and that Elder Matthew Oliver be his alternate.

16th—Motion in order that we have 800 copies of Minutes printed. That the Clerk superintend the printing and distribution of same and that he be allowed $10.00 for his services.

17th—Motion in order that we send letters and messengers to the Hiwassee Association, to-wit: Elders Henry Comer, Leonard White, and M. B. Weaver.

18th—Motion in order that Elder M. B. Weaver and Brother J. L. Drummonds write a corresponding letter to the Hiwassee Association and that the same be inserted in our Minutes.

19th—By motion be it resolved that we tender our heartfelt thanks to this dear old Church and the surrounding community for their hospitality and kind treatment throughout this Association.

20th—Motion in order to adjourn until 10 o'clock at the time and place above stated.

21st—Dismissed in order.

ELDER ALBERT DAVIS, Moderator
Post Office, Speedwell, Tenn.
SAM DAVIS, Clerk
Post Office, Luttrell, Tenn.
J. L. DRUMMONDS, Asst. Clerk
Post Office, New Tazewell, Tenn.

SUNDAY'S PROCEEDINGS

At the appointed hour Sunday a large crowd gathered at the altar and attentively listened to the well delivered Sermons of Elder U. J. Hembree from text quotation When you are tempted of evil think not of God, etc. Followed by Elder Dan Abbott and Elder Matthew Oliver. All of which was delivered in the most loving spirit and with the greatest interest to all. And a loving parting was expressed.

CORRESPONDING LETTER

We the Powells Valley Association of Primitive Baptist now in

—5—

337

Session with the Black Fox Church on August 18, 19, 20, 1939, to our Sister Association to-wit: The Hiwassee with whom we correspond, and with who we hope to revive our previous correspondence, Very dear brother in the Lord. We are sending you this letter by the hand of our messengers whom we hope you wil receive into your confidence and Christian fellowship. We are happy to acknowledge the presence of your messengers now seated among us in this conference and will be pleased to your intelligence next year when we meet with the Church next year on Friday before the third Saturday in August, 1940. Wishing you a long and happy life we remain your little sister in loving cooperation. Written by Elder M. B. Weaver and Brother J. L. Drummonds.

6

OBITUARIES

James R. Brantley

James R. Brantley was born March 27, 1882 and died December 27, 1938. Was married to Marie Brewer. To this union was born five children and later was married to Wanda Harrell, May 28, 1911. To this union was born one child. He professed faith in Christ in his early days and joined the Primitive Baptist Church at Cave Springs and was ordained Deacon of this Church and later moved his membership to Oak Grove and there lived a faithful life until death. In his sickness he often spoke of a better home. He died away and was brought back too. Then he told his companion Wanda you have made the greatest mistake you ever made in your life. He said if you could have seen the beauty I did when I was leaving this world the way is clear before me. I'm not afraid to die. He leaves to mourn his loss his companion and four children, thirteen grandchildren, four brothers, one sister, a host of friends and relatives. But we feel our loss is his eternal gain. A loving one from us is gone; The voice we love is still; A place is vacant! in our home, That never can be filled. Written by his wife, Wanda Brantley.

Sterlin Allen

Brother Sterlin Allen died December 13, 1938, being about 78 years old. He leaves to mourn his loss two children, Levie Hopson and Dan Allen and four grandchildren, three sisters. He professed faith in Christ about one year before his death. His desire was to join the Church at Meyers Grove but God saw fit to call him home before he had an opportunity. He told his daughter he had a better home waiting for him not to worry after him. He is gone but not forgotten. Home is made sad but heaven in made brighter.

Isabell Stanifer

Isabell Stanifer was born December 2, 1891, died April 11, 1939, being 47 years old. Was married to Charlie Stanifer about 1909. To this union was born 10 children, four boys, Jimmie, Georgie, Johnnie, Grover Stanifer and six girls, Lottie Earl, Pearlie Irwin, Elivee Robertson, Myree, Edith, and Ruby Stanifer. She joined the Primitive Baptist Church at Meyers Grove the 4th Saturday, 1909. She and her husband were ordained deacons, Oct. 26, 1913. Later on moved her membership to Red Hill and lived a faithful member until God saw fit to call her away. She also leaves father and mother, W. F. and Mary Robertson and four brothers, Charlie, Mannie, Oscar

and Chester Robertson and five sisters, Jasaphine Cupp, New Tazewell, Annie Earl and May Wright of Speedwell, Eva Manning, Vista
Treece and a host of friends and relatives to mourn her passing. From
us a sister is gone, A voice from us is stilled, And a vacant place in
our home, That never can be filled. Funeral services were conducted
by Elder T. G. Brantley and John Treece.

Elder Hiram Shaffner

Elder Hiram Shaffner was born May 4, 1856, died Feb. 5,
1939, making his stay on earth 83 years Profesed faith in Christ at
the age of 16 years. Joined the Primitive Baptist Church and lived a
faithful member until death. He is missed by his wife and children
and a host of friends and relatives. Ordained a deacon in the year of
1902 then in 1904 was ordained to the full work of the ministry.
Stood for the faith once delivered to the Saints. Brother Shaffner
believed in the unseen God and received many visions from the Lord.
He has gone to get his reward and we hope to meet him some sweet
day where the Saints of the most high live forever and forever. May
God bless his family and his Church is the prayer of your brother in
hope. Written by Elder T. G. Brantley.

Ham Shipley

Brother Ham Shipley was born about the year 1872. Professed
faith in Christ at an early age and joined the Primitive Baptist
Church when a young man and later moved his membership to Pleasant Point Church and lived a faithful member until God called him to
his reward March 5, 1939. We believe our loss is his eternal gain.
He will be missed by his Church and relatives and loved ones.

Sister Mary Luiza Boruff McCarty

Sister Mary Luiza Boruff McCarty was born Jan. 8, 1870, being
69 years, 5 months and 1 day old. She was married to Joushia L.
McCarty in 1888. To this union was born 8 children, one of which
preceded her in death. She has 26 grandchildren and 1 great grandchild. Her husband preceded her in death eleven months ago. Early
in her girlhood days she was saved in Christ and joined the Primitive
Baptist Church at Cave Springs, Union County, Tenn., and continued
there throughout her entire life. Sister McCarty's friends were numbered by her acquaintances, for she always had a kind word and lovely smiles for everyone. Not only will she be missed by her children
and loved ones but her death is a great loss to the whole community
in which she lived and also in Tennessee. We hope our loss is heav-

—10—

en's gain and that we will be reunited in the sweet bye and bye. She is gone from earths told and sadness to that home of joy and gladness. There with the bright angels safe in every way will be. Oh we miss her in our homes, along our ways. But soon from here we soon will be leaving to join her in endless days. Written by Elder Henry Comer.

Berry White

Berry White departed this life June 8, 1939, at the age of 69. He professed faith in Christ in early life and joined the Primitive Baptist Church at Mossy Springs and remained a member of same throughout the life of the Church which was lost in the construction of Norris Dam. To know Berry intimately meant to love him sincerely.

Sherman Ballard

Brother Sherman Ballard departed this life in the early part of 1939. He professed faith in Christ early in life and joined the Missionary Baptist and later in life he joined the Primitive Baptist at Davis Chapel and remained faithful until death. Gone but not forgotten.

James F. Lynch

Brother James F. Lynch was born Nov. 21, 1876 and died July 16, 1939. He was married to Cordelia Spangler Jan. 19, 1896. To this union was born eleven children. He professed faith in Christ early in life and united with the Church at Cave Spring in 1909, and later moved his membership to Davis Chapel where he remained a loyal member until death. Brother Lynch was dearly loved by all who knew him. Three vacant seats are left. One in the home, one in the Church and one in the car of his pastor. Aside from his family he is missed most by his unworthy pastor Leonard White.

William Brantley

Brother William Brantley was born May 15, 1868, departed this life June 6, 1939. He was married to Tilda Ellison, Dec. 3, 1882. To this union was born four children. In the year 1892 he was married to Hazie C. Boruff. He was married to Maryjane Creech, February 14, 1915. He married Mrs. Sarah Young May 13, 1933. He professed faith in Christ in early life and joined the Church at Cave Spring, and later was ordained a deacon. Later moved his membership to Strait Branch as one of the charter members, then in constitution Braden's

—11—

Chapel Church June 1938 in which he lived a faithful member until death. He is greatly missed by all who knew him and by his Church. But we hope our loss is his eternal gain. His body was laid to rest in Braden's Cemetery to await the resurrection morn. Funeral was conducted by Elder Leonard White. Gone but not forgotten. The Church.

Babara Elison Boruff

Barbara Elison, wife of Elder Alfred Boruff, age 62 years, joined the Primitive Baptist Church at Black Fox about 35 years ago of which she lived a faithful member until her death which occurred Oct. 1938. She leaves to mourn their loss husband, three children, the Church, and a host of relatives and friends. Gone but not forgotten.

Mary Louise McCarty

Mary Louis McCarty was born Jan. 8, 1870 and died June 9, 1939. She was married to Joshua McCarty in 1888. To this union 8 children were born. One of them preceded her in death. She is also survived by 26 grandchildren and one great grand child. She professed hope in Christ early in life and joined the Primitive Baptist Church of Christ at Cave Spring and remained a faithful member until death. From us a mother has gone, A voice we loved is stilled, A place is vacant in our home that never can be filled. By her son Carl and Leonard White a former pastor.

Elder J. M. Wilder

Elder J. M. Wilder was born March 24, 1882 and died May 6, 1939. He was 57 years, 1 month and 12 days old. Married to Adeline Ausmus June 13, 1903. To this union was born 6 children, 5 girls and one boy. All survive him. He leaves to mourn his loss his companion, 6 children, 1 sister, 2 brothers and a whole host of relatives and friends. He will be greatly missed by all who knew him, especially his family and Church. He professed a hope in Christ at an early age and joined the Primitive Baptist Church at Pleasant Hill and was baptised by Elder Leonard White. He was ordained to the full work of the ministry the 4th Saturday in November 1934. He was a firm believer in the Baptist doctrine and had a great power in the Church Through all his sickness he bore it patiently and without complaint and often spoke of his home in heaven. He was Moderator of the Moyer's Grove Church at his death. Funeral services were conducted at his Church by Elder Albert Davis. His body was laid to rest in the Ausmus Cemetery to await the great resurrection. "A precious

—12—

one from us is gone, A voice we loved is still, A place is vacant in our home, That never can be filled." The Family.

Linda Jane Taylor

Linda Jane Taylor was born Feb. 5, 1865, died April 15, 1939. Age, 73 years, 2 months and 10 days. Married to Elder John Ausmus To this union was born 7 children, 3 dead and 4 living. She professed hope in early age and joined the Primitive Baptist Church at Strait Branch, January 23, 1909, and lived a faithful member until she was called on the other side. We all miss her and hope our loss will be her eternal gain.

Aaron Davis

Brother Aaron Davis was born Feb. 5, 1872, departed this life December 12, 1938. Age 66 years, 19 months, 7 days. He was united in marriage to Florence Roach in 1899. To this union was born 11 children, 3 dead, 8 living. She departed this life in 1920. He was later married to Nancie Collins who still survives his death. He leaves to mourn his loss his companion, 2 brothers, 1 sister, 8 children, W. M. Davis and David Davis of LaFollette, Clyde Davis, Caryville, Lee Davis, Marley, Albert Davis, Speedwell, Mrs. Walter Presley, Mrs. Edd Miller and Mrs. Harrie Chapman of LaFollette, and 16 grandchildren, and a host of relatives and friends. He professed faith in Christ at an early age and joined the Primitive Baptist Church at Davis Chapel for which he remained a faithful member until death. He was a firm believer in God. A faithful worker in Sunday School and Church. Always striving for peace. He always had good advice for the young people. His talk was beneficial and worth listening too. Through all his sickness he bore it without complaint and often spoke of his home in heaven. He will be greatly missed by all who knew him. But we believe our loss is his eternal gain. Funeral services were conducted by Eld. Leonard White and Eld. Henry Comer and burial was at the Davis Chapel Cemetery where he will await the resurrection in the great Judgment Morning. Sleep on Dear Dad and take your rest. God called you away He knows the best. We miss you so we can say. We'll meet again some happy day. Wrote by a son, Eld. Albert Davis.

Velma Ottellee Drummonds

Velma Ottelle Drummonds, daughter of Mr. and Mrs. J. L. Drummonds, was born November 21, 1923, died March 26, 1939, being 15 years, 4 months and 5 days old. She professed faith in Christ

—13—

Feb. 24, 1938, and joined the Primitive Baptist Church at Meyers Grove the 4th Saturday in May 1938, and was baptised by Rev. Matthew Oliver. She lived a faithful member until God saw fit to call her to live with Him. She leaves to mourn her passing her parents, one brother Lloyd, one sister, Aileen, 1 nephew, Jackie Drummonds, uncles and aunts, Mr. and Mrs. J. A. Meyers, Middlesboro, Mr. and Mrs. Robert Meyers, New Tazewell, Mr. and Mrs. E. S., D. P., J. A., S. W., and G. B. Drummonds, Mr. and Mrs. W. F. Robertson all of New Tazewell. Mr. and Mrs. Thurman Poore, Knoxville, and lots of other friends and relatives. She bore her sickness with patience and just before she died she looked up at her mother and said heaven sweet heaven, oh how sweet heaven will be. Velma is greatly missed by her classmates and all who knew her. Home is made sad by her passing while heaven is made brighter. Sleep on sweet Velma and take thy rest. We all loved you dear, but God loved you best. Funeral services were conducted by Elders Matthew Oliver, T. G. Brantley, J. M. Wilder, D. P. Denton, and Hul Vance.

MINISTERIAL ROLL

Elders	Post Offices
John Ausmus	Speedwell, Claiborne County, Tennessee
T. G. Brantley	Sharps Chapel, Union County, Tennessee
Alfred Boruff	Maynardville, Union County, Tennessee
Henry Comer	LaFollette, Campbell County, Tennessee
E. S. Drummonds	New Tazewell, Claiborne County, Tennessee
Albert Davis	Speedwell, Claiborne County, Tennessee
V. H. Graves	Jamestown, Fentress County, Tennessee
John F. Keck	Goin, Claiborne County, Tennessee
W. A. Moyers	Speedwell, Claiborne County, Tennessee
M. B. Weaver	128 Jordan St., Knoxville, Knox County, Tennessee
George Mays	Goin, Claiborne County, Tennessee
Matthew Oliver	Noeton, Grainger County, Tennessee
T. J. Pierce	Speedwell, Claiborne County, Tennessee
Alfred Parks	New Market, Jefferson County, Tennessee
Leonard White	LaFollette, Campbell County, Tennessee
Carl McCarty	Speedwell, Claiborne County, Tennessee
Milton Brantley	Sharps Chapel, Union County, Tennessee

LICENTIATES

Jim Collins	New Market, Jefferson County, Tennessee
J. C. Cosby	Gibson Station, Lee County, Virginia
W. R. Petree	Sharps Chapel, Union County, Tennessee
Charlie Stanifer	New Tazewell, Claiborne County, Tennessee
J. C. Bolin	Tazewell, Claiborne County, Tennessee
Sam Miller	New Market, Jefferson County, Tennessee

344

CHURCHES	COUNTIES	PASTORS	CLERKS	CLERK'S POST OFFICE
Red Hill	Claiborne	Leonard White	Moses Treece	Speedwell, Tennessee
Gibson Station	Claiborne	Matthew Oliver	Mary Ball	Gibson Station, Virginia
		R. P. Bridges	R. P. Bridges	Sharps Chapel, Tennessee
Oak Grove	Union	T. G. Brantley	Robert England, Asst.	Goin, Tennessee
Rocky Dale	Knox	T. G. Brantley	M. C. Dunn	Corryton, Tennessee
Cedar Spring	Claiborne	T. G. Brantley	J. L. Drummonds	New Tazewell, Tennessee
Black Fox	Grainger	Matthew Oliver	Flossie Capps	Liberty Hill, Tennessee
Pleasant Point	Claiborne	V. H. Graves	Estell Heath	Goin, Tennessee
Davis Chapel	Campbell	Leonard White	O. R. Parrott	LaFollette, Tennessee
Capps Creek	Union	John F. Keck	Froney Vaughn	Goin, Tennessee
		Leonard White	Lincoln Edwards	
Pleasant Hill	Claiborne	John Ausmus, Asst.	Verlin Edwards, Asst.	Speedwell, Tennessee
New Hebron	Jefferson	Henry Comer	Cordlia Mitchell	New Market, Tennessee
Noeton	Grainger	Matthew Oliver	J. C. Oliver	Noeton, Tennessee
Black Fork	Roane	W. R. Gates	Jessie Sweat	War.burg, Tennessee
Bradens Chapel	Union	Henry Comer	Lucy Sparks	Speedwell, Tennessee

345

CHURCHES	NAMES OF DELEGATES	Rec. by Expr. Baptism	Rec. by Letter	Restored	Dismissed by Letter	Excluded	Deceased	Total Membership	Saturday Meetings	Contribution	Communion Meetings
Red Hill	Harry Patterson, Jimmie Brantley	1					1	86	1	1.00	July
Gibson Station	Elders Chas. Redmond, John Weaver, Brothers Henry Hoskins, Bill Britton		1	4			2	86	1	1.50	June
Oak Grove	Elders M. B. Weaver, T. G. Brantley, Brothers V. H. Stiner, George Shaffner, R. C. Meltibarger	8	1	3		2	2	287	1	5.20	May
Rocky Dale	Brother M. C. Dunn	1	1					74		2.25	June
Cedar Spring	Elder E. S. Drummonds, J L. Drummonds, Lee Alston, Chas. Alston, J. S. Alston, Sister Delie Drummonds	5		1			1	94	4	2.25	May
Black Fox	Elder Alfred Boruff, S. R. Cook, John Bundon, John Liford, Sam Davis, W. M. Perry, J. M. Davis	1	1					100	2	3.00	June
Pleasant Point	Elders V. H. Graves, John F. Keck, Brothers C. D. Keck, Austin Beason, J. W. Keck, Prock Beason, Estell Heath, Leatha Heath, Mertie Keck	12			1		1	143	1	5.00	July
Davis Chapel	Elders Leonard White, Albert Davis, Honry Comer				1		3	151	3	3.00	July
Capps Creek	No Letter—Come On										
Pleasant Hill	Elder W. A. Moyers, Brother Jeff Mattox	2				2		66	4	5.25	June
New Hebron	No Letter—Come On										
Noeton	Elder Matthew Oliver, Bro. J. C. Oliver, H. L. Pattrick						2	39	3	1.50	May
Black Fork	No Letter—Come On						1	15		1.00	
Bradens Chapel	Brother Brice Braden										

$22.50 for Printing Minutes

MINUTES

—— OF THE ——

ONE HUNDRED AND TWENTY-FIRST

ANNUAL SESSION

OF THE

POWELLS VALLEY
ASSOCIATION

—— OF ——

PRIMITIVE BAPTISTS

Held With the Church at
PLEASANT POINT, CLAIBORNE COUNTY, TENN.
AUGUST 16, 17, 18, 1940

The next Session will be held with the Church at Davis Chapel, Campbell County, Tennessee. Situated 2 1-2 miles Southeast of LaFollette, and 2 1-2 miles Southwest of Fincastle. To commence on Friday before the third Saturday in August, 1941

Elder Alfred Boruff to preach the Introductory Sermon and Elder John F. Keck to be his Alternate.

FRIDAY'S PROCEEDINGS

1st—According to previous arrangements the Association met pursuant to adjournment.

2nd—After singing hymns, prayer by Elder T. G. Brantley.

3rd—Praise by Elder Albert Davis by reading the 19th Psalm.

4th—Prayer by Elder John F. Keck.

5th—The Introductory Sermon was delivered by Elder M. B. Weaver from the 20th verse of the 8th chapter of Isaiah. To the law and the testimony etc., followed by Elder Matthew Oliver.

6th—After 15 minutes intermission at the sound of singing the Association reassembled and after prayer by Elder Henry Comer proceeded to organize for the transaction of business by electing Elder T. G. Brantley Moderator and Elder V. H. Graves Assistant Moderator.

7th—On motion Brother Sam Davis was reelected Clerk and Bro. J. L. Drummons, Assistant Clerk.

8th—Called for letters from Sister Churches and received ten, which were read by the Clerks.

9th—By motion all the letters were received and the delegation welcomed to seats.

10th—By motion we take the run of last years minutes. so long as it does not conflict with the business of this Association.

11th—Called for Corresponding Letters from Sister Associations and received one from the Hiwassee which was read by the Clerk.

12th—Motion that we receive said letter. Motion carried and the delegates were welcomed to seats with us, to-wit: Elders U. J. Hembree, J. J. Abbott, Brother John Edmonds.

13th—Called for newly constituted churches and received none.

14th—Called for members of our churches who were not delegates and received none.

15th—On motion the Moderator appointed all the following committees:

(a)—On Preaching—Brothers S. R. Cook, W. E. Cupp, Jim Brantley, together with this Church.

(b)—On Arrangements—Brothers Zan Goin, Windfield Keck, S. W. Drummonds.

(c)—On Correspondence—Elders M. B. Weaver, Albert Davis and Chas. Redmond.

(d)—On Request—Brothers Isaac Owens, Henry Stiner, Elder E. S. Drummonds.

(e)—On Finance—Brothers George Shoffner, Dewey Hopper, J. M. Davis.

16th—Motion in order that we adjourn until Saturday morning at 9:30.

—2—

SATURDAY'S PROCEEDINGS

1st—Saturday morning at 9:30 the Association met pursuant to adjournment. After singing and praise by Elder T. G. Brantley and prayer by Elder J. J. Abbott.

2nd—The Association was called to order by Moderator.

3rd—Called for letters from Churches which failed to get in Friday and received one which was read by the Clerk.

4th—By motion said letter was received and the delegation was welcomed to seats.

5th—Called for the report of the Committee on Arrangements.

(b)—We your Committee on Arrangements beg leave to report the following:

1st—Call the roll.

2nd—Call for the report of the Committee on Preaching.

3rd—On Correspondence.

4th—On Request.

5th—On Finance.

6th—When and where shall our next Association be held. Who shall preach the Introductory Sermon and who shall be his Alternate.

7th—How many copies of Minutes shall we have printed. Who shall superintend the print'ng and distribution of same and what shall he be allowed for his service.

Respectfully submitted,

A. C. GOIN

S. W. DRUMMONDS

WINFIELD KECK

8th—On motion the report was received and the Committee discharged.

9th—Called for the report of the Committee on Preaching.

(a)—We your Committee on Preaching beg leave to submit the following: Friday night at the Church, Elders U. J. Hembree, J. J. Abbott, Elders Albert Davis, Henry Comer. Moyers Grove, Brother John Weaver and Elder M. B. Weaver. Saturday at the Church, Elders Matthew Oliver, Oscar Moyers. Saturday night at the Church, Elders W. A. Moyers, V. H. Graves. Moyers Grove, Elders Albert Davis, Henry Comer. Sutton Carr Branch, J. J. Abbott, King. Sunday at Church Elder Leonard White. Moderator to Close.

Respectfully submitted,

BRO. JAMES BRANTLEY

BRO. W. E. CUPP

BRO. S. R. COOK

On motion report received and Committee discharged.

10th— Called for visitors from other Churches and received two from the Eastern District Association, to-wit: Elders Caleb King and Grant Sutton who were welcomed to seats with us.

—3—

11th—Called for the report of the Committee on Correspondence.

(c)—We your Committee on Correspondence beg leave to submit the following report: That we keep up our loving correspondence with the Hiwassee Association by letter and messengers to their next annual meeting.

Respectfully submitted,
ELDER M. B. WEAVER
ELDER ALBERT DAVIS
ELDER CHARLIE REDMOND

12th—By motion the report was received and the Committee discharged.

13th—By motion we send the following named Elders as Messengers to the Hiwassee Association when convened with the Church of Indian Creek, Tennessee, on Friday before the 4th Saturday in September, 1940, to-wit: Elders Henry Comer, V. H. Graves, M. B. Weaver, T. G. Brantley.

14th—Called for the report of the Committee on Request.

We your Committee on Request beg leave to report the following: That we have all obituaries printed in our Minutes that the Churches furnish. That the next annual Session of the Powells Valley Association be held with the Church at Davis Chapel, Campbell County, Tennessee, to commence on Friday before the third Saturday in August, 1941.

Respectfully submitted,
ELDER E. S. DRUMMONDS
BROTHER ISAAC OWENS
BROTHER W. H. STINER

15th—By motion the report was received and the Committee discharged.

16th—By motion the next annual Session of the Powell's Valley Association shall be held with the Church at Davis Chapel, Campbell County, Tennessee, to commence on Friday before the third Saturday in August, 1941. That Elder Alfred Boruff preach the Introductory Sermon and that Elder John F. Keck be his alternate.

17th—Called for the report of the Committee on Finance.

(e)—We your Committee on Finance beg leave to report the following:

Received from the following Churches for Printing Minutes: Pleasant Point, $5.00; Pleasant Hill $3.15; Cedar Springs, $1.50; Blackfox, $3.55; Gibson Station, $1.50; Oak Grove, $5.00; Braden's Chapel, $1.25; Capp's Creek, $1.00; Davis Chapel, $2.75; Red Hill, $1.25; Noeton, $1.50; Rocky Dale, $2.50; Total $29.95. From other sources $1.90.

Respectfully submitted,
BROTHER DEWEY HARPER
BROTHER J. M. DAVIS.

18th—By motion the report was received and the Committee discharged.

19th—Motion in order that we have 800 copies of Minutes printed, that the Clerk superintend the printing and distribution of same and that he be allowed $10.00 for his services.

20th—Called for the report of the Clerk on last year's contribution, when he reported $1.10 carried over from last year.

21st—By motion the report was received.

22nd—Motion in order that the Clerk write a Corresponding Letter to the Hiwassee Association and have the same printed in our Minutes

23rd—By motion be it resolved that we tender our heartfelt thanks to this dear old Church and the surrounding community for her generous hospitality and kind treatment to us throughout this Association. After this while singing the good old hymn and taking the parting hand. A joyful season was expressed by the shedding of tears, clapping of hands and invoking the blessings of God upon each other.

24th—Motion in order to adjourn until 10 o'clock at the place above stated.

25th—Dismissed in order by Elder Oscar Moyers.

ELDER T. G. BRANLEY, Moderator

Sharp's Chapel, Tenn.

ELDER V. H. GRAVES, Assistant Moderator

Jamestown, Tenn.

SAM DAVIS, Clerk

Luttrell, Tenn.

J. L. DRUMMONDS, Assistant Clerk

New Tazewell, Tenn.

SUNDAY'S MEETING

At the appointed hour Sunday a large congregation assembled at the altar and attentively listened to the well delivered sermon by Elder W. A. Moyers, from the 23rd Psalm. The Lord is my Shepherd, etc., followed by Elder J. J. Abbott and closing remarks by Assistant Moderator Elder V. H. Graves, all of which was delivered in a most loving spirit and with the greatest interest to all. And a joyful parting was expressed in all the congregation.

CORRESPONDING LETTER

We the Powell's Valley Association, now in session with the Church at Pleasant Point, on August 16, 17, 18, 1940, to our Sister Association with whom we correspond, to-wit: The Hiwassee: Dear Brothers and Sisters in Christ: We are sending you this our epistle of love to you for no other reason than to show you our appreciation of love and to ask a continuance of love and friendship with you and with only this in view. We have chosen these our beloved Elders as Messengers to visit you in your next Annual Meeting, when convened with the Church of Indian

—5—

351

Creek, on **Friday** before the fourth Saturday in September, 1940, to-wit: Elders Henry Comer, V. H. Graves, M. B. Weaver, T. G. Brantley. We are pleased to have your worthy Elders and Messengers seated with us now, Elder U. J. Hembree and Elder J. J. Abbott, and ask that you meet with us again next year when we meet with the Church at Davis Chapel, Campbell County, Tenn., on Friday before the third Saturday in August, 1941. Pray for this your little Sister who welcomes a loving Correspondence with **you.**

SAM DAVIS, Clerk, Powell's Valley Association.

OBITUARIES

Narcissus Treece

Narcissus Treece was born April 15, 1859, died September 24, 1939. Was married to Jefferson Treece in 1875. To this union was born 12 children. She joined the Primitive Baptist Church at Red Hill and lived a faithful member until death. She leaves to mourn her death 11 children and a host of relatives and friends.

Jacob Johnson

Jacob Johnson was born February 19, 1866, died July 20, 1940. He made his stay on earth 74 years 5 months and 1 day. He was the son of Elder T. O. Johnson. He was married to Nancy Ann Beason, January 23rd, 1887. To this union was born ten children, eight boys and two girls. W. T., J. J., B. J., H. Clay, and A. I., Theodore, Fred, J. C., preceeded death Dec. 4, 1918. Daughter Lizzie and Sarah Beatrice Johnson. He professed faith in Christ at the age of twenty three years old. He later joined the Primitive Baptist Church and was baptised in 1895 at Big Barn. Twenty two years later he and his beloved wife moved their membership by letter to Oak Grove Primitive Baptist Church from which he died a member. Father believed the Old and New Testament. Father is gone to the new home that was waiting for him that God prepared many years ago. Father has had many visions and dreams. He was loyal and loved his beloved wife and children and was loved by them. He is missed by his wife and children but we all pray to meet him in Heaven some day. Written by son Theodore Johnson and family. Funeral services conducted by his pastor, Elder T. G. Brantley.

T. J. Pierce

T. J. Pierce was born in the year 1863 and died August 12, 1940, making his stay on earth 77 years. He joined the Primitive Ministry December 1, 1908. He lived and died a strong believer in Salvation by Grace. Was powerful in exhortations and doctrine. He enjoyed going to meeting and did go as long as he was able. The funeral was conducted by Gipson, of Pruden and W. A. Moyers, of Speedwell, Oscar C. Moyers, of Crosbyton, Texas and John Ausmus of Speedwell, after which his body was laid to rest in the Wilson Cemetery beside his wife to wait the Resurrection or call of our dear Savior, to gather his redeemed home where parting will be no more. Written at the request of his friends by W. A. Moyers.

—9—

Ida Capps

Ida Capps, wife of Harrison Shelby, born Sept. 8, 1898, died Nov. 14, 1939, age 41 years and 2 months. She is survived by her husband and six children, a father, W. R. Capps, four sisters and one brother, three half-sisters and five half-brothers. She professed faith in Christ at an early age and belonged to the Rocy Dale Primitive Baptist Church.

W. R. Petree

W. R. Petree was born June 13, 1858, died November 13, 1939. Professed faith in Christ at an early age and joined the Primitive Baptist Church and was a member for 62 years. He was a deacon of said Church for many years. He leaves to mourn his passing five children,, 26 grandchildren and 16 great-granchildren and one brother, Franklin Petree. His body was laid to rest in Pleasant View Cemetery. Our loss is Heaven's gain. Funeral services were conducted by his pastor, Elder T. G. Brantley.

Arminda Kitts Roe

Arminda Kitts Roe was born March 13, 1860. Was 80 years old March 13, 1940. Was married to George Roe at the age of 20 years and to this union was born 9 children, 5 boys and 4 girls. Her husband and four of the children having passed to the Great Beyond and on Tuesday morning, July 30, 1940, at 6 o'clock the Angel of Death entered the home and carried the soul of our dear mother back to the arms of Jesus the one who gave it. She was a member of the Oak Grove Baptist Church and attended her Church sessions as long as she was able. All ministers of the Gospel found a ready welcome in her home. She was kind to her friends and neighbors and lived a quiet, peaceable life and practiced the Scripture which is taught us, "Do unto others as you would have them do unto you." She will be especially missed by her children and grandchildren. She leaves five children, Paris, of Shays Chapel, Charlie, Fonde, Ky., Murphie, of Fountain City, Lula Rutherford, Hamilton, Ohio, Ima Clawson, Monroe, Mich., and 34 grandchildren, 25 great-grandchildren to mourn their loss. There will be an empty chair at the table, a sudden break in our conversation, an empty place in our hearts that never can be filled. Yet our loss is her eternal gain. Funeral services conducted by her pastor, Elder T. G. Brantley.

Lela Dunn Ausmus

Lela Dunn Ausmus, wife of Henry Ausmus, was born March

2, 1885, and died July 12, 1940. She professed faith in Christ at an early age and joined the Church at Davis Creek and was in the Constitution of Pleasant Hill Church. She is survived by her husband, Henry Ausmus, four sons, one deceased, and six daughters, one deceased. She is also survived by her mother, Mrs .Ann Dunn and four brothers. She is also survived by her grandchildren and she was loved by all who knew her. and she will be missed by all her family and Church. Funeral services were conducted by Elder Leonard White and Elder W. A. Moyers. Gone but not forgotten.

Mrs. Sarah Elizabeth Weaver

Mrs. Sarah Elizabeth Weaver was born December 2, 1863, died December 2, 1939. She professed faith in Christ in early life and joined the Mossie Springs Baptist Church and remained a member until the Church was disbanded on account of the TVA. She then joined the Church at Oak Grove and remained there until death. She was a deaconess and a faithful Christian worker. To know her was to love her. She married Elvin Weaver in 1882. To this union was born 9 children, two of whom died in infancy. The seven others mourn their loss but realize that their loss is Heaven's gain. She died at the home of her daughter, Mrs. C. D. Welch, Maryville, Tenn.

Carlyle Marion (C. M.) and Martha Ann Reagan Cabbage

C. M. Cabbage was born March 19th, 1860, and passed away quietly, April 17, 1940, being 80 years and 29 days old.. He was married on Feb. 29th, 1880 to Martha Ann Reagan, who was born July 22, 1861, and preceeded him in death two months and 22 days, having passed away so easily on Jan. 25, 1940, being 78 years, 6 months and 2 days old. Had she lived until Feb. 29th, they would have been married 60 years. To this union was born 10 children, 3 having preceded them in death. They leave four sons, C. R., Victor, C. B., and F. A., three daughters, Coltha, Barbara, and Irene .and 17 grandchildren. In early life, before they were married they professed faith in Christ and later joined the Primitive Baptist Church at Black Fox and lived devoted members of the Church until God in His great wisdom removed them from our midst. Dad was a wonderful father, a kind and loving husband and a great neighbor. Through the years he made and maintained so many friends after mother went away it seemed he was so broken hearted he just didn't care much about this world any more. And mother had been in such poor health for the past few years she often remarked she couldn't get well and didn't want to live. She said she was not afraid to die and she calmly and peacefully awaited the summons from the Heavenly Father. She was a real mother and a wonderful woman. Her home was ever open and her services freely given for the entertainment of God's servants and other visitors who desired to enter therein. She was a devoted and helpful companion through the many years of married life. They have gone to that Heavenly Home. How we do miss them. But we do feel to know our loss is their gain and some day we hope to meet them around the Great White Throne where there will be no more parting, no more sad farewells, no vacancies that can't be filled, and God will wipe all tears from our eyes . Written by their daughter, Barbara Cabbage.

MINISTERIAL ROLL

Elders	Post Offices
John Ausmus	Speedwell, Claiborne County, Tennessee
T. G. Brantley	Sharp's Chapel, Union County, Tennessee
Alfred Boruff	Maynardville, Union County, Tennessee
Henry Comer	LaFollette, Campbell County, Tennessee
E. S. Drummonds	New Tazewell, Claiborne County, Tennessee
Albert Davis	Speedwell, Claiborne County, Tennessee
V. H. Graves	Jamestown, Fentress County, Tennessee
John F. Keck	Goin, Claiborne County, Tennessee
W. A. Moyers	Speedwell, Claiborne County, Tennessee
M. B. Weaver	128 Jordan Street, Knoxville, Knox Co., Tennessee
George Mays	Goin, Claiborne County, Tennessee
Matthew Oliver	Noeton, Grainger County, Tennessee
Leonard White	LaFollette, Campbell County, Tennessee
Milton Brantley	Sharp's Chapel, Union County, Tennessee

LICENTIATES

Jim Collins	New Market, Jefferson County, Tennessee
J. C. Cosby	Gibson Station, Lee County, Virginia
Charlie Stanifer	New Tazewell, Claiborne County, Tennessee
J. C. Bolin	Tazewell, Claiborne County, Tennessee
Sam Miller	New Market, Jefferson County, Tennessee

—13—

CHURCHES	COUNTIES	PASTORS	CLERKS	CLERK'S POST OFFICE
Red Hill	Claiborne	John F. Keck	Mose Treece	.... Speedwell, Tennessee
Gibson Station .	Claiborne	Matthew Oliver	Mary Ball	.... Gibsons Station, Virginia
Oak Grove	Union	T. G. Brantley	R. P. Bridges	..... Sharps Chapel, Tennessee
Rocky Dale	Knox	T. G. Brantley	M. C. Dunn	.... Corryton, Tennessee
Cedar Spring ..	Claiborne	T. G. Brantley	J. L. Drummonds .	... New Tazewell, Tennessee
Black Fox	Grainger	T. G. Brantley	Sam Davis	.... Luttrell, Tennessee
Pleasant Point .	Claiborne	V. H. Graves	Austin Beason	.... Goin, Tennessee
Davis Chapel ..	Campbell	Albert Davis	Charlie Smith	......., LaFollette, Tennessee
Capps Creek ...	Union	Charles Redmond	Easter Braden	........, Goin, Tennessee
Pleasant Hill ..	Claiborne	Leonard White	Lincoln Edwards .	.... Speedwell, Tennessee
New Hebron ...	Jefferson	* * *	Verlin Edwards	.... Speedwell, Tennessee
Noeton	Grainger	Matthew Oliver	Cordelia Mitchell ..	.... New Market, Tennessee
Braden's Chapel	Union	Albert Davis	J. C. Oliver	.... Noeton, Tennessee
Black Fork	Roane	W. R. Gates	Roberta Sparks	.... Speedwell, Tennessee
			Jessie Sweat	.... Wartburg, Tennessee

358

TABLE OF STATISTICS

CHURCHES	NAMES OF DELEGATES	Rec. by Expr. Baptism	Rec. by Letter	Restored	Dismissed by Letter	Excluded	Deceased	Total Membership	Saturday Meetings	Contribution	Communion Meetings
Red Hill	Bro. James Brantley, Sis. Nervil and Edith Brantley..	3	1		1		1	84	1	11.50	July
Gibson Station	Elder Chas. Redmond, Bros. John Weaver, W. E. Cupp		1			3		87	1	11.50	June
Oak Grove	Elders T. G. Brantley, M. B. Weaver, Bros. R. C. Meltibarger, Henry Stiner, R. P. Bridges					1	4	281	1	15.00	May
Rocky Dale	Brother M. C. Dunn		1		1		1	74	3	2.50	June
Cedar Spring	Elder E. S. Drummonds, Bros. J. Drummonds, S. W. Drummonds, Sisters Velta Munsey, Thelma Moyers, Delia Drummonds, Frankie Hays, Gertie Simmons, Bro. J. A. G. Drummonds							94	4	1.50	May
Black Fox	Elder Alfred Boruff, Bros. J. M. Davis, Sam Davis, S. R. Cook, John Bundon, Roy Bailey			2			3	97	2	3.55	June
Pleasant Point	Elders W. H. Graves, John F. Keck, George Mays, Bros. J. M. Cox, A. C. Goin, J. W. Keck, Milton Goin, Austin Beason, Sisters Katie Keck, Roda Lamb, Etta Keck, Myrtle Keck, Etta Hopper						2	146	1	5.00	July
Davis Chapel	Elders Albert Davis, Henry Comer, Bros. Henry Cameron, Thomas Brantley		1	1	1		1	150	3	2.75	July
Capps Creek	Bro. Charlie Collins, Sister Lizzie Weaver							25	2	1.00	
Pleasant Hill	Elder W. A. Moyers	1					1	67	4	3.15	June
New Hebron	No Letter — Come On										
Noeton	Elder Matthew Oliver							39	3	1.50	May
Black Fork	No Letter — Come On										
Braden's Chapel	Bros. Brice Bradon, Aaron Pierce	1					1	16	2	1.25	June

$22.50 for Printing Minutes

359

MINUTES

—— OF THE ——

ONE HUNDRED AND TWENTY-SECOND

ANNUAL SESSION

OF THE

POWELLS VALLEY ASSOCIATION

—— OF ——

PRIMITIVE BAPTISTS

Held With the Church at

DAVIS CHAPEL, CAMPBELL COUNTY, TENNESSEE

AUGUST 15, 16, 17, 1941

The next Session will be held with the Church at Gibson's Station,
Lee County, Virginia. To commence on Friday before the third
Saturday in August, 1942. Elder Leonard White to preach
the Introductory Sermon and that Elder V. H. Graves
be his alternate.

360

FRIDAY'S PROCEEDINGS

1st—According to previous arrangements the Association met pursuant to adjournment.

2nd—After singing hymns, and prayer by Elder Jim Abbott, the Introductory was delivered by Elder John F. Keck, by reading the 19th Psalm and commenting on the same.

3rd—After fifteen minutes intermission at the sound of singing the congregation reassembled and the Association was called to order by the Moderator, Elder T. G. Brantley.

4th—Prayer by Elder Leonard White.

5th—Motion in order to elect Elder John F. Keck, Moderator. Motion carried.

6th—Motion in order to reelect Brother Sam Davis, Clerk and Brother Josh Drummonds, Assistant Clerk. Motion carried.

7th—Called for letters from Sister Churches and received twelve which were read by the Clerks.

8th—Motion in order that we receive said letters and seat the delegation. Motion carried.

9th—Motion in order that we take the run of last year's Minutes, so long as it does not conflict with the Business of this Association.

10th—Called for Corresponding Letters from Sister Associations. Received letter from the Nolachucky Association but no messenger. Received messengers from the Hiwassee but no letter, to-wit: Elders Jim Abbott, W. R. Gates, Jack Farmer, J. N. Farmer, also received Elder J. T. McArthur from Cordele, Ga., who was welcomed to seats with us.

11th—Motion in order that the Moderator appoint all committees.

12th—On Preaching—Brothers D. P. Drummonds, Will White, Elmer Graves, together with this Church.

13th—Called for Newly Constituted Churches and received none.

14th—Called for members who were not delegates and received Brothers Jeff Mattox, Walker Edmondson, P. A. White, Sister Cordelia Lynch.

(b)—Committee on Arrangements: Elder Leonard White, Elder T. G. Brantley, Brother Jim White.

(c)—On Correspondence: Elder M. B. Weaver, Elder V. H. Graves, Elder Albert Davis.

(d)—On Request: Elder Charlie Redmond, Brother Charles Collins, Brother Thomas Brantley.

(e)—On Finance: Brothers Walker Edmondson, John Maples, George Heatherly.

15th—Motion in order to adjourn until 9:30 a. m. Saturday morning. Motion carried.

— 2 —

361

SATURDAY MORNING 9:30

1st—The Association met pursuant to adjournment.

2nd—Praise by Elder Leonard White. **Prayer by Elder Charlie Redmond.**

3rd—The Association was called to order by Moderator.

4th—Called for letters from Sister Churches that failed to get in Friday and received one which was read and received and the delegation welcomed to seats.

5th—Called for members who were not delegates, when Brother Edd McKee came forward and was welcomed to a seat with us.

6th—Called for the report of the Committee on Arrangements.

(a)—We your Committee on Arrangements beg leave to submit the following: 1st—Call the Roll 2nd—Call for the report of the Committee on Preaching. 3rd—Call for the report on Correspondence. 4th —Call for the report on Requests . 5th—Call for the report on Finance. 6th—When and where shall our next Association be held. Who shall preach the Introductory Sermon and who shall be his alternate. 7th— How many copies of Minutes shall we have printed? Who shall superintend the printing of same and what shall he be allowed for his services?

Respectfully submitted,

ELDER LEONARD WHITE,
ELDER T. G. BRANTLEY,
BROTHER JIMMIE BRANTLEY.

7th—On motion the report was received and the Committee discharged.

8th—Called for the report of the Committee on Preaching.

(b)—We your Committee on Preaching beg leave to make the following report: Friday night, Elder Farmer, Elder J. T. McArthur, Elder T. G. Brantley. Saturday morning, Elder James Abbott, Elder W. R. Gates. Saturday night, Elder Varlin Graves, Elder M. B. Weaver, Elder T. G. Brantley. Sunday, Elder Leonard White, Elder J. T. McArthur, Moderator to close.

Respectfully sumbitted,

BROTHERS D. P. DRUMMONDS,
WILLIAM WHITE,
A. R. PARROTT,
S. W. DRUMMONDS.

8th—By motion the report was received and the Committee discharged.

9th—Called for the report of the Committee on Correspondence.

(c)—We your Committee on Correspondence beg leave to make the following report: That we keep up our Correspondence with the Hiwassee and Nolachucky Associations by letter and messengers, to-wit: Elders V. H. Graves, Albert Davis and M. B. Weaver, messengers to

— 3 —

these Associations and also recommend the following letter: We the Powell's Valley Association of Primitive Baptists now in session with the Church at Davis Chapel, Campbell County, Tennessee, on August 15, 16, 17, 1941, to the Hiwassee and the Nolachucky Associations of Primitive Baptists with whom we correspond. When convened with the Churches to the Hiwassee Association, we have gladly seated your delegation with us and ask you to send us another next year. And to the Nolachucky Association, we are sorry that we have not received no letter or delegation, but are glad that we received an oral request to send messengers to your Association which we hope to do. May the Great Head of the Church be with you all in all your endeavors to worship Him.

Respectfully submitted,

ELDER V. H. GRAVES,

ELDER M. B. WEAVER,

ELDER ALBERT DAVIS.

10th—On motion the report was received and the Committee discharged.

11th—Called for the report of the Committee on Request.

(d)—We your Committee on Request beg leave to report the following: That we have all the obituaries printed in our Minutes that the Churches furnish. That the next Annual Session of the Powell's Valley Association be held with the Church at Gibson's Station, Lee County, Virginia, to commence on Friday before the third Saturday in August, 1942.

Respectfully submitted,

ELDER C. W. REDMOND,

BROTHER T. BRANTLEY,

BROTHER CHARLIE COLLINS.

11th—On motion the report was received and the Committee discharged.

12th—Motion in order that we send the following named Elders as messengers to the Hiwassee Association when convened with the Church at Lenoir City, in September 1941, to-wit: Elders M. B. Weaver, Leonard White, T. G. Brantley. Motion carried. And to the Nolachucky Association, Elders V. H. Graves, Henry Comer, when convened with the Church at Mt. Zion, Garvel's Chapel, Cosby, Tenn., to commence on Friday, before the 2nd Saturday in September, 1941.

13th—By motion the next Annual Session of the Powell's Valley Association will be held with the Church at Gibson's Station, Lee County, Virginia, to commence on Friday before the third Saturday in August, 1942.

14th—Called for the report of the Clerk on last year's contribution, when he reported a balance on hand of 45 cents.

15th—On motion the report was received.

— 4 —

16th—Called for the report of the Committee on Finance.

(e)—We your Committee on Finance beg leave to report the following: Received for Ministers expenses $8.00. Received for printing Minutes $33.25.

Respectfully submitted,

BROTHERS WALKER EDMONDSON,
JOHN MAPLES,
GEORGE HEATHERLY.

17th—On motion the report was received and the Committee discharged.

18th—Motion in order that we have 800 copies of Minutes printed, that the Clerk superintend the printing of same and that he be allowed $10.00 for his services. Motion carried.

19th—By motion be it resolved that we tender our heart felt thanks to this dear old Church and surrounding community for their generous hospitality and kind treatment to us through this Association.

20th—Motion to adjourn until 10 o'clock at the place above stated. As the farewell hymn was sung and we took the parting hand a joyful season was expressed among the congregation.

21st—Dismissed in order.

ELDER JOHN F. KECK, Moderator,
Goin, Tennessee.
SAM DAVIS, Clerk,
Luttrell, Tennessee.
JOSH DRUMMONDS, Asst.-Clerk,
New Tazewell, Tennessee.

SUNDAY'S PROCEEDINGS

At the appointed hour Sunday a large crowd assembled at the altar. First praise by Elder Henry Comer by reading the third chapter of St. Matthew. Prayer by W. A. Moyers. Sermon by Elder J. T. McArthur from text: "For I am not ashamed of the gospel of Christ, for it is the power of God, etc." Followed by Elder Leonard White from text: "There remaineth therefore a rest to the people of God." All of which was delivered in a most loving spirit and with the greatest interest to all present and a joyful parting was expressed.

— 5 —

OBITUARIES

Sister Maud Drummonds

Sister Maud Drummonds, daughter of J. M. and Lizzie King, was born December 28, 1889 and died March the 31, 1941, being 51 years, 3 months and 3 days old. She was united in marriage to George Drummonds, April the 5th, 1908. To this union 3 sons were born. She professed faith in Christ at the age of 15 years and joined the Primitive Baptist Church at Meyers Grove, April 1909 and was baptised by Uncle Jake Drummonds. She lived a faithful member until God saw fit to call her to live with Him. She leaves to mourn her passing her husband, three sons, Willie, Paskel and Ervin of Monroe, Michigan and two brothers Fred and Ernie King, Royal Oak, Michigan. Three half-brothers, Horace, Jim and Clarence King of Detroit, Michigan, three half-sisters, Mrs. Florence Masee, Detroit, Mich., Mrs. Madge Dunn, Chattanooga, Tenn., Mrs. Ruby Schultz, Los Angeles, Calif., three daughter-in-laws, Lela, Vera, and Luverne, five grandchildren, Elnora Maud, Betty Sue, Patsy Ann, Vernon and Donald B. Drummonds, all of Monroe, Mich. She bore her sickness with patience and often talked of her heavenly home. A few days before she died she talked to Velma Drummonds who passed away two years age. Home is made sad by her passing while heaven is made brighter. Sleep on sweet Maud and take thy rest. We all loved you dear but God loved you best. Funeral services were conducted by E. S. Drummonds. She was laid to rest in the Drummonds Cemetery. This done by the family.

Martin Van Buren Poore

Martin Van Buren Poore was born May 3, 1876 and died May 6, 1941, at the age of 65 years. He was married to Laura Bell Gains, February 13, 1897. He leaves his wife and 11 children, Rosa Bruce and Kenneth Poore of Sweetwater, Tenn., Lula Kitts Anna Bittner, Nancie Frantz, Pauline and Dorothy Poore of Cincinnati, Zora Spurgeon of Knoxville, Tenn., Theodore Poore, Camp Shelby, Miss., Miss Joe Poore and Emma Morris of Draper, Virginia. He also leaves 18 grandchildren and three sisters, Mary Logan, Dona Wells of Tazewell, Tenn., and Dollie Presnell of Middlesboro, two brothers Alex Monroe Poore of Tazewell, Tenn. He joined the Primitive Baptist Church at Meyers Grove in 1933 and lived a faithful member until God called him home. Funeral services were held at Goins Chapel. Burial in Moody Cemetery.

John Moyers

John Moyers was born Sept. 30, 1857, died Feb. 11, 1941. Professed faith in Christ at an early age. Joined the Primitive Baptist Church at Pleasant Point, July, 1879. Was a faithful member for 62 years. He is survived by 2 sisters, 13 sons and daughters and a host of grandchildren and relatives. To know him was to love him and he will be missed by his family and Church, but we do feel our loss is his gain and some day we hope to meet him around the Great White Throne where there will be no more parting or sad farewells.

Sister Delta Weaver

Sister Delta Weaver was born April 23, 1918, departed this life December 2, 1940, being 22 years and 7 months old. She professed faith in Christ and joined the Primitive Baptist Church at Capps Creek, May 12, 1933 and was baptised. She is survived by her mother, three brothers, five sisters, and a host of friends to mourn her loss. She left this world with a bright happy smile. Our loss is heavens eternal gain.—Her Mother.

MINISTERIAL ROLL

Elders   **Post Offices**

John Asumus .... Speedwell, Claiborne County, Tennessee

T. G. Brantley .... Sharp's Chapel, Union County, Tennessee

Alfred Boruff .... Maynardville, Union County, Tennessee

Henry Comer .... LaFollette, Campbell County, Tennessee

E. S. Drummonds .... New Tazewell, Claiborne County, Tennessee

Albert Davis .... Speedwell, Claiborne County, Tennessee

V. H. Graves .... Jamestown, Fentress County, Tennessee

John F. Keck .... Goin, Claiborne County, Tennessee

W. A. Moyers .... Speedwell, Claiborne County, Tennessee

M. P Weaver ..... 128 Jordan St., Knoxville, Knox County, Tennessee

G. W. Mays .... Goin, Claiborne County, Tennessee

Matthew Oliver .... Noeton, Grainger County, Tennessee

Leonard White .... LaFollette, Campbell County, Tennessee

Milton Brantley .... Sharp's Chapel, Union County, Tennessee

J. R. Weaver .... Gibson's Station, Lee County, Virginia

Isaac Owens .... Gibson's Station, Lee County, Virginia

Charlie Redrrond .... Gibson's Station, Lee County, Virginia

LICENTIATES

Jim Collins .... New Market, Jefferson County, Tennessee

J. C. Cosby .... Gibson Station, Lee County, Virginia

Charlie Stanifer .... New Tazewell, Claiborne County, Tennessee

J. C. Bolin .... Tazewell, Claiborne County, Tennessee

Sam Miller .... New Market, Jefferson County, Tennessee

— 10 —

CHURCHES	COUNTIES	PASTORS	CLERKS	CLERK'S POST OFFICE
Red Hill	Claiborne	John F. Keck	Mose Treece	.... Speedwell, Tennessee
Gibson Station .	Lee	Matthew Oliver	Mary Ball	...... Gibson Station, Virginia
Oak Grove	Union	T. G. Brantley	Irma Sherritze and Nelle Sherritze, Ast.	.........., Goin, Tennessee
Rocky Dale	Knox	Leonard White	M. C. Dunn	.........., Corryton, Tennessee
Cedar Spring ..	Claiborne	T. G. Brantley	J. L. Drummonds .	.... New Tazewell, Tennessee
Black Fox	Grainger	T. G. Brantley	Sam Davis	.........., Luttrell, Tennessee
Pleasant Point .	Claiborne	V. H. Graves	Austin Beason ...	.........., Goin, Tennessee
Davis Chapel ..	Campbell	Leonard White	O. R. Parrott	......, LaFollette, Tennessee
Capps Creek ...	Union	C. W. Redmond	Easter Braden ...	.........., Goin, Tennessee
Pleasant Hill ..	Claiborne	Leonard White	Lincoln Edwards, Verlin Edwards, Ast	.........., Speedwell, Tennessee
New Hebron ..	Jefferson	Henry Comer	Cordelia Mitchell .	...... New Market, Tennessee
Noeton	Grainger	Matthew Oliver	J. C .Oliver	.........., Noeton, Tennessee
Braden's Chapel.	Union	Albert Davis and Henry Comer, Asst.	Aaron Pierce, Tilda Braden, Asst.	.... Speedwell, Tennessee
Black Fork	Roane	W. R. Gates	Jessie Sweat	.... Wartburg, Tennessee

CHURCHES	NAMES OF DELEGATES	Rec. by Expr. Baptism	Rec. by Letter	Restored	Dismissed by Letter	Excluded	Deceased	Total Membership	Saturday Meetings	Contribution	Communion Meetings
Red Hill	Bro. James Brantley, Sister Nervil Brantley	1	2					84	1	1.00	July
Gibson Station	Elder J. R. Weaver, Elder Chas. Redmond, Bro. W. E. Cupp	1			1	1		94	1	3.00	June
Oak Grove	Elders T. G. Brantley, M. B. Weaver, Milton Brantley, Brother G. W. Shaffner, John Maples.	8						280	1	5.50	May
Rocky Dale	Brother Elmer Graves		4					86	3	3.00	June
Cedar Spring	Bros. J. G. S. W., G. B., D. P., Sister Delia Drummonds			1	3	1	2	89	4	3.50	May
Black Fox	Bros. Sam Davis, J. M. Davis, Roy Bailey	4			1			98	2	4.00	June
Pleasant Point	Elders V. H. Graves, John F. Keck, Bros. C. D. Keck, George Williams, Sister Myrtle Keck.			1			1	145	1	5.00	July
Davis Chapel	Elders Leonard White, Albert Davis, Henry Comer, Brothers Thomas Brantley, Charlie Smith		1	1	1	1	2	149	3	3.00	July
Capps Creek	Bros. Troy Pressley, Charlie Collins, Sister Linda Paul Elder W. A. Moyers, Bros. Neal Lambert, J. L. Edwards, Verlin Edwards.	3				1	1	27	2	1.00	June
Pleasant Hill	Brother John Hale						1	69	4	2.00	June
New Hebron	No Letter — Come On.							40	2	1.50	
Noeton	No Letter — Come On.							39	3		May
Black Fork	Brother William Sparks, Brice Braden, Aaron Pierce,										
Braden's Chapel	Sister Lucy Sparks, Tilda Braden, Venie Pierce	4						20	2	1.25	June

$22.50 for Printing Minutes

MINUTES

OF THE

ONE HUNDRED AND TWENTY THIRD

ANNUAL SESSION

OF THE

POWELLS VALLEY
ASSOCIATION
OF
PRIMITIVE BAPTIST

Held With the Church at
GIBSON STATION, LEE COUNTY VIRGINIA,
AUGUST 14-15-16, 1942.

The next Session will be held with the Church of Cedar Spring, at Myers Grove, Claiborne County Tennessee, to commence on Friday before the third Saturday in August 1943, Elder V H Graves; to preach the Introductory Sermon, and Elder John F. Keck; to be his alternate.

FRIDAY'S PROCEEDINGS

1st__ According to previous arrangements the Asscciation met persuant to adjournment.

2nd- After singing Hymns. Praise by Elder John F Keck; and prayer by Elder W A Moyers, the introductory sermon was delivred by E'der Lenord White; from Romans 1st chapter. and 16th. verse, quotation for I am not ashamed of the Gospel of Christ for it is the power of Gcd. (etc

3rd-After 15 minutes intermision the Association reconvened and after singing ard prayer by Elder Petitt; the Asscciation was called to order by mod- Elder John F Keck;

4th- By motion and second Elder T G Brantley; was Chosen mod-

5th- By motion and second E'der John F Keck; was chosen assistant moderator.

6 th- By motion and second brother Sam Davis, was reelected clerk. and brother J L Drummonds, assistant clerk.

7 th- Called for letters from sister Churches. and received 8 which was read by the clerk.

8 th By motion and second said letters was received and the delegation welcomed to seats,

9 th- By motion and second we take the run of last years minutes as our order of buisness.

10 th_ Called for corresponding letters from sister Asscciations. received letter and messengers from the Hiwassie Association, to wit Elders J J Abbott, and J F Campbell;

11 th- By motion and second said letter was received and the delegation welcomed to seats.

12 th- By motion and second the Moderator appoint all the Committees (a) on Preaching brothers Mc Henry, Jimmie Brantly, Troy Presley, together with this Church.

13 th- Called for members who were not delegates and received non

14 th- called for members of the Hiwassie Association who were not delegates and rec-Bro. R H Petitt; and wife and Grandaughter Betta, and Elder A B Green; also rec- Elder J T McArthur; of Cordele Georgia.

(B) Committee on arrangements Elder W A Moyers, Bro Jeff Maddox; and W M White; (c) on correspondence Elders Lenord White; M B Weaver, John F Keck; (d) on request Elder John Weaver, Henry Comer; Tom Brantly;

(e) on fiance, Elder E S Drummonds, Albert Davis, Bro Geo, Shoffner

15 th– Called for the report on preaching for Sat. night. said report was made. and by motion was accepted,

16 th— By motion and second that we have the confession of faith of sister E S Drummonds, printed in our minutes, also the Father of Elder T G Brantly; Obituary.

17 th- Motion in order to adjourn until 9 30, Sat. morning.

SAT. morning 9.30,

1st- The Association met persuant to adjournment.

2nd- After singing. prayer by brother Pettit,

3rd- The Association was called to order by the moderator,

4th- Called for letters that failed to get in Friday and received 3 which was read, and by motion was received, and the deligation welcomed to seats,

5'h- Called for the report of the committee on arrangements,

(B) We your committee on arrangements beg leave to submit the following order of buisness. 1st, call the roll. 2nd, call for report on preaching

3rd Call for report on correspondence. 4th, call for report on request, 5th, call for report of the committee on fiance, 6th. when and where shall our next Association be held. who shall preach the introductory sermon and who shall be his alternate, 7th. how many copies of minutes shall we have printed. and who shall superintend the printing and distribution of same, and what shall he be allowed for his service.

respectfully submited, Elder M B. Weaver,

    Brother Jeff Maddox,

    Brother W M, White,

6th- By motion the report was received and the committee discharged,

7th, Called for members who were not deligates and received none,

8th- called for letters from sister Association's that failed to get in Friday. received one from the Nolichucky, Association,

9th- By motion and second said letter was received and seated the deligation. to-wit, Elder Alen Gates;

10 th. called the roll and erased the names of absentes.

11th. Called for the report of the committee on preaching,

(c) We your committee on preaching. Beg leave to make the following report, Friday night at the Church Elder James Abbott; Elder J T McArthur; the moderator to close. Sat, morning at the Church Elder Allen Gates; Elder J F Campbell, Elder V H Graves, Saturday night. Elder A B Green, Elder James Abbott, Elder M B Weaver, Sunday at the stand Elder Lenord White, Elder W A Moyers, moderator to close,

respectfully submitted, Bro, Troy Presley,

Bro, James Brantly,

Bro, Wm McHenry,

12 th. By motion the report was received and committee discharged,

13-th, Called for the report of the committee on correspondence,

(D) We your committe on corresponden ce beg leave to make the following report, that we keep up our correspondence with the Hiwassee, and the Nolachucky, Association by letter and messenger. to wit, Elders M B Weaver; Lenord White, John F Keck, messengers to the Associations, and also reccomend the following letter.

WE the POWELS VALLEY ASSOCIATION of PRIMITIVE BAPTIST now in session with the church of Girbson Station. Lee county Virginia, on August 14-15-16, 1942. To the Hiwassee. and Nolachucky Association, of Primitive Baptist, with whome we correspond, when convened with the Churches, of the Hiwassee and Nolachucky Association's. we have gladly seated your deligation with us and ask you to send us another next year. May the great head of the Church be with you all in all your endeavers to worship Him,

Respectfully submitted Elder John F Keck;

Elder Lenord white;

Elder M B Weaver;

14th- By motion the report was received and the committee dischaged.

15th. Called for the report of the committee on Request.

(E) We your Committee on Request beg leave to make the following report, That we have all the Obituary's printed in our Minutes that the Churches furnish, and that the next Session of the Association, be held with the church at Myers Grove. Claiborne county, Tennessee. Respectfully submited

Elder John R.Weaver;

Elder Henry Comer;

Brother Thomas Brantly;

16th- By motion the report was rec- and the committee discharged.

17th- Called for the report of the committee on Finance,

We your committee on Finance, beg leave to make the following report, received from Churches for Printing Minutes, Red Hill. $2.00, Gibson Station. $3.00, Oak Grove. $10.00, Rocky Dale. $3.00, Cedar Spring, $5.25, Blackfox, $6.30, Plesant Point, $5.00, Davis Chapel, $3.00 Capps Creek, $8.00, Plesant Hill, $2.25, Noeton, $1.50, For visiting Ministers, Plesant Hill, $2.50, Davis Chapel, $2.00, Respectfully submited, Elder Albert Davis;

Elder E S. Drummonds;

Brother G W, Shoffner;

18th- By motion report was rec- and the committee discharged.

19th- By motion we send the following named messengers to the Hiwassee Association. to wit: Elder Lenord White, Elder John F. Keck, Elder M B, Weaver, when convened with the Church of Bethlehem, Cumberland co, Tenn. on Friday before the fourth Saturday in August. 1942, And to the Nolachucky, we send the following messengers to wit, Elder V H. Graves; Elder Henry Comer; when convened with the Church of Ogles Chapel, Cock Co, Tenn. to commence on Friday before the Second Sat. in September. 1942,

20th- On motion the next Annual Session of the Powels Valley Association. shall be held with the Church at Myers Grove, Claiborne County, Tenn. to commence on Friday before the Third Saturday in August. 1943. Elder V H. Graves, to preach the Introductory Sermon and Elder John F, Keck, be his alternate,

st- Called for the report of the Clerk on last years Finance, who reported a balance of $1.70 from last year.

22nd- By motion the report was received

23rd- By motion we have 800 copies of Minutes printed. that the Clerk superintend the printing and distribution of same. and that he be allowed $10.00, for his service.

24th- By motion be it resolved that we tender our heart felt thanks to this dear Old Church and her surrounding community, for their hospitality and kind treatment to us throughout this Association.

25th- Motion in order to adjourn until 10. o'clock. at the time and place above stated.

26th- Dismissed in order Elder T G. Brantly, Moderator.

Postoffice Maynardville Tenn,

Sam Davis, Clerk. Luttrell Tenn.

J L Drummonds; Assistant Clerk, New Tazewell Tenn.

Five
SUNDAY'S PROCEEDINGS

At the appointed hour Sunday a large and well behaved audiance as-sembled at the altar, and so attentatively listened to the well delivered sermon of Elder W A. Moyers; from Text: Stand fast in the Liberty wherein "CHRIST,, hath made you free; followed by Elder Lenord White; from the Text of Justification: and closing remarks by the Mod, all of which was delivered in a most loving Spirit and with the greatest intrest to all. and a loving parting was expressed by claping of hands sheding of tears. and invoking the Blessing of God upon each other.

OBTUARY'S

Mary C. Hill;

Was born Febuary 5th 1865, she was a daughter of Mr & Mrs E A. Brantly, was married to A G. Hill, Feb. 10-1887: her husband died Jan. 24- 1932 she died Jan. 30- 1942, She joined the Primitive Baptist Church at Cave Spring, and was Baptized more than 60 years ago, she later moved her membership to Lost cr ek, she was always faithful to attend her church meetings as she was able and had an oppurnity to go. sister Hill, is survived by one brother, A W. Brantley; of Los-Angeles cala. one sister Mrs J F. Miller; of Maynardville Tenn, about 27 nephews and neices, after the church at Lost Creek. was desolved, she joined the church at Oak Grove, she often shouted the praise of God and told of her hope of heaven and Immortal Glory we are sattisfied her Spirit is resting with God in the Glory World.

SARA F. MOYERS, COX;

Was born Feb 24. 1852, died Nov 9. 1941, being 89 years 11 months of age she was married to Charles R. cox; May 17, 1862 to this union was born 13 children, she joined the Primitive Baptist Church at an early age and lived a aithful member until death, Oh mother thy gentle voice is hushed, thy warm true heart is still, on thy pale and peaceful face it's resting death chill

Thy hands are clasped upon thy breast we have kissed thy marble brow, In our aking hearts we know we have no mother now.

RILDA GIVENS EVANS;

Was born March 28, 1860, died June 25, 1942, being 82 years 2 months and 27 days old, She professed faith in Christ at an early age and was a faithful member of Red Hill Primitive Baptist church, She was married to James Silus Evans, in 1876, to this union was born 8 children 4 preceded her in death, surviving are Lee and Willie Evans; Speedwell Tenn. Mrs Asberry Russell, Mrs P C. Mason; Middlesboro Ky, also 2 brothers W M. and Granvil Givens; Middlesboro Ky, she also leaves to mourn her passing 37 grand children, 35 great-grandchildren, and 4 great-great grandchildren,

We hate to give her up but God knows best.

LAURA PETERS;

Daughter of Robert and Marry Bridges; born March 26. 1880, died March 21, 1942, survivors two daughters, Mrs McKinley Roberts; of LaFollette. Mrs T R. Jarnagin; of Knoxville. one brother Ed Bridges; of Philadelphia Tenn. a sister Miss Dora Bridges; of Bloomington Ky. a step daughter Mrs Sam White; of LaFollette, she professed faith in Christ in early life and joined the church, at Cave Spring, later joined at Rocky Dale, and remained a member until death, She was a loving mother and a devout christian.

Written by a sister-inlaw Mrs Rhoda Dunn;

DANIAL BRANTLEY;

Son of John and Parlie Brantley, was born Oct. 14, 1857. died Jan. 22, 1941. age 83 years 3 months and 8 days, He was married to Amanda Cook, Nov. 1884, to this union was born 11 children. his wife and one daughter precede him to the grave. he leaves to mourn his passing 10 children, Elder T G. Brantley, Kenneth and Lonnie Brantley, and Mrs Isac Ellison. of Sharps Chapel. Mrs Verlin Farris, of LaFollette. Mrs Verlin Weaver, of Glen Mary Tenn. Mrs Will Stiner, of canton Ohio. Mrs Elvin Brantley, of Leroy Ill. Sam of Onarga Ill. and Wallace of Piper City. one brother George Brantley; of Jacksboro Tenn. also 42 grand children and 1 great grand child.

He professed a hope in Christ about the age of 18 years. Joined the Primitive Baptist church about 65 years ago.

later moved his membership to Blue Spring. he served as a Deacon of Blue Springs for a number of years. where he lived a member until death, He was loved by all who knew him. we have lost a loving father, but we feel our loss is his eternal gain.

MRS SARA JANE JOHNSON

Born January 7. 1866, died April 18. 1942, she was 76 years 3 months and 11 days old. She was a daughter of Mr & Mrs Rufus Nelson; she was married to Calvin Johnson, in their early days, He departed this life May 23, 1939. To this union 14 children were born 9 daughters and 5 sons. she leaves to mourn her loss 6 daughters: Mrs Lizzie Nelson, Balkan Ky. Mrs Lassie Thompson, Mrs Lillie Cox, Mrs Lottie Shelby, all of Kokomo Indiana. Mrs Myrtle Holliway, and Mrs Laura Dykes, of Sharps Chapel. 2 sons Mr Curtis Johnson, of Sharps chapel. and Mr Cecil Johnson, of Kokomo Indiana. 1 sister Mrs Amanda Ford, Sharps chapel. a host of grand children and great grand children with many other relations and friends. She joined the church in her early days and lived a faithful christian until her death. she made her home in her last days with Mr and Mrs Charles Dykes; near Sharps chapel. we feel our loss is her eternal gain.

OZETTA BERRY,

In loving rememberance of our dear daughter,Ozetta Berry. She was born April,28; 1912. Departeb this life, July,17; 1942.

She leaves to mourn her loss, her parents, 3 brother, 1 sister, 4 niece,s and a host of relatives and friends. She profest a hope in Christ in February,—1930. and joined the Primitive Baptist Church, at Cave Springs. And was babtised, in June follng. She was ill for 16 months. She will be greatly mis—sed,by her parents, brothers,sisters and all who knew her.

Our loss is heavens gain.while our home is made sad heaven is brighter.

A prechious one from us is gone, a voice we love is still, a vacient chain is in our home that never can be filled. sleep on dear child sleed on we hope to meet you in the sweet by and by. where we,ll never say good by.

Service held by T. G. Brantly at Blue Spring Church. Burial in cemetary there. Written by her mother.

Mrs. GEORGE GRAVES

It is with a sad heart and loving rememberance, I write this of our dear sister. Mrs George Graves: She departed this life April, 15, 1942

She proffessed a hope in Christ when quite young, and joined the Church at Pleasant Hill. of which she a faithful member. until God saw fit to call her to a home not made with hands. She had been in ill health for a number of years. and some times her suffering was almost more than she could bear. She never complained. She told her children just before she died she was not afrad to die. and her last request was for them to pray for each other.

I can only hope and pray that I too can say as sister said I am not afraid to die

although we were fiftcen hundred miles apart, I knew when the telegram came what the message was before reading it. We feel if she could speak she would tell us not to grieve for her. But to live that we may say as David said she can not come back to us. But we can go to her where there will be no crepe on our door, nor clouds to pray away but all will be peace and happiness forever She leaves her husband ten children Mrs. Everette Earl, Mrs. Andy Marrison, Beatrice, Gene and Barba Ann Graves, Everette' Clyde. Earnest. Melborne and Kermit Graves, 5 Brouthers and 5 sisters Lincoln, Verlin, Doree, Lonzo, and Jim Edward, Mrs. Wiley Duncan, Mrs. Lou Lambert, Mrs. Homer Pace, Mrs Bill Collingwrorth and Mrs. Richard Robbins and host of realitives and friends. Wrote by Mrs. Homer Pace. Velasco texas

Mr. C B WEAVER

C B Weaver. son of Orvil & Tracie weaver was born Aug. 28, 1865, Died July 4 1942. Age 76 years 10 months & 6 days. He was married to Louise Brantley Aug. 23, 1885. to this union was born nine children. One infant daughter proceded him to the grave. He leaves to mourn his passing his widow and 8 children 2 boys & 6 girls Mrs, nola Braatley, Mrs Nettie Cadle, Mrs. Beddie Dixon. All of Sharps Chapel. Tennessee. Mrs. Flossie Miller Maynardville, Tennessee, Mrs. Zinie Shoffner greenback, Tennessee, Mrs. Ora Daniles Friendsville Tennessee, Mr. Eston Weaver Knoxville Tennessee, Mr. Claud Weaver chatfield Minn. And 49 grand children, 23 great grand children, 2 brothers James Weaver greenback Tennessee, Luther Weaver Indianapolis Indinia· 3 sisters Mrs. Linda Hensley, Halls cross Roads, Mrs. Cordella Howell, Indianapolis, Ind. Mrs. Bettie Knight Indianapolis Ind. He professed a hope in Christ about the age of 18 and joined the Primitive Babtist Church at Mossy Springs about 58 years ago Later moved his membership to Oak Grove Church, Where he was a member at death. He was a kind father and loved by his neighbors and friends. we have lost a loving husband and father. But we feel our loss is his eternal gain Funeral service conducted by Elder Leonald White. Ailor's in charge·

378

There is no death to those who love the Lord. Their Stars go down to Shine on some fair Shore.

Sister Margarett Drummonds

daughter of Richard and Mary Wilson. Was borned March 1, 1875. And passed to the great beyond July 16, 1942. At The home of her son Mr. & Mrs Callie Drummonds.

She was married to E.S. Drummonds Nov. 24, 1894. To this union was borned thirteen children.

She professed a hope in Christ joined the Primitive Baptist Church at Meyers Grove and lived a faithful member until God saw fit to call her away.

She leaves besides a hoast of friends and relatives her husband and ud 10, children 5 girls Mrs. Bertha Drummonds, Mrs. Zora Patterson, Mrs· Rutha Hayes all of Monroe Mich Mrs. Mae Alston of Tazewell, Mrs Creeie Sproles of New Tazewell. 5 sons W.R.& Isom Drummonds of Va. Callie,& John Drummonds of New Tazewell, Minnie Drummonds of Monroe. Mich. Three brothers Richard & John Wilson of Ky. and Garfield of Rose Hill Va. 80, grand children 3, great grand children. She was a true Christian a devoted wife and a loving Mother and will be greatly missed in the home and community. But we feel our loss is her eternal gain.

Sleep on Dear Mother and take your rest. We loved you dearly but God loved you best.

Sleep on till the great resurection then we will meet again to never part no more. Funeral services was conducted at the Meyers Grove Church. Pall bearers were Walter & Damon Patterson Alfred & Joe Stevie Alston, Charlie & Lenord Jr. Drummonds, Coy Hayes, Doc Cox, Lou & Louie Dunesmore, Lee Joret Ford, Larn Meyers, Flower bearers were Lorene Muncey, Edna Elgie & Alieene Drummonds, Bennie Mae Toliver, Joyce Keck, Nellie & Elsie Robertson, Betty Sue Widener, Gene Treece.

The Rev's Matthew Oliver, T.G. Brantly, Richard Wilson' & MC Kinley Drummonds Officiating' With interment in the Drummonds Cemetary, Haynes Funeral Home in Charge. Written by a son Callie Drummonds.

Eleven

EXPERIENCE

Of one our beloved Sister wife of Eld. E.S. Drummonds

Just a few lines on my hope in Christ Jesus when I was a small my Sister came over home and she had met with a change and was telling my grand-father and mother, and father and mother and all what good things the Lord had done for her, I listened at her and thought I would give ever thing in this world if I only could no that I was a child of God an I went on uncern for some few years and I had a dream, I dreamed I had sired the day of grace away and I could not get forgiveness for it and then my awful trouble begin and I went on begging to the good Lord to save my poor soul and I had another dream I dreamed that me

and my father was down at old Brownies Creek Bank and was under a walnut tree they was three trees there and we was picking up walnuts and I Looked down the creek to ano her tree, and in under that tree I seen the smoke boiling up in under the tree in five different places, and I said look younder dadie. and he said that was torment, and dont go there and I clinged to him and I woke up and O I began to beg more and more I still went on in trouble for several years, and

I finally married and moved to Tennessee and went on in trouble and I was attending a revival at Meyers Grove in the old log cabin and they run two weeks meeting and I didn't think that the mourners bench was the place for me and I grew worse. The meeting broke up and I went on in trouble 12 months. I went begging and pleading and they started another meeting at the Grove and i told my Sister inlaw I didn't aim to go to the mouners bench this meeting· And the meeting went on a week or longer and it seemed like the preacher took his text on me and finally they call if there was any sinner in this congregation that felt like they wanted Gods people to pray for them and go back

to their seats and when they made that call I went and give my hand and went back to my seat. And I went the next day and when they made the call. I went and I went on to the mourners bench and I didn't think that was the place for me I thought I ought to be away from the house and I went home that night and I had another dream I dreamed I was at the foot of a high mountain in a straight path and I started up the mountain in a straight path and Just as I started up the Devil made a grab at me and I woke up and I was in so much trouble it would seem like if I would slip off some where and pray that this trouble would leave me and I kept putting off Praying till I went back to church and I went in and when meeting began they opened meeting and sung a song. While they was singing they ask if there was any mourners on the bench that wonted to be prayed for more earnest to give them their hands and I raised up and give the preacher my hand and as I went down on the bench I fell on my knees and it seemed like I wanted every body to pray for me and I never knew any thing about what the meeting done I never knew what they said but when I come to myself all of my troubles was gone and I felt like a feather I was so light I just felt like flying and brother Jeff Monroe anp aunt Jane Drummonds was standing by me and he said I know she has got religon if she will own it and I thought that I never would see any more trouble and I wonted to sing I am weak and siuful but Jesus would forgive for many little children has gone to him to live.

MINISTRIAL ROLL

Elders   Post Offices

John Ausmus————————Speedwell, Claiborne County, Tennessee

T. G. Brantley ————— Sharp's Chapel, Union County, Tennessee

Alfred Boruff —————Maynardville, Union County, Tennessee

Henry Comer —————LaFollette, Campbell County, Tennessee

E. S. Drummonds ———— New Tazewell Claidorne County, Tennessee

Albert Davis ————— Speedwell, Claiborne County Tennessee

V. H. Graves ——————Jamestown, Fentress County, Tennessee

John F. Keck —————Goin, Claiborne County, Tennessee

W. A. Moyers ————— Sdcedwell' Claiborne County, Tennessee

M. B. Weaver.———128 Jordan Street, Knoxville Knox., Co Tennessee

George Mays——————-Goin, Claiborne County, Tennessee

Matthew Olfver ————— Noeton, Grainger County, Tennessee

Leonard White————— LaFollette, Campbell County, Tennessee

Milton Brantley————— Sharp's Chapel, Union County Tennessee

J. R. Weaver——— ———— Gibson Station, Lee County. Virginia

Isaac Owens————————Gibson Station, Lee County, Virginia

Charlie Redmond———— Gibson Station Lee County, Virginia

LICENTIATES

Jim Collins ————— New Market, Jefferson County, Tennessee

Charlie Stanifer ————— New Tazewell Claiborne County, Tennessee

Sam Miller———————- New Market, Jefferson County, Tennessee

Adron Pierce——————— Speedwell, Claiborne County. Tennessee

Official Directory

CHURCHES	COUNTIES	PASTORS	CLERKS	CLERK'S POST OFFICE
Red Hill	Claiborne	John F. Keck Matthew Oliver ast.	Mose Treece	Speedwell, Tennessee
Gibson Station	Lee	John F.Keck	Mary Ball	Gibson Station, Virginia
Oak Grove	Union	T.G. Branty	Luna Sheritz	Goin, Tennessee
			Nell Sheritz ast.	
Rocky Dale	Knox	Leaord White	M.C. Dunn	Corryton, Tennessee
Cedar Springs	Claiborne	T.G. Brantly	J.L.Drummonds	New Tazewell, Tennessee
Blackfox	Grainger	T.G. Brantly	Sam davis	Luttrell, Tennessee
Pleasant Point	Claiborne	V.H.Graves	Austin Beason	Goin, Tennessee
Davis Chapel	Campbell	Leonard White Isaac Owens asst.	O.R. Parrott	LaFollette, Tennessee
Capps Creek	Union	John Weaver	Easter Braden	Goin, Tennessee
Pleasant Hill	Claiborne	Albert Davis	Lincoln Edwards	Speedwell, Tennessee
			Verlin Edwards asst.	
New Hebron	Jefferson	Henry Comer	Cordelia Mitchel	New Market, Tennessee
Noeton	Grainger	Matthew Oliver	J.C. Oliver	Noeton, Tennessee
Bradens Chapel	Union	Albert Davis Henry Comer asst.	Tilda Braden	Speedwell, Tennessee
Blackfork	Roan	W.R. Gates	Jessie Sweat	Wart Burg, Tennessee

CHURCHES	NAME OF DELEGATES	Rec by Expr Baprisim	Rec. by Letter	Restored..	Dismissed by letter	Excluded.	Deceased.	Total Membership	Saturday Meeting.	Contribution	Communion Meeting
Red Hill	Bros. Harry Patterson, Mose Treece, James Brantley, Sis. Edith Brantley.	0	0	00	000 000	000 000	1	86	1	2.00	July
Gibson Station	Elder Isaac Owens, Bro's Frank Edwards, Henry Hoskins, Marion Young. George Shoffner.	000 000 000	2	000 000	000	1	88	1	3.00	June	
Oak Grove	Elder's M B. Weaver, T G, Brantley, George Shoffner, John Mapels,	000	3	2	1	3	312	1	10.00	May	
Rocky Dale	Letter but no messenger	35 000	1	000	000	87	4	3.00	June		
Cedar Spring	Elder E. S. Drummands, Bros J. L, S , W & Isum Drummands, J. C Profit & wife, Addie Hill, Delia drummands,	3	1	000 1	000 1	90	4	5.25	May		
Black Fox	Bros Sam Davis, J. m. Davis, Tom Buckner and wife,	7	1	1 000	000 1	104	2	6.30	June		
Plesant Point	Elder V H, Graves, John F. Keck,—	3	1	1 000	000 2	144	1	5,00	July		
Davis chapel	Elder Lenord White, Henry Comer, Bro, Thomas Brantley	000 000	000	000 000	150	3	5,00	July			
	Henry cinnamon, Will White;										
Capps Creek	Elder John Weaver, Troy Presley, charlie collins, sister' Linda Braden,	1	2	000	000						
Plesnt Hill	Elder's Albert Davis, W A, moyers, Bro's Jeff maddox Verlin Edwards, Neal Lambert, W M, McHenry;	3	3	1	000 000	35	2	8,00	June		
Norton	Elder matthew Oliver, & wife; (no Letter)	8	1	000	2	74	4	2'50	June		
Braden Chapel	Will Sparks, Brice Braden, Lucy Braden, Tilda Braden,			000 000	000						
New Hebron	No Letter come on										
Black Fork	No letter come on	=	=	1,000 000 000	21	1	1,45	June			

384

1943

MINUTES

of the

One Hundred and Twenty-Fourth
ANNUAL SESSION

OF THE

POWELLS VALLEY

ASSOCIATION
of Primitive Baptists

HELD WITH

THE CHURCH OF CEDAR SPRING,
At Moyers Grove, Claiborne County, Tennessee
AUGUST 20, 21 and 22, 1943

Officers:

Elder T. G. BRANTLEY, ... Moderator
Elder JOHN F. KECK, ... Assistant Moderator
Brother SAM DAVIS, ... Clerk
Brother J. L. DRUMMONDS, ... Assistant Clerk

The next session will be held with the Church at Capps Creek, Union County, Tennessee, beginning on Friday before the Third Saturday in August, 1944. Elder W. A. Moyers to preach the Introductory Sermon, Elder Albert Davis alternate.

Ham Printing Co. Cordele. Ga.

MINUTES

FRIDAY'S PROCEEDINGS

1st. According to previous arrangements the Association met according to adjournment.

2nd. After singing hymns, prayer by Elder Henry Comer.

3rd. The Introductory Sermon was delivered by Elder V. H. Graves, from St. John 14th chapter, 6 verse. Quotation, "I am the way the truth and the light." Followed by alternate, Elder John F. Keck.

4th. After 15 minutes intermission the Association re-assembled. After singing, prayer by Elder Allen Gates. The Association was called to order for business by the Moderator, Elder T. G. Brantley.

5th. By motion, Elder T. G. Brantley was re-elected Moderator.

6th. By motion, Elder John F. Keck was elected assistant Moderator.

7th. By motion Bro. Sam Davis was re-elected Clerk, and Bro. J. L. Drummonds was re-elected assistant Clerk.

8th. Called for letters from the sister churches. Received 9, which were read by the Clerks.

9th. By motion, said letters were received, and the delegation welcomed to seats by the Moderator.

10th. Called for corresponding letters from sister Associations. Received one from the Nolachucky Association, with their messenger to-wit: Elder Allen Gates. Said letter was read by the Clerk and on motion was received, and the delegation welcomed to a seat with us.

11th. Called for letters from newly constituted churches. Received one from Monroe, Michigan, which was read by the Clerk.

12th. By motion said letter was received and the delegation welcomed to seats by the Moderator giving them the right hand of fellowship.

13. By motion the Moderator appoint all committees to arrange the business of this Association.

(A) On arrangements: Bros. John Davis, Henry Hoskins, James Edwards.

(B) On Preaching: Bros. George Shoffner, W. F. Roberson, Henry Stiner, together with the church.

(C) On Correspondence: Elders Leonard White, Albert Davis, V. H. Graves.

(D) On request: Bros. Tom Brantley, Troy Pressley, Charlie Smith.

(E) On Finance: J. M. Davis, Jim Brantley, Will White.

14th. On motion Elders M. B. Weaver, John F. Keck and Henry Comer write corresponding letters to the Hiwassee and Nolachucky Associations.

15th. On motion adjourned until Saturday morning at 10:30.

SATURDAY MORNING 10:30

1st. The Association met pursuant to adjournment.

2nd. After singing praise by Elder Leonard White, prayer by Elder Albert Davis.

3rd. The Association was called to order by the assistant Moderator, Elder John F. Keck.

4th. Called for letters from sister churches that failed to get in Friday. Received 3, which were read.

5th. By motion said letters were received and the delegates welcomed to seats.

6th. Called for members of sister churches who were not delegates. Received none.

7th. Called for the report of the committee on Preaching.

8th. We, your committee on preaching beg leave to make the following report to-wit: Friday night, Elder Leonard White, Elder Allen Gates. Saturday at the stand: Elder Oscar Moyers, Elder M. B. Weaver. Saturday night: Elder John F. Keck, W. A. Moyers. Sunday: Elder Leonard White, Moderator, to close.

Respectfully submitted,

> BROS. GEORGE SHAFFNER
> W. F. ROBERSON
> HENRY STINER.

9th. On motion the report was received and the committee was discharged.

10th. Called for the report of the committee on arrangements.

(b) We, your committee on arrangements beg leave to report the following:

1st. Call the roll. 2nd, call for the report of the committee on preaching. 3rd, call for the report of the committee on correspondence. 4th, call for the report of the committee on request. 5th, call for the report of the committee on finance. 6th, When and where shall our next Association be held. Who shall preach the introductory sermon and who shall be his alternate.

7th. How many copies of minutes shall we have printed, and who shall superintend the printing and distribution of same, and what shall he be allowed for his service.

Respectfully submitted,

> BROS. JAMES EDWARDS
> JOHN H. DAVIS
> HENRY HOSKINS.

11th. On motion the report was received and the committee discharged.

12th. Called for the report of the committee on correspondence.

(c) We, your committee on correspondence beg leave to make the following report: That we keep up our correspondence with the Hiwassee and Nolachucky Associations by letter and messengers.

Respectfully,

ELDER LEONARD WHITE
ELDER ALBERT DAVIS
ELDER V. H. GRAVES.

13th. On motion the report was received and the committee discharged.

14th. Called for the report of the committee on requests.

(d) We, your committee on requests beg leave to submit the following: That we have all the obituaries printed in our minutes, that the churches furnish, and that the next session of the Association be held with the church at Capps Creek, Union County, Tennessee.

Respectfully submitted,

BROS. CHARLIE SMITH
THOMAS BRANTLEY
TROY PRESSLEY.

15th. On motion the report was received and the committee discharged.

16th. Called for the report of the committee on finance.

(e) We, your committee on finance beg leave to make the following report: Received for printing minutes as follows: Davis Chapel, $3.50; Gibson Station $3.00; Capps Creek $5.00; Pleasant Hill $5.00; Monroe Michigan $5.00; Cedar Spring $5.00; Rocky Dale $3.00; Red Hill $2.60; Black Fox $7.00; Pleasant Point $5.00; Bradens Chapel $1.81; Oak Grove $10:00; Noeton $2.00; and for visiting ministers expenses: Rocky Dale $5.00; Capps Creek $5.00; Gibsons Station $2.00.

Respectfully submitted,

BROS. JOHN DAVIS
JAMES BRANTLEY
W. M. WHITE.

17th. On motion received the report and discharged the committee.

18th. On motion the next session of the Powells Valley Association will be held with the church at Capps Creek, Union County, Tennessee, to commence on Friday before the third Saturday in August, 1944. Elder W. A. Moyers to preach the introductory sermon and Elder Albert Davis to be his alternate.

19th. On motion we have 800 copies of minutes printed, and that the Clerk superintend the printing and distribution of same, and that he be allowed $10.00 for his services.

20th. On motion we appoint the following named Elders as messengers to the Nolachucky Association: Leonard White, Henry Comer and M. B. Weaver, V. H. Graves. To the Hiwassee Association: Elders Leonard White and V. H. Graves.

21st. On motion be it resolved that we tender our heart felt thanks to this dear old church and the surrounding community for their generous hospitality and kind treatment to us through this Association.

22nd. Motion in order to adjourn until 10:30 at the time and place above stated.

23rd. Dismissed in order.

ELD. T. G. BRANTLEY, Moderator,
Maynardville, Tenn.
ELD. JOHN F. KECK, Asst. Mod.
Goin, Tenn.
BRO. SAM DAVIS, Clerk
Luttrell, Tenn.
BRO. J. L. DRUMMONDS, Asst. Clerk,

New Tazewell, Tenn.

On Sunday of this date a large audience assembled at the altar and so attentively listened to the well delivered sermons of Elder Matthew Oliver, from text: "He that gather himself under his wings abideth forever." Followed by Elder Allen Gates from text, "I give unto thee an everlasting covenant," followed by Elder Leonard White, and closing remarks by the Moderator, all of which were delivered in a most loving spirit and with the greatest interest to all, and a loving parting was expressed.

CORRESPONDING LETTER

We, the Powells Valley Association of Primitive Baptists, now in session with the church of Cedar Spring, Claiborne County, Tenn., on August 20, 21, 22, 1943, to the Hiwassee and Nolachucky Associations of Primitive Baptists with whom we correspond and when convened with the churches of the Hiwassee and Nolachucky Associations. We have gladly seated Elder Allen Gates, of the Nolachucky and Bros. — of the Hiwassee, and ask that you send another next year. May the great head of the church be with you all in all your endeavors to worship Him.

Respectfully submitted,

ELDER HENRY COMER
ELDER M. B. WEAVER
ELDER JOHN F. KECK.

389

OBITUARIES

Bro. Glen Mitchell was born Aug. 10, 1891, died Nov. 18, 1942, joined the Primitive Baptist church in the year 1932, of which he lived a faithful member until death.

Elder Alfred Parks died December 14, 1942, joined the Primitive Baptist years ago, and was ordained an Elder, of which he lived faithful until death.

Sister Millie Brooks joined the Primitive Baptist church years ago, of which she lived a faithful member until God called her to her reward December 4, 1942. Gone but not forgotten.

Brother Aaron Pierce was born August 26, 1891, died May 1, 1943, age 51 years, 8 months, 7 days. He was first married to Betty Young. To this union was born two children, Nolon and Carl Pierce. Later, after his first wife deceased, he was married to Venie Braden. To this union was born one daughter, Betty Jane Pierce. He joined the Primitive Baptist church at Braden's Chapel, lived a faithful member until death. Funeral services were held at Flat Hollow cemetery. He leaves to mourn their loss, his wife, two sons, one daughter and four brothers, but their loss is his eternal gain.

By his wife and Henry Comer.

Sister Rozell Collins England was born Jan. 11, 1888, joined the church at Pleasant Point in 1902 and lived a faithful member until God called her to her reward in His presence Aug. 3, 1943. She was a devoted christian and a loving mother and will be missed by all who knew her.

Leonard Carl Petree, son of Mr. and Mrs. Edd Petree, was born May 28, 1940, died May 14, 1941, making his stay on earth 11 months and 15 days.

He leaves father, mother, 4 sisters, many friends and relatives. He was a sweet child and was loved by all who knew him.

Funeral services were conducted by Rev. Sam Kinsley at the Liberty Baptist church. Burial in church cemetery.

"We loved you, yes we loved you, but Jesus loved you more; He has sweetly called you to yonder's shining shore.

The Golden Gates were open, and a gentle voice said 'come,' And with farewells unspoken, you calmly entered Home."

Gone but not forgotten.

Written by a cousin: Miss Pearl A. White, Route 1, LaFollette, Tenn.

Sallie (Beeler) Kivett was born Oct. 11, 1878, died March 11, 1942, age 63 years and 5 months. She was married to James Kivett April 11, 1897. To this union was born 9 children, 5 boys, 4 girls. Two of the boys preceeded her in death, 18 grand children and 1 great grand child. She is survived by her husband, one brother and two sisters.

She professed faith in Christ and joined the Primitive Baptist church at Mossy Spring, Union County, in January 1894 (48 years ago.) where she remained a faithful member until the church disbanded on account of the waters of Norris Lake.

Sister Kivett was a loyal wife and a faithful mother, much beloved by all her neighbors in every community in which she lived.

"We cannot say, we will not say, that she is dead but just away."

Brother Isaac Newton LeMarr was born Oct. 30, 1856, died July 8, 1943. He professed faith in Christ in early life and first joined the Missionary Baptist at New Salem, about fifty five years ago. Then moved his membership to Strait Branch Primitive Baptist church some 25 years ago, where he remained until the church property was lost to Norris Lake. Then he moved his membership to Davis Chapel, where he remained a faithful member until July 8, 1943, when that noble soul of his joined God's big eternity. Dead but still living.

Sister Basie Welch, daughter of Jeff and Narcisis Treece was born February 17, 1894 and passed to the great beyond November 3, 1942 at her home. She professed faith in Christ at an early age and joined the Primitive Baptist church at Red Hill and remained a faithful member until death.

She was married to Frelon Welch October 1913. To this union was born five children, two sons and three daughters. William and Irene died in infancy.

Surviving are her husband and three children, Gene and Jeanette of Speedwell, Tenn. and Mrs. Grant Manning, of Cumberland Gap, Tenn., and Earl Treece, a nephew whom she raised and two grand sons, Jackie and Joe Manning, of Cumberland Gap Tenn. Three sisters, Mrs. J. C. Earl, of Cyril, Oklahoma, Mrs. Arnold Patterson, of Cumberland Gap, Tenn, Mrs. Lillie Siler, of Los Angeles, California and six brothers, Wylie and Mose, of Speedwell, Tenn, Luke, Bee and Jim, of Indiana and Robert Treece, of Ohio.

She was a true christian and a devoted wife and a loving mother and will be greatly missed in the home and community.

Mother was so kind and true to her children dear
But when the Lord saw fit to take her, it left us alone down here.

Our loss is heaven's gain.

Pall bearers were Edd Welch, Herzal Treece, Albert Treece and Howard Treece. Flower bearers were Beatrice Keck, Mayole McNew, Pearlie Patton, Cleo Evans, Clevia Madon, Althea Evans and Elsie Welch. The Rev. John F. Keck and Will Rose officiating with interment in the Red Hill cemetery. Agees and Walters Funeral Home in charge.

Written by a daughter, Miss Jeanette Welch.

MINISTERS ROLL

Elders	Elder's Pose Offices
John Asumus	Speedwell, Clairborne County, Tenn.
T. G. Brantley	Maynardville, Union County, Tenn.
Alfred Boruff	Maynardville, Union County, Tenn.
Henry Comer	LaFollette, Campbell County, Tenn.
E. S. Drummonds	New Tazewell, Clairborne County, Tenn.
Albert Davis	Speedwell, Clairborne County, Tenn.
V. H. Graves	Jamestown, Fentress County, Tenn.
John F. Keck	Goin, Clairborne County, Tenn.
W. A. Moyers	Speedwell, Clairborne County, Tenn.
M. B. Weaver	128 Jordan Street, Knoxville, Knox County, Tenn.
George Mays	Goin, Clairborne County, Tenn.
Matthew Oliver	Noeton, Grainger County. Tenn.
Leonard White	LaFollette, Campbell County, Tenn.
Milton Brantley	Sparks Chapel, Union County, Tenn.
J. R. Weaver	Gibson's Station, Lee County, Va.
Isaac Owens	Gibson's Station, Lee County, Va.
Charlie Redmond	Gibson's Station, Lee County, Va.

LICENTIATES

Jim Collins	New Market, Jefferson County, Tenn.
Charlie Stanifer	New Tazewell, Clairborne County, Tenn.
Sam Miller	New Market, Jefferson County, Tenn.

OFFICIAL DIRECTORY

CHURCHES	COUNTIES	PASTORS	CLERKS	CLERK'S POST OFFICE
Red Hill	Clairborne	John F. Keck	Mose Treece	Speedwell, Tenn.
Gibson's Station	Lee	Leonard White	Mary Ball	Gibson's Station, Va.
			Luna Sheritz,	
Oak Grove	Union	T. G. Brantley	Nell Sheritz, Asst.	Goin, Tenn.
Rocky Dale	Knox	Leonard White	M. C. Dunn	Carryton, Tenn.
Cedar Spring	Clairborne	T. G. Brantley	J. L. Drummonds	New Tazewell, Tenn.
			Sam Davis,	
Black Fox	Grainger	T. G. Brantley	J. M. Davis, Asst.	Lutrell, Tenn.
Pleasant Point	Clairborne	V. H. Graves	Austin Beason	Goin, Tenn.
Davis Chapel	Campbell	Charlie Redmond	O. R. Parrott	LaFollette, Tenn.
Capps Creek	Union	John Weaver	Laster Braden	Goin, Tenn.
			J. L. Edwards	
Pleasant Hill	Clairborne	Albert Davis	Virlin Edwards, asst	Speedwell, Tenn.
New Hebron	Jefferson	Henry Comer	Cordelia Mitchell	New Market, Tenn.
Noeton	Grainger	Matthew Oliver	J. C. Oliver	Noeton, Tenn.
Braden's Chapel	Union	Henry Comer	Tilda Braden	Speedwell, Tenn.
Black Fork	Roan	W. R. Gates	Jessie Sweat	Wartburg, Tenn.
Monroe Michigan		E. S. Drummonds	Maggie Sandifer	112 W. 5th St, Monroe, Mich.

Statistical Table

CHURCHES	NAMES OF DELEGATES	Rec. by Exp and Bap.	Rec. by Letter	Restored	Dis. by Letter	Excluded	Deceased	Total Membership	Saturday Meeting	Contribution	Communion Meetings
Red Hill	James Brantley, Minerva Brantley, Edith Brantley	3					1	75	2	$2.60	July
Gibson's Station	Henry Hoskins and wife, G. W. Shoffner and wife	3	2		8			87	3	5.00	July
Oak Grove	Eld. T. G. Brantley, Henry Stiner, George Shoffner, Luna Sheritz.	10	3		1	3		318	4	10.00	May
Rocky Dale	Eld. M. B. Weaver, Leola Palmer, M. C. Dunn and wife	3	2					87	4	8.00	May
Cedar Spring	Eld. E. S. Drummonds, Clay Davis, Jim Drummonds, J. L. Drummonds. John Davis.	2						92	4	5.00	May
Black Fox	John Davis, John Bundon, Sam Cook, Sam Davis	3		1	3	3½		105	2	7.00	June
Pleasant Point	Elders John F. Keck, V. H. Graves, Bros. George Williams, J. M. Cox, A. C. Goin, Edna Rossin, Allie Williams, Etta Hopper, Goldie Simmons.	4					1	150	1	5.00	July
Davis Chapel	Leonard White, Henry Comer, Thomas Brantley, Will White							149	3	3.50	July
Capps Creek	J. R. Weaver, Vada Weaver, Troy Pressley and wife,	3						35		10.00	June
Pleasant Hill	Laster Broden, Charlie and Jess Collins, Maggie Collins Albert Davis, W. A. Moyers, W. M. McHenry, James Edwards.	5		1			1	75	2	5.00	June
Noeton	Matthew Oliver and wife, John Oliver	1						21	1	2.00	June
Braden's Chapel	William Sparks, Lucy Sparks, Tilda Braden									1.80	June
New Hebron	No Letter Come on										
Black Fork	No Letter Come on										
Monroe Michigan	Sis Etna Atkinson, Maggie Stanifer						1	7	1	5.00	

1944

MINUTES

OF THE

One Hundred and Twenty-Fifth

ANNUAL SESSION

OF THE

POWELLS VALLEY

ASSOCIATION

of Primitive Baptists

HELD WITH

THE CHURCH OF CAPP'S CREEK

August 18, 19, 20, 1944

OFFICERS

Elder T. G. BRANTLEY .... Moderator
Elder JOHN F. KECK .. .. Assistant Moderator
Brother SAM DAVIS .... Clerk
Brother J. L. DRUMMONDS .... Assistant Clerk

The next Session will be held with the Church at Pleasant Point, Claiborne County, Tennessee, beginning on Friday before the third Saturday in August, 1945. Elder Albert Davis to preach the Introductory Sermon and Elder U. H. Graves to be his alternate.

FRIDAY'S PROCEEDINGS

First—According to the previous arrangements the association met pursuant to adjournment.

Second—After singing hymns, prayer by Elder Albert Davis.

Third—According to previous arrangements the introductory was delivered by Elder W. A. Moyers from twelfth chapter and second verse Hebrews, looking unto Jesus who is the author of our faith.

Fourth—After 15 minutes of intermission, the association reassembled, and after singing Hymns, prayer by Elder T. G. Brantly.

Fifth—The association was called to order for business by Moderator Elder T. G. Brantly.

Sixth—Called for letters from Sister Churches of this association received, nine of which was read by the clerks.

Seventh—On motion, all of said letters was received and the delegates welcomed to seats.

Eighth—Called for members of sister churches, who were not delegates, received from Pleasant Point: Brother B. L. Beason, Pleasant Hill; Brother Ed McBee, Gibson's Station; Sisters Susie Shoffner, Sister Mossey Cottrell.

Ninth—Called for letters from newly constituted churches, received one from Kirkwood Church, Knoxville, Tenn.

Tenth—On motion, said letter was read.

Eleventh—On motion said letter was received and the delegates welcomed to seats by the Moderator giving them the right hand of fellowship.

Twelfth—Called for corresponding letters from sister associations, received one from the Hiwassee association by the hand of Elder W. R. Gates, also one from the Nolachucky association.

Thirteenth—On motion, Said letters was received and the delegates welcomed to seats with us to-wit: Elders W. R. Gates, Elder J. F. Campbell, Elder John B. Russell, delegates from Nolachucky.

Fourteenth—On motion, Elder T. G. Brantly was reelected moderator.

Fifteenth—On motion, Elder John F. Keck was reelected assistant moderator.

16th—On motion, Brother Sam Davis was reelected clerk, and Brother J. L. Drummonds, assistant clerk.

Seventeenth—On motion, the moderator appoint all necessary committees to arrange the business of this association.

(A) On Preaching: Bros. Ike Shoffner, D. L. Beason, Sam Cook, together with this church.

(B) On Arrangements: Bros. Henry Stiner, William Sparks, H. C. Hoskins.

(C) On Correspondence: Elders J. R. Weaver, John F. Keck, Brother Tom Buckner.

(D) On Request: Bros. G. W. Williams, Charlie King, G. W. Shoffner.

(E) On Finance: Bros. George Shoffner, Troy Pressley, E. P. Drummonds.

Eighteenth—Motion in order to adjourn until 10 o'clock Saturday morning.

SATURDAY'S PROCEEDINGS

First—Saturday morning, 10 o'clock, the association met pursuant to adjournment. Prayer by Elder Albert Davis.

Second—The association was announced in order for business by the moderator.

Third—Called for letters from Sister Churches that failed to get in Friday. Received two, which was read.

Fourth—On motion, said letters was received and the delegation welcomed to seats.

Fifth—Called for members who were not delegates.

Sixth—Called for the report of the Committee on Arrangements.

(A) We your Committee on Arrangements beg leave to make the following report: First, call the roll; second, call for the report of the Committee on Preaching; third, call for the report of the Committee on Correspondence; fourth, call for the report of the Committee on Finance; sixth, when and where shall our next association be held, who shall preach the introductory sermon and who shall be his alternate. How many coppies of minutes shall we have printed, who shall superintend the printing and distribution of same, and what shall be allowed for his services.

Respectfully submitted,

> BROS. HENRY HOSKINS,
> W. M. SPARKS,
> W. H. STINER.

Seventh—On motion, the report was received and the committee discharged.

Eighth—Called the roll and erased the names of the absentees.

Ninth—Called for the report of the Committee on Preaching.

(B) We, your Committee on Preaching beg leave to submit the following report. Friday night at Oak Grove, Elder W. R. Gates; Saturday at the church, Elder Gates, Elder Russell and Elder W. A. Moyers; Sunday at the stand, Elder Matthew Oliver, Elder V. H. Graves, and Elder W. R. Gates, the moderator to close.

Respectfully submitted,

> BROS. SAM R. COOK,
> D. L. BEASON,
> IKE SHOFFNER,
> TOGETHER WITH THE CHURCH.

Tenth—On motion, the report was received and the committee discharged.

Eleventh—Called for the report of the Committee on Correspondence.

(C) We, your Committee on Correspondence, beg leave to submit the following report, that we keep up our correspondence with the Hiawassee and Nolachucky associations by letter and messengers.

Respectfully submitted,

> ELDER JOHN F. KECK,
> ELDER JOHN WEAVER,
> BRO. TOM BUCKNER.

Twelfth—On motion, the report was received and the Committee discharged.

Thirteenth—Called for the report of the Committee on Request.

(D) We, your Committee on Request, beg leave to submit the

397

following report. That we have all the obituaries printed in our minutes that the church furnish, and that the next annual session of the Powell's Valley Association be held with the church of Pleasant Point, Claiborne County, Tennessee, to commence on Friday before the third Saturday in August. 1945.

Respectfully submitted,

BROS. G. W. WILLIAMS,
CHARLIE KING,
G. W. SHOFFNER.

Thirteenth—Called for the report of the Committee on Finance.

(E) We, your Committee on Finance, make the following report received from Sister Churches for printing minutes. Davis Chapel, $6; Pleasant Point, $7; Red Hill, $2; Oak Grove, $10.25; Gibson's Station, $3; Kirkwood, $5; Blackfox, $6.50; Rockydale, $3; Cedar Spring, $6; Braden's Chapel, $3.10; Capps Creek, $3; Monroe, Mich., $3; Pleasant Hill, $6; Noeton ,$1.50; total, $63.85. Also received for visiting ministers expenses as follows: Rocky Dale, $4; Gibson's Station, $5; Capps Creek, $3; Kirkwood, $15; Monroe, Mich., $3; Pleasant Hill, $2; total, $32.00.

Respectfully submitted,

BROS. D. P. DRUMMONDS.
TROY PRESSLEY,
GEORGE SHOFFNER

Fourteenth—On motion, the report received and the Committee discharged.

Fifteenth—On motion, we have 800 coppies of minutes printed; that the clerk superintend the printing and the distribution of same, and that he be allowed 15.00 for his services.

Sixteenth—On motion, we send as messengers to the Hiwassee Association the following named elders to-wit: Elder W. H. Graves, Elder T. G. Brantly, Elder Albert Davis.

Seventeenth—On motion, we send the following named elders as messengers to the Nolachucky Association to-wit: Elder George W. Mays, Elder V. H. Graves, W. A. Moyers.

Eighteenth—On motion, Elder John F. Keck write corresponding letters to each of these associations and have the same printed in our minutes.

Nineteenth—On motion the next annual session of the Powell's Valley Association to be held with the Church at Pleasant Point, Claiborne County, Tennessee, to commence on Friday before the third Saturday in August, 1945.

Twentieth—On motion, Elder Albert Davis preach the introductory sermon, and that Elder V. H. Graves be his alternate.

Twenty-first—On motion, be it resolved that we tender our heartfelt thanks to this dear old church and the community for their generous hospitality and kind treatment through this association.

Twenty-second—Motion in order to adjourn until the time and place above stated.

Twenty-third—Dismissed in order.

ELDER T. G. BRANTLEY, Moderator,
P. O. Maynardville, Tenn.
ELDER JOHN F. KECK, Asst. Moderator,
P. O. Goin, Tenn.
BRO. SAM DAVIS, Clerk,

P. O. Luttrell, Tenn.

BRO. J. L. DRUMMONDS, Asst. Clerk,

P. O. New Tazewell, Tenn.

SUNDAY'S PROCEEDINGS

On Sunday of this date, a large and behaved audience assembled at the altar and attentively listened to the well delivered sermons of Elder W. R. Gates from text work out your own salvation with fear and trembling etc., followed by Elder Matthew Oliver and closing remarks by the moderator, all of which was delivered in a most loving spirit, and a loving parting was expressed by the shedding of tears, clapping of hands,, and invoking the blessings of God upon each other.

CORRESPONDING LETTER

We, the Powell's Valley Association of Primitive Baptist now in session with the Church of Capps Creek, Union County, Tennessee, on August 18, 19, 20, 1944, to the Hiwassee and Nolachucky Associations. We have a deep regret that you could not have a representative, especially Elder Allen Gates. We are glad to seat the Hiawassee, and ask that you send another next year. May the great head of the church be with you and guide you in all your endeavors to worship Him. This ordered by the Association. Elder John F. Keck.

OBITUARIES

MRS. NOLA WEAVER BRANTLEY

Mrs. Nola Weaver Brantley, daughter of Mr. and Mrs. C. B. Weaver, died at her home March 1, 1944, at 9:15 p. m. She was born July 7 1886, making her stay here on earth 57 years, 7 months, and 23 days.

She was married to T. G. Brantley May 29, 1904. To this union there was not any children born. She leaves to mourn her passing, her husband, Rev. T. G. Brantley of Maynardville, Tenn.; her mother Mrs. C. B. Weaver, Maynardville, Tenn; five sisters and two brothers Mrs. Zina Shoffner, Greenback, Tenn.; Mr. Claude Weaver, Chatfield, Minn.; Mrs. Charlie Cadle, Insull, Ky.; Mrs. Oscar Dixon, Sharps Chapel Tenn.; Mrs. A. C. Miller Maynardville Tenn.; Mrs. Amon Daniels, Friendsville, Tenn.; Mr. E. W. Weaver, Knoxville, Tenn, and also several nieces and nephews. She was also a foster mother of seven children one son and six daughter, Mr. Lodus Hill, Baltimore, Md.; Mrs. Izora England, Goin, Tenn.; Mrs. Pearl Cadle, Evarts Ky.; Miss Mary Spurgeon, Knoxville; Mrs. Agnes Townsend, Knoxville, and Miss Ann Franklin, Maynardville, and a host of friends to mourn her passing.

She professed hope in Christ in 1895 and joined the church at Mossy-Springs and was baptized by Elder M. B. Weaver in 1899. She later moved her membership to Oak Grove and lived a consistent member until death.

She was a devoted wife, daughter, and sister and loved by all who knew her.

We feel without any doubt that our loss is her Eternal gain. Funeral services conducted by Elder John F. Keck and Elder Leonard White. Ailors of Maynardville in charge.

MARGARET E. CAIN SMITH

Margaret E. Cain Smith, wife of Sterling Smith, was born November 1882, died February 20, 1943. She professed faith in Christ at an early age and joined the Primitive Baptist Church at Straight Branch Church and lived there until the church was took over by the TVA, after that she got her letter but never did put it in no other church. She was loved by all who knew her. She leaves her husband and a host of friends to mourn her loss, but we believe heaven is our gain.

Written by the clerk, Lussie McBee.

SISTER RACHEL DUNCAN

Sister Rachel Duncan, former wife of Elder J. D. Monroe, was born November 16, 1860, and departed this life January 4, 1944, being 83 years, one month and 19 days old. She professed faith in Christ and joined the Primitive Baptist Church at Pleasant Point at an early age and lived a faithful member until death. She leaves to mourn their loss, five grandchildren; Son, Charlie and Randa Treece of Knoxville; Pearl Phelps of Goin, and thirteen great grandchildren; one half brother, G. H. Williams, New Tazewell; one sister, Sarah Williams, Madisonville, Tenn. Dear grandmother, sleep and take your rest, we miss you but God knows best.

BROTHER M. F. KIRK

Brother M. F. Kirk was born July 14, 1879, joined the Primitive Baptist Church at Blackfox May 4, 1921, of which he lived a consistant member until God called him to his reward on March 29, 1944, and was laid to rest in the Cabbage Cemetery in Grainger County, to wait the Resurrection morning. He leaves to mourn their loss, two brothers, one half-brother and three sisters, and a host of relatives and friends.

ROSIE MOYERS EVANS

Rosie Moyers Evans was born April 18, 1875, died January 16, 1944. Joined the Primitive Baptists at an early age and later moved her membership to Pleasant Hill Church and lived a faithful member until death. She leaves husband, five sisters, three brothers and four children, and several grandchildren and great-grandchildren to mourn her loss. I hope our loss is her eternal gain.

Written by her sister, Mrs. W. A. Moyers, Speedwell, Tenn., Route No. 3.

BROTHER GEORGE WASHINGTON BRYANT

Brother George Washington Bryant was born December 18, 1867, the son of Lawson and Jane Bryant, in Claiborne County, Tennessee.

Brother Bryant departed this life January 2, 1944, at 4:25 a. m. at the age of 76 years and 18 days. He professed faith in Christ in early life, joined the Primitive Baptist Church at Gibson Station, Va., and remained a faithful member until death. Burial was at Southern Cemetery, January 3, 1944. Brother Bryant was married to Amanda Southern in 1890. To this union was born two sons and one daughter. Two sons and Mrs. Bryant preceeded him in death by several years. He is survived by one daughter, Mrs. Lela Brittain of Gibson Station; two grandchildren, Mrs. George Dalton of Appalachia, Va., George L. Brittain with the Army overseas, one great grandchild, five brothers and two sisters.

I am the resurrection and the life, saith the Lord; he that believeth in me, though he were dead, yet shall he live, and whosoever liveth and believeth in me, shall never die.

WILEY TREECE

Wiley Treece was born October 13, 1879, died June 8, 1944. He leaves to mourn his passing, his wife, 10 children, 17 grandchildren, one great-grandchildren, five brothers, three sisters, and his many friends. He professed faith in the lord in his early days joined the Primitive Baptist Church at Meyers Grove and later moved his membership to Red Hill where he remained a faithful member as long as he was able to attend.

He had not been so he could talk for a while, but his presents was company to us, but we will never forget Thursday morning, 8:30 o'clock, June 8, when the Angels come and took him away the sad and lonely hours and days we have underwent. The one we loved from earth is gone the voice we loved is still. There is a vacant place in our home that never can be filled. Funeral service was held by Bros. T. G. Brantley, Johnie Keck and Hugh Vancil. His body was laid to rest in the Red Hill Cemetery to await the resurrection. Sleep on dear daddy and take your rest. We all loved you dear but God loved you best.

By Mrs. Wiley Treece and children.

SISTER FRANCIE BRADEN

Sister Francie Braden, daughter of Sam and Catherine Duncan, was born February 25, 1899, and passed to the great beyond April 10, 1944, at Monroe, Mich. She was married to Charlie Braden June 14, 1919. To this union was born nine children, two of which have preceded her in death. She professed hope in Christ at an early age and joined the Primitive Baptist Church at Capps Creek and lived a faithful member until death. She leaves her husband, three sons and four daughters, Sherman Braden, U. S. Army; Clarence and Dewey Braden of Monroe, Mich.; Lucy, Fannie, Vina and Wanda Braden, all of Monroe, Mich.; four brothers and three sisters. We feel like our loss is Heaven's eternal gain.

Written by her niece.

DORA BELLE (JOHNSON) CAREY

Dora Belle (Johnson) Carel was born April 7, 1871, age 72 years, nine months and 25 days; died February 2, 1944. She was married to John Carey, April 9, 1891.

Surviving are her husband and ten children; six boys, Bill and Milt of Detroit, Mich.; Sherman and Johnie of Monroe, Mich.; Mitchel and Walter of Crossville, Tenn; four girls, Jannie Tompson of Detroit, Mich.; Emma Cole of Crossville, Tenn.; Ottie Mae Profit of Bonnie Blue, Va.; 52 grandchildren and 11 great-grandchildren; also four brothers, Dr. Sam Johnson of Sneedville, Tenn.; Johnie of Middlesboro, Ky.; Elsworth and Milt of Goin, Tenn.

She professed faith in Christ and joined the Primitive Baptist Church at Pleasant Point at an early age and lived a faithful member until death. She was a devoted wife and loving mother and was loved by all who knew her.

Dear mother, sleep on and take your rest. We miss you so, but God knows best.

MRS. OLIE McCHONE

Mrs. Olie McChone, 69, the wife of Sherman McChone, died at her home near Powder Spring Sunday at 6 p. m., July 16, 1944.

401

Survivors are son, John McChone, Powder Springs; two daughters, Mrs. Lulu Buckner, Luttrell, Tenn.; Mrs. Una Hunley, Powder Springs; sister, Clerce Buckner, Luttrell, Tenn.; half-brother, King David Fields, Luttrell, Tenn.; 22 grandchildren, 40 great-grandchildren. She professed faith in Christ at Crooked Creek Baptist Church and joined the church at Hamilton Grove. Funeral services conducted by her pastor, Elder T. G. Brantley.

CATHERINE WHITE ELLISON

Catherine White Ellison was born November 19, 1871, died June 5, 1944, age 72 years, seven months and 24 days. She was married to Benjamin Ellison. In their early days to this union was born seven children, four deceased. She leaves to mourn her loss her husband, Mrs. Harley Ellison, Mrs. Ivey Daniels, all of Sharps Chapel, Tenn.; 13 grandchildren, seven great-grandchildren, three brothers and two sisters; Mr. John White of Sharps Chapel, Tenn.; Mr. Henry White of LaFollette, Tenn.; Mr. Marcus White of Knoxville, Tenn.; Mrs. Marshall Ellison of Sharps Chapel, Tenn.; Mrs. Sterling Smith of Maynardville, Tenn. She professd a hope in Christ at an early age and joined the Primitive Baptist Church at Oak Grove, where she lived a member until death. We have lost a loving mother, but we feel our loss is her eternal gain. Funeral conducted by her pastor, Elder T. G. Brantley.

REBECKAH LEAH ELLISON

Rebeckah Leah Ellison was born September 11, 1943, and departed this life January 8, 1944, age three months and 28 days. Surviving are the parents, Mr. and Mrs. J. M. Ellison, and sister, Lelia Mae. We know our loss is her eternal gain, while our home is vacant without our precious babe we know that Heaven is made brighter.

A precious one from us is gone
A voice we loved is still,
A place is vacant in our home
Which never can be filled.
God loved her best, and put her to rest.
God has taken her away,
So we shall meet on that great day.
She was not with us very long,
But she's in a land where nothing is wrong.

Funeral conducted at Oak Grove Baptist Church by T. G. Brantley, pastor.

Mr. and Mrs. J. M. Ellison.

SISTER TAHITHA JANE TREECE DRUMMONDS

Sister Tahitha Jane Treece Drummonds was born August 22, 1863. She departed this life July 13, 1933, being 80 years, 10 months and nine days of age. She was united in marriage to Tandy Drummonds and to this union was born four sons, three of whom have preceeded her to the great beyond, and three daughters. She professed faith in Christ at an early age and joined the Primitive Baptist Church at Cedar Springs, April the 3rd Saturday in 1880, where she lived a faithful member until death.

Uncle Tandy preceded her in death on April 9, 1938. The deceased had been ill for several weeks.

Aunt Anne is survived by three daughters, Mrs. Bernice Welch,

Mrs. Maggie Robertson and Mrs. Veltie Munsey, and one son, Clarence Drummonds, all of New Tazewell; 20 grandchildren, five great grandchildren, and three brothers Mrs. John Treece of Knoxville, Mr. Bob Treece of Oklahoma and Mr. Jim Treece of Middlesboro; three sisters, Mrs. Betty Russell, Mrs. Martha Russell and Mrs. Mollie Snyder, all of Knoxville, and a host of friends and relatives to mourn our loss. Funeral services held by her pastor, Elder T. G. Brantley, assisted by the Rev. Charlie Williams.

MRS. EASTER ELIZABETH WEAVER
Mrs. Easter Elizabeth Weaver was born February 26, 1870, died April 19, 1943, age 73 years, 1 month, 21 days. She was married to Elder M. B. Weaver August 1887 and to this union was born 12 children: 4 boys, 8 girls; 9 survive her, 34 grandchildren, 2 great grandchildren. She professed faith in Christ when young and joined the Primitive Baptist Church and lived a faithful member until death. She was a loving mother devoted to her family and home. This final parting will ever be fresh in the memory of her children, the sweet smile that played on her face when she passed away will never be forgotten. The funeral services were conducted by Elder Dewey Jackson, Elder T. G. Brantley, Elder Leonard White, Elder J. J. Hodge. She was laid to rest in the Lynnhurst Cemetery to await the ressurection. Written by a daughter.

MRS. ELVIRA SHARP
Mrs. Elvira Sharp was born November 11, 1873, died August 14, 1944, age 70. She was married to Calvin Sharp about 1891. To this union were born 10 children, 3 sons and 7 daughters. Four daughters and husband preceded her in death. She professed a faith in Christ when young and joined the Church at Oak Grove February 1914. She was a devoted mother. During her illness she called all of her children to her bedside and asked them if they were all ready to meet her in heaven. We feel that she is at rest. Funeral was conducted by Elder T. G. Brantley and Elder Leonard White. She was buried in the Lynnhurst Cemetery. Written by a daughter-in-law, Freda Sharp.

ELDER M. B. WEAVER
Elder M. B. Weaver was a son of John and Elizabeth Hill Weaver. He was born October 12, 1866, and departed this life November 25, 1943. He was married to Miss Esther Bridges in young manhood and reared a large family of respected children. He professed faith in Christ in early boyhood and joined the Church at Mossy Spring in Union County and remained there until the Church was lost to Norris Lake. He then moved his membership to Oak Grove where he remained some five or six years, when he again transferred his membership to Rocky Dale Church in Knox County. He was licensed to preach in 1890 and was ordained to the full work of the Ministry in 1892. He was one of the greatest pastors our Association has ever produced. He was faithful until the day God gave him an honorable discharge. We can still hear the echo of his voice returning from the distant hills. His precious body sleeps in Lynnhurst Cemetery in Knoxville awaiting the glorious resurrection of the dead.

JAMES WHITE
James White was born February 17, 1878 and died July 8, 1944.

He was married to Miss Ida Allen in young manhood. He professed
faith in Christ in early life and joined the Primitive Baptist Church
at Cave Spring or Mossy Spring and remained a faithful member,
moving his membership to Davis Chapel a few years ago. Brother
White was an ideal man, truthful, honest and upright. Gone but
not forgotten.

MINISTERS ROLL

Elders	Elder's Post Offices
John Ausmus	Speedwell, Claiborne County, Tenn.
T. G. Brantley	Maynardville, Union County, Tenn.
Alfred Boruff	Maynardville, Union County, Tenn.
Henry Comer	LaFollette, Campbell County, Tenn.
E. S. Drummonds	New Tazewell, Claiborne County, Tenn.
Albert Davis	Speedwell, Claiborne County, Tenn.
V. H. Graves	Jamestown, Fentress County, Tenn.
John F. Keck	Goin, Claiborne County, Tenn.
W. A. Moyers	Speedwell, Claiborne County, Tenn.
George Mays	Goin, Claiborne County, Tenn.
Matthew Oliver	Noeton, Grainger County, Tenn.
Leonard White	LaFollette, Campbell County, Tenn.
Milton Brantley	Sharps Chapel, Union County, Tenn.
J. R. Weaver	Gibson's Station, Lee County, Va.
Isaac Owens	Gibson's Station, Lee County, Va.
Charlie Redmond	Gibson's Station, Lee County, Va.

LICENTIATES

Jim Collins	New Market, Jefferson County, Tenn.
Charlie Stanifer	New Tazewell, Claiborne County, Tenn
Sam Miller	New Market, Jefferson County, Tenn.

CHURCHES	COUNTIES	PASTORS	CLERKS	CLERK'S POST OFFICE
Red Hill	Claiborne	John F. Keck	Mose Treece	Speedwell, Tenn.
		John F. Keck,		
Gibson's Station	Lee	Matthew Oliver	Mary Ball	Gibson's Station, Va.
Oak Grove	Union	T. G. Brantley	Luna Sheritz	Goin, Tenn.
			Nell Sheritz, Asst.	
Rocky Dale	Knox	Leonard White	M. C. Dunn	Corryton, Tenn.
Cedar Spring	Claiborne	T. G. Brantley	J. L. Drummonds	New Tazewell, Tenn.
Black Fox	Grainger	T. G. Brantley	Sam Davis	Luttrell, Tenn.
Pleasant Point	Claiborne	V. H. Graves	J. M. Davis, Asst.	Powder Springs, Tenn.
Davis Chapel	Campbell	Leonard White	Austin Beason	Goin, Tenn.
Capps Creek	Union	W. R. Weaver	O. R. Parrott	LaFollette, Tenn.
Pleasant Hill	Claiborne	Albert Davis	Easter Braden	Goin, Tenn.
			Lincoln Edwards	Speedwell, Tenn.
			Austin Edwards,	
New Hebron	Jefferson		Cordelia Mitchell	New Market, Tenn.
Noeton	Grainger	Matthew Oliver	J. C. Oliver	Nocton, Tenn.
Braden's Chapel	Union	Albert Aavis	Tilda Braden	Speedwell, Tenn.
Black Fork	Roane		Jessie Sweat	Wartburg, Tenn.
Monroe, Mich.		J. S. Drummonds	Maggie Sandifer	112 W. 5th St., Monroe, Mich.
Kirkwood	Knox	Leonard White	Estella Sharp	817 Jacksboro Pk., Ft. City

405

STATISTICAL TABLE

CHURCHES	NAMES OF DELEGATES	Rec. by Expt and Bap.	Rec. by Letter	Restored	Dis. by Letter	Excluded	Deceased	Total Membership	Saturday Meeting	Contribution	Communion Meetings
Red Hill	Bros. Albert Treece, Junior Treece.	1						75	2	$2.00	July
Black Fox	Sam Cook, Sam Davis, J. M. Davis, Tom Buckner, John Bundon	1			8		2	105	1	6.5c	June
Rocky Dale	Elmer Graves, Imalee Boruff, Fay Boruff, Edith Boruff, M. C. Dunn and wife, Emma Dunn	2						79	1	3.00	May
Cedar Spring	J. L. Aileen D. P., and Jim Drummond; Clay and Fay Davis	4					1	95	4	6.00	May
Kirkwood	C. A. Fielden and wife, Estelle Petree Sharp				1			27	1	5.00	May
Braden's Chapel	W. M. Sparks, Arvel Braden, Lucy Sparks, Lucy Braden	1						22	1	3.10	June
Pleasant Point	G. W. Mays, John T. Keck, George Williams, and Austin Beason							148	1	7.00	July
Capps Creek	J. R. Weaver, Troy Pressley, Charlie and Jess Collins		1				1	24	2	3.00	May
Pleasant Hill	Albert Davis, W. A. Moyers, Jame. Edwards, Coy Edwards						1	74	2	2.00	June
Noeton	Elder Matthew Oliver and wife, Ellen Oliver									1.50	
Oak Grove	Elder T. G. Brantley, W. H. St.ner, George Shoff-ner, W. K. England	33	4		7	2	4	342	1	10.25	May
Gibson's Station	George Shoffner, Henry Hoskins, Joe Litner, Ike Shoffner							89	1	3.00	June
Monroe, Mich.	Woodrow Moyers, Sis. Edna Atkinson	2	1					8	1	3.00	Oct.
Davis Chapel	Elder Leonard White, William White	1					1	149	3	6.00	July
New Hebron	No Letter Come On										
Black Fork	No Letter Come On										

1945

MINUTES

OF THE

One Hundred and Twenty-Sixth

ANNUAL SESSION

OF THE

POWELLS VALLEY

ASSOCIATION

of Primitive Baptists

HELD WITH

THE CHURCH OF PLEASANT POINT

August 17, 18, 19, 1945.

OFFICERS

Elder T. G. BRANTLEY _____ Moderator
Elder JOHN F. KECK _____ Assistant Moderator
Brother SAM DAVIS _____ Clerk
Brother J. L. DRUMMONDS _____ Assistant Clerk

The next session will be held with the Church at Bradens Chapel Claiborne County, Tennessee, beginning on Friday before the third Saturday in August, 1946. Elder Leonard White to preach the Introductory Sermon and Elder Charlie Redmond to be his alternate.

FRIDAY'S PROCEEDINGS

1. According to the previous arrangements, the Assocation met pursuant to adjournment.

2. After singing praise, prayer by Elder Albert Davis.

3. According the previous arrangements, the introductory sermon was delivered by Elder Albert Davis from the third verse of the 11th chapter of the Pslams: "If the foundations be destroyed, what can the righteous do?" Followed by Elder Leonard White.

4. After fifteen minutes intermission, at the sound of singing the association reassembled.

5. Prayer by Elder Matthew Oliver.

6. The association was called to order by Moderator Elder T. G. Brantley.

7. Called for letters from sister churches. Received eleven, which were read by the clerks.

8. By motion and second, all said letters were received and the delegations seated.

9. Called for members from sister churches who were not delegates. Received none.

10. Called for newly constituted churches. Received none.

11. Called for corresponding letters from sister associations. Received one from the Hiwasee and one from the Nollichucky.

12. On motion said letters wer ereceived and the delegations welcomed to seats by the moderator giving them the hand of fellowship, to-wit: Elder W. R. Gates and Elder J. F. Campbell from the Hiwassee Association. and Elder Allen Gates from the Nollichucky Association.

13. On motion Elder T. G. Brantley was reelected moderator.

14. On motion Elder John F. Keck was reelected assistant moderator.

15. On motion Brother Sam Davis was reelected clerk.

16. On motion Brother J. L. Drummonds was reelected assistant clerk.

18. Motion in order to adjourn until 10 o'clock Saturday mornmittees.

(a) Committee on Preaching: Brother Jim Edwards, Brother John Bundon, Brother Troy Pressley, together with the church.

(b) Committee on Correspondence: Brother Prock Beason, Brother J. W. Keck and Brother Sam Cooke.

(c) Committee on Arrangements: Elder Leonard White, Elder John F. Keck and Elder Matthew Oliver.

(d) Committee on Request: Elder Albert Davis, Brother Henry Hoskins and Brother Dewey Hopper.

(e) Committee on Finance: Brother George Shoffner, Brother Will White and Brother Fay Keck.

17. Motion in order to adjourn until 10 o'clock Saturday morning.

SATURDAY'S PROCEEDINGS

Saturday morning at 10 o'clock the Association met pursuant to adjournment.

1. After singing praise by Elder Leonard White, prayer by Elder Matthew Oliver.

2. The association was called to order by moderator.

3. Called for letters of sister churches that failed to get in Friday. Received three, which were read by the clerks.

4. By motion the letters were all received and the delegates welcomed to seats.

5. Motion in order that we invite members of the Laurel River Association to seats with us, to-wit: Elder Carl McCarty and Bro. John Fults. Their welcome was manifested by the moderator giving them the right hand of fellowship.

6. Called for the report of the Committee on Arrangements.

We, your Committee on Arrangements, beg leave to submit the following:

1—Call of roll.

2— Call for the report on Preaching.

3—Call for the report of the Committee on Correspondence.

4—Call for the report of the Committee on Finance.

5—When and were shall the next Association be held? Who shall preach the Introductory Sermon and who shall be his alternate?

6—How many minutes shall we have printed? Who shall superintend the printing and distribution of same and what shall he be allowed for his services?

Respectfully submitted,

SAM R. COOK

D. L. BEASON

J. W. KECK

7. Motion in order that we receive the report and discharge the committee.

8. By motion and second we received the act of receiving the letter of the Church of Monroe, Michigan, as it was proved to be in disorder.

9. Called the roll and erased the names of absentees.

10. Call for the report of the Committee on Preaching.

We, your Committee on Preaching, beg leave to make the following report: Saturday at the church, Elder Matthew Oliver, Elder Allen Gates; tonight at the church, Elder Milton Brantley, Elder W. R. Gates; Saturday night at Leatherwood, Elder Henry Comer,

2

Elder Charlie Redmond; Sunday at the stand, Elder Matthew Oliver, Elder John F. Keck, and the Moderator to close.

Respectfully submitted,

JAMES EDWARDS

TROY PRESLEY

JOHN BUNDON

10. By motion the report was received and the committee discharged.

11. Called for the report of the Committee on Correspondence.

We, your Committee on Correspondence, beg leave to make the following report:

That we keep up our correspandence with the Hiwassee and Nollichucky Associations by letter and delegation, to-wit: To the Hiwassee Association, Elder Albert Davis, Elder Willie Sparks, and to the Nollichucky Association, elder Henry Comer and Elder Charlie Redmond. To the Central Union Association, Elder Leonard White and Elder John F. Keck, and also recommend the following letter to the Powells Valley Association, now in session with the Church of Pleasant Point, Claiborne County, Tennessee, on August 17, 18, 19, 1945, to the Hiwassee and Nollichucky Assocations with whom we correspond, to the Hiwassee Association, we have gladly seated your delegation with us and ask that you send another next year. To the Central Union Association, we have duly seated your worthy brothers, also have agreed to send a delegation to your association to consider a possible correspondence with you.

Respectfully submitted,

ELDER JOHN F. KECK

ELDER' LEONARD WHITE

ELDER MATTHEW OLIVER

11. On motion the report was received and the committee discharged.

12. Called for report of the Committee on Finance.

We, your Committee on Finance, beg leave to report as follows: For printing minutes and visiting ministers' expenses from various churches as follows: Rd Hill, for minutes $2.55; Gibson Station, for minutes $3.00, ministers' expenses $2.00; Oak Grove, for ministers $10.00, minutes $3.00; Rocky Dale, minutes $4.00, ministers $6.00; Cedar Springs, Minutes $5.00; Blackfox, minutes $7.00, ministers $3.35; Pleasant Point, minutes $8.00; Davis Chapel, minutes $4.00, ministers $5.00; Capps Creek, minutes $3.00, ministers $3.00; Pleasant Hill, minutes $5.40, ministers $3.00; Noeton, minutes $2.00; Bradens Chapel, minutes $3.75; Kirkwood, minutes

3

$10.00, ministers $15.00. Total for minutes $67.70, for ministers $40.35.

Respectfully submitted,
BROTHER FAY KECK
BROTHER G. W. SHOFFNER
BROTHER WILLIAM WHITE

13. Called for the report of the Committee on Request.

We, your Committee on Request, bey leave to report the following: That we have all the obituaries printed in our minutes that the churches furnish, and that the next annual session of the Powells Valley Association be held with the church at Bradens Chapel, Union County, Tennessee, to commence on Friday before the third Saturday in August, 1946.

Respectfully submitted,
ELDER ALBERT DAVIS
BROTHER HENRY HOSKINS
BROTHER DEWEY HOPPER

14. Motion in order that we received the report and discharge the committee.

15. On motion the report was received and the committee discharged.

16. On motion we have 800 copies of minutes printed, that the clerk supintend the printing and distribution of same, and that he be allowed $20.00 for his service.

17. On motion the next annual session will be held with the church at Bradens Chapel, Claiborne County, Speedwell, Tennessee, to commence on Friday before the 3rd Saturday in August, 1946.

18. On motion Elder Leanard White preach the introductory sermon, and Elder Charlie Redmond be his alternate.

19. On motion, be it resolved that we tender our heartfelt thanks to this dear old church and the surrounding community for their hospitalities and kind treatment to us throughout this association.

20. Motion in order to adjourn until 10:00 Friday morning at the place stated.

21. Dismissed in order.

ELDER T. G. BRANTLEY, Moderator
Postoffice, Maynardville, Tennessee
ELDER JOHN F. KECK, Asst. Moderator
Postoffice, Goin, Tennessee
BROTHER SAM DAVIS, Clerk
Postoffice, Luttrell, Tennessee.
BROTHER J. L. DRUMMOND, Asst. Clerk
Postoffice, New Tazewell, Tennessee.

—4—

On Sunday of this date a large and well-behaved audience assembled at the altar and so attentively listened to the well-delivered sermons of Elder Allen Gates from text, "Behold, I bring you tidings of great joy which shall be to all people," followed by Elder Matthew Oliver from the same text, and closing remarks Elder John F. Keck and the moderator, Elder T. G. Brantley, all of which was delivered in the most loving spirit and the greatest interest to all. A lovely parting was expressed by the shedding of tears, clapping of hands and invoking the blessings of God upon each other.

MINISTERS ROLL

Elders	Elders' Postoffices
John Ausmus	Speedwell, Claiborne County, Tenn.
T. G. Brantley	Maynardville, Union County, Tenn.
Henry Comer	LaFollette, Campbell County, Tenn.
E. S. Drummond	New Tazewell, Claiborn County, Tenn.
Albert Davis	Speedwell, Claiborne County, Tenn.
John F. Keck	Goin. Claiborne County, Tenn.
W. A. Moyers	Speedwell. Claiborne County, Tenn.
George Mays	Goin, Claiborne County, Tenn.
Matthew Oliver	Noeton, Grainger County, Tenn.
Leonard White	LaFollette, Campbell County, Tenn.
Milton Brantley	Sharps Chapel, Union County, Tenn.
J. R. Weaver	Gibson Station, Lee County, Va.
Charlie Redmond	Gibson Station, Lee County, Va.
R. H. Petitt	Woodlawn Pike, Knox County, Tenn.
William Sparks	Speedwell. Caliborn County, Tenn.

LICENTUATES

Jim Collins	New Market, Jefferson County, Tenn.
Charlie Standifer	Corryton, Knox County, Tenn.
Sam Miller	New Market, Jefferson County, Tenn.

—5—

and joined the Primitive Baptist Church at Pleasant Point in 1927. She lived a faithful member until death.

She was married to C. D. Keck in 1920. To ths union were born three children, Kermit, deceased; Kirby, with the U. S. Navy, and Reba of Goin.

She is missed in her home, church and community.

The Rev. John F. Keck, T. G. Brantley and V. H. Graves officiated at the funeral. Burial in the family cemetery at Pleasant Point.
—Written by Two Sisters.

McHENRY—Brother Wm. (Will) McHenry, aged 68 years, died May 30, 1945. He was married to Sister Ollie Kivette McHenry very early in life and to this union were born ten children, seven boys and three girls. He is survived by hiswife and ten children, several grandchildren, three brothers, four half-sisters and a host of relatives and friends.

He joined the Primitive Baptist Church at Pleasant Hill the 4th Saturday in July and was baptized the following day. He remained a faithful and loyal member of the church until death. He had a great desire to be at his church at the time of his death.

He is missed in the home, in his church and in the Powells Valley Assciation. His body was laid to rest in the Ausmus Cemetery near Pleasant Hill Church. Funeral services were conducted by Elder Leonard White and the pastor of the church.

This written by request of the widow.
—Elder Albert Davis.

GRAVES—Elder V. H. Graves, son of Robert H. Graves and wife, Clementine Graves, was born June 22, 1892. Deceased June 5, 1945.

On the 6th day of April, 1914, he was married to Miss Minnie Hunley. To this union no children were born. They lived happily together for three years, three months and nineteen days, when she was taken by death.

Later he was married to Miss Stella B. White. To this union six children were born. Three boys, Robert, Paul and Joe Howard; three girls, Edna, Annarine and Maxine, all living.

He professed faith in Christ at the age of twelve years. He joined the church at Hamilton's Grove in Union County, Tenn., January, 1917, but was not baptized. On the 3rd Sunday in July, 1920, he joined the Primitive Baptist Church at Kokomo, Indiana, and was baptized one month later. He started in the ministry after joining the church. In 1924 he moved back to Union County, Tenn., and was received into the church at Mossy Springs by letter, and was licensed in June, 1924, by that church to preach the Gospel of Christ and on the first Sunday in February, 1925, he was ordained to the full work of the Gospel ministry.

He has pastored the following churches: Cave Springs, Mossy Springs, Pleasant Point, Gibson Station, Black Fox, Hamilton Grove, Pleasant Hill and Beach Fork.

Brother Graves loved the churches and he served them faithfully, preaching the Gospel of Christ without fear or favor of man. He delighted especially to dwell in preaching on the Bible doctrine of Elective and Predestination and Salvation by the Sovereign Grace of God. He preached to God's children the importance of their maintaing good works.

He was pastor of Pleasant Point Church at the time of his demise. His family felt that his funeral services should be conducted at the church he so dearly loved. His body was taken to Pleasant Point Church and there it lay in state. Elders W. R. Gates, Leonard White, Theodore Brantley and Bill Myers preached the Gospel he dearly loved. Hundred of friends with his precious family paid their last respects to one they dearly loved. His body sweetly sleeps in Lynnhurst Cemetery, Knoxville, Tenn., awaiting the glorious resurrection and a sweet reunion with his loved ones in the sweet by and by.

OFFICIAL DIRECTORY

Churches	County	Pastors	Clerks	Clerk's Post Offices
Red Hill	Claiborne	J. F. Keck	Mose Treece	Speedwell, Tenn.
Gibson Station	Lee	J. F. Keck	Mary Ball	Gibson Station, Va.
Oak Grove	Union	T. G. Brantley	Luna Sheritz	Goin, Tenn.
Rocky Dale	Knox	Leonard White	Mac Dunn	Corryton, Tenn.
Cedar Springs	Claiborne	John F. Keck	J. L. Drummonds	New Tazewell, Tenn.
Black Fox	Grainger	T. G. Brantley	Sam Davis	Luttrell, Tenn.
			J. M. Davis, Ast.	Powder Springs, Tenn.
Pleasant Point	Claiborne	Matthew Oliver	Austin Beason	Goin, Tenn.
Davis Chapel	Campbell	Leonard White	O. R. Parrott	LaFollette, Tenn.
Capps Creek	Union			
Pleasant Hill	Claiborne	Albert Davis	Lincoln Edwards	Speedwell, Tenn.
			Verlin Edwards, As	Speedwell, Tenn.
New Hebron	Jefferson			
Noeton	Grainger	Matthew Oliver	J. C. Oliver	Bean Station, Tenn.
Bradens Chapel	Union	Albert Davis	Tilda Braden	Speedwell, Tenn.
		Hery Comer, Ast		
Kirkwood	Knox	Leonard White	Estelle Sharp	817 Jackson Pike, Fountain City

415

Churches	Names of Delegates	Rec. by Ex-Bap.	Rec. by Letter	Dis. by Letter	Excluded	Deceased	Total Members	Sat. Meeting	Printing Minutes	Vis. Ministers	Com. Meeting
Red Hill	James Odus, Otis Brantley, Mose Treece						86	2	$2.55	$2.00	July
Black Fox	Sam Cook, John Bundon, Tom Buckner, John Liford and wife, Sam, J. M. Davis, Myrtle Muncy	6			2		107	2	7.00	3.85	June
Rocky Dale	Elmer Graves, Edith Boruff, Vada Sharp						81	3	4.00		May
Cedar Spring	E. S., J. L., D. P., Delia Aleen Drummonds, Clay Davis Fay Davis, John Davis, Matilda Simmonds	1					95	4	5.00		May
						1	30	1	10.00	15.00	
Kirkwood	Letter but no messenger						22	1	3.75		June
Bradens Chapel	William Sparks, Lucy Sparks, Tilda Braden		4								
Pleasant Point	J. F. Keck, G. W. Mays, J. M. Cox, George Williams, J. W. Keck, Dewey Hopper, Allie Williams, Esther Hopper.						145	1	8.00		July
Capps Creek	J. R. Weaver and wife, Troy Pressley, Chas. Collins, Esther Braden						84	2	3.00	3.00	Aug.
Pleasant Hill	Albert Davis, James, Verlin Edwards, Neal Lambert, Kinley and Mossie Graves			1		1	84	4	5.40	8.00	May
Noeton	Matthew Oliver						30	8	8.00		May
Oak Grove	T. G. Brantley, Milton Brantley, Tom England, George Shoffner, Luna Sheritz, Henry Stiner		2	2			341	1	10.00	3.00	May
Gibson Station	Charlie Redmond, Joe Erwin, Henry Hoskins Leonard White, Henry Comer, Will White, Henry Cin-						95	1	8.00	2.00	June
Davis Chapel	namon, Thomas Brantley				2	2	144	8	4.00	5.00	July

1946

MINUTES

OF THE

One Hundred and Twenty-Seventh

ANNUAL SESSION

OF THE

POWELLS VALLEY

ASSOCIATION

of Primitive Baptists

HELD WITH

THE CHURCH OF BRADEN'S CHAPEL

August 16, 17, 18, 1946

OFFICERS

Elder T. G. BRANTLEY .... Moderator
Elder JOHN F. KECK .... Assistant Moderator
Brother SAM DAVIS .... Clerk
Brother J. L. DRUMMONDS .... Assistant Clerk

The next Session will be held with the Church of Oak Grove, Union County, Tenn., beginning on Friday before the third Saturday in August, 1947. Elder Albert Davis will preach the Introductory Sermon and Elbert W. M. Sparks will be his alternate.

FRIDAY'S PROCEEDINGS

First—According to the previous arrangements the association met pursuant to adjournment.

Second—After singing hymns, praise and prayer by Elder John F. Keck.

Third—According to previous arrangements the introductory sermon was delivered by Elder Leonard White from the fourteenth chapter and the fourteenth verse of Paul's letter to the Ephesians.

Fourth—After 15 minutes intermission at the sound of singing the association reassembled.

Fifth—Praise by Elder T. G. Brantly. Prayer by Elder Allen Gates.

Sixth—The association was called to order by moderator.

Seventh—Called for letters from Sister Churches of this association.

Eighth—Received nine which was read by the Clerks.

Ninth—By motion all said letters was received and the delegation welcomed to seats by the moderator.

Tenth—Called for members of Sister Churches who were not delegates, received three: Brothers Jim Brantly, Otis Brantly and John Bundon.

Eleventh—Called for newly constituted churches received none.

Twelfth—Called for corresponding letters from Sister Associations received 2 one from the Hiwassee Association with the delegation to wit: Elders John Russell and Son and Brother James Kivett; one from the Nolachucky with their delegation to wit: Elder Allen Gates.

Twelfth—On motion Said letters was received and the delegation welcomed to seats with us.

Thirteenth—Called for the report of the committee sent to investigate a possible correspondance with the Central Union Association last year when Said Committee made a good report.

Fourteenth—On motion the report was received and the committee charged.

Fifteenth—Called for the letter of the Central Union Association. Said letter was received and on motion the delegation was welcomed to seats by the moderator giving them the right hand of fellowship to wit: Elder W. R. Clark, Elder H. C. Taylor, Elder Carl McCarty.

Sixteenth—On Motion Elder T. G. Brantly was re-elected moderator and John F. Keck assistant moderator.

Seventeenth—On motion, Brother Sam Davis was re-elected clerk and Brother J. L. Drummonds assistant clerk.

Eighteenth—Motion in order that the moderator-appoint all the committees.

(A) On Preaching: Bros. Urlin Edwards, George Shoffner, Jim Brantly.

(B) On Correspondence: Elders W. M. Sparks, Albert Davis, John F. Keck.

(C) On Arrangements: Bros. James Edwards, Will White, Otis Keck.

(D) On Request: Elder Leonard White, Bros. J. S. Mattox, John Davis.

(E) On Finance: Bros. John Bundon, Orvill Braden, Neal Lambert.

Nineteenth—Motion in order to adjourn until Saturday morning, 10 o'clock.

SATURDAY'S PROCEEDINGS

Saturday Morning—10 o'clock

First—The association met pursuant to adjournment.

Second—After singing, praise by Elder Leonard White. Prayer by Elder Carl McCarty.

Third—The association was called to order by moderator.

Fourth—Called for letters of Sister Churches that failed to get in Friday. Received one which was read.

418

Fifth—On motion, Said letter was read, received, and the delegates welcomed to seats.

Sixth—Called for members who were not delegates received two Bros. Ellis Evans, J. S. Collins.

Seventh—Called for the report of the committee on arrangements.

(C) We your Committee on arrangements beg leave to make the following report: First, call the roll; second, call for the report on preaching; third, call for the report on Correspondance; fourth, call for the report of the Committee on Finance; fifth, when and where shall our next association be held who shall Preach the introductory sermon who shall be his alternate and how many minutes shall we have printed, who shall superintend the printing and distribution of the same and what shall he be allowed for his service.

Respectfully submitted,

BROS. OTIS KECK
BRO. JIM EDWARDS,
BRO. W. M. White.

Seventh—Motion in order that we are receive the report and discharge the Committee,

Eighth—Call the roll and erased the names of absentees.

Ninth—Call for the report of the Committee on Preaching.

(A) We your Committee on Preaching beg leave to report the following. Friday night at the church, Elders W. R. Clark; H. C. Taylor, Pleasant Hill Church; Elders Carl McCarty; Allen Gates Saturday at the Church Elders Billie Russell, W. R. Gates, John Russell at the Church; Saturday night at Pleasart Hill Church, Elders Allen Gates, Albert Davis; Sunday at the Church Elders Leonard White, W. R. Gates, the moderator to close.

Respectfully submited,

BRO. JAMES BRANTLY,
BRO. VERLIN EDWARDS,
BRO. GEORGE SHOFFNER.

Ninth—On motion, we receive the report and discharge the Committee.

Eleventh—Called for the report of the Committee on Correspondence.

(B) We your Committee on Correspondence beg leave to make up our Correspondence with the Hiwassee, the Nolachucky, and the Central Union Associations by letters and delegations.

Respectfully submitted,

ELDER JOHN F. KECK,
ELDER W. M. SPARKS.

Twelfth—On motion, the report was received and the Committee discharged.

Thirteenth—Call for the report of the Committee on Finance.

(D) We your Committee on Finance beg leave to make the following report. Received for Printing minutes as follows: Blackfox, $8.55; Cedar Springs, $5.00; Braden's Chapel, $5.00; Kirkwood, $5.00; Pleasant Point, $5.00; Pleasant Hill, $500; Oak Grove, $10.00; Gibsons Station, $5.00; Davis Chapel, $.75; Rockydale, $5.00; Capps Creek, $3.00; total, $64.30. For visiting ministers expenses: Braden's Chapel, $5.25; Davis Chapel, $6.00; Pleasant Hill, $5.00; Kirkwood, $10.00; Rockydale, $8.35, total, $37.60. Received from other sources for printing minutes, $32.00.

Respectfully submitted,

BROS. ORVILLE BRADEN,
BRO. JOHN BUNDON,
BRO. NEAL LAMBERT.

Fourteenth—On motion, the report was received and the Committee discharged.

Fifteenth—Call for the report of the Committee on request.

(E) We your Committee on request beg leave to make the following report. That we have all the obituary's printed in our minutes that the

419

Churches furnish, and that the next session of the Powell's Valley Association be held with the Church at Oak Grove Union County Term.

Respectfully submitted,

ELDER LEONARD WHITE,
BRO. JOHN H. DAVIS,
J. S. MATTOX.

Sixteenth—On motion, report was received and the Committee discharged.

Seventeenth—On motion, we have 1000 Copy's of minutes printed, that the Clerk Superintend the printing and distribution of the same and that he be allowed $25.00 for his services.

Eighteenth—On motion, our next session be held with the Church at Oak Grove Union County to Commence on Friday before the third Saturday in August, 1947 that Elder Albert Davis preach the introductory sermon and that Elder W. M. Sparks be his alternate.

Nineteenth—On motion, we appoint the following messengers to our Sister Associations with whom we correspond, delegates, to the Hiwassee. Elder Albert Davis, Elder W. M. Sparks when convened with the Church of Elberton September 4th, Saturday, 1946 to the Nolachucky Bros. George Shoffner, Bro. Henry Hoskins when convened with the Church of Ogle's Chapel Friday before the second Saturday, September 1946, to the Central Union Elder Albert Davis, Elder Leonard White, Bro. J. L. Edwards.

Twentieth—On motion, be it resolved that we tender our heart felt thanks to this dear old Church and the surrounding community for their generous hospitality and kind treatments throughout this association.

Twenty-first—Motion in order to adjourn until 10 a. m. at the time and place above stated.

Twenty-second—Dismissed in order.

ELDER T. G. BRANTLEY, Moderator,
P. O. Maynardville, Tenn.
ELDER JOHN F. KECK, Asst. Moderator,
P. O. Goin, Tenn.
BRO. SAM DAVIS, Clerk,
P. O. Luttrell, Tenn.
J. L. DRUMMONDS, Asst. - Clerk,
P. O. New Tazewell, Tenn.

SUNDAY'S PROCEEDINGS

On Sunday of this date, a large and well behaved audience gathered at the altar and so attentively listened to the well delivered sermon of Elder W. R. Gates, followed by Elder Leonard White, and closing remarks by the Assistant Moderator Elder John F. Keck, all of which was delivered in a most loving spirit, and with great interest to all, and a loving parting was expressed as we all took the parting hand.

MINISTERS ROLL

Elders	Elder's Post Offices
John Ausmus	Speedwell, Claiborne County, Tenn.
T. G. Brantley	Maynardville, Union County, Tenn.
Henry Comer	LaFollette, Campbell County, Tenn.
E. S. Drummonds	New Tazewell, Claiborne County, Tenn.
Albert Davis	Speedwell, Claiborne County, Tenn.
John F. Keck	Goin, Claiborne County, Tenn.
W. A. Moyers	Speedwell, Claiborne County, Tenn.
George Mays	Goin, Claiborne County, Tenn.
Matthew Oliver	Noeton, Grainger County, Tenn.
Leonard White	LaFollette, Campbell County, Tenn.
Milton Brantley	Sharps Chapel, Union County, Tenn.
J. R. Weaver	Gibson's Station, Lee County, Va.
Charlie Redmond	Gibson's Station, Lee County, Va.

R. H. Pititt .... Woodlawn Pike, Knox County, Tenn.
William Sparks .... Speedwell, Claiborne County, Tenn.
Bennie Miller .... 311 Jacksboro Pike, Fountain City, Knox County, Tenn.

LICENTIATES
Jim Collins .... New Market, Jefferson County, Tenn.
Charlie Stanifer .... Corryton, Knox County, Tenn.
Sam Miller .... New Market, Jefferson County, Tenn.
Joe Erwin .... Gibson's Station, Lee County, Va.

OBITUARIES

SISTER OLLIE KIVETTE McHENRY

Sister Ollie Kivette McHenry, age 67, widow of Wm. McHenry departed this life, Feb. 1, 1946 after a lingering illness.

Sister Ollie professed Faith in Christ and joined the Church at Pleasant Hill and was baptized Jan. 16, 1932 and was indeed a faithful member until death. She leaves to mourn her loss 10 children. 7 boys and 3 girls, one brother, one sister and several grandchildren and a host of friends and relatives. Funeral Services were conducted at Pleasant Hill Church by Elder Leonard White and pastor of Church. Her body was laid to rest by her faithful husband in Ausmus Cemetery to await the Glorious Resurrection. Wrote by Elder Albert Davis.

SISTER NANCY MINERVA CAMPBELL

Sister Nancy Minerva Campbell was borned March 24, 1876. Died December 21, 1945, being 69 years old. She was married to Harvey Lawson Alston at the age of 14 and to this Union, 10 children were born, three children preceded her in death. She is survived by her children, Mrs. E. W. Johnson, Mrs. Nora Whitmore of Middlesboro, Ky., Mrs. L. A. Johnson and Herman Alston James Alston, all of New Tazewell, Harvey of Greensboro, N. C., and Junior of Richmond, Ky. She also leaves a host of grandchildren and great grandchildren and many friends.

She joined the Primitive Baptist Church at Meyers Grove, the 4th Saturday in March, 1904 and lived a faithful members until death.

Sleep on Dear Mother take thy rest we loved you but God loved you best.

GEORGE E. HEATHERLY

With sad hearts we announce the death of beloved brother, George E. Heatherly who departed this life, Oct. 31, 1944, at the age of 72 years 10 months and 18 day old.

He was united in marriage to Cynthia Davis Jan. 21, 1894 to this Union eleven children were born, four girls and seven boys, nine of which survive him.

He professed faith in Christ in early life and joined the church at Davis Chapel where he remained a faithful member until death. We so much miss his presence but grieve not for him as one who died without hope. On the third day of Nov. 1944, at the old home church, his funeral rites were conducted by his pastor, Elder Leonard White and his body was planted in the new Sun-Rise Cemetery at Davis Chapel to await the glorious resurrection of the dead.

BEDIE ELLISON

Bedie Ellison was born Dec. 12, 1896. She was married to McKinley Ellison, Jan. 12, 1913 to this Union, 4 children were born, three boys and one girl, three of which survive her.

She professed faith in Christ in 1922 and united with the church at Davis Chapel where she remained ever faithful until death, which occurred April 1, 1946, gone from our midst but still living in our hearts.

SISTER POLLY ANN WHITE

Sister Polly Ann White, born Dec. 23, 1867 and died June 21, 1946. She joined church at Mossy Springs Jan. 1906 and was baptized some year. She lived a faithful member until church was deactivaded in the year of 1936 and later attached herself by letter to Oak Grove Church, attending that church when possible until death.

She was married to John E. White Nov. 6, 1889. To this Union was born three children, two girls and one boy. One girl and the boy preceded her in death leaving one daughter, Mrs. Stella B. Graves, the wife of the late Elder V. H. Graves and 6 grandchildren, two great grandchildren, and one sister, and a host of friends to mourn our lost.

A loved one from us has gone
A voice we loved is still
A place is vacant in our home
Which never can be filled
Sleep on dear Mother and Grandmother
—Stella Graves and Family

JAMES PRESS RUSSELL

James Press Russell was born Feb. 3, 1862, died Oct. 7 15 minutes until 11 o'clock. He professed faith in Christ at early age was a member of Oak Grove Church when the Church was organized he live a faithful member until God called him away, he was 85 yrs. 8 months 4 days old, he first married Catherine Seal this Union was born 3 children, 2 girls, 1 boy, Relda, Bill, Francie, Mrs. Francie, Monroe of California, he later married Mary Melvina Shoffner this Union was 11 children he leaves his wife and 9 children living. Mrs. Press Russell, Willoughby, Charlie Otis of Sharps Chapel, Mrs. Clema Raily of Maynardvil'e, Ditsy of the navy, Mrs. Clara Rutledge.

DR. W. S. DAVIS

Dr. W. S. Davis passed away at his home Sunday at 8 P. M. at the age of 78 years 7 months and 6 days. He was the only child of the late Elijah and Jane Capps Davis. Dr. Davis spent his entire life in this county where he was a practicing physician for fifty years.

He professed faith in Christ at an early age and was united in marriage to Ollie Lay Feb. 28, 1892. To this Union eight children were born, 3 sons. 5 daughters: Otis of Knoxville; Jeff of Indiana; Archie of Sharps Chapel; Mrs. H. G. Stiner of New Market; Mrs. John Dykes of Louisville; Mrs. Roy G. Ousley of Maynardville; Misses Irna and Winnie of Sharps Chapel. All of whom survive him.

He is also survived by 24 grandchildren, one great grandchild, and a foster daughter, Madalene Key. Dr. was confined to his bed for more than two years surrounded by his devoted family and many dear friends who mourn his passing.—by Elder T. G. Brantley.

SISTER EFFIE DAIL

Sister Effie Dail was born Nov. 23, 1881, died June 17, 1946, age 64 years 6 mo. 24 days. She professed a hope in Christ at an early age and joined the church at Mossie Springs and was baptized May 15, 1921 later moved her membership to Oak Grove where she remained a member until death about 1899 she was united in marriage to Mack Dail to this Union was born 5 children, one only daughter, and one son preceded her in death she leaves to mourn her passing her husband 3 sons, Curtis of New Market, Esco and John of Maynardvi'le, 3 sisters and 2 brothers and seven grandchildren. Services was conducted by his pastor, T. G. Brantley at Oak Grove Church, June 19.

ALICE HEATH

Alice Heath, 72, died 9 p. m. Tuesday at Claiborne Hospital, Tazewell. Death was due to a heart ailment. Mrs. Heath was the daughter of the late Josheau and Annie Goin of Goin, Tenn. and the widow of the late David P. Heath.

She was a member of the Primitive Baptist Church of Pleasant Point.

Surviving are two sons, Ott Heath of Monroe, Mich., and Park Heath of Goin, Tenn., one daughter, Mrs. Jonah Robertson of Speedwell, Tenn. She also leaves seventeen grandchildren and 5 great grandchildren.

Funeral services were held at 10:0 a. m. Friday at Pleasant Point Baptist Church with Rev. Leonard White officiating. Coffey's in charge. Pallbearers were Palmer Keck, Tobie Keck, Denver Keck, Teel Keck, and Verlin Simmons. Flower bearer were: Irene Heath, Betty Joe Heath, Peggy Robinson, Pauline Mayes, Irna Cox, Gladys Heath, Agnes Luttrell, Pauline Neely, Marie Heath and Donie Heath.

ROBERT H. GRAVES

Robert H. Graves was born in the year 1867, and deceased May 8, 1946. Was the father of the later Elder V. H. Graves, who was a minister of the Gospel of the Primitive Baptist Church many years of his life. Bro. Graves claimed a hope and although he never joined the church, the Primitive Baptist was his choice of a church.

In the late years of his life his home was in Kokomo, Ind, but he always managed to attend most of all the sessions of the Powell's Valley Association of Primitive Baptist. He was highly respected by all who knew him and his friends were numerous. He leaves behind one daughter, Mrs. Lillie M. Graves of Kokomo, Ind. and seven grandchildren, and four great grandchildren, and a host of others relatives and friends living in the states of Teennessee and Indiana. Bro. Graves left evidence of a bright hope at the end of life and we feel sure we will meet him again in the sweet bye and bye, his body was laid to us beside his wife, Mrs. Clementine T. Graves in a cemetery in Kokomo, Ind. to await the glorious resurrection.

Written by Mrs. V. H. Graves and family.

MARY ROBINSON BALL

Sister Mary Ball died March 5, 196, age 71 years 11 months 5 days. She was married to Robert H. Ball early in life and to this Union, was born, nine children: six boys and three girls. . One who proseaded her in death in 1941.

She professed faith in Christ at an early age and joined the Primitive Baptist Church at Gibson Station, Virginia, where she remained a faithful member. She was elected clerk in 1919 which she served until death. Sister Ball was loyal to her church and was loved by all who knew her. She is missed in her home and in her church.

A preasions one from us has gone

A voice we loved is still

A place is vacant in our home

Which never can be filled

God in his wisdom has called,

The bloom his love has given

And though the body slumbers here

The soul is safe in heaven.

—A daughter, Roxie Cobb

STATISTICAL TABLE

CHURCHES	NAMES OF DELEGATES	Rec. by Expt and Bap.	Rec. by Letter	Dis. by Letter	Excluded	Deceased	Total Membership	Saturday Meeting	Printing Minutes	Visiting Ministers	Communion Meetings
Red Hill	No Letter Come On	1				1	105	2	8.55		June
Black Fox	Sam Davis, J. M. Davis, John Bundon	7	1	1	1	1	87	3	5.00	8.35	May
Rocky Dale	Arvel Graves, Elmer Graves, Fay and Edith Boruff		1	1		4	94	4	5.00	5.00	May
Cedar Spring	John Davis, J. L. Drummonds	22	16	3	1	1	70	1	5.00	10.00	July
Kirkwood	Otis Keck and wife					1	28	1	5.00	5.25	June
Braden's Chapel	Elder W. M. Sparks, Edd McBee, Brice Braden, Lucy Sparks, Tilda Braden.	4	2			1	144	1	8.00		July
Pleasant Point	Elder John F. Keck					1	34	2	3.00		Aug.
Capps Creek	No Letter Come On						81	4	5.00	3.00	Aug.
Pleasant Hill	Elder Albert Davis, Bros. J. L. and Verlin Edwards, Neal Lambert, Jeff Mattox, James and Coy Edwards.	1	2	2			81	4	5.00	5.00	May
Noeton	No Letter Come On										
Oak Grove	Elder T. G. Brantley, Bros. Milton Brantley, Tom England, George Shoffner, Luna Sheritz	2	2	2			337	1	10.00	5.00	June
		2					72	1		5.00	May
Gibson's Station	Joe Erwin, George Shoffner, Henry Hoskins	2	3	3			154	3	4.75	6.00	
Davis Chapel	Elder Leonard White, Bros. Will White, O. R. arrott, Orace McCarty, Sis. J. F. Lynch, Mannie Parrot	12	3	3	1	3					

OFFICIAL DIRECTORY

CHURCHES	COUNTY	PASTORS	CLERKS	CLERKS POST OFFICE
Red Hill	Claiborne	J. F. Keck	Mose Treece	Speedwell, Tenn.
Gibsons Station	Lee	J. F. Keck	Roxie Cobb	Gibson, Station, Va.
		Matthew Oliver	Bertha Brooks	Gibson, Station. Va.
Oak Grove	Union	T. G. Brantley	Luna Sheritz	Goin, Tenn.
			Nelle Sheritz	Goin, Tenn.
Rocky Dale	Knox	Leonard White	M. C. Dunn	Corryton, Tenn.
Cedar Springs	Claiborne	John F. Keck	J. L. Drummonds	New Tazewell, Tenn.
		E. S. Drummonds		
Black Fox	Grainger	T. G. Brantley	Sam Davis	Luttrell, Tenn.
			J. M. Davis	Powder Springs, Tenn.
Pleasant Point	Claiborne	Matthew Oliver	Austin Beason	Goin, Tenn.
Davis Chapel	Campbell	Leonard White	O. R Parrott	LaFollette, Tenn.
Capps Creek	Union	J. R. Weaver		Goin, Tenn.
Pleasant Hill	Claiborne	Albert Davis	J. L. Edwards	Speedwell, Tenn.
			Verlin Edwards	Speedwell, Tenn.
Noeton	Grainger	Matthew Oliver	J. C. Oliver	Noeton, Tenn.
Braden's Chapel	Union	W. M. Sparks	Tilda Braden	Speedwell, Tenn.
Kirkwood	Knox	Leonard White	Estelle Sharp	817 Jacksboro Pk, Ft. City

1947

MINUTES

OF THE

One Hundredth and Twenty-Eighth

ANNUAL SESSION

OF THE

POWELLS VALLEY

ASSOCIATION

of Primitive Baptists

HELD WITH

THE CHURCH OF OAK GROVE

August 15, 16, 17, 1947

OFFCERS

Elder T. G. BRANTLEY	Moderator
Elder JOHN F. KECK	Assistant Moderator
Brother SAM DAVIS	Clerk
Brother J. L. DRUMMONDS	Assistant Clerk

The next Session will be held with the Church of Kirkwood, Knox County, Tenn., beginning on Friday before the third Saturday in August, 1948. Elder William Sparks will preach the Introductory Sermon and Elder T. G. Brantley will be his alternate.

FRIDAY'S PROCEEDINGS

First—According to the previous arrangements the association met pursuant to adjournment.

Second—After singing hymns, praise by Elder T. G. Brantly and prayer by Elder James Abbott.

Third—According to previous arrangements the introductory sermon was delivered by Elder Albert Davis from 10-11 verse of the 6th Chapter of Ephisians. Finally my brethren be strong in the Lord and in the power of His might.

Fourth—After 15 minutes intermission, at the sound of singing, the association reassembled.

Fifth—Remarks by Elder John F. Keck.

Sixth—Prayer by Elder W. R. Clark.

Seventh—The association was called to order for business by moderator.

Eighth—Called for letters from Sister Churches of the Powells Valley Association; received ten which were read by the clerk.

Nineth—By motion all said letters were received and the delegation welcomed to seats by the moderator.

Tenth— Called for members who were not delegates; received three James Brancolm, John Bundon and Neal Lambert.

Eleventh—Called for letter from corresponding associations; received one from the Central Union Association by Elders W. R. Clark, Carl McCarty, Robert Parton, Arthur Richmond and Brothers George Summers, Bundy Dan Miracle, C. C. Clark, Marion Clark. One from the Hiwassee Association by Messengers, Elder Bill Russell.

Twelfth—Called for members from this association who were not delegates; received Elders Alford Farmer, J. J. Abbott, A. B. Green and W. R. Gates.

Thirteenth— On motion said letters were received and the delegation welcomed to seats by the moderator.

Fourteenth—By motion Elder T. G. Grantly was re-elected moderator.

Fifteenth—By motion Elder John F. Keck was re-elected assistant moderator.

Sixteenth—By motion Bro. Sam Davis was re-elected clerk and Bro. J. L. Drummonds was re-elected assistant clerk.

Seventeenth—Motion in order that the moderator appoint all committees.

(A)   On preaching: Bros. G. B. Drummonds, Verlin Edwards and W. H. Tinnel, together with the Oak Grove Church.

(B)   On Correspondence: Bros. Tom England, James Brantly and George Shoffner.

(C)   On Arrangements: Bros. Henry Hoskins, Milton Brantly and Elder Milton Brantly.

(D)   On Request: Bros. John Bundon, Ace Sharp Lincoln Edwards.

(E)   On Finance: Bro. J. M. Davis, G. W. Williams and John Davis.

Eighteenth—Motion in order to adjourn until Saturday morning at 10 o'clock.

SATURDAY'S PROCEEDINGS

First—The association met pursuant to adjournment.

Second—After singing, praise and prayer by Elder Carl McCarty.

Third—The association was called to order by moderator Elder T. G. Brantly.

Fourth—Called for letters from Sister Churches that failed to get in Friday; received one which was read and on motion was accepted and the delegates welcomed to seats by the moderator.

Fifth—Called for members from Sister Churches that failed to get in Friday; received Bro. Ellis Evans of Capps Creek.

Sixth—Called for members who were not delegates from Sister Associations, received none.

Seventh—Called for letters from Sister Associations that failed to come in; received one from the Nolachucky Association by their messenger Elder Allen Gates.

Eighth—Call for the report of the Committee on Preaching.

(A)   We, your Committee on Preaching, beg leave to make the following report: Friday night, Cedar Grove, John F. Keck; Oak Grove, Elder W. R. Gates, Elder Clark Saturday morning, Elder Russell, Elder Carl McCarty Saturday night, Elder Brantly, Elder John F. Keck, Sunday at Stand, Elder Mathew Oliver, Elder Leonard White.   Moderator to close.

Respectfully submitted,

BRO. TENNEL
BRO. G. B. DRUMMONDS
VERLIN EDWARDS

Nineth—On motion the report was received and the committee discharged.

Tenth—Called for the report of the Committee on Correspondence.

(B)   We, your Committee on Correspondence, beg leave to make the following report: That we keep up our correspondence with the Hiwassee, the Nalachucky and Central Union Associations, by letter and messengers.

Respectfully submitted,

BRO. JAMES BRANTLY
BRO TOM ENGLAND
BRO. G. W. SHOFFNER

Eleventh—On motion the report was received and the committee discharged.

Twelfth—Call for the report of the Committee on Request.

We, your Committee on Request, beg leave to make the following report: That we have all the obituaries printed in our minutes that the churches furnish and that the next annual session of the Powells Valley Association be held with the Church of Kirkwood at Kirkwood Avenue, Knoxville, Tenn., to commence on Friday before the third Saturday in August, 1948.

Respectfully submitted,

BRO. J. L. EDWARDS
BRO. A. R. SHARP
BRO. JOHN BUNDON

Thirteenth—On motion, the report was received and the committee discharged.

Fourteenth—Call for the report of the Committee on Finance.

(D)   We, your Committee on Finance, beg leave to make the following report: Received from Sister Churches for printing minutes: Davis Chapel $5.00, Pleasant Point $10.00, Pleasant Hill $6.00, Cedar Spring $5.50, Kirkwood $5.00, Capps Creek $5.00, Gibson's Station $3.00 Blackfox $10.70, Oak Grove $10.00, Rockydale $5.00, Braden's Chapel $7.00, Noeton $2.00. Received from other sources $15.75, Total $89.25. For visiting ministers expenses: Kirkwood $5.00, Pleasant Hill $6.00, Davis Chapel $5.00, Oak Grove $5.00, Rockydale $5.00, Gibson's Station $5.00.   Total $31.00.

Fifteenth—On motion, report received and discharged the committee.

Sixteenth—Motion in order that we have 1000 copies of minutes printed.   That the clerk superintend the printing and distribution of same and that he be allowed $25.00 for his service.

Seventeenth—On motion, the next annual session of the Powells Valley Association be held with the Church of Kirkwood, Knox County, Tennessee, to commence on Friday before the third Saturday in Aug., 1948.

Eighteenth—On motion, Elder W. M. Sparks will preach the introductory sermon and that Elder T. G. Brantly will be his alternate.

Nineteenth—By motion, in the year of 1948, the moderator of the association shall be allowed a small sum for his service as moderator.

Twentieth—On motion, we send the following messengers to the following associations with which we correspond: To Hiwassee—Elder T. G. Brantly and Elder Albert Davis. To Central Union—Elder Wm. Sparks, and Albert Davis. To the Nolachucky—Elder Milton Brantly and Elder Leonard White.

Twenty-first—Motion in order that Elder John F. Keck write corresponding letters to each of these associations.

Twenty-second—Motion in order that we extend our heartfelt thanks to this dear old church and the surrounding community for their generous hospitality and kind treatment to us throughout this association.

428

Twenty-third—Motion in order to adjourn until 10 o'clock EST at the place above stated.

Twenty-fourth—Dismissed in order.

ELDER T. G. BANTLY, Moderator
P. O. Maynardville, Tenn.
ELDER JOHN F. KECK, Asst. Moderator,
P. O. Goin, Tenn.
BRO. SAM DAVIS, Clerk,
P. O. Luttrell, Tenn.
BRO. J. L. DRUMMONDS, Asst. Clerk,
P. O. New Tazewell, Tenn.

SUNDAY'S PROCEEDINGS

On Sunday of this date, a large crowd assembled at the altar and attentively listened to the well-delivered sermons by Elder Allen Gates, followed by Elder Mathew Oliver with closing remarks by the moderator and Elder W. R. Gates all of which were delivered in the most loving spirit and with great interest to all and a loving parting was expressed by the shedding of tears and clapping of hands and invoking the Blessings of God upon each other as we all took the parting hand.

MINISTERS' ROLL

Elders	Elder's Post Office
John Ausmus	Speedwell, Claiborne County, Tenn.
T. G. Brantly	Maynardville, Union County, Tenn.
E. S. Drummonds	New Tazewell, Claiborne County, Tenn.
Albert Davis	Speedwell, Claiborne County, Tenn.
John F. Keck	Goin, Claiborne County, Tenn.
W. A. Moyers	Knoxville, Knox County, Tenn.
George Mays	Goin, Claiborne County, Tenn.
Mathew Oliver	Noeton, Graiger County, Tenn.
Leonard White	LaFollette, Campbell County, Tenn.n
Milton Brantly	Sharp's Chapel, Union County, Tenn.
J. R. Weaver	Gibson's Station, Lee County, Va.
Charlie Redmond	Gibson's Station, Lee County, Va.
R. H. Pititt	Woodlawn Pike, Knox County, Tenn.
William Sparks	Speedwell, Claiborne County, Tenn.
Bennie Miller	311 Jacksboro Pike, Fountain City, Knox County, Tenn.

LICENTIATES

Jim Collins	New Market, Jefferson County, Tenn.
Charlie Stanifer	Corryton, Knox County, Tenn.
Sam Miller	New Market, Jefferson County, Tenn.
Joe Erwin	Gibson's Station, Lee County, Va.

RULES OF DECORUM

1. The churches composing the Powell's Valley Association shall not be confined to any set rules as to the specified number of Messengers they shall have in the body, but shall have the right to name in their letters as many as they choose, and in addition all orderly members of any of the churches being present be entitled to seats in the body as Messengers of their respective churches, with all the rights and privileges of the same.

2. The Messengers thus assembled shall be denominated the Powell's Valley Primitive Baptist Association.

3. For the purpose of historical information and statistical edification, the Churches are requested to state in letters, the total number of members in fellowship, the number received by Baptism, by letter, by confession of Fairth; the number dismissed, excluded and dead since last session; also the time of their meeting, their pastoral supply, and the amount of money contributed for ministers and other purposes together with any other information they deem appropriate for the edification of the saints and the glory of God.

4. This Association shall have no power to answer queries, give advice, or dictate to the Churches in any case, or to lord it over God's heritage, nor any power by which she can directly or indirectly infringe on the internal rights of the church, or censure and try any church or member in reference to faith and practice, or determine upon the validity

of gospel ordinances. These things shall rest entirely with the churches; but henceforward our annual meeting shall be only for the purpose of hearing from each other, and for the worship of God and the mutual comfort and edification of the saints. To this end we reserve the privilege annually before the Third Saturday in August and the two following days, or at such other time as may be agreed upon with any church that may invite us, having due regard to priority of claims and the good of the cause; to protect our own stand, while in session, from heresy and disorder; to recognize and invite any Primitive Baptist minister or any lay brother to worship with us, that we may deem proper; to request the brethren or our body to visit other churches or bodies in our behalf with whom we may desire to cultivate Christian fellowship; to publish in a minute of our proceedings.

5. Each session of the body shall have a Moderator and Clerk who shall be chosen according to the rules hereinafter prescribed, and who shall hold office until re-election.

6. Any orderly member of any church belonging to this body, when convened, being present, shall be eligible to election as Moderator and Clerk, or to sit on any committee appointed by the same.

7. In all elections or questions that may be necessary to determine by vote, the vote shall be taken by churches, each church being entitled to three votes for any number less than one hundred, and one additional vote for every fifty or fraction thereof above the first hundred, but the Messengers of each church a body may divide their votes as they see proper.

8. All elections of questions coming to vote shall be determined by a majority vote cast, and it shall be the duty of the minority to acquiesce in the decision thus reached.

9. If new churches desire to be admitted to this union, they shall petition by letter and Messengers, and if vouched for or recommended by one or more sister churches, for her Presbytery constituting them, or orthodox and orderly, they shall be received by the voice of the body and manifested by the Moderator giving the Messengers the right hand of fellowship.

10. Any motion or resolution introduced clearly inconsistent with the above rules shall be promptly ruled out of order unless withdrawn by the mover.

11. Any Messenger being ruled out of order by the Moderator shall have the right to appeal to the body on the question of order, and if sustained shall be allowed to proceed, but if not shall take his seat.

12. Our meetings being held in the name of Christ and the worship of God, each Messenger is expected to observe due and proper order therein.

13. It will not be considered good order for any Messenger whose name has been enrolled as such to abruptly break off or absent himself from the Association without leave.

14. The Moderator shall be entitled to the same privilege of speech as other members provided the chair is filled.

15. The Minutes of the Association shall be read and approved by the body, and signed by the Moderator before adjourning.

16. The Association shall be opened and closed by prayer.

17. Amendments to these may be made at any time by a majority of the union voting by churches, when they deem it necessary, provide such amendments do not compromise the sovereignty of the churches, nor have tendency to give this body undue power or jurisdiction over them.

OBITUARIES
ELLA MAE COLE

Ella Mae Cole was born September 28, 1909, and died June 5, 1947. She professed faith in Christ in early life and joined the Baptist Church at Blackfox where she remained a faithful member until death.

She was married to William Thomas Buckner, January 14, 1927.

She is survived by her husband, Tom Buckner; her father, Charlie Cole; mother, Mrs. Cornie Cole of New Tazewell; one sister, Mrs. Lula Heartley of Chattanooga; four brothers, Ed, Campbell, and Rev. Howard

Cole of Monroe, Michigan, and Lon Cole of Tazewell and a host of relatives and friends to mourn our loss.

She told Bro. Buckner just a few hours before she died while she was in the hospital that she would not live until morning and said she was ready to go. She smiled and looked up and said, "Heaven, sweet heaven, I long to be there."

We realize that Bro. Tom will miss her very much, however we feel that our loss is her eternal gain.

HETTIE BREWER COX

Hettie Brewer Cox was born January 1, 1884, and died April 23, 1947, being 63 years, 4 months and 22 days of age.

She was married to Jimmie Cox in 1900. To this union, one son was born, Tilman Cox of Goin.

She professed faith in Christ at an early age and joined the Primitive Baptist Church and was baptized at Pleasant Point in 1900 and later on was appointed deacon and served faithful until death.

She leaves to mourn her passing, her husband, one son, five grandchildren and four great grandchildren, four brothers, one sister and a host of friends.

Funeral services were conducted by Rev. Bill Moyers and the Pastor of the Church, Rev. Mathew Oliver.

Burial was in the Pleasant Point Cemetery.

MANDA ARMINA HARRELL BRANTLEY

Manda Armina Harrell Brantley was born July 7, 1877, and died April 23, 1947, being sixty-nine years, nine months and sixteen days old.

She was married to James Brantley in 1911. To this union, a baby was born in 1914.

She professed faith in Christ in early years and United with Davis' Creek Primitive Baptist Church, then moved her membership to Cave Springs, then to Oak Grove where she remained a faithful member until death.

She is survived by one sister, Nervy Brantley of Speedwell, Tenn.; four step-daughters, Mrs. Ludie Welch and Mrs. Martha Beeler of Maryville, Tenn., Mrs. Sherman Loy and Mrs. Bessie Loy of Clinton, Tenn. She leaves a host of friends to mourn her death.

Her death was our loss and Heaven's gain.

SARAH ELIZABETH O'DELL

Mrs. Sarah Elizabeth O'Dell, age 87 years, 11 months, and 26 days, passed away at 4 A. M., Monday, January 26, 1947, at the home of her daughter, Mrs. H. F. Coleman, Middlesboro, Ky.

She was the widow of the late Jonathan O'Dell and the daughter of John and Rebecca Keck and dear mother of John L. O'Dell Cookeville; Walter O'Dell, Monroe; B. L. O'Dell, Cumberland Gap; Mrs. A. B. Wheeler, Detroit, Mrs. E. H. Buis, New Tazewell and Mrs. H. F. Coleman, Middlesboro, Ky. There are 45 grandchildren and 12 great grandchildren.

She was a life-long member of Pleasant Point Baptist Church. Services were held at 10:00 o'clock Wednesday, January 29th at the family home by Rev. Mayo Proctor. Interment was in the Oak Grove Cemetery, New Tazewell. Coffey Funeral Home was in charge of the funeral.

LOUISA DOSSETT ELLISON

Mrs. Louisa Dossett Ellison, daughter of Maddison and Sarah Dossett, died at her home June 21, 1947, at 1:30. She was born March 20, 1876.

She was married to J. F. Ellison February 14, 1892; to this union, was born 6 sons, 7 daughters. Two sons preceeded her in death by several years.

Surviving are her husband and eleven children, Mathew Ellison, Esther McBee, Marley McBee of Kokomo, Ind, Jeff Ellison of Maryville, Bessie McCarty, Sarah Brantley, Ottie McBee, Dina Barnard, Ulyess and Swan Ellison of Sharp's Chapel, Tenn., Irene Bridges of Nashville.

Twenty eight grandchildren, one brother, J. H. Dossett of Kokomo, Ind., one sister, Mrs. Bert Ellison of Sharp's Chapel.

She professed faith in Christ at an early age and joined the church at Cave Springs; but later moved her membership to Oak Grove Primitive Baptist Church where she live a faithful member until death. We have lost a loving Companion and mother. We feel our loss is Heaven's

431

eternal gain.

A precious one from us is gone; a voice we loved is stilled; a place is vacant in our home, which never can be filled.

Funeral services conducted by Elders Leonard White and T. G. Brantley.

Ailors of Maynardville in charge.

DELIA MAE DRUMMONDS ALSTON

Mrs. Delia Mae Drummond Alston was born April 30, 1903, and died at her home September 11, 1946, age 44 years, 4 months and 11 days old. She professed faith in Christ at an early age and joined the Primitive Baptist Church at Myers Grove, January 4, in 1914.

She. lived faithful until death. She was united in marriage to Lee Alston, October 20, 1921, and to this union six children were born—five sons, Joe Steve, Alfred Alva, Andrew, and David; one daughter, Reva, all of Tazewell, two grandchildren, Loretta and Pearlie Mae Alston of Tazewell. Other survivors are her father, E. S. Drummonds of New Tazewell, Four sister, Mrs. Bertha Drummond, Mrs. Zora Patterson, Mrs. Ruth Hayes, Mrs. Creedie Sproles all of Monroe, Mich., and five brothers, W. R. and John Drummonds of Royal Blue, Tenn., Isom Drummonds, New Tazewell and Callie Drummonds, Morristown, and Mannie Drummonds, Monroe, Mich.

Funeral services were held at the Myers Grove Primitive Baptist Church on Sunday, September 15th with the Rev. Mathew Oliver officiating. Burial was in the Drummonds Cemetery. Buckner and Haynes Funeral Home, Tazewell, had charge of the funeral.

A loved one from us has gone, a voice we loved is still, a place is vacant in our home that never can be filled. Sleep on Dear mother, take your rest, we loved you. God loved you best.

NINNIE ALSTON JOHNSON

Ninnie Alston Johnson, daughter of the late Harvey L. and Nancy M. Alston, was born June 24, 1897. She professed faith in Christ in early life and jointed the Primitive Baptist Church at Myers Grove, February 4, 1913.

She was united in marriage to Levi Johnson and to this union was born one son, John W. Johnson.

She is survived by husband, Levi Johnson; son, John Johnson; sister, Nora Whitmore, Middlesboro, Ky.; brothers Harvey Alston, Greensboro, N. C., Herman James and Jr. Alston all of Tazewell; one granddaughter, Darles Johnson, New Tazewell.

Coffey Funeral Home, Tazewell, was in charge.

BROTHER W. F. MADDOX

Brother W. F. Maddox died at his home in Jamestown, Tennessee, October 19, 1946, at 1:00 P. M.. He was born August 14, 1873, age 73 years, 2 months and 5 days.

He was married to Margaret Williamson July 29, 1894. To this union was born 17 children—8 boys and 9 girls.

He is survived by his wife, Mrs. W. F. Maddox; one son, Clyde Maddox, three daughters, Mrs. Edd Fowler of Jamestown, Tenn., Mrs. J. B. Sluck of Sevierville, Tenn., and Mrs. C. H. Dunkelberg of Alhardt, Tenn.; also ten grandchildren, one great grandchild, one brother, one half sister and three half brothers.

He joined the Primitive Baptist Church at Pleasant Hill the 4th Saturday in June, 1943, and was baptized the following day and lived a faithful member until death.

JACOB ROBERT COLLINS

Jacob Robert Collins, son of the late Mathew and Mary Collins, was born March 28, 1873 and departed this life December 18, 1946, being seventy-three years, eight months and twenty days old.

He was married to Annie Vandelie Sowder, August 16, 1894. To this union nine children were born; one son Walter Mathew, preceeding him in death. The living Rachel, Eva, Esco, Arlis and Dewey Collins, Francis Rosson, Allie Williams, Lennie Keck all of Goin, Tenn.

He professed faith in Christ in early life and joined the Primitive Baptist Church at Pleasant Point and lived a faithful member until death. He leaves his wife, three sons, five daughters, sixteen grandchildren, nine great grandchildren, one brother, Willie Collins, and a host of relatives and friends to mourn their loss. But our loss is heaven's gain.

The Rev. T. G. Brantley and Mathew Oliver officiated. Coffey's had charge of the funeral. Burial was in the church cemetery.

A precious one from us in gone
A loving voice is stilled
A place is vacant in our home
That never can be filled

BROTHER WILLIAM RICHARD DRUMMONDS

Brother William Richard Drummonds, born July 18 1896, passed away at him home in Royal Blue, Tenn., on June 17, 1947, at 10:30 P. M. of a heart attack.

He professed faith in Christ, January, 1912, and joined the Primitive Baptist Church at Myers Grove.

He is survived by his wife, Mrs. Nellie Drummonds and three daughters, Mrs. Bill Hamby of Pennington, Gap, Va., Route 1, Mrs. Harry Jenkins, 836 Reisig St., Monroe, Mich., and Mrs. Bill Rush, 829 Walnut St., Monroe, Mich., also four grandchildren. He leaves his father, the Elder E. S. Drummonds, New Tazewell, Tenn., four brothers, Isom and John of Royal Blue, Tenn., Rev. Callie Drummonds, Morristown, Tenn., Manie of Monroe, Mich., four sister Mrs. Jake Drummonds, Mrs. Fred Patterson, Mrs. Sam Hayes and Mrs. Otis Sprales, Monroe, Mich., and a host of relatives and friend.

Funeral services were held at Myers Grove Church, and burial was in Drummonds' Cemetery. Rev. Mathew Oliver and Johnnie Keck officiating.

CORDELIA MEYERS DRUMMONDS

Cordelia Meyers Drummonds, daughter of the late Vincent and Rachel Meyers, was born December 10, 1891, died July 25, 1947, being fifty-five years, seven months, and fifteen days of age.

She was married to J. L. Drummonds May 26, 1912 and to this union three children were born.

She professed faith in Christ when very young and joined the Primitive Baptist Church at Myers Grove, June, 1910. She was ordained as deaconess November 23, 1913. She lived a faithful member until death.

She is survived by her husband, J. L. Drummonds; one son, Lloyd Drummonds; one daughter, Aileen Drummonds; three grandchildren, Jackie, Glenn and Pansy Drummonds, all of New Tazewell; two brothers, Alfred Meyers of Middlesboro, Ky., and Robert Meyers of Knoxville, Tenn.; a daughter velma preceeded her in death march 26, 1939.

A loved one from us is gone
A voice we love is still
A place is vacant in our home
Which never can be filled.

She leaves a host of relatives and friends to mourn her passing. She was loved by all who knew her and will be greatly missed by her family and friends.

Services were conducted at Myers Grove Baptist Church by Elders Mathew Oliver, T. G. Brantley and John F. Keck.

Pall bearers were Lonnie Meyers, James Drummonds, Carlie Drummonds, Ray Drummonds, Lawrence Meyers and Raymond Poore. Honorary pall bears were Odra Drummonds, Isam Drummonds, John Drummonds, Ewin Drummonds, Roy Meyers, Earl Poore, Leon Holt, Henry Ford, Steve Poore and Doc Cox.

Flower girls were Lenore Meyers Carr, O'Doskey Meyers, Doro Drummonds, Hazel Drummonds, Trula Poore Conner, Stella Gray Drummonds, Blanche Cox, Beth Dunsmore, Irene Simmons, Edna Drummonds, Elgie Drummonds, Reva Alston, Dorothy Drummonds Neely, Evelyn Keck, Jessie Standifer, Norma Jean Simmons, Elaine Drummonds, Algean Dunsmore, Jean Hipshire, Robbie Sue Keck, Velta Drummonds Munsey, Betty Sue Widner and Trula Watson Drummonds.

Burial was in Drummonds' Cemetery, with Coffey Funeral Home in charge.

MARY FRANCES DAY DRUMMONDS

Mary Frances Day Drummonds, born November 22, 1884, to the late Will and Martha Day, was married to James A. Drummonds, February 28, 1904.

Mollie, as she was affectionately called by friends, died on October 2, 1946. She is survived by her husband; three daughters, Mrs. Frankie Hayes of Washburn, Tenn., Mrs. Gertrude Zwack of Monroe, Mich., Mrs. Dona Drummonds of New Tazewell, Tenn.; three sons, Willie E. Drummonds of New Tazewell, Tenn., Carlie W. Drummonds of Monroe, Mich., Virgil L. Drummonds of New Tazewell, Tenn.; Six grandchildren; two sisters, Mrs. Robert Meyers of Knoxville, Tenn., Mrs. J. L. Bartlett of Phoenix, Ariz.; one brother, Mr. Robert Day of Middlesboro, Ky.

She professed a hope in Christ at an early age and joined the Primitive Baptist Church at Myers Grove the fourth Saturday in January of 1908, living a faithful member until death.

Flower girls were Mrs. Cleo Neely, Miss Edna Drummonds, Mrs. Beatrice Cox, Miss Lillian Hayes, Miss Alma Welch, Miss Mary Lou Neely, Miss Laurene Munsey, and Mrs. Nell Wright.

Pall bears were Isam Drummonds, James Drummonds, John Drummonds, Lloyd Drummonds, Ray Drummonds, and Odra Drummonds.

Funeral services were conducted at Myers Grove Primitive Baptist Church, October 4, 1946, by Rev. T. G. Brantley and Rev. John F. Keck. Burial was in the Drummonds' Cemetery.

CYNTHIA DAVIS HEATHERLY

Sister Cynthia Davis Heatherly, wife of the late George E. Heatherly, was born March 7, 1876, and died Dec. 6, 1946. She professed faith in Christ in early life and joined the church at Davis Chapel where her membership remained until death. She always filled her place in church and was an active member. Her faithfulness still beckons us on, and her prayers still echo in our memories. The funeral oration was delivered by her pastor, Elder Leonard White. The body was interred in Sunrise Cemetery by her loyal husband, awaiting the resurrection of the dead.

BROTHER THOMAS BRANTLEY

Brother Thomas Brantley, departed this life March 19, 1947, age seventy-five years. He professed faith in Christ in early life and joined the Church at Cave Spring where he remained a faithful member until the church was lost to Norris Lake. He then joined the Church at Davis Chapel where re remained a loyal member,. always filling his place.

Uncle Tom, as everyone called him, was honest, upright, and true.

Funeral services were held by Elders T. G. Brantley and Leonard White with burial in Fincastle Cemetery.

GLADYS WHITE CHADWELL

Sister Gladys White Chadwell, died March 23, 1947 at the age of thirty-eight. She was a loyal wife, faithful mother and a consecrated Christian. She professed faith in Christ in her girlhood days and joined the Church at Davis Chapel where her membership remained until death.

She was kind, gentle and loving and patiently bore her prolonged suffering, with Christian courage. God bless her loyal husband, father and mother who so gently cared for her. The funeral was conducted by her pastor, Elder Leonard White.

MRS. ALICE GRAVES DOSSETT

Mrs. Alice Graves Dossett was born October 13, 1879 and died September 5, 1947. She leaves her husband, ten children,, six boys, 4 girls, and twenty grandchildren and three great grandchildren; also two brothers, W. C. Graves and Andy Graves, and a host of friends.

She professed faith in Christ in early life and joined the Primitive Baptist Church at Case Springs and was baptized. She was a faithful member when able to go.

A loved one from us is gone, a vacant place is in our home which can never be filled.

J. H. DOSSETT
Husband

434

CHURCHES	NAMES OF DELEGATES	Rec. by Expt. and Bapt.	Rec. by Letter	Dism. by Letter	Excluded	Deceased	Total Membership	Saturday Meetings	Printing Minutes	Visiting Ministers	Communion Meetings
Red Hill	No Letter Come On										
Black Fox	Sam Davis, J. M. Davis, John Liford, Walton Cabbage, Myrtle Muncy, Roy Bailey, Cora Muncy						105	2			June
Rocky Dale	Bros. McDunn, Sis. Rhoda Dunn, Lola Palmer					2	103	2	10.70		June
Cedar Springs	John and Clay Davis, J. L, G. B, G. A. and Sister Aileen Drummonds						80	4	5.00	5.00	May
Kirkwood	Hobart Tinnell and wife, Asa Sharp and wife, Otis Kack and wife	2				5	80	4	5.50		May
Braden's Chapel	Elder William Sparks, Bro. Edd McBee, Charlie Cain, Sister Hallie Russell	2		2		1	68	1	5.00	5.00	July
Pleasant Point	Elder John F. Keck, Bros. J. W. Keck, Austin Beason, George Williams, Sisters Alleen Williams, Laura Keck	2	1				31	1	7.00		June
Capps Creek	Emmon Browning, Troy Presley, Charlie Collins		1			3	142	1	10.00		July
Pleasant Hill	Elder Albert Davis, Bros. Verlin, James, Coy and Lincoln Edwards, James, Adus and Otis Brantly	2	5				34	2	4.00		May-Oct.
Noeton	No Letter Come On								2.00		
Oak Grove	Elder T. G. Brantley, Milton Brantly, George Shoffner, Tom England, Verlin Hopper	3		1			86	4	6.00	6.00	June
Gibson's Station	Joe Irwin, George Shoffner and wife, Willie White, Henry Hokins	6	7			2	337	1	10.00	5.00	May
							96	1	8.00		June
Davis Chapel	Elder Leonard White, McKinley Ellison, J. M. Kivett, Sister Cordelia Lynch, Willie White	5	3	1		3	160	3	5.00	5.00	June

CHURCHES	COUNTY	PASTORS	CLERKS	CLERK'S POST OFFICES
Red Hill	Claiborne	J. F. Keck	Mose Treece	Speedwell, Tenn.
Gibson's Station	Lee	Matthew Oliver	Roxey Cobb	
Oak Grove	Union	T. G. Brantley	Bertha Brooks	Gibson's Station, Va.
			Luna Sheritz	
			Nelle Sheritz	
Rock Dale	Knox	Leonard White	M. C. Dunn	Goin, Tenn.
Cedar Springs	Claiborne	John F. Keck		Corryton, Tenn.
Black Fox	Grainger	T. G. Brantley	E. S. Drummonds	New Tazewell, Tenn.
			J. L. Drummonds	Luttrell, Tenn.
			Sam Davis	
			J. M. Davis	Powder Springs, Tenn.
Pleasant Point	Claiborne	Matthew Oliver	Austin Beason	Goin, Tenn.
Davis Chapel	Campbell	Leonard White	O. R. Parrott	LaFollette, Tenn.
Capp's Creek	Union	J. R. Weaver		
		George Mays	Easter Braden	Goin, Tenn.
Pleasant Hill	Claiborne	Albert Davis	Lincoln Edwards	
			Verlin Edwards	Speedwell, Tenn.
Noeton	Grainger	Matthew Oliver	J. C. Oliver	Noeton, Tenn.
Braden's Chapel	Union	W. M. Sparks	Dean Clawson	Speedwell, Tenn.
Kirkwood	Knox	Leonard White	Estelle Sharp	819 Jacksboro Pk., Ft. City

436

1948

MINUTES

OF THE

One Hundred and Twenty-Ninth

ANNUAL SESSION

OF THE

POWELLS VALLEY
ASSOCIATION

of Primitive Baptists

HELD WITH

THE CHURCH OF KIRKWOOD

August 20, 21, 22, 1948

OFFICERS

Elder JOHN F. KECK ....Moderator
Elder ALBERT DAVIS ....Assistant Moderator
Brother SAM DAVIS ... .Clerk
Brother J. L. DRUMMOND .... Assistant Clerk

The next Session will be held with the Church at Black Fox, Grainger County, Tenn., beginning on Friday before the third Saturday in August, 1949. Elder Leonard White to preach the Introductory Sermon and Elder J. R. Weaver to be his alternate.

FRIDAY'S PROCEEDINGS

First—According to the previous arrangements the Association met pursuant to adjournment.

Second—After singing. Prayer by Elder A Richmond.

Third—The introductory sermon was delivered by Elder Matthew Oliver, from the text "They Hated Me Without A Cause," followed by Elder Albert Davis.

Fourth—After 15 minutes intermission at the sound of singing the association re-assembled.

Fifth—Remarks by Elder Leonard White. Prayer by Elder Canady.

Sixth—The association was called to order by Assistant Moderator, Elder J. F. Keck.

Seventh—Called for letters from Sister Churches of this association, received eleven, which were read by Clerks.

Eighth—On motion all said letters was received and the delegation was welcomed to seat by the Moderator.

Ninth—On motion the letter of the newly consolidated church, to wit: Brantly's Chapel was received and their delegates welcomed to seats with us.

Tenth—Called for members who were not delegates, received one, C. N. Petree, from Rock Dale, who was welcomed to a seat.

Eleventh—Called for corresponding letters from Sister Associations, received one, from the Nolichuckey Association with their delegate, to wit: Elder Allen Gates.

On motion said letter was received and the delegate welcomed to a seat. Also one from Central Union Association, with their delegates, to wit: Elders W. R. Clark and Arthur Richmond.

Twelfth—On motion said letter was received and the delegates welcomed to seats.

Thirteenth—On motion Elder John F. Keck was elected Moderator, and Elder Albert Davis, Assistant Moderator.

Fourteenth—On motion Bro. Sam Davis was re-elected Clerk, and Bro. J. L. Drummonds was re-elected Assistant Clerk.

Fifteenth—On motion that the Moderator appoint all committees.

(A) On Preaching: Bros. George Shoffner, Will White and W. I. Browning.

(B) On Correspondence: Bros. Tom England, Lincoln Edwards and Elmer Graves.

(C) On Arrangements: Elder Milton Brantly, Estelle Heath, and Elder Matthew Oliver.

(D) On Request: Elder R. H. Petitt, Bros. George Williams, and John Bundon.

(E) On Finance: Brothers A. R. Sharp, Harve Rogers, and Clifford Brantley.

Sixteenth—Called for the report of the Committee on Preaching.

(A) We your Committee on Preaching beg leave to report the following: Friday afternoon—Elders Albert Davis, Carl McCarty, and Arthur Richmond. Friday night—Elders Kennedy, Weaver and Meyers. Saturday morning—Allen Gates, Arthur Richmond. Saturday afternoon—Elders R. H. Petitt, William Sparks, John F. Keck. Saturday night—Elders Leonard White, Charlie Myers, Carl McCarty. Sunday—Elders Oliver, Keck, and Weaver. Moderator to close.

Respectfully submitted,
BRO. WILL WHITE,
BRO. GEORGE SHOFFNER,
BRO. W. J. BROWNING.

Seventeenth—On motion, called for the report and discharge the committee.

Eighteenth—Motion in order to adjourn until Saturday morning at 10 o'clock.

First—According to the previous arrangements the Association met pursuant to adjournment.

Second—Praise by Elder John F. Keck and Elder Leonard White. Prayer by Elder R. H. Petitt.

Third—Called for the letter of the Hiawassee Association, received none.

Fourth—Called for the report of the Committee on Arrangements.

(B) We your Committee on Arrangements beg leave to report the following: First, call the roll; second, call for the report on preaching; third, call for the report on correspondence; fourth, call for the report of the Committee on Finance, when and where shall our next Association be held. Who shall preach the introductory sermon and who shall be his alternate; how many minutes shall we have printed, who shall superintend the printing of same and what shall be allowed for his services.

Respectfully submitted,
BRO. ESTELLE HEATH
ELDER MATTHEW OLIVER
ELDER MILTON BRANTLY

Fourth—On motion report received and the committee discharged.

Fifth—Called for the report of the Committee on Correspondence.

(C) We your Committee on Correspondence beg leave to make the following report: That we keep up our correspondence with the Hiawassee, Nolachuckey and Central Union Associations, by letter and messengers.

Respectfully submitted,
BRO. LINCOLN EDWARDS
BRO. ELMER GRAVES,
BRO. TOM ENGLAND

Sixth—Called for the report of the Committee on Request.

(D) We your Committee on Request beg leave to make the following report: That we have all the obituaries printed in our minutes, that the churches furnish, and our next session of the Association be held with the Blackfox Church.

Respectfully submitted,
ELDER R. h. PETITT,
BRO. JOHN BUNDON.
BRO. GEORGE WILLIAMS,

Seventh—On motion the report was received, and the Committee discharged.

Eighth—Called for the report of the Committee on Finance.

We your Committee on Finance beg leave to report the following report: Received for printing of Minutes and Ministers' expenses: Caps Creek Minutes $4.00; Pleasant Point, $10.00; Gibson's Station, minutes, $4.00, Minister $4.00; Rocky Dale, minutes, $3.00, Ministers, $7.00; Blackfox, minutes, $9.00; Braden's Chapel, minutes, $4.00, Ministers, $4.00; Brantly's Chapel, minutes $8.86; Pleasant Hill, minutes $5.00, Ministers $10.00; Oak Grove, minutes $10.00, Ministers $5.00; Cedar Spring, minutes $6.00; Davis Chapel, minutes $3.00, Ministers $7.00; Kirkwood, minutes $5.00, Ministers $20.00.

Ninth—Call the roll and erased the names of absentees.

Tenth—On motion we have 1,000 Minutes printed, that the Clerk superintend the printing and distribution of same, and that he be allowed $25.00 for his service.

Eleventh—On motion the next Annual Session of the Powell's Valley Association will be held with the church at Blackfox, Grainger County,

439

Tennessee. To commence on Friday before the third Saturday in August, 1949.

Twelfth—On motion Elder Leonard White shall preach the introductory sermon, and the Elder R. H. Weaver be his alternate.

Thirteenth—On motion the act of 1947, Article nineteen as to paying the Moderator of the Association, was rescinded.

Fourteenth—On motion we send Messengers to the following Associations; to the Hiawassee, Elders R. H. Petitt, and Kennedy; to the Central Union, Elders Albert Davis, Leonard White, and William Sparks; to the Nolachuckey, Elders J. R. Weaver, Leonard White and John F. Keck.

Fifteenth—On motion that the Clerk write corresponding letters to each of these Associations.

Sixteenth—On motion we extend our' heartfelt thanks to this dear church and the surrounding community for generous hospitalities, and kind treatment to all of us throughout this Association. May the bountiful Giver of good gifts reward you.—The Clerk.

Seventeenth—Motion in order to adjourn until the time and place above stated, at 10:30 (EST).

Eighteenth—Dismissed in order.

ELDER JOHN F. KECK, Moderator,

P. O. Goin, Tenn.

ELDER ALBERT DAVIS, Asst. Moderator,

P. O. Speedwell, Tenn.

On Sunday a large audience assembled at the altar and attentively listened to the well delivered sermons of Elder J. R. Weaver, from the text "Verily-Verily I Say Unto You, The Hour is Come When The Dead Shall Hear The Voice Of The Son Of God, And They That Hear Shall Live." Followed by Elder Matthew Oliver, and closing remarks by the Moderator. All of which was delivered in a most loving spirit, and a loving parting was expressed, by the clasping of hands and the shedding of of tears, and invoking the Blessings of God upon each other.

BRO. SAM DAVIS, Clerk,
P. O. Luttrell, Tenn.
BRO. J. L. DRUMMONDS, Asst. Clerk,
P. O. New Tazewell, Tenn.

MINISTERS ROLL

Elders	Elder's Post Office
John Ausmus	Speedwell, Claiborne County, Tenn.
E. S. Drummonds	New Tazewell, Claiborne County, Tenn.
Albert Davis	Speedwell, Claiborne County, Tenn.
John F. Keck	Goin, Claiborne County, Tenn.
W. A. Moyers	Knoxville, Knox County, Tenn.
Matthew Oliver	Noeton, Grainger County, Tenn.
Leonard White	LaFollette, Campbell County, Tenn.
Milton Brantly	Sharp's Chapel, Union County, Tenn.
J. R. Weaver	Gibson's Station, Lee County, Va.
Charlie Redmond	Gibson Station, Lee County, Va.
R. H. Petitt	Woodlawn Pike, Knox County, Tenn.
William Sparks	Speedwell, Claiborne County, Tenn.
L. J. Moyers	New Tazewell, Claiborne County, Tenn.
V. M. Kennedy	

OBITUARIES

JEFFERSON SCHOEFIELD MADDOX

Jefferson Schoefield Maddox, born February 11, 1886, died June 17, 1948, age 62 years, 4 months, and 6 days. He was the son of George W. and Martha Jane Maddox.

He professed faith in Christ at an early age and joined the Church of Pleasant Hill, and was a faithful member until death.

He is survived by one daughter, Hassie Redmon, Speedwell, Tenn.; one son, John Leonard Maddox, Gibson Station, Virginia; 8 grandchildren; three brothers, John Maddox, Knoxville, Tenn; G. W. and Charlie Maddox, of Speedwell, Tenn; one sister, Mrs. C. H. Rogers, of Middlesboro, Ky.

He is missed and mourned by a host of friends and his church and relatives.

At peace with God he lies at rest. Funeral services wereheld at his home church by Elder John Ausmus and Elder Albert Davis, officiating. His body was laid to rest in the Ausmus Cemetery near the church.

AGGIE MIRACLE GRAVES

Aggie Miracle Graves, born January 18, 1889, died January 1, 1948. Being 57 year, 11 month, and 14 days old. She leaves to mourn her loss her husband, James Graves; one brother, James Miracle; two sisters, Mrs. George Roberts and Mrs. George Toliver, all of Speedwell, Tenn. One daughter born to this union, died in infancy.

She professed faith in Christ at an early age and joined the church at Pleasant Hill and lived a faithful member until death. She was bedfast for 30-years or more and she bore her sickness with patience and often spoke of her home in Heaven and loved to talk of the love of God

She leaves a host of friends to mourn her loss, but we believe our loss is her eternal gain. Gone but not forgotton.

GEORGE MAYES

Brother George Mayes was born December 5, 1891, and departed this life in 1948. He was married to Perlie Harrison May 20, 1923.

He professed faith in Christ in 1911, and was ordained to preach in 1922. He served the following churches as assistant pastor, Pleasant Point and Capps Creek.

REV. D. A. BRANSON

Rev. D. A. Branson was born January 5, 1854, passed away August 10, 1948. He professed faith in Christ, September 5, 1873, and joined the Missionary Church, December 1874.

Rev. Branson married Mary E. England, August 1, 1874 and to this union were born eleven children, seven boys and four girls Mrs. Mary E. Branson passed away May 15, 1920. Rev. Branson later married Mary L. Hensley. She passed away April 27, 1940.

Surviving are: one son, Levi Branson, Middlesboro, Ky.; two daughters, Mrs. James Duncan, Noeton, Tenn., and Mrs. Ida Willis, Hazel Park, Mich.; 28 grandchildren; some great grandchildren and great, great, grandchildren.

Funeral services were held at Meyers Grove Primitive Baptist Church, by Elder E. S. Drummonds, Rev. England and Rev. Carmony, and Sister Louella Treece. The body was laid to rest in the Drummonds Cemetery.

CAROLINE KECK GRAVES

Sister Caroline Keck Graves, daughter of Andrew and Katie Keck, died November 22, 1947, age 81 year.

She was united in marriage to Eli Graves, to this union was born twelve children, seven boys and five girls, eleven surviving, also 54 grand-children and 25 great grand-children.

She professed faith in Christ at the age of fourteen, and joined the Big Barn Church, later uniting with Rocky Dale Primitive Baptist church and lived a faithful life until death.. She was loved by all who knew her our loss is heaven's gain.

Funeral services were conducted by T. G. Brantley. We all loved you dear, but God loved you best, this is done by the family.

JAMES P. TAYLOR

James P. Taylor was born June 19, 1870, died September 12, 1947, age 77 years, 2 months, 23 days.

He was married in early life to Elizabeth Medley and to this union was born 10 children, 9 of whom survive him.

He professed faith in Christ in early life and joined the Primitive Baptist church at Strait Branch. He later moved his membership to Oak Grove where he was a member until his death.

Burial at Zion Chapel, in Blount County, with Rev. T. G. Brantley and A. J. Pellam officiating.

Gone but not forgotten.

CHARLEY BUSSELL

Charley Bussell was born May 17, 1886, died February 27, 1947. Charley Bussell was married to Laura Dixon July 3, 1898.. He is survived by his widow, Laura Bussell; 8 children; 17 grandchildren.

He joined the Primitive Baptist Church in 1904. Was a Mason since 1902. living faithful to his church and order until death. Leaving his family who was so devoted to him to mourn his absence and many friends who mourn his loss, he is gone but not forgotten and his memory will live in their hearts forever. He was a devoted husband and father and dearly beloved by all who knew him.

A precious one from us is gone.
A voice we loved, is still,
A place is vacant in our home
Which can never be filled.

Written by his wife—Laura Bussell.

ELDER T. G. BRANTLEY

Elder Theodore Godfrey Brantley was born October 13, 1385, died May 20, 1948. Age 62 years, 7 month, and 7 days. He was united in marriage to Miss Nola Weaver Brantley, May 29,1904. No children were born to this union but seven children were nurtured in the home to wit: Mrs. Izora England, Mrs. Pearl Codle, Miss Mary Spurgeon, Mrs. Agnes Townsend, Mrs. Edith Carpenter, Miss Ann Franklin, and Mr. Lodus Hill.

On the 7th day of January, 1945, he was again united in marriage to Miss Virgie Gilbert Brantley. To this union two children have been born: daughter, Mary Ruth, and son T. G.,Jr.

He is survived by his wife and children; four sisters, Mrs. Verlin Farris, of LaFollette; Mrs. Verlin Weaver, of Knoxville; Mrs. Elvin Brantley, of Cissna Park, Ill.; Mrs. Will Steiner, of Canton, Ohio; four brothers, Kenneth of Sharp's Chapel; Lonnie, of Knoxville; Sam and Wallace of Onarga, Ill.

He professed faith in Christ in January of 1903 at the age of 17. At the age of 13 he felt the call to preach the gospel. Joined the church at Mossy Spring, April 10, 1909. Was baptized May 8, 1909. Was ordained to the full work of the gospel ministry May 12, 1917. After moving to Sharp's Chapel he moved his membership to Oak Grove church, July 4, 1941. He was one of the outstanding ministers of East Tennessee and

442

the favorite of the Powell's Valley Association, which he served as Moderator 17 years. The length of his ministeral life was thirty-one years and eight days. During that time he baptized 576, married 134 couples, officiated in 884 funerals, his last funeral being conducted May 18, 1948.

At the date of his death he was pastor of three churches; Oak Grove, which he served as pastor his entire ministry; Black Fox and Poplar Springs in Roane County. He had also served Cave Springs, Mossy Spring, Red Hill, Rocky Dale, Hamilton Grove, Myers Grove.

He would often talk to his companion of the time when he would be called to leave her and the children, making request of the ministers to officiate and singers to sing his favorite songs he wished to be sung at his funeral. He was faithful and loving husband and a loving and understanding father.

His funeral was conducted May 23, 1948, at the Oak Grove Church, with Elder Leonard White, Elder John F. Keck and Elder Matthew Oliver officiating. The large crowd overflowing the church, and the many beautiful floral offerings told of the high esteem that his friends and churches he had pastored held his labor of love among them.

His body was laid to rest in the church cemetery to await the morning of the resurrection. We shall see again the face we have loved, and lost for awhile.

His Wife

ANDREW CURTIS MILLER

Andrew Curtis Miller was born August 4, 1896, died April 20, 1948. Age 51 years, 8 month, 16 days.

He confessed faith in Christ when a boy but never joined any church. He was a strong believer in Primitive Baptist faith.

He leaves to mourn his loss the widow, Mrs. Nellie Flossie Miller; three sons, Lee, Chalmer and Delone Miller; three daughters, Mrs. Claude Hankins, Misses Evelyn and Dorothy Miller, all of Maynardville; five grandchildren; three brothers, H. L., of Maynardville, George E. and W. R. Miller, of Knoxville; three sisters, Mrs. H. M. Loy and Mrs. L. L. Walton, of Knoxville, Mrs. J. E. Alfrey of Maynardville.

A host of friends and relatives to mourn his passing. Our loss is his eternal gain. Pallbearers were his nephews.

—By his wife and children

BOB CAPPS

Brother Bob Capps was born May 3, 1875, departed this life July 10, 1948.

He was married to Sarah Marrion, to this union 6 children were born. He later married Oma Grose, to this union 8 children were born.

He professed faith in Christ at an early age, and joined the Primitive Baptist church at Black Fox, and lived faithful until death.

He is survived by his widow, 13 children, one brother, Samuel Capps, and a host of grandchildren, and many friends to mourn his passing.

Funeral services by Rev. Saylor and Rev. Matthew Oliver. Burial in Pennington Chapel Banriff Cemetery.

SISTER ELIZABETH WEAVER

Sister Elizabeth Weaver was born August 15, 1869, deceased November 21, 1947.

She was married to Lafayette Weaver April 11, 1887, to this union 14 children were born of which 8 survive. She joined the Mossy Springs church at the age of 16 years. Her membership was at Capps Creek at the time of her death. She enjoyed going to church until her death. We miss her so much, but we believe our loss is her eternal gain.

—Her children

LICENTIATES

Jim Collins.. New Market, Jefferson County, Tenn.
Charlie Stanifer .... Corryton, Knox County, Tenn.
Sam Miller .... New Market, Jefferson County, Tenn.
Joe Erwin .... Gibson's Station, Lee County, Va.

CORRESPONDING LETTER

We the Powell's Valley Association of Primitive Baptists now in Session at Kirkwood, August 20-21-22-1948, send its greetings to the Hiawassee, Nolachuckey and the Central Union Associations, with whom we correspond:

Very Dear Brothers: We desire to keep up our long cherished correspondence with you and have chosen these our beloved Elders, delegates to your Associations. To the Hiawassee Association: Elders R. H. Petitt and Elder Kennedy; Central Union Association: Elders Albert Davis, Elder Leonard White and Elder Will Sparks; Nolachuckey: Elders Leonard White, John F. Keck, H. R. Weaver. Having seated all your delegates in our assembly we heartily invite another next year. Pray for this your little sister.—The Clerk of the P. V. A.

444

CHURCHES	NAMES OF DELEGATES	Rec'd by Baptism	Rec. by Letter	Dism. by Letter	Excluded	Deceased	Total Membership	Sat. Meetings	Printing Minutes	Visiting Minister's Exp.	Communion Meetings
Red Hill	No Letter. Came on										
Blackfox	Bro. John Bundon and Wife, Bros. San Davis, J. M. Davis										
Rocky Dale	Bros. Elmer Graves, M. C. Dunn, Sisters Bessie Graves, Rhoda Dunn, Vada Sharp, Leola Palmer						1 102	3	9.00		June
Cedar Spring	Bros. J. L., S. W., G. B. Drummonds, Elder L. I. Movers	1				1	79	3	3.00	7.00 May	May
Kirkwood	Elder R. H. Pettitt and Wife, Elder V. M. Kennedy, Bros. Asa Sharp and Wife, Sisters Frieda Sharp, Nell Sharp, Anna Culvahouse						81	4	6.00		May
Braden's Chapel	Elder William Sparks, Bro. Edd McBee	4		3			69	1	5.00	20.00 Aug.	Aug.
Pleasant Point	Elder John F. Keck, Bro. George Williams and wife, Sisters Francie Rossin, Oma Rossin	1	1				33	1	4.00	4.25 June	June
Capp's Creek	John R. Weaver, Bros. Troy Pressley, N. C. Browning,						1 142	1	10.00		July
Pleasant Hill	Charlie Collins, Sister Cora Weaver, Elder Albert Davis, Bros. Curlin, J. L. Edwards, Kinley Graves, James Branscomb	2				1	38	2	4.00		
Noeton	No Letter. Came on					2	86	4	10.00	5.00 June	June
Oak Grove	Elder Milton Brantley, Bros. Dewey Ellison, George Shoffner, Tom England										
Gibson's Station	Bros. Joe Erwin, Henry Hoskins	7	3		1		97	1	4.00	4.00 June	June
Davis Chapel	Elder Leonard White, Bros. Henry Cinnamon, Raymond Heatherly						342	1	10.00	5.00 May	May
Brantley's Chapel	Bros. Jeff Ellison, Everett Brantley, Milton Welch, V. A. Beason	1	2	2	11		1 149	3	3.00	7.00 June	July
							12	3	8.56		July

OFFICIAL DIRECTORY

CHURCHES	COUNTY	PASTORS	CLERKS	CLERK'S POST OFFICES
Red Hill............	No Letter. Came on.	John F. Keck.	Sam Davis................	Luttrell, Tenn.
Blackfox.........	Union............	Asst. Matthew Oliver	Asst.—J. M. Davis....	Powder Springs, Tenn.
Rocky Dale.......	Knox............	Leonard White.........	Leola Palmer.........	Corryton, Tenn.
Cedar Springs....	Claiborne.........	John F. Keck....	J. L. Drummonds........	New Tazewell, Tenn.
		Asst.—Clay Davis.....		
Kirkwood.......	Knox.	Leonard White.........	Estelle Sharp.........	819 Jacksboro Pk. Ftn. City
Braden's Chapel.	Union....	Wm. Sparks...........	Dean Clawson...........	Speedwell, Tenn.
Pleasant Point....	Claiborne.........	Matthew Oliver..........	Austin Beason.	Goin, Tenn.
Capps Creek....	Union...........	John R. Weaver.........	Ester Braden............	Goin, Tenn.
		Asst. Matthew Oliver		
Pleasant Hill......	Claiborne............	Albert Davis....	Lincoln Edwards.	Speedwell, Tenn.
			Asst.—Verlin Edwards.	Speedwell, Tenn.
Noeton............	No Letter. Came on.	....	....	....
Oak Grove...........	Union.........	Albert Davis...........	Luna Sheritz.	Goin, Tenn.
			Asst.—Nelle Sheritz	Goin, Tenn.

446

1949

MINUTES

OF THE

One Hundred and Thirtieth

ANNUAL SESSION

OF THE

POWELLS VALLEY

ASSOCIATION

of Primitive Baptists

HELD WITH

THE CHURCH OF BLACKFOX

Grainger County, Tennessee

August 19-20-21, 1949

OFFICERS

Elder JOHN F. KECK..Moderator
Elder ALBERT DAVIS .... Assistant Moderator
Brother SAM DAVIS ... .Clerk
Brother J. L. DRUMMONDS....................................Assistant Clerk

The next Session will be held with the Church of Pleasant Hill, Claiborne County, Tennessee, beginning on Friday before the third Saturday in August 1950. Elder Lenville Moyers will preach the introductory sermon and Elder Matthew Oliver will be his alternate.

FRIDAY'S PROCEEDINGS

First—According to the previous arrangements the Association met pursuant to adjournment.

Second—After singing and prayer by Elder Will Campbell the introductory sermon was delivered by Elder W. R. Weaver, from third chapter, fourteenth verse Exodus. And God said unto Moses, I am that I am. Followed by Elder Leonard White from St. Luke, first chapter, first and second verse. For as much as many have taken in hand to set forth in order a Declaration of those things which are most surely believed among us.

Third—After fifteen minutes intermission the Association reassembled. Prayer by Elder Lenville Moyers and Elder W. M. Sparks.

Fourth—The Association was called to order by the Moderator.

Fifth—Called for letters from Sister Churches. Received eleven which were read by the clerks.

Sixth—On motion all the said letters were received and the Deligation was welcomed to seats by Moderator.

Seventh—Called for letters from corresponding Associations. Received one from Hiwassee and one from Central Union.

Eighth— On motion, said letters were received and the Delegates welcomed to seats by the Moderator. Delegates from the Hiwassee Association were Elders J. F. Campbell and John Russell. Delegate from Central Union, Carl McCarty.

Ninth—On motion we received the corresponding request of the Nolochucky Association by proxy.

Tenth—On motion Elder John F. Keck was re-elected Assistant Moderator and Bro. Albert Davis was re-elected Assistant Moderator.

Eleventh—On motion Bro. Sam Davis was reelected Clerk and Bro. J. L. Drummonds reelected assistant Clerk.

Twelfth—On motion the Moderator appoint all the committees on arrangements, Bros. Elmer Graves, George Shoffer and Sam Cook.

B—On preaching, Bros. Lincoln Edwards, Von Beason and George Shoffner.

C—On Correspondence, Elder Matthew Oliver, Elder Lenville Moyers and Elder Milton B. Brantly.

D—On request, Bros. Brice Braden, Everett Brantly and John Davis.

E—On finance, Bros. Roy Baily, J. M. Davis and Millard Welch.

Thirteenth—On motion we adjourned until 10 A. M. Saturday morning.

SATURDAY'S PROCEEDINGS

First—Call for the report of the Committee on arrangement.

A—We, your committee on arrangements beg leave to make the following report:

1—Call the roll.

2—Call for the report on preaching.

3—Call for the report on correspondence.

4—Call for the report on finance. When and where shall our next Association be held. Who shall preach the introductory sermon. Who shall be his alternante. How many copies of the minutes shall we have printed. Who shall superintend the printing and distribution of same. What shall he be allowed for his services.

Respectfully submitted,
BRO. SAM COOK
BRO. G. W. SHOFFNER
BRO. ELMER GRAVES

Second—On motion the report was received and the committee discharged.

Third—Call the roll and erase the names of absentees.

Fourth—Call for the report on the committee on preaching.

B—We, your committee on preaching, beg leave to report the following: Friday afternoon Elders Albert Davis, Carl McCarty, and Friday night, Elders Campbell and Russel. Saturday morning Elder Mathew Oliver, Elder Lenvil Moyers. Sat. night Farmer and Milton Brantly. Sunday, Elder Leonard White, Elder Mathew Oliver.

Respectfully submitted,
BRO. VON BEASON
BRO. G. W. SHOFFNER

Fifth—On motion we received the report and discharged the committee.

Sixth—Called for the report of the committee on correspondence.

C—We your committee on correspondence beg leave to make the following report: That we keep our correspondence with the Hiwassee, Nolochucky and Central Union Associations by letter and messengers.

Respectfully submitted,
ELDER LENVIL MOYERS
ELDER MILTON BRANTLEY

Seventh—On motion the report was received and the committee discharged.

Eighth—Called for the report of the committee on request.

D—We your committee on request beg leave to make the following report: That we have all the obituaries printed in our minutes which the churches furnish. That our next session be held with the Church of Pleasant Hill.

Respectfully submitted,
BRO. JOHN DAVIS
BRO. EVERETT BRANTLY

Ninth—On motion the report was received and the committee discharged.

Tenth—Call for the report of the committee on finance.

E—We, your committee on finance, beg leave to make the following report. Received from the sister churches the following contributions for ministers and minutes.

For ministers: Kirkwood, $6.00; Davis Chapel, $6.00; Bradens Chapel, $6.12; Pleasant Hill, $5.00; Oak Grove, $5.00; Brantleys Chapel, $4.00. For Minutes: Kirkwood, $4.00; Rocky Dale, $5.00; Davis Chapel, $4 00; Cedar Spring, $8.50; Capps Creek, $5.00; Bradens Chapel, $6.00; Pleasant Hill, $10.00; Gibson Station, $8.00; Noeton, $2.00; Black Fox, $9.00; Oak Grove, $11.00; Pleasant Point, $10.00; Brantleys Chapel, $5.00.

Respectfully submitted.
BRO. MILLAN WELCH
BRO. ROY BAILY

Eleventh—Called for letters from Sister churches that failed to get in Friday and received two.

Twelfth—On motion said letters were received and the Delegation welcomed to seats by the Moderator.

Thirteenth—On motion we have one thousand copies of the minutes printed. That the Clerk superintend the printing of same and that he be paid $25.00 for his services.

Fourteenth—On motion, the next annual Association be held with the church of Pleasant Hill, Claiborne County, Tennessee, Commence on Friday before the third Saturday in August, 1950.

Fifteenth—On motion, Elder Lenvil Moyers, preach the Introductory sermon and that Elder Mathew Oliver be his alternate.

Sixteenth—On motion, we send Elders J. R. Weaver and Mathew

449

Oliver as messengers to the Nolochucky Association. Elders Albert Davis, Mathew Oliver and Milton Brantly to the Central Union Association. Elders Albert Davis and W. M. Sparks.

Seventeenth—On motion, the clerk write each delegate letters of correspondence to the Associations.

Eighteenth—On motion, we extend to this dear old church and the people of the surrounding community, our sincere appreciation for the generous hospitality and kindness shown us through the Association.

Ninteenth—On motion, we adjourn until 10:30 A. M. EST at the place above stated.

Twentieth - Dismissed in order.

Respectfully submitted,
ELDER JOHN F. KECK,
Moderator, Goin, Tennessee.
ELDER ALBERT DAVIS,
Asst. Mod. Speedwell, Tenn.
BRO. SAM DAVIS,
Clerk, Luttrell, Tenn.
BRO. J. L. DRUMMONDS,
Asst. Clk, New Tazewell, Tenn.

SUNDAY'S PROCEEDINGS

On Sunday a large audience assembled at the alter and attentively listened to the well delivered sermons of Elder Leonard White from first chapter of John, thirty-sixth verse. He was followed by Elder Mathew Oliver with closing remarks by the Moderator. All sermons were delivered in a most loving spirit and a loving parting was expressed.

MINISTERS' ROLL

John Ausmus	Speedwell, Tenn.
E. S. Drummonds	New Tazewell, Tenn.
Albert Davis	Speedwell, Tenn.
John F. Keck	Goin, Tenn.
W. A. Moyers	Knoxville, Tenn.
Mathew Oliver	Bean Station, Tenn.
Leonard White	LaFollette, Tenn.
Milton Brantly	Sharps Chapel, Tenn.
J. R. Weaver	Gibson Station, Va.
Charlie Redmond	Gibson Station, Va.
R. H. Petit	Knoxville, Tenn.
William Sparks	Speedwell, Tenn.
Lenvil Moyers	Speedwill, Tenn.
V. W. Kennedy	Knoxville, Tenn.
Dewey Ellison	Sharps Chapel, Tenn.

LICENTIATES

Jim Collins	New Market, Tenn.
Charlie Stanifer	Corryton, Tenn.
Sam Miller	New Market, Tenn.
Joe Erwin	Gibson Station, Va.

Corresponding letter

We, the Powels Valley Association of Primitive Baptist now in Session at Blackfox Church on August 19-20-21, 1949, sendeth greetings to the Hiwassee, Nolachuckey and Central union associations with whom we correspond: Very dear Brothers and Sisters, we desire to keep up our cherished correspondence with you and have chosen these, our beloved Elders to bear this Epistle of love to you. To your associations, to the Hiwassee Elders, Albert Paris, Mathew Oliver, Milton Brantly; to the Nolachucky Elders, J. R. Weaver, Mathew Oliver; to the Central Union Elders, Albert Paris, W. M. Sparks, James Brancome. Having seated all your delegations in our assembly, we heartly invite another next year. When Convened with the church of Pleasant Hill, Claiborne County, Tenn., on Friday before the third Saturday in August, 1950.

OBITUARIES

DORA L. BRADEN BERRY

Sister Dora L. Braden Berry, was born Nov. 20, 1891, and died Oct. 10, 1948. She was married to B. F. Berry, June 21, 1908, to this union, five children were born, two girls and three boys.

She professed faith in Christ at an early age and joined the church at Cave Spring in 1908. She remained a faithful member until the church was lost to Norris Lake.

Sister Dora was an ideal lady, a loyal wife, a faithful mother, a generous neighbor and a kind friend. She is so much missed by the husband and children. The body is sweetly resting in the Cemetery at New Market, Tenn., awaiting the resurrection of the dead.

W. H. WEAVER

Brother W. H. Weaver was born April 12, 1885, and died Sept. 20, 1948. He was a son of the late Alvin Weaver and Elizabeth Anderson Weaver.

He was married to Miss Janie White, Dec. 24, 1905. To this union, two sons were born, Lincoln and Leon Weaver. He professed faith in Christ at an early age and joined the church at Mossy Spring where he remained a member until the church was lost to Norris Lake. He then moved his letter to Davis Chapel, where he remained a faithful member until his death. Henry was always an ideal boy, a loyal husband, a faithful father, a precious brother, an obedient son and a generous neighbor, loved and respected by all who knew him, equaled by few and surpassed by none. Sweetly sleeping, awaiting the resurrection of the dead.

JEFFERSON WINFIELD KECK

Jefferson winfield Keck, son of T. C. and Malinda Francis Keck, was born Sept. 19, 1885. Died Feb. 7, 1949. Age 63 years, 4 mo. and 18 days.

He was united in marriage to Miss China Mayes on Nov. 8, 1914. To this union, one son was born. Both wife and son died in 1915.

On March 27th, 1921, he was united in marriage to Miss Laura Gray. To this union, 4 sons were born. Homer, Edward, Bryan and Corum.

Edward and Bryan preceded him in death.

He is survived by his widow and two sons. Homer of Goin, Tenn; and Corum of Knoxville. One sister, Mrs. Dona Cole of Canton, Ohio. Two half sisters, Mrs. Bessie Collins of Goin and Mrs. China Cox of Knoxville. Four half brother, R. G. Keck, J. N. Keck, C. D. Keck and E. M. Keck all of Goin. His step-mother, Mrs. T. C. Keck and one uncle, Dr. John Francisco, of Enid, Oklahoma.

He professed faith in Christ at an early age, but declined to join the church until after his children were large enough to follow in his footsteps. He then joined the Primitive Baptist Church at Pleasant Point and was an outstanding member of the church. He was serving as a deacon of the church at his death.

He bore his illness patiently and always wanted the family near him. He called for his sons just a few hours before he died. When they came to his bedside, he looked upon them and shed tears. If he could have spoken his heart's desire to them, he probably would have said similar words of the Psalmist David to his son. "I go the way of all the earth, you be strong and show yourselves men, keep the charge of the Lord God, walk in his ways, keep his commandments and his testimonies, as it is written in the law of Moses, that you may prosper in all that you do".

His funeral was conducted Feb. 8, 1949 at Pleasant Point, with the pastor Elder Mathew Oliver and Elder John F. Keck officiating. The large crowd attending the funeral and the many beautful floral offerings showed the high esteem he was held by his relatives and friends.

His body was laid to rest in the Pleasant Point Cemetery Members of the Masonic Lodge gave a beautiful ceremony at the grave.

His wife.

LUVENA BAKER BORUFF

Luvena Baker Boruff, daughter of Mr. and Mrs. W. S. Baker was born July 19, 1886 in Union county, died May 12, 1946 in El wood, Ind.

She was married to Louis Boruff in November, 1910, to this union was born two children, Mrs. Pearl Deford of Curtisville, Ind., and Jamerson Boruff of Elwood, Indiana. She has eight grandchildren, four sisters, Mrs. Victor Kitts and Mrs. Vaughn Waddington of Maynardville, Tenn.; Mrs. Maggie Kitts of Corryton, Tenn.; and Mrs. C. O. Bridges of Knoxville, two brothers, Walter and Berton Baker of Maynardville, Tenn.

She joined the church at Rockydale, Corryton, Tenn., Aug. 5, 1922, and was a faithful member as long as she lived near it. We lost a "good neighbor" when she moved to Indiana in 1933. The days never got too hot nor the night too cold for her to go sit by a sick bedside and help take care of the sick or help out in time of distress. She is gone but her good works live on.

A neighbor.

LOUIS LaFAYETTE BORUFF

Louis LaFayette Boruff, son of Mr. and Mrs. Frank Boruff, was born July 19, 1888 in Union County, Tenn., died April 27th 1949 at Elmwood, Indiana. He was married to Luvena Baker in Nov. 1910. She died May 12, 1946. He was then married to Bessie Ann Barnes in Feb. 1949. He is survived by his widow, two children, Jamerson, of Elmwood, Ind.; Mrs. Pearl Deford of Curtisville, Ind; eight grandchildren; three brothers, John of Kokomo; P. O. of Windfall, and Author, of Elmwood and two sisters, Mrs. Rohda Smith of Elmwood, and Mrs. William Loy of Leesburg, Ind. He joined the church at Rockydale, Corryton, Tenn. on Aug. 5, 1922 and made a good member. He always enjoyed meeting his many friends and visiting with them.

ARMINTY, MELVINA GRAVES EVANS-GREEN

Arminty, Melvina Graves, Evans-Green, was born July 22nd, 1858. Departed this life, July 5th, 1949, making her stay here on earth 90 years, 11 month, 13 days. She united with Riley Evans in her early life. To this union was born six children. Three daughters and three sons of which husband and two daughters preceeded her in death. In 1906 she married the late Thomas Green who also preceeded her in death. She professed faith in Christ in her early life and joined the Primitive Baptist church at Union. Later, she moved her membership to Capps Creek where she remained a faithful member and a true believer in the saving grace of God until her death. She leaves to mourn her passing away, one daughter, three sons and a large number of grand and great-grandchildren; one sister; two brothers and a host of friends and relatives.

MRS. ADDILINE BERRY BRANTLEY

Mrs. Addiline Berry Brantley, age 57, departed from this life on August 5th at 10 p. m.

She professed faith in Christ at a middle age and joined the church at Mossie Springs, later moving her membership to Oak Grove Church.

She was the wife of Milton Brantley and the mother of seven children, four dead and three living, Sylvia Brantley, Cra Brantley Williams and Coran Brantley.

She also leaves three sisters: Mrs. Tishie Creech, Miss Rhoda Berry, Sharps Chapel, and Mrs. Mary Harron of New Market; Three brothers, Millard and Frank Berry of New Market, and Bud Berry of Shraps Chapel. Six grandchildren and a host of friends and relatives who mourn their loss to heavens eternal gain.

BART NICELY

Bart Nicely was born Feb. 13, 1889 and departed this life Aug. 8, 1949. Age 60 years six months and 26 days. Professed faith in Christ a few years ago but never joined a church. He leaves to mourn him, his widow, Lizzie Nicely, four daughters, Truly, Beatric, Marry, and Gracie; one brother, Eck Nicely, ten sisters, Marry Muncy, Cardilia Muncy, Francis Rosenbalm, Mildred Rosenbalm, Liddie Muncy, Orlione Collins, Ettie Rosenbalm, Myrtle Muncy, Carrie Larmer, and Gracie Loy. He leaves a testimony with us to brighten his crossing. He was a loving father and a devoted husband, a loving brother and was loved by all who knew him. He was dear to us all. How we will miss him, but we hope to meet him in heaven where there will be no more sad farewells, no tear dimmed eyes. Sleep on, dear brother, and take your rest. We all have loved you, but God loved you best.

Sister Carrie.

DEWEY HOPPER

Dewey Hopper was born Feb. 9, 1889, died Feb. 25, 1949 being 50 years and 16 days of age. He was united in marriage to Etta Shipley July 11, 1920. He is survived by his wife, Mrs. Etta Hopper, Goins, parents, Mr. and Mrs. Henry Hopper, Goin, Tenn. sister, Mrs. Lottie Lynch, Knoxville. He professed faith in Christ and joined the Primitive Baptist church in the year 1939 at Pleasant Point. He was baptized the first Sunday in August 1939 and lived a faithful member until his death. He also leaves to mourn his passing, several nieces and nephews. He will be missed and mourned by a host of relatives and friends and his church. He is gone but not forgotten and his memory will live in their hearts forever. He was a devoted husband and son and dearly beloved by all who knew him. Funeral services were conducted at 1:00 p. m. Sunday at the Pleasant Point Baptist church with Elder Leonard White and Elder Mathew Oliver officiating. Interment in the Hopper cemetery.
Coffey—Stubblefield Funeral Home in charge.

MR. AND MRS. JOHN BUNDON

John Berry Bundon, 68, died at 12:30 p. m. yesterday at Fort Sanders Hospital, exactly 18 hours after the death of his wife, Mrs. Laura Elizabeth Bundon, 60.
Mrs. Bundon died at 6:30 p. m. Thursday at the couple's home in Tazewell. Both had been ill for some time.
Survivors include three sons, Nimmon and Hubert Bundon, both of Maryville, and Lennon Bundon of New Tazewell; 12 grandchildren; and a great-grandson. Mr. Bundon is survived by a sister, Mrs. Cynthia Gray of Monroe, Mich, and Mrs. Bundon leaves a half-brother, Ion Merritt of Knoxville, and a half-sister, Mrs. Lennie Hayes of Blaine.
Both Mr. and Mrs. Bundon were members of Black Fox Primitive Baptist Church.
Double funeral services were held at Carr's Branch Baptist Church in Claiborne County, at 2 p. m. Saturday.

DANIEL PLESANT DRUMMONDS

Daniel Plesant Drummonds, son of W. A. and Sibby Drummonds was born Sept. 20, 1877, and died Oct. 6, 1948. Age 71 years and 16 days.
He was united in marriage to Cardie Chumbley, Nov. 24, 1907. To this union three children were born.
Leaving to mourn his passing are his wife, Mrs. Cordie Drummonds; two daughters, Miss Hazel Drummonds, New Tazewell, Mrs. Dorothy Neely, Monroe, Mich; one son, Ray Drummonds, New Tazewell; three grandchildren, Durward, Elaine and Janice Drummonds; brothers, E. S. Drummonds, J. A. Drummonds, S. W. Drummonds, and J. L. Drummonds all of New Tazewell, G. B. Drummonds, Monroe, Mich. Sisters, Mrs. Mary Robertson, Speedwell, Tenn. and Mrs. Kate Poore, Maynardville, Tenn. A host of other relatives and friends mourn his loss.
He professed faith in Christ and joined the Primitive Baptist church at Meyers Grove, Nov. 1892, was baptized by Elder E. M. Branson. He lived a faithful member until death.
Funeral services were conducted at Meyers Grove Baptist church by Rev. John F. Keck and Rev. Charlie Meyers.
Pall bearers were: James Drummonds, Earl Poore, Steve Poore, Lloyd Drummonds, Ward Chumley and John Drummonds.
Flower girls were: Dora Drummonds, Frankie Hayes, Marjorie Watson, Mary Lou Neely, Ethel England, O'Doskie Meyers, Ann Chumley, Mrs. Bob Meyers, Aileen Drummonds, Beatrice Cox, Nelle Wright, and Dessie Chumley.
Interment in the Drummonds Cemetery with Coffey-Stubblefield Funeral Home, Tazewell in charge.

CHURCHES	NAMES OF DELEGATES	Rec. by Baptism	Rec. by Letter	Dism. by Letter	Excluded	Deceased	Total Membership	Saturday Meeting	Printing Minutes	Visiting Ministers	Communion Meetings
Red Hill	No Letter Come On										
Black Fox	Bros. Ray Bailey, Sam Cook, J. M. Davis, Sam Davis, W. M. Perry, Sis. Roma Baily, Myrtle Muncy, Sallie Davis, John Liford and wife	1	1			2	102	2	9.00		June
Rocky Dale	Bros. Elmer Graves, Sis. Bessie Graves, Leala Palmer, Rhoda Dunn	5	11	1	4	1	86		5.00	5.00	June
Cedar Spring	Bros. J. C. Bolin, John Davis, J. L.-G. B. Drummonds, Elders Lenvel Moyers	1				1	82	4	8.50	6.00	May
Kirkwood	Bros. Harry Chambers, J. L. Sharp, Sis. Evelyn Sharp—		5	2			72	1	4.00	6.00	Aug.
Braden's Chapel	Elder W. M. Sparks, Bros. Brice Braden, Edd McBee, Sis. Hallie Russell	1					34	1			
Pleasant Point	Elder John F. Keck, G. W. Williams—					2	144	1	6.00	6.16	June
Capps Creek	Elder John R. Weaver and wife, Bros. W. I. Browning, Troy Presley, Sis. Vergie Browning, Fannie Russell, Charlie Collins	1			2		35	1	10.00		July
Pleasant Hill	Elder Albert Davis, Bros. Verlin-Roy Edwards and wife, James Brantly	1					87	3	5.00	5.00	Apr.
Noeton	Elder Mathew Oliver, Bro. John Oliver.						35	4	10.00	5.00	June
Oak Grove	Elders Dewey Elison, Milton Brantly, Bros. George Shoffner, Sis. Vesta Elison, Lillie Shoffner					3	332	3	2.00		
Gibson's Station	Bro. George Shoffner and wife, Bro. Henry Hoskins.	1		8			80	1	10.00	5.00	May
Brantly's Chapel	Bros. Jipp Elison, Everett Brantly, W. M. Welch, Plumer McBee, Sis. Mildred Brantly, Luda Welch, Otie McBee			2			14	3	8.00	5.00	
Davis Chapel	Elder Leonard White, O. R. Parrott, Raymond Heatherly	2		1	1	1	148	3	4.00	6.00	July

455

CHURCHES	COUNTY	PASTORS	CLERKS	CLERK'S POST OFFICES
Red Hill	Grainger	John F. Keck	Sam Davis	Luttrell, Tenn.
Black Fox		Asst.— Mathew Oliver	Asst.—J. M. Davis	Powder Springs, Tenn.
Rocky Dale	Knox	Leonard White	Leaia Palmer	Rt. 13, Fountain City, Tenn.
Cedar Springs	Claiborne	W. M. Sparks	J. L. Drummonds	New Tazewell, Tenn.
Kirkwood	Knox	Leonard White	Estelle Sharp	819 Jacksboro Pk., Fountain City, Tenn.
Braden's Chapel	Union	W. M. Sparks	Hallie Russell	Speedwell, Tenn.
Pleasant Point	Claiborne	Matthew Oliver	Austin Beason	Goin, Tenn.
Capps Creek	Union	J. K. Weaver	Easter Braden	Goin, Tenn.
Pleasant Hill	Claiborne	Albert Davis	Asst.—Fannie Pressley Lincoln Wards	Speedwell, Tenn.
			Asst.—Verlin Edwards	
Noeton	Grainger	Matthew Oliver	John Oliver	Bean Station, Tenn.
Oak Grove	Union	Albert Davis	Luna Sheritz	Goin, Tenn.
			Asst.—Nelle Sheritz	
Gibson's Station	Lee	Mathew Oliver	Ropie Cobb	Gibson's Station, Va.
Brantly's Chapel	Blount	John F. Keck	R. P. Bridges	Maryville, Rt. 8, Tenn.
			Asst.—Mildred Brantly	
Davis Chapel	Campbell	W. M. Sparks	Mannie Kitts	Lafollette, Tenn.

456

1950

MINUTES

OF THE

One Hundred and Thirty-First
ANNUAL SESSION

OF THE

Powells Valley Association

of Primitive Baptists

HELD WITH

The Church At Pleasant Hill

Claiborne County, Tennessee

August 18-19-20, 1950

OFFICERS

Elder Albert Davis_____ Moderator
Elder John F. Keck _____ Assistant Moderator
Brother J. L. Drummonds_____ Clerk
Brother W. E. Browning _____ Assistant Clerk

The next session will be held with the Church of Brantley's Chapel, Blount County, Tennessee, beginning on Friday before the third Saturday in August, 1951. Elder Leonard White to preach the introductory sermon and Elder W. M. Sparks will be his alternate.

J. L. DRUMMONDS AND SAM DAVIS

Brother Sam Davis was released from the Clerkship after a service of many years. Brother J. L. Drummonds was elected Clerk at the 131st session of the Association, held at Pleasant Hill, August 18-20, 1950.

Friday's Proceedings

First—According to the previous arrangements the Association met pursuant to adjournment.

Second—After singing and prayer by Elder Charlie Redmond the introductory sermon was delivered by Elder Linville Meyers, from Third Chapter of Timothy, seventh verse. "Ever learning and never able to come to the knowledge of the truth."

Third—After ten minutes intermission, the association reassembled. Prayer by Brother Jimmie Brantley and Elder Allen Gates.

Fourth—The association was called to order by the Moderator, Elder John F. Keck.

Fifth—Called for letters from Sister Churches. Received eleven which were read by the clerks.

Sixth—On motion all said letters were received and the Delegation was welcomed to seats by the Moderator.

Seventh—Called for letters from corresponding Associations. Received one from Hiwassee and one from Central Union.

Eighth—On motion, said letters were received and the Delegates welcomed to seats by the Moderator. Delegates from the Hiwassee, Elder Allen Gates. Delegates from the Central Union was Elder Carl McCarty.

Ninth—On Motion, Elder Albert Davis was elected Moderator and Elder John F. Keck was elected Assistant Moderator.

Tenth—Brother Sam Davis was released from the position as Clerk on his request since he was getting old, on motion.

Eleventh—On motion Brother J. L. Drummonds was elected Clerk and Brother W. I. Browning was elected Assistant Clerk.

Twelfth—On motion the Moderator appoint all the committees.

A—On arrangements, Brother Ellis Evans, George Williams, and John Davis.

B—On preaching, Brothers Verlin Edwards, Brice Breden, and Henry Hoskins.

C—On correspondence, Elders W. A. Moyers, W. R. Weaver, and Brother George Shoffner.

D—On request, Elder W. M. Sparks, Brother J. L. Edwards, and G. B. Drummonds.

E—On finance, Brothers John Davis, Jimmie Brantley, and G. W. Shoffner.

Thirteenth—On motion, we adjourned until 10:00 a. m., Saturday morning.

Saturday's Proceedings

After singing praise, scripture reading by James Branscome from Epheseans 6.

First—Call for the report of the Committee on arrangements.

A. We, your Committee on arrangements beg leave to make the following report:

1. Call the roll
2. Call for the report of the Committee on preaching.
3. Call for the report of the Committee on correspondence.
4. Call for the report of the Committee on finance. When and where shall our next Association be held. Who shall preach the introductory sermon and who shall be his alternate. How many copies of the Minutes shall we have printed and who shall superintend the printing and distribution of the same. What shall he be allowed for his services?

Respectfully submitted,
BROTHER ELLIS EVANS
BROTHER GEORGE WILLIIAMS
BROTHER JOHN DAVIS

Second—On motion the report was received and the committee discharged.

Called the roll and erased the names of the absentees.

Fourth—Called for the report of the committee on Preaching.

B. We, your committee on preaching. beg leave to make the following report:

Friday night at the Church, Elders Allen Gates, W. A. Moyers Braden's Chapel, Elder W. M. Sparks and Elder Carl McCarty. Saturday night at the Church, Elder Linville Meyers, Elder Albert Davis. At Bradens Chaple, Elder Allen Gates. Sunday, Elders Leonard White, Matthew Oliver, Moderator to close.

Respectfully submitter,

BRO. VERLIN EDWARDS

BRO. BRICE BRADEN

BRO. HENRY HOSKINS

Fifth—On motion, we received the report and discharged the committee.

Sixth—Called for the report of the committee on correspondence.

C. We, your committee on correspondence, beg leave to make the following report:

That we keep up our correspondence with the Hiwassee and Central Union Associations with letter and messengers.

Respectfully submitted,

ELDER JOHN WEAVER

ELDER W. A. MOYERS

BROTHER GEORGE SHOFFNER

Seventh—on motion, the report was received and the committee discharged.

Eighth—Called for the report of the committee on request.

D. We, your committee on request beg leave to make the following report:

The we publish all the obituaries that the churches furnish and that our next Association be held with the Church at Brantley's Chapel, Blount County, Tennessee, to commence on Friday before the third Saturday in August, 1951, and two days following.

Respectfully submitted,

ELDER W. M. SPARKS

BROTHER G. B. DRUMMONDS

BROTHER J. L. EDWARDS

Ninth—On motion, the report was received and the committee discharged.

Tenth—Called for the report of the committee on Finance.

E. We, your committee on finance, beg leave to make the following report:

Received from Sister Churches the following for the printing of the Minutes and for visiting ministers:

For Minutes—Rocky Dale, $5.00; Brantley's Chapel, $4.00; Kirkwood, $4.00; Oak Grove, $10.00; Cedar Springs, $7.00; Pleasant Hill, $12.00; Noeton, $2.00; Capps Creek, $5.00; Pleasant Point, $5.00; Black Fox, $9.00; Gibson Station, $3.00; Bradens Chapel, $5.00; Davis Chapel, f3.00. Total $74.00.

For Ministers—Rocky Dale, $5.00; Brantley's Chapel, $7.42; Kirkwood, $6.00; Pleasant Hill, $5.00; Pleasant Point, $5.00; Gibson Station, $5.00; Bradens Chapel, $5.00; Davis Chapel, $7.00. Total, $45.42.

Respectfully submitted,

BROTHER JOHN DAVIS

BROTHER JIMMIE BRANTLEY

BROTHER G. W. SHOFFNER

Eleventh—Called for letters from Sister Churches that failed to get in Friday and received one.

Twelfth—On motion, said letters were received and the delegation was welcomed to seats by the Moderator.

Thirteenth—On motion, we have one thousand copies of the Minutes printed. That the clerk superintend the printing and distribution of the same and that he be allowed $25.00 for his services.

Fourteenth—On motion, the next annual session of the Association be held with the Church of Brantley's Chapel, Blount County, Tennessee, to begin on Friday before the third Saturday in August, 1951.

Fifteenth—On motion, Elder Leonard White will preach the introductory sermon and that Elder W. M. Sparks will be his alternate.

Sixteenth—On motion, we send Elders W. A. Moyers, Leonard White, and J. R. Weaver to the Hiwassee Association as messengers. To the Central Union, Elders W. M. Sparks, Charlie Redmond, and Albert Davis.

Seventeenth—On motion, the clerk write each delegate letters of correspondence to the Association.

Eighteenth—On motion, the Association stood one minute in honor of Brother Sam Davis, retired clerk.

Nineteenth—On motion, we extend to this dear old church and the people of the surrounding community, our sincere appreciation for the generous hospitality and kindness shown us through this Association.

Twentieth—On motion, we adjourn until 10:30 a. m. EST at the place above stated.

Twenty-First—Dismissed in order.

Respectfully submitted,
ELDER ALBERT DAVIS,
Moderator, Speedwell, Tennessee
ELDER JOHN F. KECK,
Assistant Moderator, Goin, Tennessee
BROTHER J. L. DRUMMONDS,
Clerk, New Tazewell, Tennessee
BROTHER W. I. BROWNING,
Assistant Clerk, Sharps Chapel, Tennessee

Sunday's Proceedings

On Sunday a large audience assembled at the altar and attentively listened to the well delivered Sermon of Elder Matthew Oliver from Deuteronomy, 32 chapter, 11 verse. "As an eagle stirreth up her nest, fluttereth over her young, spread abroad her wings, taketh them, beareth them on her wings." He was followed by Elder Leonard White, with a few remarks. The closing remarks were made by the Moderator. All sermons were delivered in a most loving spirit and a loving parting was expressed.

Licentiates

Jim Collins	New Market, Tenn.
Charlie Standifer	Corryton, Tenn.
Sam Miller	New Market, Tenn.
James Branscome	Speedwell, Tenn.
Tony Easteridge	Knoxville, Tenn.
George Shoffner	Goin, Tenn.

Corresponding Letters

We, the Powell Valley Association of Primitive Baptists now in session at Pleasant Hill Church, on August 18-19-20, 1950 sendeth greetings to the Hiwassee and Central Union Associations with whom we now correspond: Very dear brothers and sisters, we desire to keep up our cherished correspondence with you and have chosen these, our beloved Elders to bear this Epistle of love to you. To the Central Union we send Elders W. M. Sparks, Albert Davis, and Charlie Redmond. The Hiwassee we send Elders J. R. Weaver, Leonard White, and W. A. Moyers. Having seated all your delegation, we heartily invite another next year. When convened with the Church at Brantley's Chapel, Blount County, Tennessee, on Friday before the third Saturday in August, 1951.

Obituaries

LIZZIE NICELY

Lizzie Nicely was born January 8, 1896, departed this life March 20, 1950. Age 54 years, two months, twelve days.

She professed faith in Christ at an early age and joined the Primitive Baptist Church at Black Fox, and lived a faithful Christian until death.

She leaves to mourn her passing her four daughters, Trula, Beatrice, Mary, and Gracie, her mother Jane Baily, three sisters Nerva Nicely, Hazel Munsey, Zena Munsey, three brothers, James, Herbert, and Roy Bailey.

She leaves a testimony with us to brighten her crossing. She was a loving mother and was loved by all who knew her. She was dear to us and oh how we miss her, but we will meet her again in Heaven where there will be no more sad farewells and no tears.

Sleep on, dear mother and take thy rest. We all love you and hope to live together again in Heaven some sweet day.

The daughters

CORDIE CHUMLEY DRUMMONDS

Cordie Chumley Drummonds, daughter of Mary and J. F. Chumley, was born October 14, 1873, died September 16, 1949, being 75 years, 11 months, and 2 days of age.

On November 24, 1907, she was united in marriage to D. P. Drummonds, and to this union three childern were born.

Survivors are daughters, Hazel Drummonds, New Tazewell, Tenn. Mrs. Dorothy Neely, Monroe, Mich. Son, Ray Drummonds, New Tazewell. Father, J. F. Chumley, Middlesboro, Ky. Broothers, J. W. and J. R. Chumley, New Tazewell. Sisters: Mrs. Ida Mink, Evarts, Ky. Mrs Mabel Watson, New Tazewell, Three grandchildren, Durward, Phyllis Elaine, and Janice Drummonds of New Tazewell. And a host of other relatives and friends.

She professed faith in Christ at an early age and joined the Meyers Grove Methodist Church, where she remained a faithful member until death.

Pall bearers were: Loyd Drummonds, Kelsie Watson, Ward Chumley, Milton Goin, Raymond Poore, and J. C. Chumley.

Flower girls were: Beatrice Cox, Mary Lou Neely, Aileen Drummonds, Marjorie Watson, Delta Chandler, Blanche Cox, Aileen Drummonds, Vonue Goin, Ida Beeler, Mildred Leffler, Ethel England, Florabelle Poore, Pauline Shoffner, Jewell Hurley, Myrna and Rylyn Hurley.

A loved one from us is gone,
A voice we loved is still,
A place is vacant in our home
Which never can be filled.

Funeral was conducted by Rev. George Buchanan and Rev. John F. Keck. Interment in Drummonds Cemetery with Coffy-Stubblefield Funeral Home in charge.

W. M. PERRY

W. M. Perry was born October 25, 1871, departed this life March 3, 1950, being 78 years, 4 months, and 8 days old.

He professed faith in Christ in early life and joined the Primitive Baptist Church at Black Fox, where he remained a faithful member until death. He also served as deacon of that church.

He was first united in marriage to Sarah Hamilton Perry, who proceeded him in death. On September 15, 1940, he was united in marriage to Mossie Goin Perry.

He is survived by his widow, Mossie Perry, three step-daughters, Ethel, Bonnie, and Laura Goin, three sisters, Mrs. Hala Hindrex, Knovville, Tennessee. Mrs. Mary Hendrix, Liberty Hill, Tennessee, Mrs. Lundie Yadon, Blain, Tennessee, several nieces and nephews and a host of friends to mourn his passing. But we deeply feel our loss is Heaven's gain.

A dear friend from us is gone,
A voice we loved is still,
A place is vacant in our home
Which never can be filled.
His Wife.

GACIE LENOR NICELY LAY

Sister Gacie Lenor Nicely Lay was born December 2, 1913, July 8, 1950, age 36 years, 7 months, 6 days.

She professed faith in Christ at an early age and later joined the Primitive Baptist Church at Black Fox and lived a faithful member until death.

Left to mourn her passing are her husband, Easton Lay and two daughters, Anna Lee and Eula Lay of Liberty Hill. One brother, Eck Nicely, nine sisters, Mary Mincy, Cordelia Munsey, Carry Larmer, Myrtle Munsey, Mildred Rosenbalm, of New Tazewell, Francis Rosenbalm, Clinton. Twenty-nine nieces, 21 nephews, and a host of friends and relatives.

Our loss is her Eternal gain. While we are made sad, Heaven is made glad.

> A loved one from us is gone,
> A voice we loved is still,
> A place is vacant in our home
> Which never can be filled.
> In rememberance of a loving sister,
> By sisters, Myrtle and Carris

ELDER JOHN AUSMUS

Elder John Ausmus passed away in September, 1949, being about 78 years old. He married Jane Taylor, and to this union five children were born, three boys and two girls.

His companion departed this life about ten years before he was called away.

Brother Ausmus professed faith in Christ forty years ago, and joined the Church at Straight Branch the 4th Saturday in January, 1909. He was ordained to the full work of the ministry the 1st Saturday in March 1921.

Brother Ausmus remained a member of Straight Branch Church until it was covered by Norris Lake. Then he moved his membership to Pleasant Hill Church where he remained a faithful member until death.

He has served as Moderator of some of our Churches.

Uncle Johnny was a fine preacher and a firm believer in the Primitive Baptist Faith.

He is missed by his loved ones and his church and his friends.

MRS. MARY F. ROBBERTSON

Mrs. Mary Robertson, daughter of the late W. A. and Sibby Drummonds, was born August 1, 1873, and died November 4, 1949, being 76 years, 3 months, and 3 days of age.

On February 8, 1891, she was united in marriage to W. F. Robertson. To this union 13 children were born, four having preceeded here in death She professed faith in Christ at an early age and joined the Red Hill Primitive Baptist Church in 1893.

She leaves to mourn her passing, her husband, daughters, Josephine Cupp. Knoxville, Mrs. Annie Earls, Cumberland Gap, Mrs. Mae Wright Speedwell, Vesa Treece, LaFayette, Ind., Mrs. Eva Blankenship, Detroit, Mich. Sons: Charlie Robertson, LaFayette, Ind., Minnie and ChesterRobertson, St. Charles, Va., Oscar Robertson, Middlesboro, Ky. Sister, Mrs. Kate Poore, Maynardville, brothers, E. S. and G. B. Drummonds, Monroe, Mich., S. W., J. L. and J. A. Drummonds, New Tazewell. Ninty-one grandchildren and a host of other relatives and friends.

Funeral services were held at 10 A. M. Monday at Meyers Grove, with Elder Matthew Oliver and Elder Leonard White officiating. In terment in the Drummonds Cemetery.

Pall Bearers: Otis Robertson, Roscoe Robertson, Loyd Treece, Josh Stapleton, Sam Earl, and Lee Robertson. Flower girls were the granddaughters.

Coffey-Stubblefield Funeral Home in charge of the funeral.

Statistical Table

CHURCHES	NAMES OF DELEGATES	Received by Relationship	Received by Baptism	Received by Letter	Dis. by Letter	Excluded	Deceased	Total Membership	Saturday Meeting	Printing Minutes	Visiting Ministers	Communion Meeting
Black Fox	Sam Davis, J. M. Davis		1			2	3	98	2	$ 9.00		June
Braden's Chapel	Brice Braden, Edd McBee, Elder W. M. Sparks		8			4		37	1	5.00	$ 5.00	July
Brantley's Chapel	Everett Brantley, Jeff Ellison, Clifford Brantley, Mildred Brantley							14	4	4.00	4.42	July
Capps Creek	Elder J. R. Weaver, W. I. Browning, Mrs. W. I. Browning, Mr. and Mrs. Ellis Evans							29	3	5.00		April
Cedar Spring	J. L. Drummond, G. B. Drummond, S. W. Drummond, Aileen Drummonds, John Davis, Velta Munsey	4		1	6		1	83	4	7.00		May
Davis Chapel	Raymond Heatherly, McKinley Ellison, Ollie Heatherly, Jim Kivett, Elder Leonard White, Lessie Ellison, Mollie McCarty					5		144	3	3.00	7.00	July
Gibson's Station	Elder Charlie Redmond, Elder Joe Erwin, George Shoffner, Henry Hoskins	2		3	3	8	3	78	1	3.00	5.00	July
Kirkwood	Otis Keck, Flossie Keck, J. L. Sharp, Evelyn Sharp		1			1	2	75	1	4.00	6.00	Aug.
Noeton	No Letter. Come on.									2.00		
Oak Grove	Elder Dewey Ellison, Tom England, George Shoffner		5		2		2	333	1	10.00		May
Pleasant Hill	Elder Albert Davis, Kinley Graves, Kate Ausmus, James Edwards, Mossie Graves, James Branscome		3				1	87	4	12.00	5.00	June
Pleasant Point	George Williams, Allie Williams, Oma Rosson, Elder John F. Keck							144	1	10.00		July
Red Hill	No Letter. Come on.											
Rocky Dale	Elmer Graves, Everette Berry, Avrell Graves, Bessie Graves, Trula Berry							86	1	5.00	5.00	June

CHURCHES	COUNTY	PASTORS	CLERKS	CLERK'S POST OFFICE
Red Hill	Grainge:	Elder Matthew Oliver	John Oliver	Bean Station, Tenn.
Noetou		Elder W. M. Sparks	J. L. Drumponds	New Tazewell, Tenn.
Cedar Springs	Claiborn:	Elder W. A. Moyers		
Pleasant Point	Claiborn:	Elder J. R. Weaver, Asst.	Austin Beason	Goin, Tennessee
Oak Grove	Union	Elder Albert Davis	Luna Sherritze Nelle Sherritze, Asst.	Goin, Tennessee Luttrell, Tennessee
Blac: Fox	Grainge:	Elder Dewey Ellison	Sam Davis John Davis, Asst.	Powder Springs, Tenn.
Capp's Creek	Unio:	Elder John Weaver	W. I. Browning	Sharps Chapel, Tenn.
Braden's Chapel	Unio:	Elder W. M. Sparks	Arvel Braden	Speedwell, Tennessee
Davis Chapel	Campbell	Elder W. M. Sparks	Lassie Ellison	LaFollette, Tennessee
Pleasan. Hill	Claiborne	Elder Albert Davis	Lincoln Edwards	Speedwell, Tennessee
Rocky Dale	Knox	Elder Leonard White	Verlin Edwards Leola Palmer	Route 13, Fountain City, Tenn.
Brantley's Chapel	Blour:	Elder John F. Keck	Faye Baruff, Asst. Mildred Brantley, Asst. R. F. Bridges	City 10, Maryville, Tenn. Rt. 8, Maryville, Tenn.
Kirkwood	Kno:	Elder Leonard White Elder Matthew Oliver	Estelle F. Sharp	819 Jacksboro Pk. Fountain City, Tenn.
Gibson Station	Lee	Elder Joe Irwin, Asst.	Roxie Cobb	Gibson Station, Va.

466

1951

MINUTES

OF THE

ANNUAL SESSION

OF THE

Powells Valley Association

of Primitive Baptists

HELD WITH

The Church at Brantley's Chapel

Blount County, Tennessee

August 17-18-19, 1951

OFFICERS

Elder Albert Davis..Moderator
Elder John F. Keck.. Assistant Moderator
Brother J. L. Drummonds..Clerk
Brother W. I. Browning................................... Assistant Clerk

The next session will be held with the church at Gibson Station, Lee County, Virginia, beginning on Friday before the third Saturday in August, 1952. Elder W. A. Moyers to preach the introductory sermon and Elder Henry Comer to be his alternate.

Friday's Proceedings

First—According to the previous arrangements the Association met pursuant to adjournment.

Second—After singing and prayer by Elder Henry Comer, Amazing Grace was sung and an old fashioned handshake was had. The introductory sermon was delivered by Elder W. M. Sparks, from the sixth chapter Ephesians followed by Elder Tonie Eastridge.

Third—After ten minutes intermission, the association reassembled. Scripture lesson was read by Elder Albert Davis from the twenty-third Psalm. Prayer by Brother Phelps and Elder Charlie Redmond.

Fourth—The assiciation was called to order by the moderator, Elder Albert Davis.

Fifth—Called for letters from sister churches. Received eleven which were read by the clerks.

Sixth—On motion all said letters were received and the delegates were welcomed to seat by the moderator.

Seventh—Called for members who were not delegates and received Brother Ellis Evans who was welcomed to a seat by the moderator.

Eighth—Called for letters from corresponding associations. Received one from the Central Union Association. On motion said letter was received and the delegates were welcomed to seats by the moderator. Delegates were Sister Cora Hill, Elder E. B. Earl, and Elder Robert Feltner.

Ninth—Called for members of the corresponding associations who were not delegates and received Brother Jeff Lemley, Crosbyton, Texas, and Elder O. C. Moyers, Texas.

Tenth—On motion, Elder Albert Davis was reelected Moderator and Elder John F. Keck was reelected Assistant Moderator.

Eleventh—On motion, Brother J. L. Drummonds was reelected Clerk and Brother W. I. Browning was reelected assistant clerk.

Twelfth—On motion the Moderator appoint the committees.

A—On arrangements, Brother Milton Brantley, G. B. Drummonds, and George Shoffner.

B—On preaching, Brothers J. M. Ellison, Ellis Evans, and Henry Hoskins, together with this church.

C—On correspondence, Elders W. M. Sparks, Henry Comer, and Brother James Kivett.

D—On request, Brothers James Edwards, Charlie Redmond, and Millard Welch.

E—On finance—Brothers Lincoln Edwards, Edd McBee, and Plumer McBee.

Thirteenth—On motion, we adjourn until 10:00 a. m. Saturday morning.

Saturday's Proceedings

After singing praise, scripture reading by Elder John F. Keck from Psalms 116.

First—Called for the report of the committee on arrangements.

A. We, your committee on arrangements beg leave to submit the following report:

1. Call the roll
2. Call for the report of the committee on preaching
3. Call for the report of the committee on correspondence
4. Call for the report of the committee on finance.

When and where shall our next association be held. Who shall preach the introductory sermon and who shall be his alternate. How many copies of the minutes shall we have printed and who shall superintend the printing and distribution of the same. What shall he be allowed for his services?

Respectfully submitted,
BROTHER G. W. SHOFFNER
BROTHER MILTON BRANTLEY
BROTHER G. B. DRUMMONDS

Second—On motion the report was received and the committee discharged.

Third—Called the roll and erased the names of the absentees.

Fourth—Called for the report of the committee on preaching.

B. We, your committee on preaching beg leave to submit the following report:

Friday night at the church. Elder Oscar Moyers and Elder Henry Comer. Saturday morning at the church Elder Robert Feltner and Elder Allen Gates. Sunday Elder Leonard White, Elder Matthew Oliver, Elder Charlie Redmond, and the moderator to close.

Respectfully submitted,
BROTHER ELLIS EVANS
BROTHER HENRY HOSKINS
BROTHER J. M. ELLISON

Fifth—On motion, we received the report and discharged the committee.

Sixth—Called for the report of the committee on correspondence.

C. We, your committee on correspondence, beg leave to submit the following report:

That we keep up our correspondence with the Hiwassee and Central Union association by letter and messengers.

Respectfully submitted,
ELDER HENHY COMER
ELDER W. M. SPARKS
BROTHER J. M. KIVETT

Seventh—On motion, the report was received and the committee discharged.

Eighth—Called for the report of the committee on request.

D. We, your committee on request beg leave to submit the following report:

That we publish all the obituaries that the churches furnish and that our next association be held with the church at Gibson Station, Lee County, Virginia to commence on Friday before the third Saturday in August, 1952, and two days following.

Respectfully submitted,
ELDER C. W. REDMOND
BROTHER JAMES EDWARDS
BROTHER MILLARD WELCH

Ninth—On motion the report was received and the committee discharged.

Tenth—Called for the report of the committee on finance.

E. We, your committee on finance beg leave to submit the following report:

Received from sister churches the following for the printing of the minutes and for visiting ministers:

	Visiting Ministers	Minutes
Brantley's Chapel	$ 4.83	$ 7.00
Gibson Station	7.00	3.00
Capps Creek	2.00	3.00
Kirkwood	6.00	4.00
Rockydale	5.00	5.00
Davis Chapel	5.00	3.00
Braden's Chapel	3.00	7.00
Pleasant Hill	5.00	10.00
Pleasant Point		10.00
Monroe, Michigan		5.00
Cedar Springs		8.00
Black Fox		8.60
Oak Grove		10.00
Donation at Church		9.00
Total amount	$37.83	$92.60

Respectfully submitted
BROTHER J. L. EDWARDS
BROTHER PLUMER McBEE
BROTHER EDD McBEE

Eleventh—On motion, the report was received and the committee discharged.

Twelfth—Called for letters from sister churches that failed to get in Friday and received one which was read by the clerk.

Thirteenth—On motion said letter was received and the delegation was welcomed to seats by the moderator.

Fourteenth—Called for the letters from corresponding association and received one from the Hiwassee Association by Elder Allen Gates which was read and received.

Fifteenth—Called for members of that association who were not delegates and received Elder C. C. Oliver who was welcomed to seat by the moderator. Elder Carl McCarty from the Central Union.

Sixteenth—On motion, we have one thousand copies of the minutes printed. That the clerk superintend the printing and distribution of the same and that he be allowed $25.00 for his services.

Seventeenth—On motion the next annual session of the Association be held with the church at Gibson Station, Lee County, Virginia, to begin on Friday before the third Saturday in August, 1952, and two days following.

Eighteenth—On motion, Elder W. A. Moyer will preach the introductory sermon and Elder Henry Comer will be his alternate.

Nineteenth—On motion, we send Elders W. M. Sparks and Henry Comer to the Central Union Association as messengers and Elders Tonie Eastridge, Matthew Oliver, and John F. Keck to the Hiwassee Association.

Twentieth—On motion, the clerk write each delegate letters of correspondence.

Twenty-First—On motion, we extend to this dear old church and the people of the surrounding community, our sincere appreciation for the kindness and generous hospitality shown us through this Association.

Twenty-Second—On motion, we adjourn until 10:30 a. m. EST at the place above stated.

> Respectfully submitted,
> ELDER ALBERT DAVIS,
> Moderator, Speedwell, Tennessee
> ELDER JOHN F. KECK,
> Assistant Moderator, Goin, Tennessee

Twenty-Third—Dismissed in order.

> BROTHER J. L. DRUMMONDS,
> Clerk, New Tazewell, Tennessee
> BROTHER W. I. BROWNING,
> Assistant Clerk, Sharps Chapel, Tennessee

Sunday's Proceedings

On Sunday a large audience assembled at the altar and attentively listened to the well delivered Sermon of Elder R. H. Pettit from John, fifth chapter. He was followed by Elder Matthew Oliver and Elder Carl McCarty. The closing remarks were made by the assistant moderator. All sermons were delivered in a most loving spirit and a loving parting was expressed.

Licentiates

James Branscome	Speedwell, Tennessee
Jim Collins	New Market, Tennessee
Sam Miller	New Market, Tennessee
Charlie Standifer	Corryton, Tennessee
Clay Davis	New Tazewell, Tennessee

Ministers

Elder Leonard White_____ _____ LaFollette , Tennessee
Elder E. S. Drummonds_____ 606 Kentucky Ave., Monroe, Michigan
Elder J. R. Weaver_____ Harrogate, Tennessee
Elder George Shoffner_____ Sharps Chapel, Tennessee
Elder W. A. Moyers_____ 826 Arthur St., Knoxville, Tennessee
Elder T. I. Eastridge_____ 1320 Brookside Ave., Knoxville, Tennessee
Elder R. H. Pettit _____ Woodlawn Pike, Knoxville, Tennessee
Elder W. M. Sparks _____ Speedwell, Tennessee
Elder Henry Comer_____ Speedwell, Tennessee
Elder Matthew Oliver_____ Bean Station, Tennessee
Elder Joe Irwin_____ Gibson Station, Virginia
Elder Dewey Ellison_____ Sharps Chapel, Tennessee
Elder Albert Davis_____ Speedwell, Tennessee
Elder John F. Keck _____ Goin, Tennessee
Elder Lenvil Meyers _____ Monroe, Michigan

Corresponding Letters

We, the Powell Valley Association of Primitive Baptists now in session at Brantley's Chapel Church, on August 17, 18, and 19, 1951, send the greetings to the Hiwassee and Central Union Associations with whom we now correspond: Very dear brothers and sisters, we desire to keep up our cherished correspondence with you and have chosen these our beloved Elders to bear this Epistle of love for you. To the Central Union we send Elders W. M. Sparks and Henry Comer. To the Hiwassee we send Elders Tonie Eastridge, John F. Keck, and Matthew Oliver. Having seated all your delegation, we heartily welcome another one next year. When convened with the church at Gibson Station, Lee County, Virginia to begin on Friday before the third Saturday in August, 1952.

Rules of Decorum

1. The churches composing the Powell's Valley Association shall not be confined to any set rules as to the specified number of Messengers they shall have in the body, but shall have the right to name in their letters as many as they choose, and in addition all orderly members of any of the churches being present be entitled to seats in the body as Messengers of their respective churches, with all the rights and privileges of the same.

2. The Messengers thus assembled shall be denominated the Powell's Valley Primitive Baptist Association.

3. For the purpose of historical information and statistical edification, the Churches are requested to state in letters, the total number of members in fellowship, the number received by Baptism, by letters, by confession of Faith; the number dismissed, excluded and dead since last session; also the time of their meeting, their pastoral supply, and the amount of money contributed for ministers and other purposes together with any other information they deem appropriate for the edification of the saints and the glory of God.

4. This Association shall have no power to answer queries, give advice, or dictate to the Churches in any case, or to lord it over God's heritage, nor any power by which she can directly or indirectly infringe on the internal rights of the church, or censure and try any church or member in reference to faith and practice or determine upon validity of gospel ordinances. These things shall rest entirely with the churches; but henceforward our annual meetings shall be only for the purpose of hearing from each other, and for the worship of God and the mutual comfort and edification of the saints. To this end we reserve the privilege annually before the Third Saturday in August and the two following days, or at such other time as may be agreed upon with any church that may invite us having to protect our own stand, while in session, from heresey and disorder; to recognize and invite any Primitive Baptist minister or any lay brother to worship with us, that we may deem proper; to request the brethren or our body to visit other churches or bodies in our behalf with whom we may

471

desire to cultivate Christian fellowship; to publish in a minute of our proceedings.

5. Each session of the body shall have a Moderator and Clerk who shall be chosen according to the rules herein after prescribed, and who shall hold office until re-election.

6. Any orderly member of any church belonging to this body, when convened, being present shall be eligible to election as Moderator and Clerk, or to sit on any committee appointed by the same.

7. In all elections or questions that may be necessary to determine by vote, the vote shall be taken by churches, each church being entitled to three votes for any number less than one hundred, and one additional vote for every fifty or fraction thereof above the first hundred, but the Messengers of each church a body may divide their vote as they see proper.

8. All elections of questions coming to vote shall be determined by a majority vote cast, and it shall be the duty of the minority to acquiesce in the decision thus reached.

9. If new churches desire to be admitted to this union, they shall petition by letter and Messengers, and if vouched for or recommended by one or more sister churches for her Presbytery constituting them, or orthodox and orderly, they shall be received by the voice of the body and manifested by the Moderator giving the Messengers the right hand of fellowship.

10. Any motion or resolution introduced clearly inconsistent with the above rules shall be promptly ruled out of order unless withdrawn by the mover.

11. Any Messenger being ruled out of order by the Moderator shall have the right to appeal to the body on the question of order, and if sustained shall be allowed to proceed, but if not take his seat.

12. Our meeting being held in the name of Christ and the worship of God, each Messenger is expected to observe due and proper order therein.

13. It will not be considered good order for any Messenger whose name has been enrolled as such to abruptly break off or absent himself from the Association without leave.

14. The Moderator shall be entitled to the same privilege of speech as other members provided the chair is filled.

15. The minutes of the Association shall be read and approved by the body. and signed by the Moderator before adjourning.

16. The Association shall be opened and closed by prayer.

17. Amendments to these may be made at any time by a majority of the union voting by churches, when they deem it necessary, provide such amendments do not compromise the sovereignty of the churches, nor have tendency to give this body undue power or jurisdiction over them.

Obituaries

ELLA KAY EDWARDS BRADEN

Mrs. Ella Kay Edwards Braden, born June 18, 1925, departed this life November 15, 1950, at the age of 25 years, 4 months, and 27 days.

She was united in marriage to Arvel Braden January 15, 1944. To this union was born five children, three girls, Evelyn, Ruth, and Mildred, and two boys, Lee Roy and James Fred.

She professed a hope in Christ at an early age and joined the church at Pleasant Hill where she lived a faithful member until death.

She leaves to mourn their loss, her husband, and five children, her father, step-mother, three brothers, nine sisters, and a host of relatives and friends.

We feel our loss is Heaven's gain.

TIMOTHY ESAU WILLIAMS

Timothy Esau Williams was born September 30, 1882, and passed away at his home near Goin on January 17, 1951.

He professed faith in Christ at an early age. He lived a Christian life but never joined any church.

He is survived by his wife, Mrs. Frella Williams, Goin, daughters,

Mrs. J. E. Heath, Knoxville; Mrs. Roy Robertson, Crossville; Mrs. Parlin Simmons, Neuberts, Tennessee; Mrs. Verlin Simmons, Goin, Tennessee; 16 grandchildren, and five great-grandchildren; one half brother, J. P. Goins, Goin, Tennessee.

Funeral services were held at 11:00 a. m. Friday at the Pleasant Point Church with Elders Leonard White and John F. Keck officiating. Interment in the church cemetery.

The Coffey-Stubblefield Funeral Home in Charge.

SARAH HOPPER SHARP (AUNT SADE)

Sarah Hopper Sharp, widow of the late James W. Sharp, was born April 9, 1867, died December 15, 1950, being 83 years, 8 months and 6 days of age.

At the age of 17 she was united in marriage to James W. Sharp and to this union eleven children were born.

She leaves to mourn her passing three daughters: Linda Sharp and Myrtle Taylor of Knoxville, Tennessee and Alta Snodderly of Maryville, Tennessee. Six sons: R. E., B. E., L. O., C. A., M. D., and Claude Sharp all of Knoxville, Tennessee and a host of other relatives and friends.

She professed faith in Christ at an early age and joined the Cave Springs Primitive Baptist Church. Later she became a charter member of the Kirkwood Primitive Baptist Church, Knoxville, Tennessee and showed her devotion to her Church by being a faithful member until death. Our loss is her Eternal gain.

Funeral services were held at 2 p. m., Sunday at Kirkwood Primitive Baptist Church, with Elder Leonard White and Elder R. H. Pettit officiating. Interment in Lynnhurst Cemetery.

Rose Funeral Home in charge of the funeral.

W. HOBERT TINNELL

W. Hobert Tinnell was born September 17, 1904, died July 28, 1951, being 46 years, 10 months and 11 days of age.

He was united in marriage to Virginia Anderson and to this union three children were born.

He is survived by his wife, Virginia Anderson Tinnell, two daughters, Joyce and Alice, one son, James Tinnell, his mother, Mrs. Jane Tinnell and one grandchild and a host of other relatives and friends.

He professed faith in Christ at an early age and joined the Lenoir City Primitive Baptist Church. Later he moved his letter to the Kirkwood Primitive Baptist Church of Knoxville where he remained a faithful member until death.

Funeral services were held at 1 p. m., Monday at Kirkwood Primitive Baptist Church, with Elder Leonard White, Elder R. H. Pettit and Elder James Tilley officiating. Interment in Lenoir City Cemetery.

Rose Funeral Home in charge of the funeral.

LOUISA BRANTLEY WEAVER

Louisa Brantley Weaver was born July 18, 1867 and died May 14, 1951, being 83 years, 9 months, and 26 days old.

She was married to C. B. Weaver on Aug. 23, 1885. To this union 9 children were born, 7 daughters, and 2 sons of which 2 daughters preceded her in death. Her husband also preceded her in death almost 9 years.

She professed faith in Christ at an early age and joined the Primitive Baptist Church at Mossy Springs. She later moved her membership to Oak Grove, Union Co., when the Mossy Springs Church was disbanded because of the Norris Lake Reservoir. She remained a faithful member until death.

Funeral Services were held at Blue Springs Baptist Church at 2:00 p. m., on May 17, 1951. Rev. Leonard White and Rev. John F. Keck officiated. Interment in church cemetery.

She was survived by 5 daughters, Mrs. Zinie Shoffner of Maryville; Mrs. Nettie Cadle and Mrs. Ora Daniels of Greenback; Mrs. Bedie Dixon of Kingston and Mrs. Flossie Miller of Maynardville. Two sons, Claude Weaver of Byron, Minn., and Eston Weaver of Knoxville. One sister, Mrs. Pheobe Bridges of Knoxville and leaves 49 grandchildren, 58 great-grandchildren, 4 great great grandchildren and a host of neices, nephews and friends to mourn her passing. Our loss is her Eternal gain.

Her children

CHURCHES	NAMES OF DELEGATES	Restored	Received by Relationship	Received by Baptism	Received by Letter	Dis. by Letter	Excluded	Deceased	Total Membership	Saturday Meeting	Printing Minutes	Visiting Ministers	Communion Meeting
Rocky Dale	Elmer Graves, Everette Berry, Maston Dunn, Bessie Graves, Trula Berry, Rhoda Dunn, Leola Palmer								70	3	$5.00	$5.00	June
Braden's Chapel	W. M. Sparks, Edd McBee			2	6	2	18		42	1	7.00	3.00	July
Brantley's Chapel	Elijah Ferguson, Milton Brantly, Plummer McBee, Millard Welch, Corum Berry, Raymond Miller, Clifford Brantley, Jess Brantley, Everette Brantley		70	9	9				39	1	7.00	4.83	July
Cedar Springs	S. W. Drummond, Clay Davis G. B. Drummond, J. L. Drummond, Alleen Drummond, Esther Miracle			4	2	2	2	2	74	1	8.00	Aug.	May
Davis Chapel	Henry Comer, W. M. Kivett, Jim Heatherly, McKinley Ellison			2	1	2	1	3	76	1	10.00		July
Gibson's Station	George Shoffner, Henry Hoskins, Charlie Redmon, R. H. Pettit, Mollie Pettie, Ambrose Sharp, Frieda Sharp, J. L. Sharp, Evelyn Sharp, Estella Sharp			4		1	2	1	152	3	8.00		July
Kirkwood	No Letter. Come. on.	1							80	4	8.00		May
Noeton	Toni Eastridge, George Shoffner, Belle Moore, Luna Sherritz,			1	1	5	2	3	325	1	10.00	10.00	May
Oak Grove	Tom England,	1		1	1				141	1	10.00	1.00	July
Pleasant Point	John F. Keck					1	1	1	93	4	10.00	5.00	June
Pleasant Hill	Albert Davis, James Edwards, J. L. Edwards, Lonzo Edwards												
Red Hill	No Letter. Come on.												
Black Fox	J. M. Davis, Sam Davis	1		1		1		2	97	2	8.60		June
Capps Creek	W. I. Browning, Cora Weaver				1	5		1	20	3	3.00	2.00	April

474

Official Directory

CHURCHES	COUNTY	PASTORS	CLERKS	CLERK'S POST OFFICE
Kirkwood	Knox	Elder Leonard White	Edelle P. Sharp	819 Jackboro Pt. Fountain City, Tenn.
Capps Creek	Union	Elder John Weaver, Elder Joe Irwin, Asst.	W. L. Browning	Sharps Chapel, Tenn.
Davis Chapel	Campbell	Elder W. M. Sparks	Lassie Kilson	LaFollette, Tenn.
Gibson Station	Lee	Elder Leonard White, Elder Matthew Oliver, Asst.	Roxie Cobb	Gibson Station, Va.
Cedar Springs	Claiborne	Elder W. M. Sparks	J. L. Drummond	New Tazwell, Tenn.
Pleasant Point	Claiborne	Elder W. A. Moyers	Austin Beason	Goin, Tennessee
Braden's Chapel	Union	Elder W. M. Sparks, Elder Henry Comer, Asst.	Arvel Braden	Speedwell, Tennessee
Black Fox	Grainger	Elder Dewey Ellison	Sam Davis, J. M. Davis	Luttrell, Tennessee Powder Springs, Tenn.
Brantley's Chapel	Blount	Elder Carl McCarty, Elder Tonie Eastridge	R. P. Bridges	Rt. 8, Maryville, Tenn.
Oak Grove	Union	Elder Tonie Eastridge	Luna Sherritz	Goin, Tennessee
Rocky Dale	Knox	Elder Leonard White	Leola Palmer	Rt. 13, Fountain City, Tenn.
Pleasant Hill		Elder Albert Davis	Lincoln Edwards, Verlin Edwards, Asst.	Speedwell, Tennessee Speedwell, Tennessee

475

1952

MINUTES

OF THE

One Hundred and Thirty-third

ANNUAL SESSION

OF THE

Powells Valley Association

— OF —

PRIMITIVE BAPTISTS

HELD WITH

The Church at Gibson Station

Lee County, Virginia

August 15-16-17, 1952

OFFICERS

Elder Albert Davis_____Moderator
Elder John F. Keck_____Assistant Moderator
Brother J. F. Drummonds_____Clerk
Brother W. I. Browning_____Assistant Clerk

The next session will be held with the Church of Oak Grove, Union County, Tennessee, beginning on Friday before the third Saturday in August, 1953. Elder Leonard White to preach the introductory sermon and Elder John F. Keck will be his alternate.

Friday's Proceedings

First—According to the previous arrangements, the Association met pursuant to adjournment.

Second—After singing praise and prayer by Brother Taylor, How Firm a Foundation was sung. The introductory sermon was delivered by Elder Henry Comer from the 19th verse of the 2nd chapter of 2nd Timothy followed by Elder Albert Davis.

Third—After ten minutes intermission, the association reassembled. Scripture lesson was read by Elder Albert Davis from the 12th chapter of Romans. Prayer by Elder Clark and Elder Allen Gates. One verse of "Am I a Soldier of the Cross" was sung.

Fourth—The Association was called to order by the Moderator, Elder Albert Davis.

Fifth—Called for letters from sister churches. Received 12 which were read by the clerks. Also received an oral statement from Noeton by Elder Matthew Oliver.

Sixth—On motion, all said letters were received and the delegates were welcomed to seats by the moderator.

Seventh—Called for members who were not delegates and received Brother Edd McBee from Braden's Chapel, who was welcomed to a seat by the Moderator.

Eighth—Called for letters from corresponding associations. Received one from the Hiwassee and one from the Central Union. On motion, said letters were received and the delegates were welcomed to seats by the moderator. Delegates were Elder Allen Gates, Elder Clyde McGee, and Elder John Russell from the Hiwassee. Elder Marvin Clark, Elder Carl McCarty, Elder Walter Clark, Elder Edd Earls, Elder Oscar Smith, Elder Henry C. Taylor, and Brother Dave Phelps from the Central Union.

Ninth—On motion, Elder Albert Davis was re-elected Moderator and Elder John F. Keck was re-elected Assistant Moderator.

Tenth—On motion, Brother J. L. Drummonds was re-elected Clerk and Brother W. I. Browning was re-elected Assistant Clerk.

Eleventh—On motion, the Moderator appoint the committees.

A. On arrangements, Brothers J. L. Edwards, John Davis, and Brice Braden.

B. On preaching, Brothers Henry Hoskins, Bud Branscome, and Otis Keck, together with this church.

C. On correspondence, Elder Henry Comer, W. M. Sparks, and Milton Brantley.

D. On request, Brother Silas Drummonds, Brother George Shoffner, and Elder Joe Irwin.

E. On finance, Brothers Von Beason, J. M. Davis, and Everett Brantley.

Twelfth—On motion, we adjourn until 10 a. m. Saturday morning.

Saturday's Proceedings

After singing praise, scripture reading by Elder John F. Keck from the 14th chapter of Saint John. Prayer by Brother Ellis Evans.

First—Called for the report of the committee on arrangements.

A. We, your committee on arrangements beg leave to submit the following report:

1. Call the roll.
2. Call for the report of the committee on request.
3. Call for the report of the committee on preaching.
4. Call for the report of the committee on correspondence.
5. Call for the report of the committee on finance.

When and where shall our next association be held. Who shall preach the introductory sermon and who shall be his alternate. How many copies of the minutes shall we have printed and who shall superintend the printing and distribution of the same. What shall he be allowed for his services?

Respectfully submitted,
BRICE BRADEN
J. L. EDWARDS
JOHN H. DAVIS

Second—On motion, the report was received and the committee discharged.

Fourth—Called for the report of the committee on preaching.
B. We, your committee on preaching beg leave to submit the following report:

Friday night at the stand Elder Carl McCarty and Elder Allen Gates. Elder Clyde McGee and Elder W. R. Clark at the stand Saturday morning. Elder W. M. Sparks and Elder Clyde McGee at the church tonight. At Pleasant Hill Elder Carl McCarty and Elder Allen Gates. Sunday at the stand Elder Matthew Oliver, with the Moderator to close.

Respectfully submitted,
HENRY HOSKINS
BUD BRANSCOME
OTIS KECK

Fifth—On motion, the report was received and the committee discharged.

Sixth—Called for the report of the committee on correspondence.
C. We, your committee on correspondence, beg leave to submit the following report:

That we keep up our correspondence with the Hiwassee and the Central Union Associations by letter and messengers.

Seventh—On motion, the report was received and the committee discharged.

Eighth—Called for the report of the committee on request.
D. We, your committee on request, beg leave to submit the following report:

That we publish all the obituaries that the churches furnish and that our next association be held with the church at Oak Grove, Union County, Tennessee, to commence on Friday before the third Saturday in August, 1953, and two days following.

Respectfully submitted,
G. W. SHOFFNER
SILAS DRUMMONDS
ELDER JOE IRVING

Ninth—On motion, the report was received and the committee discharged.

Tenth—Called for the report of the committee on finance.
E. We, your committee on finance, beg leave to submit the following report:

Received from sister churches the following for the printing of the minutes and for visiting ministers:

	Visiting Ministers	Minutes
Rocky Dale	$ 5.00	$ 5.00
Noeton	1.00	1.00
Kirkwood	10.00	5.00
Braden's Chapel		7.00
Brantley's Chapel	5.68	7.00
Cedar Springs		8.50
Davis Chapel	5.00	5.00
Gibson Station	4.00	4.00
Oak Grove		10.00
Pleasant Point		10.00
Black Fox		10.00
Capps Creek		3.00
Pleasant Hill	5.00	10.00
Monroe, Michigan		5.00
	———	———
Total amount	$35.68	$90.50
Balance from last year		3.85
		———
Total		$94.35
Received from other sources		1.50
		———
Total		$95.85

Respectfully submitted,
VON BEASON
J. M. DAVIS
EVERETT BRANTLEY

Eleventh—On motion, the report was received and the committee discharged.

Twelfth—On motion, we have one thousand copies of the minutes printed. That the clerk superintend the printing and the distribution of the same and that he be allowed $25.00 for his services.

Thirteenth—On motion, the next annual session be held with the church at Oak Grove, Union County, Tennessee, to begin on Friday before the third Saturday in August, 1953, and two days following.

Fourteenth—On motion, Elder Leonard White will preach the introductory sermon and that Elder John F. Keck will be his alternate.

Fifteenth—On motion, we send Elder Henry Comer and Elder Leonard White to the Central Union Association as messengers, and Elder Albert Davis and Elder W. M. Sparks to the Hiawassee.

Sixteenth—On motion, the clerk write each delegate letters of correspondence.

Seventeenth—On motion, we extend to this dear old church and the people of the surrounding community, our sincere appreciation for the kindness and generous hospitality shown us through this Association.

Eighteenth—On motion, we adjourn until 10:30 EST at the place above stated.

Ninteenth—Dismissed in order.

ELDER ABLERT DAVIS,
Moderator, Speedwell, Tennessee
ELDER JOHN F. KECK,
Asst. Moderator, Goin, Tennessee
BROTHER J. L. DRUMMONDS,
Clerk, New Tazewell, Tennessee
BROTHER W. I. BROWNING,
Asst. Clerk, Sharps Chapel, Tennessee

Sunday's Proceedings

On Sunday a large audience assembled at the altar and attentively listened to the well delivered sermon of Elder Matthew Oliver from the 1st verse of the 91st Psalm, "He that dwelleth in the secret place of the most High shall abide under the shadow of the Almighty." He was followed by Elder Albert Davis. Both sermons were delivered in a most loving spirit. Wonderful testimonies were given by many of God's children and a great blessing was received by all. A most loving parting was expressed.

Licentiates

James Branscome ———— 325 Winchester St., Monroe, Mich.
Jim Collins———— New Market, Tennessee
Sam Miller———— New Market, Tennessee
Charlie Standifer———— Corryton, Tennessee
Clay Davis ———— New Tazewell, Tennessee

Ministers

Elder Leonard White ———— LaFollette, Tennessee
Elder E. S. Drummonds ———— 606 Kentucky Ave., Monroe, Michigan
Elder J. R. Weaver ———— Harrogate, Tennessee
Elder George Shoffner———— Sharps Chapel, Tennessee
Elder W. A. Moyers ———— 828 Arthur St., Knoxville, Tennessee
Elder T. I. Eastridge———— 1320 Brookside Ave., Knoxville, Tennessee
Elder R. H. Pettit ———— 107 Jacksboro Pike, Fountain City, Tennessee
Elder W. M. Sparks ———— Speedwell, Tennessee
Elder Henry Comer———— Route 4, LaFollette, Tennessee
Elder Matthew Oliver———— Bean Station, Tennessee
Elder Joe Irwin———— Gibson Station, Virginia
Elder Dewey Ellison———— Sharps Chapel, Tennessee
Elder Milton Brantley———— Sharps Chapel, Tennessee
Elder Albert Davis ———— Speedwell, Tennessee
Elder Charlie Redmond———— Gibson Station, Virginia
Elder John F. Keck———— Goin, Tennessee
Elder Lenvil Meyers———— Monroe, Michigan

Corresponding Letters

We, the Powell Valley Association of Primitive Baptists now in session at Gibson Station Church on August 15, 16, and 17, 1952, send greetings to the Hiwassee and Central Union Association with whom we now correspond: Very dear brothers and sisters, we desire to keep up our long cherished correspondence with you and have chosen these our beloved Elders to bear this Epistle of love to you. To the Hiwassee, Elder Albert Davis and Elder W. M. Sparks, and to the Central Union, Elder Leonard White and Elder Henry Comer. Having seated all your delegation this year, we heartily welcome another next year, when convened with the church at Oak Grove, Union County, Tennessee, to begin on Friday before the third Saturday in August, 1953.

Obituaries

MRS. LILLIE LYNCH CLAWSON

Mrs. Lillie Lynch Clawson was born November 13, 1875 and departed this life December 24, 1951. being 76 years. 1 month, and 13 days old. She was married to Jahue Clawson May 11, 1889. She leaves to mourn her loss eight children: Linnie Beeler, Sharps Chapel,· Tenn.; Donnie Clawson, Speedwell. Tenn.; Mrs. W. E. Braden, Speedwell, Tenn.; Charlie Clawson, Liggett, Ky.; Hubert Clawson, Speedwell, Tenn.; Clara Turner, Monroe, Mich.; Arletta Leach, Speedwell, Tenn. and Sebern Clawson, Speedwell, Tenn. Her husband and one daughter precedes her in death. She professed faith in Christ at an early age and joined the Methodist Church. She lived a faithful life until death. Our loss is Heaven's gain. Funeral services were conducted by Elder W. M. Sparks. She was laid to rest in the Braden's Cemetery.

NANCY CUPP MIRACLE

Nancy Cupp Miracle was born November 1, 1868 and departed this life May 8, 1952, being 83 years, 3 months, and 27 days old. She professed faith in Christ at an early age and joined the Primitive Baptist Church at Cedar Springs. She was married to Pless Miracle who preceded her in death. Three sons, Mac, Peter, and Harvey preceded her in death. Survivors include 9 children: Nathan. Billy, Andy. New Tazewell, Tenn.; Tom Jeff, Liberty Hill; Rufus, Speedwell; Mrs. Katie Cupp and Mrs. Rossie Tuttle, Crossville, Tenn.; Mrs. Melda Paul, Harrogate, Tenn.; 71 grandchildren; 42 great grandchildren; 2 brothers, Jim Cupp and Harrison Cupp; one sister, Mrs. Mary Greene, all of Bell County, Ky.; and a host of other relatives and friends. Funeral services were held at Meyers Grove with Elders Proctor Edwards and Graves officiating. Burial was in the Drummonds Cemetery.

MISS MARGARET HAMILTON

Miss Margaret· Hamilton, age 82, died at the home of her nephew, Frank Hubbs, of Mascot. Survivors: sister, Mrs. Ollie Beeler of Liberty Hill and Mrs. Nancy Weaver of Knoxville, and a host of nieces and nephews. Funeral at Beeler's Chapel, Liberty Hill, Rev. Roy Shelton officiating. Interment in church cemetery. She was a member of Black Fox Primitive Baptist Church.

MRS. MARGARET WILLIAMS

Mrs. Margaret Williams, 75, died at the home of her son, James Williams, Knoxville. Survivors: three daughters and one step-daughter, Mrs. Lillie McDaniel, Mrs. Betsy Acuff, Mrs. Edna Shelton, and Mrs. Gertie West;

five sons, James, Knoxville; Elvin, Washburn· Rector, Liberty Hill; Bill Washburn; and Herman, Powder Springs; 35 grandchildren, several great-grandchildren; a sister, Mrs. Sally Davis, Luttrell; and a brother, Jack Kirk, Kentucky. Services at Black Fox Primitive Baptist Church, Revs. Andy Vance and Loy Shelton officiating. Burial in the Cabbage Cemetery.

MRS. R. D. BORUFF

Mrs. R. D. Boruff, age 59, died at her home near Sweetwater. Survivors: husband; three daughters, Mrs. Earl Richesin of Maryville, Mrs. Buck Emerson and Lucille Boruff of Sweetwater; five sons, Elvin, Robert, Claude, R. D. Jr., and Carl, all of Sweetwater; three sisters, Mrs. Arthur Boruff of Maryville, Mrs. James Shelby, Goin, Mrs. West Sweet of Fountain City; three brothers, Will Southerland of Knoxville, Robert Southerland of Liva, Ky.; Loren Southerland of Fountain City; 20 grandchildren and one great-grandchild. She was a member of the Black Fox Primitive Baptist Church. She was for 20 years a member of the Daughters of America at Halls Cross Roads Lodge. Funeral at the family residence. Further services at the Clapps Chapel Methodist Church. Revs. Thomas Franks and Leonard White officiating. Burial in Clapps Chapel Cemetery.

MRS. CHINA ADLINE AUSMUS WILDRE

Mrs. China Adline Ausmus Wildre was born at Speedwell, Tenn., on April 25, 1882, and passed away at Auburn Heights, Michigan on August 24, 1951, at the age of 69 years, 3 months, and 29 days. She was the daughter of Joseph and PollyAnn Hunter Ausmus and was a member of Pleasant Hill Church. She joined the church May 1913. She leaves to mourn her passing a son, Elbert H. Wilder, Pontiac, Michigan; five daughters, Mrs. Claudia Brewer, Auburn Heights, Michigan· Mrs. Bertha Harrison and Mrs. Claudia Bognor of Pontiac, Michigan; and Mrs. Uritha Washam of Detroit, Michigan; and Mrs. Bennie Shackleforth of Rochester, Michigan; two brothers, Henry Ausmus, Speedwell, Tenn.; and Oscar Ausmus, Cincinnati, Ohio; 15 grandchildren and 2 great-grandchildren. She was laid to rest in the Ausmus Cemetery.

MRS. BEDIE JANE WEAVER

Mrs. Bedie Jane Weaver was born March 11, 1897 and died April 27, 1952, being 55 years, 1 month, and 16 days of age. She was united in marriage to J. O. Dixon and to this union was born 2 daughters and 2 sons, of which one son preceded her in death. She is survived by her husband, one daughter, Fern Dison; both of Kingston; 2 sons, Otis Dixon, Saint Petersburg, Fla.; J. B. Dixon, Greenback, Tenn.; sisters, Mrs. Zinnie Shoffner, Mrs. Ora Daniels, Greenback; Mrs. Flossie Miller Maynardville; Mrs. Nettie Cadle, Rockford; brothers, Claude Weaver Bryon, Mich.; Eston Weaver, Greenback; five grandchildren and a host of relatives and friends to mourn her passing. She professed faith in Christ at an early age and joined the Primitive Baptist Church at Mossy Springs, later moved her membership to Oak Grove. She remained a faithful member until death. Funeral services were held at Oak Grove at 1:30 p. m. April 30, 1952. Elder Leonard and Elder Tony Eastridge officiating. Interment in church cemetery. Our loss is her eternal gain.

MR. SAMUEL S. CAPPS

Mr. Samuel S. Capps was born March 14, 1869 and departed this life September 8, 1951, being 82 years, 5 months, and 24 days of age. He professed faith in Christ when he was 16 years old and has been a member of Black Fox Church for 65 years and a deacon for 40 years. He was first united in marriage to Mary Jane Marion in 1889 and to this union was born 11 children. She and three children preceded him in death. He later married Carlie Snyder in 1923 and to this union no children were born. He is survived by his widow, Mrs. Carlie Capps, 3 sons, Albert of Luttrell, Tenn.; Jesse of Powder Springs, Tenn.; and Calvin of Liberty Hill, Tenn.; 5 daughters, Mrs. Dolly Helton, Mrs. Katie Loy, and Mrs. Iva Davis of Liberty Hill; Mrs. Gertrude Greene, Rutledge; and Mrs. Lula Campbell of Morristown. 48 grandchildren and 36 great-grandchildren and a host of other relatives and friends.

JAHUE S. CLAWSON

Jahue S. Clawson was born March 13, 1872 and departed this life October 7, 1951. He was united in marriage to Lillie Lynch Clawson May 11,

481

1890 and to this union there was born nine children: Lennie Beeler, Sharps Chapel, Tennessee; Sarah Vennie Braden, Speedwell; Clara Turner, Monroe, Mich.; Arlettie Leach, Speedwell; Donnie Clawson, Speedwell; Charlie Clawson, Legett, Ky.; Hubert Clawson, Speedwell; Sebern Clawson, Speedwell. He leaves to mourn his passing his wife, 8 children, 1 brother, 2 sisters 37 grandchildren, 60 great-grandchildren and a host of other relatives and friends. He professed faith in Christ at an early age and lived faithful until death. He was loved by all who knew him. Our loss is Heaven's gain.

MRS. LINDA BRADEN PAUL

Mrs. Linda Braden Paul was born March 24, 1861, died April 5, 1952 at the home of her son, Mack Braden. She professed faith in Christ at an early age and was a member of the Capps Creek Church. She is survived by 4 sons, Harvie Braden, Corryton, Tenn.; Mack Braden, Goin, Tenn.; Charlie Braden, Speedwell, Tenn.; and Issac Braden, Monroe, Mich. Two step-children. Sarah Shoffner, Monroe, Mich.; and John Dave Braden, Speedwell, Tennessee. 37 grandchildren, 56 great-grandchildren and 15 great-great-grandchildren and a host of other relatives and friends. Mother is gone and we miss her. Her voice is lying still, her vacant place in her home no one else can ever fill. We feel our loss is Heaven's gain. The children.

ANDREW WEAVER

Andrew Weaver was born December 5, 1890 and departed this life January 27, 1952, being 61 years, 1 month, and 22 days old. He professed faith in Christ in 1912 and was a great lover of the Primitive Baptist Church. He leaves to mourn his passing, his wife, Mrs. Cora Weaver, Knoxville, 2 sons and 5 daughters, 2 brothers and five sisters and a host of other relatives and friends.

MARTHA LYONS BROWN

Martha Lyons Brown, was born October 8, 1896, died June 23, 1952, being 55 years, 8 months and 15 days of age. She was united in marriage to J. A. Lyons, in June,1911, and to this union 3 children were born. And in the year 1947 she married J. R. Brown. She professed faith in Christ at an early age and joined Oak Grove Primitive Baptist Church, later she moved her letter to Kirkwood Primitive Baptist Church, where she remained until death. She is survived by her husband, J. R. Brown; one daughter, Mrs. Hattie Cook; two sons, Walter and Harley Lyons; two sisters, Mrs. Bernice Bean, Mrs. Mabel Brockman; and two brothers, R. A. and W. A. Monroe grandchildren and 4 step-children.

Funeral services were held at 11:00 a. m. Wednesday, June 25, at Kirkwood Primitive Baptist Church, with Elder Leonard White and Elder R. H. Pettit officiating. Interment in Lynn Hurst Cemetery. Rose Funeral Home in charge of the funeral.

Statistical Table

CHURCHES	NAMES OF DELEGATES	Restored	Received by Relationship	Received by Baptism	Received by Letter	Dis. by Letter	Excluded	Deceased	Total Membership	Saturday Meeting	Printing Minutes	Visiting Ministers	Communion Meeting
Brantley's Chapel	Jeff Ellison, Corum Berry, Plun.er McBee, Von Beason, Jess Brantley, Everett Brantley, Mildred Brantley	1		5		3			48	1	$ 7.00	$ 5.68	Aug.
Pleasant Hill	Albert Davis, Bud Branscome, J. L. Edwards, Kinley Graves			1			2	1	90	4	10.00	5.00	June
Rocky Dale	Audra Davis			1		1			72	3	5.00	5.00	June
	Everett Berry, Trula Berry			1					78	1	4.00	4.00	June
	Charlie Redmond, Joe Irwin and wife, Roxie Cobb, Roxie												
Gibson Station	Cadle, Mossie Cotrell			5			4	1	321	1	10.00		May
Oak Grove	George Shoffner, Luna Sheritze, Tom England												May
Noeton	Elder Matthew Oliver and wife			7		1	1	4	99	3	1.00	1.00	Sept.
Black Fox	J. M. Davis, George Campbell, Sam Davis									2	10.00		June
Capps Creek	W. I. Browning, Cora Weaver, Virgie Browning					1	1	1	20	3	3.00		April
	J. L. Drummonds, S. W. Drummonds, John Drummonds, John												
Cedar Springs	Davis, Mary Lee Davis, Esther Miracle, Roxie Drummonds, Aileen Drummonds			2				1	81	4	8.50		May
Braden's Chapel	W. M. Sparks, Brice Braden, Buster Clawson, Lucy Sparks				1	1	2		41	1	7.00		July
	George Williams, C. D. Keck, Charlie Smith, John F. Keck	1				2			139	1	10.00		July
Pleasant Point	Allie Williams, Oma Rosson, Edna Rosson			3		1	1		150	3	5.00	5.00	July
Davis Chapel	Henry Comer, Leonard White, Cordelia Lynch							1	80	1	5.00	10.00	Aug.
Kirkwood	Otis Keck, Flossie Keck, Vernie Culvohouse												

483

CHURCHES	COUNTY	PASTORS	CLERKS	CLERK'S POST OFFICE
Kirkwood	Knox	Elder Leonard White	Hugh Brumint, Ruby Brumint, Asst.	109 Brown Ave., Knoxville, Tenn.
Capps Creek	Union	Elder John R. Weaver, W. I. Browning	W. I. Browning	Sharps Chapel, Tenn.
		Elder Joe Irwin, Asst.		
Davis Chapel	Campbell	Elder W. M. Sparks	Lassie Ellison	LaFollette, Tenn.
Gibson Station	Lee	Elder Leonard White, Elder Mathew Oliver, Asst.	Roxie Cobb	Gibson Station, Va.
Cedar Springs	Claiborne	Elder W. M. Sparks	J. L. Drummonds	New Tazewell, Tenn.
Pleasant Point	Claiborne	Elder Milton Brantley	Austin Beason	Goin, Tenn.
Braden's Chapel	Union	Elder W. M. Sparks, Elder Henry Comer, Asst.	Arvel Braden	Speedwell, Tenn.
Black Fox	Grainger	Elder Albert Davis	Sam Davis	Luttrell, Tenn.
			J. M. Davis	Powder Springs, Tenn.
Brantley's Chapel	Blount	Elder Carl McCarty, Elder Toni Eastridge	R. B. Bridges	Route 8, Maryville, Tenn.
Oak Grove	Union	Elder Toni Eastridge	Mamie Shoffner, Ruth Shoffner	Sharps Chapel, Tenn.
Rocky Dale	Knox	Elder Leonard White	Leola Palmer	Route 13, Fountain City, Tenn.
Pleasant Hill		Elder Albert Davis	Lincoln Edwards, Verlin Edwards	Speedwell, Tenn.
Noeton	Grainger	Elder Matthew Oliver	John Oliver	Bean Station, Tenn.

484

1953

MINUTES

of the

One Hundred and Thirty-fourth
ANNUAL SESSION

of the

Powells Valley Association

of

PRIMITIVE BAPTISTS

Held With

The Church at Oak Grove

Union County, Tennessee

August 14-15-16, 1953

OFFICERS

Elder Albert Davis .... Moderator
Elder John F. Keck .... Assistant Moderator
Brother J. L. Drummonds .... Clerk
Brother W. I. Browning .... Assistant Clerk

The next session will be held with the church at Cedar Springs, Claiborne County, Tennessee, to begin on Friday before the third Saturday in August, 1954. Elder W. M. Sparks will preach the introductory sermon and Elder John F. Keck will be his alternate.

CHURCHES	DELEGATES	Restored	Received By Relationship	Received By Baptism	Received By Letter	Dis. By Letter	Excluded	Deceased	Total Membership	Sat. Meeting	Printing Minutes	Visiting Ministers	Communion Meeting
Kirkwood	Eld. R. N. Pettit & wife; Bro. John Sharp & wife; Sister Estelle Sharp; Lucy Norton; Hugh Brummitt & wife				2			1	78	1	$5.00	$5.00	Aug
Pleasant Hill	Albert Davis, James Brantley, James Branscome, Lonzo Edwards, J. L. Edwards, Ed McBee.			4	1			1	94	4	10.00	5.00	Jun
Capps Creek	John R. Weaver, W. I. Browning, Vada Weaver, Cora Weaver, Myrtle Weaver, Veechie Browning.		1	2				1	20	3	5.00		Jul
Brantley's Chapel	Everett Brantley, Ellis Evans, Plummer McBee, Clifford Brantley, Mildred Brantley, Lottie Evans, Brasha Brantley		3	3	1	3		3	50	2	7.25	6.50	Jul
Davis Chapel	Leonard White, Henry Comer, Gains Irwin, Florence Irwin, Cordelia Lynch, McKinley Ellison		1	2	1		1	2	151	3	5.00	5.00	Jul
Davis Chapel	Arvell Graves, Elmer Graves, Everett Berry, Trula Berry, Bessie Graves, Leola Palmer			5					70	3	4.00	4.00	Jun
Rocky Dale	Leecy Sparks, W. M. Sparks, Brice Braden, Buster Clawson			2					41	1	8.00		Jul
Braden's Chapel	Jimmy Oliver, Noe Collins and wife, John Oliver and wife					1			18	3	2.00		May
Noeton	George Shoffner, Harve Rogers, Loe Ray, Jim Shelby, Tishie Creech						2	2	325	1	10.00		May
Oak Grove	Charlie Redmond, Joe Irwin, George Shoffner, Henry Hoskins, Mossie Cottrell, Mollie Irwin.								78	1	10.00		Jun
Gibson Station	J. L. Drummonds, S. W. Drummonds, John Drummonds, Isom Drummonds, John Davis and wife, Mary Lee Davis							1	81	4	3.00		May
Cedar Spring	J. M. Davis, Sam Davis, Roy Bailey, George Campbell, Clayton Davis, Roma Bailey, Flossie Capps, Pearlie Larmer								96	2	8.00		Jun
Black Fox	Linvil Meyers, James Drummonds and wife, Sister Evans, Elder Isaac Owens							1	17	3	10.00		Jun
Monroe, Mich.	J. M. Cox, George Williams, C. D. Cox, Allie Williams, Lucy Cox, Oma Rosson, Edna Rosson, Fracie Rosson, Laurie Keck, John F. Keck								139	1	5.00		Jul
Pleasant Point											10.00		

Friday's Proceedings

First — Acording to previous arrangements, the Association met pursuant to adjournment.

Second — After singing praise and prayer by Elder Charlie Redmond, Amazing Grace was sung. The introductory sermon was delivered by Elder Leonard White from the first chapter of Saint Luke, followed by Elder John F. Keck.

Third — After ten minutes intermission, the Association reassembled. Scripture leson was the twenty-third Psalms by Elder Albert Davis. Prayer by Brother Jimmy Brantley. One verse of Leaning on the Everlasting Arms was sung. Prayer by Elder Gates.

Fourth — The Association was called to order by the Moderator, Elder Albert Davis.

Fifth — Called for letters from sister churches. Received twelve, which were read by the clerks.

Sixth — On motion, all said letters were received and the delegates were welcomed to seats by the Moderator.

Seventh — Called for members who were not delegates and received Brother James Edwards and Brother Verlin Edwards from Pleasant Hill, who were welcomed to a seat by the Moderator.

Eighth — Called for letters from corresponding associations. Received one from the Hiwassee Association by Elder Allen Gates. Delegates were Elder Clyde McGhee and Eller Robert Campbell. The Delegates wede welcomed to seats by the Moderator.

Ninth — On motion, Elder Albert Davis was re-elected Moderator and Elder John F. Keck was re-elected Assistant Moderator.

Tenth — On motion, Brother J. L. Drummonds was re-elected Clerk and Brother W. I. Browning was re-elected Assistant Clerk.

Eleventh — On motion, the Moderator appoint the committees.

A. On arrangements, Brothers: Hugh Brummitt, Jim Edwards, and George Shoffner.

B. On preaching. Brothers: Brice Braden, James Brantley and Henry Hoskins, together with this church.

C. On correspondence, Elders: Matthew Oliver, John Weaver, and Henry Comer.

D. On request, Brother John Davis, Brother J. L. Edwards, and Elder Charlie Redmond, and Brother Plummer McGhee.

E. On finance, Brothers: S. W. Drummonds, Everett Brantley, and H. E. Rogers.

Twelvth — On motion, we adjourn until 10 a. m. on Saturday.

Saturday's Proceedings

After singing praise, scripture reading was by Elder John F. Keck. Prayer by Elder Carl McCarty.

First — Called for letters from sister churches that failed to get in Friday. Received two, which were read by the clerks.

Second — Moved and seconded that we receive the letters and welcome the delegates to seats.

Third — Called for members who were not delegates. Received Brother James Drummond and wife, Sister Evans and Elder Linvel Meyers from Monroe, Michigan.

Fourth — Called for the report of the committee on arrangements.

A. We, the committee on arrangements beg leave to submit the following report:

1. Call the roll.
2. Call for the report of the committee on request.

487

3. Call for the report of the committee on preaching.
4. Call for the report of the committee on correspondence.
5. Call for the report of the committee on finance.

When and where shall our next Association be held. Who shall preach the introductory sermon and who shall be his alternate. How many copies of the minutes shall we have printed and who shall superintend the printing and distribution of the same. What shall he be allowed for his services?

Respectfully submitted,
HUGH BRUMMITT
JAMES EDWARDS
GEORGE SHOFFNER

Fifth — On motion, the report was received and the committee discharged.
Sixth — Called the roll and erased the names of the absentees.
Seventh — Called for the report of the committee on preaching.
B. We, your committee on preaching, beg leave to submit the following report:

Friday night at the stand Elder Allen Gates and Elder Henry Comer. Saturday morning Elder Linvel Meyers and Elder Carl McCarty. Saturday night Elder W. M. Sparks and Elder John F. Keck, and Elder Charlie Redmond. Sunday morning Elder Leonard White and Elder Matthew Oliver, Moderator to close.

Respectfully Submitted,
BRICE BRADEN
JAMES BRANTLEY
Henry Hoskins

Eighth—On motion, the report was received and the committee discharged.
Ninth — Called for the report of the committee on correspondence.
C. We, your committee on correspondence, beg leave to submit the following report:

That we keep up our correspondence with the Hiwassee and Central Union Associations by letter and messengers.

Respectfully submitted,
MATTHEW OLIVER
JOHN WEAVER
HENRY COMER

Tenth — On motion the report was received and the committee discharged.
Eleventh — Called for the report of the committee on request.
D. We, your committee on request, beg leave to submit the following report:

That we publish all the obituaries that the churches furnish and that our next Association be held with the church at Cedar Springs, Claiborne County, Tennessee, to begin on Friday before the third Saturday in August, 1954, and two days following.

Respectfully submitted,
PLUMMER McGHEE
J. L. EDWARDS
C. W. REDMOND
JOHN DAVIS

Twelvth — On motion the report was received and the committee discharged.

Thirteenth — Called for the report on the committee on finance
E. We, your committee on finance, beg leave to submit the following report:

Received from sister churches the following for printing of the minutes and fod visiting ministers.

	Visiting Ministers	Minutes
Brantley's Chapel	$ 6.50 .	$ 7.25
Pleasant Hill	5.00	10.00
Rocky Dale	4.00	4.00
Gibson Station	3.00	5.00
Oak Grove		10.00
Noeton		2.00
Black Fox		8.00
Capps Creek		5.00
Monroe		5.00
Cedar Springs		8.00
Bradens Chapel		10.00
Pleasant Point		10.00
Davis Chapel	5.00	5.00
Kirkwood	5.00	5.00
Total Amount	$28.50	$94.25
Balance from last year		4.60
Received from other sources		.50
Total Amount		$99.65

Respectfully submitted,
H. E. ROGERS
EVERETT BRANTLEY
S. W. DRUMMONDS

Fourteenth — On motion the report was received and the committee discharged.

Fifteenth — On motion, we have one thousand copies of the minutes

printed. That the clerk superintend the printing and distribution of the sam and that he be allowed $25.00 for his services.

Sixteenth — On motion, the next annual session be held with the church at Cedar Springs, Claiborne County, Tennessee, to begin on Friday before the third Saturday in August, 1954, and two days following.

Seventeenth — On motion Elder W. M. Sparks will preach the introductory sermon and Elder John F. Keck will be his alternate.

Eighteenth — On motion we will send Elders Henry Comer and W. M. Sparks to the Central Union Association and Elders John F. Keck and Henry Comer to the Hiwassee Association.

Nineteenth — On motion, the clerk write each delegate a letter of correspondence.

Twentieth — On motion, we extend to this dear old church and the people of the surrounding community, our sincere appreciation for the kindness and generous hospitality shown us through this Association.

Twenty-First — On motion, we adjourn until 10:30 EST at the place above

stated.

Twenty-Second — Dismissed in order.

ELDER ALBERT DAVIS,

Moderator, Speedwell, Tennessee
ELDER JOHN F. KECK,
Assistant Moderator, Goin, Tennessee
BROTHER J. L. DRUMMONDS,
Clerk, New Tazewell, Tennessee
BROTHER W. I. BROWNING,
Assistant Clerk. Monroe. Michigan

489

Sunday's Proceedings

On Sunday a large crowd assembled at the altar and attentively listened to the well delivered sermon of Elder Matthew Oliver from the 17th chapter of Jeremiah, "The sin of Judah is written with a pen of iron and with the point of a diamond." He was followed by Elder Leonard White from the 13th chapter of The Acts of the Apostles. Both sermons were delivered in a most loving spirit. Wonderful testimonies were given by many of God's children and a great blessing was received by all. The Moderator, Elder Albrt Davis made the closing remarks. Elder Allen Gates gave the benediction. A most loving parting was expressed.

Licentiates

James Branscome	325 Winchester St., Monroe. Mich.
Jim Collins	New Market. Tennessee
Sam Miller	New Market, Tennessee
Charlie Standifer	Corryton, Tennessee
Clya Davis	New Tazewell, Tennessee

Ministers

Elder Leonard White	LaFollette. Tennessee
Elder E. S. Drummonds	606 Kentucky Ave., Monroe. Mich.
Elder J. R. Weaver	Harrogate. Tennessee
Elder George Shoffner	Sharps Chapel, Tennessee
Elder W. A. Moyers	828 Arthur St., Knoxville, Tennessee
Elder T. I. Eastridge	1320 Brookside Ave., Knoxville, Tennessee
Elder R. H. Pettit	107 Jacksboro Pike, Fountain City, Tennessee
Elder W. M. Sparks	Speedwell, Tennessee
Elder Henry Comer	Route 4, LaFollette, Tennessee
Elder Matthew Oliver	Bean Station, Tennessee
Elder Joe Irwin	Gibson Station, Virginia
Elder Dewey Ellison	Sharps Chapel, Tennessee
Elder Milton Brantley	Sharps Chapel, Tennessee
Elder Albert Davis	Speedwell, Tennessee
Elder Charlie Redmond	Gibson Station, Virginia
Elder John F. Keck	Goin, Tennessee
Elder Lenvil Meyers	521 E. Elm St., Monroe, Mich.
Elder Isaac Owens,	2932 North Custer Rd., Monroe, Mich.

Corresponding Letters

We, the Powell Valley Association of Primitive Baptists now in session at Oak Grove Church on August 14, 15, 16, 1953, send greetings to the Hiwasee and Central Union Associations with whom we correspond: very dear brothers and sisters, we desire to keep our long cherished correspondence with you and have chosen these our beloved Elders to bear this Epistle of love to you. To the Hiwasee, Elders John F. Keck and Henry Comer. To the Central Union, Elders W. M. Sparks and Henry Comer. Having seated all your delegation this year, we heartily welcome another next year, when convened with the church at Cdar Springs. Claiborne County, Tennessee, to begin on Friday before the third Saturday in August, 1954.

Obituaries

MRS. MANNIE DRUMMONDS NEAL

Mrs. Mannie Drummonds Neal, age 76, of Tazewell Pike, Fountain City, passed away at Fort Sanders Hospital. A member of Myers Grove Baptist Church. Survivors: daughters, Mrs. Susan Lett, Knoxville; Mrs. Roy Mingle, Tazewell Pike, Fountain City; Mrs. N. C. Ward, Johnson City; sons, A. L. Neal, Fountain City; Victor Neal, Knoxville; James Neal, Newport; I. W. Neal, Jefferson City; Otto Neal, Copperhill; R. E. Neal, Houston, Texas; sisters, Mrs. Vesta Freeman, Fountain City; Mrs. Scott DeBusk, Tampa, Fla.; brother, John Drummonds, Four Mile, Ky.; 13 grand children; six great-grandchildren. Service held at Gentry's Chapel, Rev. Effert Snodderly and Rev. Charles Hood officiating. Interment Shipe's Cemeterey, Millertown Pike. Active pallbears, nephews. Ralph, Elmer and Glen Underwood, Anderson Munsey, Jimmy DeBusk, Wade Drummonds. Honorary pallbearers: Walter E. Ford. Luster R. Ford. Dr. P. H. Cardwell, O. Y. Brandon, Harry Meek, Charlie Hubbs, Andy Draper. Homer Webster. Gentry's in charge.

JEFFERSON D. KECK

Jefferson (Jeffie) D. Keck, was born August 1, 1886, passed away at his home August 1, 1953. He was married to Lunda Cox, January 23, 1908 and to this union six children were born. Conley and Kenneth Peck of Concord, Lydia Owens and Carl Keck of Inskip, Walter and Patrick Keck, Knoxville. He professed faith in Christ at an early age and joined the church at Pleasant Point Baptist Church and remained a member until death. Funeral services were held August 3rd at Roses Chapel and he was laid to rest in the Lynnhurst Cemetery. We feel our loss is heaven's gain.   Wife and family.

MRS. RINDIA COX

Mrs. Rindia Cox was born February 4, 1871 and died at the age of 82 years 2 months and 12 days. Married to L. C. Cox 1893 who preceeded her to the grave eleven years ago. To this union four children were born. Two sons and two daughters.

She professed faith in Christ at an early age and joined the Primitive Baptist Church at Pleasant Point. She was a faithful member and was loved by all who knew her. During her brief illness she suffered untold agonies but bore it patiently and begged the children not to mourn her departure. She said it only meant rest for her. She was laid to rest in the church cemetery. We miss her so much but we believe our loss is her eternal gain.

Her Children

MA LISSIE PUGH

Sister Ma Lissie Pugh, departed this life June 10, 1953, at about the age of 104 years.

She was formerly a member of Gibson Station Church, but moved to La-Follette, a number of years ago and joined the Church at Davis Chapel where her membership remained until the long life came to a close.

Gone but not forgotten.

W. M. WHITE

W. M. White was born March 17, 1861, died May 5, 1963. He was united in marriage to Miss Jane Ellison in 1883. To this union three children were born, two girls and one boy, one of the girls survive.

He was again united in marriage to Miss Ollie Kivett, August 23, 1923. To this union two children were born, one girl and one boy, both survive.

He professed faith in Christ at a nearly age and joined the church at Mossy Spring where he remained a member until the church was lost to Norris Lake, he then moved his membership to Davis Chapel where he remained a faithful member until death. Uncle Will, as every one called him, was much loved and is greatly missed. He sleeps in the beautiful Sunrise Cemetery at Davis Chapel awaiting the glorious ressurection of the dead.

RUBY LEE COX WELCH

Ruby Lee Cox Welch was born July 16, 1933, died July 6, 1953, being 21 years, 11 months and 20 days old. She was married to Arnell Welch December 24, 1951. She professed faith in Christ at an early age and joined the church at Brantley's Chapel where she remained a faithful member until death. We deeply feel our loss is Heaven's gain.

491

J. M. KIVETT

J. M. Kivett was born February 20, 1873, died February 10, 1953. He was married to Miss Sallie Beeler April 11, 1879. To this union nine children were born, five boys and four girls.

He professed faith in Christ at an early age and joined the church at Mossy Spring in September 1884 and remained a member of this church until it was lost to Norris Lake. He later moved his membership to Davis Chapel where it remained until death called him away.

He was living alone when he became very sick and spent the first night alone, but he said I was not alone, I could see a circle of unknown friends standing around my bed which gave me much comfort.

His body is interred in Davis Chapel Cemetery to sleep until Jesus comes

JOHN DAVE BRADEN

John Dave Braden was born January 15, 1874 and departed this life March 1st, 1953, being 79 years, one month and 13 days of age. He professed faith in Christ at an early age and joined the Primitive Baptist Church at Oak Grove in Union County and later moved his membership to Pleasant Hill Church. He lived a faithful member until death. He bore his sickness with patience and often spoke of his Heavenly home. We feel our loss is Heaven's gain.

The home has lost a good father and husband. The church has lost a good member.

Sleep on dear father until resurrection morn
We're sure he's gone to rest
We loved him oh so dearly
But Jesus loved him best.
We love to walk the pathways
His dear feet have trod
Because those paths will lead us all home
Around the throne of God.
In memory of our dear husband and father by his wife and children.

JOSEPH L. MONROE

Joseph L. Monroe was born in Claiborne County, Tennessee, July 14, 1882, died March 26, 1953. He was the son of Elder Jeff Monroe and Nancy Sharp Monroe. He professed faith in Christ and joined hte Kirkwood Primitive Baptist Church, March 17, 1946. He had one son Harry Conway Monroe who preceded him in death in 1946. He left to mourn his wife, Mary Heath Monroe, and one brother Horace Maynard Monroe, West Point, New York.

Funeral service was held at Mynatt's Chapel, Elder Leonard White, officiating, burial in Lynn Hurst Cemetery.

MRS. CHINA ADLINE AUSMUS WILDER

Mrs. China Adline Ausmus Wilder was born at Speedwell, Tennessee, April 25, 1882, and passed away at Auburn Heights, Michigan, August 24, 1951, being 69 years, 3 months and 29 days old. She was united in marriage to J. M. Wilder and to this union was born one son and five daughters, all are residents of Michigan. Her husband who was an Elder in our church passed away about 15 years ago. She is also survived by two brothers.

Sister Adline professed a hope in Christ and joined the Primitive Baptist Church at Pleasant Hill, May 1913, where she remaineed a loyal member until death. Our church suffered a great loss when Sister Adline passed away. Funeral services were held at Pleasant Hill by Elders Leonard White and Albert Davis. Her body was laid to rest by her faithful husband in the Ausmus Cemeter to await the glorious resurrection of the dead.

HENRY VEWELL BORUFF

Henry Vewell Boruff was born August 31, 1863 and departed this life January 14, 1953, being 89 years, four months, and 13 days old. He professed faith in Christ in the early part of his life and at the time of his death was a member of Rocky Dale Church. He was married to Emma Dyer in 1882. Eight children were born to this union. Mrs. Borruff and four children preceeded him in death. Funeral services wer held at Gntry's Mortuary with Rev. Nick Warren and Walter Henderlight officiating. Burial in the Lynnhurst Cemetery.

JAMES MARION BORRUFF

James Marion Borruff, son of the late Mr. and Mrs. M. C. Boruff, was born July 28, 1896 and died August 31, 1952. He was married to Lucy Foust and to this union was born eight children, seven girls and one boy. He is survived by his wife and eight children, step mother, one sister, six half brothers, nine grandchildren and a host of other relatives and friends. He professed faith in Christ at an early age and soon joined the Rocky Dale Church. He was baptized June 1923. He remained a faithful member, except during his illness, until death. He was also a faithful member to the Halls Cross Roads Jr. OUAM. He is missed by all who knew him. His body was laid to rest in Clapps Chapel Cemetery. Funeral services were conducted at Rocky Dale by the pastor, Elder Lonard White.

A lovd one from us is gone,
A vacant place in our home
Which never can be fulfilled.
Oh, Dad, though we know you
Are in your heavenly home
We miss your sweet face and the touch of your hand.
But we know you are happy
In a much fairer land.
Lord, help us to bear our burdens
Until we meet Dad
In that beautiful land.

Wife and Children

HILDA YADON LIFORD

Hilda Yadon Liford was born January 28, 1884, and departed this life August 15, 1952, at the age of 68 years, 6 months, and 19 days. She professed faith in Christ at the age of 16 and joined the church at Black Fox January 31, 1921 and was baptized the fourth Saturday in 1921 by Elder T. G. Brantley. She was married to John Liford and to this union was born six children. four daughters and two sons. One daughter preceeded her in death, leaving three daughters, Roma Bailey, Alma Munsey and Clara Carver. Two sons, Fred and Claude Liford; twelve grandchildren, one great grandchild, two sisters, Tilda Guy and Frances Liford, three brothers, Robert, John and Eck Yadon. A host of friends and relatives. Our loss is her eternal gain. Funeral services were conducted by Elders Dewey Ellison and Clarence Janeway.

Written by her daughter, Roma Bailey

GEORGE BENTON DRUMMONDS

George Benton Drummonds, son of the late W. A. and Sibby Drummonds, was born January 30, 1886· died October 23, 1952, being 66 years, 8 months, and 23 days old. He was united in marriage to Maude King in 1908. To this union three sons were born. He professed faith in Christ at an early age and joined the Primitive Baptist Church at Cedar Springs the 4th Saturday in January, 1905, and remained a faithful member until death. Survivors include, three sons, James, Paskel, and Ewin Drummonds all of Monroe, Michigan; seven grandchildren, Eleanor, Betty, Patsy Ann, Georgetta, Vernon, Donald, and Arnold Drummonds, all of Monroe. One sister, Mrs. Kate Poore, Maynardville, four brothers, J. L., S. W., New Tazewell; E. S. and J. A., Monroe; and a host of other friends and relatives. Funeral services were conducted October 26, 1952 at 2:30 p. m. at the Meyers Grove Church by Elders Linvel Meyers, John F. Keck, and W. M. Sparks. Pallbearers were Willie Drummonds, Ray Drummonds, Isom Drummonds, Steve Poore, Theodore Drummonds, and Ellice Ford. Flower bearers were Elaine Drummonds, Beth and Algean Dunsmore, Clara and Nancy Drummonds, Eleanor and Patsy Ann Drummonds, Loretta Richards. Margaret Widner, Pearlie Holt, Velta Munsey Billie Ann and Janice Drummonds, Francis Poore, Nelle Wright, Edna and Pansy Drummonds, Mrs. Ray Drummonds, and Mrs. Odra Drummonds. Interment in the Drummonds Cemetery. Ailor's, Maynardville, in charge.

CHURCHES	COUNTY	Pastors	CLERKS	CLERK'S POST OFFICE
Kirkwood	Knox	Elder Leonard White	Hugh Brummitt, Ruby Brummitt, Asst't.	1329 Brown Ave, Knoxville, Tenn.
Capps Creek	Union	Elder John R. Weaver; Elder Joe Irwin, Asst.; Elder W. M. Sparks	Vada Weaver	Harrogate, Tenn.
Davis Chapel	Campbell	Elder Leonard White, Elder Mathew Oliver, Asst.	Lassie Ellison	LaFollette, Tenn.
Gibson Station	Lee	Elder W. M. Sparks	Roxie Cobb	Gibson Station, Va.
Cedar Springs		Elder Milton Brantley	Mossie Cottrell	New Tazewell, Tenn.
Pleasant Point	Claiborne	Elder W. M. Sparks, Elder Henry Comer, Asst.	J. L. Drummonds	Coin, Tenn.
Braden's Chapel	Claiborne	Elder Albert Davis	Austin Beason	Speedwell, Tenn.
Black Fox	Union	Elder Carl McCarty, Elder H. C. Taylor	Arvel Braden	Luttrell, Tenn.
Brantley's Chapel	Grainger		Sam Davis	Route 3, Maryville, Tenn.
Oak Grove	Blount	Elder Albert Davis	J. M. Davis	Sharps Chapel, Tenn.
Rocky Dale	Union	Elder Leonard White	R. B. Bridges	Route 13, Fountain City, Tenn.
Pleasant Hill	Knox	Elder Albert Davis	Belle Moore, Ruth Shoffner	Speedwell, Tenn.
Noeton	Grainger	Elder Matthew Oliver	Leola Palmer, Lincoin Edwards, Verlin Edwards, John Oliver, Maggie Sandifer	Bean Station, Tenn.
Monroe, Mich.	Monroe	Elder Linvil Meyers	Gertrude Zwack	1825 Spalding Road, Monroe, Mich.

1954

MINUTES

OF THE

ONE HUNDRED AND THIRTY-FIFTH

ANNUAL SESSION

OF THE

Powells Valley Association

OF

PRIMITIVE BAPTISTS

HELD WITH

THE CHURCH AT CEDAR SPRINGS

Claiborne County, Tennessee

August 20-21-22, 1954

OFFICERS

Elder Albert Davis _____ Moderator
Elder John F. Keck _____ Assistant Moderator
Brother J. L. Drummonds _____ Clerk
Brother Sam Davis _____ Assistant Clerk

The next session will be held with the church at Pleasant Point, Claiborne County, Tennessee, to begin on Friday before the third Saturday in August, 1955. Elder Leonard White will preach the introductory sermon and Elder W. M. Sparks will be his alternate.

STATISTICAL TABLE

CHURCHES	DELEGATES	Restored	Received By Relationship	Received By Baptism	Received By Letter	Dis. By Letter	Excluded	Deceased	Total Membership	Sat. Meeting	Printing Minutes	Visiting Ministers	Communion Meeting
Black Fox	J. M. Davis, Sam Davis, Herbert Perry, Roy Bailey and wife, George Campbell		1	3	2			1	95	2	$ 9.25	$	Jun
Braden's Chapel	Elder W. M. Sparks, Brice Braden, Buster Clawson, Leecy Sparks,		1					1	43	1	5.00	3.00	Jul
Brantley's Chapel	Everette Brantley, Ellis Evans, Von Beason, Corum Berry, Plumner McBee, Fate McBee, Jr., S. F. Torbett, Mildred Brantley, Lottie Evans, Gennette Beason, Twila Berry, Ottie McBee, Ada McBee			6	2		1		57	2	8.00	4.20	Jul
Capps Creek	No delegates present									3	5.00		
Cedar Springs	S. W. Drummonds, J. L. Drummonds, John Davis, Velta Munsey, Mary Treece, Matilda Simmons, Pearlie Holt, Mary Lee Davis, Cleo Davis			1	1			1	81	4	8.00		May
Davis Chapel	Elder Henry Comer, Elder Leonard White, Cordelia Lynch, Gains Irwin, O. R. Parrot	1				1		1	151	3	5.00	5.00	Jul
Gibson Station	Elder Joe Irwin, Elder Charlie Redmond, George Shoffner, Henry Hoskins	1	1		3		1		84	1	4.00	4.00	Jun
Kirkwood	Ambrose Sharp, Freida Sharp, Hugh Brummitt, Ruby Brummitt,	1	1	5	1				86	1	5.00	5.00	Aug
Monroe, Mich.	Elder Linvil Meyers, Elder E. S. Drummonds, John Drummonds, James Drummonds, Lela Drummonds, Martha Ann Evans	1			3	2			20	3	5.00	3.00	Jun
Norton	Jimmy Oliver, Bessie Collins, John Oliver and wife					2		2	16	3	2.00		May
Oak Grove	George Shoffner, Lillie Shoffner, Lassie Rogers, Harve Rogers, Cillis Shoffner	1				4	2	2	317	1	10.00		May
Pleasant Hill	Elder Albert Davis, Kinley Graves, Edd McBee, Lincoln Edwards, Verlin Edwards			1	2	1	1	1	91	4	10.00	5.00	Jun
Pleasant Point	Elder John F. Keck, George Williams, Allie Williams, Oma Rosson, Edna Rosson, C. D. Keck, Etta Williams		1		1	1		3	136	1	10.00		Jul
Rocky Dale	Elmer Graves, Everette Berry, Trula Berry				1		1	1	70	3	5.00	5.00	Jun

FRIDAY'S PROCEEDINGS

First — According to previous arrangements, the Association met pursuant to adjournment.

Second — After singing praise and prayer by Elder Carl McCarty, the introductory sermon was delivered by Elder W. M. Sparks from the thirteenth chapter of John, verse 35, followed by Elder John F. Keck.

Third — After ten minutes intermission, the Association reassembled. Scripture lesson was by Elder Albert Davis from the 6th chapter of Psalms. Prayer by Elder Leonard White. Amazing Grace was sung. Prayer by Brother Hugh Brummett.

Fourth — The Association was called to order by the Moderator, Elder Albert Davis.

Fifth — Called for letters from sister churches. Received thirteen which were read by the clerks.

Sixth — On motion, all said letters were received and the delegates were welcomed to seats by the moderator.

Seventh — Called for members who were not delegates and received none.

Eighth — Called for letters from corresponding Associations and received one from Central Union. On motion said letter was received and the delegates were welcomed to a seat.

Ninth — On motion Elder Albert Davis was reelected Moderator and Elder John F. Keck was reelected assistant moderator.

Tenth — On motion, Brother J. L. Drummonds was reelected clerk and Brother Sam Davis was elected assistant clerk.

Eleventh — On motion, the moderator appoint all the committees.

A. Arrangements — Brothers Henry Hoskins, J. W. Drummonds, and Elder Henry Comer.

B. Preaching — Brothers O. R. Parrott, Lincoln Edwards, and Everrette Brantley, together with the church.

C. Correspondence — Elder Linvil Meyers, Brothers George Shoffner and McKinley Graves.

D. Request — Brothers John Davis, Hugh Brummitt, and Charlie Redmond.

E. Finance — Brothers John Drummonds, George Shoffner, and Plummer McBee.

Twelfth — On motion, we adjourn until 10 a. m. on Saturday.

SATURDAY'S PROCEEDINGS

After singing praise, scripture reading was by Elder John F. Keck from 1st Peter. Prayer by Brother Hugh Brummitt.

First — Called for letters from sister churches that failed to get in Friday and received none.

Second — Called for letters from corresponding Associations that failed to get in Friday and received one from the Hiwassee Association, which was read and received. The delegates were welcomed to seats.

Third — Called for the report of the committee on arrangements.

A. We, the committee on arrangements, beg leave to submit the following report:

1. Call the roll.
2. Call for the report of the committee on request.
3. Call for the report of the committee on preaching.
4. Call for the report of the committee on correspondence.
5. Call for the report of the committee on finance.

When and where shall our next Association be held. Who shall preach the introductory sermon and who shall be his alternate. How many copies of the minutes shall we have printed and who shall superintend the printing and distribution of the same. What shall he be allowed for his services.

Respectfully submitted,

JAMES W. DRUMMONDS
HENRY HOSKINS
HENRY COMER

Fourth — On motion, the report was received and the committee discharged.

Fifth — Called the roll and erased the names of the absentees.

Sixth — Called for the report of the committee on Preaching.

B. We, the committee on preaching, beg leave to submit the following report:

Friday night, Elder Carl McCarty and Elder H. C. Taylor. Saturday morning, Elder L. I. Meyers and Elder W. A. Moyers. Saturday night, Elder Allen Gates and Elder Henry Comer. Sunday, Elder T. I. Eastridge and Elder Leonard White with the moderator to close.

Respectfully submitted,

LINCOLN EDWARDS
O. R. PARROTT
EVERETTE BRANTLEY

Seventh — On motion, the report was received and the committee discharged.

Eighth — Called for the report of the committee on correspondence.

C. We, your committee on correspondence beg leave to submit the following report:

That we keep up our correspondence with the Hiwasse and Central Union Associations by letter and messengers.

Respectfully submitted,

LINVIL MEYERS
GEORGE SHOFFNER
McKINLEY GRAVES

498

Ninth—On motion the report was received and the committee discharged.

Tenth — Called for the report of the committee on request.

D. We, the committee on request, beg leave to submit the following report:

That we publish all the obituaries that the churches furnish and that our next Association be held with the church at Pleasant Point, Claiborne County, Tennessee, to begin on Friday before the third Saturday in August 1955, and two days following.

Respectfully submitted,

JOHN DAVIS
HUGH BRUMMITT
CHARLIE REDMOND

Eleventh — On motion, the report was received and the committee was discharged.

Twelfth — Called for the report of the committee of finance.

E. We, the committee on finance, beg leave to submit the folliwing report:

Received from sister churches the following for printing of the minutes and for visiting ministers:

	Visiting Ministers	Printing Minutes
Braden's Chapel	$ 3.00	$ 5.00
Davis Chapel	5.00	5.00
Oak Grove		10.00
Capps Creek		5.00
Black Fox		9.25
Brantley's Chapel	4.20	8.00
Cedar Springs		8.00
Pleasant Hill	5.00	10.00
Kirkwood	5.00	5.00
Pleasant Point		10.00
Monroe, Michigan	3.00	5.00
Rocky Dale	5.00	5.00
Gibson Station	4.00	4.00
Noeton		2.00
Total Amount	$34.20	$91.25
Balance From Last Year		7.53
Total Amount		$98.78

Respectfully submitted,

JOHN DRUMMONDS
GEORGE SHOFFNER
PLUMMER McBEE

499

Thirteenth — On motion, the report was received and the committee discharged.

Fourteenth — On motion, we have 1,000 copies of the minutes printed and that the clerk superintend the printing and distribution of the same and that he be allowed $25.00 for his services.

Fifteenth — On motion, the next annual session be held at Pleasant Point, Claiborne County, Tennessee, to begin on Friday before the third Saturday in August, 1955, and two days following.

Sixteenth — On motion, Elder Leonard White will preach the introductory sermon and Elder W. M. Sparks will be his alternate.

Seventeenth — On motion, we send Elders W. M. Sparks and Henry Comer to the Central Union Association and Elders Leonard White, W. A. Moyers, and Albert Davis to the Hiwassee Association.

Eighteenth — On motion, the clerk write each a letter of correspondence.

Nineteenth — On motion, we extend to this dear old church and the people of the surrounding community our sincere appreciation for the kindness and generous hospitality shown us throughout this Association.

Twentieth — On motion, we adjourn until 10:30 EST at the above stated place and date.

Twenty-first — Dismissed in order.

ELDER ALBERT DAVIS,
Moderator, Speedwell, Tennessee
ELDER JOHN F. KECK,
Assistant Moderator, Goin, Tennessee
J. L. DRUMMONDS,
Clerk, New Tazewell, Tennessee
SAM DAVIS,
Assistant Clerk, Luttrell, Tennessee

SUNDAY'S PROCEEDINGS

On Sunday a large crowd assembled at the altar and attentively listened to the well delivered sermon of Elder T. I. Eastridge from Matthew 27:37-53. He was followed by Elder Leonard White from the eleventh chapter of Revelations, verse 15, 2nd clause. Both sermons were delivered in a most loving spirit. Wonderful testimonies were given by many of God's children and several special songs were rendered. A great blessing was received by all. The Moderator, Elder Albert Davis, gave the closing remarks. The benediction was given by Elder Allen Gates.

LICENTIATES

Hugh Brummitt .... 1329 Brown Ave., Knoxville, Tennessee
James Branscome .... 325 Winchester St., Monroe, Mich.
Charlie Standifer .... Corryton, Tennessee
Clay Davis .... New Tazewell, Tennessee
George Shoffner .... Sharps Chapel, Tennessee

MINISTERS

Elder Leonard White .... LaFollette, Tennessee
Elder E. S. Drummonds .... 606 Kentucky Ave., Monroe, Mich.
Elder J. R. Weaver .... Harrogate, Tennessee

500

Elder W. A. Moyers _____ 828 Arthur St., Knoxville, Tennessee
Elder R. H. Pettit _____ 107 Jacksboro Pike, Fountain City, Tennessee
Elder W. M. Sparks _____ Speedwell, Tennessee
Elder Henry Comer _____ Route 4, LaFollette, Tennessee
Elder Matthew Oliver _____ Bean Station, Tennessee
Elder Joe Irwin _____ Gibson Station, Virginia
Elder Dewey Ellison _____ Sharps Chapel, Tennessee
Elder Milton Brantley _____ Sharps Chapel, Tennessee
Elder Albert Davis _____ Speedwell, Tennessee
Elder Charlie Redmond _____ Shawanee, Tennessee
Elder John F. Keck _____ Goin, Tennessee
Elder Lenvil Meyers _____ 521 E. Elm St., Monroe, Mich.
Elder Isaac Owens _____ 2932 North Custer Rd., Monroe, Mich.
Elder T. I. Eastridge _____ Rt. 2, Louisville, Tennessee

CORRESPONDING LETTERS

We, the Powell Valley Association of Primitive Baptists now in session at Cedar Springs, Claiborne County, Tennessee on August 20, 21, 22, 1954, send greetings to the Hiwasse and Central Union Associations with whom we correspond: Very dear brothers and sisters, we desire to keep up our long cherished correspondence with you and have chosen these our beloved Elders to bear this Epistle of love to you. To the Hiwassee, Elders Leonard White, Albert Davis, and W. A. Moyers. To the Central Union, Elders Henry Comer and W. M. Sparks. Having seated all your delegation, we heartily welcome another next year when convened with the church at Pleasant Point, Claiborne County, Tennessee, to begin on Friday before the third Saturday in August, 1955.

OBITUARIES

WILLIAM ANDREW SHOFFNER

William Andrew Shoffner was born in Union County, Tennessee, August 4, 1895. Died in Middlesboro, Kentucky, June 28, 1954. He was united in marriage January 26, 1919 to Stella Sharp. To this union 4 children were born. One preceded him in death. He professed faith in Christ and joined the Primitive Baptist Church at Oak Grove some 30 years ago and remained a faithful member until death. He leaves to mourn his loss his wife, 3 children, 4 sisters, and 3 brothers. We are longing to meet him on that beautiful shore where separation will be no more.

Wife and Children

BARBARA P. HOPPER

Barbara P. Hopper was born October 21, 1877, and departed this life December 18, 1953, being 76 years, 1 month, and 26 days old. She was united in marriage to Henry Hopper June 21, 1894. To this union was born six children. Five boys preceded her in death. She leaves to mourn: her husband, Henry Hopper, and one daughter, Lottie Lynch, and one brother, J. A. Rosson. Ten grandchildren, and sixteen great grandchildren. She professed faith in Christ at an early age and joined the Primitive Baptist Church at Pleasant Point and lived a faithful member until death.

A precious one from us is gone, a voice we loved is still, a chair is vacant in our home which never can be filled.

HALLIE COLUMBIA RIDINGS SOWDER

Hallie Columbia Ridings Sowder, age 66, passed away at Fort Sanders Hospital in Knoxville at 1:45 p. m. Jnuary 16, 1954. Survivors, husband, Marvel Sowders, Goin; sister, Vice Ann Keck, Goin; brothers, Jonce Ridings, White Oak, Tennessee, Crockett Ridings, Tazewell. She professed faith in Christ at an early age and joined the Pleasant Point Primitive Baptist Church where funeral services were held 10:00 a. m. Monday with Rev. Loyd England, Rev. Johnnie Keck, and Rev. Bernice Hooper officiating. Interment in the church cemetery. Pallbearers: Clearance Ridings, Andrew Ridings, Junior Billingsley, Arlis Collins, Dick Hopper, and Lawrence Rosson. Coffey, Tazewell, in charge.

MRS. REBECCA MAYES

Mrs. Rebecca Mayes, age 84, of Detroit, Michigan, died at 9 p. m. Tuesday. She was a member of Pleasant Point Church. Survivors: one son, Oda Charles Mayes, Detroit; four daughters, Mrs. R. H. Wolfenbarger, Mrs. E. D. Miller of Knoxville; Mrs. Clarence Dyer, Detroit, and Mrs. Jim Ford, Goin; Twenty grandchildren and fourteen great grandchildren. The body was returned to Roberts Funeral Home in Knoxville. Service 2:30 p. m. Saturday at Roberts Chapel. Interment in Highland Memorial Cemetery.

MARY ELLA OLIVER

Sister Mary Ella Oliver, age 68, wife of Elder Matthew Oliver, went to her reward April 14, 1954. She was the mother of eight children, three sons, and five daughters. Her remains were laid to rest in the church cemetery on April 16, 1954. Our loss is Heaven's gain.

NOE J. COLLINS

Brother Noe J. Collins, husband of Sister Bessie Collins, passed to the great beyond January 17, 1954. He was the father of six children, 4 sons and 2 daughters. His remains were laid to rest in the church cemetery.

502

MRS. DELLA MUNSEY

Mrs. Della Munsey was born March 27, 1884 and departed this life March 10, 1954. She professed faith in Christ at an early age and joined the Primitive Baptist Church at Blackfox where she remained a member until death. She leaves to mourn her passing four children, one son, Edd Munsey, U. S. Army, Fousine Clay, Lissie, and Ruth Munsey, all at home. We feel our loss is Heaven's gain.

Written by Her Foster Daughters

MR. RAYMOND HEATHERLY

Mr. Raymond Heatherly, age, 49 years, 23 days, was born January 31, 1904, and died January 23, 1954. He professed faith in Christ at an early age and joined the Primitive Baptist Church at Davis Chapel. He is survived by his widow, Mrs. Ollie Carroll Heatherly. His only daughter, Mildred, preceded him in death August 26, 1945. He also leaves three sisters, five brothers to mourn his loss. He remained a faithful member of the church till death. Funeral services were held January 25 at 2 p. m., Tuesday, 1954, at Davis Chapel Primitive Church with Elder Leonard White and Elder W. M. Sparks and Elder Henry Comer officiating. Interment in Davis Chapel Sunrise Cemetery.

JAMES R. BRANTLEY

James R. Brantley was born April 8th, 1900 in Union County, Tennessee and passed away at his home in Speedwell, Tennessee July 21st, 1954 at 1:30 p. m. at the age of 54 years, 3 months and 13 days.

Mr. Brantley was the son of the late Freeman Brantley and Minerva Harrell Brantley of Union County, Tennessee. He moved to Claiborne County where he was widely known in 1936. He was united in marriage to the former Miss Ada Mayes and was the father of three children, all of whom survive. Mr. Brantley was a member of the Pleasant Hill Baptist Church and 32nd Degree Mason of the Powell Valley Lodge No. 443 F. & A. M.

Left to mourn his passing are his wife, Mrs. Ada Brantley, two sons: Odus Brantley and Ottis Brantley, and one daughter, Miss Edith Brantley, all of Speedwell, Tennessee. Also his mother, Mrs. Minerva Brantley of Speedwell, Tennesse.

After the service here, burial will be in the Red Hill Cemetery where the Masons will confer their last rites at the graveside.

JOHN CALVIN DRUMMOND

John Calvin Drummond, age 87, passed away September 25, 1953, at the home of his son, W. W. Drummond, Four Mile, Ky., Survivors: wife, Maude Ellen Drummond; sons, R. L. Drummond, Jackson, Mich., N. J. Drummond, Atlanta, Ga., C. H. Drummond, Oak Ridge, Tennessee, W. W. Drummond, Four Mile, Ky., Mrs. J. H. Childs, Jackson, Mich., Mrs. W. H. Barton, Atlanta, Ga., Mrs A. E. Derrick, Atlanta, Ga., Mrs. C. R. Stacks, Atlanta, Ga., 16 grandchildren and 8 great great grandchildren; sisters, Mrs. I. T. Freeman, Fountain City, Tenn., Mrs. Tom DeBusk, Tampa, Fla. He was a member of the Meyers Grove Baptist Church. Funeral services were held 11:00 a. m. Sunday at the River Side Baptist Church in Four Mile, Ky. Rev. Vorsbee, Rev. George Buchanan, Rev. Arch Buchannan, officiating. Interment in the Family Cemetery in Lonesome Valley near Tazewell. Coffey in charge.

OFFICIAL DIRECTORY

CHURCHES	COUNTY	PASTORS	CLERKS	CLERK'S POST OFFICE
Kirkwood	Knox	Elder Leonard White	Hugh Brummitt, Ruby Brummitt, Asst.	1329 Brown Ave., Knoxville, Tenn.
Capps Creek	Union	Elder J. P. Weaver, Elder Joe Irwin, Asst.	Vada Weaver	Harrogate, Tenn.
Davis Chapel	Campbell	Elder W. M. Sparks	Lassie Ellison	LaFollette, Tenn.
Gibson Station	Lee	Elder Leonard White, Elder Matthew Oliver, Asst.	Roxie Cobb, Mossie Cottrell, Asst.	Gibson Station, Va.
Cedar Springs	Claiborne	Elder W. M. Sparks	J. L. Drummonds	New Tazewell, Tenn.
Pleasant Point	Claiborne	Elder Milton Brantley	Austin Beason	Goin, Tenn.
Braden's Chapel	Claiborne	Elder W. M. Sparks, Elder Henry Comer, Asst.	Arvel Braden	Speedwell, Tenn.
Black Fox	Grainger	Elder Albert Davis	Sam Davis, J. M. Davis	Luttrell, Tenn. Powder Springs, Tenn.
Brantley's Chapel	Blount	Elder Carl McCarty, Elder H. C. Taylor	R. B. Bridges	Maryville, Tenn., Route 8
Oak Grove	Union	Elder Albert Davis	Belle Moore, Ruth Shoffner, Asst.	Sharps Chapel, Tenn.
Rocky Dale	Knox	Elder Leonard White	Trula Berry, Wilma Shelton, Asst.	Fountain City, Tenn. Route 13 Corryton, Tenn.
Pleasant Hill	Campbell	Elder Albert Davis	Lincoln Edwards, Verlin Edwards, Asst.	Speedwell, Tenn.
Norton	Grainger	Elder Matthew Oliver	John Oliver, Bessie Collins, Asst.	Bean Station, Tenn.
Monroe, Mich.	Monroe	Elder Linvil Meyers	Ditsy Russell	325 Winchester St. Monroe, Mich.
			Gertrude Zwack, Asst.	1825 Spawdling Rd. Monroe, Mich.

504

1955

MINUTES

OF THE

ONE HUNDRED AND THIRTY-SIXTH

ANNUAL SESSION

OF THE

Powells Valley Association

OF

PRIMITIVE BAPTISTS

HELD WITH

THE CHURCH AT PLEASANT POINT

Claiborne County, Tennessee

August 19-20-21, 1955

OFFICERS

Elder Albert Davis .... Moderator
Elder Tona Eastridge .... Assistant Moderator
Brother Austin Beason .... Clerk
Brother Sam Davis .... Assistant Clerk

The next session will be held with the church at Davis Chapel, Claiborne County, Tennessee, to begin on Friday before the third Saturday in August, 1956. Elder Leonard White will preach the introductory sermon and Elder W. M. Sparks will be his alternate.

Church	DELEGATES	Restored	Received By Relationship	Received By Baptism	Received By Letter	Dis. By Letter	Excluded	Deceased	Total Membership	Sat. Meeting	Visiting Ministers	Communion Meeting	Printing Minutes
Black Fox	George Campbell, John Davis, Sam Davis			1					94		8.00	4.00	Jun
Bradens Chapel	Elder W. M. Sparks, Brice Braden, J. C. Monday, Leecy Sparks, Lola Braden				1				44	1	4.00	4.00	Jul
Brantley's Chapel	Everett Brantley, Plumer McBee, Corum Berry, Mildred Brantley, Attie McBee, Trudy Berry							3	57	2	8.00	5.00	Jul
Capps Creek	Elder John R. Weaver, Cora Weaver, Vada Weaver			1			1	1	82	3	5.00	5.00	Jul
Cedar Springs	S. W. Drummonds, J. L. Drummonds, John Davis, Cleo Davis, Velta Munsey, Mary Treece		2	6		2	2		157	4	5.00	5.00	May
Davis Chapel	Elder Leonard White, Cordelia Lynch					2			82	3	4.00	4.00	Jul
Gibson Station	George Shoffner, Henry Hoskin, Joe Irwin, Mollie Irwin				3			1	86	1	5.00	4.00	Jun
Kirkwood	Elder Hugh Brummet and wife, Asa Sharp and wife		1	1				3	16	1	5.00	20.00	Aug
Monroe, Mich.	John Drummonds								26	1	3.00	3.00	May
Norton	Elder Gilbert Adkins, Jimmy Adkins, Charlie Collins and wife.							2		1	3.00		May
Oak Grove	Elder Milton Brantley, Dewey Ellison, Tony Eastridge, George Shoffner, orace Rodgers, Veda Cole, Francis Eastridge, Mantie Brantly			1	6	2	2	2	317	1	10.00		May
Pleasant Hill	Elder Albert Davis, W. A. Moyers, J. L. Edwards, Kinley Graves, Verlin Edwards, Bud Branscome, William Branscome			2			1	1	93	4	15.00	5.00	Jun
Pleasant Point	Elder John F. Keevk, J. M. Cox, George Williams and wife, Oma Rosson, Edna Rosson, C. D. Keck, Etta Williams						21	3	134	1			Jul
Rocky Dale	Everett Berry and wife						1	3	85	3	5.00	5.00	Jun

FRIDAY'S PROCEEDINGS

First—According to previous arrangements, the Association met pursuant to adjournment.

Second—After singing praise and prayer by Elder John Russell, the introductory sermon was delivered by Elder Leonard White, followed by W. M. Sparks. Text: 5 Chapter Cor., "Is There a Cause?"

Third—After ten minutes intermission, the Association reassembled. Scripture lesson was by Elder Albert Davis, 27 Psalms. Prayer by Elder Hugh Brummet and Elder John Weaver.

Fourth—The Association was called to order by the Moderator, Elder Albert Davis.

Fifth—Called for letters from sister churches. Received 14, which were read by the clerks.

Sixth—On motion, all said letters were received and the delegates welcomed to seats by the moderator.

Seventh—Called for members who were not delegates. Received one from Davis Chapel, O. D. Macartie.

Eighth—Called for letters from corresponding associations. Received from Hiwassee Messenger John Russell from Central Union letter.

Ninth—On motion said delegates were welcomed to a seat after the letters were received.

Tenth—On motion Elder Elbert Davis reelected moderator, Elder Toney Eastridge, assistant moderator.

Eleventh—On motion Brother Austin Beason elected clerk, and Brother Sam Davis, assistant clerk. On motion that we rate confidence to Brother J. L. Drummonds, Clerk.

Twelfth—On motion, the Moderator appoint all the committees.

    A. Arrangements—Brothers Everet Berry, Johnnie Davis, J. C. Monday.

    B. Preaching—Brothers Brice Braden, John Drummonds, Verlin Edwards.

    C. Correspondence—Brothers Leonard White, John R. Brewer, Hugh Brummitt.

    D. Request—Brothers Lincoln Edwards, George Shoffner, George Williams.

    E. Finance—Brothers John M. Davis, W. M. Sparks, Everett Brantley.

Thirteenth—On motion, we adjourn until 10 a. m. on Saturday.

SATURDAY'S PROCEEDINGS

First—After singing praise, scripture lesson was by Elder Toney Eastridge, 17th Chapter First Kings, prayer by Elder McCarty.

Second—Called for letters from sister churches that failed to get in Friday, and received none.

Third—Called for the report of the committee on arrangements.

    A. We, the committee on arrangements, beg leave to submit the following report:

        1. Call the roll.

        2. Call for the report of the committee on request.

        3. Call for the report of the committee on preaching.

        4. Call for the report of the committee on correspondence.

        5. Call for the report of the committee on finance.

    When and where shall our next Association be held? Who shall preach the introducing sermon, and who shall be his alternate?

How many copies of the minutes shall we have printed? Who shall superintend the printing and distribution of the same? What shall be allowed for his services?

Respectfully submitted,

EVERETT BERRY

J. H. DAVIS

J. C. MONDAY

Fourth—On motion, the report was received and the committee discharged.

Fifth—Called the roll and erased the names of the absentees.

Sixth—Called for the report of the committee on preaching.

We, the committee on preaching, beg leave to submit the following report:

Friday night at the Church, Elder Toney Eastridge and Elder John Russell. At Oak Grove Church, Elder John Weaver and Elder Hugh Brummitt. Saturday morning at the Church, Elder Taylor and Elder Carl McCarty.

Saturday night at the Church, Elder Willie Sparks and Elder John Weaver. Saturday night at Oak Grove, Elder John Russell. Sunday, Elder Leonard White, the moderator to close.

Respectfully submitted,

BRICE BRADEN

JOHN L. DRUMMONDS

VERLIN EDWARDS

Seventh—On motion the report was received and the committee discharged.

Eighth—Called for the report on the committee of correspondence.

We, your committee on correspondence, beg leave to submit the following report:

That we keep up our correspondence with the Hiwassee and Central Union Association by letter and messenger.

Respectfully submitted,

LEONARD WHITE

JOHN R. WEAVER

HUGH BRUMMITT

Ninth—On motion the report was received and the committee discharged.

Tenth—Called for the report of the committee on request.

We, the committee on request, beg leave to submit the following report:

That we published all the obituaries that the churches furnish and that our next association be held with the churcn at Davis Chapel, Campbell, Tennessee, to begin on Friday before the third Saturday in August, 1956, and two days following.

Respectfully submitted,

LINCOLN EDWARDS

GEORGE SHOFFNER

GEORGE WILLIAMS

Eleventh—On motion, the report was received and the committee was discharged.

Twelfth—Called for the report on the committee of finance.

2

We, your committee on finance, respectfully submit the following report:

Churches	Minutes	Ministers
Capp's Creek	$ 5.00	$ .00
Davis Chapel	5.00	5.00
Pleasant Hill	15.00	.00
Braden Chapel	4.00	4.00
Gibson Station	4.00	4.00
Kirkwood	5.00	20.00
Brantleys Chapel	8.00	5.00
Rocky Dale	5.00	5.00
Oak Grove	10.00	.00
Pleasant Point	10.00	.00
Cedar Springs	5.00	.00
Black Fox	8.00	.00
Noeton	3.00	.00
Monroe, Michigan	5.00	.00
Received for	$92.00	$46.00
Balance Carried Over From 1954		38.00
Total		$176.00

Respectfully submitted,

JOHN M. DAVIS
W. M. SPARKS
EVERETT BRANTLEY

Thirteenth—On motion the report was received and the committee discharged.

Fourteenth—On motion we have 1,000 copies of the minutes printed and that the clerk superintend the printing and distribution of the same, and that he be allowed $22.00 for his services.

Fifteenth—On motion the next annual session be held at Davis Chapel, Campbell County, Tennessee, to begin on Friday before the third Saturday in August 1956, and two days following.

Sixteenth—On motion, Elder Leonard White will preach the introductory sermon and Elder W. M. Sparks will be his alternate.

Seventeenth—On motion, we send Elders W. M. Sparks and Toney Eastridge, Ellis Evans to the Central Union, and Elders John F. Keck, Albert Davis and Hugh Brummitt to the Hiwassee Association.

Eighteenth—On motion, the clerk write each a letter of correspondence.

Nineteenth—On motion, we extend to the dear old church and the people of the surrounding community our sincere appreciation for the kindness and generous hospitality shown us throughout this association.

Twentieth—On motion we adjourn until 10:30 E.S.T. at the above stated place and date.

Twenty-First—Dismissed in order.

ELDER ALBERT DAVIS
Moderator, Speedwell, Tenn.
ELDER TONEY EASTRIDGE
Moderator, Route 2, Louisville, Tenn.
AUSTIN BEASON
Clerk, Goin, Tenn.
SAM DAVIS
Assistant Clerk, Luttrell, Tenn.

SUNDAY'S PROCEEDINGS

On Sunday a large crowd gathered at the altar. Services were opened by Elder John F. Keck. Prayer by Ellis Evans. Then there was a wonderful sermon delivered by Elder Leonard White from the 15th Chapter of First Cor. of the 24th verse. It was enjoyed by all and the loving spirit and a loving parting was expressed by the clapping of hands and invoking the blessings of God upon each other and closing remarks by the Moderator Elder Albert Davis. Benediction by Elder Johnnie Adkins.

LICENTIATES

James Branscome .... 325 Winchester St., Monroe, Michigan
Charlie Standifer .... Corryton, Tennessee
Clay Davis .... New Tazewell, Tennessee
George Shoffner .... Sharps Chapel, Tennessee

MINISTERS

Elder Leonard White .... LaFollette, Tennessee
Elder E. S. Drummonds .... 606 Kentucky, Ave., Monroe, Mich.
Elder J. R. Weaver .... Harrogate, Tennessee
Elder W. A. Moyers .... 828 Arthur St., Knoxville, Tennessee
Elder R. H. Pettit .... 107 Jacksboro Pike, Fountain City, Tenn.
Elder W. M. Sparks .... Speedwell, Tennessee
Elder Henry Comer .... Route 4, LaFollette, Tennessee
Elder Joe Irwin .... Gibson Station, Virginia
Elder Dewey Ellison .... Sharps Chapel, Tennessee
Elder Milton Brantley .... Sharps Chapel, Tennessee
Elder Albert Davis .... Speedwell, Tennessee
Elder Charlie Redmond .... Shawanee, Tennessee
Elder John F. Keck .... Goin, Tennessee
Elder Lenvil Moyers .... 512 E. Elm St., Monroe, Michigan
Elder Isaac Owens .... 2932 North Custer Rd., Monroe, Michigan
Elder T. I. Eastridge .... Route 2, Louisville, Tennessee
Hugh Brummitt .... 1329 Brown Ave., Knoxville, Tennessee

CORRESPONDING LETTERS

We, the Powell Valley Association of the Primitive Baptists now in session at Pleasant Point, Claiborne County, Tennessee, on August 19, 20, 21 in 1955 send greetings to the Hiwassee and Central Union Associations with whom we correspond: Very dear brothers and sisters, we desire to keep up our long cherished correspondence with you and have chosen these our beloved Elders to bear this Epistle of love to you. To the Hiwassee, Elder John F. Keck, Elder Albert Davis, Elder Hugh Brummitt. To the Central Union, Elder W. M. Sparks, Elder Toney Eastridge, Ellis Evans. Having seated all your delegation, we heartily welcome another next year when convened with the church at Davis Chapel, Campbell County, Tennessee, to begin on Friday before the third Saturday in August 1956.

510

such amendments do not compromise the sovereignity of the churches nor have tendency to give this body undue power or jurisdiction over them.

OBITUARIES

MRS. MANERVIE BRANTLEY

Mrs. Manervie Brantley was born in Claiborne County, Tennessee on December 10, 1883, and passed away at Middlesboro, Kentucky, on July 5, 1955, at the age of 71 years, 6 months and 25 days. Mrs. Brantley was the daughter of the late James and Ollie Moyers Harrell. She was united in marriage to Freeman Brantley 56 years ago, nd to this union was born one son, James. Her husband preceded her in death on April 28, 1936, and her son passed away on July 21, 1954. Mrs. Brantley had lived in Claiborne County all of her life, and she was a member of the Pleasant Hill Primitive Baptist Church. Left to mourn her passing are two grandsons, Ottis and Odus Brantley, and one granddaughter, Miss Edith Brantley. Her daughter-in-law, Mrs. James Brantley, all of Speedwell, Tenn. Also four nieces and one nephew, Mrs. Mable Partin, Mrs. Annie Rose, Mrs. Gertie Anderson, all of Jellico, Tenn., Mrs. Opal Bell, Bloomington, Ind., Mr. Tilman Bryant, Cincinnati, Ohio.

ROY OTIS KECK, SR.

Roy Otis Keck, Sr., passed away at 12:45 p. m. at his home, 2316 McCroskey Ave., September 7, 1755. He was born March 23, 1897 at Sharps Chapel, Tenn. He was a deacon and member of Kirkwood Baptist Church. He is survived by his wife, Mrs. Flossie Yadon Keck; daughter, Mrs. E. A. Strader; three sons, Roy O. Jr., and James Frank of Knoxville, and W. B. of Gastonia, N. C.; one sister, Mrs. T. G. Waggoner of Knoxville and seven grandchildren. Funeral services were held at Roberts Funeral Home September 9, at 2:00 p. m. with Elder Leonard White and Rev. David Walker officiating. Interment was at Lynn Hurst Cemetery.

MISS ETHA MONROE

Miss Etha Monroe, born May 16, 1892 at Sharps Chapel, Tennessee. She was the daughter of Arnold and Ida Belle McDonald Monroe. She professed faith in Christ at an early age and joined the Church at Oak Grove. She lead a faithful Christian life, attending Church regularly as long as she was able to do so. Though an invalid most of her life, the faith she found in Christ, early in life sustained her to the nd. She was always happy to see her friends and greeted them with a smile.

Miss Monroe passed away May 3, 1955, at the home of her devoted niece and nephew, Mr. and Mrs. John Rensler, with whom she had made her home for the past 20 years. She leaves to mourn her passing: three brothers, A. B. of California, J. O. of Knoxville and Scott, Sharps Chapel; three nieces and two nephews.

Funeral services were conducted by Elder Leonard White at Berry's Chapel in Knoxville. She was buried in the family cemetery by the side of her father.
Mabel Monroe Brockman

BENJAMIN FRANKLIN (FRANK) BERRY

Benjamin Franklin (Frank) Berry was born April 8, 1887, and passed away January 29, 1955, following an auto accident, at the age of 67 years, 9 months and 21 days. He professed faith in Christ at an early age and joined Cave Springs Primitive Baptist Church in Union County. Later moved his letter to Rockydale where he remained a faithful member until death. Funeral services were held Wednesday, February 2, 1955, at 2:30 p. m. and was laid to rest at New Market Cemetery.

He was married to Dora L. Braden, June 20, 1908. He is survived by three sons, Willard, Clyde, Avia; one daughter, Mrs. Dorothy (Berry) Kivett; 10 grandchildren; three sisters and two brothers. He was preceded in

6

death by his wife, Dora; daughter, Ozetta; and gronddaughter, Wanda Sue Kivett. Also left to mourn are a host of relatives and friends.

Dear Dad, we all miss you so much since you went away. You went so quick and unexpected to us all. We can't understand your leaving, but Jesus does. We know you're happy up there with Jesus and loved ones where the roses never fade. We all hope to meet you some sweet day.

Written by daughter, Dorothy Kivett

MARY THOMAS MUNCEY

Mary Thomas Muncey was born September 16, 1889. Died February 1, 1955. She professed faith in Christ 35 years ago, and joined the Primitive Baptist Church at Black Fox, Tennessee. She was baptized by Rev. F. G. Brantley and lived a faithful member until death. She was married to Herman Muncey 36 years ago. Survivors are: husband; 9 sisters; 2 brothers. Services were held at the Mount Eagan Baptist Church, February 3, 1955 at 2:00 p. m. by the Rev. Dewey Ellison and Rev. Loy Shelton. Burial was in the Needham Cemetery.

M. F. MINCY

M. F. Mincy (Uncle Bill) as he was called, was born July 30, 1871. He professed a hope in Christ in early life and joined the Black Fox Primitive Baptist Church about the year 1895, and lived a faithful member until God called him to his reward on June 27, 1955. He leaves to mourn their loss: one brother, J. L. Mincy and 7 children who reside in Kentucky and Indiana. He was laid to rest in the Cabbage Cemetery in Grainger County June 29, 1955. Gone but not forgotten.

JAMES A. GARFIELD DRUMMONDS

James A. Garfield Drummonds was born September 30, 1879 and departed this life August 18, 1955 at the home of his son, Carlie Drummonds, being 75 years, 10 months and 18 days of age.

He professed faith in Christ at an early age and joined the Primitive Baptist Church at Cedar Springs the 4th Saturday in September 1899, and lived a faithful member.

He was united in marriage to Mary Frances Day, February 28, 1903, who preceded him in death October 2, 1946. Six children were born to this union, all of whom survive: 3 sons, Willie, New Tazewell, Carlie, Monroe, Michigan, Virgil, Knoxville; 3 daughters, Mrs. Gertrude Zwack and Dora of Monroe, Michigan, Mrs. Frankie Hayes, Washburn; 8 grandchildren and one great-grandchild; 3 brothers, E. S., Monroe, Michigan, S. W., Middlesboro, Ky., J. L., New Tazewell; one sister, Mrs. Kate Poore, Knoxville, and a host of other relatives and friends.

Funeral services were held at the Meyers Grove Baptist Church with Elder Linvil Meyers officiating. Ailor's, Maynardville, in charge.

ELDER MATHEW OLIVER

Elder Mathew Oliver, age 76, died October 13, 1954. He was the father of eight children, three sons and five daughters. He was a Primitive Baptist minister for 40 years. His remains were laid to rest in the Noeton Church Cemetery on October 15, 1954. We are longing to meet him on that beautiful shore, where separation will be no more.

MRS. MARY LONG RITCHIE

Mrs. Mary Long Ritchie, age 81, died July 14, 1955. She was a sister of Elder Mathew Oliver. She was a member of the Noeton Primitive Baptist Church. She was the mother of four sons and one daughter. Her remains were laid to rest in the Harrell Cemetery July 16, 1955. Our loss is Heaven's gain.

7

MRS. DOROTHY REDMOND

Mrs. Dorothy Redman, age 58, passed away at her home, Goin, 2:00 a. m. Sunday, November 21, 1954.

Survivors: husband, Mr. Oscar Redman, Goin; daughters, Mrs. Ott Williams, Erie, Tenn., Mrs. John F. Morris, Herlong, Calif.; son, Curtis Redman, Knoxville; mother, Mrs. Bill Dunsmore, New Tazewell; sisters, Mrs. Herbert Treece, Tazewell, Mrs. Otis Simmons, New Tazewell, Mrs. Rose Russell, Middlesboro, Ky.; brothers, Horace Wilcox, Monroe, Mich., Walter Wilcox, New Tazewell. She was a member of the Pleasant Point Baptist Church, where funeral services were held 10:00 a. m. Tuesday, November 23, 1954 with Rev. Johnnie Keck officiating. Interment in the Keck Cemetery. Coffey in charge.

EASTER KECK DUNSMORE

Easter Keck Dunsmore, age 79, passed away at her home near New Tazewell July 15, 1955.

She was born in Claiborne County April 15th, 1876, the daughter of J. L. and Rachel Keck. She was married to Melvin Jackson Wilcox, 1895, and to this union was born eleven children. Mr. Wilcox and six children preceded her in death. She later married Mr. W. C. Dunsmore. She is survived by her husband, Mr. W. C. Dunsmore, New Tazewell; sons, Horace Wilcox, Monroe, Mich., Walter Wilcox, New Tazewell; daughters, Mrs. Herbert Treece and Mrs. Otis Simmons, New Tazewell, Mrs. R. V. Russell; brothers, Essau, Matt, Arlis and Lee Keck, all of Goin. She was a member of the Pleasant Point Baptist Church where funeral services were held 10:00 a. m. Sunday with Rev. Tip Coleman and Lonnie Dunsmore officiating. Interment in the church cemetery. Coffey in charge.

MRS. MARGARET FORTNER

Mrs. Margaret Fortner, 81, formerly of Goin, Tenn., passed away at her home, 3030 East Fifth Avenue, Knoxville, at 11:45 a. m. Tuesday. She was a member of Pleasant Point Baptist Church.

Survivors: one daughter, Mrs. I. C. Russell; 3 sons, H. O. Fortner, Twin Falls, Idaho, Curtis Fortner, Powell, Tenn., Ray Fortner, Knoxville; 3 sisters, Mrs. Jake Shelton, New Market, Mrs. George Gibbs and Mrs. Floyd Cox of Texas; 2 brothers, Rev. John F. Keck, Goin, and Haskell Keck, Crossville; 14 grandchildren and 13 great-grandchildren. Funeral Thursday, 1:00 p. m. at Mynatt's Chapel, with graveside service 3:00 p. m. at Lily Grove Cemetery in Claiborne County, Rev. George Tusler and Dr. James Wilder officiating. The family received friends at Mynatt's 3 to 5 and 7 to 9 p. m. Wednesday.

CHURCHES	COUNTY	PASTORS	CLERKS	CLERK'S POST OFFICE
Kirkwood	Knox	Elder Leonard White	Dola Webb	3815 Buffett Road Knoxville, Tenn.
Capps Creek	Union	Elder J. P. Weaver, Elder Joe Orwin, Asst.	Vada Weaver	Harrogate, Tenn.
Davis Chapel	Campbell	Elder Hugh Brummett	Lassie Ellison	LaFollette, Tenn.
Gibson Station	Lee	Elder Leonard White, Elder Char. Redmond, Asst.	Roxie Cobb, Mossie Cottrell, Asst.	Gibson Station, Va.
Cedar Springs	Claiborne	Elder W. M. Sparks	J. L. Drummonds	New Tazewell, Tenn.
Pleasant Point	Claiborne	Elder Milton Brantley	Austin Beason	Goin, Tenn.
Bradens Chapel	Claiborne	Elder W. M. Sparks, Elder Henry Coner, Asst.	Arvel Braden	Speedwell, Tenn.
Black Fox	Grainger	Elder Albert Davis	Sam Davis, J. M. Davis	Luttrell, Tenn. Powder Springs, Tenn.
Brantley's Chapel	Blount	Elder Carl McCarty, Elder H. C. Taylor	R. B. Bridges	Maryville, Tenn., Route 8
Oak Grove	Union	Elder Albert Davis	Belle Moore, Ruth Shoffner, Asst.	Sharps Chapel, Tenn.
Rocky Dale	Knox	Elder Leonard White	Trula Berry, Wilma Shelton, Asst.	Fountain City, Route 13 Corryton, Tenn.
Pleasant Hill	Campbell	Tony Eastridge	Lincoln Edwards, Verlin Edwards, Asst.	Speedwell, Tenn.
Norton	Grainger	Elder Gilbert Adkins	John Oliver, Bessie Collins, Asst.	Bean Station, Tenn.
Monroe, Mich.	Monroe	Elder Linvil Meyers	Ditsy Russell	325 Winchester St. Monroe, Mich.

1956

MINUTES

OF THE

One Hundred and Thirty-Seventh

ANNUAL SESSION

OF THE

Powells Valley Association

OF

PRIMITIVE BAPTIST

HELD WITH

THE CHURCH AT DAVIS CHAPEL

Campbell County, Tennessee

August 17-18-19, 1956

OFFICERS

Elder Albert Davis _____ Moderator
Elder Tona Eastridge _____Assistant Moderator
Brother Austin Beason _____ Clerk
Brother Sam Davis _____ Assistant Clerk

The next session will be held with the church at 325 Winchester St., Monroe, Michigan, to begin on Friday before the third Saturday in August, 1957. Elder Tona Eastridge will preach the introductory sermon and Elder Hugh Brummit will be his alternate.

STATISTICAL TABLE

	DELEGATES	Restored	Received by relationship	Received by baptism	Received by letter	Dis. by letter	Excluded	Deceased	Total Membership	Communion Meeting	Minutes	Visiting Ministers	Saturday Meeting
Black Fox	George Campbell, Sam Davis, J. M. Davis; Elder W. M. Sparks, Henry Comer, J. C. Monday,	1	0	0	1	1	1	1	93	Jun	9.00	.00	2
Braden's Chapel	Elder Braden; Brice Braden	0	0	0	0	1	1	1	43	Jul	4.00	4.00	1
Brantley's Chapel	Jeff Ellison, Lelia Ellison, Plumer McBee, Clifford Brantley, Corum Truila, Berry Bailey		0	15	0	0	3	1	68	Jul	5.00	.00	2
Capps Creek	Elder John R. Weaver, Immon Browning	0	0	0	0	0	0	1		Apr	5.00	.00	3
Cedar Springs	John H. Davis, Cleo Davis, Kenneth Osborne, Veltie Munsey, Gladys Davis, Roxie Drummonds, Alva Davis		3	0	0	0	0	1	84	May	7.00	.00	4
Davis Chapel	Coudeia Lynch, Elder Mr. and Mrs. Leonard White, Mr. and Mrs; Gaines Irwin, Mr. and Mrs. Hugh Hill	0	0	0	0	2	0	5	50	Aug	5.00	5.00	3
Gibson Station	George Shoffner, Henry Hoskin; Elder Hugh Brummit, M. A. Norton, Lucy Norton	0	1	6	0	0	0	1	82	Aug	4.00	4.00	3
Kirkwood	John Drummons, Hallie Russell	0	8	6	2	0	0	1	93	Apr	10.00	10.00	3
Monroe, Mich.	Elder Gilbert Adkins, Charlie Collins and wife	0	0	2	2	0	0	1	19	Jul	5.00	.00	3
Noeton	Elder Tonie Eastridge, George Shoffner, Francis Eastridge; Milton Brantley	0	6	6	0	0	0	1	30	Aug	3.00	.00	3
Oak Grove	Elder Albert Davis, James H. Branscomb, Jim Edwards; Kinley Graves	0	8	8	0	1	4	3	310	Aug	10.00	.00	1
Pleasant Hill	C. D. Keck	0	0	1	1	2	2	1	91	Jun	12.00	.00	4
Pleasant Point	Elmer Graves, Everett Berry, Trula Berry, Parmilia Shelton, Wilma Shelton		0	1	1	2	2	2	130	Jul	10.00	.00	1
Rocky Dale			5	7	0	1	0	2	77	Jul	5.00	5.00	4

FRIDAY'S PROCEEDINGS

First-According to previous arragements, the Association met pursuant to adjournment.

Second-After singing praise and prayer by Elder Hugh Brummit, the introductors sermon was delivered by Elder Leonard White followed by Elder W. M. Sparks. Text: 4 Chapter Thessalonia, "Wherefore comfort ye one another."

Third-After ten minutes intermission, the Association reassembled. Scripture lesson was by Elder Albert Davis. Prayer by Elder Henry Comer and Elder John Russell.

Fourth-The Association was called to order by the Moderator, Elder Albert Davis.

Fifth-Called for letters from sister churches. Received 14, which were read by the Clerks.

Sixth-On motion, all said letters were received and the delegates welcomed to seats by the moderator.

Seventh-Called for members who were not delegates. Received one from Pleasant Hill, Shermon Pierce.

Eight-Called for letters from corresponding associations. Received from Hiwassee Messenger John Russell from Central Union Carl McCarty.

Ninth-On motion said delegates were welcomed to a seat after the letters were received.

Tenth-On motion Elder Elbert Davis reelected moderator, Elder Toney Eastridge, assistant moderator.

Eleventh-On motion Brother Austin Beason elected clerk and Brother Sam Davis, assistant clerk.

Twelfth-On motion, we adjourn until 10 a.m. on Saturday.

SATURDAY'S PROCEEDINGS

First-After singing praise, scripture lesson was by Elder Albert Davis, 1st Chapter Psalmist David. Prayer by Elder Allen Gates.

Second-Called for letters from sister churches that failed to get in on Friday, and received none.

Third-Called for the report of the committee on arrangements.

We the committee on arrangements beg leave to submit the following report.

1. Call the roll.
2. Call for the report of the committee on request.
3. Call for the report of the committee on preaching.
4. Call for the report of the committee on correspondence.
5. Call for the report of the committee on finance.

When and where shall our next association be held? Who shall preach the introductory sermon, and who shall be his alternate? How many copies of the minutes shall we have printed? Who shall superintend the printing and distribution of the same? What shall be allowed for his services?

Respectfully submitted,
Brice Braden
Hugh Hill
Plumer McBee

Fourth-On motion, the report was received and the committee discharged.

Fifth-Called the roll and erased the names of the absentees.

Sixth-Called for the report of the committee on preaching.

We the committee on preaching beg leave to submit the following report:

Friday evening at the church Elder John Russell and Milton Brantley. Friday night at the church, Elder Toney Eastridge.

At Pleasant Hill Church Elder Hugh Brummitt and Elder Albert Davis. Saturday morning at church, Elder Adkins and Elder Allen Gates. Saturday

1

night at church, Elder Hugh Brummitt, Elder John Weaver. At Braiden Chapel, Elder Toney Eastridge and Elder W. M. Sparks.

Sunday, Elder Leonard White, the moderator to close.

Respectfully submitted,
John H. Davis
O. D. McCarty
Verlin Edwards

Seventh-On motion the report was received and the committeee discharged.

Eigth-Called for the report on the committe of correspondence.

We, your committee on correspondence, beg leave to submit the following report:

That we keep up our correspondence with the Hiwassee and Central Union Association by letter and messenger.

Respectfully submitted,
Hugh Brummitt
John R. Weaver
James H. Branscomb

Ninth-On motion the report was received and the committee discharged.

Tenth-Called for the report of the committee on request.

We, the committee on request, beg leave to submit the following report: That we publish all the obituaries that the churches furnish and that our next association be held with the church in Monroe, Michigan, 325 Winchester St., to begin on Friday before the third Saturday in August, 1957 and two days following.

Respectfully submitted
George Campbell
Kinley Graves
G. W. Shoffner

Eleventh-On motion, the report was received and the committee was discharged.

Twelfth-Called for the report on the committee of finance.

We your committee on finance, respectfully submit the following report:

Churches	Minutes	Ministers
Capps Creek	$ 5.00	$ .00
Davis Chapel	5.00	5.00
Pleasant Hill	12.00	.00
Braden Chapel	4.00	4.00
Gibson Station	4.00	4.00
Brantleys Chapel	5.00	5.00
Kirkwood	10.00	10.00
Rocky Dale	5.00	5.00
Oak Grove	10.00	.00
Pleasant Point	10.00	.00
Cedar Springs	7.00	.00
Black Fox	9.00	.00
Noeton	3.00	.00
Monroe, Michigan	5.00	.00
Total received for	$94.00	$33.00
Amount carried over from 1955		51.00
Total		$178.00
Total Amount Paid Out		133.00
Total left in treasury at this date		$ 45.00

Respectfully submitted,
John M. Davis
Junior McBee
Henry Comer

2   518

Thirteenth-On motion the report was received and the committee discharged.

Fourteenth-On motion we have 1,000 copies of the minutes printed and the clerk superintend the printing and distribution of the same, and that he be allowed $25.00 for his services.

Fifteenth-On motion the next annual session be held at 325 Winchester St., Monroe, Michigan, to begin on Friday before the third Saturday in August 1957, and two days following.

Sixteenth-On motion, we send Elder Tona Eastridge will preach the introductory sermon and Elder Hugh Brummit will be his alternate.

Seventeenth-On motion, we send Elders Leonard White, Gilbert Adkins, Henry Comer and W. M. Sparks to the Central Union, and Elders Milton Brantley, Albert Davis, Tona Eastridge and Hugh Brummitt to the Hiwassee Association.

Eighteenth-On motion, the clerk write each a letter of correspondence.

Nineteenth-On motion, we extend to the dear old church and the people of the surrounding community our sincere appreciation for the kindness and generous hospitality show us throughout this assiciation.

Twentieth.-This association sends a letter of regret to the following which were unable to attend, Elder John F. Keck, Brothers Lincoln Edwards and J. L. Drummonds.

Twenty-first-On motion, we adjourn until 10:30 E. S. T. at the above stated place and date.

Twenty-second-Dismissed in order.

ELDER ALBERT DAVIS
Moderator, Speedwell, Tenn.
ELDER TONEY EASTRIDGE
Moderator, Route 2, Louisville, Tenn.
AUSTIN BEASON
Clerk, Goin, Tenn.
SAM DAVIS
Assistant Clerk, Luttrell, Tenn.

SUNDAY'S PROCEEDINGS

On Sunday a large crowd gathered at the altar. Services were opened by Elder Leonard White. Text: 3rd. Chapter, 1st. Timothy, that though contest know how to behave in the house of the lord. Then there was wonderful sermon delivered by Leonard White. It was enjoyed by all and the loving spirit and a loving parting was expressed by the clapping of hands and invoking the blessings of God upon each other and closing remarks by the Moderator, Elder Albert Davis.

MINISTERS

Elder Leonard White _____ LaFollette, Tennessee
Elder J. R. Weaver _____ Harrogate,Tennessee
Elder W. A. Moyers _____ Route 7, Ball Camp Pike, Knoxville, Tennessee
Elder R. H. Pettit _____ 107 Jacksboro Pike, Fountain City, Tennessee
Elder W. M. Sparks _____ Speedwell, Tennessee
Elder Henry Comer _____ Route 4, LaFollette, Tennessee
Elder Joe Irwin _____ Gibson Station, Virginia
Elder Dewey Ellison _____ Sharps Chapel, Tennessee
Elder Milton Brantley _____ Sharps Chapel, Tennessee
Elder Albert Davis _____ Speedwell, Tennessee
Elder Charlie Redmond _____ Shawanee, Tennessee
Elder John F. Keck _____ Goin, Tennessee
Elder Lenvil Moyers _____ 512 E. Elm. St., Monroe, Michigan
Elder Isaac Owens _____ 2932 North Custer Rd., Monroe, Michigan
Elder T. I. Eastridge _____ Route 2, Louisville, Tennessee
Hugh Brummitt _____ 1329 Brown Ave., Knoxville, Tennessee
Gilbert Adkins _____ Bean Station, Tennessee

3

LICENTIATES

CORRESPONDING LETTERS

We, the Powell Valley Association of the Primitive Baptists now in session at Davis Chapel, Campbell County, Tennessee on August 17-18-19, 1956, send greetings to the Hiwassee and Central Union Associations with whom we correspond: Very dear brothers and sisters, we desire to keep up our long cherished correspondence with you and have chosen these our beloved Elders to bear this Epistle of love to you. To the Hiwassee, Elders Milton Brantley, Albert Davis, Tona Eastridge and Hugh Brummitt. To the Central Union, Elders Leonard White, Gilbert Adkins, Henry Comer and W. M. Sparks. Having seated all your delegation, we heartily welcome another next year when convened with the church at 325 Winchester Street, Monroe, Michigan, to begin on Friday before the third Saturday in August, 1957.

OBITUARIES

MR. JOHN F. CAREY

Mr. John F. Carey, age 88, passed away Saturday morning at the home of his son, Milton Carey, Crossville. Survivors: sons, Milton, Shurman D. M. Walter and William Carey, all of Crossville, Johnny Carey, Monroe, Mich., daughters, Mrs. Gladys Keck, Mrs. Emma Cole, and Mrs. Ottie Proffitt, all of Crossville, Mrs. Janie Thompson, Detroit, Mich. brothers, Floyd Carey, Goin, Dan Carey. Middlesboro, George Carey, Goin, Speedwell; sister, Mrs. Sarah Earls, Middlesboro. Funeral services were held 11:00 a. m. Monday from the Pleasant Point Primitive Baptist church with Elder Comer and Rev. H. B. Harris officiating. Interment in the Hopper cemetery.

Coffey in charge.

MR. CHARLES A. FIELDEN

Charles A. Fielden was born November 9, 1889, the son of the late Jilson Fielden and Della Maples Fielden, in Grainger County, Tennessee.

He professed Faith in Christ at an early age, joining the Indian Ridge Baptist Church and later joining the Kirkwood Primitive Baptist Church, of which he was a member at the time of his death.

Mr. Fielden was married August 22, 1913 to the former Emma Sharp, who survives him along with his mother, one son, J. H. Fielden and one granddaughter, Elaine Kay Fielden.

Services were conducted April 22, 1956 by Elder Leonard White at Rose Chapel with burial in LynnHurst Cemetery.

MISS ODOSKEY RUBY MEYERS

Miss Odoskey Ruby Meyers, age 41, pasesd away at her home near Hall Cross Roads August 1, 1956. Survivors: parents, Mr. and Mrs. Robert Meyers, Halls X Rds. sister, Mrs. Yadon Howard, Monroe, Mich., brother, Mr. Lonnie Meyers, Knoxville, Funeral service 11:00 a.m. at Meyers Grove

5

Baptist church with Rev. Clyde Gideon, and Rev. W. M. Sparks officiating. Interment in the Drummon cemetery. Pallbearers: Porter Mathews, Howard Neeley, Jake Smith, Carl Ford, Dock Cox, and Brisco Relford.

Coffey in Charge.

ELISHA FERGUSON

Elisha Ferguson, was born January 23, 1876, died May 22, 1956. He was united in marriage to Miss Charlotte Butler in January, 1897. To this union 7 children were born, three boys and four girls. One boy was killed in World War II. He professed faith in Christ at an early age and joined the Missionary Baptist Church and on November 19, 1950, he joined the Primitive Baptist Church at Brantley's Chapel where he remained a faithful member until death. We deeply feel our loss is Heaven's gain.

JOHN ATKINS

John Atkins was born August 3, 1891 and departed this life January 24, 1954. He leaves to mourn his passing his wife, Ida Atkins; 2 sons, Macy Atkins, and Tandy Atkins; 3 daughters, Rosa, Sally and Shirley Atkins; 2 step children, Martha Collins and James Collins, and a host of relatives and friends.

No pen can write, no tongue can tell our sad and bitter loss. God alone has helped so well to bear our heavy cross. His place at home is vacant, his toils of life are o're, he has gone to be at rest on God's eternal shore.

Written by wife, Ida Atkins.

MISS FLAXIE LYNCH

Miss Flaxie Lynch, age 46, died 10:55 p.m. Saturday at the East Tennessee Baptist Hospital. Her residence was 513 East Fifth Avenue.

She was a member of the Oak Grove Baptist Church.

Survivors: sisters, Mrs. W. C. Robertson, Knoxville, Mrs. James Maples, Mrs. Pearl Welch, Mrs. Louise Roe, all of Sharps Chapel; brother, John Lynch of Kentucky; several nieces and nephews.

Funeral services 2 p.m. Monday at Oak Grove Baptist Church. Rev. Leonard White and Rev. Hugh Burnett officiated. Interment at rest in church cemetery.

We saw you fading like a flower,
But you tried so hard to stay.
We nursed you with tender care
Until God called you away.
Although the world in which you live
Is free from care and pain
Our world would be like Heaven
If we had you back again.
It's only human to want you back,
But this we know is true,
You never can return to us,
But we can come to you.
Her Sisters

BROTHER CALVIN DOYLE EDWARDS

Brother Calvin Doyle Edwards was born August 13, 1940. He departed this life January 4, 1956, being 15 years, 4 months and 21 days of age.

He is survived by his parents, Jim and Emma Edwards of Speedwell; one brother Glen Edwards; 4 sisters, Ruby Gean, Barbara Sue, Bernice and Mary Jane Edwards, all of Speedwell; 3 half brothers, Matthew Edwards, Ivo Brantley and Delmer Brantley of Monroe, Michigan; 6 half sisters, Alda Clawson, Alberta Leach and Margie Monday of Monroe, Michigan, Betty Joe Clawson, Dayton Ohio, Helen Clawson, Speedwell, and Ella Kay Braden, who preceeded him in death; and a host of relatives and friends.

He professed faith in Christ and joined the Church at Braden's Chapel in February, 1950 and lived a faithful member until death. We feel our loss is Heaven's eternal gain.   The Family.

6

MRS KATY JEAN KECK

Mrs. Katy Jean Keck, age 94 years, and widow of the late T. C. Keck, passed away at the home of her son, C. D. Keck, Goin, Tenn., on May 6, 1956.

She professed faith in Christ at an early age and joined the Primitive Baptist Church at Pleasant Point, of which she was an active member for about 70 years. She served as Deaconeer of the church for several years.

She leaves to mourn her passing 3 sons, Grover, Jim and Clarvel, all of Goin; 2 daughters, Mrs. Bessie Collins of Goin and Mrs. China Cox of Knoxville, Tenn.; 15 gradchildren and 27 great-grandchildren.

Funeral services were conducted at Pleasant Point Church. Elders Henry Comer, W. M. Sparks and Lloyd England participated. Interment in Keck's Cemetery.

W. H. HENRY STINER

W. H. Henry Stiner, age 88, pased away at his home in Sharps Chapel, May 7th, 3 p.m. He was a member of the Oak Grove Primitive Baptist Church.

Survivors: wife, Florence Graves Stiner; daughters, Rena Stiner, Sharps Chapel, Mrs. Hattie Simmons, Monroe, Michigan, Mrs. Jane Moyers, Goin, Tenn.; sons, Willie Stiner, Sharps Chapel, James tSiner, Goin, Tenn.; one brother, G. S. Stiner, Fountain City; 23 grandchildren; 37 great-grandchildren, and a host of relatives and friends to mourn his loss. We are longing to meet him on that beautiful shore where separations will be no more.

Wife and Children.

MRS. ALICE SHOFFNER

Mrs. Alice Shoffner, age 74, of Sharps Chapel, passed away June 11, 1956 at Oak Ridge Hospital at 4 p.m. Monday.

Survivors: husband, W. I. Shoffner; daughters, Mrs. P. V. Shoffner, Mrs. Bertha Cox, Sharps Chapel, Mrs. Paris Shoffner, California, Mrs. Ottis Bratcher, Ohio; sons, Rhynie Shoffner and Kenneth Shoffner, Maynardville, Aaron Rouse, Michigan, James Rouse, Kokomo, Indiana; sisters, Mrs. Martha Bailey, Mrs. Trula Walker, Knoxville, Mrs. James Dyke, Sharps Chapel; brothers, Kyle, Earl and Wonna Welch, Knoxville, Francis Welch, Sharps Chapel, Carl Welch of Michigan.

Funeral services at Oak Grove Baptist Church of which she was a member. Interment in the church cemetery. Rev. Leonard White and Rev. Albert Davis officiated. She was loved by all who knew her.

Husband and children.

LETHA VIOLA BEELER HAMIC

Letha Viola Beeler Hamic was born November 3, 1885, and departed this life March 11, 1956, being 69 years and 4 months old. She was married to Aberham Beeler November 7, 1907.

She leaves to mourn her loss four children and her husband.

She professed faith in Christ at an early age and joined the church at Black Fox in 1926 where she was a member at death.

We hope to meet her some day in the sweet by and by

Written by her daughter, Estie Capps.

ELDER E. S. DRUMMONDS

Elder E. S. Drumonds was born September 10, 1875 in Claiborne County, Tenn. He united with the Primitive Baptist Church at Cedar Spring, Claiborne County, Tenn., when a young man but later moved his membership to the Primitive Baptist Church of Monroe, Michigan where he remained a faithful member until he departed this life on January 1, 1956.

He was united in marriage to Miss Margaret Wilson on November 26,

7

1892. To this union 13 children were born, eight of which survive. His loving wife preceeded him in death, departing this life July 16, 1942.

He was ordained to the full work of the ministry on March 23, 1930 and served as pastor in the following churches, Black Fox, New Hebeon and the church at Monroe, Michigan, where he worked so faithful to get organized.

Elder Drummonds is greatly missed by the family and also by his preaching brethern, but our loss is Heaven's gain.

Funeral services were conducted at the Meyers Grove Church. Elder Linvel Meyers assisted by C. A. Meyers officiated. Interment in the Drummonds cemetery.

HASSIE MADDOX REDMOND

Hassie Maddox Redmond was born April 18, 1918. She departed this life January 24, 1956, being 37 years, 9 months and 6 days of age.

Sister Hassie is survived by her six children, her mother and stepfather, Mr. and Mrs. Robert Sexton, and one brother, John Maddox, of Newport, Michigan, also a host of relative and friends.

Sister Hassie professed a hope in Christ at an early age and joined Pleasant Hill Church in May, 1935, where she remained a member until death.

Funeral services were held at her home church. Elder Robert Davis and Elder Lonzo Waggoner had charge of the funeral. She was laid to rest in the Ausmus Cemetery close to the church.

We feel our loss is Heaven's gain.

Written by Mrs. Albert Davis.

CHURCHES	COUNTY	PASTORS	CLERKS	CLERK'S POST OFFICE
Kirkwood	Knox	Elder Leonard White	Estelle Petree Sharp	5313 Jacksboro, Pike Fountain City, Tenn.
Capps Creek	Union	Elder J. P. Weaver, Elder Joe Orwin, Asst.	Vada Weaver	Harrogate, Tenn.
Davis Chapel	Campbell	Elder Hugh Brummett	Lassie Ellison	LaFollete, Tenn.
Gibson Station	Lee	Elder Leonard White, Elder Char. Redmond, Asst.	Roxie Cobb Mossie Cottrell, Asst.	Gibson Station, Va.
Cedar Springs	Claiborne	Elder W. M. Sparks	J. L. Drummonds	New Tazewell, Tenn.
Pleasant Point	Claiborne	Elder Henry Comer	Austin Beason	Goin, Tenn.
Bradens Chapel	Claiborne	Elder W. M. Sparks	Arvel Braden	Speedwell, Tenn.
Black Fox	Grainger	Elder Albert Davis	Sam Davis J. M. Davis	Luttrell, Tenn. Powder Springs, Tenn.
Brantley's Chapel	Blount	Elder Carl McCarty Elder H. C. Taylor	R. B. Bridges	Maryville, Tenn., Route 8
Oak Grove	Union	Elder Albert Davis	Belle Moore Ruth Shoffner, Asst.	Sharps Chapel, Tenn.
Rocky Dale	Knox	Elder Hugh Brummitt	Trula Berry Wilma Shelton, Asst.	Fountain City, Tenn. Route 13 Corryton, Tenn.
Pleasant Hill	Campbell	Tony Eastridge	William Branscomb Verlin Edwards, Asst.	Speedwell, Tenn.
Noeton	Grainger	Elder Gilbert Atkins	John Oliver Bessie Collins, Asst.	Bean Statton, Tenn.
Monroe, Mich.	Monroe	Elder Linvil Meyers	Ditsy Russell	324 Winchester St. Monroe, Mich.

1957

MINUTES

of the

One Hundred and Thirty-Eighth

ANNUAL SESSION

of the

POWELLS VALLEY ASSOCIATION

of

PRIMITIVE BAPTISTS

held with

THE CHURCH AT ROCKY DALE

Knox County, Tennessee

AUGUST 16-17-18, 1957

OFFICERS

Elder Albert Davis _____ Moderator
Elder Tony Eastridge _____ Assistant Moderator
Brother Austin Beason _____ Clerk
Brother J. L. Drummonds _____ Assistant Clerk

The next session will be held with the church at Bradens Chapel, Union County, Tennessee, to begin on Friday before the third Saturday in August, 1958. Elder Hugh Brummit will preach the introductory sermon and John B. Weaver will be his alternate.

	DELEGATES	Restored	Received by Relationship	Received by Baptism	Received by Letter	Dismissed by Letter	Excluded	Deceased	Total Membership	Visiting Ministers	Printing Minutes	Saturday Meeting	Communion Meeting
Black Fox	Elder George Campbell, J. M. Davis, Sam Davis, Walton Cabbage and Wife		2	9				2	93	10.00		2	2 Jun
Braden's Chapel	Elder W. M. Sparks, Elder Henry Comer, J. C. Monday, Leecy Sparks, Winnona Monday, Lola Braden			1					44	5.00	5.00	1	1 Jul
Brantley's Chapel	Plumer McBee, Corum Berry, Everett Brantley, Ellis Evans Ollie McBee, Twila Berry, Mildred Brantley, Lottie Evans			2	1		1		70	5.00	5.00	2	2 Jul
Cripps Creek	Elder John R. Weaver, Vada Weaver		4					1	18	5.00	7.00	3	3 May
Cedar Springs	J. L. Drummonds, J. H. Davis, Gladys Davis							1	87	7.00	7.00	3	3 April
David Chapel	Elder Leonard White, O. R. Parrot & Wife, O. D. McCarty & Wife		1	3					154	5.00	5.00	3	3 Jul
Gibson Station	Elder Charlie Redmond, George Shoffner, Mossie Cottrell, Henry Hoskins & Wife		1	1				2	98	4.00	4.00	3	1 Aug
Kirkwood	Elder Hugh Brummit, R. O. Taylor, Myrtle Taylor		1	9	3		1		104	10.00	10.00	1	Last Apr
Monroe, Michigan	Letter Tabled												
New Hebron	Received by letter								24		6.00	4	4 Sept
Norton	Joe Long & Wife, Charlie Collins & Wife			5				1	35		3.00	3	3 Jul
Oak Grove	Elder Tony Eastridge, George Shoffner, Francis Eastridge							2	308	5.00	5.00	4	1 May
Pleasant Hill	Elder James H. Branscomb & Wife, Elder Albert Davis & Wife Shermon Pierce	1				1	1		90	5.00	7.00	4	4 Jun
Pleasant Point	George Williams and Wife, C. D. Keck, Oma Rosson, Etta Williams								130	5.00	5.00	1	Jul
Rocky Dale	Parnick Shelton, Wilma Shelton, Everett Berry, Trula Berry, Charlie Myers, Velva Myers							2	86	5.00	5.00	2	4 Jul

FRIDAY'S PROCEEDINGS

First—According to previous arrangements, the Association met pursuant to adjournment.

Second—After singing there was prayer by Elder Robert Campbell of the Hiwassee Association. The introductory sermon was delivered by Elder Tony Eastridge. Text: 32 Chapter, 11 Verse of Deuteronomy—The Wisdom and Promises of God. He was followed by Elder Leonard White. Text: Knowledge and Goodness of God.

Third—After ten minutes intermission, the Association reassembled. Scripture lesson was by Elder Albert Davis, 12 Chapter, Paul's letter to the Romans. Prayer by Elder George Campbell and Elder Henry Comer.

Fourth—The Association was called to order by the Moderator, Elder Albert Davis.

Fifth—Called for letters from sister churches. Received 13, which were read by the clerks.

Sixth—On motion, all said letters were received and the delegates welcomed to seats by the moderator.

Seventh—Called for members who were not delegates. Received none.

Eighth—Called for letters from corresponding associations. Received from Hiwassee: Elder Allen Gates. John Russell, Clyde McGee, Robert Campbell, Claude Thomas, Harrison Green, John Lively and wife. Received from Central Union: Letter.

Ninth—On motion said delegates were welcomed to a seat after the letters were received.

Tenth—On motion Elder Albert Davis reelected moderator Elder Tony Eastridge, assistant moderator.

Eleventh—On motion Brother Austin Beason elected clerk, and Brother J. L. Drummonds, assistant clerk.

Twelfth—On motion, the Moderator appointed all the committees.

   A. Arrangements—Brothers Corum Berry, John Oliver, John H. Davis.

   B. Preaching—Brothers John M. Davis, Sherman Pierce, O. D. McCarty.

   C. Correspondence—Elders Hugh Brummitt, James H. Branscomb, and W. M. Sparks.

   D. Request—Bothers J. C. Monday, Plumer McBee, Parnick Shelton.

   E. Finance—Brothers Everett Berry, W. E. Hamilton, C. A. Meyers.

Thirteenth—On motion, we adjourned until 10 a.m., on Saturday. We were dismissed by Elder Leonard White.

SATURDAY'S PROCEEDINGS

First—After singing the Scripture lesson was given by Elder Tony Eastridge 5 Chapter Acts—By the Hands of The Apostles. Prayer by Elder Henry Comer.

Second—Called for the letters from sister churches, that failed to get in Friday and received one from Gibson Station. The letter was read and the delegates were welcomed to their seats.

Third—Called for the report of the committee on arrangements.

   We, the Committee on Arrangements, beg leave to submit the following report:

      1. Call the roll.
      2. Call for the report of the Committee on Request.
      3. Call for the report of the Committee on Peaching.
      4. Call for the report of the Committee on Correspondence.
      5. Call for the report of the Committee on Finance.

   When and where shall our next association be held? Who shall preach the introductory sermon, and who shall be his alternate?

1

How many copies of the minutes shall we have printed? Who shall superintend the printing and distribution of the same? What shall be allowed for his services?

Respectfully submitted,
CORUM BERRY
JOHN OLIVER
JOHN H. DAVIS

Fourth—On motion, the report was received and the committee discharged

Fifth—Called the roll and erased the names of the absentees.

Sixth—Called for the report of the committee on preaching.

We, the committee on preaching, beg leave to submit the following report:

Friday night at the Church, Elder Robert Campbell and Elder John Russell.

Saturday morning at the Church, Elder W. M. Sparks and Elder Hugh Brummitt.

Saturday night at the Church, Elder Allen Gates and Elder Henry Comer.

Sunday at the Church, Elder Leonard White. Moderator to close.

Respectfully submitted,
JOHN M. DAVIS
SHERMAN PIERCE
O. D. McCARTY

Seventh—On motion the report was received and the committee discharged.

Eighth—Called for the report of the committee of correspondence.

We, your committee on correspondence, beg leave to submit the following report.

That we keep up our correspondence with the Hiwassee and Central Union Associations by letter and messenger.

Respectfully submitted,
HUGH BRUMMITT
JAMES H. BRANSCOMB
W. M. SPARKS

Ninth—On motion the report was received and the committee discharged.

Tenth—Called for the report of the committee on request.

We, the committee on request beg leave to submit the following report.

That we publish all the obituaries that the churches furnish and that our next association be held with the Church at Braden's Chapel, Union County, Tennessee. It will begin on Friday before the third Saturday in August 1958 and two days following.

Respectfully submitted,
J. C. MONDAY
PLUMER McBEE
PARNICK SHELTON

Eleventh—On motion, the report was received and the committee was discharged.

Twelfth—Called for the report of the committee of finance.

We your committee on finance, respectfully submit the following report:

Church	Minutes	Ministers
Capp's Creek	$ 5.00	$ 0.00
Davis Creek	5.00	5.00

2   528

```
Pleasant  Hill  ------------------------------------------------- 7.00      5.00
Braden's  Chapel  ---------------------------------------------- 5.00      0.00
Gibson  Station  ----------------------------------------------- 4.00      4.00
Brantley's Chapel  --------------------------------------------- 5.00      5.00
Kirkwood  ------------------------------------------------------10.00     10.00
Rocky  Dale  -------------------------------------------------- 5.00      5.00
Oak  Grove  --------------------------------------------------- 5.00      5.00
Pleasant  Point  ---------------------------------------------- 5.00      5.00
Cedar  Springs  ----------------------------------------------- 7.00      0.00
Black  Fox  ---------------------------------------------------10.00      0.00
Noeton  ------------------------------------------------------- 3.00      0.00
New  Hebron  -------------------------------------------------- 6.00      0.00
Monroe, Michigan Letter tabled, Money returned.
```

Received for --$82.00 $44.00
Balance carried over from 1956 --------------------------------   45.00
Total --- $171.00
Total Expense --- $135.00

Balance in Treasury -- $ 36.00

ence.

Respectfully submitted,

EVERETT BERRY

W. E. HAMILTON

C. A. MEYERS

Thirteenth—On motion the report was received and the committee discharged.

Fourteenth—On motion we have 1,000 copies of the minutes printed and that the clerk superintend the printing and distribution of the same and that he be allowed $25.00 for his services. Elder Leonard White is to assist the clerk.

Fifteenth—On motion the next annual session be held at Braden's Chapel, Union County, Tennessee, to begin on Friday before the third Saturday in August 1958, and two days following.

Sixteenth—On motion Elder Hugh Brummitt will preach the introductory sermon and Elder John R. Weaver will be his alternate.

Seventeenth—On motion, we sent Elder Leonard White and Elder Tony Eastridge to the Hiwassee Association; Elder Hugh Brummitt and Elder W. M Sparks to the Central Union Association.

Eighteenth—On motion, the clerk wrote each a letter of correspondence.

Nineteenth—On motion, we extended to the dear old Church and the people of the surrounding community our sincere appreciation for the kindness and generous hospitality shown us throughout the Association.

Twentieth—After the preceeding business, services were opened by Elder Hugh Brummitt. Prayer was by Brother George Shoffner. Elder W. M. Sparks followed with the text from the 4th Chapter, 16th Verse of Corinthians. Services were closed by Elder Hugh Brummitt speaking from the

3

5th chapter, 17th verse of Galatians. Elder Charlie Redmond dismissed the services.

Twenty-first—On motion, we adjourned until 10:30 E. S. T. at the above stated place and date.

Twenty-second—Dismissed in order by Elder George Campbell.

Elder Albert Davis, Moderator
Speedwell, Tennessee
Elder Tony Eastridge, Assistant Moderator
Route 2, Louisville, Tennessee
Austin Beason, Clerk
Goin, Tennessee
J. L. Drummonds, Assistant Clerk
New Tazewell, Tennessee

SUNDAY'S PROCEEDINGS

On Sunday a large crowd gathered at the altar. After singing services were opened by Elder Hugh Brummitt. Prayer by Brother Sherman Pierce. Elder Leonard White followed with a sermon from the 2nd chapter, 9th verse of Philippians—Paul's writing. wherefore God has also highly exalted him, and given him a name which is above every name. Benediction was given by Elder James H. Branscomb.

LICENTIATES

Clay Davis _____ New Tazewell, Tennessee
George Shoffner _____ Sharps Chapel, Tennessee
J. C. Monday _____ Speedwell, Tennessee
Jim Oliver _____ Bean Station, Tennessee
Blain Cupp _____ New Tazewell, Tennessee
Kenneth Osborne _____ New Tazewell, Tennessee
Everett Berry _____ Fountain City, Tennessee
Charlie A. Meyers _____ Fountain City, Tennessee

MINISTERS

Elder Leonard White _____ LaFollette, Tennessee
Elder J. R. Weaver _____ Harrogate, Tennessee
Elder W. A. Moyers _____ Route 7, Ball Camp Pike Knoxville, Tennessee
Elder R. H. Pettit _____ 107 Jacksboro Pike Fountain City, Tennessee
Elder W. M. Sparks _____ Speedwell, Tennessee
Elder Henry Comer _____ Route 4, LaFollette, Tennessee
Elder Joe Irwin _____ Gibson Station, Virginia
Elder Dewey Ellison _____ Sharps Chapel, Tennessee
Elder Milton Brantley _____ Sharps Chapel, Tennessee
Elder Albert Davis _____ Speedwell, Tennessee
Elder Charlie Redmond _____ Shawanee, Tennessee
Elder John F. Keck _____ Goin, Tennessee
Elder Lenvil Moyers _____ 512 E. Elm St., Monroe, Michigan
Elder Isaac Owens _____ 2932 North Custer Rd., Monroe, Michigan
Elder T. I. Eastridge _____ Route 2, Louisville, Tennessee
Elder Hugh Brummitt _____ 1329 Brown Ave., Knoxville, Tennessee
Elder Gilbert Adkins _____ Bean Station, Tennessee
Elder George Campbell _____ Fountain City, Tennessee
Elder James H. Branscomb _____ Speedwell, Tennessee

CORRSPONDING LETTERS

We, the Powell Valley Association of the Primitive Baptist now in session at Rocky Dale, Knox County, Tennessee on August 16-17-18, 1957, send greetings to the Hiwassee and Central Union Associations with whom

4

we correspond: Very dear brothers and sisters, we desire to keep up our long cherished correspondence with you and have chosen these our beloved Elders to bear this Epistle of love to you. To the Hiwassee, Elders Leonard White and Tony Eastridge. To the Central Union, Elders Hugh Brummitt and W. M. Sparks. Having seated all your delegation, we heartily welcome another next year when we convene with the Church at Braden's Chapel. Union County, Tennessee, to begin on Friday before the third Saturday in August, 1958.

OBITUARIES

MARCUS WEAVER

Marcus Weaver, age 72 died suddenly Tuesday July 2, 5:45 p.m. He was a member of Rocky Dale Primitive Baptist Church. He leaves to mourn, his passing his wife, Della, of Maynardville, Tenn., Daughters, Mrs. Harry Stroh, Sibley, Illinois, Mrs. Opal Wills, Waloon Lake, Michigan; Mrs. Jessie Finn, Gibson City, Illinois. Brothers, Andy Weaver, Knoxville, James, Milan, Michigan.; Chalmer, Detroit, Michigan; sister, Mrs. Dorothy Stoll, Ann Arbor, Michigan; stepmother, Mrs. Henry Weaver, Ann Arbor, Michigan. Funeral was 3 p.m., Wednesday at Ailor's Chapel, with Elder H. E. Brummitt, and Elder Leonard White officiating. Burial was in Gibson City, Illinois.

JAMES ESTLE HEATH

James Estle Heath was born July 2, 1904 passed away March 6, 1957, at Saint Mary's Hospital. He was married to Letha Williams, December 31, 1922, to this union 4 children were born, 2 sons. and 2 daughters. He professed faith in Christ at an early age, and joined the Primitive Baptist Church at Pleasant Point, after moving to Knoxville. he later moved his membership to Kirkwood Primitive Baptist, where funeral services were conducted by Elder Leonard White, A. R. Kitts and Andy Vance. His body was laid to rest in Lynn Hurst Cemetery to sleep until Jesus comes.

MRS. LIZA ATKINS WHITE

Mrs. Liza Atkins White was born December 8, 1881 and departed this life June 11, 1957. She professed faith in Christ at an early age, and was a faithful member of Noeton Primitive Baptist Church She was the widow of the late Martin White, who passed away June 6, 1951. To this union was born five children. She leaves a host of relatives and friends to mourn her passing.

6

EMMA DUNN FARRIS

Emma Dunn Farris was born at Speedwell, Tennessee, April 30, 1872. Departed this life November 17, 1956, at the age of 84.

She was the widow of William S. Farris. Survived by three daughters: Mrs. Edna Giles, Lake Monroe, Florida; Mrs. Mayme Bridges, Knoxville, Tennessee; Mrs. Bessie Summitt, Lenoir City, Tennessee; and one son Varley Farris, Lenoir City, Tennessee; one sister, Mrs. Vonia Wilson, Middlesboro, Kentucky (who followed her in death eight days later); one half sister Mrs. Flossie Hill, Loudon, Tennessee; one brother Maston Dunn, Corryton, Tennessee; two half brothers, Elvin Hopper, Loudon, Tennessee and Newton Hopper, Indiana; eleven grandchildren and seven great grandchildren.

She professed faith in Christ at an early age and united with the Davis Creek Primitive Church. On November 22, 1921, she joined Rocky Dale Church where she remained a member until her death.

In later years, she was not able to hear but little of the preaching, even with the help of a hearing aid, but would enjoy going to church to hear the singing and to enjoy the fellowship of God's people. She often said she could get a blessing by watching others as they listened to the preaching of His Word. Aunt Emma does not need a hearing aid now to enjoy the singing of the angels, or to receive the blessings of her Savior.

Funeral services were held at Cumberland Presbyterian Church at Lenoir City, Tennessee, by Elders Leonard White and Hugh Brummitt. Burial in church cemetery.—Written by a Niece, Emma Dunn.

OFFICIAL DIRECTORY

CHURCHES	COUNTY	PASTORS	CLERKS	CLERKS' POST OFFICE
Black Fox	Grainger	Elder Albert Davis	Sam Davis J. M. Davis	Lutrell, Tenn. Corryton, Tenn.
Bradens Chapel	Union	Elder W. M. Sparks Elder Henry Comer, Asst.	Arvel Braden	Speedwell, Tenn.
Brantley's Chapel	Blount	Elder W. M. Sparks	R. B. Bridges	Maryville, Tenn. Route 8
Capps Creek	Union	Elder J. R. Weaver Elder Joe Irwin, Asst.	Vada Weaver	Harrogate, Tenn.
Cedar Springs	Claiborne	Elder W. M. Sparks	John H. Davis	New Tazewell, Tenn.
Davis Chapel	Campbell	Elder Hugh Brummitt Elder Leonard White, Asst	Lassie Ellison	LaFollette, Tenn
Gibson Station	Lee, Va.	Elder Leonard White Elder C. Redmond, Asst.	Roxie Cobb Mossie Cottrell, Asst.	Gibson Station, Va.
Kirkwood	Knox	Elder Leonard White Elder R. H. Pettit, Asst.	Estelle Petree Sharp	5313 Jacksboro Pk. Fountain City, Tenn.
Monroe, Mich.	Monroe	Elder Linvil Meyers	Ditsy Russell	324 Winchester St. Monroe, Mich.
New Hebron	Jefferson	Elder Milton Brantley	Viola M. Ingle	New Market, Tenn. Route 3
Noeton	Grainger	Elder Allen Gates	John Oliver Bessie Collins, Asst.	Bean Station, Tenn.
Oak Grove	Union	Elder Albert Davis	Belle Moore Ruth Shoffner, Asst.	Sharps Chapel, Tenn.
Pleasant Hill	Claiborne	Elder Tony Eastridge	William Branscomb Verlin Edwards, Asst.	Speedwell, Tenn.
Pleasant Point	Claiborne	Elder Tony Eastridge	Austin Beason	Goin, Tenn.
Rocky Dale	Knox	Elder Hugh Brummitt	Trula Berry Wilma Shelton, Asst.	Fountain City Corryton, Tenn. Route 13

1958

MINUTES

of the

One Hundred and Thirty-Ninth

ANNUAL SESSION

of the

POWELLS VALLEY ASSOCIATION

of

PRIMITIVE BAPTISTS

held with

THE CHURCH AT BRADEN'S CHAPEL

Union County, Tennessee

AUGUST 15-16-17, 1958

OFFICERS

Elder Albert Davis _____ Mcderator
Elder Tony Eastridge _____ Assistant Moderator
Brother Austin Beason _____ Clerk
Brother Jim Edwards _____ Assistant Clerk

The next session will be held with the church at Brantley's Chapel, Blount County, Tennessee, to begin on Friday before the third Saturday in August, 1959. Elder Everett Berry will preach the introductory sermon and Elder J. C. Monday will be his alternate.

Churches	Delegates	Restored	Received by Relationship	Received by Baptism	Received by Letter	Dismissed by Letter	Excluded	Deceased	Total Membership	Visiting Ministers	Printing Minutes	Saturday Meeting	Communion Meeting
Black Fox	George Campbell, John Davis, Walton Cabbage, Jessie Cabbage.							2	91		10.00	2	2 Jun
Braden's Chapel	Brice Braden, J. C. Monday, Arvel Braden, Mathew Edwards, Noble Lee Clawson, Helen Clawson, Winona Monday, Ruby Edwards, Henry Comer, W. M. Sparks, Leecy Sparks, Lola Braden, Barbara Clawson.					1			42		5.00	1	1 Jul
Brantley's Chapel	Clifford Brantley, Ellis Evans, Plumer McBee, Corum Berry, Everett Brantley, Junior McBee, Truman Brantley, Dennis Brantley, Barsh Brantley, Lottie Evans Ottie McBee, Twila Berry, Mildred Brantley.				2			1	71	5.00	5.00	2	2 Jul
Capps Creek	No Letter												
Cedar Springs	Blaine Cupp, Helen Cupp, Isam Drummonds, Velta Munsey, Ester Drummonds, Tilda Simmons, John H. Davis, Pearlie Holt, Mary Treece, Nora Treece.					1		1	66		7.00	3	3 May
Davis Chapel	Leonard White, Mr. and Mrs. O. R. Parrot, Cordelia Lynch, Ollie White, O. D. McCarty.	1		2				1	156	5.00	5.00	3	3 Jul
Gibson Station	Charlie Redmond, Franklin Jones, Lucille Ball, Fannie Jones.				1				83		5.00	1	1 Aug
Kirkwood	Hugh Brummitt, Melvin Norton, Lucy Norton.		1		1	3			103	10.00	10.00	1	last Apr
Monroe Michigan	Lenvil Meyers, Ditsy Russell, Hallie Russell, John Drummonds, Roxie Drummonds, Mr. and Mrs. Millard Thompson.							1	12		5.00	3	3 Jul
New Hebron	Received by letter								25		2.00	4	4 Sept
Nocton	Johnnie Adkins, Gilbert Adkins, John Oliver		1						36	5.00	3.00	3	3 May
Oak Grove	George Shoffner, Tony Eastridge, Francis Eastridge, W. E. Hamilton			2				4	304		10.00	1	1 May
Pleasant Hill	Mr. and Mrs. James H. Branscomb, Mr. and Mrs. Albert Davis, Mr. and Mrs. W. A. Moyers, Verlin Edwards, Bud Branscomb, Jim Edwards, Kinley Graves, Sherman Pierce.			1				1	90	4.50	6.50	4	4 Jun
Pleasant Point	George Williams, Allie Williams, C. D. Keck, Oma Rosson.					2		1	127	5.00	5.00	1	1 Jul
Rocky Dale	Everett Berry, Parnick Shelton, Elmer Graves, Wilma Shelton, Grace Graves.			5					91	5.00	5.00	2	4 Jul

FRIDAY'S PROCEEDINGS

First—According to previous arrangements, the Association met pursuant to adjournment.

Second—After singing there was prayer by Elder Leonard White. The introductory sermon was delivered by Elder Hugh Burmmitt. The text: Jude 1st verse: The Servant of Jesus Christ, Mercy Unto You and Peace and Love Be Multiplied. Since the alternate was absent, complimentary words, were given by Elder Leonard White.

Third—After ten minutes intermission, the Association reassembled. Scripture lesson was by Elder Albert Davis, 13th chapter of Paul's Writings to first Corinthians. I speak with the Tongues of men and of angels. Prayer by Elder Johnnie Adkins and Elder John Russell.

Fourth—The Association was called to order by the Moderator, Elder Albert Davis.

Fifth—He called for letters from sister churches. Received 13, which were read by the clerks.

Sixth— On motion, all said letters were received and the delegates were welcomed to seats by the moderator.

Seventh—Called for members who were not delegates. Received two, W. E. Hamilton, Oak Grove and Nora Treece, Cedar Springs.

Eighth—Called for letters from corresponding association. Received from Hiwassee: Elder John Russell, Elder Allen Gates, Robert Campbell, George Pickard, and Mattie Russell.

Ninth—(A) On motion said delegates were welcomed to a seat after the letters were received.

(B) There was a move and second to lift the letters tabled last year.

(C) There was a move and second to receive Elder Lenvil Meyers' Church in the association.

Tenth—On motion Elder Albert Davis was re-elected moderator and Elder Tony Eastridge assistant moderator.

Eleventh—On motion Brother Austin Beason was re-elected clerk, and Brother Jim Edwards was elected assistant clerk.

Twelfth—On motion the Moderator appointed the following committees.

(A) Arrangements—Brothers Clifford Brantley, Ditsy Russell, and Elmer Graves.

(B) Preaching—Brother Sherman Pierce, John Drummonds, and W. E. Hamilton.

(C) Correspondence—Elders Henry Comer, Noble Lee Clawson, and W. M. Sparks.

(D) Request—Elder Johnnie Adkins, Brother Plumer McBee, and Brother Sam Drummonds

(E) Finance—Borthers John Davis Verlin Edwards, and Everett Berry.

Thirteenth—On motion we adjourned until 10 a.m. on Saturady. We were dismissed by Elder Henry Comer.

SATURDAY'S PROCEEDINGS

First—After singing, the Scripture lesson was given by Elder Tony Eastridge, 5th Chapter of Romans. Prayer was by Elder W. A. Moyers.

Second—There was a call for the letters from sister churches that failed to get in Friday. One was received from Cedar Springs. The letter was read and the delegates were welcomed to their seats.

Third—A call was made for the report of the Committee on Arrangements.

1

536

We the Committee on Arrangements, beg leave to submit the following report:

1. Call the roll.
2. Call for the report of the Committee on Request.
3. Call for the report of the Committee on Preaching.
4. Call for the report of the Committee on Correspondence.
5. Call for the report of the Committee on Finance.

When and where shall our next assoc'ation be held. Who preach the introductory sermon? Who shall be his alternate? How many copies of the minutes shall we have printed? Who shall superintend the printing and distribution of them? What shall be allowed for his services?

Respectfully submitted,
CLIFFORD BRANTLEY
DITSY RUSSELL
ELMER GRAVES

Fourth—On motion the report was received and the committee discharged.

Fifth—The roll was called and the names of the absentees erased.

Sixth—A call was made for the report of the Committee on Preaching.

We, the committee on Preaching, beg leave to submit the following report:

1. Friday Night
   At the Church—Elder Tony Eastridge and Elder J. C. Monday.
   At Pleasant Hill Church—Elder Hugh Brummitt and Elder Noble Lee Clawson.
2. Saturday Morning
   At the Church—Elder W. M. Sparks and Elder Leonard White.
3. Saturday Night
   At the Church—Elder W. A. Moyers and Elder Henry Comer.
   At Pleasant Hill Church—Elder J. C. Monday and Elder Lenvil Meyers.
4. Sunday Morning
   At the Church—Elder Lenvil Meyers.
   The Moderator is to close.

Respectfully submitted,
SHERMAN PIERCE
JOHN DRUMMONDS
EARNEST HAMILTON

Seventh—On motion the report was received and the committee discharged.

Eighth—A call was made for the report of the Committee on Correspondence.

We, the Committee on Correspondence, beg leave to submit the following report:

We shall keep up our correspondence with the Hiwassee Association by letter and messenger.

Respectfully submitted,
ELDER HENRY COMER
ELDER NOBLE LEE CLAWSON
ELDER W. M. SPARKS

Ninth—On motion the report was received and the committee discharged.

2

Tenth—A call was made for the report of the Committee on Request.

We, the Committee on Request, beg leave to submit the following report:

That we publish all the obituaries that the churches furnish and that our next association be held with the Church at Brantley's Chapel. Blount County, Tennessee. It will begin on Friday before the third Saturday in August 1959 and two days following.

Respectfully submitted,
ELDER JOHNNIE ADKINS
PLUMER McBEE
SAM DRUMMONDS

Eleventh—On motion the report was received and the committee discharged.

Twelfth—A call was made for the report of the Committee of Finance.

We, the Committee on Finance, beg leave to submit the following report:

Church	Printing Minutes	Visiting Ministers
Davis Chapel	$ 5.00	$ 5.00
Monroe, Michigan	5.00	0.00
Gibson Station	5.00	0.00
Norton	3.00	5.00
Kirkwood	10.00	10.00
Brantley's Chapel	5.00	5.00
Oak Grove	10.00	0.00
Braden's Chapel	5.00	0.00
Pleasant Hill	6.50	4.50
Pleasant Point	5.00	0.00
New Hebron	2.00	5.00
Rocky Dale	5.00	5.00
Black Fox	10.00	0.00
Cedar Springs	7.00	0.00
Total Received	$83.50	$39.50
Balance Carried Over From 1957		36.00
Complete Total		$159.00
Total Expense		115.00
Balance in Treasury		$ 44.00

Respectfully submitted,
JOHN DAVIS
VERLIN EDWARDS
EVERETT BERRY

Thirteenth—On motion the report was received and the committee discharged.

Fourteenth—On motion we passed to have 1,000 copies of the minutes printed and that the clerk superintend the printing and distribution of them. He is to be allowed $25.00 for his services.

Fifteenth—On motion the next annual session is to be held at Brantley's Chapel. Blount County, Tennessee. It is to begin on Friday before the third Saturday in August. 1959. and two days following.

Sixteenth—On motion Elder Everett Berry will preach the introductory sermon and Elder J. C. Monday will be his alternate.

Seventeenth—On motion we send Elder Albert Davis and Elder Everett Berry to the Hiwassee Association.

3

Eighteenth—On motion the clerk will write a letter of correspondence to the Hiwassee Association.

Nineteenth—On motion we extended to the dear old Church and the people of the surrounding community our sincere appreciation for the kindness and generous hospitality shown us throughout the association.

Twentieth—On motion we adjourned our business until 10:30 a.m. of the following year at the above stated place and date.

Twenty-first—We were dismissed in order by Elder James H. Branscomb.

Elder Albert Davis, Moderator
Speedwell, Tennessee
Elder Tony Eastridge, Assistant Moderator
Route 2, Louisville Tennessee
Austin Beason, Clerk
Go'n, Tennessee
Jim Edwards. Assistant Clerk
Speedwell, Tennessee

Twenty-second—After a ten minute intermission the association reassembled. Services were opened by singing. Prayer was by Ellis Evans. Elder W. M. Sparks spoke from Paul's writings: Let your request be known unto God. He was followed by Elder Leonard Wh'te. who spoke from the 5th chapter, 9th verse of Romans: Much more than being now justified by His Blood. We were dismissed by Parnick Shelton.

SUNDAY'S PROCEEDINGS

On Sunday a large crowd gathered at the altar. Services were opened by Elder J. C. Monday. Prayer was by Brother Ellis Evans. Elder Lenvil Meyers followed with a sermon from St. Luke 10th chapter 42nd verse: Mary hath chosen that good part which shall not be taken away from her. Part of the text also was from First Peter. chapter 2 verse 9: A chosen generation. This was a wonderful sermon that was enjoyed by all. Closing remarks were made by Elder Albert Davis.

LICENTIATES

Charlie A. Meyers _____ Fountain City, Tennessee
Jim Oliver _____ Bean Station, Tennessee
Parnick Shelton _____ Corryton, Tennessee
Clay Davis _____ New Tazewell, Tennessee
George Shoffner _____ Sharps Chapel, Tennessee

MINISTERS

Elder Leonard White _____ Lafollette, Tennessee
Elder J. R. Weaver _____ Harrogate, Tennessee
Elder W. A. Moyers _____ Route 7, Ball Camp Pike Knoxville, Tennessee
Elder R. H. Pettit _____ 107 Jacksboro Pike Fountain City, Tennessee
Elder W. M. Sparks _____ Speedwell, Tennessee
Elder Henry Comer _____ Route 4, LaFollette, Tennessee
Elder Joe Irwin _____ Gibson Station. Virginia
Elder Dewey Ellison _____ Sharps Chapel, Tennessee
Elder Milton Brantley _____ Sharps Chapel. Tennessee
Elder Albert Davis _____ Speedwell, Tennessee
Elder Charlie Redmond _____ Shawanee. Tennessee
Elder John F. Keck _____ Goin, Tennessee
Elder Lenvil Meyers _____ 512 E. Elm St., Monroe, Michigan

4

Elder T. I. Eastridge _____ Route 2, Louisville, Tennessee
Elder Hugh Brummitt _____ 1329 Brown Ave., Knoxville, Tennessee
Elder Gilbert Adkins _____ Bean Station Tennessee
Elder George Campbell _____ Fountain City, Tennessee
Elder James H. Branscomb _____ Speedwell Tennessee
Elder Johnnie Adkins _____ Bean Station, Tennessee
Elder Everett Berry _____ Fountain City, Tennessee
Elder J. C. Monday _____ Speedwell, Tennessee
Elder Noble Lee Clawson _____ Speedwell, Tennessee
Elder Blaine Cupp _____ New Tazewell, Tennessee
Elder Kenneth Osborne _____ Maynardville, Tennessee

CORRESPONDING LETTER

We, the Powell Valley Association of the Primitive Baptist. now in session at Braden's Chapel, Union County Tennessee, on August 15, 16, 17, 1958 send greetings to the Hiwassee Association with whom we correspond. Very dear Brothers and Sisters, we desire to keep up our long cherished correspondence with you. We have chosen these our beloved Elders to bear this episle of love to you. We send to you as our delegates Elder Albert Davis and Elder Everett Berry. Having seated all your delegates, we heartly welcome more next year when we convene with the Church at Brantley's Chapel. Blount County Tennessee, to begin on Friday before the third Saturday in August, 1959.

OBITUARIES

MRS. VICIE ANN KECK

Mrs. Vicie Ann Keck, age 80, passed away at the home of her son Ausbin of Goin, Tennessee on March 22, 1958

Survivors: husband, Delbert of Goin; sons, Ausbin of Goin and David of Sharps Chapel; daughters: Emaline Mayes of Middlesboro. Kentucky and Gladys Tinnel of Speedwell, Tennessee; brothers, Jonce Riding of White Oak, Tennessee and Crockett Riding of Tazewell Tennessee; 23 grandchildren and 6 great grandchildren. She was a member of Pleasant Point Baptist Church where funeral services were held. Elder Everett Berry and Elder Tony Eastridge officiated. Interment in Keck's cemetery.

6

5

MRS. JANE PETERS

Mrs. Jane Peters, age 89, passed away at the home of her son Zeno of Sharps Chapel. Survivors: son, Zeno of Sharps Chapel; daughters, Mrs. Mossie Dykes and Mrs. Mamie Johnson both of Sharps Chapel; 23 grandchildren, 48 great grandchildren, and 9 great-great-grandchildren. She was a member of Oak Grove Primitive Baptist Church where services were held. Services were conducted by Elder Leonard White. Burial in Stiner cemetery.

MRS. LASSIE SHARPE ROGERS

Mrs. Lassie Sharpe Rogers was borned April 14, 1880. She professed faith in Christ January 1, 1894, and joined the Primitive Baptist Church the first Sunday in January 1895. She was married to Isaac Shoffner March 18, 1901. Born to their union were five children: Lillas, Lucas, Petters, Rosa, and Desalina. She was married to H. E. Rogers March 5, 1916. She departed this life May 20 1958.

"Gone but not forgotton."

SUSAN MYRTLE MUNSEY

Susan Myrtle Munsey was borned October 9, 1901, and departed this life November 10, 1957. She leaves to mourn her passing two sons Frank of Powder Springs and J. C. of Corryton; three grandchildren, Pamela, Carolyn, and Susan; seven sisters, Carrie Larman, Cordelea Muncey Lyda Mincey, Arleone Collins all of Liberty Hill, Tennessee, Ettia Rosenbalm of N w Tazewell. Mary Mincey of Knoxville and Frances Rosenbalm of Hieskell; one brother Eck Nicely of Liberty Hill. She joined the Primitive Baptist Church of Black Fox in 1939 and lived a faithful member until her death.

She was a loving mother and how we will miss her. She was loved by all who knew her, but God loved her best. Our loss is his Eternal gain. A loving mother from us is gone and a voice we loved is still. Sleep on dear mother and take your rest. We all loved you, but God loved you best.
—Written by her sons, Frank and J. C. Munsey.

MRS. LOVE LARMER MUNSEY

Mrs. Love Larmer Munsey, age 71, passed away suddenly Friday, September 27, 1957. She professed faith in Christ at an early age and later joined the Black Fox Primitive Baptist Church where she remained a faithful member until death. She leaves to mourn her passing her husband Farley; four daughters Mrs. Clayton Bailey of Powder Springs, Mrs. Joe Starnes of Washburn, Mrs. Ora Bailey and Mrs. Millard Munsey both of Liberty Hill; four sons, Clarence, Luther, and James of Powder Springs and Paul of Liberty Hill; three sisters, Miss Pearlie Larmer of Powder Springs. Mrs. Charlie Russell of Goin, and Mrs. A. M. Marrion of Ritchey, Missouri; 36 grandchildren; 32 great-grandchildren. Funeral services were held at Black Fox Primitive Baptist Church by Elder Albert Davis and Elder Lay Shelton and laid to rest in Cabbage cemetery.

A Brighter Home

Lone are the paths and sad the bowers,
Whence thy dear smile is gone:
But a brighter home than ours,
In Heaven is now thine own.

Gone but not forgotten.
—Written by a granddaughter, Mrs. Dorothy Bailey.

7

BETTY JEAN KIRPATRICK

Betty Jean Kirpatrick was born at Maryville, Tennessee November 21, 1939. She departed the life August 19, 1957, at Bacon's Hospital at Alma, Georgia following a car accident. She was 17 years-10 months-and 2 days old. She professed faith in Christ and joined Brantley's Chapel Baptist Church in January, 1956. She leaves to mourn her passing her mother Mrs. Lucy Payne sister Mary Evelyn, and brother Jam s all of Maryville; father, McKinley Kirpatrick of Bambridge, Georgia; grandmother, Mrs. Susie Evans of Rockford; and a host of relatives, friends, and classmates. Funeral services were held at Brantley's Chapel by Elder Carl M. McCarty and Elder Lonnie Dotson. She was laid to rest in Grandview cemetery to sleep til Jesus comes.

> The sweetest are the first to fade;
> The fondest one of all peaceful rest is laid;
> She is waiting for us only where no pain can ever mar;
> Our dear one who left us lonely; watches through the gates ajar.

—Written by Twila J. Berry.

JAMES W. DRUMMONDS

Brother James W. Drummonds, son of the late Mr. and Mrs. George Drummonds, was borned January 30, 1909. At death he was 48 years-7 months-17 days old. He was married to Miss Lela Simmons July 19 1935. To this union was born three daughters; Eleanor, Betty Sue, and Georgetta. He joined the Primitive Baptist Church at Cedar Springs the 4th Saturday in December, 1922. He later became a Deacon. He moved his membership to Monroe, Michigan where he lived a faithful member ti'l God called him home to rest on September 17, 1957, at Monroe. He leaves to mourn his passing his wife, Lela; three daughters, Mrs. Norma Miller Mrs. Glen Monday, and Georgetta Drummonds; one grandchild, Norma Mae Miller; two brothers, Pat and Ewin of Monroe, Michigan; grandmother, Mrs. Jim King of Arthur, Tennessee; and a host of relatives and friends.

> We saw you fading like a flower
> But you tried so hard to stay.
> We nursed you with tender care
> Until God called you away.

Others the world in which you live is free from care and pain
  Our world would be like Heaven if we had you back again.
It's only human to want you back, but this we know is true,
  You never can return to us, but we can come to you.

—Written by The Family.

WILLIAM BRYANT

William Bryant passed away May 15, 1958. He was 87 years old. He was married to Miss Thellie Bowman on December 12, 1897. To this union was born 10 children, 4 sons and 6 daughters. Several years ago he professed a hope in Christ and joined the Primitive Baptist Church at Pleasant Hill September 27, 1914 and remained a member until death.

> "Our loss is his eternal gain."

—Written by Elder Albert Davis.

8

JAMES NEWTON DYKE

James Newton Dyke was borned October 19, 1889. He passed away June 17, 1958 at the age of 68. He professed faith in Christ at an early age and jo ned the Church at Oak Grove. He leaves his wife. Mrs. Clotis Welch Dyke; four sons, Lonnie and Jay of Sharps Chapel, Robert of Nashville, and Carl of Detroit, Michigan; three daughters, Mrs. Esco Dale of Maynardville, Mrs. Clyde Ellison of Sharps Chapel, and Mrs. Emerson Ellison of Walton, Indiana; four brothers, Emmit and Charles of Sharps Chapel, John of Knoxville and Mana of Maynardville; two sisters, Mrs. Leslie Graves of Maynardville and Mrs. Aaron Rouse of Monroe Michigan; 21 grandchildren; 1 great-grandchild; and a host of friends to mourn his loss.

"Our loss is his eternal gain."

—Written by His Family.

WILLIAM ISSAC SHOFFNER

William Issac Shoffner was born November 15, 1883. He passed away June 9, 1958. He was married to Alice Welch Rouse. To this union three children were born; daughter, Bertha Cox of Sharps Chapel; sons, Rina and Kenneth of Maynardville. His step-children included stepdaughters, Nila Shoffner of Sharps Chapel. Mrs. Ottis Bratcher of Ohio, and Lillis Shoffner of California; stepsons Aaron Rouse of Michigan and James Rouse of Indiana. He had 27 grandchildren, 10 great-grandchildren, and one brother George of Sharps Chapel. He was a member of Oak Grove Primitive Baptist Church.

> He was a cripple here on earth
> But he won't be in Heaven.

Our loss is Heaven's gain.

—Written by His Family.

CHURCHES	COUNTY	PASTORS	CLERKS	CLERK'S POST OFFICE
Black Fox	Grainger	Elder Albert Davis / Elder Geo. Campbell, asst.	Sam Davis / J. M. Davis, asst.	Luttrell, Tenn. / Corryton, Tenn.
Braden's Chapel	Union	Elder J. C. Monday / Elder N. L. Clawson, asst.	Leecy Sparks	Speedwell, Tenn.
Brantley's Chapel	Blount	Elder W. M. Sparks	R. B. Bridges	Maryville, Tenn. Route 8
Capps Creek	Union	Elder J. R. Weaver / Elder Joe Irwin, asst.	Vada Weaver	Harrogate, Tenn.
Cedar Springs	Claiborne	Elder W. M. Sparks	John H. Davis	New Tazewell, Tenn.
Davis Chapel	Campbell	Elder Hugh Brummitt / Elder Leonard White, asst.	Lassie Ellison	LaFollette, Tenn.
Gibson Station	Lee, Va.	Elder Leonard White / Elder C. Redmond, asst. / Elder Everett Berry, asst.	Roxie Cobb / Mossie Cottrell, asst.	Gibson Station, Va.
Kirkwood	Knox	Elder Leonard White / Elder R. H. Pettit, asst.	Estell Petree Sharp	5313 Jacksboro Pk. Fountain City, Tenn.
Monroe, Mich.	Monroe	Elder Lenvil Meyers	Ditsy Russell	324 Winchester St. Monroe, Mich.
New Hebron	Jefferson	Elder Milton Brantley	Viola M. Ingle	New Market, Tenn. Route 3
Noeton	Grainger	Elder Allen Gates	John Oliver / Bessie Collins, asst.	Bean Station, Tenn.
Oak Grove	Union	Elder Albert Davis	Belle Moore / Ruth Shoffner, asst.	Sharps Chapel, Tenn.
Pleasant Hill	Claiborne	Elder Tony Eastridge	William Branscomb / Verlin Edwards, asst.	Speedwell, Tenn.
Pleasant Point	Claiborne	Elder Tony Eastridge	Austin Beason	Goin, Tenn.
Rocky Dale	Knox	Elder Hugh Brummitt	Trula Berry / Wilma Shelton, asst.	Fountain City, Tenn / Corryton, Tenn.

1959

MINUTES

of the

One Hundred and Fortieth

ANNUAL SESSION

of

PRIMITIVE BAPTISTS

held with

THE CHURCH AT BRANTLEY'S CHAPEL

Blount County, Tennessee

AUGUST 14-15-16, 1959

OFFICERS

Elder Albert Davis _____ Moderator
Elder Tony Eastridge _____ Assistant Moderator
Brother Austin Beason _____ Clerk
Brother Jim Edwards _____ Assistant Clerk

    The next session will be held with the church at Kirkwood, Knoxville, Tennessee to begin on Friday before the third Saturday in August, 1960. Elder J. C. Monday will preach the introductory sermon. Elder James H. Branscomb will be his alternate.

STATISTICAL TABLE

CHURCHES	DELEGATES	Restored	Received by Relationship	Received by Baptism	Received by Letter	Dismissed by Letter	Excluded	Deceased	Total Membership	Visiting Ministers	Printing Minutes	Saturday Meeting	Communion Meeting
Black Fox	George Campbell, John Davis, Walton Cabbage, Jessie Cabbage.			3			2	1	90		10.00	2	2 Jun
Braden's Chapel	Elder J C Monday, Buster Clawson, W. M. Sparks, Henry Conner, Harrison Sparks, Leecy Sparks, Winoma Monday.			10					53		5.00	1	1 Jul
Brantley's Chapel	Corum Berry and wife, Von Beason and wife, Everett Brantley and wife, Rina Johnson and wife, Plumer McBee and wife, Hollis Evans and wife.		1	1					73		5.00	2	2 July
Cedar Springs	John Davis, J. L Drummonds, Alvia Davis, Ester Drummonds, Frankie Hayes.			1			2		66		7.00	3	3 May
Davis Chapel	Elder Leonard White, O R Parrot, O. D. McCarty, Cordia Lynch, Mayne Parrot, Mollie McCarty.			5		4	2	2	154	5.00	5.00	3	3 July
Gibson Station	Lucille Ball, Mollie Irwin, Roxie Cobb.	2	1	5		4			82	2.00	3.00	3	3 Aug
Kirkwood	Elder R. H. Pettit, Millie Pettit, H. E. Burnmitt, J. L. Sharp, Evelyn Sharp.			1					103	12.00	8.00	1	lastApr
Monroe, Mich.	John Drummonds, Ditsy Russell, Hallie Russell, Lloyd Keller, Mary Lee Keller.								12		5.00	3	3 July
New Hebron	Elder Gilbert Adkins.			1					25	2.00	2.00	4	4 Sept
Noeton	Elder Johnnie Adkins, Charlie Collins.		1			1			37	3.00	5.00	3	3 May
Oak Grove	George Shoffner, Tony Eastridge, Tesa Creech, Francis Eastridge.			1	1	3	2	4	300	2.00	8.00	1	1 May
Pleasant Hill	Verlin Edwards, James Edwards, Elder James H Branscomb			5		2		4	90		10.00	4	4 Jun
Pleasant Point	Elder and Mrs Albert Davis, Claude Rosson.		1	3		3		1	131	5.00	5.00	1	1 July
Rocky Dale	Everett Berry, Parruick Shelton, Elmer Graves, Trula Berry, Wilma Shelton, Grace Graves, Besie Graves.			2		1		1	92	5.00	5.00	2	2 May

FRIDAY'S PROCEEDINGS

First—According to previous arrangements the association met pursuant to adjournment..

Second—After singing there was prayer by Elder Leonard White. The introductory sermon was delivered by Elder Everett Berry, text 6th Chapter John, 61st Verse also from the 16th Chapter of Ezekiel. He was followed by Elder J. C. Monday who spoke from the 38th Chapter of Isaiah—Set Your House In Order.

Third—After a ten minute intermission the association reassembled. Scripture lesson was by Elder Albert Davis, 1st Chapter of the Book of Psalms—The Ungodly Is Like The Chaff Which The Wind Driveth Away. Prayer by Elder Henry Comer and also by Elder Carl McCarty.

Fourth—The association was called to order by the Moderator, Albert Davis.

Fifth—The Moderator called for letters from sister churches. Thirteen were received. They were read by the clerks.

Sixth—On motion all said letters were received and the delegates were welcomed to seats by the moderator.

Seventh—A call was made for members who were not delegates. None were received.

Eighth—A call was made for letters from corresponding association. None were received.

Ninth—On motion Capps Creek Church was dismissed from the association.

Tenth—On motion Elder Albert Davis was re-elected moderator and Elder Tony Eastridge, assistant moderator.

Eleventh—On motion Brother Austin Beason was re-elected clerk and Brother Jim Edwards, assistant clerk.

Twelfth—On motion the moderator appointed the following committees:
1. Arrangements—John L. Drummonds, John H. Davis, Parnick Shelton.
2. Preaching—Verlin Edwards, Millard Welch, W. E. Hamilton.
3. Correspondence—George Campbell, Henry Comer, Johnnie Adkins.
4. Request—Johnnie Davis, J. H. Branscomb, Brother Norton.
5. Finance—Von Beason, J. C. Monday, Lloyd Keller.

Thirteenth—On motion we adjourned until 10:00 a.m. on Saturday. We were dismissed by Elder Noble Lee Clawson.

SATURDAY'S PROCEEDINGS

First—After singing, the scripture lesson was given by Elder Albert Davis, 12th Chapter 1st Verse of Romans. Prayer was by Brother Parnick Shelton.

Second—There was a call for the letters that failed to get in Friday. One was received from Gibson Station. The letter was read and the delegates were welcomed to their seats.

Third—A call was made for the report of the Committee on Arrangements.

We, the Committee on Arrangements, beg leave to submit the following report:
1. Call the roll.
2. Call for the report of the Committee on Request.
3. Call for the report of the Committee on Preaching.
4. Call for the report of the Committee on Correspondence.
5. Call for the report of the Committee on Finance.

1

547

When and where shall our next Association be held? Who shall preach the introductory sermon? Who shall be his alternate? How many copies of the minutes shall we have printed? Who shall superintend the printing and distribution of them? What shall be allowed for his services?

Respectfully submitted,
JOHN L. DRUMMONDS
JOHN H. DAVIS
PARNICK SHELTON

Fourth—On motion the report was received and the committee discharged.

Fifth—The roll was called and the names of the absentees erased.

Sixth—A call was made for the report of the Committee on Preaching.

We, the Committee on Preaching, beg leave to submit the following report:

1. Friday night, at the church, Elder Hugh Brummitt and Elder Carl McCarty.
2. Saturday morning, at the church, Elder Johnnie Adkins and Parnick Shelton.
3. Saturday night, at the church, Elder Clifford Brantley and Elder J. H. Branscomb.
4. Sunday morning, at the church, Elder Tony Eastridge and Elder Leonard White.

The Moderator is to close.

Respectfully submitted,
W. E. HAMILTON
MILLARD WELCH
VERLIN EDWARDS

Seventh—On motion the report was received and the committee discharged.

Eighth—A call was made for the report of the Committee on Correspondence.

We, the Committee on Correspondence, beg leave to submit the following report:

We shall keep up our correspondence with the Hiwassee Association by letter and messengers.

Respectfully submitted,
ELDER HENRY COMER
ELDER GEORGE CAMPBELL
ELDER JOHNNIE ADKINS

Ninth—On motion the report was received and committee discharged.

Tenth—A call was made for the report of the Committee on Request.

We, the Committee on Request, beg leave to submit the following report:

That we publish all the obituaries that the churches furnish and that our next association be held with the church at Kirkwood in Knoxville, Tennessee. It will begin on Friday before the third Saturday in August, 1960, and the two days following.

Respectfully submitted,

JOHN M. DAVIS
ELDER J. H. BRANSCOMB
BROTHER NORTON

2

Eleventh—On motion the report was received and the committee discharged.

Twelfth—A call was made for the report of the Committee on Finance.
We, the Committee on Finance, beg leave to submit the following report:

Church	Printing Minutes	Visiting Ministers
Rocky Dale	$ 5.00	$ 5.00
Davis Chapel	5.00	5.00
Bradens Chapel	5.00	0.00
Kirkwood	8.00	12.00
Pleasant Hill	10.00	0.00
Cedar Springs	7.00	0.00
Black Fox	10.00	0.00
Pleasant Point	5.00	5.00
New Hebron	2.00	0.00
Noeton	5.00	3.00
Oak Grove	8.00	2.00
Monroe	5.00	0.00
Brantley's Chapel	5.00	5.00
Gibson Station	3.00	2.00
Total Received	$83.00	$39.00
Balance Carried Over From 1958		44.00
Complete Total		$166.00
Total Expense		85.00
Balance in Treasury		$81.00

Respectfully submitted,

ELDER J. C. MONDAY
VON BEASON
LLOYD KELLER

Thirteenth—On motion the report was received and the committee discharged.

Fourteenth—On motion we passed to have 1,000 copies of the minutes printed and that the clerk superintend the printing and distribution of them. He is to be allowed $25.00 for his services.

Fifteenth—On motion the next annual session is to be held at Kirkwood in Knoxville, Tennessee. It is to begin on Friday before the third Saturday in August, 1960, and last the two following days.

Sixteenth—On motion Elder J. C. Monday will preach the introductory sermon. Elder James H. Branscomb will be his alternate.

Seventeenth—On motion we agreed to send Elder Leonard White, Elder Hugh Brummitt, and Elder Everett Berry to the Hiwassee Association.

Eighteenth—On motion the clerk will write a letter of correspondence to the Hiwassee Association.

Nineteenth—On motion we extend to the dear old church and the people of the surrounding community our sincere appreciation for the kindness and generous hospitality shown us throughout the Association.
the following year at the above stated place and date.

3

Twenty-first—We were dismissed in order by Elder George Campbell.

> Elder Albert Davis, Moderator
> Speedwell, Tennessee
> Elder Tony Eastridge, Assistant Moderator
> Route 2, Louisville, Tennessee
> Austin Beason, Clerk
> Goin, Tennessee
> Jim Edwards, Assistant Clerk
> Speedwell, Tennessee

Twenty-second—After a ten minute intermission that association reassembled. Services were opened by singing. After that, some complimentary words were said by Elder Tony Eastridge. He was followed by Brother Parnick Shelton whose text was from 23rd Chapter Psalms, 1st Verse—The Lord Is My Shepherd, I Shall Not Want. He was followed by Elder Johnnie Adkins, first Episle of Peter, The Suffering of Christ and The Glory To Follow. We were dismissed by Brother Charles Collins.

SUNDAY'S PROCEEDINGS

On Sunday a large crowd gathered at the altar. Services were opened by Elder W. M. Sparks. His text was from Psalms, Chapter 51. Prayer was by Elder Henry Comer. Preaching was by Elder Tony Eastridge. His text was the 3rd Chapter, 12th Verse from the Book of James—Can The Fig Tree, My Brethern Bear Olive Berries. He was followed by Elder Leonard White who spoke from the Book of Leviticus, Chapter 16, Verse 25—And the Fat of The Sin Offering Shall Be Burned Upon the Altar.

LICENTIATES

Charlie A. Meyers	Fountain City, Tennessee
Jim Oliver	Bean Station, Tennessee
Parnick Shelton	Corryton, Tennessee
Clay Davis	New Tazewell, Tennessee
George Shoffner	Sharps Chapel, Tennessee
Claude Rosson	Goin, Tennessee
Odell Carpenter	Maryville, Tennessee

MINISTERS

Elder Leonard White	LaFollette, Tennessee
Elder W. A. Moyers	Route 7, Ball Camp Pike, Knoxville, Tennessee
Elder R. H. Pettit	107 Jacksboro Pike, Fountain City, Tennessee
Elder W. M. Sparks	Speedwell, Tennessee
Elder Henry Comer	Route 4, LaFollette, Tennessee
Elder Joe Irwin	Gibson Station, Virginia
Elder Dewey Ellison	Sharps Chapel, Tennessee
Elder Milton Brantley	Sharps Chapel, Tennessee
Elder Albert Davis	Speedwell, Tennessee
Elder Charlie Redmond	Shawanee, Tennessee
Elder John F. Keck	Goin, Tennessee
Elder Lenvil Meyers	512 E. Elm St., Monroe, Michigan
Elder T. I. Eastridge	Route 2, Louisville, Tennessee
Elder Hugh Brummitt	1329 Brown Ave., Knoxville, Tennessee
Elder Gilbert Adkins	Bean Station, Tennessee
Elder George Campbell	Fountain City, Tennessee

4

Elder J. H. Branscomb _____ Speedwell, Tennessee
Elder Johnnie Adkins _____ Bean Station, Tennessee
Elder Everett Berry _____ Fountain City, Tennessee
Elder J. C. Monday _____ Speedwell, Tennessee
Elder Noble Lee Clawson _____ Speedwell, Tennessee
Elder Blaine Cupp _____ New Tazewell, Tennessee
Elder Kenneth Osborne _____ Maynardville, Tennessee
Elder Clifford Brantley _____ Maryville, Tennessee

CORRESPONDING LETTER

We, the Powell Valley Association of the Primitive Baptist, now in session at Brantley's Chapel, Blount County, Tennessee on August 14, 15, 16, 1959, send greetings to the Hiwassee Association, with whom we correspond. Very dear Brothers and Sisters, We desire to keep up our long cherished correspondence with you. We have chosen these our beloved Elders to bear this epistle of love to you. We send you as our delegates Elder Leonard White, Elder Hugh Brummitt, and Elder Everett Berry. Having seated all your delegates, we heartily welcome more next year when we convene with the Church at Kirkwood, Knoxville, Tennessee, to begin on Friday before the third Saturday, in August, 1960.

.

OBITUARIES
MRS. THELLIE BRYANT

Thellie Bryant, the former Miss Thellie Bowman, passed away at her home in Knox County, January 12, 1959 She was married to William Bryant December 12, 1897. To this union was born ten children, four sons and six daughters. She professed a Hope in Christ several years ago and was united with the Primitive Baptist Church at Pleasant Hill, September 27, 1914 where she remained a member until death.

Our loss is her Eternal gain.

MRS. MAE BELLE (DAMEWOOD) RUSSELL

Mae Belle (Damewood) Russell was born July 4th., 1917. She departed this life July 14, 1959. She was united in marriage to Sylvester Russell in November 1940. To this union was born nine children, four of which preceded her in death. She is survived by her husband, two daughters and three sons; Velva and Patsy Sue, Clifton Forrester, Leroy, and Robert Esco, all of Speedwell, Tennessee. She has two sisters, Mrs. Zettie Taylor and Miss Rose Damewood, also two brothers, Goldie Damewood and Elbert Damewood.

Twentieth—On motion we adjourned our business until 10:30 A.M. of

6

She professed Hope in Christ and joined Capp's Creek Church. She later moved to Plesant Hill Church where she remained a loyal member. We feel our loss is her Eternal Gain.

MR. NEAL LAMBERT

Neal Lambert was born February 25, 1872. He departed this life September 2, 1958 being 86 years old. Brother Lambert was united in marriage to Matilda Ausmus November 6, 1898 and to this union was born eight children, five girls and three boys. He is survived by his companion and all the children, namely; Mrs. Floy Ausmus. Mrs. Etta McCoy, Mrs. Hattie Miracle, Mrs. Lottie Berry, Mrs. Audra Davis, Bill, Charlie and Ben Lambert. Brother Lambert has one sister and one brother still living, Mrs. Rosa Leach and Sam Lambert. He has twenty nine grandchildren and nineteen great grandchildren. Brother Lambert professed Hope in Christ and united with the Church at Pleasant Hill in June, 1921. Later he was ordained as a Deacon and served this office faithfully. He is missed at home, at church and in his neighborhood but we know God knows best and we are sure that our loss is his Eternal gain.

A daughter—Mrs. Albert Davis

MR. WILLIAM W. GRAVES

William W. Graves was born April 17, 1892. He departed this life March 26, 1959. He was married to Abbie Braden and to this union was born eight children, one of which preceded him in death. Those surviving are his companion, Mrs. Abbie Graves and seven children; Mrs. Dallas Dunn, Mrs. Francis Dunn, Mrs. Helen Edwards, Mrs. Ruby Maddox. Ebra, Edward and Boyd Graves, and several grandchildren. He had one sister Mrs. Sarah Branscomb, and two brothers Mr. James Graves and Mr. Kinley Graves.

Brother William professed Hope in Christ in early life. He joined Pleasant Hill Primitive Baptist Church in 1951 and lived a faithful member until God called him away. Brother William was a bright light in our church. He was blind for more than thirty years, but thank God he could feel God's good Spirit down in his heart. He would rejoice and tell of the goodness of God so many times. Our Church has suffered a great loss, but our loss is his Eternal gain.

MR. W. H. (HESS) WHITE

W. H. (Hess) White, a retired farmer, died Sunday Morning, July 5, at his home at the age of 84.

He leaves to mourn his loss his wife, four daughters, and five sons, He also leaves two brothers, 31 grandchildren and 17 great grandchildren.

He professed faith in Christ at an early age and joined the Cave Springs Church in Union County, then later he moved to LaFollette and moved his membership to Davis Chapel Primitive Baptist Church.

Funeral services were held at Davis Chapel Primitive Baptist Church at LaFollette, Tennessee by Elder Leonard White and Elder Brown. Burial in the church cemetery.

MR. JAMES DOSSETT

James Dossett was born February 2, 1876, and passed away August 4, 1959, at his home at Corryton, Tennessee. He was a member of Davis Chapel Primitive Baptist Church LaFollette, Tennessee.

Survivors: wife, Beulah Dossett, Corryton; four sons W. R., J. E., and

7

Clarence of Fountain City, Tennessee and H. E. of Gary, Indiana; one stepson Howard Lambert, Fountain City, Tennessee; 3 stepdaughters Mrs. David Keyes, Dandridge, Tennessee, Mrs. H. W. Miller, Fountain City, Tennessee, and Mrs. H. L. Oaks, Corryton, Tennessee; one brother Fletcher Dossett, Dayton, Ohio; 7 grandchildren; one great grandchild.

Funeral services were held at Mynatt's Chapel at 11 A.M. August 6, 1959 by Elder Leonard White and Reverend Johnny Jones. Brief graveside services were held at Davis Chapel Cemetery at 1:30 P.M. where he was laid to rest.

MRS. NOLA STARNES ATKINS

Mrs. Nola Starnes Atkins was born December 20, 1885. She departed this life December 2, 1958. She professed faith in Christ at an early age and joined the Black Fox Church where she remained a faithful member until death. She leaves to mourn her passing away: husband, Kester Atkins; one son, Robert Starnes and his wife; one granddaughter Imogene Starnes.

We saw you fading like a flower
But we tried so hard to keep you.
We nursed you with tender care
Until God called you away.

Written by the Family.

ARTICLES OF FAITH

Article 1. We believe in only one true and living God, as He is revealed to us in the Holy Scriptures—Father, Son and Holy Ghost.

Article 2. We believe that the Scriptures of the old and new Testaments are the words of God and the only rule of all-saving knowledge and obedience.

Article 3. We believe in the doctrine of election according to the foreknowledge of God.

Article 4. We believe in the doctrine of orginal sin.

Article 5. We believe in man's importency to rescue himself from the fallen state he is in by his own will or ability.

Article 6. We believe that sinners are justified in the sight of God only by the imputed righteousness of Jesus Christ.

Article 7. We believe the elect according to the foreknowledge of God will be called, converted, regenerated and sanctified by the Holy Spirit.

Article 8. We believe the Saints will preserve and never fall finally away.

Article 9. We believe that baptism, the Lord's Supper, and feet washing are ordinances of Jesus Christ, and that true believers are the only subject of these ordinances, and that the true mode of baptism is by immersion.

Article 10. We believe in the Resurrection of the dead and the General Judgement.

Article 11. We believe that the punishment of the wicked will be everlasting and that the joys of the righteous will be eternal.

Article 12. We believe that no minister has the right to administer the ordinances, except those who have been regularly baptized and called of God, and come under the imposition of hands of the Presbytery.

8

CHURCHES	COUNTY	PASTORS	CLERKS	CLERK'S POST OFFICE
Black Fox	Grainger	Elder Albert Davis, Elder Geo. Campbell, asst.	J. M. Davis	Corryton, Tenn.
Braden's Chapel	Union	Elder J. C. Monday, Elder N L. Clawon, asst.	Arvil Braden	Speedwell, Tenn.
Brantley's Chapel	Blount	Elder W. M. Sparks	R. B. Bridges	Maryville, Tenn.
Cedar Springs	Claiborne	Elder W. M. Sparks, Elder Blaine Cupp, asst.	John H. Davis	New Tazewell, Tenn.
Davis Chapel	Campbell	Elder Hugh Brummitt, Elder Leonard White, asst.	Lassie Ellison, Ruth Heatherly, asst.	LaFollette, Tenn.
Gibson Station	Lee, Va.	Elder Leonard White, Elder Everett Barry, asst.	Roxie Cobb, Mossie Cottrell, asst.	Gibson Station, Va.
Kirkwood	Knox	Elder Leonard White, Elder R. H. Pettit, asst.	Estell Petree Sharp	5313 Jacksboro Pike Fountain City, Tenn.
Monroe, Mich.	Monroe	Elder Lenvil Meyers	Ditsy Russell	324 Winchester St, Monroe, Michigan
New Hebron	Jefferson	Elder Gilbert Adkins	Viola M. Ingle	New Market, Tenn.
Noeton	Grainger	Elder Allen Gates	John Oliver, Bessie Collins, asst.	Bean Station, Tenn.
Oak Grove	Union	Elder W. M. Sparks	Belle Moore, Ruth Shoffner, asst.	Sharps Chapel, Tenn.
Pleasant Hill	Claiborne	Elder Tony Eastridge, Elder J. H Branscomb, A.	William Branscomb, Verlin Edwards, asst.	Speedwell, Tenn.
Pleasant Point	Claiborne	Elder Tony Eastridge	Austin Beason	Goin, Tenn.
Rocky Dale	Knox	Elder Hugh Brummitt	Trula Berry, Wilma Shelton, asst.	Fountain City, Tenn. Corryton, Tenn.

554

1960

MINUTES

of the
ONE HUNDRED AND FORTY-FIRST

ANNUAL SESSION
of the

POWELLS VALLEY ASSOCIATION

of

PRIMITIVE BAPTIST

held with

THE CHURCH AT KIRKWOOD

Knox County, Tennessee

AUGUST 19-20-21, 1960

OFFICERS

Elder Albert Davis -- Moderator
Elder Tony Eastridge ---------------------------- Assistant Moderator
Brother Austin Beason -- Clerk
Brother O. R. Parrot ------------------------------------ Assistant Clerk

The next session will be held with the church at Black Fox, Grainger County, Tennessee. It will begin on Friday before the third Saturday in August, 1961. Elder Leonard White will preach the Introductory Sermon. Elder Clifford Brantley will be his alternate.

CHURCHES	DELEGATES	Restored	Received by Relationship	Received by Baptism	Received by Letter	Dismissed by Letter	Excluded	Deceased	Total Membership	Visiting Ministers	Prnting Minutes	Saturday Meeting	Communion Meeting
Black Fox	Martha Thompson, Jesse Cabbage, Roma Bailey, George Campbell, John Davis, William Thompson, Roy Bailey Walton Cabbage, Bill Munsey.								91	$ $10.00	5.00	1	2 June
Braden's Chapel	J. C. Monday, W. M. Sparks, Henry Comer.								53		5.00	1	1 July
Brantley's Chapel	Mr. and Mrs. Clifford Brantley, Mr. and Mrs. Ellison Evans Plumer McBee. Mr. and Mrs. Everett Brantley, Mr. and Mrs. Jeff Ellisor	1			2			2	72	4.00	6.00	2	2 July
Cedar Springs	John Davis, J. L. Drummonds, Alvia Davis.		1		2		1	1	61		7.00	4	4 May
Davis Chapel	Leonard White, Cordlia Lynch, Mr. and Mrs. O. R. Parror					2		1	152	5.00	5.00	3	3 June
Gibson Station	Mr. and Mrs. Franklin Jones, Lucille Ball, Roxie Cobb	2	4					1	90	4.00	4.00	1	1 August
Kirkwod	Mr. and Mrs. R. H. Pettit, Mr. and Mrs. H. E. Burmmitt, Melvn Norton, Lucy Norton.	4	1			2	2	1	104	10.00	10.00	1	Last April
Monroe, Michigan	Lenvil Meyers, Roxie Drummonds, Hallie Russell, Millard Thompson, Fay Thompson, John Drumonds.								12		5.00	3	3 July
New Hebron	Gilbert Adkins, Ray Mitchell.								25		1.00	4	4 May & Sept.
Noeton	Mr. and Mrs. Jonnnie Adkins, Mr. and Mrs. Charlie Collins Mrs. Joe Long.	2						1	36		5.00	3	3 May
Oak Grove	George Shoffner, Tony Eastridge, Francis Eastridge, Mr. and Mrs. Alfred Relford.							4	296		8.00	1	1 May
Pleasant Hil	Mr. and Mrs. James H Branscomb, Mr. and Mrs. Albert Davis, Verlin Edwards.				1			1	90		12.00	1	1 June
Pleasant Point	George Williams, Allie Williams, Claude Rosson, Doris Rosson.							3	128		10.00	1	1 July
Rocky Dale	Everett Berry, Trula Berry, Parncik Shelton, Wilma Shelton, Elmer Graves, Bessie Graves, Grace Graves, Wanda Clapp.	1						1	92	5.00	5.00	2	2 May

556

FRIDAY'S PROCEEDINGS

First—According to previous arrangements the Association met pursuant to adjournment.

Second—After singing, Elder Albert Davis spoke from the 13th Chapter of Paul's writings to the 1 Corinthians. Prayer was led by Elder Leonard White. The Introductory Sermon was delivered by Elder J. C. Monday, who spoke from the 16th Chapter of Eekiel the 6th Verse. Elder James H. Branscomb spoke from Isaiah—40th Chapter the 1st and 2nd Verses. Dismissal was by Elder W. M. Sparks.

Third—After a ten minute intermission, the Association reassembled. Singing the following by prayer by Elder R. H. Pettit and Brother O. R. Parrot.

Fourth—The Association was called to order by Elder Albert Davis, Moderator.

Fifth—The Moderator called for letters from sister churches.

Sixth—On motion all said letters were received and the delegates were welcomed to seats by the Moderator.

Seventh—A call was made for members who were not delegates. One was received—Verlin Edwards of Pleasant Hill.

Eighth—A call was made for letters from Corresponding Associations. Two were received—one from Hiwassee and one from New Bethlem.

Ninth—After the letters were read the delegates were welcomed to seats by the Moderator. The Hiwassee delegates were Claude Thomas, Henry Chamberlin, Estie Chamberlin, and Mrs. Ben Fields. Those from New Bethlem were W. O. Walker, W. M. Lawson, Carl McCarty, and Lester Bundy.

Tenth—On motion Elder Albert Davis was re-elected Moderator, and Elder Tony Eastridge was re-elected Assistant Moderator.

Eleventh—On motion Brother Austin Beason was re-elected Clerk, and Brother O. R. Parrot was elected Assistant Clerk.

Twelfth—On motion the Moderator appointed the following committees:
1. Arrangements—W. A. Norton, Plumer McBee, Millard Thompson.
2. Preaching—J. L. Sharp, Ellis Evans, Bill Munsey.
3. Correspondence—W. M. Sparks, Everett Berry, Hugh Brummitt.
4. Request—Alfred Relford, J. L. Drummonds, Everett Brantley.
5. Finance—John Drummonds, R. H. Pettit, Henry Comer.

Thirteenth—On motion we adjourned until 10:00 a.m. on Saturday, August 20, 1960. We were dismissed by Elder Carl McCarty.

SATURDAY'S PROCEEDINGS

First—After singing, Elder Tony Eastridge read the scripture lesson from the 8th chapter of Romans Prayer was led by Elder Clifford Brantley.

Second—There was a call for letters that failed to get in Friday. None were received.

Third—A call was made for the report of the Committee on Arrangements.

We, the Committee on Arrangements, beg leave to submit the following report:
1. Call the roll.
2. Call for the report of the Committee on Request.
3. Call for the report of the Committee on Preaching.
4. Call for the report of the Committee on Correspondence.
5. Call for the report of the Committee on Finance.

When and where shall our next Association be held? Who shall preach the Introductory Sermon? Who shall be his alternate? How many copies of the Minutes shall we have printed? Who shall superintend the printing and distribution of them? What shall be allowed for his service.

Respectfully submitted,
W. A. NORTON
PLUMER McBEE
MILLARD THOMPSON

Fourth—On motion the report was received and the committee discharged.
Fifth—The roll was called and the names of the absentees erased.
Sixth—A call was made for the report of the Committee on Preaching.
We, the Committee on Preaching, beg leave to submit the following report:

1. Friday night at the church—Elder Tony Eastridge and Elder Lenvil Meyers.

2. Saturday morning at the church—Elder Carl McCarty and Elder Clifford Brantley.

3. Saturday night at the church—Elder Hugh Brummitt and Elder Claude Thomas

4. Saturday night at Brantleys Chapel—Elder Tony Eastridge, Elder Carl McCarty, and Elder Clifford Brantley.

5. Sunday at the church—Elder Everett Berry and Elder Leonard White.

The Moderator is to close.

Respectfully submitted,
J. L. SHARP
ELLIS EVANS
BILL MUNSEY

Seventh—On motion the report was received and the committee discharged.
Eighth—A call was made for the report of the Committee on Correspondence.
We, the Committee on Correspondence, beg leave to submit the following report:

We shall keep up our correspondence with the Hiwassee and New Bethlem Associations.

Respectfully submitted,
HUGH BRUMMITT
W. M. SPARKS
EVERETT BERRY

Ninth —On motion the report was received and the committee discharged.
Tenth—A call was made for the report of the Committee on Request.

We, the Committee on Request, beg leave to submit the following report:
We shall publish all the obituaries that the church furnishes. Our next Association will be held with the church at Black Fox in Grainger County, Tennessee. It will begin on Friday before the third Saturday in August, 1961 and continue the two following days.

Respectfully submitted,
ALFRED RELFORD
J. L. DRUMMONDS
EVERETT BERRY

2

558

Eleventh—On motion the report was received and the committee discharged.

Twelfth—A call was made for the report of the Committee on Finance. We, the Committee on Finance, beg leave to submit the following report:

Church	Printing Minutes	Visiting Ministers
Black Fox	$10.00	$ 0.00
Braden's Chapel	5.00	0.00
Brantley's Chapel	6.00	4.00
Cedar Springs	7.00	0.00
Davis Chapel	5.00	5.00
Gibson Station	4.00	4.00
Kirkwood	10.00	10.00
Monroe, Michigan	5.00	0.00
New Hebron	1.00	0.00
Noeton	5.00	0.00
Oak Grove	8.00	0.00
Pleasant Hill	12.00	0.00
Pleasant Point	10.00	0.00
Rocky Dale	5.00	5.00

	Printing Minutes	Visiting Ministers
Total Received	$93.00	$28.00
Balance Carried over from 1959		$81.00
Complete Total		202.00
Total Expense		110.00
Balance in Treasury		$92.00

Respectfully submitted,

R. H. PETTIT
JOHN DRUMMONRS
HENRY COMER

Thirteenth—On motion the report was received and the committee discharged.

Fourteenth—On motion we passed to have 1,000 copies of the Minutes printed and that the Clerk superintend the printing and distribution of them. He is to be allowed $25.00 for his services.

Fifteenth—On motion the next Annual Session is to be held at Black Fox Church Grainger County,T ennessee. It is to begin on Friday before the third Saturday in August, 1961 and continue the two following days.

Sixteenth—On motion Elder Leonard White will preach the Introductory Sermon Elder Clifford Brantley will be his alternate.

Seventeenth—On motion we agreed to send Elder R. H. Pettit, Elder Hugh Brummitt, and Elder Everett Berry to the Hiwassee Association. We also agreed to send Elder Lenvil Meyers, Elder Henry Comer, and Brother John Drummonds to the New Bethlem Association.

Eighteenth—On motion the Clerk will write each a letter of Correspondence.

Nineteen—On motion we extend to the old church and the people of the surrounding community our sincere appreciation for the kindness and generous hospitality shown us throughout the association at the above stated place and date.

3

Elder Albert Davis, Moderator
Speedwell, Tennessee
Elder Tony Eastridge, Assistant Moderator
Rt. 2, Louisville, Tennessee
Austin Beason, Clerk
Goin, Tennessee
O. R. Parrot, Assistant Clerk
LaFollette, Tennessee

Twenty-first—After a ten minute intermission the Association reassembled. Services opened by singing. Then Elder Carl McCarty spoke from 1st John 4th Chapter—"Ye are God's Little Children." Then Elder Clifford Brantley spoke from Joshua, 3rd Chapter and 11th Verse. We were dismissed by Elder Everett Berry.

SUNDAY'S PROCEEDINGS

On Sunday a large crowd gathered at the altar. Since the Moderator was absent. Elder Tony Eastridge presided. Prayer was by Brother Charlie Meyers. Elder Everett Berry spoke from 1st Corinthians—Chapter 85 Verse 6. He was followed by Elder Leonard White who spoke from 2nd Corinthians —4th Chapter 5th Verse. Closing was by Elder Tony Eastridge.

LICENTIATES

Charlie A. Meyers	Fountain City, Tennessee
Jim Oliver	Bean Station, Tennessee
Parnick Shelton	Corryton, Tennessee
George Shoffner	Sharps Chapel, Tennessee
Claude Rosson	Goin, Tennessee
Odell Carpenter	Maryville, Tennessee

MINISTERS

Elder Leonard White	LaFollette, Tennessee
Elder R. H. Pettit	107 Jacksboro Pike, Fountain City, Tennessee
Elder W. M. Sparks	Speedwell, Tennessee
Elder Henry Comer	Route 4, LaFollette, Tennessee
Elder Joe Irwin	Gibson Station, Virginia
Elder Dewey Ellison	Sharps Chapel, Tennessee
Elder Milton Brantley	Sharps Chapel, Tennessee
Elder Albert Davis	Speedwell, Tennessee
Elder Charlie Redmond	Shawanee, Tennessee
Elder John F. Keck	Goin, Tennessee
Elder Lenvil Meyers	512 E. Elm St., Monroe, Michigan
Elder T. I. Eastridge	Route 2, Louisville, Tennessee
Elder Hugh Brummitt	1329 Brown Ave., Knoxville, Tennessee
Elder Gilbert Adkins	Bean Station, Tennessee
Elder George Campbell	Blaine, Tennessee
Elder J. H. Branscomb	Speedwell, Tennessee
Elder Johnnie Adkins	Bean Station, Tennessee
Elder Everett Berry	Fountain City, Tennessee
Elder J. C. Monday	Speedwell, Tennessee
Elder Nobie Lee Clawson	Speedwell, Tennessee
Elder Clifford Brantley	Maryville, Tennessee

4

CORRESPONDING LETTER

We, the Powell Valley Association of the Primitive Baptist, now in session at Kirkwood in Knox County, Tennessee, on August 19-20-21, 1960, send greetings to the Hiwassee and New Bethlem Associations with whom we correspond. Very dear Brothers and Sisters, We desire to keep our long correspondence with you. We have chosen these our beloved Elders to bear this episle of love to you. Our messengers to the Hiwassee Association are Elder R. H. Pettit, Elder Hugh Brummit, and Elder Everett Berry. To the New Bethlem Association we send Elder Lenvil Meyers, Elder Henry Comer, and Brother John Drummonds. Having seated your delegates we heartily welcome more next year when we convent with the church at Black Fox in Grainger County, Tennessee. We will begin on Friday before the third Saturday in August, 1961.

5

OBITUARIES

MRS. MARTHA JANE BRUMMITT

Mrs. Martha Jane Brummitt was born September 24, 1868 and died February 8, 1960. She was married to Andy Brummitt April 18, 1886. To this union was born 16 children of which 7 survive, 2 girls and 5 boys.

She professed faith in Christ at an early age and joined Caves Springs Church where she remained a member until the Church was lost to Norris Lake. She then moved her membership to Oak Grove where she remained a faithful member until death.

Granny as everyone called her was much loved and is greatly missed. She sleeps in the beautiful Blue Springs Cemetery at Sharps Chapel awaiting the glorious resurrection of the dead.

Funeral services were held at Blue Springs Church by Elder Leonard White and Elder Hugh Brummitt.

MRS. MARY L. WILDER BOWEN

Mrs. Mary L. Wilder Bowen was born March 24, 1876, passed away January 27, 1960. She was 83 years, 10 months, and 3 days old at her death. She professed faith in Christ at an early age and joined the Primitive Baptist Church at Oak Grove and remained a member until her death. Survivors:

6

561

daughters Mrs. Lettie Bowen of Goin, Tennessee and Mrs. David Keck of Sharps Chapel, Tennessee; sons—Jim Wilder of Middlesboro, Kentucky, Earnest Wilder of Goin, Tennessee, Herbert Bowen of Knoxville, Tennessee, and Argo Bowen of Goin, Tennessee; sister Mrs. J. P. Graves of Maryville, Tennessee; a host of relatives and friends.

MRS. SARAH BEASON

Mrs. Sarah Beason, age 76, wife of Mr. Proctor Beason, Goin, Tennessee, passed away November 5, 1959, in Monroe, Michigan. She was a member of Pleasant Point Church.

Survivors: husband; sons—Jeff, Mannie, and Dewey Beason of Monroe, Michigan, Austin and Paris Beason of Goin; daughters—Mrs. Herbert Keck and Mrs. Frank McBee of Monroe, Michigan; sisters—Mrs. Maggie Simmons of Monroe, Michigan and Mrs. Martha Clark of Middlesboro, Ky; brothers—Lloyd and Willie Lambert of Florida, and Tilmon Lambert of Monroe, Michigan.

Funeral services were held at 10:00 a.m. Sunday at the Pleasant Point Primitive Baptist Church with Rev. Lloyd England and Elder Albert Davis officiating. Pall bearers were grandsons.

ELDER WILLIAM ABERHAM MOYERS

Elder William Aberham Moyers, son of the late John Calvin Moyers and Annie Dossett Moyers, passed away Thursday, January 21, 1960, at 3:20 p.m. He was born September 21, 1888, at Goin, Tennessee. At death he was 71 years and 4 months old. He was married to Lucinda Moyers April 20, 1914. To this union was born 12 children, 8 deceased and 4 living. He is survived by his wife—Lucinda; daughter—Mrs. Nadine Gibby of Knoxville, Tennessee; sons—Earl Ray of Monroe, Michigan, Robert Lee and Kenneth Bruce of Knoxville, Tennessee; sisters—Mrs. Milton Evans of Cumberland Gap, Tennessee and Mrs. Ida Gent of Knoxville, Tennessee; brothers— Oscar of Crosbyton, Texas, Claude and Levi of Monroe, Michigan, Hughie of Knoxville, Tennessee; Ten grandchildren.

He professed faith in Christ at the age of 14. He was united with Pleasant Hill Baptist Church of Speedwell, Tennessee in January, 1931. He was ordained as full minister the 4th Sunday in July, 1931. He lived a faithful and devout christian until death.

He leaves a lot of relatives and friends. Our loss is his eternal gain. Funeral services were at 2 p.m. Sunday, January 24 at Pleasant Hill Baptist Church with Elder Leonard White, Elder Tony Eastridge, and Elder Hugh Brummitt officiating. Interment in the Greasy Hollow Cemetery.

G. M. IRWIN

Brother G. M. Irwin was born January 12, 1879 and died January 29, 1960 at the age of 81. He was married to Florence Ford in 1901. To this union was born 8 children, 2 boys and 6 girls. Three of the girls preceeded him in death. He professed faith in Christ early in life and joined the Methodist Church where he remained a member for several years. In 1953, he joined the Primitive Baptist Church at Davis Chapel and on June 21 of that year he was baptized by Elder Leonard White. The funeral oration was given by Elder Leonard White assisted by Elder H. E. Brummitt and Elder W. M. Sparks. Brother Irwin was much loved by all who knew him. His body was lain to rest in Sunrise Cemetery to await the glorious resurrection of the dead.

7

NORIA ROACH DEWEESE

Noria Roach Deweese, daughter of David Roach, was born January 20, 1897 and died February 21, 1960 at the age of 63. She professed faith in Christ at an early age and joined the church at Davis Chapel where her membership remained until death. Noria was an ideal lady and much loved by all who knew her. She died in the full triumphs of a living faith. She had been away from Davis Chapel Community since the date of her marriage to Mr. Deweese. She was brought back to the old home church for funeral services and burial. The funeral oration was given by Elder Leonard White. Her body now rests in the old church cemetery awaiting the glorious resurrection of the dead.

DELONE DOSSETT

Delone (Pete) Dossett, age 48, Route 2, Corryton, Tennessee passed away September 12, 1959. He was a member of the Kirkwood Primitive Baptist Church, The American Legion Post No. 2, and a Veteran of World War II.

Survivors: Wife, Mrs. Ora White Dossett; Father, John Dossett; sisters— Mrs. Hobert White, Mrs. Eva Gayer both of Kokomo, Indiana, Mrs. K. J. Brantley of Sharps Chapel, Tennessee; brothers—Joseph, Cornelilus, and Vaughn of Kokomo, Indiana and Matthew of Galyon, Ohio.

Funeral services were held at Kirkwood Primitive Baptist Church by Elder Leonard White. Burial in Lynnhurst Cemetery.

MASTON C. DUNN

Maston C. Dunn was born at Speedwell, Tennessee July 13, 1869 and passed away at his home at Corryton, Tennessee on February 26, 1960, at the age of 90 years and 7 months.

He married his first wife, Martha Belle Petree in 1900 and his present wife Mrs. Rhoda Bridges in 1937. Besides his present wife, he is survived by three daughters—Mrs. Virgie Collins, Murphysboro, Illinois, Mrs. Fern Whited and Emma Dunn of Corryton, Tennessee; a son Elmer C. Dunn, Johnson City, Tennessee; three stepsons, six grandchildren, four great grandchildren, one half sister and two half brothers.

Mr. Dunn joined the Primitive Baptist Church at Mossey Springs in 1905 and remained a faithful member until he became a charter member of Rocky Dale Church at Corryton in 1922. He served as clerk of Rocky Dale for 2 years and as deacon until his death.

Mr. Dunn will long be remembered for his service as rural mail carrier and trustee of Union County, his loyalty and service to his present community, his faithfulness to his church, and his deep devotion to his family. His life is an inspiration to all who knew him. His seat is vacant at his church and home but another place has been occupied in that Celestial City.

Funeral services were held at Gentry's Chapel on February 28, 1960 by Elder Leonard White and Elder Hugh Brummitt. Burial was in Lynnhurst Cemetery in Fountain City.

MRS. MARTHA WHITAKER

Mrs. Martha Whitaker, known as Martha Southern, departed this life February 20, 1960 at the age of 86. She professed faith in Christ at an early age and joined the Gibson Station Church where she remained a faithful member until her death. She leaves several friends and cousins to mourn her loss. She was laid to rest in Florida.

8

WILLIAM FRANK ROBINSON

Mr. William Frank Robinson, age 90, formerly of Speedwell passed away at the home of his son Chester in Pennington Gap, Virginia May 19, 1960.

Survivors: sons—Chester of Pennington Gap, Charlie of California, Mannie of Chevrolet, Kentucky, and Oscar of Middlesboro, Kentucky; daughters—Mrs. Josephine Cupp and Mrs. Vesta Treece of Indiana, Mrs. May Wright of Ohio, Mrs. Annie Earls and Miss Eva Robinson of Cumberland Gap, Tennessee.

Funeral services were held at 2:30 p.m. Saturday at Meyers Grove Baptist Church with Reverend Hobert Irwin and Reverend H. M. Sparks officiating. Interment in the Drummonds Cemetery. Pall bearers: George Stanifer, Tommy Stapleton, Luther, Lee, and Clifford Robinson, and Leonard Manning.

MRS. BERNCEY ETTA WELCH

Mrs. Berncey Etta Welch, age 68, passed away in a Knoxville hospital April 12, 1960.

Survivors: husband—M. M. Welch of New Tazewell, Tennessee; daughters—Mrs. Beulah Buchanan, Mrs. Tilda Fortner of New Tazewell, Mrs. Laura Hutchins and Mrs. Ruby Burkhart of Monroe, Michigan, Mrs. Alma Day of Grand Prairie, Texas, Mrs. Bonnie Johnson of Lawton, Oklahoma; son—Lee Roy of Knoxville, Tennessee; 13 grandchildren; sisters—Mrs. A. N. Munsey of New Tazewell and Mrs. Maggie Robertson of Lake City, Florida; brother—Mr. C. H. Drummonds of New Tazewell.

She was a member of the Meyers Grove Primitive Baptist Church where funeral services were held at 10:30 a.m. Thursday with Elder Charlie Meyers and Elder Virgil Simmons officiating. Interment in the Drummonds Cemetery. Pall bearers: Clifford and Hollis Robinson, Odra, Claude, Isom, and Willie Drummonds.

To the dear people of Meyers Grove I would like to take this opportunity to thank you all for the love you showed to my dear sister, Mrs. Berncey Etta Welch, while she was spending her last night at home. It was so hard for us all and Marson and the children. My heart is so heavy, my eyes are full of tears but I know God needed a jewel and sis was it. I know she is a jewel in Heaven and we must go there to see her. Marson don't weep for you will meet her again in the sweet by and by.

Love,
Maggie

MRS. ADELINE CAMPBELL

Mrs. Adeline Campbell, age 88, passed away at her home at Bean Station, Tennessee. She was a member of the Noeton Primitive Baptist Church.

Survivors: four daughters—Mrs. Sallie Helton, Mrs. Pate Atkins, Miss Vbara Campbell, all of Bean Station, Mrs. Laura Wolfenbarger of Knoxville, Tennessee; two sons—John and Will of Bean Station. Funeral services were held at the Noeton Church with Elder John Adkins and Elder Gilbert Adkins officiating. Interment in the Church Cemetery.

9

MRS. SARAH ALICE BRIDGES

Mrs. Sarah Alice Bridges, age 89, passed away December 23, 1959, at her home in Corryton, Tennessee. She professed faith in Christ at an early age and joined the Primitive Baptist Church. She was a member of the Kirkwood Church of Knoxville, Tennessee at the time of her death. She was the widow of John R. Bridges.

Survivors: daughters—Mrs. Tandy Monday, Mrs. A. L. Satterfield, Mrs. Y. L. Gregg, Mrs. J. R. Simpon all of Knoxville, Tennessee and Mrs. A. L. Huber of Akron, Ohio; stepdaughters—Mrs. Phoebe Clark and Mrs. Cordele Crich both of Nashville, Tennessee; sons—E. T. and A. R. Bridges of Knoxville and J. L. of Akron, Ohio; brother—M. M. Weaver of Kankaku, Illinois; 27 grandchildren; 41 great grandchildren.

Funeral services were held at Rose Funeral Home Saturday at 2:00 p.m. by Elder Leonard White and Elder Hugh Brummitt. Interment in the Lynnhurst Cemetery.

SEELY LYNCH FORD

Seely Lynch Ford was born November 30, 1888, and departed this life July 19, 1960, being 71 years 8 months and 19 days old. She professed faith in Christ at an early age and later joined the Pleasant Point Church where she lived a faithful member until death.

She was married to Jasper Hopper January 12, 1911. He preceeded her in death. She was married to G. F. Ford November 10, 1919. To this union was born one son Billy Sunday Ford. Both her husband and son preceeded her in death. She is survived by three stepdaughters—Mrs. Della Carroll of Four Mile, Kentucky, Mrs. Laura Heath of Burchard, Nebraska, Mrs. Mossie Griffith of Hazard, Kentucky; one sister—Mrs. Sherman Russell of Goin, Tennessee; one brother—B M. Lynch of Goin, Tennessee; a host of relatives and friends. "Our loss is Heaven's Gain."

MR. MADISON C. KECK

Mr. Madison C. (Matt) Keck, age 79, of Goin, Tennessee passed away May 25, 1960.

Survivors: wife—Mrs. Mary Jane Keck of Goin; sons— Curtis, Fay, and Russell of Goin, Fred of Miami, Florida; daughters—Mrs. Loallea Robinette of Kingston, Tennessee, Mrs. Cecil Carey of Goin, Mrs. Roberta Carr and Mrs. Hughes Barnes both of New Tazewell, Mrs. Lovetta Crawford of Powells; brothers—Esau, Lee, and Arlis all of Goin; 13 grandchildren, 6 great grandchildren.

He was a retired farmer and prominent citizen of Claiborne County, a member of Pleasant Point Baptist Church, a member of Evening Star Lodge No. 180, F. & A. M. of Tazewell for 58 years, a member of the Tazewell Chapter No. 162 of Royal Arch Mason, former member of the Independent Order of Odd Fellows and Junior Order of American Mechanics, former assistant treasurer of Claiborne County, former member of Claiborne County Board of Education, Doctor of Veterinary Science, and one of the founders of Tazewell Tobacco Markets.

Funeral services were held at 3:00 p.m. Saturday at the Pleasant Point Baptist Church with Elder Leonard White and Elder Johnnie Keck officiating. Interment in the family cemetery. Masons rendered honors at the grave.

10

CHURCHES	COUNTY	PASTORS	CLERKS	CLERK'S POST OFFICE.
Black Fox	Grainger	Elder Albert Davis Elder Geo. Campbell, A.	J. M. Davis	Corryton, Tenn.
Braden's Chapel	Union	Elder J. C. Monday Elder N. . Clawson, asst.	Arvil Braden	Speedwell, Tenn.
Brantley's Chapel	Blount	Elder Clifford Bratley	R. P. Bridges	Maryville, Tenn. Route 8
Cedar Springs	Claiborne	Elder J. C. Monday	John H. Davis	New Tazewell, Tenn.
Davis Chapel	Campbell	Elder Hugh Brummitt Elder Leonard White, A.	Ruth Heatherly Lasie Ellison, asst.	LaFollette, Tenn. LaFollette, Tenn.
Gibson Station	Lee, Virginia	Elder Leonard White Elder Everet Berry, asst.	Roxie Cobb Mossie Cottrell, asst.	Gibson Station, Va. Gibson Station, Va.
Krkwood	Knox	Elder Leonard White Elder R. H. Pettit, asst.	Estelle Petree Myrtle Taylor, asst.	5313 Jacksboro Pk. Fountain City, Tenn. 5311 Jacksboro Pk. Fountain City, Tenn.
Monroe, Michigan	Monroe	Elder Lenvil Meyers	Ditsy Russell	324 Winchester St. Monroe, Michigan
New Hebron	Jefferson	Elder Gilbert Adkins	Ray Mitchell	New Market, Tenn.
Noeton	Grainger	Elder Johnny Adkns Elder Gilbert Adkins, A.	John Oliver Bessie Collins, asst.	Bean Station, Tenn. Morristown, Tenn.
Oak Grove	Union	Elder W. M. Sparks Elder Clifford Brantley, A.	Relle Moore Ruth Shoffner, asst.	Sharps Chapel, Tenn.
Pleasant Hill	Claiborne	Elder Tony Eastridge Elder J. H. Branscomb, A.	William Branscomb Verlin Edwards, asst.	Speedwell, Tenn. Speedwell, Tenn.
Pleasant Point	Claiborne	Elder Tony Eastridge	Austin Beason	Goin, Tenn.
Rocky Dale	Knox	Elder Hugh Brummitt	Avrell Graves Roy Clapp, asst.	Corryton, Tenn. Knoxville, Tenn.

566

1961

MINUTES

of the

One Hundred and Forty-Second

ANNUAL SESSION

of the

POWELLS VALLEY ASSOCIATION

of

PRIMITIVE BAPTISTS

held with

THE CHURCH AT BLACK FOX

Grainger County, Tennessee

AUGUST 18-19-20, 1961

OFFICERS

Elder Albert Davis --- Moderator
Elder Hugh Brummitt -------------------------------- Assistant Moderator
Brother Austin Beason --- Clerk
Brother O. R. Parrot --------------------------------------- Assistant Clerk

The next session will be held with the church at Pleasant Hill in Claiborne County, Tennessee. It will begin on Friday before the third Saturday in August, 1962. Elder George Campbell will preach the Introductory Sermon. Elder Parnick Shelton will be the alternate.

STATISTICAL TABLE

CHURCHES	DELEGATES	Restored	Received by Relationship	Received by Baptism	Received by Letter	Dismissed by Letter	Excluded	Deceased	Total Membership	Visiting Ministers	Printing Minutes	Saturday Meeting	Communion Meeting
Black Fox	Flossie Capps, Jesse Cabbage, Roma Bailey, George Campbell, John Davis, William Thompson, Roy Bailey, Walton Cabbage.	0	0	0	0	0	1	2	88	$0.00	$10.00	2	2, June
Braden's Chapel	J. C. Monday, W. M. Sparks, Henry Comer, Buster Clawson, Lessie Sparks, Winona Sparks.	0	0	12	0	0	0	0	67	0.00	5.00	1	1, July
Brantley's Chapel	Jeff Ellison, Leila Ellison, Von Beason, Everett Brantley, Mildred Brantley, Ellis Evans, Lottie Evans, Clifford Brantley, Barsha Brantley.	0	3	1	2	0	0	0	79	5.00	5.00	2	2, July
Cedar Springs	J. L. Drummonds, Velta Munsey, Pearlie Holt.	0	0	0	0	0	0	1	60	0.00	7.00	4	4, June
Davis Chapel	Leonard White, Cordelia Lynch, O. R. Parott, Mamie Parott, Millie McCarty.	0	3	5	0	0	1	2	159	5.00	5.00	3	3, June
Gibson Station	Mr. and Mrs. Franklin Jones, Lucille Ball, Mossie Cottrell.	0	4	3	2	0	0	2	96	4.00	4.00	1	1, Aug.
Kirkwood	Hugh Brummitt, Ruby Brummitt	1	4	4	0	1	1	5	110	10.00	10.00	Every Sun.	Last April
Monroe, Michigan	John Drummonds, Roxie Drummonds.	0	3	1	0	0	0	0	14	0.00	2.00	3	3, July
New Hebron	Gilbert Adkins	0	0	1	0	0	0	0	19	0.00	1.00	4	4, May & Sept.
Noeton	Johnny Adkins, Gilbert Adkins, Jake Overley, Charlie Collins.	0	1	0	0	0	0	0	38	0.00	3.00	3	3, May
Oak Grove	George Shoffner, Tony Eastridge, Francis Eastridge, Lillie Shoffner.	0	0	9	0	2	0	5	300	3.00	7.00	1	1, May
Pleasant Hill	James H. Branscomb, Helen Ruth Branscomb, Albert Davis, Audrey Davis, Lucinda Moyers, Sarah Branscomb.	0	1	1	0	1	0	2	88	0.00	10.00	4	4, June
Pleasant Point	George Williams, Allie Williams, Claude Rosson, Doris Rosson, Everett Berry, Trula Berry, Parnick Shelton, Wilma Shelton.	0	1	0	0	0	1	1	130	0.00	10.00	1	1, July
Rocky Dale	Grace Graves.	0	1	8	0	1	1	0	99	5.00	5.00	2	2, May

FRIDAY'S PROCEEDINGS

First—According to previous arrangements the Association met pursuant to adjournment.

Second—After singing, Elder Albert Davis spoke from the 18th Chapter of St. Matthew. Prayer was by Elder George Campbell. After Elder Leonard White spoke some complimenary words, Elder Clifford Brantley spoke from 2nd Kings—Chapter 18 Verse 29. We were dismissed by Elder Henry Comer.

Third—After intermission, there was more singing. Prayer was by Elder Thomas of Hiwassee.

Fourth—The Association was called to order by Elder Albert Davis.

Fifth—The Moderator called for letters from sister churches.

Sixth—On motion all said letters were received and the delegates were welcomed to seats by the Moderator.

Seventh—A call was made for members who were not delegates. One was received, James Edwards of Pleasant Hill.

Eighth—A call was made for letters from Corresponding Associations. One was received from New Bethlem. In absence of a letter, Hiwassee was received by delegation.

Nineth—the letter was read from New Bethlem and received, Hiwassee delegates were welcomed to seats. They were Claude Thomas, Roy Thomas, Henry Chamberlain, Mattie Thomas, Ella Fields, Mayme Thomas, Hazel Thomas, and Estie Chamberlain.

Tenth—On motion the second Elder Albert Davis was re-elected Moderator. Elder Hugh Brummitt was elected Assistant Moderator.

Eleventh—On motion the second Brother Austin Beason was re-elected Clerk. Brother O. R. Parrot was re-elected Associate Clerk.

Twelfth—On motion the moderator appointed the following committees:
1. Arrangements—Jeff M. Ellison, W. M. Sparks, Parnick Shelton.
2. Preaching—Jim Edwards, Everett Brantley, Walton Cabbage.
3. Correspondence—Everett Berry, Johnny Adkins, Henry Comer.
4. Request—J. C. Monday, Bill Munsey, J L. Drummonds.
5. Finance—Clifford Brantley, George Shoffner, Von Beason.

Thirteenth—On motion we adjourned until 10:00 a.m. on Saturday August 19, 1961. We were dismissed by Elder Johnny Adkins.

SATURDAY'S PROCEEDINGS

First—After singing, Elder Hugh Brummitt spoke from the 12th Chapter of Ecclesiastes. Prayer was by Elder Tony Eastridge.

Second—There was a call for letters that failed to get in Friday. None were received.

Third—A call was made for the report of the Committee on Arrangements.

We, the Committee on Arrangements, beg leave to submit the following report:

1. Call the roll
2. Call for the report of the Committee on Request
3. Call for the report of the Committee on Preaching
4. Call for the report of the Committee on Correspondence
5. Call for the report of the Committee on Finance

When and where shall our next Association be held? Who shall preach the Introductory Sermon? Who shall be his alternate? How many copies or the Minutes shall we have printed. Who shall superintend the printing and distribution of them? What shall be allowed for his services?

Respectfully submitted,
JEFF ELLISON
W. M. SPARKS
PARNICK SHELTON

Fourth—On motion the report was received and the Committee discharged.

Fifth—The roll was called and the names of the absentees erased.

Sixth—A call was made for the report of the Committee on Preaching.

We the Committee on Preaching beg leave to submit the following report:

1. Friday night at the Church—Elder Henry Comer and Elder Claude Thomas.

2. Friday night at Brantley's Chapel—Elder Hugh Brummitt and Elder Everett Berry

3. Saturday morning at the Church—Elder J. C. Monday and Elder Johnny Adkins.

4. Saturday night at the church—Elder George Campbell and Elder Parnick Shelton.

5. Saturday night at Brantley's Chapel—Elder Tony Eastridge.
6. Sunday at the Church — Elder Everett Berry and Elder Leonard White.

The Moderator is to close.

Respectfully submitted,
JIM EDWARDS
EVERETT BRANTLEY
WALTON CABBAGE

Secenth—On motion the report was received and committee discharged.
Eighth—A call was made for the report of the Committee on Correspondence.

We, the Committee on Correspondence, beg leave to submit the following report:
We shall keep up our correspondence with the Hiwassee and New Bethlem Associations.

Respectfully submitted,
EVERETT BERRY
JOHNNY ADKINS
HENRY COMER

Ninth—On motion the report was received and the committee discharged
Tenth—A call was made for the report of the Committee on Request.
We, the Committee on Request, beg leave to submit the following report:
We shall publish all the obituaries that the churches furnish. Our next Association will be held with the Church at Pleasant Hill in Claiborne County, Tennessee. It will begin on Friday before the third Saturday in August, 1962, and continue the two following days.

Respectfully submitted,
J. C. MONDAY
BILL MUNSEY
J. L. DRUMMONDS

2

Eleventh—on motion the report was received and the committee discharged.

Twelfth—A call was made for the report of the Committee on Finance. We, the Committee on Finance, beg leave to submit the following report:

CHURCH	PRINTING MINUTES	VISITING MINISTERS
Black Fox	$10.00	$ 0.00
Braden's Chapel	5.00	0.00
Brantley's Chapel	5.00	5.00
Cedar Springs	7.00	0.00
Davis Chapel	5.00	5.00
Gibson Station	4 00	4.00
Kirkwood	10.00	10.00
Monroe, Michigan	2.00	0.00
New Hebron	1.00	0.00
Noeton	3 00	0.00
Oak Grove	7.00	3.00
Pleasant Hill	10.00	0 00
Pleasant Point	10.00	0.00
Rocky Dale	5 00	5.00
Total Received	$84.00	$32.00
Balance carried over from 1960		92.00
Complete Total		$208.00
Total Expense		115.00
Balance in Treasury		$ 93.00

Respectfully submitted,

CLIFFORD BRANTLEY
GEORGE SHOFFNER
VON BEASON

Thirteenth—On motion the report was received and the committee discharged.

Fourteenth—On motion we passed to have 1,000 copies of the Minutes printed, and the clerk will superintend the printing and distribution of them He is to be allowed $25.00 for his services.

Fifteenth—On motion the next annual session is to be held at Pleasant Hill Church in Claiborne County, Tennessee. It is to begin on Friday before the third Saturday in August, 1962, and continue the two following days.

Sixteenth—On motion Elder George Campbell was selected to preach the Introductory Sermon. Elder Parnick Shelton will be his alternate.

Seventeenth—On motion we agreed to send Elder Everett Berry and Elder J. C. Monday to the Hiwassee Association, and Elder W. M. Sparks and Elder Johnny Adkins to the New Bethlehem Association.

Eighteenth—On motion the clerk will write each a Letter of Correspondence.

Nineteen—On motion we extended to the old Church and the people of the surrounding community our sincere appreciation for the kindness and generous hospitality shown us throughout the Association at the above stated place and date.

Twentieth—There was a move and second that we adjourn our business until 10:30 a.m. at the above stated place and date. We were dismissed by Elder Noble Lee Clawson.

3

Elder Albert Davs, Moderator
Speedwell, Tennessee
Elder Hugh Brummit,
Assisant Moderator
1329 Brown Avenue
Knoxville, Tennessee
Austin Beason, Clerk
Goin, Tennessee
O. R. Parrot, Assistant Clerk
LaFollette, Tennessee

Twenty-first— After a ten m i n u t e intermission, the Association re-assembled. After singing there was prayer by Mrs. T G. Brantley. Elder J. C. Monday spoke from the first chapter 18th verse of Isaiah and also from the 5th chapter of St. Mark. "Saying come now let us reason togethehr." He was followed by Elder Johnny Adkins who spoke from the same subject. We were dismissed by Brother Claude Rosson.

SUNDAY'S PROCEEDINGS

On Sunday a large crowd gathered at the altar. There was singing with the Moderator presiding. Prayer was by Elder James H. Branscomb. Elder Everett Berry spoke from Isaiah—55th Chapter, 11th Verse. He was followed by Elder Leonard White who spoke from Hebrews—1st Chapter and 8th Verse. The closing was by the Moderator. Singing followed. We were dismissed by Brother Ellis Evans.

LICENTIATES

Jim Oliver .... Bean Station, Tennessee
George Sholfner .... Sharps Chapel, Tennessee
Claude Rosson .... Goin, Tennessee
Odell Carpenter .... Maryville, Tennessee

MINISTERS

Elder Leonard White .... LaFollette, Tennessee
Phone 562 5667
Elder R. H. Pettit .... 107 Jacksboro Pike, Fountain City, Tennessee
Phone 689 5581
Elder W. M. Sparks .... Speedwell, Tennessee
Phone 562 7997
Elder Henry Comer .... Poute 4, LaFollette, Tennessee
Phone 562 3952
Elder Joe Irwin .... Gibson Station, Virginia
Elder Dewey Ellison .... Sharps Chapel, Tennessee
Elder Albert Davis .... Speedwell, Tennessee
Phone 3667
Elder Lenvil Meyers .... 512 E Elm St., Monroe, Michigan
Elder T. I. Eastridge .... Route 2, Louisville, Tennessee
Phone 98 3108
Elder Hugh Brummitt .... 1329 Brown Ave., Knoxville, Tennessee
Elder Gilbert Adkins .... Bean Station, Tennessee
Phone 525 3583
Elder George Campbell .... Blaine, Tennessee
Elder J. H. Branscomb .... Speedwell, Tennessee
Elder Johnnie Adkins .... Bean Station, Tennessee
Elder Everett Berry .... Fountain City, Tennessee
Phone 922 4241

4

Elder J. C. Monday ------------------------------- Speedwel', Tennessee
Elder Noble Lee Clawson -------------------------- Speedwell, Tennessee
Elder Clifford Brantley ------------------------- Maryville, Tennessee
                                                  Phone 982 3735
Elder Parnick Shelton ------------------------- Corryton, Tennessee
                                                  Phone 689 6183
Elder Roy Oliver -------------------------------- Bean Station, Tennessee
Elder R. B. Brantley ------------ 200 Hermitage Road, Knoxville, Tennessee
                                                  Phone 577 8362

CORRESPONDING LETTER

We, the Powells Valley Association of the Primitive Baptist, now in session at Black Fox Church in Grainger County, Tennessee on August 18, 19, 20, 1961, send greetings to the Hiwassee and New Bethlem Associations with whom we correspond. Very Dear Brothers and Sisters, we desire to keep our long correspondence with you. We have chosen these our beloved Elders to bear this episte of love to you. Our messengers to the Hiwassee Association are Elder Everett Berry and Elder J. C. Monday. Our messengers to the New Bethlem Association are Elder W M. Sparks and Elder Johnny Adkins. Having seated all your delegales we heartily welcome more next year when we convene with the Church at Pleasant Hill in Claiborne County, Tennessee. We will begin on Friday before the third Saturday in August, 1962.

OBITUARIES

EMMA FLORENCE RUSSELL

S'ster Emma Florence Russell was born March 5, 1871 and passed away June 10, 1961, being 90 years, 3 months, and 4 days old. She was united with Pleasant Hill Primitive Baptist Church some years ago. She lived a member until God called her away. She was united in marriage to Jesse Russell at an early age and to this union was born 16 children; 10 of whom still are surv vors: Lottie Ellison, Nolia Harrison, Fred Russell, Bill Russell, and Harriet Brewer all of Speedwell, Tennessee; Charlie Russell of LaFollette; Claude Russell of Cumberland Gap; M a l i n d a Owens of Ashland, Kentucky; Annette Ellison and Frank Russell of Michi·gan. She has two sisters: Matilda Lambert ad Maggie Easterly; one brother—J'm Ausmus; one half sister—Gillie Brantley; one half brother—

6

573

Conley Ausmus; 24 grandchildren; 35 great grandchildren; some great great grandchildren; and a host of relatives and friends "Gone To Rest— Our Loss Is Heaven's Gain." —Written by the Children.

EDGAR McBEE

Brother Edgar McBee was born September 9, 1880 and departed this life July 1, 1961. He was a faithful member of the Pleasant Hill Baptist Church at the time of death. He leaves to mourn his passing his wife Lussie Pierce and a host of relatives and friends. Our church has suffered a great loss as well as the family has. We all feel that—"Our Loss Is Heaven's Gain." —Written by the Famiy.

CLYDE ELLISON

Clyde Ellison, born January 3, 1923, died suddenly at his home July 12, 1961 at 11 p.m. He leaves to mourn his loss his wife—Mrs. Mary Dyke Ellison, one son—Gary Lynn, his parents—Mr. and Mrs. Dewey Ellison of Sharps Chapel, grandparents—Mr. and Mrs W. H. Berry of Speedwell. He professed faith in Christ at an early age and joined the church at Oak Grove where he remained a faithful member. He was a teacher in Union County for 15 years. He was a charter member of Oak Grove Sunday School and the teacher of class number 3. He was dearly loved by all who knew him. "Our Loss Is His Eternal Gain."

"We cannot say—
We will not say—
That he is dead.
He's Just away."
Written by his wife and son.

MAGGIE LEONA LARMER

Maggie Leona Larmer was born March 6, 1930, and departed this life April 23, 1960, being 30 years, 1 month and 17 days old. She leaves to mourn her passing: Two sisters Lizzie Bailey of Powder Springs, Mary Jones of Washburn, Five brothers Oak Larmer of Liberty Hill, Ruben Larmer, Garfield Larmer, Austin Larmer all of Powder Springs, Odra Larmer of Straw Plains. She professed faith in Christ at an early age, but nevr did join any church. She left a testimony to brighten her crossing. She often talked of her passing. She said the way was clear and she had nothing to fear. She was loved by all who knew her. We all loved her, but God loved her best God needed a jewel to decorate Heaven and Maggie was His precious jewel. While we are made sad, Heaven was made glad. Our lost is her eternal gain. Written by brother Oak Larmer, in rememberance of a loving sister Maggie Leona Larmer.

JOHN LIFORD

Mr. John Liford was born February 16, 1880, and died December 22, 1960. He professed faith in Christ at an early age. Later joined Black Fox Prim'tive Baptist Church where he was elected a deacon and remained a member until death. He left to mourn his loss 5 children, three daughters, Mrs. Roy Bailey of Liberty Hill, Mrs. James Munsey and Mrs. Bruce Carver of Powder Springs, two sons Fred Liford of Greenback, Claude Liford of Liberty Hill, 18 grandchildren. His wife Hila Yadon Liford proceeded him in death 8 years ago. Funeral services were held at Black Fox Bap-

7

574

tist Church with interment in Cabbage Cemetery with Rev. Clarence Janeway and Rev. Loy Shelton officiating

Sleep on Dear Father till Resurrection morn.
We're sure he's gone to rest
We loved him, oh, so dearly
But Jesus loved him best
We love to walk the pathways
His dear feet have trod
Because those paths will lead us all home
Around the white throne.

Written by daughter & Grand-daughter.

MARY KATHERN MINCEY

Mary Kathern Mincey was born July 5, 1881, and passed away Sunday, October 2, 1960. She had been a member of Black Fox Baptist Church for 50 years. Survivors included son, Frank Mincey, daughters, Mrs. Roy Jones, Mrs. Percy Lay, Mrs. Lester Thomas, step-sons, Robert and Amos Mincey, step-daughters, Mrs. Dan Brannen, 18 grandchildren, 11 great-grandchildren. Brother, Alex Nicely, sisters, Mrs. Lydia Mincey, Mrs. Carrie Larmer, Mrs. Cordelia Muncey, Mrs. Orlene Collins, Mrs. Frances Rosenbalm, and Mrs. Etta Rosenbalm. She was a wonderful Mother and Grandmother. She has gone to a better home, and will never be forgotten by her loved ones and many friends.

RUBY SHARP BRIDGES

Mrs. Ruby Sharp Wood Bridges was born January 19, 1901 and passed away November 18, 1960. She was the daughter of the late Brice M. and Emma Browning Sharp. She was formerly connected with the Fort Sanders Presbyterian Hospital and later with the Baptist Hospital.

She professed faith in Christ at an early age and was a member of the Kirkwood Primitive Baptist Church.

Survivors, husband, Lloyd Bridges of Macedonia, Ohio; one daughter, Mrs. Winifred Cantrell of Knoxville, Tennessee; two sons, Jack M. Wood of Witchita, Kansas and Roy E. Wood of Jacksonville, Florida; eight grandchildren.

Services were held at Rose Funeral Home with Elder Leonard White officiating. Interment in Lynnhurst Cemetery.

MANNA DILLO SHARP

Manna Dillo Sharp was born April 15, 1906 and passed away June 11, 1961. He was the son of the late James W. and Sarah Hopper Sharp.

He was a member of the Kirkwood Primitive Baptist Church.

Survivors, wife, Mrs. Alva Satterfield Sharp; two daughters, Mrs. E. G. Cheek and Mrs. Douglas Shoffner, both of Knoxville, Tennessee; two grandchildren; three sisters, Mrs. Linda Sharp, Mrs. R. O. Taylor and Mrs. S. B. Snodderly, all of Knoxville; three brothers, R. E., B. E. and L. O. Sharp of Knoxville.

Funeral services were held at Gentry's Chapel on June 13, 1961 by Elder Leonard White. Burial was in Lynnhurst Cemetery.

VESTA DRUMMONDS FREEMAN

Mrs. Vesta Drummonds Freeman, age 89, passed away August 22, 1960 at her home, 5336 North Broadway, Fountain City, Tennessee. She was a member of Myers Grove Baptist Church. Survivors: daughter—Mrs. J. M. Inklebarger, Fountain City; granddaughters—Mrs. Charles Walker, Miami,

8

575

Florida, and Mrs. Joe Haynes, Mountain City; grandson—T. J. Inklebarger, Atlanta, Georgia; 8 great-grandchildren; sister—Mrs. Scott DeBusk, Tampa, Florida. Services were at Gentry's Chapel with Dr. Charles S. Bond officiating. Interment in Lynnhurst cemetery. Pallbearers: nephews—Wade Drummonds,, James DeBusk, Anderson Munsey, Archie L. Neal, Elmer Underwood, and Isaac Neal.

SARAH SHOFFNER

Mrs. Sarah Shoffner, age 84, passed away at the home of her daughter Mrs. John Atkinson of Monroe, Michigan June 5, 1961. She leaves to mourn her passing: three sons—Paris and Rufus of Monroe, Michigan, Dewey of St. Clair Shores, Michigan; four daughters—Mrs. Clifford Brown, Middlesboro, Kentucky, Mrs. Joe Cottrell of Harrogate, Tennessee, Mrs. Promer Sandifer and Mrs. John Atkinson of Monroe, Michigan; step-son—George Shoffner of Middlesboro, Kentucky; step-daughters—Mrs. Oscar Cadle and Mrs. James Ramsey of Harrogate; four brothers—Harry Braden of Corryton, Tennessee, Mack Braden of Sharps Chapel, Tennessee, Isaac and Charlie Braden of Monroe, Michigan; 13 grandchildren; 24 great-grand-children. She was a member of Gibson Station Primitive Baptist Church where funeral services were held with Elder Leonard White and Elder Everett Berry officiating. Interment in the Shoffner cemetery. "Sleep on dear mother and take your rest. We all loved you but God loved you best. Our loss is his eternal gain."

ELDER CHARLIE W. REDMOND

Elder Charlie W. Redmond, age 79, died Tuesday, January 31, 1961, at the Claiborne County Hospital. Survivors: wife—Mary of Shawanee; daughter—Millie Thompson of Shawanee; two grandchildren; one great-grandchild; half sister— Rebecca Helton of Barbourville, Kentucky; seven step children. Funeral services were held at the Gibson Station Primitive Baptist Church with Elder Leonard White, Elder Everett Berry, and Elder Albert Davis officiating. Interment in the Southern Cemetery. Uncle Charlie is missed by the churches and friends.

ANNA VANDELIE SOWDER COLLINS

Anna Vandelie Sowder Collins was born July 4, 1878 and departed this life February 15, 1961 being 82 years, 7 months, and 11 days old. She professed faith in Christ and joined the Big Barren Primitive Baptist Church. She was married to Jacob Collins in 1894 and to this union was born nine children: four sons and five daughters. One son, Walter, preceeded her in death. She is survived by three sons—Esco, Arlis, and Dewey; five daughters—Mrs. Francie Rosson, Mrs. Allie Williams, Mrs. Lennie Keck, Rachel and Eva Collins all of Goin, Tennessee; 16 grandchildren; 31 great-grandchildren; 4 great-great-grandchildren; two brothers—Marvil Sowder of Goin and Tilmon Sowder of Knoxville; 5 sisters—Mrs. Mary Haley of Middlesboro, Kentucky, Mrs. Dessie Hopper of Cumberland Gap, Tennessee, Mrs. Cedilla Keck of Monroe, Michigan, Hassie and Carie Sowder of Knoxville, Tennessee; many relatives and friends. "Our Loss Is Heaven's Gain "

"A loved one from us is gone.
A voice we loved is stilled—
A place is vacant in our home—
A place that can't be filled."

Elder Alonzo Wagoner, Elder Leonard White, and Elder Tony Eastridge officiated. Interment was in Pleasant Point Cemetery.

9

ELDER JOHN F KECK

Elder John F. Keck, age 74 passed away at his home near ~~oin~~, December 8, 1960. Survivors: wife—Minnie Watson Keck of ~~oin~~; sons—Norris and Forres of Goin, Ross of Waterville, Ohio; daughter—Mrs. H. C. Weiger of Chicago, Illinois; six grandchildren; brother—Haskel Keck of Crossville; sister—Mrs. F. P. Cox of Henderson, Texas. Elder Keck was a well known and beloved minister of the Baptist Church. He served as pastor of many churches in Claiborne and surrounding counties of some 35 years. Funeral services were held at the Pleasant Point Church with Elder Leonard White, Elder Virgil Simmons, and Elder Andy Vance officiating. Interment in the Drummonds Cemetery. Pallbearers: Fay Keck, Russell Keck, Vaughn Widner, White Collins, Woodrow Keck, and Claude Rosson.

ZINIE KIVETT SHOFFNER

Mrs. Zinie Kivett Shoffner age 71 died suddenly at her home in Sharps Chapel, Tennessee at 11:00 p.m , Monday, October 31, 1960. She is survived by: husband— Claude; daughter—Mrs. Flora Shoffner of Sharps Chapel; sons—Deward Divett of Maryville, Carlos Kivett of Knoxville, James Kivett of Toledo, Ohio, Richard Kivett of Sharps Chapel; Sisters—Mrs. Flossie Miller of Maynardville, Mrs. Nettie Cadle of Sevierville, Mrs. Ora Daniels of Greenback; brother—Claude Weaver of Byron, Minnesota; 19 grandchildren; one great-grandchild. She joined the Mossie Springs Primitive Bap'ist Church where she remained a faithful member until the church was disbanded. She then joined the Church at Oak Grove where she remained a member until her death. Funeral services were held at Oak Grove with Elder Leonard White and Elder Bill Sparks officiating. Interment in the church cemetery.

ARTICLES OF FAITH

Article 1. We believe in only one true living God, as He is revealed to us in the Holy Scriptures—Father, Son and Holy Ghost.

Article 2. We believe that the Scriptures of the old and new Testaments are the words of God and the only rule of all-saving knowledge and obedience.

Article 3. We believe in the doctrine of election according to the foreknowledge of God.

Article 4. We believe in the doctrine of original sin.

Article 5. We believe in man's importency to rescue himself from the fallen state he is in by his own will or ability.

Article 6. We believe that sinners are justified in the sight of God only by the imputed righteousness of Jesus Christ.

Article 7. We believe the elect, according to the foreknowledge of God will be called, converted, regenerated and sanctified by the Holy Spirit.

Article 8. We believe the saints will preserve and never fall finally away.

Article 9. We believe that baptism, the Lord's Supper, and feet washing are ordinances of Jesus Christ, and that true believers are the only subject of these ordinances, and that the true mode of baptism is by immersion.

Article 10. We believe in the Resurrection of the dead and the General Judgement.

Article 11. We believe that the punishment of the wicked will be everlasting and that the joys of the righteous will be eternal.

Article 12. We believe that no minister has the right to administer the ordinances, except those who have been regularly baptized and called of God, and come under the imposition of hands of the Presbytery.

10

CHURCHES	COUNTY	PASTORS	CLERKS	CLERK'S POST OFFICE
Black Fox	Grainger	Elder Albert Davis Elder Geo. Campbell, A.	Bennie Capps Flossie Capps	Liberty Hill, Tenn. Liberty Hill, Tenn.
Braden's Chapel	Union	Elder J. C. Monday Elder N. L. Clawson, A.	Arvil Braden	Speedwell, Tenn.
Brantley's Chapel	Blount	Elder Clifford Brantley	Rina Johnson Rina Johnson, Jr., asst	Eagleton Village, Maryville, Tenn. Maryville, Tenn.
Cedar Springs	Claiborne	Elder J. C. Monday	Pearlie Holt	New Tazewell, Tenn.
Davis Chapel	Campbell	Elder Hugh Brummitt Elder Leonard White, A.	Ruth Heatherly Lassie Ellison, asst.	LaFollette, Tenn. LaFollette, Tenn.
Gibson Station	Lee, Virginia	Elder Leonard White Elder Everett Berry, asst.	Roxie Cobb Mossie Cottrell, asst.	Gibson Station, Va. Gibson Station, Va.
Kirkwood	Knox	Elder Leonard White Elder R. H. Pettit, asst.	Estelle Petree Sharp Myrtle Taylor, asst.	5313 Jacksboro Pk., Fountain City, Tenn. 5311 Jacksboro Pk. Fountain City, Tenn.
Monroe, Michigan	Monroe	Elder Lenvil Meyers	Ditsy Russell	324 Winchester St. Monroe, Michigan
New Hebron	Jefferson	Elder Gilbert Adkins	Ray Mitchell	New Market, Tenn.
Noeton	Grainger	Elder Gilbert Adkins	John Oliver Bessie Collins, asst	Bean Station, Tenn. Morristown, Tenn.
Oak Grove	Union	Elder W. M. Sparks Elder Clifford Brantley, a.	Belle Moore Ruth Shoffner, asst.	Sharps Chapel, Tenn. Sharps Chapel, Tenn.
Pleasant Hill	Claiborne	Elder Tony Eastridge Elder J. H. Branscomb, A.	William Branscomb Verlin Edwards, asst.	Speedwell, Tenn. Speedwell, Tenn.
Pleasant Point	Claiborne	Elder Tony Eastridge	Austin Beason	Goin, Tenn.
Rocky Dale	Knox	Elder Hugh Brummitt Elder Parnick Shelton, a.	Arvell Graves Roy Clapp, asst.	Corryton, Tenn. Knoxville, Tenn.

578

1962

MINUTES

of the

One Hundred and Forty-Third

ANNUAL SESSION

of the

POWELLS VALLEY ASSOCIATION

of

PRIMITIVE BAPTISTS

held with

THE CHURCH AT PLEASANT HILL

Claiborne County, Tennessee

AUGUST 17-18-19, 1962

OFFICERS

Elder Albert Davis .... Moderator
Elder Hugh Brummitt .... Assistant Moderator
Brother Austin Beason .... Clerk
Brother O. R. Parrot .... Assistant Clerk

The next session will be held with the church at Gibson Station in Lee County, Virginia. It will begin on Friday before the third Saturday in August, 1963. Elder Parnick Shelton will preach the Introductory Sermon. Elder James H. Branscomb will be the alternate.

CHURCHES	DELEGATES	Restored	Received by Relationship	Received by Baptism	Received by Letter	Dismissed by Letter	Excluded	Deceased	Total Membership	Visiting Ministers	Printing Minutes	Saturday Meeting	Communion Meeting
Black Fox	Flossie Capps, Roma Bailey, George Campbell, John Davis, Roy Bailey, W-lton Cabbage, Bill Muncey, Bennie Capps.	0	0	0	0	0	0	0	88	$ 0.00	$10.00	2	2, June
Braden's Chapel	J. C. Monday, W. M. Sparks, Henry Comer N. L. Clawson.	0	0	0	0	0	0	0	67	0.00	5.00	1	1, July
Brantley's Chapel	Von Beeson, Everett Brantley, Mildred Brantley, Corum Berry, Twila Berry, Rina Johnson, Plumer McBee.	0	2	8	2	1	3	1	84	0.00	10.00	2	2, July
Cedar Springs	J. L. Drummonds, Velta Muncey, Pearlie Holt, Clifford Robertson, Ida Robertson, Frankie Haze, Mary Treece.	0	0	2	4	0	0	0	58	0.00	4.00	4	4, May
Davis Chapel	Leonard White, Cordelia Lynch, O. R. Parott, Mamie Parott, Naomi White, Lassie Ellison.	0	0	1	0	0	1	1	151	4.00	4.00	3	3, June
Gibson Station	Mr. and Mrs. Franklin Jones, Lucille Ball, Mossie Cottrell, Mollie Irwin, Henry Hoskins.	1	0	1	0	2	0	0	89	4.00	4.00	1	1, Aug.
Kirkwood	Hugh Brummitt, Ruby Brummitt, M. A. Norton, Lucy Norton, Walter Lyons Callie Lyons.	0	1	0	0	0	0	0	109	10.00	10.00	Every Sun.	Last April
Monroe, Michigan	John Drummonds, Roxie Drummonds, Lenvil Meyers, Mr. and Mrs. Millard Thompson.	0	1	0	0	0	0	0	14	0.00	5.00	3	3, July
New Hebron	Gilbert Atkins, Roy Mitchell.	0	0	0	0	0	0	0	25	0.00	1.00	4	4, May & Sept.
Noeton	Johnny Atkins, Gilbert Atkins, Jake Overley.	0	0	0	0	0	0	0	38	0.00	3.00	3	3, May
Oak Grove	George Shoffner, Tony Eastridge, Francis Eastridge, Lillie Shoffner, Mr and Mrs. Alfred Relford, Veda Cole.	0	3	1	0	0	0	1	304	0.00	9.00	1	1, May
Pleasant Hill	James H. Branscomb, Helen R. Branscomb, Albert Davis, Audrey Davis, Lucinda Meyers, Bud Branscomb, Ohian Edwards Lottie Berry.	0	0	0	0	0	0	1	87	4.00	5.00	4	4, June
Pleasant Point	Claude Rosson Doris Rosson.	0	0	0	0	0	0	2	128	0.00	10.00	1	1, July
Rocky Dale	Everett Berry, Trula Berry, Patrick Shelton, Wilma Shelton, Elmer Graves.	0	0	1	0	1	0	2	97	5.00	5.00	2	2, May

First—According to previous arrangements the Association met pursuant to adjournment.

Second—After singing, Elder Albert Davis read the 133rd Chapter of Psalms. Prayer was by Elder Thomas of Hiwassee. Elder George Campbell spoke from the 1st Chapter of the Epistle of John. After singing, we were dismissed by Elder Johnnie Atkins.

Third—After intermission there was more singing. Prayer was by Elder Lenvil Meyers and Elder Leamon Branscum of New Bethlem.

Fourth—The Association was called to order by Elder Albert Davis.

Fifth—The Moderator called for letters from sister churches.

Sixth—On motion all said letters except one were received and the delegates were welcomed to seats by the Moderator.

Seventh—A call was made for members who were not delegates. None were received.

Eighth—A call was made for letters from Corresponding Associations. Two were received—one from New Bethlem and one from Hiwassee.

Ninth—The letter from New Bethlem was read and received. Their delegates were welcomed to seats with us. They were Elder Leamon Branscum and wife, Elder Jim Hublin, Elder H. C. Taylor and wife, Elder Carl McCarty and wife, Dave Phelps and wife, Sylvan Gilbert and wife. The letter from Hiwassee was read and received. Their delegates were welcomed to seats with us. They were Elder John Russell, Elder Henry Vonn, Elder Claude Thomas, and Sister Mrs. Ben Fields.

Tenth—On motion and second Elder Albert Davis was re-elected Modera-. tor. Elder Hugh Brummitt was elected Assistant Moderator.

Eleventh—On motion and second Brother Austin Beason was re-elected Clerk. Brother O. R. Parrot was re-elected Assistant Clerk.

Twelfth—On motion the Moderator appointed the following committees:
1. Arrangements—John Davis, Plumer McBee, Elmer Graves.
2. Preaching—J. L. Drummonds, Bud Branscomb, Vaughn Beason.
3. Correspondence—Elder George Campbell, Elder Everett Berry, Elder Clifford Brantley.
4. Request—Elder Henry Comer, Johnnie Davis, Walter Lyons.
5. Finance—Elder James H. Branscomb, Elder N. L. Clawson, Elder Tony Eastridge.

Thirteenth—On motion we adjourned until 10:00 a.m. on Saturday, August 18, 1962. We were dismissed by Elder W. M. Sparks.

SATURDAY'S PROCEEDINGS

First—After singing Elder Hugh Brummitt spoke from the 13th Chapter of First Corinthians. Prayer was by Elder W. M. Sparks.

Second—There was a call for letters that failed to get in Friday. One was received from Gibson Station. The delegates were welcomed to seats by the Moderator.

Third—A call was made for the report of the Committee on Arrangements.

We, the Committee on Arrangements, beg leave to submit the following report:
1. Call the roll.
2. Call for the report of the Committee on Request.
3. Call for the report of the Committee on Preaching.
4. Call for the report of the Committee on Correspondence.
5. Call for the report of the Committee on Finance.

When and where shall our next Association be held? Who shall preach the Introductory Sermon? Who shall be his alternate? How many copies of the Minutes shall we have printed? Who shall superintend the printing and distribution of them? What shall be allowed for his services?

Respectfully submitted,
PLUMER MCBEE
ELMER GRAVES
JOHN L. DAVIS

Fourth—On motion the report was received and the Committee discharged.

Fifth—The roll was called and the names of the absentees erased.

Sixth—A call was made for the report of the Committee on Preaching.

We the Committee on Preaching beg leave to submit the following report:
1. Friday night at the Church—Elder Carl McCarty and Elder Parnick Shelton.

2. Saturday morning at the Church—Elder Clifford Brantley and Elder Everett Berry.

3. Saturday night at the Church—Elder Claude Thomas and Elder J. H. Branscomb.

4. Saturday night at Davis Chapel—Elder Tony Eastridge and Elder Everett Berry.

5. Sunday morning at the Church—Elder J. H. Branscomb and Elder Lenvil Meyers.

The Moderator is to close.

Respectfully submitted,
BUD BRANSCOMB
J. L. DRUMMONDS
VAUGHN BEASON

Seventh—On motion the report was received and the Committee discharged.

Eighth—A call was made for the report of the Committee on Correspondence.

We, the Committee on Correspondence, beg leave to submit the following report:

We shall keep up our correspondence with the Hiwassee and New Bethlem Associations.

Respectfully submitted,
ELDER EVERETT BERRY
ELDER CLIFFORD BRANTLEY
ELDER GEORGE CAMPBELL

Ninth—On motion the report was received and the Committee discharged.

Tenth—A call was made for the report of the Committee on Request.

We, the Committee on Request, beg leave to submit the following report:

We shall publish all the obituaries that the churches furnish. Our next Association will be held with the Church at Gibson Station in Lee County, Virginia. It will begin on Friday before the third Saturday in August, 1963, and continue the two following days.

Respectfully submitted,
ELDER HENRY COMER
JOHN M. DAVIS
WALTER LYONS

2

Eleventh—On motion the report was received and the Committee discharged.

Twelfth—A call was made for the report of the Committee on Finance. We the Committee on Finance beg leave to submit the following report:

CHURCH	PRINTING MINUTES	VISITING MINISTERS
Black Fox	$10.00	$ 0.00
Braden's Chapel	5.00	0.00
Brantley's Chapel	10.00	0.00
Cedar Springs	4.00	0.00
Davis Chapel	4.00	4.00
Gibson Station	4.00	4.00
Kirkwood	10.00	10.00
Monroe, Michigan	5.00	0.00
New Hebron	1.00	0.00
Noeton	3.00	0.00
Oak Grove	9.00	0.00
Pleasant Hill	5.00	4.00
Pleasant Point	11.00	2.00
Rocky Dale	5.00	5.00
Total Received	$86.00	$29.00
Balance carried over from 1961		93.00
Complete Total		$208.00
Total Expense		115.00
Balance in Treasury		$93.00

Respectfully submitted,
ELDER J. H. BRANSCOMB
ELDER TONY EASTRIDGE
ELDER N. L. CLAWSON

Thirteenth—On motion the report was received and the Committee discharged.

Fourteen—On motion we passed to have 1,000 copies of the Minutes printed, and the clerk will superintend the printing and distribution of them. He is to be allowed $25.00 for his services.

Fifteenth—On motion the next annual session is to be held at the Gibson Station Church in Lee County, Virginia. It is to begin on Friday before the third Saturday in August, 1963, and continue the two following days.

Sixteenth—On motion Elder Parnick Shelton was selected to preach the Introductory Sermon. Elder James H. Branscomb will be his alternate.

Seventeenth—On motion we agreed to send Elder Henry Comer, Elder Albert Davis, and Elder W. M. Sparks to the Hiwassee Association, and Elder Henry Comer, Elder James H. Branscomb, and Elder N. L. Clawson to the New Bethlem Association.

Eighteenth—On motion the Clerk will write each a Letter of Correspondence.

Nineteenth—On motion we extended to the old Church and the people of the surrounding community our sincere appreciation for the kindness and generous hospitality shown us throughout the Association at the above stated place and date.

Twentieth—There was a move and second that we adjourn our business until 10:30 a.m. at the above stated place and date. We were dismissed by Elder Everett Berry.

3

Respectfully submitted,
Elder Albert Davis, Moderator
Speedwell, Tennessee
Elder Hugh Brummitt, Asst. Moderator
1329 Brown Avenue
Knoxville, Tennessee
Austin Beason, Clerk
Goin, Tennessee
O. R. Parrot, Asst. Clerk
LaFollette, Tennessee

Twenty-First—After intermission, the Association re-assembled. After singing there was prayer by Elder Leonard White. Elder Clifford Brantley spoke from the 1st Chapter of Malachi. He was followed by Elder Everett Berry who spoke from the 8th Chapter of Ezekiel. We were dismissed by Elder J. C. Monday.

SUNDAY'S PROCEEDINGS

On Sunday a large crowd gathered at the altar. There was singing and then consoling words from Elder Tony Eastridge. Prayer was by Elder Johnnie Atkins. Elder J. H. Branscomb spoke a few words. Elder Lenvil Meyers spoke from the 21st Chapter of St. Luke. The Meeting seemed to be enjoyed by all. The closing was by the Moderator. We were dismissed by Elder Tony Eastridge.

LICENTIATES

Jim Oliver -- Bean Station, Tennessee
George Shoffner --------------------------------- Sharps Chapel, Tennessee
Claude Rosson --- Goin, Tennessee
Odell Carpenter ------------------------------------ Maryville, Tennessee

MINISTERS

Elder Leonard White ----------------------------- LaFollette, Tennessee
                                                   Phone 562-5667
Elder R. H. Pettit ---------------------------- 107 Jacksboro Pike
                                               Fountain City, Tennessee
                                                   Phone 689-5581
Elder W. M. Sparks ---------------------------- Speedwell, Tennessee
                                                   Phone 562-7997
Elder Henry Comer ---Route 4
                                               LaFollette, Tennessee
                                                   Phone 562-3952
Elder Joe Irwin ------------------------------- Gibson Station, Virginia
Elder Dewey Ellison --------------------------- Sharps Chapel, Tennessee
Elder Albert Davis ---------------------------- Speedwell, Tennessee
                                                   Phone 3667
Elder Lenvil Meyers ----------------------------------- 512 E. Elm St.
                                               Monroe, Michigan
Elder T. I. Eastridge ------------------------------------- Route 2
                                               Louisville, Tennessee
                                                   Phone 983-1068
Elder Hugh Brummitt --------------------------------- 1329 Brown Ave.
                                               Knoxville, Tennessee
                                                   Phone 525-3583
Elder Gilbert Atkins ------------------------------------- Route 3
                                               Rutledge, Tennessee
Elder George Campbell -------------------------- Blaine, Tennessee

4

584

Elder J. H. Branscomb ------------------------------ Speedwell, Tennessee
Elder Johnnie Atkins ------------------------------ Bean Station, Tennessee
Elder Everett Berry ------------------------------ Fountain City, Tennessee
                                                        Phone 992-4241
Elder J. C. Monday ------------------------------ Speedwell, Tennessee
Elder Noble Lee Clawson ------------------------------ Speedwell, Tennessee
Elder Clifford Brantley ------------------------------ Brown School Road
                                                   Maryville, Tennessee
                                                        Phone 982-3735
Elder Parnick Shelton ------------------------------ Corryton, Tennessee
                                                        Phone 689-6183
Elder Roy Oliver ------------------------------ Bean Station, Tennessee

CORRESPONDING LETTER

We, the Powell Valley Association of the Primitive Baptist, now in session at the Pleasant Hill Church in Claiborne County, Tennessee on August 17-18-19, 1962, send greetings to the Hiwassee and New Bethlem Associations with whom we correspond. Very dear Brothers and Sisters, We desire to keep our long cherished correspondence with you. We have chosen these our beloved Elders to bear this epistle of love to you. Our messengers to the Hiwassee Association are Elder Henry Comer, Elder Albert Davis, and Elder W. M. Sparks. Our messengers to the New Bethlem Association are Elder James H. Branscomb, Elder Henry Comer, and Elder Noble Lee Clawson. Having seated all your delegates, We heartily welcome more next year when we convene with the Church at Gibson Station in Lee County, Virginia. We will begin on Friday before the third Saturday in August, 1963.

5

OBITUARIES

MARY E. HUNSUCKER

Mrs. Mary England Hunsucker, age 58, passed away January 15, 1962, at Claiborne County Hospital. She was a member of the Pleasant Point Baptist Church.

Survivors: husband—Ray of Goin; daughter—Cue Williams of Knoxville; son—Emerson of Goin; one Grandson; sister—Mrs. M. C. Killion of Goin; brothers— Matt England of Powells, Bill and Walter England of Knoxville; several nieces and nephews.

Funeral services were held at the Lily Grove Baptist Church with Elder Hugh Brummitt and Reverend Lloyd England officiating. Burial was in the Church cemetery. Pallbearers were Carl and Glenn England, Bradley Keck, Roy Killian, Hubert Herrell, Clyde Heath.

6

MANDA HURST

Manda Hurst, age 68, passed away April 1, 1955. She professed faith in Christ at an early age and joined the Black Fox Primitive Baptist Church.

Survivors: two daughters—Mrs. Fred Liford and Mrs. Buck Russell, one son—Edward Hurst, all of Greenback; nine grandchildren and one great-grandchild; four brothers—Alex and John Marion of Missouri, Don of Martel, and Robert of Greenback; one sister—Dosh Collingsworth of Texas.

Funeral services were at Axley's Chapel Church. Rev. B. T. Loveday and Rev. Harley Ramey officiated. Interment in the Church cemetery. "Our loss is Heaven's gain."

Written by Daughter, Mrs. Fred Liford

CHINA O. COX

Mrs. China O. Cox passed away at her home at 514 Redford Place, Knoxville, Tennessee on June 5, 1962.

Survivors: husband—Sillus Cox; daughter—Mrs. Irene Bates; grandson—W. C. Bates Jr.; granddaughter—Gail Bates. All are from Knoxville. Three brothers—Grover, Jim, and C. D. (Gob) Keck all of Goin. A sister—Mrs. Bessie Collins of Goin. A host of relatives and friends.

She bore her illness with never a word of complaint and with such courage that it was amazing to the family and the ones who cared for her so tenderly. She joined the Pleasant Point Primitive Baptist Church on May 6, 1939, and remained a faithful member until her death. She was very much interested in the Church. She spoke of it on the afternoon before she died. She expressed a hope that the Church would continue and grow in grace and knowledge. Her faith in God and the Resurrection was so strong that she had no fear, even as she passed through the shadow of death. At the last moment of life when she could no longer talk she opened her eyes smiled at her husband who so patiently watching by her bedside.

The funeral was conducted at the Rose Funeral Home by Elder Charles Ausmus. The large crowd that attended and the beautiful flowers showed that her relatives and friends held her in high esteem. The body was lain to rest in the Lynnhurst Cemetery.

FRANK H. SMITH

Frank H. Smith was born April 14, 1897, and died April 25, 1962, being 65 years and 10 days old. He leaves to mourn his passing: wife—Mrs. Grace Boles Smith of Corryton; one son— Sgt. Harold H. Smith of Fort Hood Texas; three daughters— Mrs. Bobbye Satterfield and Mrs. Maxine McKelvy of Corryton and Mrs. Nadine Powell of Atlanta, Georgia; four sisters—Mrs. Tina Daniel, Mrs. Cleo Wood, and Mrs. Mary Clapp of Corryton, Mrs. Harriet Hobby of Knoxville; four brothers—John and Roscoe of Corryton, Carl of Knoxville, and Bruce of Luttrell; several nieces and nephews; many relatives and friends. He professed faith in Christ at an early age and later in life, joined Rocky Dale Church where he remained a faithful member. Funeral services were held at Stevens' Chapel with Elder Leonard White and Elder Hugh Brummitt officiating. Interment in Lynnhurst Cemetery.

"There's an open gate at the end of the road
Through which each must go alone,
And there is a light we cannot see
Our Father claims His own;
Beyond the gate our loved one
Finds happiness and rest,
And there is comfort in the thought
That a Loving God knows best."

Written by his wife and daughter

7

LOCKIE W. SHELTON

Lockie Webster Shelton, age 74, passed away at a Convalescence Home in Knoxville on August 8, 1962. She leaves two sons Elder Parnick Shelton and Ross Shelton both of Corryton, Tennessee. One brother—Curtis Webster of Knoxville. Five grandchildren.

She was a member of Rocky Dale Primitive Baptist Church. Funeral services were held at Stevens' Chapel, with Elder Hugh Brummitt, Elder Leonard White, and Elder Everett Berry officiating. Interment in Troutt Cemetery. She is greatly missed by the family and church.

MELVINA S. RUSSELL

Mary Melvina Shoffner Russell was born May 14, 1877, and died in the home of her daughter, Mrs. Clemma Raley on July 14, 1962. She married James Press Russell April 9, 1894. To this union was born 11 children, 9 of which are living.

Survivors: 2 daughters—Mrs. Clemma Raley of Maynardville and Mrs. Clara Rutledge of Morton, Mississippi; 7 sons—Willoughby, Charles, and Denzil of Sharps Chapel, Otis of Maynardville, Ditsy of Monroe, Michigan, Milburn and Lloyd of Speedwell; 32 grandchildren; 47 great-grandchildren; one sister of Knoxville; one step-daughter, Francis Monroe of California; one brother of Kansas; one half sister, Myrtle Cox.

She was one of the first members when Oak Grove Church was ordained. She was lain to rest in the Oak Grove Cemetery. We hope to meet her on that beautiful shore. Our loss is Heaven's gain.

Written by daughters Clemma and Clara

MAMIE O. HAMILTON

Mamie Ousley Hamilton was born October 21, 1891, and passed away June 11, 1961. She professed faith in Christ at an early age and joined the Primitive Baptist Church at Hamilton Grove where she was a member until the water of Norris Dam came. She then became a member of Oak Grove. She was married to Forrest Hamilton March 14, 1914. Born to this union were 2 children.

Survivors: husband—Forrest Hamilton; son—Fate; daughter—Icie Myers; 3 grandchildren—Bobby, Bracley, and Barbara Hamilton; 2 sisters—Emma Craig and Lillis Hamilton.

Funeral services were held at McCammons and Ammon with Elder Ralph Cline and Elder Tommy Lynch officiating. Interment in Grandview Cemetery. Gone but not Forgotten. "When darkness seems to hide his face I rest on His unchanging grace. In every high and stormy gale, my anchor holds within the vale."

MARY M. SEXTON

Mary Melissa Hunter Maddox Sexton was born in 1892. She was the daughter of the late John and Rachel Hunter. She was united in marriage to the late Jefferson Scoffield Maddox and to this union was born a son John Leonard and a daughter Hassie Cloe who preceded her in death.

Sister Lissie was united with the Church at Pleasant Hill in April, 1911, and was a member until God called her away on May 9, 1962. She often spoke of her Home in Heaven, and we feel our loss is Heaven's gain.

Survivors: her second husband—Robert Sexton of Gibson Station, Virginia; son John Maddox; 9 grandchildren; one great-grandchild; one brother—Jess Hunter of Speedwell, Tennessee; one sister—Grace Bolinger of Monroe, Michigan; a host of relatives and friends.

8

MILTON BRANTLEY

Daniel Milton Brantley was born February 16, 1886 and died September 10, 1961, at his home. He was 75 years, 6 months, and 25 days old. He married Sarah M. Ellison on March 5, 1912. To this union was born three sons and two daughters. Clifford, Everett, and Doyle of Maryville—Mrs. Norma Jean Bush of Corryton and Mrs. Juanita Brantley of Kokomo, Indiana. There are 13 grandchildren.

He professed faith in Christ at an early age and joined Mossie Springs Primitive Baptist Church. He later moved his membership to Oak Grove, and after moving to Maryville moved his membership to Brantley's Chapel where he remained a faithful member until his death. He leaves a host of relatives and friends to mourn his passing.

Funeral services were held at Brantley's Chapel Primitive Baptist Church at Maryville by Elder Leonard White and Elder W. M. Sparks. Interment in the church cemetery.

> "No pen can write, no tongue can tell
> our sad and bitter loss.God alone
> has helped so well to bear our heavy
> bross. His place at home and church
> is vacant, his trials of life are o're
> he's now at rest on God's eternal shore."

Written by the family

ARTICLES OF FAITH

Article 1. We believe in only one true living God, as He is revealed to us in the Holy Scriptures—Father, Son and Holy Ghost.

Article 2. We believe that the Scriptures of the old and new Testaments are the words of God and the only rule of all-saving knowledge and obedience.

Article 3. We believe in the doctrine of election according to the foreknowledge of God.

Article 4. We believe in the doctrine of original sin.

Article 5. We believe in man's importancy to rescue himself from the fallen state he is in in his own will or ability.

Article 6. We believe that sinners are justified in the sight of God only by the imputed righteousness of Jesus Christ.

Article 7. We believe the elect, according to the foreknowledge of God will be called, converted, regenerated and sancified by the Holy Spirit.

Article 8. We believe the saints will preserve and never fall finally away.

Article 9. We believe that baptism, the Lord's Supper, and feet washing are ordinances of Jesus Christ, and that true believers are the only subject of these ordinances, and that the true mode of baptism is by immersion.

Article 10. We believe in the Resurrection of the dead and the General Judgment.

Article 11. We believe that the punishment of the wicked will be ever lasting and that the joys of the righteous will be eternal.

Article 12. We believe that no minister has the right to administer the ordinances, except those who have been regularly baptized and called of God, and come under the imposition of hands of the Presbytery.

9

CHURCHES	COUNTY	PASTORS	CLERKS	CLERK'S POST OFFICE
Black Fox	Grainger	Elder Albert Davis Elder George Campbell, asst.	Bennie Capps Flossie Capps, asst.	P. O. Box 91 Maynardville, Tenn. Liberty Hill, Tenn.
Braden's Chapel	Union	Elder N. L. Clawson Elder J. C. Monday, asst.	Arvil Braden	Speedwell, Tenn.
Brantley's Chapel	Blount	Elder Clifford Brantley	Rina Johnson Rina Johnson, Jr., asst.	9 Douglas Avenue Maryville, Tenn. 14 Houston Street Maryville, Tenn.
Cedar Springs	Claiborne	Elder J. C. Monday Elder N. L. Clawson, asst.	Pearlie Holt	New Tazewell, Tenn.
Davis Chapel	Campbell	Elder Hugh Brummitt Elder Leonard White, asst.	Ruth Heatherly Lassie Ellison, asst.	LaFollette, Tenn. LaFollette, Tenn.
Gibson Station	Lee Virginia	Elder Leonard White Elder Everett Berry, asst.	Roxie Cobb Mossie Cottrell, asst.	Gibson Station, Va. Gibson Station, Va.
Kirkwood	Knox	Elder Leonard White Elder R H Petit, asst.	Estelle Petree Sharp Myrtle Taylor, asst.	5313 Jacksboro Pike Fountain City, Tenn. 5311 Jacksboro Pike Fountain City, Tenn.
Monroe, Michigan	Monroe	Elder Lenvil Meyers	Ditsy Russell	5177 Plum Creek Monroe, Michigan
New Hebron	Jefferson	Elder Gilbert Atkins	Rachel Mitchell	New Market, Tenn.
Noeton	Grainger	Elder Gilbert Atkins	John Oliver Bessie Collins, asst.	Bean Station, Tenn. Morristown, Tenn.
Oak Grove	Union	Elder W. M. Sparks Elder Clifford Brantley, asst.	Belle Moore Ruth Shoffner, asst.	Sharps Chapel, Tenn. Sharps Chapel, Tenn.
Pleasant Hill	Claiborne	Elder Tony Eastridge Elder J. H. Branscomb, asst.	William Branscomb Verlin Edwards, asst.	Speedwell, Tenn. Speedwell, Tenn.
Pleasant Point	Claiborne	Elder Tony Eastridge	Austin Beason	Goin, Tenn.
Rocky Dale	Knox	Elder Hugh Brummitt Elder Parnick Shelton, asst.	Arvell Graves Roy Clapp, asst.	Corryton, Tenn. 2331 Washington Ave Knoxville, Tenn.

1963

MINUTES

of the

One Hundred and Forty-Fourth

ANNUAL SESSION

of the

POWELLS VALLEY ASSOCIATION

of

PRIMITIVE BAPTISTS

held with

THE CHURCH AT GIBSON STATION

Lee County, Virginia

AUGUST 16-17-18, 1963

OFFICERS

Elder Albert Davis -- Moderator
Elder Hugh Brummitt --------------------------- Assistant Moderator
Brother Austin Beason -- Clerk
Brother O. R. Parrott ------------------------------ Assistant Clerk

The next session will be held with the church at Oak Grove in Union County, Tennessee. It will begin on Friday before the third Saturday in August, 1964. Elder James H. Branscomb will preach the Introductory Sermon. Elder Noble Lee Clawson will be the alternate.

CHURCHES	DELEGATES	Restored—No	Received by Relationship	Received by Baptism	Received by Letter	Dismissed by Letter	Excluded	Deceased	Total Membership	Visiting Ministers	Printing Minutes	Saturday Meeting	Communion Meeting
Black Fox	George Campbell, John Davis, Bill Muncey, Bennie Capps, Terree Cabbage, Flossie Capps.	0	0	0	0	0	0		88	$0.00	$10.00	2	2, June
Braden's Chapel	N. L. Clawson, J. C. Monday, W. M. Sparks, Leecy Sparks, Henry Conner.	0	5	0	0	0		1	72	$0.00	$5.00	1	1, July
Brantley's Chapel	Corun Berry, ...ila Berry, Von Beason, Ellis Evans, Lottie Evans, Clifford Brantley.	0	0	0	0	0		1	78	$0.00	$5.00	2	2, July
Cedar Springs	Clifford Robertson, Ida Robertson, Peggy Robertson, Maggie Robertson, Mattie Wilson, Pearlie Holt, Mary Treece, Joan Good.	0	0	5	0	0	0		60	$0.00	$3.00	4	4, May
Davis Chapel	Mr. and Mrs. Leonard White, Earl White, Mr. and Mrs. Orice McCarty, Mr. and Mrs. Onie Parrott, Cordela Lynch.	0	2	0	0	2		1	150	$4.00		3	3, June
Gibson State	Henry Hoskins, Harve Rhymer, Sid Steg...l, Fr...	0	5	0	0	0		0	94	$4.00		1	1, June
Kirkwood	Hugh Brummitt, Ruby Brummitt, Walter Lyons, M. A. Norton, Lucy Norton, Bill Taylor, Lou Emma Taylor.	2	3	0	0	2		3	109	$10.00	$10.00	Eve. Sun.	Last Sun. April
Monroe, Michigan	Lenvil Meyers	0	1	0	2	0	2	0	14	$0.00	$5.00	3	3, July
New Hebron	Ray Mitchell	0	0	0	0	0		1	24	$0.00	$1.00	4	4, May & Sept.
Noeton	Roy Oliver	0	1	0	0	0	0		39	$0.00	$3.00	3	3, May
Oak Grove	Johnnie Adkins, Gilbert Adkins, Jake Overbay, Charles Collins.												
Pleasant Hill	Tony Eastridge, Lillie Shottner.	0	0	0	0	0		1	89	$0.00	$10.00	4	4, June
Pleasant Point	Mr. and Mrs. Albert Davis, Verlin Edwards, Mr. and Mrs. James H. Branscomb, Bud Branscomb, Sarah Branscomb. C. D. Keck, Cleo Beason	0	3	0	2	0		1	125	$0.00	$10.00	1	1, July
Rocky Dale	Everett Berry, Trula Berry, Parnick Shelton, Wilma Shelton, Richard Livingston, Della Weaver.	5	12	1	0	0		2	113	$5.00	$5.00	2	2, May

FRIDAY'S PROCEEDINGS

First—According to previous arrangements the Association met pursuant to adjournment.

Second—After singing Elder Albert Davis read the 5th chapter of St. Matthew. Prayer was by Elder Walter Lyons. Then Elder Parnick Shelton spoke from the 3rd chapter of 1st. Corinthians. After singing we were dismissed by Elder Everett Berry.

Third—After interm'ssion there was more singing. Prayer was by Elder W. M. Sparks and Elder Carl McCarty.

Fourth—The Association was called to order by Elder Albert Davis.

Fifth—The Moderator called for letters from sister churches.

Sixth—On motion all said letters except one were received and the delegates were welcomed to seats by the Moderator.

Seventh—A call was made for members who were not delegates. One was received—Elder Roy Oliver of Noeton.

Eighth—A call was made for letters from Corresponding Associations. One was received from New Bethlem.

N:nth—The letter from New Bethlem was read and received. Their delegates were welcomed to seats with us. They were Elder Carl McCarty, Sylvan Gilbert, Morin Gilbert, Mayme Napier, and Jim Humblin. There was no letter from Hiwassee.

Tenth—On motion and second Elder Albert Davis was re-elected Moderator. Elder Hugh Brummitt was re-elected Assistant Moderator.

Eleventh—On motion and second Brother Austin Beason was re-elected Clerk. Brother O. R. Parrott was re-elected Assistant Clerk.

Twelfth—On motion the Moderator appointed the following committees:
  1. Arrangements—Earl White, Frankl'n Jones, Von Beason.
  2. Preaching—Corum Berry, H. C. Hoskins, Melvin Norton.
  3. Correspondence—Clifford Brantley, Walter Lyons, Everett Berry.
  4. Request—N. L. Clawson, Verlin Edwards, Harve Rhymer.
  5. Finance—Henry Comer, Parnick Shelton, Bud Branscomb.

Thirteenth—On motion we adjourned until 10:00 A.M. on Saturday, August 17, 1963. We were dismissed by Elder Henry Comer.

SATURDAY'S PROCEEDINGS

First—After singing Elder Hugh Brummitt spoke from the 51st Chapter of Psalms. Prayer was by Elder Tony Eastridge.

Second—There was a call for letters that failed to get in Friday. One was received from New Hebron. The delegates were welcome to seats by the Moderator.

Third—A call was made for the report of the Committee on Arrangements.

We, the Committee on Arrangements, beg leave to submit the following reports:

  1. Call the roll.
  2. Call for the report of the Committee on Request.
  3. Call for the report of the Committee on Preaching.
  4. Call for the report of the Committee on Correspondence.
  5. Call for the report of the Committee on Finance.

When and where shall our next Association be held? Who shall preach the Introductory Sermon? Who shall be his alternate? How many copies of the Minutes shall we have printed? Who shall superintend the printing and distribution of them? What shall be allowed for his services?

Respectfully submitted,

EARL WHITE

FRANKLIN JONES

VON BEASON

Fourth—On motion the report was received and the Committee discharged.

Fifth—The roll was called and the names of the absentees erased.

Sixth—A call was made for the report of the Committee on Preaching.

We, the Committee on Preaching, beg leave to submit the following report:

1. Friday night at the Church—Elder J. H. Branscomb and Elder W. M. Sparks.

2. Saturday morning at the Church—Elder Carl McCarty and Elder Walter Lyons.

3. Saturday night at the Church—Elder George Campbell and Elder Albert Davis.

4. Sunday morning at the Church—Elder J. C. Monday and Elder Hugh Brummitt.

The Moderator is to close.

Respectfully submitted,

CORUM BERRY

H. C. HOSKINS

MELVIN NORTON

Seventh—On motion the report was received and the Committee discharged.

Eighth—A call was made for the report of the Committee on Correspondence.

We, the Committee on Correspondence, beg leave to submit the following report:

We shall keep up our correspondence with the Hiwassee and New Bethlem Association.

Respectfully submitted,

CLIFFORD BRANTLEY

WALTER LYONS

EVERETT BERRY

Ninth—On motion the report was received and the Committee discharged.

Tenth—A call was made for the report of the Committee on Request.

We, the Committee on Request, beg leave to submit the following report: We shall publish all the obituaries that the churches furnish. Our next Association will be held with the Church at Oak Grove in Union County, Tennessee. It will begin on Friday before the third Saturday in August, 1964, and continue the two following days.

Respectfully submitted,

N. L. CLAWSON

VERLIN EDWARDS

HARVE RHYMER

2

Eleventh—On motion the report was received and the Committee discharged.

Twelfth—A call was made for the report of the Committee on Finance We, the Committee on Finance, beg leave to submit the following report:

CHURCH	PRINTING MINUTES	VISITING MINISTERS
Gibson Station	$ 4.00	$ 4.00
Braden's Chapel	5.00	0.00
Pleasant Hill	10.00	0.00
Monroe. Michigan	5.00	0.00
Davis Chapel	4.00	4.00
Black Fox	10.00	0.00
Noeton	3.00	0.00
Brantley's Chapel	5.00	0.00
Cedar Springs	3.00	0.00
Oak Grove	8.00	0.00
Kirkwood	10.00	10.00
Pleasant Point	10.00	0.00
Rocky Dale	5.00	5.00
New Hebron	1.00	0.00

Total Received	$83.00	$ 23.00
Balance carried over from 1962		93.00
Complete Total		$199.00
Total Expense		120.00
Balance in Treasury		$79.00

Respectfully submitted.
HENRY COMER
PARNICK SHELTON
BUD BRANSCOMB

Thirteenth—On motion the report was received and the Committee discharged.

Fourteenth—On motion we passed to have 1,000 copies of the Minutes printed, and the clerk will superintend the printing and distribution of them. He is to be allowed $50.00 for h's services.

Fifteenth—On motion the next annual session is to be held at the Oak Grove Church in Union County, Tennessee. It is to begin on Friday before the third Saturday in August, 1964, and continue the two following days.

Sixteenth—On motion Elder James H. Branscomb was selected to preach the Introductory Sermon. Elder N. L. Clawson will be his alternate.

Seventeenth—On motion we agree to send Elder Henry Comer, Elder Parnick Shelton, and Elder Tony Eastridge to the H wassee Association and Elder Henry Comer, Elder W. M. Sparks, and Elder N. L. Clawson. to the New Bethlem Association.

Eighteenth—On motion the Clerk will write each a Letter of Correspondence.

Nineteenth—On motion we extend to the old Church and the people of the surrounding community our sincere appreciation for the kindness and generous hospitality shown us throughout the Association at the above stated place and date.

3

Twentieth—-There was a move and second that we adjourn our business until 10:30 A.M. at the above stated place and date. We were dismissed by Elder George Campbell.

Respectfully submitted,
ELDER ALBERT DAVIS, Moderator
Speedwell, Tennessee
ELDER HUGH BRUMMITT, Asst.
Moderator
1329 Brown Avenue
Knoxville, Tennessee
AUSTIN BEASON, Clerk
Goin, Tennessee
O. R. PARROT, Asst. Clerk
LaFollette, Tennessee

Twenty-First—After intermission, the Association re-assembled. After singing there was prayer by Elder Lenvil Meyers. He was followed by Elder Carl McCarty who spoke from 2nd Timothy. Then Elder Walter Lyons spoke a few consoling words. We were dismissed by Elder N. L. Clawson.

SUNDAY'S PROCEEDINGS

On Sunday a large crowd gathered at the altar. There was singing and then Elder Everett Berry read from the 23rd Psalms. Prayer was by Elder R. B. Brantley, Elder J. C. Monday spoke from the 22nd Chapter of Genesis. He was followed by Elder Hugh Brummitt who spoke from 1st Peter the 3rd verse. The closing was by the Moderator. We were dismissed by Elder Roy Oliver.

MINISTERS

Elder Gilbert Atkins ------------------------------Route 3
Rutledge, Tennessee
Elder Johnnie Atkins ----------------------------Bean Station, Tennessee
Elder Everett Berry ------------------------------Fountain City, Tennessee
Phone 922-4241
Elder J. H. Branscomb --------------------------Speedwell, Tennessee
Phone 86-3392
Elder Clifford Brantley ------------------------Brown School Road
Maryville, Tennessee
Phone 982-3735
Elder Hugh Brummitt -------------------------1329 Brown Ave.
Knoxville, Tennessee
Phone 525-3583
Elder George Campbell ----------------------Route 2
Corryton, Tennessee
Elder Nobel Lee Clawson --------------------Speedwell, Tennessee
Elder Albert Davis ---------------------------Speedwell, Tennessee
Phone 86-3667
Elder Henry Comer --------------------------Route 4
LaFollette, Tennessee
Phone 562-3952
Elder T. I. Eastridge ------------------------Route 2
Louisville, Tennessee
Phone 983-1068
Elder Dewey Ellison ------------------------Sharps Chapel, Tennessee
Elder Joe Irwin -----------------------------Gibson Station, Virginia

4

```
Elder Walter Lyons -------------------------------1602 Garfield Street
                                                  Alcoa, Tennessee
                                                  Phone YU 33222
Elder Lenvil Meyers -----------------------------512 East Elm Street
                                                  Monroe, Michigan
Elder J. C. Monday ------------------------------Speedwell, Tennessee
Elder Roy Oliver --------------------------------Bean Station, Tennessee
Elder R. H. Pettit ------------------------------107 Jacksboro Pike
                                                  Fountain City, Tennessee
                                                  Phone 689-5581
Elder Parnick Shelton ---------------------------Corryton, Tennessee
                                                  Phone 689-6183
Elder George Shoffner ---------------------------Sharps Chapel, Tennessee
Elder W. M. Sparks ------------------------------Speedwell, Tennessee
                                                  Phone 562-7997
Elder Leonard White -----------------------------LaFollette, Tennessee
                                                  Phone 562-5667
```

LICENTIATES

```
Odell Carpenter ---------------------------------Maryville, Tennessee
Jim Oliver --------------------------------------Bean Station, Tennessee
Claude Rosson -----------------------------------Goin, Tennessee
```

CORRESPONDING LETTER

We, the Powells Valley Association of the Primitive Baptist, now in session at the Gibson Station Church in Lee County, Virginia on August 16-17-18, 1963, send greetings to the Hiwassee and New Bethlem Associations with whom we correspond. Very dear Brothers and Sisters, We desire to keep our long cherished correspondence with you. We have chosen these our beloved Elders to bear this epistle of love to you. Our messengers to the Hiwassee Association are Elder Henry Comer, Elder Parnick Shelton, and Elder Tony Eastridge. Our messengers to the New Bethlem Association are Elder Henry Comer, Elder W. M. Sparks, and Elder N. L. Clawson. Having seated all your delegates, we heartily welcome more next year when we convene with the Church at Oak Grove in Union County, Tennessee. We will begin on Friday before the third Saturday in August, 1964.

OBITUARIES

ETTA HOPPER KECK

Mrs. Etta Hopper Keck was born July 15, 1883, being 79 years, 3 months and 17 days.

She was united in marriage to Manuel Keck in the year 1900. To this union was born seven children. Six children preceded her in death. Left to mourn her passing is her husband, Manuel and son Lawrence Keck, both of Goin, Tennessee; five grandchildren and five great-grandchildren; sisters, Lou Miller, Cincinnati, Ohio, Nina Perry, Vesta Tolliver and Saby Weaver all of Knoxville, Tennessee.

She joined the Pleasant Point Prim'tive Baptist Church at an early age and lived a faithful member until death.

LASSIE GRAVES SHARP

Lassie Graves Sharp was born September 11, 1889 and passed away August 4, 1963 at St. Mary's Hospital at Knoxville. She was the daughter of the late Patrick and Parlie Graves. She was a member of the Kirkwood Primitive Baptist Church. She was married to Ed Sharp March 8, 1914 and to this union two children were born.

Survivors: husband—Ed; daughter—Mrs. Nellie Norriss; son—D. O.; sister—Mrs. Hershell Ousley; brother—Cleon; Virgil, and Rush Graves. She bore her illness with great courage and without complaint. A devoted wife, loving mother, and christian neighbor is gone from this world to God's eternal shore. We will miss her but our loss is Heaven's gain.

Funeral services were conducted at the Rose Funeral Home by her pastor Elder Leonard White. Interment in the Lynnhurst Cemetery.

MILLARD L. BRIDGES

Millard L. Bridges was born May 27, 1888, and passed away November 7, 1962 at the home of his daughter, Mrs. Lillian Bridges Moore of Byington, Tennessee. He was converted at an early age and joined the White Hollow Primitive Baptist Church. Later he moved his letter to the Kirkwood Primitive Baptist Church where he rema'ned a member until the end. He was married to Della Davis and to this union was born eight children.

Survivors sons—James E. of Morristown Indiana, Clyde, Claude, and Paul of Knoxville; daughter—Mrs. Jack Stell of California, Mrs. Mary Lillian Moore of Knoxville; 15 grandchildren and 3 great-grandch'ldren. We feel that our loss is His eternal gain. Funeral services were conducted at the Weaver Funeral Home by Elder Leonard White, Reverend Roy Arwood, and Reverend Ben Whaley. Interment in New Mossy Springs Cemetery.

MRS. VADA PETREE SHARP

Mrs. Vada Petree Sharp was born December 18, 1907 and passed away February 27, 1963. She professed faith in Christ at an early age and joined Mossy Springs Baptist Church. Later she became a charter member of Rocky Dale Church. She was an active member as long as her health perm'tted her and had a great interest in the Church as long as she l'ved. She is survived by sisters—Mrs. Ethel Feagins, Bristol, Tennessee and Mrs. Reva Zachary of Corryton; brother—Cecil Petree of Akron, Ohio.

Funeral services were conducted at Steven's Chapel in Knoxville by Elder Hugh Brummitt and Elder Parnick Shelton. Interment in Lynnhurst Cemetery.

7

MRS. MARY JANE KECK

Mrs. Mary Jane Keck, of Goin, wife of the late M. C. Keck, passed away July 25, 1963.

Survivors: sons. Curtis, Fay and Russell Keck all of Goin, Fred Keck of Middlesboro, Ky ; daughters, Mrs. Cecil Carey, Go'n, Mrs. Loalles Robinette, Kingston, Mrs. Lavetta Crawford, Powell Station, Mrs. Roberta Carr and Mrs. Rowena Barnes, New Tazewell; sisters, Mrs. Ollie Bolinger, New Tazewell, Mrs. Ida Cole, Goin Mrs. Mossie Russell, Fountain City, Mrs. Fluta Baird, York, S. C.; 14 grandchildren; 11 great-grandchildren.

For more than fifty years she has been a member of Pleasant Point Baptist Church where funeral services were held. Interment in fam ly cemetery, Elder Leonard White and Rev. Willie Newman officiated.

JESSE LINCOLN EDWARDS

Jesse Lincoln Edwards was born October 1, 1890. He passed away September 13, 1962 at the Veterans Hospital at Mountain Home, Tennessee. He was married to Hassie Harmon on July 25, 1917.

Survivors: wife—Mrs. Hassie Edwards; sons—Virgil and Roy of Speedwell, Harold of Dayton, Ohio; brothers—Verlin, David. Lonzo, and Jim of Speedwell; sisters—Mrs. Cinda Duncan of Deer Loodge, Tennessee, Mrs. Lou Lambert of Speedwell, Tennessee, Mrs. Homer Pace of Dallas, Texas; Mrs. Minnie Collinsworth of Greenboro, North Carolina, and Mrs. Edna Robins of Madisonville, Tennessee. He joined the Primitive Baptist Church at Pleasant Hill in 1917. He was a faithful member until death and served as clerk for 35 years. He was a member of F. A. M. Lodge No. 577.

Funeral services were held at Pleasant Hill Baptist Church by Elder W. M. Sparks and Elder Tony Eastridge. Interment in Hunter Cemetery. Pallbearers were Kelburn Edwards, Condis Edwards, Mathew Edwards Carl Edwards, and Edward Graves.

MARTHA LEONA HENEGAR

Martha Leona Henegar was born September 9, 1899 and died November 10, 1962. She was 63 years 2 months and one day old. She leaves to mourn her passing her husband Hiriam E. Henegar and nine children. She professed faith in Christ at an early age and joined the church at White Hollow. In later years she joined the church at Brantley's Chapel. She always had a testimony. She was loved by all who knew her. We all loved her but God loved her best. She has gone to a better home and w'll never be forgotten by her loved ones. She was laid to rest in Brantley's Chapel Cemetery.

VERNIE SHARP CULVAHOUSE

Vernie Sharp Culvahouse was born in Union County at Sharps Chapel, November 12, 1905. She passed away at St. Mary's Hospital in Knoxville July 7, 1963, after a long illness. She was converted at an early age and joined the Oak Grove Primitive Baptist Church of which she was a member until the Kirkwood Church was organized. She then moved her membership to that church where she was an active and fa thful member until the end. She was married to C. S. Culvahouse May 22, 1935. She leaves her husband, three sons, and five grandchildren. We feel that our loss is His eternal gain.

Funeral services were conducted at the Rose Funeral Home by Elder Leonard White. Interment in Woodlawn Cemetery.

8

SILAS W. DRUMMONDS

Silas W. Drummonds, son of the late W. A. and Sibby Drummonds. was born February 19, 1883 and departed this life November 22, 1962. He was 79 years 9 months, and 3 days old. He was a native of Claiborne County and a long time resident of New Tazewell. At the time of death he was res d- ing in Kentucky.

Survivors: wife—Mrs. Roxie Drummonds of Middlesboro, Kentucky; daughter—Mrs. Nona Wilson of Middlesboro; sons—Paris of Grays, Ken- tucky, Theodore of Perrysburg, Ohio, Willard of Toledo, Ohio; 10 grand- children; 20 great-grandchildren; one brother—J. L. Drummonds of Ply- mouth, Michigan.

Funeral services were held at Meyers Grove Baptist Church where he was a member. Elder Charlie Meyers and Elder J. C. Monday officiated. Interment in the Drummonds Cemetery. Pallbearers were Ray Drum- monds, Lester England, Bill Poore Mannie Drummonds, John Drum- monds, and W. E. Drummonds.

MRS. TILDA LEDFORD MCFARLAND

Mrs. Tilda Ledford McFarland was born November 18, 1878 and died November 12, 1962. She was a member of the Davis Chapel Primitive Baptist Church.

Survivors: husband—Sil McFarland; 2 step daughters—Mrs. Mary Bruce of LaFollette and Mrs. Geneva Smith of Knoxville; step-son James, Knox- ville. Services were held at Dav s Chapel Church by Elder Leonard White. Burial in the Church cemetery.

JOSIE R. SMITH

Josie R. Smith was born May 9, 1889 and died January 2, 1963, at her home on Nancy Ferrie Road Near Jefferson City. She was 73 years 3 months and 29 days old. She was the widow of Andrew P. Smith. She professed faith in Christ at an early age and was in the service of the Lord at every opportunity. She lived her life as an open book. I know she is at rest. She left four ch'ldren who will always think of her as not dead but just away. She was a faithful member of New Hebron Church from August, 1949, until her death. Reverend Minnis Lamb, Reverend J. B. Cross, and Reverend B. C. Cochran officiated at the funeral services. Interment was in West View Cemetery. "I cannot say that she is dead. She is just away. With the wave of the hand she has wondered into an unknown land. She left us dreaming how very fair it must be since she lingers there. I think of her as the same. She is not dead. She is just away."

Her daughter—Georgia Grind Staff

VERLIE HOPPER

Verl'e Hopper, age 78, passed away at 3:30 P.M. Wednesday, at his home near Sharps Chapel.

Survivors: wife—Alice, daughter—Ophelia Wilson of Knoxville, son—Levi Hopper of Maynardville, six grandchildren. He was a Deacon at Oak Grove Church.

Funeral was at 2:00 P.M. Friday at Oak Grove Baptist Church where he was a member. Elder Albert Davis and Elder Bill Sparks offic ated. He was laid to rest in the Oak Grove Cemetery. He was born January 26, 1885 and died April 10, 1963. Lee Cooke Funeral Home was in charge. He is gone but not forgotten. We hope to meet him in Heaven.

Wife, children, and grandchildren.

9

MRS. BELLE GRAVES KECK

Mrs. Belle Graves Keck, age 89, wife of the late M. M. Keck, passed away Thursday at the home of her daughter Mrs. I. N. Shoffner of Harrogate.

Survivors: daughters—Mrs. Shoffner of Harrogate, Mrs. Leonard Stanley of Harrogate, Mrs. Aaron Cole of Piney Flats, Mrs. Fred Druillard of Monroe, Michigan, Mrs. Charl'e T. Baker of New Market; sons—Londy Keck of Monroe, Michigan and Esten Keck of Detroit; 20 grandchildren; 24 great-grandchildren; and one great-great-grandchild. She was a member of the Primitive Baptist Church at Gibson Station, Virginia.

Funeral services were held at Coffey Funeral Home Chapel. Elder Leonard White and Elder Everett Berry offic'ated. Interment in Pleasant View Cemetery at Maynardville, Tennessee.

JOHN GRAVES

John Graves, age 83, passed away at the home of his niece Mrs. Ruby Johnson.

Survivors: sisters—Miss Dorothy Graves; nephew—Nolan Graves of Baltimore, Maryland; brother—Wanna Graves of Goin; niece—Mrs. Ruby Johnson of Maynardville.

Funeral services were held at the Irwin's Chapel. Elder Leonard White officiated.

FLORENCE F. STINER

Mrs. Florence F. Stiner age 90, passed away Tuesday morn'ng. She was a member of Oak Grove Baptist Church.

Survivors: sons—Willie of Sharps Chapel and James of Goin; daughters—Rena Stiner of Sharps Chapel, Jane Moyers of Goin, and Hattie Simmons of Monroe. Michigan.

Funeral services were held at the McNeil Funeral Home Chapel with Elder Albert Davis officiating. Nephews served as pallbearers. Interment in the St'ner Ridge Cemetery.

EZRA GRAVES

Ezra Graves was born December 19, 1888 and passed away September 18, 1962. He professed faith in Christ at an early age. Later he joined Rocky Dale Primitive Baptist Church. His love for his church and his faithful attendance was an inspiration for all who knew him. He left to mourn his passing: daughter—Mrs. Emma Cleveland of Corryton; sons—Truman of Corryton and Tracy of Knoxville; one grandson; 6 granddaughters. Services were held at Mynatt's Chapel with Elder Hugh Brummitt and Elder Parnick Shelton officiating. Burial in Fairview Cemetery. The understanding, advice, and patience our father gave us children has sustained us this far and will be remembered by us throughout our lives. Our loss is Heavens gain.

By his daughter, Emma Cleveland

ELDER W. A. PINKSTAFF

Elder W. A. Pinkstaff passed away at h's home in Fayetteville, Tennessee on June 9, 1963 at the age of 84. Elder Pinkstaff has been in the ministery for 66 years. He had visited and preached several of the Powells Valley Churches in the last few years.

Funeral services were conducted in Fayetteville by h's grand on, Elder Kenneth Pinkstaff.

10

CHURCHES	COUNTY	PASTORS	CLERKS	CLERK'S POST OFFICE
Black Fox	Grainger	Elder Albert Davis	Bennie Capps Flossie Capps	P. O. Box 91, Maynardville, Tenn. Liberty Hill, Tenn.
Braden's Chapel	Union	Elder N. L. Clawson Elder J. C. Monday, asst.	Arvil Braden	Speedwell, Tenn.
Brantley's Chapel	Blount	Elder Clifford Brantley Elder Everett Berry, asst.	Rina Johnson Rina Johnson, Jr. asst.	9 Douglas Avenue, Maryville, Tenn. 14 Houston Street, Maryville, Tenn.
Cedar Springs	Claiborne	Elder J. C. Monday Elder N. L. Clawson, asst.	Pearlie Holt	New Tazewell, Tenn.
Davis Chapel	Campbell	Elder Hugh Brummitt Elder Leonard White, asst.	Ruth Heatherly Lassie Ellison, asst.	LaFollette, Tenn. Rt. 1, LaFollette, Tenn.
Gibson Station	Lee, Virginia	Elder Leonard White Elder Everett Berry, asst.	Roxie Cobb Mossie Cottrell, asst.	Gibson Station, Va. Harrogate, Tenn.
Kirkwood	Knox	Elder Leonard White Elder R. H. Pettit, asst.	Estelle Petree Sharp Myrtle Taylor, asst.	5313 Jacksboro Pike, Fountain City, Tenn. 5311 Jacksboro Pike, Fountain City, Tenn.
Monroe, Michigan	Monroe	Elder Lenvil Meyers	Disty Russell	5177 Plum Creek, Monroe, Mch.
New Hebron	Jefferson	Elder Gilbert Atkins	Cordie Mitchell Rachel Mitchell, asst.	New Market, Tenn.
Noeton	Grainger	Elder Gilbert Atkins	John Oliver Bessie Collins, asst.	Bean Station, Tenn. Morristown, Tenn.
Oak Grove	Union	Elder W. M. Sparks Elder Clifford Brantley, asst.	Belle Moore Ruth Shoffner, asst.	Sharps Chapel, Tenn. Sharps Chapel, Tenn.
Pleasant Hill	Claiborne	Elder Tony Eastridge Elder J. H. Branscomb, asst.	William Branscomb Verlin Edwards, asst.	Speedwell, Tenn. Speedwell, Tenn.
Pleasant Point	Claiborne	Elder Tony Eastridge	Austin Beason	Goin, Tenn.
Rocky Dale	Knox	Elder Hugh Brummitt Elder Parnick Shelton, asst	Arvell Graves Roy Clapp, asst.	Corryton, Tenn. 2231 Washington Ave., Knoxville, Tenn.

1964
MINUTES
of the

One Hundred and Forty-Fifth

ANNUAL SESSION
of the

POWELLS VALLEY ASSOCIATION
of

PRIMITIVE BAPTISTS
held with

THE CHURCH AT OAK GROVE
UNION COUNTY, TENNESSEE

AUGUST 14-15-16, 1964

OFFICERS
Elder Albert Davis .... Moderator
Elder Hugh Brummitt ....Assistant Moderator
Brother Austin Beason ....Clerk
Brother O. R. Parrott .... Assistant Clerk
    The next session will be held with the Church at Lenoir City in Loudon County, Tennessee. It will begin on Friday before the third Saturday in August, 1965. Elder Noble Lee Clawson will preach the Introductory Sermon. Elder Claude Rosson will be the alternate.

CHURCHES	DELEGATES	Restored	Received by Relationship	Received by Baptism	Received by Letter	Dismissed by Letter	Excluded	Deceased	Total Membership	Visiting Ministers	Printing Minutes	Saturday Meeting	Communion Meeting
Black Fox	George Campbell, John Davis, Walton Cabbage, Bennie Capps, Jessie Cabbage, Roma Bailey, Flossie Capps, Roy Bailey	0	0	2	0	0	0	2	88	$ 00.00	$ 10.00	2	2, June
Braden's Chapel	J. C. Monday, N. L. Clawson, W. M. Sparks, Henry Comer, Leecy Sparks, Winona Monday	0	3	2	0	0	0	1	76	00.00	5.00	1	1, July
Brantley's Chapel	Wayne Brantley, Mayme Brantley, Ellis Evans, Lottie Evans, Everett Brantley, Mildred Brantley	0	0	0	0	3	3	0	77	00.00	5.00	2	2, July
Cedar Springs	Clifford Robertson, Ida Robertson, Maggie Robertson, Velta Munsey, Mary Treece	0	0	3	0	0	0	0	63	00.00	3.00	4	4, May
Davis Chapel	Mr. and Mrs. Leonard White, Earl White, Mr. and Mrs. Onle Parrott, Cordela Lynch	0	0	0	0	0	0	3	147	4.00	4.00	3	3, June
Gibson Station	Franklin Jones, Brenda Jones, Mellie Thompson	0	4	0	0	0	1	1	96	4.00	4.00	1 Eve.	1, June
Kirkwood	Hugh Brummitt, Ruby Brummitt, Walter Lyons, W. H. Taylor, Lou Emma Taylor, M. A. Norton, Lucy Norton, Jack Cook, Dottie Cook	0	3	2	3	0	0	2	117	5.00	10.00	Sun.	Last April
Lenoir City	Mr. and Mrs. Chamberlain, Mr. and Mrs. Caney Key, Cora Hill	0	0	0	0	0	0	0	212	5.00	5.00	3	3, May
Monroe, Michigan	Mr. and Mrs. John Drumonds, Mr. and Mrs. Ditsy Russell, Mrs. Katie Cupp, Mrs. Marie Evans, Mrs. Gertrude Zwak	0	0	1	1	0	0	0	46	00.00	5.00	3	3, July
New Hebron	Gilbert Atkins	0	0	0	0	0	0	0	25	00.00	1.00	4	4 & Sept.
Noetown	Johnny Atkins, Gilbert Atkins, Jake Overbay, John Oliver	0	0	3	0	1	0	3	38	00.00	3.00	3	3, May
Oak Grove	George Shoffner, Tony Eastridge, Mr. and Mrs. Malcolm Walker, Mr. and Mrs. Alfred Relford, Mr. and Mrs. Aaron Cole, Mr. and Mrs. Lowell Relford, Mr. and Mrs. Manie Shoffner, Cills Shoffner, Hodge Walker, Lillie Shoffner, Tessie Creech, Francis Eastridge, Belle Moore, Floy Cole, Ruth Edwards	0	0	8	1	0	0	4	308	00.00	8.00	1	1. May
Pleasant Hill	Mr. and Mrs. J. H. Branscomb, Mr. and Mrs. Albert Davis, Verlin Edwards, Sarah Branscomb	0	0	6	0	0	0	0	95	00.00	10.00	4	4, June
Pleasant Point	Mr. and Mrs. Claude Rosson, Mr. and Mrs. George Williams, C. D. Keck	0	0	0	0	0	0	3	122	60.00	10.00	1	1, July
Rocky Dale	Everett Berry, Trula Berry, Parnick Shelton, Wilma Shelton, Elmer Graves, Bessie Graves, Arvell Graves, Joe Graves, Joe Bush, Jean Bush	0	0	2	0	0	2	0	113	5.00	5.00	2	2, May

FRIDAY'S PROCEEDINGS

First—According to previous arrangements the Association met pursuant to adjournament.

Second—After singing, Elder Albert Davis read the 13th chapter of the I Corinthians. Prayer was by Elder Claude Rosson. Then Elder James H. Branscomb spoke from the 10th Chapter, 9th Verse of Romans. After singing, we were dismissed by Elder R. H. Pettit.

Third—After intermission there was more singing. Prayer was by Elder Tony Eastridge and Elder John Russell.

Fourth—The Association was called to order by Elder Albert Davis.

Fifth—The Moderator called for letters from sister churches.

Sixth—On motion all said letters except one were received and the delegates were welcomed to seats by the Moderator.

Seventh—A call was made for members who were not delegates. None were received.

Eighth—There was a call for petitionary letters from other churches. Lenoir City was received by move and second. The delegates were welcomed to seats by the Moderator.

Ninth—A call was made for letters from Corresponding Associations. Two were received—from New Bethlem and Hiwassee.

Tenth—The letters were read and the delegates were welcomed to seats with us. The Hiwassee delegates were Elder John Russell and Elder and Mrs. Claude Thomas. The New Bethlem delegate was Elder Carl McCarty.

Eleventh—On motion and second Elder Albert Davis was re-elected Moderator and Elder Hugh Brummitt was re-elected Assistant Moderator.

Twelfth—On motion and second Brother Austin Beason was re-elected Clerk, and Brother O. R. Parrott was re-elected Assistant Clerk.

Thirteenth—On motion the Moderator appointed the following committees:

1. Arrangements—A. G. Relford, Ditsy Russell, Caney Key.
2. Preaching—M. A. Norton, Ellis Evans, Verlin Edwards.
3. Correspondence—J. H. Branscomb, Tony Eastridge, Parnick Shelton.
4. Request—W. H. Taylor, John Davis, Elmer Graves.
5. Finance—Everett Berry, Claude Rosson, John L. Drummonds.

Fourteenth—On motion we adjourned until 10:00 A.M. on Saturday, August 15, 1964.

SATURDAY'S PROCEEDINGS

First—After singing, Elder Hugh Brummitt spoke from the 16th Chapter of Ezekiel. Prayer was by Elder Carl McCarty.

Second—There was a call for letters that failed to get in Friday. One was received from Cedar Springs. The delegates were welcomed to seats by the Moderator.

Third—A call was made for the report of the Committee on Arrangements.

We, the Committee on Arrangements, beg leave to submit the following report:

1. Call the roll.
2. Call for the report of the Committee on Preaching.
3. Call for the report of the Committee on Correspondence.
4. Call for the report of the Committee on Request.
5. Call for the report of the Committee on Finance.

—1—

When and where shall our next Association be held? Who shall preach the Introductory Sermon? Who shall be his alternate? How many of the copies of the Minutes shall we have printed? Who shall superintend the printing and distribution of them? What shall be allowed for his services?

Respectfully submitted,
A. G. RELFORD
DITSY RUSSELL
CANEY KEY

Fourth—On motion the report was received and the Committee discharged.

Fifth—The roll was called and the names of the absentees erased.

Sixth—A call was made for the report of the Committee on Preaching.

We, the Committee on Preaching, beg leave to submit the following report:

1. Friday night at the Church—Elder Claude Thomas and Elder Noble Lee Clawson.
2. Friday night at Blue Springs—Elder Leonard White.
3. Saturday morning at the Church—Elder Clifford Brantley and Elder Hugh Brummitt.
4. Saturday night at the Church—Elder Carl McCarty.
5. Saturday night at Gibson Station—Elder Hugh Brummitt.
6. Sunday morning at the Church—Elder Everett Berry.

The Moderator is to close.

Respectfully submitted,
M. A. NORTON
ELLIS EVANS
VERLIN EDWARDS

Seventh—On motion the report was received and the Committee discharged.

Eighth—A call was made for the report of the Committee on Correspondence.

We, the Committee on Correspondence, beg leave to submit the following report:

We shall keep up our correspondence with the Hiwassee and the New Bethlem Associations.

Respectfully submitted,
JAMES H. BRANSCOMB
TONY EASTRIDGE   ·
PARNICK SHELTON

Ninth—On motion the report was received and the Committee discharged.

Tenth—A call was made for the report of the Committee on Request.

We, the Committee on Request, beg leave to submit the following report:

We shall publish all the obituaries that the churches furnish. Our next Association will be held with the Church at Lenoir City in Loudon County, Tennessee. It will begin on Friday before the third Saturday in August, 1965 and continue the two following days.

Respectfully submitted,
W. H. TAYLOR
JOHN DAVIS
ELMER GRAVES

—2—

Eleventh—On motion the report was received and the Committee discharged.

Twelfth—A call was made for the report on the Committee on Finance. We, the Committee on Finance, beg leave to submit the following report:

Church	Printing Minutes	Visiting Ministers
Gibson Station	$ 4.00	$ 4.00
Braden's Chapel	5.00	0.00
Pleasant Hill	10.00	0.00
Monroe, Michigan	5.00	0.00
Davis Chapel	4.00	4.00
Black Fox	10.00	0.00
Cedar Springs	3.00	0.00
Noeton	3.00	0.00
Brantley's Chapel	5.00	0.00
Oak Grove	8.00	0.00
Kirkwood	10.00	5.00
Pleasant Point	10.00	0.00
Rocky Dale	5.00	5.00
New Hebron	1.00	0.00
Lenoir City (East Side)	5.00	5.00
Total Received	$88.00	$23.00
Balance Carried Over From 1963		79.00
Complete Total		$190.00
Total Expense		$150.00
Balance in Treasury		$ 40.00

Respectfully submitted,
EVERETT BERRY
CLAUDE ROSSON
JOHN L. DRUMMONDS

Thirteenth—On motion the report was received and the Committee discharged. (B) On motion the clerk is to pay the visiting ministers.

Fourteenth—On motion we passed to have 1,000 copies of the Minutes printed, and the clerk will superintend the printing and distribution of them. He is to be allowed $50.00 for his services.

Fifteenth—On motion the next annual session is to be held at the Lenoir City Church in Loudon, County, Tennessee. It is to begin on Friday before the third Saturday in August, 1965, and continue the two following days.

Sixteenth—On motion Elder Noble Lee Clawson was selected to preach the Introductory Sermon. Elder Claude Rosson will be his alternate.

Seventeenth—On motion we agreed to send Elder Albert Davis, Elder Henry Comer, and Elder Tony Eastridge to the Hiwassee Association and Elder W. M. Sparks, Elder J. C. Monday, Elder George Campbell, and Elder Henry Comer to the New Bethlem Association.

Eighteenth—On motion the Clerk will write a letter of Correspondence to each.

Nineteenth—On motion we extend to the old Church and the people of the surrounding community our sincere appreciation for the kindness

—3—

and generous hospitality shown us throughout the Association at the above stated place and date.

Twentieth—There was a move and second that we adjourn our business until 10:30 A.M. at the above stated place and date. We were dismissed by Elder Henry Vann.

Respectfully submitted,

ELDER ALBERT DAVIS, Moderator
Speedwell, Tennessee
ELDER HUGH BRUMMITT, Asst. Moderator
1329 Brown Avenue
Knoxville, Tennessee
AUSTIN BEASON, Clerk
Goin, Tennessee
O. R. PARROTT, Asst. Clerk
LaFollette, Tennessee

Twenty-First—After intermission, the Association re-assembled. After singing there was prayer by Elder Henry Comer. He was followed by Elder Clifford Brantley who spoke from the 3rd Chapter-7th Verse of Malachi. Then Elder Hugh Brummitt spoke from the 12th Chapter, 1st and 2nd Verses of Hebrews. We were dismissed by Elder J. C. Monday.

SUNDAY'S PROCEEDINGS

On Sunday a large crowd gathered at the altar. There was singing then Elder W. M. Sparks spoke some consoling words. Prayer was by Elder Clifford Brantley. Elder Everett Berry spoke from the first chapter and 16th verse of the Book of Ruth. This was enjoyed by all. The closing was by the Moderator. We were dismissed by Elder Johnnie Atkins.

MINISTERS

Elder Gilbert Atkins .... Route 3
Rutledge, Tennessee
Elder Johnnie Atkins .... Bean Station, Tennessee
Elder Everett Berry .... Fountain City, Tennessee
Phone 922-4241
Elder J. H. Branscomb .... Speedwell, Tennessee
Phone 86-3392
Elder Clifford Brantley .... Brown School Road
Maryville, Tennessee
Phone 982-3735
Elder Hugh Brummitt .... 1329 Brown Avenue
Knoxville, Tennessee
Phone 525-3583
Elder George Campbell .... Route 2
Corryton, Tennessee
Elder Nobel Lee Clawson .... Speedwell, Tennessee
Elder Albert Davis .... Speedwell, Tennessee
Phone 86-3667
Elder Henry Comer .... Route 4
LaFollette, Tennessee
Phone 562-3952

—4—

Elder T. I. Eastridge ....Route 2
Louisville, Tennessee
Phone 983-1068
Elder Dewey Ellison ....Sharps Chapel, Tennessee
Elder Joe Irwin   ....Gibson Station, Virginia
Elder Walter Lyons ....1602 Garfield Street
Alcoa, Tennessee
Phone YU 33222
Elder Lenvil Meyers ....512 East Elm Street
Monroe, Michigan
Elder J. C. Monday ....Speedwell, Tennessee
Elder Roy Oliver ....Bean Station, Tennessee
Elder R. H. Pettit ....107 Jacksboro Pike
Fountain City, Tennessee
Phone 689-5581
Elder Claude Rosson ....Goin, Tennessee
Phone 626-3168
Elder Parnick Shelton ....Corryton, Tennessee
Phone 689-6183
Elder George Shoffner ....Sharps Chapel, Tennessee
Elder W. M. Sparks ....Speedwell, Tennessee
Phone 562-7997
Elder Leonard White ....LaFollette, Tennessee
Phone 562-5667

LICENTIATES

Odell Carpenter ....Maryville, Tennessee
Jim Oliver ....Bean Station, Tennessee

CORRESPONDING LETTER

We, the Powells Valley Association of the Primitive Baptist, now in session at the Oak Grove Church in Union County, Tennessee on August 14-15-16, 1964, send greetings to the Hiwassee and New Bethlem Associations with whom we correspond. Very Dear Brothers and Sisters, We desire to keep our long cherished correspondence with you. We have chosen these our beloved Elders to bear this epistle of love to you. Our messengers to the Hiwassee Association are Elder Albert Davis, Elder Tony Eastridge, and Elder Henry Comer. Our messengers to the New Bethlem Association are Elder W. M. Sparks, Elder J. C. Monday, Elder Henry Comer, and Elder George Campbell. Having seated all your delegates, we heartily welcome more next year when we convene with the Church at Lenoir City in Loudon County, Tennessee. We will begin on Friday before the third Saturday in August, 1965.

OBITUARIES

MRS. LOU ATKINS

Mrs. Lou Atkins, age 73, died suddenly Tuesday, July 9, 1963, at Morristown-Hamblem Hospital. She professed faith in Christ at an early age and joined the Primitive Baptist Church where she remained a faithful member until death. She leaves to mourn her loss: husband—Richard Atkins, Thorn Hill, Tennessee; three daughters—Mrs. Bertha Branton and Mrs. Lizzie Coffey both of Morristown and Mrs. Dora Long, Rutledge; two sons— Archie, Rutledge and Nelson, Thorn Hill; three brothers—Jim Oliver, Washburn, Doyle Oliver, Thorn Hill, and Roy Oliver, Bean Station; one sister—Mrs. Relda Hurst, Morristown; 16 grandchildren; 8 great-grand- children. "Our loss is her eternal gain. So sleep on Dear Wife and Mother. We know when Jesus comes to gather his elect, you will be in that blessed number." Funeral services were conducted at the home with Elder Johnnie Atkins and Elder Gilbert Atkins officiating. Burial in Atkins Cemetery.

JOHN HENRY CINNAMON

John Henry Cinnamon, age 73, of Route 3, LaFollette, died at 4:25 A.M. Wednesday, January 8, 1964, at the LaFollette Community Hospital. The survivors are: the wife—Eva Cinnamon; daughter—Mrs. Joyce Green of Jacksboro; sons—Edward, Lincoln Park, Michigan and Floyd, LaFollette; sisters—Mrs. M. J. White, LaFollette and Mrs. Adeline Rakestraw, Oak- ford, Indiana; half - sister—Mrs. Nellie Letner, Knoxville; half-brother— Amon Boruff, LaFollette and Eprin Boruff, Kenvir, Kentucky; 7 grand- children. He was a member of the Davis Chapel Primitive Baptist Church. Funeral services were held Friday afternoon, January 10, at Midway Bap- tist Church, LaFollette. Reverend Ernest Goins and Reverend Ralph Cordell officiated. Burial was in the Davis Chapel Cemetery.

JAMES MILTON COX

James Milton Cox was born January 5, 1876 and departed this life February 5, 1964. He was 88 years and one month old. He was preceded in death by his wife Hettie Brewer Cox in 1947. Survivors: son—Tilmon, Goin; 5 grandchildren; 10 great-grandchildren; one great-great-grandchild; brothers—Charlie Cox of Dayhoit, Kentucky, General Cox of Middlesboro, Kentucky; sisters—Mrs. Frelia Williams and Mrs. Sally Johnson both of Goin, Tennessee, Mrs. Mossie Haley of Middlesboro, Kentucky, and Mrs. Lunda Keck of Knoxville, Tennessee. He joined the Pleasant Point Primitive Baptist Church and remained a member until death. Funeral services were conducted by Elder Tony Eastridge and Elder John R. Weaver. Burial was in the church cemetery.

—7—

SAMUEL NATHAN DAVIS

Samuel Nathan Davis was born June 27, 1878, and passed from this life May 11, 1964. He was 85 years-10-months-14 days old. He professed faith in Christ about sixty years ago and joined the Black Fox Primitive Baptist Church where he remained a faithful member until death. He was clerk of the Powells Valley Association for thirty-seven years. In the year nineteen hundred he was united in marriage to Sallie Kirk. To this union eleven children were born. Flossie, a daughter, preceded him in death. Survivors: the widow, eight sons, two daughters, three sisters, many other relatives, and a host of friends. All will miss him and mourn his passing.

EMIT DYKE

Emit Dyke, age 75, of Sharps Chapel, died at St. Mary's Hospital at 2:00 A.M. Wednesday. He was a member of the Oak Grove Baptist Church. Survivors: wife—Mossie Dyke; daughters—Mrs. Clayton Sheckles of Monroe, Michigan, Mrs. Mana Moyers of Knoxville, Tennessee; sons—Otis and Frank of Monroe, Michigan, Noble and Edward of Halls Cross Roads, Pete of Sharps Chapel, Tennessee, Willard (Pat) of San Francisco, California; sisters—Mrs. Erin Rouse of Monroe, Michigan, Mrs. Leslie Graves of Maynardville, Tennessee; 38 grandchildren. Funeral services were at 2:00 P.M. at the Oak Grove Church. Elder W. M. Sparks and Elder Albert Davis officiated. Interment was in the Oak Grove Cemetery.

FOREST S. HAMILTON

Forest S. Hamilton was born May 30, 1895, and passed away April 5, 1964. He professed faith in Christ at an early age and joined the Hamilton Grove Primitive Baptist Church where he was a member until the water of Norris Dam came. He then became a member of Oak Grove where he remained until death. He was married to Mammie Ousley Hamilton March 14, 1914. There were two children. Survivors: son—Fate Hamilton of Greenback, Tennessee; daughter—Icie Hamilton Myers of Maryville, Tennessee; three grandchildren; one great-grandchild; two brothers—Ernest Hamilton of Maryville, Tennessee and Murphy Hamilton of Philadelphia, Tennessee; sister—Sallie Hamilton Riley of Kentucky. Funeral services were held at Smiths Chapel in Maryville. Reverend Thomas Lynch, Reverend F. S. Fuller, and Elder Tony Eastridge officiated. Interment was in Grandview Cemetery. "Gone but not Forgotten."

JAMES MERTON KITTS

James Merton Kitts, age 72, died June 28, 1964, at Veterans Hospital, Mountain Home, Tennessee. Survivors: wife—Nannie; daughters—Mrs. Joseph McCoin of Cleveland, Tennessee and Mrs. Roy Bentley of LaFollette; sons—Jesse L. and George E both of Dayton, Ohio; seven grandchildren. Funeral services were held at Davis Chapel Baptist Church, of which he was a member. Elder Leonard White and Elder J. E. Ledbetter officiated. Interment in the Sunrise Cemetery.

AMOS OAK LARMER

Amos Oak Larmer was born January 5, 1912, and passed away at his home near Liberty Hill after a lingering illness January 18, 1964. He leaves to mourn his passing: wife—Carrie N. Larmer; daughter—Bernice Larmer of Liberty Hill; sisters—Lizzie Bailey and Mary Jones of Powder Springs;

—8—

brothers—Ruber and Odra both of Washburn and Austin and Garfield both of Powder Springs; 19 neices; 9 nephews; a host of friends and relatives. He professed hope in Christ at an early age and later joined the Black Fox Primitive Baptist Church where he remained a faithful member until death. We want to thank our friends and all the community for their kindness in this bereaved hour.

"While we are sad, Heaven was made glad,
You are not forgotten, nor will you ever be,
As long as life and memory last, we will remember thee,
Your loving smile and gentle face,
No one will ever take your place."

Written by wife and daughter

JOSEPH WESLEY LONG

Joseph Wesley (Joe) Long was born May 30, 1904. He passed away suddenly at his home in Morristown February 9, 1964. He was the son of the late Joe Frank and Elizabeth Oliver Long of Morristown and the son-in-law of the late Elder Mathew Oliver. He was married to Zella Oliver and to this union was born five children two of which died in infancy. Survivors: wife—Zella; son—Raymond of Morristown; daughters—Mrs. Fayrene Reed and Mrs. Opal Woods both of Morristown; sisters—Mrs. Parlea Shannon and Mrs. Ruth Bunch both of Morristown and Miss Pearl Long of Maryland; 9 grandchildren; brothers—Hubert, Mathew, and Ernest all of Morristown. He professed faith in Christ and joined the Noeton Primitive Baptist Church in May, 1957. He lived a faithful member until death. The funeral services were conducted by his pastor Elder Gilbert Atkins assisted by Elder Johnny Atkins and Elder Olaf Atkins. He was laid to rest in the Hamblen Memorial Gardens in Hamblen County, Tennessee at 2 P.M. Wednesday February 12, 1964. Pallbearers were nephews and the neices served as flower girls.

"Your gentle face and patient smile
    with sadness we recall.
You had a kindly word for each
    and died beloved by all.
Ah bitter was the trial to part
    from one as good as you.
You are not forgotten loved one
    nor will you ever be.
As long as life and memory last
    we will remember thee.
We miss you now, our hearts are sore.
As time goes by, we miss you more.
Your loving smile, your gentle face,
No one can fill your vacant place."

Wife and Children

PARIS HAYNES OUSLEY

Paris Haynes Ousley, age 94, of Route 3, Emory Road, Powell, Tennessee, passed away at his home Sunday. A member of Oak Grove Church, he was a retired farmer and former merchant in Union and Meigs Counties. He was sheriff of Union County from 1900 to 1902. Survivors: daughters—Mrs. K. D. Lively of Witchita, Kansas, Miss Delta Ousley of Powell, Mrs. A. V. Edwards of Kokomo, Indiana, Mrs. H. E. Anderson of Knoxville, Tennessee, Mrs. E. B. Edgemon of Ten Mile, Tennessee; sons—Herbert F. Ousley of

Hartford City, Indiana, Ott C. Ousley of Maynardville, Tennessee, Osbern Ousley of Sharps Chapel, Tennessee, Herchel Ousley of Route 2, Powell, Tennessee, Durard Ousley of Athens, Tennessee, Winslow T. Ousley of Kokomo, Indiana; 25 grandchildren; 23 great-grandchildren; 4 great-great-grandchildren. Funeral services were at 2:00 P.M. Wednesday at Gentry's Chapel. Reverend John Wilder officiated. Interment was in the Bethel Church Cemetery.

LAFAYETTE RUTHERFORD

Lafayette Rutherford, age 84, of 122 Ault Street, Knoxville, Tennessee, passed away at 11:00 A.M., Saturday, April 11, 1964, after a lingering illness. He was a member of Kirkwood Primitive Baptist Church and had been a christian for almost seventy years. Survivors: wife—Mrs. Beulah Cody Rutherford; daughter—Mrs. George Von Wahlde of Cincinnati, Ohio; brother—Frank Rutherford of Knoxville; half-brother and three half-sisters all of LaFollette. Funeral service were at 2:00 P.M. Monday, April 13, 1964, at McCammon-Ammons Chapel in Maryville, Tennessee. Elder Leonard White and Reverend John Steiner officiated. Interment was in the Zion Chapel Cemetery in Blount County.

LILLIE SHOFFNER

Mrs. Lillie Shoffner, the wife of George Shoffner, passed away November 2, 1963, at the home of her daughter in Louisville, Tennessee. She was 87 years old. She was a member of the Oak Grove Primitive Baptist Church. Survivors: husband—George Shoffner; daughters—Mrs. Ebb Moore of Sharps Chapel, Mrs. Luna Sherritze of Goin, and Mrs. Tony Eastridge of Louisville; sons—Charlie, Mannie, and Cillis all of Sharps Chapel. "She bore her illness with patience. She always wanted to help someone else. She attended church as long as she was able. She is gone from this world to Gods eternal shore. She was a devoted wife and loving mother. Our loss is Heaven's gain." Funeral services were held at 11:00 A.M. Monday, November 4, 1963, at the Oak Grove Baptist Church. Elder Bill Sparks and Elder J. H. Branscomb officiated. Interment was in the Rush Strong Cemetery.

Husband and Children

JAMES H. STANFORD

James H. Stanford, age 87, died at 4:00 A.M. Tuesday, December 24, 1963, at Mormont Rest Home in Norris, after a lingering illness. He was a member of Kirkwood Primitive Baptist Church. Survivors: son—Charles of Avon Park, Florida; daughters—Mrs. W. E. Heatherly and Mrs. Ollie Armstrong both of Knoxville and Mrs. W. S. Pritchard of Oak Ridge; brothers—John and Ranson both of LaFollette; sisters—Mrs. Nettie Davis and Mrs. Rushia O'Rick both of LaFollette; 9 grand-children; 16 great-grandchildren. Funeral services were held at 2:00 P.M. Thursday, December 26, 1963, at Davis Chapel in LaFollette, Tennessee. Elder Leonard White officiated. Interment in Davis Chapel Cemetery.

—10—

CARL STUBBLEFIELD

Carl Stubblefield was born May 25, 1885 and passed away at his home February 10, 1964. He lived near Bean Station, Tennessee. He had been ill for eight years. He professed faith in Christ at an early age and was a member of Noeton Primitive Baptist Church. Survivors: wife—Henrietta; daughters—Kate Stubblefield and Mrs. Hattie Mae Overbay; son—Muscoe Stubblefield; two granddaughters—Helen Stubblefield and Mrs. Estes Johnson; one great-grandson—Terry Dean Johnson; (All of the above survivors are of Bean Station.) sister—Mrs. Ada Blair of Morristown; several neices and nephews; a host of friends. Services were held at Noeton Baptist Church with Elder Gilbert Atkins, Elder Olaf Atkins, and Elder Clarence Crews officiating. Interment was in the church cemetery.

ALF WHITE

Alf White, age 84, passed away at his home in LaFollette, Tennessee June 25, 1964. He professed faith in Christ at an early age. He was a member of the Davis Chapel Primitive Baptist Church. He was married to Louisa Berry and to their union seven children were born. Two children preceded him in death. Survivors: wife—Louisa; daughters—Mrs. Beatrice Nelson of Holyoke, Massachusetts and Mrs. Orebell Miller of LaFollette; sons—Clarence of Holyoke, Massachusetts and Forest and Walter both of LaFollette; brother—Louis; 11 grandchildren; 4 great-grandchildren. We feel our loss is his eternal gain. Funeral services were held at Davis Chapel Church by Elder Hugh Brummitt and Elder Everett Berry. Interment was in the Sunrise Cemetery at Davis Chapel.

BESSIE PROFFIT WILSON

Bessie Proffit Wilson was born May 11, 1889, and departed this life June, 1963. Survivors: daughter—Lois Kennedy; 3 grandchildren—Wilma, Sonny, and Judy all of Knoxville; sisters—Sadie Rouse and Loumae Keck both of Goin and Etter Keck of Knoxville; brothers—Porter Proffit of Crossville and Theodore Proffit of Georgetown, Ohio. She joined the Pleasant Point Church in 1915. She left a testimony that she was all right. She was loved by those who knew her. She moved to Knoxville and could not attend her church as she wanted to, but she went to other churches and lived faithful to Christ. "While we were made sad—Heaven was made glad." Our loving sister, Bessie.

—11—

CHURCHES	COUNTY	PASTORS	CLERKS	CLERK'S POST OFFICE
Black Fox	Grainger	Elder Parnick Shelton	Bennie Capps Flossie Capps	P. O. Box 91 Maynardville, Tenn. Liberty Hill, Tenn.
Braden's Chapel	Union	Elder J. C. Monday, Mod. Elder N. L. Clawson, asst.	Arvil Braden	Speedwell, Tenn.
Brantley's Chapel	Blount	Elder Clifford Brantley Elder Everett Berry, asst.	Rina Johnson Rina Johnson, Jr., asst.	9 Douglas Avenue Maryville, Tenn. 14 Houston Avenue Maryville, Tenn.
Cedar Springs	Claiborne	Elder N. L. Clawson, Mod. W. M. Sparks, asst.	Pearlie Holt	New Tazewell, Tenn.
Davis Chapel	Campbell	Elder Hugh Brummitt Elder Parnick Shelton, asst.	Ruth Heatherly Lassie Ellison, asst.	Davis Chapel Road R-1 LaFollette, Tenn. Rt. 1, LaFollette, Tenn.
Gibson Station	Lee, Virginia	Elder Leonard White Elder Everett Berry, asst.	Roxie Cobb Mossie Cottrell, asst.	Gibson Station, Va. Harrogate, Tenn.
Kirkwood	Knox	Elder Leonard White Elder R. H. Pettit, asst.	Estelle Petree Sharp Shirley S. Bowden, asst.	5313 Jacksboro Pike, Knoxville, Tenn. 811 Banks Ave., N.E. Knoxville, Tenn.
Lenoir City	Loudon	Elder Walter Lyons	Mary Parris	Rt. 4, Box 283-B Lenoir City, Tenn.
Monroe, Michigan	Monroe	Elder Lenvil Meyers	Disty Russell	5177 Plum Creek, Monroe, Mich.
New Hebron	Jefferson	Elder Gilbert Atkins	Cordie Mitchell Rachel Mitchell, asst.	New Market, Tenn. New Market, Tenn.
Noetown	Grainger	Elder Gilbert Atkins	John Oliver Bessie Collins, asst.	Bean Station, Tenn. Morristown, Tenn.
Oak Grove	Union	Elder W. M. Sparks Elder L. C. Monday, asst.	Belle Moore Ruth Shoffner, asst.	Sharp's Chapel, Tenn. Sharp's Chapel, Tenn.
Pleasant Hill	Claiborne	Elder Tony Eastridge Elder J. H. Branscomb, asst.	William Branscomb Verlin Edwards, asst.	Speedwell, Tenn. Speedwell, Tenn.
Pleasant Point	Claiborne	Elder Tony Eastridge	Austin Beason	Goin, Tenn.
Rocky Dale	Knox	Elder Hugh Brummitt Elder Parnick Shelton, asst.	Arvell Graves Roy Clapp, asst.	Corryton, Tenn. 2331 Washington Ave., Knoxville, Tenn.

1965
MINUTES
of the
One Hundred and Forty-Sixth
ANNUAL SESSION
of the
POWELLS VALLEY ASSOCIATION
of
PRIMITIVE BAPTISTS
held with
THE CHURCH AT LENOIR CITY
LOUDON COUNTY, TENNESSEE
AUGUST 20-21-22, 1965

OFFICERS

Elder Albert Davis .... Moderator
Elder Hugh Brummitt .... Assistant Moderator
Brother W. H. Taylor .... Clerk
Brother O. R. Parrott .... Assistant Clerk
    The Next Session will be held with the Church at Pleasant Point in Claiborne County, Tennessee. It will begin on Friday before the 3rd Saturday in August, 1966. Brother Claude Rosson will preach the introductory sermon, and Elder Walter Lyons will be the Alternate.

CHURCHES	DELEGATES	Restored	Received by Letter	Received by Baptism	Received by Relationship	Dismissed by Letter	Excluded	Deceased	Total Membership	Visiting Ministers	Printing Minutes	Meeting	Communion
Black Fox	Bonnie Capps, Jessie Cabbage, George Campbell, John Davis, Roma Bailey, Rachel Bailey, Sue Terry, Mary Terry, Debbie Terry	0	0	9	0	0	0	1	96	$0.00	$10.00	2nd Sat.	2nd June
Braden Chapel	Henry Comer, Wm. Sparks, J. C. Clawson and Buster Clawson	0	1	4	2	0	0	0	82	0	5.00	1st Sat.	1st June
Brantley's Chapel	Ellis Evans, Lottie Evans, Von Beeson, Genette Beeson, Mildred Brantley, Plumer McBee, Ottie McBee, Junior McBee, Clifford Brantley and Barsha Brantley	0	0	0	0	0	1	0	76	0	10.00	2nd Sat.	2nd July
Cedar Springs	Clay Widner, Wanda Widner, N. L. Clawson, Clifford Robertson and Maggie Robertson.	0	0	2	1	1	0	0	64	0	3.00	4th Sat.	4th May
Davis Chapel	Leonard White, Mrs. White, Earl White, Bro. and Sister Orlee McCarty and Cordelia Lynch	0	0	1	0	0	0	3	145	4.00	4.00	1 & 3 Sun. Night Sun.	1st Sat. June
Gibson Chapel	Franklin Jones, Floyd Warf, Fannie Jones, Brenda Jones and Birtha Turner	0	0	7	2	0	0	0	119	4.00	4.00	1st Sat.	1st Sun.
Kirkwood	Hugh Brummitt, Ruby Brummitt, Walter Lyons, Callie Lyons, R. H. Petitt, Mollie Petitt, M. A. Norton, Lucy Norton, W. H. Taylor, Louemma Tayor and Nellie Simer.	0	0	0	0	0	0	0	117	5.00	10.00	Each Sun.	Last Sun.
Lenoir City	Mr. and Mrs. Carey Key and Annie Spoon	0	0	2	1	4	4	4	205	5.00	5.00	3rd Sun.	3rd April
Monroe, Michigan	Lenvil Myers and John Drummonds	0	0	0	2	2	0	0	14	0	3.00	3rd Sun.	3rd July
Noeton	Jonnie Atkins and Wife, John Oliver and Jake Overbay	0	0	0	0	0	1	0	35	0	3.00	1st Sat.	1st May
New Hebron	George Shoffner, Tonie Eastridge, Francis Eastridge, Alfred Relford, Maggie Relford, Mannie Shoffner, Ruth Shoffner, Tishie Creech, Lillie Shoffner, Aaron Cole, Veda Co'e and Bell Moore. Gilbert Atkins	0	0	0	0	0	1	0	303	0	8.00	1st Sat.	1st May
Oak Grove	Elder George Shoffner, Elder Tony Eastridge, Sister Francis Eastridge, Bro. Alfred Relford, Sister Maggie Relford, Bro. Mannie Shoffner, Sister Ruth Shoffner, Sister Tishie Creech, Sister Lillie Shoffner, Bro. Aaron Cole, Sister Veda Cole and Sister Belle Moore.	0	0	0	0	0	0	0	25	0	0	4th Sat.	4th Sat. May & Sept.
Pleasant Hill	Mr. and Mrs. J. H. Branscomb, Mr. and Mrs. Albert Davis, Verlin Edwards and Sarah Branscomb	0	0	3	0	2	0	0	96	0	10.00	4th Sat.	4th June
Pleasant Point	George Williams, Claude Rosson, Doris Rosson and Allie Williams.	0	0	0	0	0	0	3	192	0	10.00	1st Sun.	1st July
Rocky Dale	Everett Berry, Trula Berry, Darnuck Shelton, Wilma Shelton, Elmer Graves, Arvell Graves, Joe Bush and Norma Bush.	0	0	0	2	0	1	2	112	0	0	Each Sun.	2nd Sun. May

FRIDAY, AUGUST 20, 1965

First—According to previous arrangements, the Association met pursuant to adjournment, with moderator, Elder Albert Davis presiding.

Second—After song service Moderator Albert Davis read from the 1st Chapter of Psalmist David. Followed by prayer by Elder Clifford Brantley.

Then Bro. Noble Lee Clawson preached the introductory sermon, taking as his text, the 122nd Psalm. After singing we were dismissed by Elder Walter Lyons.

Third—After intermission and more singing, and prayer, the moderator called the Association to order and asked for the letters of the sister churches. Letters were received from all sister churches except one. On motion and second the letters were received and the delegates were seated.

Fourth—Call was made for members from sister churches who were not delegates. Bros. Roy Oliver and Claude Thomas came.

Fifth—Motion carried to seat the delegation from Davis Chapel Church, pending arrival of their letter the following day.

Sixth—Call by moderator for petitionary letters, none were received.

Seventh—Call by moderator for letters from corresponding Associations. One was received from the Hiwassee Association. By motion their letter was received and their delegates were seated.

Eighth—Call for members who were not delegates and none came.

Ninth—By regular motion Bro. Albert Davis was reelected Moderator; Bro. Hugh E. Brummitt, Assistant Moderator. W. H. Taylor elected Clerk and Bro. O. R. Parrott, Assistant Clerk. Motion carried to send a letter of sympathy and appreciation for the splendid work of Bro. Austin Beason as clerk of the owell Valley Association.

Tenth—Motion carried for the moderator to appoint the following committees:

1. Arrangements
   M. A. Norton
   Ellis Evans
   Alvin Graves

2. Preaching
   John Davis
   John Oliver
   Henry Chamberlain

3. Correspondence
   R. H. Petitt
   Gilbert Atkins
   Parnick Shelton

4. Request
   Walter Lyons
   Henry Comer
   George Shoffner

5. Finance
   Earl White
   Cancy Key
   Clifford Brantley

Eleventh—By order the Association was adjourned until Saturday at 10:30.

SATURDAY, AUGUST 21, 1965

First—After a real good song service the Saturday session was introduced by Elder Hugh Brummitt reading from the 53rd Chapter of Isiah. This was followed by prayer by Elder William Sparks.

Second—Call for letters not received Friday. Two were received, the one delayed from Davis Chapel and one from the Church at Monroe, Michigan. The letter from these two churches were received and the delegation from Monroe, Michigan was seated. The delegation from Davis Chapel having been seated the previous day.

Third—By motion letter from the New Bethel Association was received and the delegation seated.

— 1 —

Fourth—By motion the Committee on Arrangements was released after submitting the following report:

1. Roll call of delegates.
2. Call for report of Committee on Preaching.
3. Call for report of Committee on Correspondence.
4. Call for report of Committee on Request.
5. Call for report of Committee on Finance.
6. When and where will the next Association be held? Who shall preach the introductory sermon and who shall be the alternate? How many copies of minutes shall we print and who shall supervise the printing and distribution of same? And, how much shall be allowed for this service?

Respectfully submitted,
E. N. Evans
M. A. Norton
Alvin Graves

Fifth—Call was made for report of Committee on Preaching. We the Committee on Preaching present the following report:

For Saturday—Elder Henry Comer and Elder Carl McCarty.

For Saturday Night—Elder Tony Eastridge and Elder Everett Berry.

For Sunday—Elder Leonard White and Elder Hugh Brummitt.

John Oliver
John Davis
Henry Chamberlain

Sixth—On motion the report was received and the committee realeased.

Seventh—A call was made for the report of the Committee on Correspondence. We the Committee on Correspondence beg to submit the following report: We shall keep our correspondence with the Hiwassee and New Bethel Associations.

R. H. Petitt
Parnick Shelton
Johnnie Atkins

Eighth—The report was received and the committee released.

Ninth—A call for the report of Committee on Request. We the Committee on request wish to make this report:

That we print all obituaries furnished by the churches. That our next Association be held with the church at Pleasant Point in Claiborne County, Tennessee, beginning on Friday before the 3rd Saturday in August 1966 and to continue the two following days.

Henry Comer
George Shoffner
Walter Lyons

Tenth—On motion the report was received and the committee released.

Eleventh—A call for the report of the Committee on Finance. We the Committee on Finance beg to submit the following report:

— 2 —

Church	Printing Minutes	Visiting Ministers
Black Fox	$10.00	
Bradens Chapel	5.00	
Brantleys Chapel	10.00	
Cedar Springs	3.00	
Davis Chapel	4.00	
Gibson Station	4.00	$ 4.00
Kirkwood	10.00	4.00
Monroe, Michigan	5.00	5.00
Noeton	3.00	
Lenoir City	10.00	
Oak Grove	8.00	
Rocky Dale	5.00	
Pleasant Hill	10.00	5.00
New Hebron		
Total	$92.00	$23.00
Collection	85.00	
Carried Over	40.00	
	23.00	
Total in Bank	$240.00	
Paid out	$193.00	
Balance	$ 47.00	

SUNDAY, AUGUST 22, 1965

After singing, Elder Lyons, Pastor of the church at Lenoir City, welcomed the people back to Lenoir City, then read the 23rd Psalm. This was followed by Elder Leonard White who gave a wonderful sermon from the 2nd Chapter and 21st Verse of Jashua. This was followed by Elder Hugh Brummitt, Assistant Moderator, who closed out the last service of the Association.

Respectfully submitted,
Elder Albert Davis,
Moderator
Elder Hugh Brummitt,
Assistant Moderator
W. H. Taylor,
Clerk
O. R. Parrott,
Assistant Clerk

MINISTERS

Elder Gilbert Atkins................................ Route 3
Rutledge, Tennessee
Elder Johnnie Atkins............................. Bean Station, Tennessee
Elder Everett Berry................................ Fountain City, Tennessee
Phone 922-4241
Elder J. H. Branscomb;........................... Speedwell, Tennessee
Phone 86-3392
Elder Clifford Brantley........................... Brown School Road
Maryville, Tennessee
Phone 982-3735
Elder Hugh Brummitt.............................. 1329 Brown Avenue
Knoxville, Tennessee
Phone 525-3583

Elder George Campbell.................................... Route 2
Corryton Tennessee
Elder Nobel Lee Clawson...... .... Speedwell, Tennessee
Elder Albert Davis.............................. Speedwell, Tennessee
Phone 86-3667
Elder Henry Comer.................................... Route 4
LaFollette, Tennessee
Phone 562-3952
Elder T. I. Eastridge................................... Route 2
Louisville, Tennessee
Phone 983-1068
Elder Dewey Ellison............................. Sharps Chapel, Tennessee
Elder Alvin Graves................................. Lenoir City, Tennessee
Elder Joe Irwin.................................... Gibson Station, Virginia
Elder Walter Lyons............................. 1602 Garfield Street
Alcoa, Tennessee
Phone YU 33222
Elder Lenvil Meyers................................ 512 East Elm Street
Monroe, Michigan
Elder J. C. Monday.......................... Speedwell, Tennessee
Elder Roy Oliver.................................... Bean Station, Tennessee
Elder R. H. Pettit................................. 107 Jacksboro Pike
Fountain City, Tennessee
Phone 689-5581
Elder Claude Rosson.............................. Goin, Tennessee
Phone 626-3168
Elder Parnick Shelton.......................... Corryton, Tennessee
Phone 689-6183
Elder George Shoffner............................ Sharps Chapel, Tennessee
Elder W. M. Sparks............................... Speedwell, Tennessee
Phone 562-7997
Elder Leonard White............................. LaFollette, Tennessee
Phone 562-5667

LICENIATES

Odell Carpenter.. Maryville, Tennessee
Jim Oliver.. Bean Station, Tennessee

September 13, 1965

We, the Powells Valley Association of Primitive Baptist, now in session with the church at Lenoir City, Tennessee, convening August 20, 21, and 22, send greetings to the Hiwassee Association with whom we correspond.

Our very dear Brothers and Sisters, we desire to keep our long cherished correspondence with you. We have chosen as messengers to bear the epistle of love to you, our beloved Elders: Elder George Campbell, Elder Tony Eastridge and Elder Henry Comer. Having seated and welcomed your delegation, we look forward to having more of you next year when we convene with the church at Pleasant Point in Claiborne County, Tennessee, beginning on Friday before the 3rd Saturday in August 1966.

Elder Albert Davis
Moderator
Elder Hugh Brummitt
Assistant Moderator
W. H. Taylor
Assoc. Clerk
O. R. Parrott
Assistant Clerk

— 4 —

September 13, 1965

We the Powell Valley Association of Primitive Baptist, now in session with the church at Lenoir City, Tennessee, on August 20, 21, and 22, hereby send greetings to the New Bethel Association with whom we correspond.

Dear Brothers and Sisters in Christ, we desire to keep our loving correspondence with you.

We have chosen to bear our message of love to you, the following: Elder Henry Comer, Elder Alvin Graves, Elder Clifford Brantley, Elder Noble Clawson and Elder Wm. Sparks. We trust you will seat these our beloved Brothers, and having seated and welcomed your delegation, we look forward to having more of you next year when we meet with the church at Pleasant Point in Claiborne Count, Tennessee, beginning on Friday before the 3rd Saturday in August 1966.

Elder Albert Davis,
Moderator
Elder Hugh Brummitt,
Assistant Moderator
W. H. Taylor,
Clerk
O. R. Parrott,
Assistant Clerk

September 29, 1965

Dear Sister Beason,

We the people and churches of the Powell Valley Association of Primitive Baptist, while in session with the church at Lenoir City, Tennessee, wish to extend to Mrs. Austin Beason, our deepest sympathy in her bereavement, caused by the passing of her dear husband and our good Clerk, Brother Austin Beason. We hereby extend to you, our Love, Prayers, and Sympathy of the Powell Valley Association.

Elder Albert Davis,
Moderator
Elder Hugh Brummitt,
Assistant Moderator
W. H. Taylor,
Clerk
O. R. Parrott,
Assistant Clerk

— 5 —

OBITUARIES
MRS. SALLIE WALLACE

Mrs. Sallie Wallace, age 97, passed away August 14, 1965 at the home of her daughter, Rt. 2 Maynardville. Survivors: daughters, Mrs. Ama Sexton, Mrs. Grace Graves of Corryton. Mrs. Eva Gose of Cincinnati, Ohio; sons, James Chesney of Knoxville, Tom Chesney of Cincinnati, Ohio. She was head of a five-generation family. 18 Grand-children; 47 great-grandchildren and 13 great-great-grandchildren.

She was a member of Rocky Dale Primitive Baptist Church. Funeral services were conducted by Elder Leonard White, who was Pastor of the church when she joined, and Rev. Curtis Carr. Interment in Pleasant View Cemetery.

She was an inspiration to all who knew her for her love of God, love of life; family and friends. The sincere patience she bore throughout her long life, and the tender smile she possessed.

Written by Grand-daughter
Wilma Shelton

SARAH ELIZABETH LAMB

Sarah Elizabeth Lamb was born April 29th, 1888, and departed this life April 21st, 1965. Age 76 years 11 months and 22 days. She is survived by daughters, Sarah Cooper, Esther Craig, Mollie McCarty; Sons, Louis Lamb, Frank Lamb, and Archie Lamb. One brother Charlie Thacher. She joined the church at Mossy Springs and later moved to Davis Chapel where she remained until death. Funeral services were held by Elder Leonard White and Elder W. M. Sparks. Interment in Sunrise Cemetery.

HERBERT E. GRAVES

Herbert E. Graves was born October 15, 1892. Passed away suddenly at his home in Anderson County September 14, 1964. He was the son of the late Eli and Caroline Keck Graves. Professed faith in Christ at an early age and joined the Primitive Baptist Church at Rocky Dale, Corryton, Tenn. He was also a vetran of World War One. He leaves to mourn his loss his wife Lucy, 5 sons, 7 daughters. Sons: J. C. Graves of Andersonville; Vinson of Heiskell; Herbert E., Jr. of Indiana; Elery and Harold of Florida. Daughters: Carolyn Fielden of Clinton; Naomi Demarcus, Barbara Hutchison of Knoxville; Sharon Hale of Norris; Rubylee Fielden of Andersonville; Deane Pointer and Charlotte Bell of Heiskell. 30 Grandchildren. 5 Brothers and 3 sisters. Many other relatives and a host of friends. Funeral services were conducted at Ailors Funeral Home. Elder Hugh Brummitt and Rev. Esco Hale officiated. Interment in Rocky Dale Cemetery.

A Patient Face.
A Loving Smile.
A voice from us is still.
Your vacant chair is in our home that never
    can be filled.

We miss you more our hearts are sad.
Your smile we cannot see.
But the memories of your gentle voice with
    us will ever be.

Written by Wife and Children
July 22, 1965

— 7 —

622

JAMES FRANKLIN CADLE

James Franklin Cadle age 76, of 7 Douglas Avenue, Maryville passed away September 5, 1964. He was a member of Brantley's Chapel Primitive Baptist Church. Survivors, wife, Malissie Cadle, one daughter Mrs. Hazel Johnson of Maryville, three sons, Riley Cadle of Maryville. J. C. and Alfred Cadle of New Market, Six Grandchildren and five great-grandchildren. Stepmother Katherine Blakley of Oneida; Six brothers, George of Speedwell, Charlie of Sevierville, Bill and Willard of Jamestown, Thomas and Clint of New Mexico. Three half-brothers; Warl and Elvin of Illinois, Roy of Oneida.

Funeral services were held at Brantley's Chapel Primitive Baptist Church. Elder Clifford Brantley and Elder Tony Eastridge officiating. Interment in Church Cemetery.

> They say time heals all sorrows and helps us to forget.
> But time so far has only proved how much we miss you yet.
> God gave us strength to face it and courage to bare the blow.
> But what it meant to lose you no one will ever know.

Mother and Children.

MRS. MYRTLE MUNSEY

Mrs. Myrtle Munsey was born November 21, 1907, died March 7, 1965, professed faith in Christ at an early age, joined the Primitive Baptist Church at Black Fox. She remained a member until her death. She is survived by four daughters; Miss Faustine Clay, Mrs. Lissia Arnwine, Mrs. Ruth Dalton and Mrs. Judy Dalton, one son, Carl P. Munsey of the U. S. Army.

We loved you but Jesus loved you more. He has sweetly called you to yonders shining shore.

Written by a daughter, Mrs. Ruth Dalton.

MRS. CORA MAYES KECK

Mrs. Cora Mayes Keck, 70, passed away at her home, Goin, Tennessee on March 5, 1965. Survivors: husband, Grover Keck, Goin Son, Woodrow Keck, Goin; Daughter, Mrs. Leva Claxton, Knoxville; nine Grandchildren, four great grandchildren and one foster great grandson. Brothers, Audie Mayes of Goin and Cletis Mayes, Monroe, Michigan. Sister, Mrs. Effie Beason and Mrs. Letta Gregg, Monroe, Michigan. Mrs. Emma Cox, Middlesboro, Kentucky and Mrs. Syble Simmons of Knoxville, Tennessee, and a host of relatives and friends.

She joined the Primitive Baptist Church at Pleasant Point in 1927 and was baptized by Elder Virlin Graves. She loved the church and was a faithful member. She spoke of death frequently during her illness and said she was not afraid to die and at the last moment of life she smiled and just seemingly went to sleep.

The funeral was held at the Pleasant Point Church with the Elders Claude Rasson, Lloyd England and Albert Davis officiating.

The large crowd and beautiful flowers showed that she was held in high esteem by relatives and friends.

She was laid to rest in the Keck Cemetery at Pleasant Point.

— 8 —

623

JAMES A. BEASON

James A. Beason, age 59, died at his home August 4. He was a member of Pleasant Point Primitive Baptist Church and served as Church clerk for 26 years. He was clerk of the Powell Valley Association for 10 years.

Survivors: Wife, Cleo Beason, New Tazewell; Sons, Bruce Beason, New Tazewell; Hollis Beason, Kokomo, Indiana. Daughters: Wilma Gibson and Carol Duncan, Tazewell. Eleven Grandchildren. Brothers: Jeff, Mannie and Dewey Beason, Monroe, Michigan. Paris Beason, New Tazewell.

Sister Pearl McBee, Monroe, Michigan.

ELDER ARCH PACKETT

Elder Arch Packett was born April 13, 1903, passed away Feb. 8, 1965. He was suddenly called away after preaching his final sermon about 7:30 p.m.

He had been a member of the Primitive Baptist Church in Lenoir City for over twenty-five years. He had been pastor of the church at one time and was assistant pastor at the time of his death.

Suvivors are his wife, Edith Farmer Packett, and four children: Cecil Packett, Bill J. Packett, Pauline Littleton and Alverine Voiles all of Lenoir City.

Funeral services were held at the Primitive Baptist Church with Elder Leonard White officiating. Interment was in the Lakeview Cemetery.

DAVID LEANDER BEASON

David Leander (Prock) Beason, 80 of Goin, died at Claiborne Hospital, October 8. He had been engaged in farming and was a member of the Pleasant Point Baptist Church.

Survivors: sons, Jeff, Dewey and Mannie Beason all of Monroe, Michigan, J. F. and Paris Beason of Goin; daughter, Mrs. Pearl McBee of Monroe, Michigan; 25 grandchildren.

Funeral Services were held at the Pleasant Point Baptist Church Sunday at 10 a.m. with the Revs. Lloyd England and Albert Davis officiating. Burial was in the Hopper cemetery.

Grandsons served as pallbearers. Coffey, in charge.

CURTIS RALPH DeFORD

Curtis Ralph DeFord was born May 30, 1914.
Passed away in Atlanta, Georgia, April 24, 1965.
He leaves a wife, Shannah; two sons, Ted of Nederland, Texas and Dan of San Francisco, California. His mother, Mrs. Chas. DeFord.
He joined the Primitive Church in Lenoir City and had many friends.

CHURCH	COUNTY	PASTOR	CLERK	ADDRESS
Black Fox	Grainger	Elder Parnick Shelton	Bennie Capps Flossie Capps, Asst.	P. O. Box 91 Maynardville, Tenn. Liberty Hill, Tenn.
Braden's Chapel	Union	Elder J. C. Mondax Assist. Buster Clawson	Arvil Braden	Speedwell, Tenn.
Brantley's Chapel	Blount	Elder Everett Berry	Rina Johnson Rina Johnson, Jr., Asst.	9 Douglas Ave. Maryville, Tenn. 14 Houston Ave. Maryville, Tenn.
Cedar Springs	Claiborne	E'der N. L. Clawson Assistant Elder W. M. Sparks	Pearlie Holt Ida Robertson, Asst.	New Tazewell, Tenn.
Davis Chapel	Campbell	Elder W. M. Sparks Assistant Elder Leonard White	Ruth Heatherly Lassie Ellison	Rt. 1, LaFollette, Tenn. Rt. 1, LaFollette, Tenn.
Gibson Station	Lee, Co. Va.	Elder Leonard White Assistant Elder Everett Berry	Roxie Cobb Mossie Cottrell, Asst.	Gibson Station, Va. Harrogate, Tenn.
Kirkwood	Knox	Elder Leonard White	Estelle Petree Sharp Shirley Bowden, Asst.	5313 Jacksboro Pike Knoxville, Tenn. 811 Banks Ave. NE Knoxville, Tenn.
Lenoir City	Loudon	Elder Walter Lyons	E. H. Scarbrough	Lenoir, Tenn.
Monroe, Michigan	Monroe	Elder Lervil Myers	Ditsy Russell	5177 Plum Creek Dr. Monroe, Michigan
Noeton	Grainger	Eder Gilbert Atkins	John Oliver Bessie Collins, Asst.	Bean Station, Rt. 2 Morristown, Tenn. Rt. 5
Oak Grove	Union	Elder M. M. Sparks J. C. Monday, Asst.	Belle Moore Ruth Shoffner, Asst.	Sharps Chapel, Tenn. Sharps Chapel, Tenn.
Pleasant Hill	Claiborne	Elder Tony Eastridge Elder J. H. Branscomb	Wm. Branscomb Verlin Edwards, Asst.	Speedwell, Tenn. Speedwell, Tenn.
Pleasant Point	Claiborne	Elder Tony Eastridge	Claude Rosson, Asst.	New Tazewell, Tenn.
Rocky Dale	Knox	Elder Hugh Brummitt	Arvel Graves Roy Clapp, Asst.	Corryton, Rt. 3 Knoxville, Tenn., Rt. 12
No Letter 1965				

1966
M̶INUTES
OF THE
ONE HUNDRED AND FORTY-SEVENTH
Annual Session
OF THE
POWELL VALLEY ASSOCIATION
OF
PRIMITIVE BAPTIST
held with
THE CHURCH AT PLEASANT POINT
IN CLAIBORNE COUNTY, TENN.
AUGUST 19-20-21st, 1966

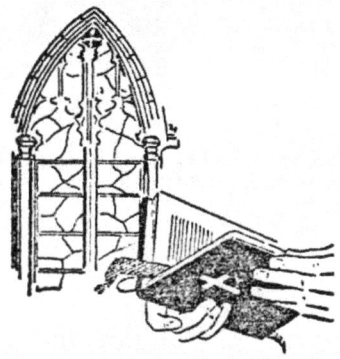

The next session to be held with the sister church at Brantley's Chapel in Blount County, Tenn. To begin at 10:30 A.M. on Friday before the 3rd. Saturday in August, 1967 and continue the two following days.

Elder Walter Lyons to preach the introductory Sermon with Elder William Sparks to be the alternate.

OFFICERS

Elder Albert Davis .... Moderator
Elder Hugh Brummitt .... Assistant Moderator
Brother W. H. Taylor .... Clerk
Brother R. O. Parrott .... Assistant Clerk

STATISTICAL TABLE

CHURCHES	DELEGATES	Restored	Received by Letter	Received by Baptism	Received by Relationship	Dismissed by Letter	Excluded	Deceased	Total Membership	Visiting Ministers	Printing Minutes	Meeting
Black Fox	Elder George Campbell, Bros. Arthur Terry, Stevie Terry, Roy Bailey, John Davis, Herbert Davis, Herbie Davis, Bennie Capps, Dale Capps, Sisters Sue Terry, Debby Terry, Mary Terry, Roma Bailey, Mary Ruth Bailey and Edith Davis.	0	0	4	0	0	0	3	97		$10.00	Each Sun &
Braden's Chapel	Elders W. M. Sparks, Noble Clawson, J. C. Monday, Henry Comer, Sisters Helen Clawson, Winona Monday, Leacy Sparks, Minnie Wilson.	0	1	11	2	0	0	1	95		$10.00	1st & Night Sat &
Brantley's Chapel	Elder Clifford Brantley, Bros. Corum Berry, Von Beason, Plumer McBee, Ellis Evans, Sisters Barsha Brantley, Twila Berry, Lottie Evans, Mildred Brantley.	0	0	2	0	0	3	0	75		$10.00	2nd Sat & Sun
Cedar Springs	Brothers Bill Good, Clifford Robinson, Sisters Belta Munsey, Pearie Holt, Maggie Robinson and Mrs. Bill Good.	0	0	3	0	0	0	0	63		$ 4.00	4th Sun
Davis Chapel	Elder Leonard White, Bros. Earl White, O. R. Parrott, Orice McCarty, Sisters Mamie Parrott, Mollie McCarty, Cordelia Lynch.	0	0	1	0	1	1	0	144	$3.00	$ 7.00	Sat & Sun 4th 1 & 3
Gibson Station	Bros. Franklin Jones, Harve Rhymer, Sisters Fannie Jones, Brenda Jones and Mellie Thompson.	0	0	1	0	0	0	1	85	$4.00	$ 4.00	Sun Night 1st
Kirkwood	Elders Hugh Brummitt, Walter Lyons, R. H. Pettit, Brothers M.A. Norton, W. H. Taylor, Ambrose Sharp, Sisters Ruby Brummitt, Callie Lyons, Mollie Pettit, Lucy Norton, Lou Emma Taylor, Freda Sharp, Nellie Simerly and Helen Johnson.	0	0	0	0	1	1	0	117	$5.00	$10.00	Sat & Sun Eo. M Every
Lenoir City	Bros. Henry Chamberlain, Caney Key, Hubert Spoon, Sisters Esta Chamberlain, Annie Key, Annie Spoon, Ella Fields.	0	0	0	0	0	0	0	205		$10.00	Every Sun Mon.
Monroe, Mich.	Elder Lenvil Meyers, Bro. John Drummonds, Sister Lela Drummonds, and Sister Gertrude Zwak.	0	0	0	0	0	2	0	14		$ 5.00	Every Sun & Night
Noeton	Bros. John Oliver, James Oliver, Charlie Collins, Elder Gilbert Atkins, Sisters Ruth Oliver, Eunice Oliver, Doshia Collins, Bessie Collins.	0	0	0	0	0	0	0	30		$ 3.00	Sun Night Each
Oak Grove	Elders George Shoffner, Tony Eastridge, Bros. Alford Relford, Aaron Cole, Mannie Shoffner, Malcolm Walker, Sisters Francis Eastridge, Maggie Relford, Lillie Shoffner, Veda Cole, Belle Moore, Ruth Shoffner, Laura Lou Walker, Ruth Edwards and Bobby Beason.	0	2	0	0	1	0	3	300		$10.00	3rd Sat & Sun
New Hebron	The New Hebron Church Lettered to the Association but gave no statistics. Their church burned down, but they are rebuilding. Elder Gilbert Attni pastor, and Sister Cardie Mitchell, clerk, New Market, Tenn. Rt. 1.											1st Sat & Sun
Pleasant Hill	Elders Albert Davis, J. H. Brangcomb, Brother Verlin Edwards, Sister Audrey Davis, Bertha Edwards and Faye Davis.	0	0	4	0	1	0	2	97		$10.00	4th Sat & Sun
Pleasant Point	Bros. George Williams, Sister Allie Williams, Elder Claude Rasson and Si Darris Rasson, Brother C. D. Keck, Brother Arilis Collins and Sister Mena Keck.	0	0	0	0	0	2	2	---		$10.00	1st Sun
Rocky Dale	Elders Everett Berry, Pernick Shelton, Bros. Elmer Graves, Arvell Graves, Joe Bush, Dewey Graves, Sisters Trula Berry, Wilma Shelton, Norma Jean Bush.	0	1	2	0	1	2	2	112	$5.00	$ 5.00	Each Sun & Night

FRIDAY, AUGUST 19, 1966

The one hundred and forty seventh annual session of the Powell Valley Association of Primitive Baptist met with the sister church of Pleasant Point in Claiborne County, Tennessee on August 19, 1966 with Moderator Elder Albert Davis presiding.

The service was begun by the congregation singing "Amazing Grace". Then Elder Davis read from the 19th chapter of the Psalmist David and then called on Elder Henry Comer who prayed an humble and spiritual prayer.

Elder Claude Rosson preached the introductory sermon taking as his text the 1st verse of the 6th chapter of Jobe. This was followed by Alternate Elder Walter Lyons preaching from the 2nd chapter of Ephesians.

After song and handshake, intermission in prayer by Elder Leonard White.

After intermission the Association was called to order by Moderator Davis, who pleaded for peace, cooperation, love and spirit throughout the entire time. He then called for the opening prayer by Elder Carl McCarty of the corresponding New Bethel Association.

First — Call by moderator for letters of the sister churches. Letters were received from all sister churches except Oak Grove whose letter was delayed.

Second — Motion carried to receive the letters of the sister churches and seat their delegates.

Third — The moderator call for members of the sister churches who were not delegates to be seated, none came.

Fourth — Motion carried to seat the delegates from Oak Grove pending the arrival of their letter on Saturday.

Fifth — The call for petitionary letters and there was none.

Sixth — Moderator called for letters of the corresponding associations, one was received from the New Bethel Association which was read and accepted and delegates seated.

Seventh — Call for any member of the corresponding associations not delegated. Elder Claude Thomas came and was seated.

Eighth — Motion carried that the association re-elect the following officers for the next year:

Elder Albert Davis	Moderator
Elder Hugh Brummitt	Assistant Moderator
Bro. W. H. Taylor	Clerk
Bro. O. R. Parrott	Assistant Clerk

Ninth — The association voted for the moderator to appoint all those who are to serve on the various committees and appointed them as follows:

1. *Arrangements*
   Bro. Corum Berry
   Bro. Elmer Graves
   Bro. Arlis Collins

3. *Committee on Correspondence*
   Elder W. M. Sparks
   Elder Clifford Brantley
   Bro. John Oliver

—1—

2. *Committee on Preaching*
    Bro. M. A. Norton
    Bro. Arvel Keck
    Bro. Von Beason

4. *Committee on Request*
    Elder Johnnie Atkins
    Bro. George Williams
    Bro. Earl White

5. *Committee on Finance*
    Elder Claude Rosson
    Elder Walter Lyons
    Bro. John Davis

Tenth — Voted to adjourn until 10:00 A.M. the following morning, Saturday, August 20, 1966.

SATURDAY, AUGUST 20, 1966

First — After a good song service, a nice welcome and spiritual talk by the Assistant Moderator Elder Hugh Brummitt. He then read a lesson from the 17th verse of the 20th chapter of The Acts and called for prayer by Elder Charles Taylor of Maryville.

Second — Moderator Davis called for any letters from sister churches not received Friday. One was read and received from the sister church of Oak Grove.

Third — Call for letters of any corresponding association not received Friday. One was received from the Hiwassee Association which was read and accepted and the delegates seated.

Fourth — Call for the report of the Committee on Arrangements who submitted the following report which was accepted and the committee released.

Arrangements

1. Roll call of delegates.
2. Call for the report of Committee on Preaching.
3. Call for report of Committee on Correspondence.
4. Call for report of Committee on Requests.
5. Call for report of Committee on Finance.
6. When and where shall the next association be held? Who shall preach the introductory sermon and who shall be the alternate? How many copies of minutes shall we print, and who shall supervise the printing and distribution of them and how much shall he receive for his service?

                    Respectfully submitted,
                    Bro. Corum Berry
                    Bro. Elmer Graves
                    Bro. Arlis Collins

Fifth — Call was made for a report of the Committee on Preaching, who gave the following report, which was accepted and the committee released.

Report:
We the Committee on Preaching recommend the following:

—2—

Friday Night	Elder Ernest Thomas
	Elder Henry Comer
Saturday	Elder Charles Taylor
	Elder Carl McCarty
Saturday Night	Elder Clifford Brantley
	Elder Henry Comer
Sunday	Elder W. M. Sparks
	Elder Leonard White

Respectfully submitted,
Bro. M. A. Norton
Bro. Von Beason
Bro. Arvil Keck

Sixth — Called for a report of the Committee on Correspondence, who gave the following report which was accepted and the committee released.

Report:

We the Committee on Correspondence recommend that we keep our correspondence with the beloved Hiwassee and New Bethel Associations and that we letter and delegate to each.

Submitted by,
Elder Clifford Brantley
Elder W. M. Sparks
Bro. John Oliver

Seventh — Called for report of Committee on Request who submitted the following report which was accepted and the committee released.

Report:

We the Committee on Request wish to recommend that we print in the minutes all obituaries furnished the clerk and that our next Association be held with the sister church at Brantley's Chapel in Blount County beginning on Friday before the third Saturday in August and continue the two following days.

Submitted by,
Elder Johnnie Atkins
Bro. Earl White
Bro. George Williams

Eighth — Call for report of Committee on Finance, who gave the following report which was accepted and the committee released.

Finance Report:

Church	Printing Minutes	Visiting Ministers
Black Fox	$10.00	
Bradens Chapel	10.00	
Brantleys Chapel	10.00	
Cedar Springs	4.00	

—3—

Church	Printing Minutes	Visiting Ministers
Davis Chapel	7.00	$ 3.00
Gibson Station	4.00	4.00
Kirkwood	10.00	5.00
Monroe, Michigan	5.00	
Noeton	3.00	
Lenoir City	10.00	
Oak Grove	10.00	
Rocky Dale	5.00	5.00
New Hebron	1.00	1.00
Pleasant Hill	10.00	
Pleasant Point	10.00	
Total	$109.00	$18.00
	18.00	
By Congregation	55.00	
Collection Total for the day	$182.00	

Respectfully submitted by,
Elder Claude Rosson
Elder Walter Lyons
Bro. John Davis

Association Report:

Balance in Bank	$ 40.00
Collection of the day	182.00
TOTAL	$222.00
Expense	130.00
Balance in Bank	$ 92.00

Ninth — Motion carried the Association request the clerk to have printed 1,000 copies of the Association minutes and distribute them to the sister churches and to be paid ($50.00) fifty dollars for this service.

Tenth — The Association voted to hold our next annual session with the sister church at Brantleys Chapel in Blount County, Tennessee beginning on Friday (at 10:30) before the third Saturday in August 1967.

Eleventh — Elder Walter Lyons was elected to preach the introductory sermon with Elder W. M. Sparks as the alternate.

Twelfth — Motion carried that we letter and delegate to the two corresponding associations, namely the New Bethel Association and the Hiwassee Association, and that we authorize the clerk to prepare an Association letter for the delegates to carry with them.

Thirteenth — The Association delegated to represent our Association in the Hiwassee, Elder Henry Comer and Elder W. M. Sparks. Our delegates to the New Bethel Association are Elder Henry Comer, Elder

George Campbell and Elder Tony Eastridge.

Fourteenth — The Powell Valley Association of Primitive Baptist while in session voted to extend to the sister church at Pleasant Point and the entire community for every expression of love, kindness and hospitality shown to us while in your church and community, our thanks, love and our prayers.

Fifteenth — Motion carried that the business session of the Association be adjourned until Friday before the third Saturday in August 1967 when it will meet with the sister church at Brantley's Chapel at 10:30 A. M. Closed by prayer by Elder Parnick Shelton.

Elder Albert Davis, Moderator
Elder Hugh Brummitt, Assistand Moderator
W. H. Taylor, Clerk
R. O. Parrott, Assistant Clerk

SUNDAY, AUGUST 21, 1966

After singing some good spiritual songs, the Sunday service was introduced by the Assistant Moderator, Elder Hugh Brummitt, who made a nice talk and called for prayer by Elder Luther Abrams of the New Bethel Association. This was followed by Elder W. M. Sparks who spoke from the Psalmist David.

The service continued with Elder Leonard White bringing a wonderful spiritual message, using as his lesson the 1st verse in the 6th chapter of Paul's letter to the Philippians.

After several spiritual demonstrations and testimonies, Elder Brummitt closed out the service and called for the parting prayer by Elder J. C. Monday.

This bringing to a close one of the most spiritual and harmonious Associations, with peace and love abounding throughout the entire Association.

Elder Albert Davis, Moderator
Elder Hugh Brummitt, Assistant Moderator
W. H. Taylor, Clerk
R. O. Parrott, Assistant Clerk

ORDAINED MINISTERS

Elder Gilbert Atkins . . . . Route 3
                                         Rutledge, Tennessee
Elder Johnnie Atkins . . . . Bean Station, Tennessee
Elder Everett Berry . . . . Fountain Cith, Tennessee
                                         Phone 922-4241
Elder J. H. Branscomb . . . . Speedwell, Tennessee
                                         Phone 86-3392
Elder Clifford Brantley . . . . Brown School Road
                                         Maryville, Tennessee
                                         Phone 982-3735

Elder Hugh E. Brummitt .... 1329 Brown Avenue
                                        Knoxville, Tennessee
                                        Phone 525-3583
Elder George Campbell .... Route 2
                                        Corryton, Tennessee
                                        Phone 687-5754
Elder Noble Lee Clawson .... Speedwell, Tennessee
Elder Henry Comer .... Route 4
                                        LaFollette, Tennessee
                                        Phone 562-3952
Elder Albert Davis .... Speedwell, Tennessee
                                        Phone 86-3667
Elder Tony Eastridge .... Route 2
                                        Louisville, Tennessee
                                        Phone 983-1068
Elder Dewey Ellison.................... Sharps Chapel, Tennessee
Elder Alvin Graves .... Lenoir City, Tennessee
Elder Joe Irwin .... Gibson Station, Virginia
Elder Walter Lyons .... 1602 Garfield Street
                                        Alcoa, Tennessee
                                        Phone YU3-3222
Elder Lenvil Meyers .... 512 E. Elm Street
                                        Monroe, Michigan
Elder J. C. Monday .... Speedwell, Tennessee
Elder Roy Oliver .... Bean Station, Tennessee
Elder R. H. Pettit .... 107 Jacksboro Pike
                                        Knoxville, Tennessee
                                        Phone 689-5581
Elder Claude Rosson .... Goin, Tennessee
                                        Phone 626-3168
Elder Parnick Shelton.................. Corryton, Tennessee
                                        Phone 689-6183
Elder George Shoffner.................. Sharps Chapel, Tennessee
Elder W. M. Sparks .... Speedwell, Tennessee
                                        Phone 562-7997
Elder Leonard White .... LaFollette, Tennessee
                                        Phone 562-5667
Elder Clay Widner .... 101 West Norris Street
                                        Norris, Tennessee

LICENTIATES

Bro. Joe Bush .... Corryton, Tennessee
Bro. Odell Carpenter.................... Maryville, Tennessee
Bro. Jim Oliver .... Bean Station, Tennessee

We, the Powell Valley Association of Primitive Baptist now in session with the sister church at Pleasant Point in Claiborne County, Tennessee August 19, 20, and 21, send our love and greetings to the New Bethel Association.

Our dearly beloved Brothers and Sisters in Christ, we desire to keep our long cherished correspondence with your association.

We have chosen as messengers to bear to you our love, fellowship and humble prayers the following Elders whom we hope you will receive to sit with you in your Godly conversions:

Elder Tony Eastridge
Elder Henry Comer
Elder George Campbell

Having corresponded with you this year, we look forward to seeing some of you next year when we convene with the church at Brantley's Chapel in Blount County, Tennessee on Friday before the third Saturday in August 1967 at 10:30 A.M.

Elder Albert Davis, Moderator
Elder Hugh Brummitt, Asst. Moderator
Bro. W. H. Taylor, Clerk
Bro. R. O. Parrott, Asst. Clerk

September 1966

We, the Powell Valley Association of Primitive Baptist, while in session with the sister church at Pleasant Point in Claiborne County, Tennessee, convening August 19, 20, and 21, send greetings to the Hiwassee Association.

Our dearly beloved Brothers and Sisters in Christ, we desire to continue our cherished correspondence with you. We letter and delegate to your association by sending to you our beloved Elders Henry Comer and W. M. Sparks to represent our association. We hope you will accept them in love and fellowship. Having corresponded with you this year we look forward to having some of you with us next year when we meet with the church at Brantley's Chapel in Blount County on Friday before the third Saturday in August 1967.

This done while the association was in session.

Elder Albert Davis, Moderator
Elder Hugh Brummitt, Asst. Moderator
Bro. W. H. Taylor, Clerk
Bro. R. O. Parrott, Asst. Clerk

—7—

OBITUARIES

JANE MUNSEY BAILEY

Mrs. Jane Munsey Bailey was born September 25, 1880, passed from this life April 7, 1966. She was 85 years old. She professed faith in Christ at an early age and joined Black Fox Baptist Church, where she remained a member until death. She was united in marriage to Frank Bailey. To this union ten children were born, six who preceded her in death. Survivors: sons James Bailey and Roy Bailey of Liberty Hill, Tennessee, daughters Mrs. Hazel Munsey and Mrs. Clarence Nicely of Liberty Hill, Tennessee. Thirty-five grandchildren. Many other relatives and a host of friends. Elders Parnick Shelton and Loyd Shelton officiated.

Sleep on, Dear Mother, 'til resurrection morn.
We're sure she's gone to rest,
We loved her, oh so dearly,
But Jesus loved her best.

We love to walk the pathway
Her dear feet have trod
Because those paths will lead us
All home around the White Throne.

Written by granddaughter

ARTHUR BOURFF

Arthur Bourff, 71, Route 2, Tipton, Indiana, died Friday morning at 5:30 o'clock at the Tipton County Hospital.

Born in Union County, Tennessee, April 9, 1895, he was the son of Frank and Cordelia Lamb Bourff. He was married November 5, 1916 to Mary Damewood. The family had lived in Tipton County for 35 years. He was a member of the Rocky Dale Primitive Church. He joined Rocky Dale Church October 21, 1922.

Survivors include the widow; a son, Henry of Route 2, Tipton; a a brother, John of St. Petersburg, Florida; a sister, Mrs. Rhoda Smith of Knoxville, Tennessee, and one grandchild.

The body was at the Mitchell Funeral Home in Tipton where friends called after 2 o'clock Sunday afternoon.

Funeral rites were held on Tuesday at 2 o'clock at the Mitchell Funeral Home. Rev. Chester Mitchell officiated.

BARBARA CAIN BRADEN

Barbara Cain Braden was born February 3, 1886; departed this life March 13, 1966. She leaves to mourn her passing, husband Fred R. Braden, sons Brice, Obie, and Arvil of Speedwell, Tennessee, Mack of Maynardville, Tennessee, Milt of Monroe, Michigan, daughters Venie Pierce, Jane Edwards and Betty Braden of Speedwell, Tennessee, brother Dan

—10—

Cain of Monroe, Michigan, sister Ella Smith of Deerlodge, Tennessee, 26 grandchildren. She professed faith in Christ at an early age, was a member of Straight Branch Church until abandoned by the T.V.A. She then moved her membership to Bradens Chapel Church where she remained a faithful member until her death.

> Mom went to heaven one dreary Sunday eve,
> Jesus called for her, so she took her leave.
> The home place is so lonely since mom went away,
> But if we'll all be faithful, we'll meet her some sweet day.
>
> Lord, she's in your loving care,
> There's no more now that we can do,
> But help us Lord to meet her there,
> In heaven when this life is through.

Sadly missed by family and friends.

CARLIE CAPPS

Mrs. Carlie Capps was born December 9, 1882, and departed this life July 30, 1966, being 83 years, 7 months, and 21 days old. She was the widow of the late Samuel Capps. She is survived by a brother Rome Carter and a sister, Mrs. I. B. Powell; two step sons, Albert and Calvin Capps; five step daughters, Mrs. Iva Davis, Mrs. Kate Lay, Mrs. Dollie Helton, Mrs. Lula Campbell, and Mrs. Gertrude Greene. She was a member of the Black Fox Primitive Baptist Church. Funeral Services were conducted August 2nd at the Towners Funeral Chapel in Ottawa, Kansas.

MATTHEW COLLINS

Matthew Collins was born July 12, 1896 and passed from this life June 28, 1966. He professed faith in Christ in early age and joined Noeton Primitive Baptist Church. Survivors, his wife, four daughters, one son, twelve grandchildren and one great-grandson.

Interment in the church cemetery.

A. C. ZAN GOIN

A. C. Zan Goin passed away Wednesday, March 16, at Claiborne County Hospital. He was 94 years and 10 months of age. He was united in marriage to Nora Rouse and to this union was born 7 children: Verlin Goin, New Market, Tennessee; Josh Goin, Baltimore, Maryland; Walter Goin, Knoxville, Tennessee; Lillie Maddux, Riverton, Wyoming; Eva Keck, Monroe, Michigan; Cleo Beason, New Tazewell, Tennessee; and Edna Johnson, Gary, Indiana. 22 grandchildren, 72 great-grandchildren, and 11 great-great-grandchildren.

His wife and one son, Walter, preceded him in death. He was later married to Ida Quesenberry. He was a retired farmer and a member of Pleasant Point Primitive Baptist Church.

—11—

MRS. BESSIE (CARDWELL) GRAVES

Mrs. Bessie (Cardwell) Graves, age 71, passed away at 1:45 Monday, September 6, 1965 at the home on Emory Road, Corryton, Tennessee.

She was a member of Rocky Dale Primitive Baptist Church. She professed faith in Christ August 5, 1922 and joined Rocky Dale Church. She was baptized in Little Flat Creek by Elder Theodore Brantley.

She leaves her husband, Elmer H. Graves; daughters, Mrs. Betty Graves, Miami Shores, Florida; Mrs. John Clapp, Mrs. Elmer Hubbs, Mrs. Dan Clapp, all of Corryton. Mrs. Bruce Perrin, Knoxville. Sons Avrell and Harry Graves of Corryton. Fourteen grandchildren and six great-grandchildren.

Services were at 3:00 P.M. on Wednesday at Rocky Dale Primitive Baptist Church. Elder Parnick Shelton and Elder H. E. Brummitt officiating. Interment in Rocky Dale Cemetery.

"We saw our dear mother fading like a flower,
But she tried so hard to stay.
We nursed her with tender care
Until God called her away.
Although the world in which she lives
Is free from care and pain,
Our world would be like heaven
If we had her back again.

It is only human to want her back,
but this we know is true, she can never
return to us but we can go to her. We feel
like our loss is heaven's gain."

Written by Lorene Hubbs
Her daughter

ELIZABETH (BETTY) BRATCHER JONES

Elizabeth (Betty) Bratcher Jones was born in 1883. She lived to be 82 years of age.

She professed a hope in Christ many years ago and joined the Primitive Baptist Church at Straight Branch in Union County. When Norris Lake came up, that church was disbanded and she came to Pleasant Hill Primitive Baptist Church and joined in 1934 and remained a member until her death June 8, 1966.

She was first married to Sil Bratcher who passed away several years ago then later she married Granvil Jones who still survives her. She had no children but has one sister still living and several nieces and a host of friends.

She was laid to rest in Taylor's Grove Cemetery in Union County. Funeral conducted by Elder Albert Davis.

FRED L. KECK

Fred L. Keck, 58, passed away 1:45 P.M. Tuesday at Memorial Mission Hospital, Asheville, North Carolina. Survivors: wife, Mrs. Dallie

—12—

Keck of Asheville; son, Raymond of Asheville; daughter, Mrs. Johnnie Polly of Waynesville, Ohio; granddaughter, Susan Keck, Asheville; grandsons, Scottie Keck, Asheville, Gregory Polly, Waynesville; brothers, F. G., Russell, and Curtis Keck all of New Tazewell. Tennessee; sisters, Mrs. Cecil Carey, Mrs. Rowena Barnes, Mrs. Roberta Carr of New Tazewell, Mrs. Lovetta Crawford, Powell, Tennessee, Mrs. Loalles Robinett, Kingston, Tennessee.

He was engaged in the mobile home business in Asheville.

Funeral 2:00 P.M. Thursday at Coffee Funeral Home Chapel. Interment Keck Cemetery. Body will lie in state one hour before service. Family will receive friends 7 to 9 Wednesday.

SPENCER MONROE KECK

Spencer Monroe Keck was born June 12, 1906, passed away August 1, 1966. He professed faith in Christ in 1934. Survivors, wife Lennie Keck; daughter, Mrs. Joe Lakin of Knoxville, one grandson, David Lakin of Knoxville. Funeral services were held at Pleasant Point Primitive Baptist Church August 1966. Elder Leonard White and Elder Tony Eastridge officiated. Burial in Keck cemetery. Coffee of Tazewell in charge.

MARGARET CUMY WILLIAMSON MADDOX

Margaret Cumy Williamson Maddox, born March 13, 1877, died October 21, 1965. She was married to the late William Franklin Maddox on July 29, 1894. To this union were born seventeen children. Fourteen preceded her in death. She left three children: Mrs. Cairletta Monday, Clarkrange, Tennessee; Sibyl Dunkelberg, Allardt, Tennessee; and Clyde Maddox, Jamestown, Tennessee. She left ten grandchildren and fifteen great grandchildren. She joined the Primitive Baptist Church at Pleasant Hill in May, 1910 and was a faithful member thereafter.

Funeral services were held at the Primitive Baptist Church at Pleasant Hill. Elder Albert Dabis officiated. Interment was in the Ausmus Cemetery October 23, 1965.

May she rest in peace.

WILLIAM ALFORD MUNCEY

William Alford Muncey, age 69, passed away May 31, 1966, at the home of his brother, Herman Muncey. He leaves to mourn his loss wife, Lucy, brother Herman, three half brothers, Rector, Elvin, and James Williams; three half sisters, Mrs. Edna Shelton, Mrs. Lillie McDaniel, and Mrs. Betsie Acuff. He was a member of the Black Fox Primitive Baptist Church. Funeral services were conducted at Black Fox Baptist Church with Rev. Andy Vance and Elder Parnick Shelton officiating. Interment in Cabbage Cemetery.

Gone but not forgotten.

> Written by Brother
> Herman Muncey

—13—

JAKE OVERBAY

Jake Overbay was born September 27, 1929, passed away suddenly at his home April 13, 1966, Bean Station, Tennessee.

He was the son of Annie Hurst Overbay and the late Harry Overbay. On January 15, 1950 he was married to Edith Travis, and to this union was born two daughters.

Survivors: Wife, Edith; daughters, Peggy and Phyllis Overbay at home; mother, Annie Hurst Overbay, Bean Station, Tennessee; two sisters, Miss Minnie Overbay and Mrs. Moscoe Stubbelfield, Bean Station. He professed faith in Christ and later became a member and deacon of Noeton Primitive Baptist Church. He lived a faithful member until his death. Funeral services were conducted by his pastor Elder Gilbert Atkins and Elder Johnny and Olof Atkins on Saturday afternoon April 16 at Noeton Primitive Baptist Church and laid to rest in the Noeton Cemetery.

A place is vacant in our home
A voice we loved to hear is still
There's an empty place within our hearts
That no one here can fill.

Wife and Daughters

SIDNEY STIGALL

With bowed heads and sad hearts, Gibson Station Church announces the death of our beloved brother Sidney (Sid) Stigall, who departed this life August 3, 1966 at the age of 76 years. He had been a member of the church for only five or six years, but his faithfulness to attend and his willingness to bear his part of the burdens, and hold his tongue while others talked, has endeared him to the church and pastors alike. Funeral services were conducted by Elders Everett Berry and Leonard White at the old home church, and under cloudy skies the body was planted in the soil of old Virginia to sleep til Jesus comes. God bless his loved ones.

His Pastor,
Elder Leonard White

HERZEL TREECE

Herzel Treece was born May 4, 1907, passed away May 11, 1966.

He professed a hope in Christ at an early age and joined the Primitive Baptist Church. His father, one brother, and a daughter preceded him in death. He is survived by his wife Dora, his mother Nora, one daughter, and one son, four brothers and five sisters.

Written by Mother
Nora Treece

DORA WATTS

Dora Watts, age 73, died at M-H Hospital April 11, 1966, after a long illness. She was a member of Noeton Primitive Baptist Church. Survivors, one brother, Matthew Collins, and several nieces and nephews, and a host of friends. Services were held at Noeton Primitive Baptist Church. Interment in the church cemetery.

—14—

OFFICIAL DIRECTORY

CHURCH	COUNTY	PASTOR	CLERK	ADDRESS
Black Fox	Grainger	Elder Parrick Shelton	Bennie Capps	P.O. Box 91 Maynardville, Tenn.
Braden's Chapel	Union	Elder J. C. Monday, Asst. Noble Clawson	Flossie Capps, Asst. Arvil Braden, Asst.	Rt., 2, Washburn, Tenn. Speedwell, Tenn.
Brantley's Chapel	Blount	Elder Everett Berry	Rina Johnson,	9 Douglas Ave. Maryville, Tenn. 14 Houston Ave. Maryville, Tenn.
Cedar Springs	Claiborne	Elder N. L. Clawson. Elder W. M. Sparks	Rina Johnson, Jr., Asst. G. Good	New Tazewell, Tann.
Davis Chapel	Campbell	Elder W. M. Sparks Elder Leonard White, Asst.	Ruth Heatherly Katherine Hill, Asst.	Rt., 1, LaFollette, Tenn. Rt., 4, LaFollette, Tenn.
Gibson Station	Lee County,	Elder Leonard White Elder Everett Berry, Asst.	Roxie Cobb Mossie Cottrell, Asst.	Gibson Station, Va.
Kirkwood	Knox	Elder Leonard White	Estelle Petree Sharp Shirley Bowden, Asst.	5313 Jacksboro Pike Knoxville, Tenn. 811 Banks Ave., N.E. Knoxville, Tenn.
Lenoir City	Loudon	Elder Walter Lyons	E. H. Scarbrough	Lenoir City, Tenn.
Monroe, Mich.	Monroe	Elder Lenvil Meyers	Ditsy Russell	5177 Plum Creek Fr. Monroe, Mich. 1825 Spaulding Rd. Monroe, Mich.
Noeton	Grainger	Elder Gilbert Atkins	Gertrude Zwok, Asst. John Oliver Bessie Collins, Asst.	Bean Station, Tenn. Rt. 5, Morristown, Tenn.
Oak Grove	Union	Elder W. M. Sparks J. C. Monday, Asst.	Belle Moore Ruth Shoffner, Asst.	Sharps Chapel, Tenn. Sharps Chapel, Tenn.
Pleasant Hill	Claiborne	J. C. Monday	William Branscomb Verlin Edwards, Asst.	Speedwell, Tenn. Speedwell, Tenn.
Pleasant Point	Claiborne	Elder Tony Eastridge Elder Claude Rosson, Asst.	Claude Rosson Menada Keck, Asst.	New Tazewell, Tenn. New Tazewell, Tenn.
Rocky Dale	Knox	Elder Hugh Brummitt	Avrell Graves	Rt. 3, Corryton, Tenn. Phone 689-3668 Corryton, Tenn.
New Hebron	Jefferson	Elder Gilbert Atkins	Roy Clapp, Asst. Cordie Mitchell	New Market, Tenn.

640

1967 Minutes

OF THE
ONE HUNDRED FORTY-EIGHTH
Annual Session

of the
POWELL VALLEY ASSOCIATION
OF PRIMITIVE BAPTIST
held with
THE CHURCH AT BRANTLEY'S CHAPEL
BLOUNT COUNTY, TENNESSEE
AUGUST 18, 19, and 20, 1967

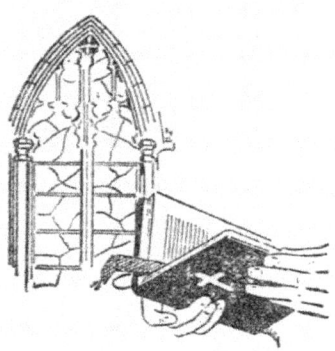

The next session to be held with the sister church at Cedar Springs in Claiborne County, Tennessee. To begin on Friday before the third Saturday in August, 1968 and continue the two following days.

Elder Hugh E. Brummitt will preach the introductory sermon and Elder Henry Comer will be the alternate.

OFFICERS

ELDER ALBERT DAVIS .... Moderator
    Speedwell, Tenn. Phone 869-3596
ELDER HUGH BRUMMITT .... Assistant Moderator
    1329 Brown Ave., Knoxville, Tenn. Phone 525-3583
BROTHER W. H. TAYLOR .... Clerk
    Route 13, Knoxville, Tenn. Phone 922-2143
BROTHER O. R. PARROTT .... Assistant Clerk
    LaFollette, Tennessee

CHURCHES	DELEGATES	Restored	Received by Letter	Received by Baptism	Received by Relationship	Dismissed by Letter	Excluded	Deceased	Total Membership	Visiting Ministers	Printing Minutes	Meeting	Communion
Black Fox	Elder George Campbell, Bros. Dale Capps, Calvin Capps, Stevie Terry, Arthur Terry, John Davis, Bennie Capps; Sisters Mary Ruth Capps, Mary Terry, Flossie Capps and Debbie Terry.	0	1	2	0	0	2	1	97	$10.00	$10.00	2nd Sun	Sun after 1st Sat
Braden's Chapel	Elders J. C. Monday, Noble Lee Clawson, Wm. Sparks, Henry Comer; Sisters Helen Clawson, Winona Monday, Leecy Sparks.	0	2	16	0	0	0	0	111	$10.00	$10.00	1st Sat & 1st Sun June	1st Sun June
Brantley's Chapel	Elder Clifford Brantley, Bro. Corum Berry, Rims Johnson, Millard Welch; Everett Brantley, Sisters Twila Berry, Hazel Johnson, Bartha Brantley, Luda Welch, Ottie McBee and Mildred Brantley.	0	0	2	2	0	2	0	77	$20.00	$20.00	2nd Sun July	2nd Sun July
Cedar Springs	Bro. Johnny Ayers, Sisters Gray Good and Patricia Good.	0	0	0	0	0	0	4	56		$10.00		
Davis Chapel	Elder Leonard White, Bros. Oties McCarty, Hugh Hill, Onie Parrott, Gene Hobbs; Sisters Cordelia Lynch, Mollie McCarty, Ruby Hill and Mamie Parrott.	0	2	0	1	0	3	3	144	$5.00	$10.00	3rd Sun & June	3rd Sun June
Gibson Station	Bros. Franklin Jones, Harve Thymer, Spurgeon Thompson; Sisters Millie Thompson, Mossie Cottrell, and Sister Jones.	0	0	0	0	0	0	0	110	$5.00	$10.00	1st Sat & Sun Night	1st Sun June
Kirkwood	Elders R. H. Pettis, Hugh E. Brummitt, Walter Lyons; Brothers M. A. Norton, and W. H. Taylor; Sisters Lou Emma Taylor, Lucy Norton, Ruby Brummitt, and Callie Lyons.	0	0	0	3	2	0	2	113	$5.00	$10.00	Every Sun	Last Sun April
Lenoir City	Elders Charles Taylor, Alvin Graves; Bros. Henry Chamberlain, Caney Key, Hubert Spoons; Sisters Ettie Chamberlain, Annie Spoons and Cora Hill.	0	0	1	3	0	0	1	208		$15.00	Each Sun Night	3rd Sun May
Monroe, Mich.	Elder Luluel Meyers, Bro. John Drummonds and Sister Roxie Drummonds.	0	0	0	0	0	0	0	14		$5.00	3rd Sun	3rd Sun July
Norton	Elder Gilbert Atkins, Bros. John Oliver, Charlie Collins; Sisters Doshia Colline, and Ruth Oliver.	0	0	5	0	0	0	0	35		$3.00	Each Sun	Sun May & Sept.
Oak Grove	Elder George Shaffner, Tony Eastridge, Bros. Alfred Relford, Aaron Cole; Sisters Margie Relford, Francis Eastridge, Belle Moore, Lillie Shaffner, Veda Cole and Tishie Creech.	0	0	5	0	0	3	5	297	$12.00		1st Sun	1st Sun May
New Hebron	No Letter, Church Burned.												
Pleasant Hill	Elders James Henry Beuscomb, Albert Davis; Sisters Audra Davis, Lucinda Meyers and Nadine Mayes Gibby.	0	0	2	0	0	0	3	96	$13.00		4th Sat & Sun June	4th Sun June
Pleasant Point	Elder Claude Rosson, Bro. George Williams, Sisters Doris Rosson and Allie Williams.	0	0	0	0	0	2	2	118	$10.00		1st Sun	1st Sun July
Rocky Dale	Elders Everett Berry, Patrick Shelton, Bros. Elmer Graves, Avcel Graves; Sisters Trula Berry, Wilma Shelton and Norm Jean Bush.	0	0	2	1	0	2	2	112	$5.00	$10.00	Sun after Sat	Sun After Sat May

642

FRIDAY, AUGUST 18, 1967

The one hundred and forty eighth session of the Powell Valley Association of Primitive Baptist met with the Sister Church of Brantley's Chapel in Blount County, Tennessee, on August 18th 1967, with Moderator Elder Albert Davis presiding.

The service began by congregational singing, directed by Bro. Von Beason. Then Elder Davis read the 12th chapter of Romans and called for prayer by Elder Charles Taylor, pastor cf Lenoir City Church.

After more singing, the introductory sermon was preached by Elder Wm. Sparks. Reading from the book of Ephesians and using the theme, "Endure to keep the Unity of the Spirit and the Bonds of Peace".

After preaching, called for a song, then was dismissed for intermission, in prayer by Elder Clifford Brantley.

After intermission the congregation was called back by singing.

Moderator, Elder Davis then called the Association to order with prayer by Elder Charles Abrams of the New Bethel Association.

Elder Davis made a short talk and pleaded for peace, harmony and love to prevail in the Association.

BUSINESS OF ASSOCIATION

First — Moderator called for letters of the sister churches. Letters were recieved from all the churches except New Hebron.

Second — The Association voted to recieve the letters and seat their delegations.

Third — Call for members present who were not named as delegates, but wish to be seated as such. Two came, Bro. Spurgeon Thompson and Sister Minnie Wilson.

Fourth — Called for petitionary letters and there were none.

Fifth — Moderator called for letters of corresponding associations, one was recieved from the New Bethel Association, which was read and accepted and their delegation seated.

Sixth — Called for any one from the sister association not delegated and none came.

Seventh — Next came the election of officers for the coming year as follows:

Elder Albert Davis	Moderator
Elder Hugh E. Brummitt	Assistant Moderator
Bro. W.H. Taylor	Clerk
Bro. O.R. Parrott	Assistant Clerk

Eighth — Motion and seconded that the Moderator be authorized to appoint all the committees who are to serve during this association.

Ninth — The Committees were named as follows:

1. *Committee on Arrangements*
   Elder Henry Comer
   Elder Geroge Campbell
   Bro. Millard Welch

2. *Committee on Correspondence*
   Elder Charles Taylor
   Elder Claude Rosson
   Bro. Everett Brantley

—1—

643

3. *Committee on Preaching*   4. *Committee on Request*

Bro. John Oliver   Elder W. M. Sparks
Bro. John Drummonds   Elder George Shoffner
Bro. Ellis Evans   Bro. Corum Berry

5. *Committee on Finance*

Bro. Henry Chamberlain
Bro. John Davis
Bro. Von Beason

— After completing the appointment of all the committees, voted to adjourn until 10:30 A.M. Saturday, morning, August 19, 1967.

SATURDAY, AUGUST 19, 1967

First   — After a good spiritual song service the Assistant Moderator Elder Hugh E. Brummitt welcomed the Association back with a very good humble and spiritual talk then read from the 2nd chapter of Ephesians then called for an opening prayer by Elder J.C. Monday.

Second   — Moderator Davis called the Association to order for business and asked for letters from sister churches not recieved Friday and none came.

Third   — Called for any corresponding letters not recieved Friday and none came.

Fourth — Called for report on Committee on Arrangements, who submitted the following report, which was recieved and the committee released.

Arrangements

1. Roll call of delegates.
2. Call for the report of Committee on Preaching
3. Call for report of Committee on Correspondence.
4. Call for report of Committee on Requests.
5. Call for report of Committee on Finance.
6. When and where shall the next association be held? Who shall preach the introductory sermon and who shall be the alternate? How many minutes of the association shall we have printed, and who shall supervise the printing and distribution of them. and how much shall he recieve for his service?

Respectfully submitted,

Bro. Millard Welch
Elder George Campbell
Elder Henry Comer

Fifth   — Call for report of committee on preaching who submitted the following report which was accepted then the committee released.

—2—

Report:

We the Committee on Preaching wish to recommend the following Elders for preaching services:

Friday Night	Elder Charles Abrams Elder Charles Taylor
Saturday	Elder Claude Rosson Elder Linvel Myers
Saturday Night	Elder George Campbell Elder Raymond Brantley
Sunday	Elder Tony Eastridge Elder Leonard White

Respectfully submitted,

Bro. E.N. Evans
Bro. John Drummonds
Bro. John Oliver

Sixth — Called for a report of the Committee on Correspondence, who submitted the following report which was recieved and the committee realesed.

Report:

We the Committee on Correspondence recommend that we keep our good relationship and beloved correspondence, and that we letter and delegate to the beloved New Bethel Association. But since we have not recieved any correspondence or any delegation from the Hiwassee Association we assume that they no longer wish to letter or delegate so we recommend that we discontinue our relationship with same.

Respectfully submitted,

Elder Claude Rosson
Elder Charles Taylor
Bro. Everett Brantley

Seventh—Call for report of Committee on Request who gave the following report which was accepted and the committee released.

Report:

We the Committee on Request wish to recommend that the clerk have all obituaries given him printed and that we have (1000) one thousand copies of minutes made and distributed by the clerk and that he recieve $50.00 for his service. We also request that the next session of the Association be held with the sister church at Cedar Springs (Myers Grove) in Claiborne County, Tennessee to begin at 10:30 on Friday before the 3rd Saturday in August 1968 and continue three days.

Respectfully submitted,

Elder George Shoffner
Elder W.M. Sparks
Bro. Corum Berry

—3—

Eighth — Call for report of Finance Committee who gave the follow
ing report which was accepted and committee released.

Church	Printing Minutes	Visiting Ministers
Black Fox..............................	$10.00	
Bradens Chapel.........................	10.00	
Brantleys Chapel	20.00	
Cedar Springs	10.00	
Davis Chapel	10.00	$ 5.00
Gibson Station.........................	5.00	5.00
Kirkwood	10.00	5.00
Monroe, Michigan	5.00	
Noeton	3.00	
Lenoir City	15.00	
Oak Grove	12.00	
Rocky Dale	5.00	5.00
New Hebron		
Pleasant Hill	13.00	
Pleasant Point	10.00	
	$138.00	$20.00
	20.00	
Total	$158.00	

Association Report for the Year:

Total for day....................	$158.00	
Bal. in Bank....................	92.00	
TOTAL	$250.00	
Expenses for year.....................	90.00	
Bal. in Bank........................	$160.00	

Respectfully submitted,
Bro. Henry Chamberlain
Bro. John Davis
Bro. Von Beason

Ninth — Motion carried that we print all obituries and have 1000
minutes printed by clerk and distributed and that he recieve $50.00 for
his service, and that the next Association be held with the sister church
at Cedar Springs (Myers Grove) in Claiborne County, Tennessee on
Friday before the third Saturday in August 1968 at 10:30 A.M. That
Assistant Moderator, Elder Hugh E. Brummitt, preach the introductory

—4—

sermon and that Elder Henry Comer be the alternate.

Tenth —Motion carried that we letter and delegate to the New Bethel Association, and that we delegate Elder Henry Comer, Elder J.C. Monday, Elder Tony Eastridge and Elder W.M. Sparks to represent our Association when they convene in September. That we authorize the clerk to prepare a letter for the delegates to carry with them.

Eleventh—Motion and seconded that the Association extend to the Brantleys Chapel Church and community our heart felt thanks for the welcome, hospitality and kindness shown to all of us and that you have our love and prayers hoping that God will graceously bless you all.

Twelfth—Motion carried to adjourn until next year when we meet with the sister church of Cedar Springs on Friday before the third Saturday in August 1968 at 10:30.

This bringing to a close one of the most spiritual and harmoneous Associations we can remember.

Elder Albert Davis, Moderator
Bro. W.H. Taylor, Clerk

SUNDAY, AUGUST 20, 1967

The Sunday service was begun by congregation singing several good old songs.

Elder Clifford Brantley furthered introduced the service by reading the Bible lesson and calling for prayer by Elder Johnny Atkins.

Elder Tony Eastridge was to preach next, but so graciously and humbly gave his time to Elder Leonard White to take the entire time.

Elder White read from the 4th, 5th and 6th verses of Paul's letter to Tytus and from the 9th chapter of Romans. Then preached a wonderful sermon on Regeneration.

After a song and hand shake, the Association was closed out by Assistant Moderator Elder Hugh E. Brummitt then called for a closing prayer by Elder Walter Lyons.

ORDAINED MINISTERS

Elder Gilbert Atkins .... Route 3
Rutledge, Tennessee
Elder Johnnie Atkins .... Bean Station, Tennessee
Elder Everett Berry .... Fountain City, Tennessee
Phone 922-4241
Elder J. H. Branscomb .... Speedwell, Tennessee
Phone 86-3392
Elder Clifford Brantley .... Brown School Road
Maryville, Tennessee
Phone 982-3735

—5—

Elder Hugh E. Brummitt .... 1329 Brown Avenue
                                          Knoxville, Tennessee
                                          Phone 525-3583
Elder George Campbell .... Route 2, Fritts Rd.
                                          Concord, Tennessee

Elder Noble Lee Clawson .... Speedwell, Tennessee
Elder Henry Comer .... Route 4
                                          LaFollette, Tennessee
                                          Phone 562-3952
Elder Albert Davis .... Speedwell, Tennessee
                                          Phone 869-3596
Elder Tony Eastridge .... Route 2
                                          Louisville, Tennessee
                                          Phone 983-1068
Elder Dewey Ellison..................... Sharps Chapel, Tennessee
Elder Alvin Graves .... Lenoir City, Tennessee
Elder Joe Irwin .... Gibson Station, Virginia
Elder Walter Lyons .... 1602 Garfield Street
                                          Alcoa, Tennessee
                                          Phone YU3-3222
Elder Lenyil Meyers .... 512 E. Elm Street
                                          Monroe, Michigan
Elder J. C. Monday .... Speedwell, Tennessee
Elder Roy Oliver .... Bean Station, Tennessee
Elder R. H. Pettit .... 4907 Jacksboro Pike
                                          Knoxville, Tennessee
                                          Phone 689-5581
Elder Claude Rosson .... Goin, Tennessee
                                          Phone 626-3168
Elder Parnick Shelton................... Corryton, Tennessee
                                          Phone 689-6183
Elder George Shoffner................... Sharps Chapel, Tennessee
Elder W. M. Sparks .... Speedwell, Tennessee
                                          Phone 562-7997
Elder Leonard White .... LaFollette, Tennessee
                                          Phone 562-5667
Elder Clay Widner .... 101 West Norris Street
                                          Norris, Tennessee

Bro. Jim Oliver .... Bean Station, Tennessee

Elder Charles Taylor .... 212 E. Pinecrest
                                          Maryville, Tennessee

LICENTIATES

Bro. Joe Bush .... Corryton, Tennessee
Bro. Odell Carpenter........................ Maryville, Tennessee

—6—

648

August, 1967

We, the Powell Valley Association of Primitive Baptist while in session with the sister church at Brantley's Chapel in Blount County, Tennessee convening August 18, 19, 20, send these greetings to the New Bethel Association.

Our dearly beloved Brothers and Sisters in Christ, we desire to continue our correspondence with you. We hereby letter and delegate to your association by sending to you our beloved Ministers, Elder Henry Comer, Elder J.C. Monday, Elder Wm. Sparks and Elder Tony Eastridge. We hope you will accept them in love and fellowship. Having enjoyed your delegation this year, we look forward to seeing some of you when we convene with the sister church at Cedar Springs in Claiborne County, Tennessee on Friday before the third Saturday in August 1968.

May the Lord bless you all is our prayer.

Elder Albert Davis, Moderator
Elder Hugh E. Brummitt, Asst. Moderator
Bro. W.H. Taylor, Clerk
Bro. O.R. Parrott, Asst. Clerk

OBITUARIES

MRS. MELDA (JOHNSON) DAVIS

Mrs. Melda (Johnson) Davis was born April 20, 1876 passed from this life October 3, 1966. She was 90 years. She professed faith in Christ at an early age, and later joined the Primitive Baptist Church at Davis Chapel and remained a member until death. She was married to Thomas E. Davis, to this union was born six children - Juanita proceeded her in death. Survivors are two daughters, Marie Davis of LaFollette, Tennessee, and Mrs. Grace Lang, Dunellen, New Jersey; three sons, Mack Davis of St. Louis, Missouri, Richard Davis of Columbus, Ohio and Lewis Davis of LaFollette, Tennessee. Funeral services were October 5, 1966 at the Primitive Baptist Church at Davis Chapel, Elder Leonard White and Elder Wm. Sparks officiated. Burial in the old Davis Chapel Cemetery.

MRS. CINDA EDWARDS DUNCAN

Mrs. Cinda E. Duncan was born November 5th in the year of our Lord 1891 and passed away April 5, 1967. She is survived by her husband, Wiley of the Glades Community. She is also survived by seven children, 4 sons; Troy of Andover, Ohio, Charles of Sunbright, Tennessee, Harley of Deer Lodge, Tennessee, Ted of Miamiasburg, Ohio; three daughters, Nellie Lankford of Centerville, Tennessee, Mossie Beasley of Centerville, Tennessee, Ruth Beshears of San Deigo, California. She is also survived by 31 grandchildren and 15 great-grandchildren. Among her survivors are 4 brothers; Verlin, Dave, Lonzo and James Edwards all of Speedwell, Tennessee, 4 sisters; Mrs. Lou Lambert of Speedwell, Tennessee, Mrs. Mae Pace of Dallas, Texas, Mrs. Minnie Collingsworth of Greensboro, North Carolina, and Mrs. Edna Robbins of Madisonville, Tennessee.

She was born Cinda Edwards, the daughter of the late Jefferson and Jane Ausmus Edwards of Claiborne County.

She became a Christian and joined the Primitive Baptist Church in 1910. She lived a full life in the service of our Lord. At the time of her passing she was a member of the Pleasant Hill Primitive Baptist Church of Speedwell, Tennessee. Our great loss is Heaven's gain.

The Family

MRS. LERTIE DYKES

Mrs. Lertie Dykes, age 47, passed away Friday, December 2nd at St. Mary's Hospital.

She leaves to mourn her loss five daughters, Mrs. Betty Rutherford, Corryton, Tennessee, Mrs. Peggy Russell, Miss Brenda Dykes, Mrs. Phyllis Dykes, Mrs. Patsy Kitts all of Maynardville. One son, Billy Joe

Dykes, Maynardville. Parents, Mr. & Mrs. Harve Longmire, Tazewell. Three brothers, Lou and Ted Longmire of Tazewell, Kenneth Longmire of Knoxville, one grandson, Michael Russell.

She professed faith in Christ at an early age and joined the church at Oak Grove where she remained a faithful member. We feel our loss is her eternal gain.

Sleep on dear Mom
And take your rest
We loved you dearly
But God loves you best.

LEE ELLISON

Lee Ellison was born May 12, 1933, passed away September 17, 1965 at St. Mary's Hospital in Knox County. He was the son of Mr. & Mrs. Lonnie Ellison. Professed faith in Christ and joined Oak Grove Primitive Baptist Church. Survived by parents, Mr. & Mrs. Lonnie Ellison, two sisters, Mrs. Annie Ford and Mrs. Ima Bridges, five nieces two nephews and a host of relatives and friends. Funeral services were conducted at the church. Elder W.M. Sparks and Elder J.C. Monday officiated.

We miss you more, our hearts are sad,
Your smile we cannot see.
But, the memories of your gentle voice
With us will ever be.

Written by father & mother
August 31, 1966

MRS. ANNIE BELLE FORD

Mrs. Annie Belle Ford was born August 5, 1931. Passed away January 14, 1967 at a Knoxville hospital.

She was the daughter of Mr. & Mrs. Lonnie Ellison. Survived by one daughter, Lona Ford and one son, L.E. Ford, parents, Mr. & Mrs. Lonnie Ellison and one sister Mrs. Ima Bridges.

She professed faith in Christ and joined Oak Grove Baptist Church. She lived a faithful member until death. Funeral services were conducted by Elder W.M. Sparks and Elder J.C. Monday. She will be greatly missed by her parents, sister and children and all who knew her. She was laid to rest in the church cemetery.

A place is vacant in our home.
A voice we loved to hear is still.
There's an empty place within our hearts.
That no one here can fill

Written by father and mother
Mr. & Mrs. Lonnie Ellison

MRS. INA HALE

Mrs. Ina Hale was born in April 1882 and passed away on October 19, 1966 at the age of 84. Her membership was at Hamilton Grove Church and was later moved to Rocky Dale Church where she remained faithful until death.

She was survived by one sister, Mrs. Amy Moore of Knoxville and a host of relatives and friends.

Funeral services were held at Mynatts Chapel by Elder Hugh Brummitt and Elder Leonard White.

Interment in Pleasant View Cemetary.

FATE C. HAMILTON

Fate C. Hamilton, age 51, of Route 1, Maryville, passed away at Blount Memorial Hospital at 11:45 a.m. Wednesday. Survivors: wife, Rowena Lamdin Hamilton; daughters, Mrs. Barclay Ogle, Maryville, Mrs. Barbara McGhee, Lenoir City; son, Bobby Hamilton, Maryville; two grandchildren, Tommy Ogle, Debbie Ogle; sister, Mrs. Arlie Myers, Maryville. Funeral 3 p.m. Friday at Smith Mortuary Chapel, Rev. Willie Newman, Rev. Tommy Lynch officiating. Interment, Grandview Cemetary.

JOHN H. HARRISON

John H. Harrison, 76, passed away at the Middlesboro Hospital Tuesday, October 4, 1966. He was married in 1912 to Nancy Haynes, she passed away in the early 20's. He was married to Nolia Russell about 40 years ago. He joined the church at Pleasant Hill In June 1960, and attended as long as he was able.

He is survived by his wife Nolia Harrison; three sons: Joe, Pontiac, Michigan; Clyde, Monroe, Michigan; and Oakie, Speedwell, Tennessee; eight grandchildren and twelve great-grandchildren; one sister Mrs. Emmie Burton, Harlan, Kentucky; one brother Verlin Harrison, Harlan, Kentucky, and host of relatives and friends to mourn his passing.

Our loss is his Eternal Gain.

—12—

652

MRS. IDA RICE HILL

Mrs. Ida Rice Hill, wife of the late Bart Hill, was born September 19, 1878 and passed away July 10, 1967. She was the last member of the Rice family.

She is survived by two daughters, Nrs. Stella Clapp, and Mrs. Faye Anderson both of Corryton, Tennessee, and ¢e son, Clun Hill, Knoxville, Tennessee. She had nine grandchildren and 16 great-grandchildren.

In August 1955, she joined Rocky Dale Primitive Baptist Church where she remained a faithful member until death.

Funeral services were held at Gentry's Chapel by Elder Leonard White and Elder Hugh Brummitt. Interment Clalps Chapel Cemetary. Our loss is heavens gain.

LILBURN MILTON JOHNSON

Lilburn Milton Johnson was born September 4, 1883. He passed away on April 3, 1967. He was preceded in death by his wife, Sally Cox Johnson October 10, 1966. He is survived by his sons: Ted and Arthur Johnson of New Tazewell, Tennessee; Roy Johnson of Monroe, Michigan; daughters: Mrs. Madie Keck and Mrs. Evelyn Brewer of Monroe, Michigan; Mrs. Edna Stiner of Fort Wayne, Indiana; Mrs. Hazel Keck of New Tazewell, Tennessee; Mrs. Nelle Tolliver of Knoxville, Tennessee. One daughter who preceded him in death. 26 grandchildren and 8 great-grandchildren; one brother Johnny Johnson of Wyndotte, Michigan.

He professed faith in Christ and wanted his children to live close to the Lord. He was a loyal faithful husband and father and a wonderful neighbor.

Dear God the circle is broken here,
But only for awhile.
Help us to live to meet again
Where we will never say good-bye.

Funeral services were held Wednesday April 5, at 10:30 A.M. at Pleasant Point Church. Elder Tony Eastridge and Elder Claude Rosson officiated. Interment in Hopper's Cemetary.

"For I reckon that the sufferings of this present time are not worthy to be compared with the glory which shall be revealed to us".

Romans 8:18

PARALEE SHARP JOHNSON

Paralee Sharp Johnson was born May 30, 1895 and departed this life June 5, 1967.

She leaves to mourn her loss four daughters, Mrs. Jayette McDonnell, Chicago, Illinois; Mrs. Fern Parsley, Liberty Center, Ohio; Mrs. Bobbie Weeks, Oak Ridge and Mrs. Delores Seneker, Knoxville, Tennessee; three sons, Jacob C. and Jefferson, Knoxville and Gordon L. Johnson,

—13—

Atlanta, Georgia, 15 grandchildren and eight great grandchildren; four brothers, Isaac, Asa, Ambrose and Robert Sharp; two sisters, Mrs. Ida Lowe and Mrs. Alice Keck.

One son Titus C. Johnson is deceased.

She was a member of Kirkwood Primitive Baptist Church of Knoxville where she was a faithful member until illness prevented.

She was the daughter of the late Calvin and Elvira Sharp.

Funeral services were conducted at the Rose Funeral Home by Elder Leonard White and Rev. B. Calvin Thomas. Interment in Lynnhurst Cemetery.

MRS. SARAH E. JOHNSON

Mrs. Sarah E. (Sally Cox) Johnson was born May 10, 1887. Passed away October 10, 1966. She was the wife of L.M. Johnson for 61 years. Nine children were born to them, one preceded her in death.

She was a member of the Pleasant Point Primitive Baptist Church which she joined at an early age. She bore her long suffering illness with patience and wore a smile to hide her sorrow. I am sure, "our loss is Heavens gain".

She leaves to mourn her husband L.M. Johnson, three sons; Ted and Arthur of New Tazewell, Tennessee; Roy of Monroe, Michigan. Five daughters; Edna Stiner of Fort Wayne, Indiana; Madie Keck and Evelyn Brewer of Monroe, Michigan; Hazel Keck of New Tazewell, Tennessee; and Nelle Tolliver of Knoxville, Tennessee; 26 grandchildren and seven great-grandchildren; sisters: Mrs. Frellie Williams, New Tazewell, Tennessee; Mrs. Mossie Haley of Middlesboro, Kentucky; Mrs. Lunda Keck, Knoxville, Tennessee: brothers; Charlie Cox of Harlan Kentucky; General Cox of Middlesboro, Kentucky.

Funeral services were held Wednesday October 12, 10:30 A.M. at Pleasant Point Church. Elder Leonard White and Elder Claude Rosson officiated. Interment at Hopper's Cemetary.

GRAVES McKINLEY

Graves McKinley was born June 24, 1897, departed this life October 12, 1966. He was united in marriage to Mossie Jones in the year of 1920. To this union was born four sons and one daughter. One son preceded him in death in World War II.

Brother McKinley professed a hope in Christ and united with the church at Pleasant Hill March of 1942 and lived a loyal, faithful member until death. He is greatly missed by his family, his church and his community.

He leaves to mourn his loss his wife and four children 15 grandchildren, one sister, one brother and a host of relatives and friends, but we feel our loss is Heaven'S gain.

He was layed to rest in the Aumus Cemetery in Speedwell, Tennessee to await the Glorious Resurrection.

Written by Elder & Mrs. Albert Davis

—14—

JOHN MAPLES

John Maples, 71, of Route 1, Sharp's Chapel, passed away at Claiborne County Hospital. Survivors: wife, Mrs. Nancy L. Maples; son Ernest, Knoxville, Herman, Sharp's Chapel; daughters, Mrs. Helen Clark, LaSalle, Michigna, Mrs. Ella Franks, Knoxville, Mrs. Idella Mazingo, Sharp's Chapel, Mrs. Anna Lee Rowe, Kokomo, Ind., 14 grandchildren; brothers, Ed and Robert, Sharp's Chapel. Sister, Mrs. Gertie Wilson, Knoxville. He was a World War I veteran. Funeral at Oak Grove Primitive Baptist Church where he was a member. Elder Albert Davis officiating. Interment in Church Cemetery. Cocke Funeral Home in charge.

MRS. EMMA C. MEYERS

Emma C. Meyers, wife of the late Robert Meyers, passed away at the Claiborne County Hospital February 13, 1967.

Survivors: son, Lonnie Meyers, Knoxville; daughter, Mrs. Yadon Howard, of New Tazewell; three grandchildren; two great-grandchildren; brother; Bob Day, of Middlesboro, Kentucky.

Funeral services were held 2:00 P.M. Wednesday at Coffey Chapel. The body laid in state one hour before services. Interment in Drummonds Cemetary. Coffey, Tazewell in charge.

NATHAN MIRACLE

Nathan Henry Miracle, age 74, died at his home April 20, 1967. New Tazewell. Survivors: brothers; Billy and Andy Miracle, of New Tazewell, Tennessee; T.J. Miracle, Tazewell; Rufus Miracle, of Lexington, Kentucky. Sisters: Mrs. Lonnie Paul, Speedwell; Mrs. Roie Tuttle, Crossville, and Mrs. Matie Cupp, Flat Rock, Michigan.

Funeral services were held at 10:00 A.M. Sunday at Cedar Springs Primitive Baptist Church, Rev. Harold Hunt officiating. Burial in Drummonds Cemetery. Pallbearers: Otis Cupp, Elisha Lundy, Isaac Miracle, Rev. Glen Cupp, Matthew Miracle and Conley Miracle. Coffey Mortuary in charge.

MRS. EDNA RAWSON MORGAN

Mrs. Morgan passed away at her home in Rutledge, Route 3, on Monday. Survivors: husband, James H. Morgan, Rutledge; son, Charles Morris Morgan, Rutledge; mother, Mrs. Frances Rawson, New Tazewell; sisters, Mrs. Oma McCann, Rutledge, Mrs. Eula Gray Cupp, New Tazewell; brothers Billy, Lawrence, Claude Rawson, New Tazewell, Carl Rawson, Fountain City. Funeral at New Blackwell Baptist Church. Interment in church cemetery.

MRS. PARIE (HEATHERLY) MYERS

Mrs. Parie (Heatherly) Myers, Age 69, died 8:10 a.m. Friday, July 14, 1967, at the ORINS Hospital, Oak Ridge, Tennessee. She professed faith in Christ at an early age and joined the Primitive Baptist Church at Davis Chapel. She was the daughter of the late George E. and Cynthia Heatherly. She was the wife of the late Otto Myers who died in 1961. To this union was born 3 children: daughters, Mrs. Mae Oma Dossett and Mrs. Dorothy Black, son, Carl all of LaFollette, Tennessee. Brothers, James S. and Jesse Heatherly of LaFollette; Homer of Dayton, Ohio; Edgar of Monroe, Michigan. Sisters, Mrs. Elsie Carroll of Dayton, Ohio; Mrs. Nannie Kitts of Centerville, Ohio. 5 grandchildren. Funeral services were held at Davis Chapel Church by Elder Wm. Sparks and Elder Leonard White. Interment was in the Sunrise Cemetery at Davis Chapel.

OUSLEY, HERCHEL

Herchel Ousley, age 63, Route 2, Powell, passed away at 4:35 A.M. at St. Mary's Hospital. Member at Oak Grove Baptist Church, Union County. Member of Fleet Reserve Association, Branch No. 194, and Member of Powell Lions Club. Survivors: wife, Mrs. Lola Graves Ousley; sisters, Mrs. K. D. Lively, Wichita, Kansas, Mrs. Victor Edwards, Kokomo, Ind., Mrs. H. E. Anderson, Knoxville, Miss Delta Ousley, Halls, Mrs. E. B. Edgemon, Erie, Tenn; brothers, Herbert and Winslow of Kokomo, Ind., Ott C. and Osbern of Sharp's Chapel, Furard, Athens; several neices and nephews. Rev. W. H. Parrott and Rev. Leonard White officiated at the funeral. Interment in Lynnhurst cemetery.

MOLLIE WIGGINS PETTIT

Mollie Wiggins Pettit was born May 8, 1886 and departed this life December 27, 1966.
She was married to Rufus H. Pettit August 2r, 1907 and to this union

She was married to Rufus H. Pettit August 24, 1907 and to this union two sons were born. She leaves to mourn her loss her husband and one son, Cliff H. Pettit of Knoxville, five grandchildren and six great grandchildren, two sisters and four brothers.
She was a member of Kirkwood Primitive Baptist Church of Knoxville and was an active and faithful member until illness prevented shortly before death. We feel that our loss is her gain.
Funeral services were conducted at the Rose Funeral Home by Elder Leonard White. Interment in Lynnhurst Cemetery.

CHARLIE LEE ROBERTSON

Charlie Lee Robertson, was born September 8, 1897, died at age 69 years 9 month old. He professed faith in Christ at an early age and join the Primitive Baptist Church at Cedar Springs.

He was married to Maggie Drummonds May 13, 1913 and to this union was born 10 children. One preceded him in death leaving 5 sons and 4 daughters. Mrs. Mattie Holt, Mrs. Bill Good, both of New Tazewell. Mrs. Ester Good, and Mrs. T.S. Elliott, both of Michigan. Sons Clifford Robertson, of New Tazewell; Larwence, Otis, Claude, Hoy Robertson all of Michigan.

Five sisters, three brothers, one uncle, 25 grandchildren, 11 great-grandchildren and a host of friends.

Funeral services were held at the Primitvei Baptist Church at Cedar Springs. Elder Lester Bundy and Claude Rosson, officiated. Interment was in the Drummonds Cemetery, June 23, 1967. Coffey of Tazewell, in charge.

May he rest in peace.

Written by children

ROGERS, HARVEY E.

Harvey E. Rogers, age 85, died at 8:20 at Claiborne County Hospital. He was a member of Oak Grove Baptist Church and was a member of Union County Court for several years. He was a 50-year Mason in Blazing Star Lodge No. 455, F&AM. Survivors: sister, Mrs. Kate Browning, Niota; several nieces and nephews; stepdaughters, Misses Rosa and Dessilena Shoffner; stepsons, Pettus and Lucas Shoffner; step-grandson, Sammy Don Shoffner; four step-great-grandchildren, all of Sharp's Chapel. Funeral at Oak Grove Baptist Church with Elders Albert Davis, William Sparks, and Leonard White officiating. Cooke Funeral Home, Maynardville, in charge.

JOHN A. SHOFFNER

John A. (Moody) Shoffner, age 88, died 4 p.m. Saturday at his home Sharp's Chapel. Survivors: wife, Mrs. Cynthia Shoffner; daughters, Mrs. Florence Settles, Speedwell, Mrs. Frances Hopper, Sharp's Chapel; sons, Claude, Jim, Tilmon, and Bill, Sharp's Chapel, Jess, Andersonville. Funeral 11 a.m. Monday at Oak Grove Baptist Church, Elder Paris Graves and Elder Albert Davis officiating. Interment church cemetary. Cooke Funeral Home, Maynardville, in charge.

SARAH JANE WHITE WEAVER

Sarah Jane White Weaver departed this life February 24, 1967, age 89.

She was married to W.H. Weaver avout 1905. To this union two sons were born, Lincoln and Leon, which survive her. Her husband passed away in 1948. She later married Wheeler Lambert whom she also survived.

She professed faith in Christ in early life and joined the Primitive Baptist Church at Mossy Spring, Union County, Tennessee where she remained a faithful member until the church was lost to Norris Lake'. She then transferred her membership to Davis Chapel where she remained until released by death.

She now sleeps by her first husband in the beautiful garden of death at Kempton, Illinois, peacefully awaiting the resurection of the dead.

MARRISON MONROE WELCH

Marrison Monroe Welch, age 80, New Tazewell, died December 19, 1966 at Claiborne Hospital. He was a member of the Primitive Baptist Church at Cedar Springs.

Survivors, son, Lee Roy Welch, Knoxville, daughters, Mrs. Beulad Buchanan, New Tazewell, Mrs. Tillie Fortner, Tazewell. Mrs. Alma Day, Chouteau, Oklahoma; Mrs. Ruby Pnibyl, and Mrs. Laura Lirschner both of Michigan and Mrs. Bonnie Johnson, of Knoxville; 15 grandchildren; brother, Frilon Welch,' Speedwell; half-brothers, Ralph and Ed Welch, both of Speedwell and Lon Welch of Anderson, Maryland.

Funeral services were held at 2:00 P.M., Wednesday at Coffey Funeral Home Chapel with Rev. Yadon Howard and William Simmon officiating. Burial in Drummonds Cemetary.

Pallbearers: Grant Manning, Pat, Ditt, and Ditt Thomas Welch, Jr., Toby Welch and Warren G. Welch. Coffey Mortuary in charge.

PEARLIE LAVERNE WYRICK

Pearlie Laverne Wyrick, age 62, New Tazewell, died at Claiborne Hospital November 10.

Survivors: daughter, Mrs. Opal Keck, New Tazewell: sons, Willard and John Wyrick Jr., Powells; seven grandchildren; stepmother, Mrs. Myrtle Cox, Sharps Chapel; sisters, Mrs. Nola Berry, Mrs. Nancy Brewer, Powells, Mrs. Hattie Shoffner, Maryville; brothers, Dewey Cox New Tazewell, Hughie and Sillus Cox, Sharps Chapel; half-brother, Bobby Cox, Knoxville.

Funeral services were held Friday at 10:30 A.M., at Oak Grove Baptist Church, Union County. Burial in church cemetary.

Rev. Lloyd Endland officiated.

Pallbearers: J.C. and Bob Cox, Clondis White, Dennis Bastic, Paul Nelson and Austin Shoffner. Coffey, in charge.

—18—

THOMAS ALEXANDER YADON

Thomas Alexander Yadon, born January 28, 1884, departed this life January 28, 1967. He was 83 years old. He professed faith in Christ at an early age and joined the Primitive Baptist Church at Black Fox and remained a member until death. He was married to Lundie Perry Yaden who preceded him in death. To this union were born three children, Mabel Lee of Mascot, Elmer Yaden of Charlotte, North Carolina, and Oscar Yaden deceased. Four grandchildren and five great-grandchildren. Two sisters, Matilda Guy of Powder Springs and Francis Liffarel of Washburn.

Services were conducted at the Black Fox Church January 31, 1967. Elder Parnick Shelton and Elder Ralph Muncy officiating. Smith's Funeral home in charge.

Sadly missed by family and friends.

CHURCH	COUNTY	PASTOR	CLERK	ADDRESS
Black Fox..............	Grainger	Elder Parnick Shelton...............	Bennie Capps	P.O. Box 91 Maynardville, Tenn.
Braden's Chapel........	Union	Elder J. C. Monday, Asst. Noble Clawson	Flossie Capps, Asst.	Rt. 2, Washburn, Tenn. Speedwell, Tenn.
Brantley's Chapel......	Blount	Elder Clifford Brantley .... Elder Everett Berry, Asst.	Arvil Braden.............. Rina Johnson,..............	9 Douglas Ave. Maryville, Tenn. Rt. 8, Brown School Rd. Maryville, Tenn.
Cedar Springs	Claiborne	Elder Claude Rosson"........ Elder Claude Widner, Asst.	Rina Johnson, Jr., Asst. .... Eula Gray Good	New Tazewell, Tenn.
Davis Chapel...........	Campbell	Elder W. M. Sparks .... 562-7997, Speedwell	Ruth Heatherly .... Lassie Ellison, Asst.	Rt. 1, LaFollette, Tenn. Rt. 1, LaFollette
Gibson Station	Lee County, Va.......	Elder Leonard White......... Elder Everett Berry, Asst.	Roxie Cobb .... Lucille Freeman, Asst.	Gibson Station, Va.
Kirkwood	Knox	Elder Leonard White.........	Estelle Petree Sharp .... Shirley Bowden, Asst.	5313 Jacksboro Pike Knoxville, Tenn. 811 Banks Ave., N.E. Knoxville, Tenn.
Lenoir City .... Monroe, Mich.	Loudon .... Monroe................	Elder Chas. Taylor ''..... Elder Alvin Graves, Asst ...... Elder Lenvil Meyers..........	E. H. Scarbrough .... Ditsy Russell .... Gertrude Zwak, Asst.	Lenoir City, Tenn. 5177 Plum Creek Fr., Monroe, Mich. 1825 Spaulding Rd. Monroe, Mich.
Noeton	Grainger	Elder Gilbert Atkins.............	John Oliver................. Bessie Collins, Asst.	Bean Station, Tenn. Rt. 5, Morristown, Tenn.
Oak Grove.............	Union.................	Elder W. M. Sparks .... J. C. Monday, Asst.	Belle Moore Ruth Shoffner, Asst.	Sharps Chapel, Tenn. Sharps Chapel, Tenn.
Pleasant Hill	Claiborne	J. C. Monday .... Elder Albert Davis, Asst.	William Branscomb .... Verlin Edwards, Asst.	Speedwell, Tenn. Speedwell, Tenn.
Pleasant Point........	Claiborne	Elder Tony Eastridge .... Elder Claude Rosson, Asst.	Claude Rosson .... Menada Keck, Asst.	New Tazewell, Tenn. New Tazewell, Tenn.
Rocky Dale............	Knox	Elder Hugh Brummitt	Avrell Graves	Rt. 3, Corryton, Tenn. Phone 689-3668
New Hebron	Jefferson	Elder Gilbert Atkins.................	Charles Bryant, Asst. Cordia Mitchell	Rt. 4, Corryton New Market, Tenn.

660

1968 MINUTES
of the
ONE HUNDRED FORTY-NINTH
ANNUAL SESSION
of the
POWELL VALLEY ASSOCIATION
OF PRIMITIVE BAPTIST
held with THE SISTER CHURCH
at
CEDAR SPRINGS
Claiborne County, Tennessee
August 16, 17, 18, 1968

The next session to be held with the Sister Church at Davis Chapel in Campbell County, Tennessee, to begin at 10:30 on Friday before the third Saturday in August 1969, and continue the following two days.

Elder Henry Comer will preach the introductory sermon with Elder J. C. Clawson as alternate.

OFFICERS

ELDER ALBERT DAVIS .... Moderator
　　　　　Speedwell, Tenn. Phone 869-3596

ELDER HUGH E. BRUMMITT .... Assistant Moderator
　　　1329 Brown Ave., Knoxville, Tenn. Phone 525-3583

BRO. W. H. TAYLOR .... Clerk
　　　　　Route 13, Knoxville, Tenn. Phone 922-2143

BRO. O. R. PARROTT .... Assistant Clerk
　　　　　LaFollette, Tennessee

661

STATISTICAL TABLE

CHURCHES	DELEGATES	Restored	Rec'd by Let.	Rec'd by Baptism	Rec'd by Relationshp	Dismissed by Letter	Excluded	Deceased	Total Membership	Visiting Ministers	Ptg. Minutes	Meeting	Communion
Black Fox	Elder George Campbell, Bros. Arthur Terry, Walter Cabbage, Dale Capps, Stevie Terry, Calvin Capps, Roy Bailey, Bennie Capps; Sisters Flossie Capps, Debbie Terry, Roma Bailey, Sandra Capps, Mary Terry, Mary Ruth Terry.	0	0	2	0	0	0	2	97	0	$10.00	1st Sat & Sun.	1st Sun. & Sun. July
Brodens Chapel	Elders J. C. Monday, Noble Lee Clawson, W. M. Sparks, Henry Comer; Sisters Leecy Sparks, Helen Clawson, Winnona Monday, Genifer Sparks, Glenda Wilson and Minnie Wilson.	0	0	7	0	0	0	1	117	0	$10.00	2nd Sun & Sat. July	2nd Sun July
Brantley's Chapel	Elder Clifford Brantley, Bros. Corum Berry, Von Beason, Plummer McBee, Everett Brantley; Sisters Twila Berry, Mildred Brantley, Barsha Brantley.	0	0	4	2	0	0	1	82	0	$20.00	4th Sun.	4th Sun July
Cedar Springs	Bros. J. L. Drummonds, Johnny Ayers, Clifford Robertson, Bill Good; Sisters Ida Robertson, Maggie Robertson, Eula Gray Good, Ailene Campbell, Jippy Ayers, Velt Munsey, Joan Noah, Mary Treace, Ellen Good, Patricia Good, Gloria Good, Agnes Alston.	0	0	0	0	1	0	1	54	0	$10.00	4th Sun	4th Sun June
Davis Chapel	Elder Leonard White; Bros. Orice McCarty, Onie Parrott, Gene Hobbs, Hugh Hill; Sisters Mollie McCarty, Mamie Parrott, Ruby Hill	0	0	4	0	0	0	4	144	0	$10.00	3rd Sat Nite Sun, Ea Sun Nite	3rd Sun June
Gibson Station	Bros. Spurgin Thompson, Harve Rhymer, Floyd Cobb, Franklin Jones; Sisters Fannie Jones, Mellie Thompson	0	0	1	0	0	0	1	116	0	$5.00	1st Sun	1st Sun June
Kirkwood	Elders R. H. Petitt, Hugh E. Brummitt, Walter Lyons; Bros. M. A. Norton, W. H. Taylor, John L. Sharp; Sisters Callie Lyons, Ruby Brummitt, Lucy Norton, Evelyn Sharp, Lou Emma Taylor	0	0	0	0	0	1	1	111	0	$10.00	Earch Sun	Last Sun April
Lenoir City	Elders Charles Taylor, Alvin Graves; Bros. Hubert Spoons, Henry Chamberlain; Sisters Estie Chamberlain, Annie Spoons, Cora Hill	0	0	0	0	0	3	0	205	0	$15.30	Ea. Sun Sun Nite	3rd Sun May
Benton, Michigan	Elder Lenvil Meyers; Bro. John Drummonds; Sisters Roxie Drummond, Lela Drummond, Gertrude Swack	0	0	0	0	0	0	0	14	0	$5.00	Ec. Sun Nite	3rd Sun July
Newton	Bro. John Oliver; Sisters Ruth Oliver, Bessie Collins	0	0	0	0	0	0	0	35	0	$3.00	3rd Sun	3rd Sun May & Sept.
Oak Grove	Elders George Shoffner, Tony Eastridge; Bros. Aaron Cole, Alford Relford, Lowell Relford; Sisters Frances Eastridge, Maggie Relford, Veda Cole, Carol Telford, Tishie Creech, Lillie Shoffner	0	0	4	0	3	3	2	304	0	$12.00	1st Sat & Sun	1st Sun May
Pleasant Hill	Elders Albert Davis, J. H. Branscomb; Bro. Verlin Edwards; Sisters Audra Davis, Nadine Gibby, Lucinda Moyers	0	0	0	0	0	0	0	96	0	$12.00	4th Sat & Sun	4th Sun June
Pleasant Point	Elder Claude Rosson; Bros George Williams, C. D. Keck; Sisters Doris Rosson, Francie Rosson, Allie Williams, Menada Keck	0	0	0	0	0	0	0	119	0	$10.00	1st Sun	1st Sun July
Rocky Dale	Elders Everett Berry, Patrick Shelton; Bros. Joe Bush, Ralph Clopp, Elmer Graves, Avrel Graves, Dewey Graves; Sisters Trula Berry, Wilma Shelton, Wanda Clapp, Norma Jean Bush	0	0	0	2	0	0	1	111	0	$5.00	Sun after 2nd Sat	Sun after 2nd Sat May
Cave Creek	Elder Raymond Brantley; Bros. Alfred Farmer, Floyd Farmer, Clarence Johnson, Zekie Johnson, Elmer Guetner, Estie Guettner, Elizabeth Johnson, Linda Johnson, Rose Guettner, Loraine White, Margaret Rother, Frankie Howard, Edra Calfee	0	0	0	0	0	0	0	40	0	$5.00	3rd Sat.	3rd Sat.

FRIDAY, AUGUST 16, 1968

The Powell Valley Association of Primitive Baptist having been blessed of the Lord and privileged to meet again in love, peace and harmony with the Sister Church at Cedar Springs in Claiborne County, Tennessee, on August 16, 17, and 18 for the one hundred and forty-ninth session.

After singing the good old songs of Zion, the Moderator introduced the service by reading from the first chapter of the book of James, verses one to thirteen. Then called for the opening prayer by Elder Tony Eastridge.

Elder Hugh E. Brummitt, Assistant Moderator, then preached the introductory sermon, using for the lesson verses 14-15 of the 24th chapter of Joshua, using the theme "Choose ye this day whom you will serve, as for me and my house we will serve the Lord". This sermon was perhaps one of Elder Brummitt's best.

The Moderator then called for a song, handshake and intermission for fifteen minutes.

After intermission and a spiritual song service, Moderator Davis called the Association to order, pleading to all Sister Churches for continued love, peace and harmony. Then after reading a very dedicated poem composed by himself, called for prayer by Elder Carl McCarty of the New Bethel Association.

ORDER OF BUSINESS

First —Moderator called for letters of the Sister Churches. Letters were received from all the 14 churches of the Association.

Second —Motion carried to receive the letters and seat the delegates named in the letters.

Third —Called for members present but not delegated who wish to be seated and four came: Elder Johnny Atkins, Sister Halie Atkins, Brother John Oliver and Sister Brantly of Oak Grove.

Fourth —Called for petitionary letters and one was received from Cave Creek in Roane County, Tennessee, asking to be admitted to the Powell Valley Association of Primitive Baptist.

Fifth —The Association unanimously voted to receive and welcome the Cave Creek Church and seat the good delegation in their letter.

Sixth —Call for letters of corresponding Associations. One received from the New Bethel Association. Their letter was received and delegates seated. Letter received from the original Hiwassee Association composed of three churches, to take up correspond-

-1-

ence with the Powell Valley Association. The Association voted to accept their petition, take up correspondence with them and seat their delegation.

Seventh — Call for any others who wish to be seated as delegates who were not named. None came.

Eighth — Call for the election of officers for the coming year. Motion carried that the Association re-elect Elder Albert Davis as Moderator and re-elect Elder Hugh E. Brummitt as Assistant Moderator. Motion carried that the Association re-elect Bro. W. H. Taylor as Clerk and Bro. O. R. Parrott as Assistant Clerk.

Ninth — Motion adopted to authorize the Moderator to appoint all the committees to serve for the session.

Tenth — The Moderator appointed the committees as follows:

1. *Committee on Arrangements*

Elder Raymond Brantly
Elder Parnick Shelton
Bro. J. C. Johnson

2. *Committee on Correspondence*

Elder Tony Eastridge
Elder Clifford Brantley
Elder W. M. Sparks

3. *Committee on Preaching*

Bro. Henry Chamberlain
Bro. Clifford Robertson
Bro. M. A. Norton

4. *Committee on Request*

Elder Claude Rosson
Bro. John Oliver
Bro. Verlin Edwards

5. *Committee on Finance*

Elder Henry Comer
Elder Walter Lyons
Bro. Corum Berry

After completing the appointment of all the committees the Association voted to adjourn until 10:30 A. M. Saturday Morning, August 17, 1968.

SATURDAY, AUGUST 17, 1968

First — After a good song service directed by Elder Charles Taylor and Assistant Moderator, Hugh E. Brummitt, making a welcome talk and then reading the 116th Psalm, he called for prayer by Elder C. C. Oliver, of the Original Hiwassee Association.

Second — The Moderator then called the Association to order for business and called for any letters from Sister Churches not received Friday. There were none.

Third — Call for any corresponding letters not received Friday. None.

Fourth — Call for the report of the Committee on Arrangements, who gave the following report, which was received and the committee released.

—2—

Committee on Arrangements

1. Call for roll call of delegates.
2. Call for the report of Committee on Preaching.
3. Call for report of Committee on Correspondence.
4. Call for report of Committee on Request.
5. Call for report of Committee on Finance.
6. When and where shall the next Association be held? Who shall preach the introductory sermon and who shall be the alternate? How many minutes of the Association shall we have printed, and who shall supervise the printing and distribution of them, and how much shall he receive for his service?

Submitted by
Elder Parnick Shelton
Elder Raymond Brantley
Bro. J. C. Johnson

Fifth — Call for report of Committee on Preaching, who submitted the following report which was received and the committee released.

Preaching Committee recommends:

Friday Night	— **Elder Charles Taylor**
Saturday	— **Elder Raymond Brantley**
Saturday Night	— **Elder Parnick Shelton** — **Elder Lenvil Myers**
Sunday	— **Elder Leonard White**

Respectfully submitted,

Bro. Henry Chamberlain
Bro. M. A. Norton
Bro. Clifford Robertson

Sixth — Call for report of Committee on Correspondence who gave the following report which was received and the committee released.

Report of Committee:

We, the Committee on Correspondence, recommend that we keep our correspondence with the beloved New Bethel Association and also the ones we now correspond with, the Original Hiwassee Association and that we letter and delegate to each of these Associations.

Respectfully submitted,

Elder Tony Eastridge
Elder W. M. Sparks
Elder Clifford Brantley

Seventh—Call for report of Committee on Request, who gave the following report which was accepted and the committee released.

Report:

We, the Committee on Request, recommend that we request the Clerk to have printed 1,000 copies of the minutes and distributed to the Sister Churches. And that he have printed all obituaries given to him, and that he receive $50.00 for his services. We also request that the next session of the Association be held with the Sister Church at Davis Chapel in Campbell County, Tennessee, to begin at 10:30 on Friday before the third Saturday in August 1969.

Respectfully submitted,

Elder Claude Rosson
Bro. John Oliver
Bro. Verlin Edwards

Eighth – Call for report of Committee on Finance, who gave the following report which was accepted and the committee released.

Report:

Church	Printing Minutes	Visiting Ministers
Black Fox	$10.00	
Bradens Chapel	$10.00	
Brantleys Chapel	$20.00	
Cedar Springs	$10.00	
Davis Chapel	$10.00	$5.00
Gipson Station	$ 5.00	$5.00
Kirkwood	$10.00	$5.00
Lenoir City	$15.00	
Monroe, Mich.	$ 5.00	
Noeton	$ 3.00	
Oak Grove	$12.00	
Pleasant Hill	$12.00	
Pleasant Point	$10.00	
Rocky Dale	$ 5.00	$5.00
Cave Creek	$ 5.00	

TOTAL PRINTING MINUTES	$142.00	
TOTAL VISITING MINISTERS	$ 20.00	
GRAND TOTAL		$162.00
BALANCE IN BANK		$117.00
		$279.00
PRINTING OF MINUTES		130.00
BALANCE IN BANK		$149.00

Respectfully submitted,

Elder Walter Lyons
Elder Henry Comer
Bro. Corum Berry

Ninth — Motion carried that we have printed all obituaries, and that we have printed 1,000 minutes and that the Clerk supervise the printing and distribution of same and that he receive $50.00 for his service. Also that the next session be held with the Sister Church at Davis Chapel in Campbell County, Tennessee, beginning at 10:30 on Friday before the third Saturday in August 1969. And that Elder Henry Comer preach the introductory sermon and Elder J. C. Monday be the alternate.

Tenth — Motion approved that we letter and delegate to the New Bethel Association our beloved Elder George Campbell, Elder Henry Comer and Elder Walter Lyons to represent us in that Association. And that we delegate Elder Charles Taylor, Elder Raymond Brantley and Elder Henry Comer to the Original Hiwassee Association and that the Clerk prepare a letter for each delegation to take along with them.

Eleventh — Motion that the Association give a standing vote to the church and to the entire community for the good hospitality, love and kindness shown to all of us while in your community. And that you have our love and prayers and hoping that God will graciously bless you all.

Twelfth — Motion carried to adjourn until next year when we meet with the Sister Church at Davis Chapel on Friday before the third Saturday in August 1969.

Elder Albert Davis
Elder Hugh E. Brummitt,
Assistant Moderator
Bro. W. H. Taylor, Clerk
Bro. O. R. Parrott,
Assistant Clerk

SUNDAY, AUGUST 18, 1968

The Sunday service opened by congregational singing and two special songs by Bro. Johnny Ayers; the pastor, Elder Claude Rosson, welcomed the crowd and made a short talk, then called for prayer by Elder Noble Clawson.

Elder Leonard White reading from the third, fourth, and fifth verses of the second chapter of First Timothy and bringing a wonderful message. After song and handshake and short testimony by several, the Association was closed by prayer by Elder J. H. Branscomb.

–6–

ORDAINED MINISTERS

NAME	ADDRESS
Elder Gilbert Atkins	Route 3, Rutledge, Tennessee
Elder Johnnie Atkins	Bean Station, Tennessee
Elder Everette Berry	Fountain City, Tennessee Phone: 922-4241
Elder J. H. Branscomb	Speedwell, Tennessee Phone: 86-3392
Elder Clifford Brantley	Maryville, Tennessee Brown School Road Phone: 982-3735
Elder Hugh E. Brummitt	Knoxville, Tennessee 1329 Brown Avenue Phone: 525-3583
Elder George Campbell	Concord, Tennessee Fritts Road Phone: 966-5340
Elder Noble Lee Clawson	Route 4 Speedwell, Tennessee
Elder Henry Comer	LaFollette, Tennessee Phone: 562-3952
Elder Albert Davis	Speedwell, Tennessee Phone: 869-3596
Elder Tony Eastridge	Louisville, Tennessee Route 2 Phone: 983-1068
Elder Dewey Ellison	Sharps Chapel, Tennessee
Elder Alvin Graves	Lenoir City, Tennessee
Elder Joe Irwin	Gibson Station, Virginia
Elder Walter Lyons	Alcoa, Tennessee 1602 Garfield Street Phone: YU 3-3222
Elder Lenvil Meyers	Monroe, Michigan 715 Scott Street
Elder J. C. Monday	Speedwell, Tennessee
Elder Roy Oliver	Bean Station, Tennessee
Elder R. H. Petitt	Knoxville, Tennessee 4907 Jacksboro Pike Phone: 689-5581

-7-

669

Elder Claude Rosson	New Tazewell, Tennessee
	Phone: 626-3168
Elder Parnick Shelton	Corryton, Tennessee
	Phone: 689-6183
Elder George Shoffner	Route 2
	Louisville, Tennessee
Elder W. M. Sparks	Speedwell, Tennessee
	Phone: 562-7997
Elder Leonard White	LaFollette, Tennessee
	Phone: 562-5667
Elder Clay Widner	Norris, Tennessee
	101 W. Norris Street
Elder James Oliver	Bean Station, Tennessee
Elder Charles Taylor	Maryville, Tennessee
	212 E. Pinecrest
Elder Raymond Brantley	Loudon, Tennessee
	Route 3

LICENTIATES

Bro. Joe Bush	Corryton, Tennessee
Bro. Odell Carpenter	Maryville, Tennessee
Bro. Johnny Ayers	New Tazewell, Tennessee

August 22, 1968

We, the Powell Valley Association of Primitive Baptist, while in Session with the Sister Church at Cedar Springs in Claiborne County, Tennessee, convening August 16, 17 and 18, 1968, send greetings and love to the New Bethel Association.

Our dearly beloved Brothers and Sisters in Christ, we desire to keep our correspondence with you. We hereby letter and delegate to you by sending to you some of our beloved Elders, who are in good standing and fellowship with us; Elder Henry Comer, Elder George Campbell and Elder Walter Lyons, whom we hope you will accept to sit with you.

Having enjoyed the good fellowship of your delegation this year, we look forward and pray that it will be repeated next year when we meet with the Sister Church at Davis Chapel in Campbell County, Tennessee, on Friday before the third Saturday in August 1969.

Elder Albert Davis, Moderator

Bro. W. H. Taylor, Clerk
Route 13
Knoxville, Tennessee

August 23, 1968

We the Powell Valley Association of Primitive Baptist, while in session with the Sister Church at Cedar Springs in Claiborne County, Tennessee, convening August 16, 17 and 18, 1968, send greetings and love to the Original Hiwassee Association.

Our dearly beloved Brothers and Sisters in Christ, we desire to keep our correspondence with you. We hereby letter and delegate to you by sending to you some of our beloved Elders, who are in good standing and fellowship with us; Elder Henry Comer, Elder Charles Taylor and Elder Raymond Brantley, whom we hope you will accept to sit with you.

Having enjoyed the good fellowship of your delegation this year, we look forward and pray that it will be repeated next year when we meet with the Sister Church at Davis Chapel in Campbell County, Tennessee, on Friday before the third Saturday in August 1969.

Elder Albert Davis, Moderator

Bro. W. H. Taylor, Clerk
Route 13
Knoxville, Tennessee

671

In Memoriam

LIZZIE CLAWSON

Mrs. Lizzie Clawson, age 74, died at her home in Speedwell, Friday afternoon, October 13, 1967. Survivors: husband, Donnie Clawson, Speedwell; daughters, Miss Edith Clawson, Mrs. Mell Berry, Mrs. Lon Bullard, Speedwell, Mrs. Dean Owens, West Carrollton, Ohio. Sons, Johnnie and P. J. Clawson, Monroe, Michigan. Earl and Roy Clawson of Dayton, Ohio. Rev. Noble Lee Clawson and Ray, Speedwell. Brother, John Foust, Coaliron, Kentucky. 41 grandchildren and 21 great-grandchildren. A host of other relatives and friends. Funeral services were held at Bradens Chapel Baptist Church where she was a faithful member. Revs. Bill Sparks and J. C. Monday officiating. Burial in Bradens Cemetery.

We loved her much but God loved her more, called her home to suffer no more.

By a Son,

Noble Lee Clawson

JAMES P. ALSTON

James P. Alston, born November 15, 1904, passed away September 11, 1967. He was a Primitive Baptist. He leaves to mourn his loss, wife, Agnes; two daughters, Mrs. Helen Dumpus of Monroe, Michigan, and Phyllis Southern of New Tazewell. Two sons, Robert and Edward both of Monroe, Michigan. One sister, Zora Whittmore of Middlesboro, Kentucky. Two brothers, Herman of New Tazewell, Tennessee and Harvey of Greensboro, North Carolina. One son preceded him in death.

Burial in Drummond Cemetery September 13, 1967.

MRS. ETTA WILLIAMS

Mrs. Etta Williams, age 63, of Sharps Chapel, passed away at 9 a.m. Tuesday in Claiborne County Hospital after a lingering illness. Survivors: husband, Rector Williams; step-mother, Mrs. Effie Walker, foster daughter, Mrs. Beverly Rottman; three grandchildren, Utica, Michigan; brother, Malcolm H. Walker, Sharp's Chapel; sisters, Mrs. O. L. Woods, Maynardville, Mrs. Dan Cain, Monroe, Michigan, Mrs. Hazel Wiggins, Greenfield, Indiana, Mrs. Opal McBride, Brooklyn, New York, Mrs. Roy Clawson, Dayton, Ohio. Funeral 2 p.m. Thursday at Oak Grove Baptist Church, of which she was a member, Elder Albert Davis, Elder William Sparks officiating. Interment in Stiner Cemetery. Pallbearers: Nephews. Cooke Funeral Home, Maynardville, in charge.

MRS. MAGGIE ROE

Mrs. Maggie Roe, age 83, of Sharps Chapel, passed away at 3:15 p.m. Wednesday. Survivors: husband, Paris Roe, Sharps Chapel; daughter, Mrs. Pearl Dykes, Kokomo, Indiana; sons, Vibe and A. L., Kokomo, Indiana, Clatis, Speedwell, Roy, Sharps Chapel, Clyde, Maynardville, sisters, Mrs. Lula Shipley, Mrs. Clara Woodson, Mrs. Bertha Stiner, LaFollette, Mrs. Mossie Flemming, Knoxville, Mrs. Alice Irwin, California; brother, Lonnie King, LaFollette; 23 grandchildren; 40 great-grandchildren. Funeral, 2 p.m. Friday, Oak Grove Church, Rev. Albert Davis, Rev. Claude Roe, Rev. Claude Brooks officiating. Burial in church cemetery. Ailor's, Maynardville, in charge.

MRS. CORDELIA MUNCEY

Mrs. Cordelia Muncey, age 85, passed away at 5:50 p.m. Thursday at Hillcrest Nursing Home. Residence 910 Camp Street. She was the widow of Milton Muncey. Member of Fox Primitive Baptist Church. Survivors: daughter, Mrs. Allie Beller; son, Dewey Muncey, all of Knoxville; 38 grandchildren; 42 great-grandchildren; 11 great-great-grandchildren; sisters, Arlene Collins, Carrie Larmer, of Liberty Hill, Etta Rosenbaum, New Tazewell, Lyda Mincey, Liberty Hill, Francis Rosenbaum, Heiskell; several nieces and nephews. Services at Black Fox Baptist Church at 2 p.m. Sunday, Rev. John Atkins, Rev. Charles Thomas officiating. Interment Beeler Cemetery, Liberty Hill. Active pallbearers will be grandsons. The body will lie in state at the church one hour before services. Friends will be received 7 to 9 p.m. Saturday at Rose Mortuary.

ELLIS NEWMAN EVANS

Ellis Newman Evans, age 74, Route 1, Greenback, Tennessee passed away August 2, 1968, at his home. He was a member of Brantley's Chapel Primitive Baptist Church where he served the Lord faithfully. He leaves to mourn his wife, Lottie Evans; daughters, Mrs. Lillian Wilder, Knoxville; Mrs. Walter Owens, Maryville; sons, Rev. Everett and Kenneth of Ohio; Roy, Rev. Owen, Ellis, Jr., Clarence, Coy, and Lee, all of Greenback. 35 grandchildren; 17 great-grandchildren.

Funeral was August 4 at Brantley's Chapel Primitive Baptist Church. Elder Clifford Brantly, Rev. William Deakin and Rev. Grady Hill officiated. Burial was at Morganton Cemetery. Miller's of Maryville in charge.

With one last farewell said,
He closed his eyes and then was dead.
But to live on in eternity's shore,
Where farewells and death will be no more.

Written by his son Owen.

JOHN MARION DAVIS

John Marion Davis was born August 6, 1903, passed away July 9, 1968, He was 64 years, 9 months and 3 days of age.

He professed faith in the Lord in early manhood, and joined the Primitive Baptist Church at Black Fox. He was a trustee of the church and at the time of his death was also treasurer. As he grew in years he also grew in faith and grace, and became a great pillar of strength to the church.

Survivors are his widow and his mother, seven brothers and two sisters who mourn him. We loved him for he had the love of Christian Fellowship in his heart.

Written by his widow

MRS. LINDA SHARP

Mrs. Linda Sharp was born March 16, 1891 and departed this life September 12, 1967. She was united in marriage to Worth Sharp in the year of 1919. To this union was born two sons and one daughter. One son preceded her in death. She lived a loyal and faithful life to her family and is greatly missed by all who knew her. She was a member of Kirkwood Primitive Baptist Church.

She leaves to mourn her loss two children, one grandson, three brothers, two sisters, other relatives and a host of friends. We feel our loss is Heaven's gain.

Funeral services were conducted at the Gentry Mortuary by Elder Leonard White. Interment in Lynnhurst Cemetery.

LOU SHOFFNER

In loving memory of our dear beloved sister, **Lou Shoffner**. She was born March 15, 1884, died May 3, 1968. She was married to the late Henry Shoffner and to this union seven children were born - four girls and three boys, all of which survive her. Several grandchildren and great-grandchildren and two great-great-grandchildren.

She professed faith in Jesus Christ early in life and was one of Gibson Station's first members. Funeral services were conducted by her pastor, Elder Leonard White, assisted by her assistant pastor, Elder Everett Berry, at Coffey's Funeral Home in Tazewell, Tennessee. Then the body was taken to the old Shoffner Cemetery and under fair skies was placed by her husband to await the coming of Jesus.

CORDELIA SPANGLER LYNCH

With sad hearts and lingering memories we announce the departure of Sister Cordelia Spangler Lynch. She was born October 22, 1876 and died June 6, 1968. She was married to James F. Lynch January 19, 1896. To this union eleven children were born, of which four preceded her in death. She professed faith in Christ at an early age and joined the Methodist Church, but in 1908 she joined the Church at Cave Spring and remained a faithful member for a number of years. Later transferred her membership to Davis Chapel Primitive Baptist Church where she remained faithful until God discharged her from the Army of the faithful.

On the 9th day of June, 1968, her body was returned to the old consecrated altar at Davis Chapel Church where floral offerings and loving memories over-shadowed the altar while the funeral oration was delivered by Elder Leonard White (who 60 years before had buried her body in the sparkling waters of old Powells River) assisted by her last pastor, our dear beloved Elder W. M. Sparks. Then her body was transferred to old Glade Spring Cemetery to sleep by her beloved husband, under a disturbed atmosphere, flashing lightning, rolling thunder and bleeding hearts, her body was lowered to its last resting place to await the coming of Jesus. She died in the full triumphs of a living faith.

FLORENCE FORD IRWIN

With sad hearts we announce the passing of our beloved sister, Mrs. Florence Ford Irwin. She was born September 1, 1884, and died January 6, 1968. She was married to Mr. Gains Irwin on May 21, 1901. To this union eight children were born of which five survive.

She professed faith in Christ in her girlhood days and joined the Methodist Church where she remained for a number of years, but on February 17, 1953, joined the Primitive Baptist Church at Davis Chapel and was baptised June 21, 1953, by Elder Leonard White.

On January 9, 1968, her body was removed to the Church which she so dearly loved and the funeral was conducted by Elders W. M. Sparks and Leonard White and under grey skies and a beautiful white carpet of snow her body was lain to rest in the beautiful Sunrise Cemetery to sleep until Jesus comes.

MRS. LOUISE WHITE

Mrs. Louise White, age 81, died suddenly at 11 a.m. Wednesday, November 8, 1967. She was the daughter of the late Wm. White and Jane Ellison White and the wife of Harve White, who died in 1943.

Survivors: one son, Clive White, Uniontown, Ohio; half brother, Reba White of LaFollette; half sister, Mrs. Clyde Lynch of Taylor, Michigan;

2 grandchildren; 1 niece, Wanda Lynch; 1 nephew, David K. Lynch.

She brought her letter in March 1947 to Davis Chapel Church where she remained a member until death. She joined Mossy Springs in White Hollow at an early age and remained there until Norris Dam was built.

Funeral services were held Friday morning, November 10, 1967, at Fincastle Methodist Church with Elder Leonard White and the pastor of the church officiating. Burial was in the church cemetery.

MRS. BERTHA J. RAY

Mrs. Bertha J. Ray (Bertha Comer) was born July 4, 1897, passed away March 18, 1968, at Miami Valley Hospital in Dayton, Ohio, where the family has resided for the past several years.

She was a member of the Davis Chapel Primitive Baptist Church at the time of her death.

She leaves to mourn her husband Robert W. Ray; 2 sons, Albert and J. T.; 3 daughters, Thelma, Lois and Georgia; one sister, Mrs. Delia Heatherly; 3 half brothers and 3 half sisters and step-mother, Mrs. Dovie Comer Stanford all of LaFollette.

Funeral services were held March 21, at Davis Chapel Primitive Baptist Church, burial in Sunrise Cemetery. Services were conducted by Elder Leonard White. She was a devout Christian from an early age.

CHURCH	COUNTY	PASTOR	CLERK	ADDRESS
Black Fox	Grainger	Elder Patrick Shelton	Bennie Capps / Flossie Capps, Asst.	P. O. Box 91, Maynardville, Tenn. / Rt. 1 Maynardville, Tenn
Braden's Chapel —	Union	Elder L. C. Monday / Elder Noble Clawson, Asst.	Arvil Braden	Speedwell, Tenn.
Brantley's Chapel	Blount	Elder Everett Berry / Elder Clifford Brantley, Asst.	Rina Johnson / Daniel Brantley, Asst.	9 Douglas Ave., Maryville, Tenn. / Maryville, Tennessee
Cedar Springs	Claiborne	Elder Claude Rosson / Elder Noble Clawson, Asst.	Eula Gray Good	New Tazewell, Tenn.
Davis Chapel	Campbell	Elder W. M. Sparks / Elder Leonard White, Asst.	Ruth Heatherly / Lassie Ellison, Asst.	Rt. ?, LaFollette, Tenn. / Rt. 1, LaFollette, Tenn.
Gibson Station	Lee County, Va.	Elder Leonard White / Elder Everett Berry, Asst.	Roxie Cobb / Lucille Freeman, Asst.	Ewing, Va.
Kirkwood	Knox	Elder Leonard White	Estelle Sharp / Alice T. Powers, Asst.	5313 Jacksboro Pk., Knoxville, Tenn / 2923 Clearview Ave., Knoxville, Tenn.
Lenoir City	Loudon	Elder Charles Taylor / Elder Alvin Groves, Asst.	E. H. Scarbrough	Rt. 4, Box 283, Lenoir City, Tenn
Monroe, Mich.	Monroe	Elder Lenvil Meyers	Ditsy Russell / Gertrude Swok, Asst.	5177 Plumb Creek Ci., Monroe, Mich. / 1825 Spaulding Rd., Monroe, Mich.
Noeton	Grainger	Tony Eastridge Elder	John Oliver / Bessie Collins, Asst.	Bean Station, Rt. 2 / Morristown, Tenn. Rt. 5
Oak Grove	Union	Elder W. M. Sparks / Elder J. C. Monday, Asst.	Belle Moore / Ruth Shoffner, Asst	Sharps Chapel, Tenn. / Sharps Chapel, Tenn.
Pleasant Hill	Claiborne	Elder J. C. Monday / Elder Albert Davis, Asst.	William Branscomb / Verlin Edwards, Asst.	Speedwell, Tenn. / Speedwell, Tenn.
Pleasant Point	Claiborne	Elder Tony Eastridge / Elder Claude Rosson, Asst.	Elder Claude Rosson / Menada Keck, Asst.	New Tazewell, Tenn. / New Tazewell, Tenn.
Rocky Dale	Knox	Elder Hugh E. Brummitt	Elder Lee Collett / Charles Bryant, Asst.	Rt. 1, Luttrell, Tenn. / Rt. 4, Corryton, Tenn.
Cave Creek	Roane	Elder Raymond Brantley	J. C. Johnson	Rt. 3, Loudon, Tenn.

1969 MINUTES

Of The

ONE-HUNDRED FIFTIETH

ANNUAL SESSION

Of The

POWELL VALLEY ASSOCIATION

OF PRIMITIVE BAPTIST

Held With The SISTER CHURCH

At DAVIS CHAPEL

Campbell County, Tennessee

August 15, 16, 17, 1969

DAVIS CHAPEL CHURCH

The next session to be held with the Sister Church at Rocky Dale in Knox County, Tennessee, to begin at 10:30 on Friday before the 3rd Saturday in August 1970, and Elder Charles Taylor will preach the introductory sermon and Elder R. B. Brantley will be the alternate.

OFFICERS

ELDER ALBERT DAVIS ....Moderator
Speedwell, Tennessee-Phone 869-3596

ELDER HUGH E. BRUMMITT .... Assistant Moderator
1329 Brown Avenue, Knoxville, Tenn.-Phone 525-3583

BRO. W. H. TAYLOR ....Clerk
Route 13, Knoxville, Tenn.-Phone 922-2143

BRO. O. R. PARROTT ....Assistant Clerk
LaFollette, Tennessee

FRIDAY, AUGUST 15, 1969

The Powell Valley Association of Primitive Baptist having been blessed of the Lord and privileged to meet with the Sister Church at Davis Chapel, in Campbell County, Tennessee, August 15, 16 and 17, 1969, for the one hundred and fiftieth session.

After a good spiritual song service, directed by Brother Alfred Farmer of Cave Creek Church, Elder Raymond Brantley was called on for prayer.

Following prayer, Elder Henry Comer delivered the introductory sermon, reading from the 104th Psalm and using as his theme "The Sacrifices God Made for His Children." He preached a wonderful sermon.

Then after a song the congregation was dismissed for intermission by Elder Tony Eastridge.

After a short recess the congregation reconvened and after a song, the Moderator, Elder Davis, called the Association to order for whatever business the Association might have, with a plea for Love, Peace and Harmony to continue throughout the entire session. He then called for the opening prayer by Elder Walter Lyons, Pastor of Davis Creek Church. There was also a prayer by Elder Carl McCarty of the corresponding Association, New Bethel.

ORDER OF BUSINESS

1. Moderator called for the letters of the Sister Churches. Letters were received from all the fifteen churches of the Powell Valley Association.
2. Motion carried to receive the letters and seat the delegation from all the churches.
3. Called for anyone who was not delegated but present and wished to be seated, and none came.
4. Moderator called for any petitionary letters and none were presented.
5. Call for letters of corresponding Associations and two were received. One from the New Bethel Association and one from the original Hiwassee Association.
6. Motion carried to receive the letters of the two corresponding Associations and seat their delegates.
7. Call for any from the Associations who were not delegated in the letter but present and desired to be seated. Two came, Bro. Frank Barnes and Sister Martha Barnes of New Bethel.
8. Moderator called for the delegation to come forward and take the hand of fellowship and be officially accepted by the Association.
9. Moderator called attention to the election of officers for the coming year.
10. Association voted to re-elect Elder Albert Davis, Moderator and re-elect Elder Hugh E. Brummitt as Assistant Moderator.
11. Motion carried to re-elect Bro. W. H. Taylor, Clerk, and Bro. O. R. Parrott as Assistant Clerk.
12. Motion carried to authorize the Moderator, Eider Davis, to appoint all of the Committees.
13. The Moderator appointed the following committees to serve this session.

COMMITTEE ON ARRANGEMENTS
Elder George Campbell
Elder Alvin Graves
Bro. Alfred Farmer

COMMITTEE ON PREACHING
Bro. Verlin Edwards
Bro. Henry Chamberlain
Bro. Orice McCarty

COMMITTEE ON CORRESPONDENCE
Elder Raymond Brantley
Elder Johnnie Ayers
Elder Claude Rosson

—1

COMMITTEE ON REQUEST
Bro. James Heatherly
Bro. John Oliver
Bro. Franklin Jones

COMMITTEE ON FINANCE
Bro. Everett Brantley
Elder Charles Taylor
Bro. Bennie Capps

14. After completing the appointment of the committees, the Association adjourned until 10:30 A.M., Saturday Morning, August 16, 1969.

SATURDAY, AUGUST 16, 1969

1. The Saturday service, after a good song service, was introduced by the Assistant Moderator, Elder Hugh E. Brummitt. Bro. Brummitt read the 23rd Chapter of Psalms and made a wonderful humble talk and called for the opening prayer by Elder Joe Bush of Rocky Dale Church.
2. The Moderator called the Association to Order for business and asked for any letters from Sister Churches not received Friday. None were given.
3. Called for any corresponding letters not received Friday. There were none.
4. Moderator called for the report of the Committee on Arrangements who gave the following report, which was accepted and the committee released in order.

5. Report of Committee on Arrangements.

REPORT OF COMMITTEE ON ARRANGEMENTS

1. Call for the roll call of delegates
2. Call for a report of Committee on Preaching
3. Call for report of Committee on Correspondence
4. Call for report of Committee on Request
5. Call for report of Committee on Finance.
6. How many minutes of the Association shall we have printed? Who shall supervise the printing and distribution of the same, and what shall he be paid for his services? When and where shall the next Association be held and who shall preach the introductory serman and who shall be the alternate?

Respectively submitted,
Bro. James Heatherly
Bro. John Oliver
Bro. Frank Jones

6. Call for the report of the Committee on Correspondence, who submitted the following report, which was accepted and the committee release in order.

REPORT OF COMMITTEE ON CORRESPONDENCE

We the Committee on Correspondence recommend that we keep our correspondence with the Association with which we now correspond, namely: The New Bethel and Original Hiwassee. We further recommend that we send messengers and letters to these Associations.

Respectively submitted,
Elder Raymond Brantley
Elder Claude Rosson
Elder Johnnie Ayers

7. Call for report of Committee on Preaching who gave their report which was accepted and the committee released in order.

REPORT OF COMMITTEE ON PREACHING

Friday Night	Elder Carl McCarty
Saturday	Elder Raymond Brantley
Saturday Night	Elder Hugh E. Brummitt
Saturday Night	Elder Charles Taylor
Sunday	Elder Leonard White

Respectfully submitted,
Bro. Henry Chamberlain
Bro. Verlin Edwards
Bro. O. D. McCarty

8. Call for the report of the Committee on Request which was adopted and the committee released.

REPORT OF COMMITTEE ON REQUEST

We the Committee on Request request that the Clerk have printed in the minutes all obituaries made available to him. Also, that he have 1,000 copies of the minutes printed and distributed to the Sister Churches and that he receive $50 for his services.
We also request that the next session of the Association be held with the Sister Church at Rocky Dale in Knox County, Tennessee, to begin at 10:30 on Friday before the third Saturday in August, 1970.

Respectfully submitted,
Bro. James Heatherly
Bro. John Oliver
Bro. Franklin Jones

9. Call for report of Committee on Finance which was accepted and the committee released.

REPORT OF COMMITTEE ON FINANCE

REPORT OF COMMITTEE

We the Finance Committee beg to submit the following report:

Church	Printing Minutes	Visiting Ministers
Black Fox	$10.00	
Bradens Chapel	$10.00	
Brantleys Chapel	$20.00	
Cedar Springs	$10.00	
Davis Chapel	$10.00	$5.00
Gibson Station	$8.00	
Kirkwood	$10.00	$5.00
Lenoir City	$15.00	
Monroe, Michigan	$5.00	
Noeton	$5.00	
Oak Grove	$10.00	
Pleasant Hill	$13.00	
Pleasant Point	$10.00	
Rocky Dale	$5.00	$5.00
Cave Creek	$17.00	
	$158.00	$15.00
TOTAL	$173.00	

Respectfully submitted,
Bro. Bennie Capps
Bro. Everett Brantley
Elder Charles Taylor

CLERK'S FINANCIAL STATEMENT

Balance in Bank	$149.00
Receipts	173.00
TOTAL	$322.00
Expenses for 1969	185.00
BALANCE IN BANK	$137.00

10. Motion carried that we authorize the Clerk to have printed in the minutes all obituaries of deceased members made available to him and that he have printed 1,000 copies of the minutes and distribute same to the Sister Churches and that he receive $50.00 for his services.

11. Motion approved that the next session of the Association be held with the Sister Church at Rocky Dale to begin on Friday before the third Saturday in August 1970. Service to begin at 10:30 A.M. and that Elder Charles Taylor preach the introductory sermon and Elder Raymond Brantley be the alternate.

12. Motion carried that we letter and delegate to the New Bethel Association and the Original Hiwassee Association, and that we delegate to the Hiwassee Association, Elder Charles Taylor and Elder Raymond Brantley and that we delegate to the New Bethel Association, Elder W. M. Sparks, Elder Henry Comer and Elder Alvin Graves.

13. Motion that the Association authorize the Clerk to prepare a letter of correspondence for each of the delegates to carry to the respective Associations.

14. Motion that we reinstate in the Articles of Faith the clause "That the washing of feet is an example of Jesus Christ and that we should follow this example."

15. Motion that we, as the Powell Valley Association, extend to the Davis Chapel Church and to the entire community our heart felt thanks for the Love, Kindness and Hospitality shown us while in your community.

16. Motion carried that the Association adjourn until next year when we meet with the Sister Church at Rocky Dale in Knox County, Tenn., on Friday 10:30 before the third Saturday in August 1970.

Association dismissed in prayer by Elder W. M. Sparks.

Elder Albert Davis, Moderator
Elder Hugh E. Brummitt, Assistant Moderator
Bro. W. H. Taylor, Clerk
Bro. O. R. Parrott, Assistant Clerk

SUNDAY, AUGUST 17, 1969

The Sunday service was introduced by Elder Walter Lyons, pastor of Davis Chapel Church, who gave a welcome greeting and called for prayer by Elder Abram of New Bethel Association.

This was followed by Elder Leonard White's reading from the 16th Chapter of Leviticus and the 34th verse. Elder White preached a wonderful sermon staying close with thought of the sacrifice and atonements Christ made for His people.

After singing and much rejoicing, the service was closed with prayer by Elder Noble Lee Clawson.

ORDAINED MINISTERS

Elder Gilbert Atkins
Route # 3
Rutledge, Tennessee

Elder Johnnie Atkins
Bean Station, Tennessee

Elder Everett Berry
Fountain City, Tennessee
Phone: 922-4241

Elder J. H. Branscomb
Speedwell, Tennessee
Phone: 869-3392

Elder Clifford Brantley
Brown School Road
Maryville, Tennessee
Phone: 982-3735

Elder Hugh E. Brummitt
1329 Brown Avenue
Knoxville, Tennessee
Phone: 525-3583

Elder George Campbell
Fritts Road
Concord, Tennessee
Phone: 966-5340

Elder Noble Lee Clawson
Route #4
Speedwell, Tennessee

Elder Henry Comer
La Follette, Tennessee
Phone: 562-2812

Elder Albert Davis
Speedwell, Tennessee
Phone: 869-3596

Elder Tony Eastridge
Louisville, Tennessee
Phone: 983-1068

Elder Alvin Graves
Lenoir City, Tennessee
Phone: 986-5548

Elder Joe Irwin
Gibson Station, Virginia

Elder Walter Lyons
1602 Garfield Street
Alcoa, Tennessee
Phone: 982-1183

Elder Lenvil Meyers
715 Scott Street
Monroe, Michigan

Elder J. C. Monday
Speedwell, Tennessee

Elder Roy Oliver
Bean Station, Tennessee

Elder R. H. Petitt
Jacksboro Pike
Knoxville, Tennessee
Phone: 689-5581

Elder Claude Rosson
New Tazewell, Tennessee
Phone: 626-3168

Elder Parnick Shelton
Corryton, Tennessee
Phone: 689-6183

Elder George Shoffner
Route #2
Louisville, Tennessee

Elder W. M. Sparks
Speedwell, Tennessee
Phone: 562-7997

Elder Leonard White
La Follette, Tennessee
Phone: 562-5667

Elder Clay Widner
101 West Norris Street
Norris, Tennessee

Elder James Oliver
Bean Station, Tennessee

Elder Charles Taylor
212 E. Pinerest
Maryville, Tennessee
Phone: 982-4929

Elder Raymond Brantley
Route #3
Loudon, Tennessee
Phone: 1-376-7147 Kingston Exchange

Elder Joe Bush
Corryton, Tennessee

Elder Johnnie Ayers
New Tazewell, Tennessee

LICENTIATES

Bro. Odell Carpenter
Maryville, Tennessee

PREACHING RECORD

FRIDAY, AUGUST 15, 1969

The Introductory sermon was delivered by Elder Henry Comer.

Elder Comer preached a very good sermon from the 104th Psalm, using as his theme, "The Sacrifices of God for His Children."

SATURDAY, AUGUST 16, 1969

Elder Raymond Brantley of Cave Creek Church brought the message Saturday reading from the 3rd Chapter of Genesis, and preaching a wonderful sermon on the 1st, 2nd, 3rd, and 4th Rivers.

SATURDAY NIGHT, AUGUST 16, 1969

Elder Hugh E. Brummitt of Rocky Dale Church gave a very spiritual lesson Saturday night, reading from the 40th Chapter of Psalms, the 1st, 2nd, and 3rd verses.

Also, Elder Charles Taylor of Lenoir City Church gave a wonderful lesson, using the 9th Chapter and the 6th Verse of Romans as the subject.

SUNDAY, AUGUST 17, 1969

The Sunday Service introduced by Elder Walter Lyons, pastor of Davis Chapel Church, called for prayer by Elder Abrams of New Bethel Association.

Elder Leonard White followed with a wonderful sermon. The lesson from the 16th Chapter of Leviticus and the 34th Verse. Staying with the everlasting sacrifices and atonements Christ made for his Children.

Service dismissed in prayer by Elder Noble Lee Clawson.

685

August 25, 1969

Letter to New Bethel Association

We the Powell Valley Association of Primitive Baptist Churches, while in session with the Sister Church at Davis Chapel in Campbell County, Tennessee, do hereby send greetings of Love and Fellowship to the New Bethel Association.

Our dearly beloved Brothers and Sisters in Christ, we desire to keep our correspondence with you and we hereby letter and delegate to you our beloved Elders, W. M. Sparks, Alvin Graves and Henry Comer, who are in good standing and fellowship and whom we trust you will accept to sit with you.

Having enjoyed the good fellowship of your delegation at Davis Chapel, we look forward to seeing more of you next year at Rocky Dale on the third Friday, August 1970.

Remember us in your prayers.

Elder Albert Davis, Moderator
Elder Hugh E. Brummitt, Asst. Moderator
Bro. W. H. Taylor, Clerk
Bro. O. R. Parrott, Asst. Clerk

August 25, 1969

Letter to Original Hiwassee Association

We the Powell Valley Association of Primitive Baptist Churches, while in regular session with the Sister Churches, convened at Davis Chapel Church in Campbell County, Tennessee, August 15, 16 and 17, 1969, do hereby send greetings of Love and Fellowship.

Dearly beloved Brothers and Sisters we desire to continue our correspondence with you and do hereby letter and delegate to you our beloved Elder Charles Taylor and Elder Raymond Brantley, who are in good standing and fellowship, whom we hope you will accept to sit with you.

Having enjoyed the good fellowship of your delegation this year, we hope to see more of you when we convene again with the church at Rocky Dale in August on Friday before the 3rd Saturday 1970.

We desire your prayers.

Elder Albert Davis, Moderator
Elder Hugh E. Brummitt, Asst. Moderator
Bro. W. H. Taylor, Clerk
Bro. O. R. Parrott, Asst. Clerk

—8—

In Memoriam

HENRY (UNCLE HENRY) HOSKINS

Henry (Uncle Henry) Hoskins, age 90, departed this life November 15, 1968. He was one of the soldiers who kept watch at the front of San Juan Hill while Teddy Roosevelt with a colored regiment climbed the back of the mountain and captured the Spanish in 1898.

He was a faithful member of Gibson Station Church. Funeral orations were delivered by: Elders Leonard White and Everette Berry. Interment in Shoffner Cemetery.

LILLY YOUNG

With sad hearts we announce the death of our much beloved sister, Lilly Stigall Young, age 71.

She joined Gibson Station Church in early life and lived a faithful member until God discharged her. She was much loved by her family, church and community. Aunt Lilly, we all loved you.

MISS ADELINE McFARLAND

Miss Adeline McFarland, age 78, passed away Saturday 2 a.m., June 14 1969, at her home, 2919 Johnston Street, Knoxville, Tennessee. She was a member of the Kirkwood Primitive Baptist Church.

She leaves to mourn her loss three sisters, Miss Mary McFarland, Mrs. Mellie Norris, Mrs. Arletta Shoffner; one brother, Emmitt McFarland, 4 grandsons and a host of other relatives and friends.

Funeral services were conducted at the Rose Mortuary by Elder Leonard White and Elder Everett Berry. Interment in Lynnhurst Cemetery.

MEALIE JANE (CINNAMON) WHITE

Mrs. Mealie Jane (Cinnamon) White widow of the late Hess White 79, of 1138 Circle Drive, LaFollette, died Monday, Jan. 26, 1969. Survivors: daughters, Mrs. Tilda Chadwell, Mrs. Reva Ivy, Mrs. Eva Ivy, LaFollette; Mrs. Pauline Johnson, Holy Oak, Mass.; sons, Don, Willard, LaFollette; Amos, Paxton, Ill.; Coolidge, Monroesville, Ohio; Ulyss, Garden City, Mich.; Sisters, Mrs. Nellie Letner, Knoxville; Mrs. Adeline Ellison, Kokomo, Ind.; brothers, Lonnie Boruff, Kokomo, Ind.; Ephiram Boruff, Black Mountain, Ky.; 36 grandchildren; 47 great-grandchildren; one great-great-grandchild. She was a member of the Davis Chapel Primitive Baptist Church. Services 2 p.m. Thursday, Davis Chapel Primitive Baptist Church, Rev. Leonard White officiating. Interment, Sunrise Cemetery.

—11—

EASTER WEAVER RUSSELL

Easter Weaver Russell passed away in January of 1969 being about 85 years old.

Sister Russell was united to John Russell in marriage at an early age and to this union was born 7 children. Two of which preceeded her in death. Also her husband preceeded her in death.

Sister Russell joined Capp's Creek Church some several years ago and later moved her membership to Pleasant Hill Church where she remained a faithful member until death.

Our loss is her eternal gain.

MRS. LUELLA SHELBY

Mrs. Luella Shelby, age 73, of Route 4, New Tazewell, passed away at Claiborne County Hospital at 3 p.m., Saturday, Oct. 12, 1968. Survivors: Husband, James Shelby, Route 4, New Tazewell; daughters, Mrs. Anna Mae Davis, New Tazewell, Mrs. Gracie Shoffner, Sharps Chapel, Tenn.; son, Willis Shelby Belvue, Ohio; 10 grandchildren; seven great grandchildren; sisters, Mrs. Bertha Sweet, Knoxville, Mrs. Allie Borff, Friendsville; brothers, Will Sutherland and Loren Sutherland, both of Knoxville. Funeral services 2 p.m. Tuesday at Edwards Baptist Church. Interment, Stinner Cemetery. The body remains at Coffey Funeral Home, where the family will receive friends 7 to 9 p.m. Monday. Coffey, Tazewell, in charge.

MRS. MARTHA VIOLA BORUFF

Mrs. Martha Viola Boruff, age 79, residence 1608 Maryville Pike, passed away 11 a.m. Thursday, Aug. 27, 1968 at Hillcrest Nursing Center. She was a member of the Rockydale Baptist Church. Survivors: daughter, Mrs. Mildred M. Meadows; son Robert E. Boruff; nine grandchildren; 14 great-grandchildren all of Knoxville; brother George Hasten Petree of LaSalle, Mich.; sister, Mrs. Margaret Magnolia Miller, Rockford, Tenn.; one step-sister, Mrs. Brenda Boruff, several nieces and nephews. Services 2 p.m. Thursday at Rose Chapel, Rev. Fred Harbin officiating. Interment in Lynnhurst Cemetery. Friends will be received Wednesday from 7 to 9 p.m. at Rose Mortuary.

ELDER C. D. ELLISON

Elder C. D. Ellison, born July 4, 1898, died Nov. 26, 1968 was married to Vestie England June 11, 1916. Joined Oak Grove Church of Sharps Chapel, Feb. 1927. Ordained for Deacon Dec. 1931 ordained for Minister Jan. 7, 1949. He is missed by his family and friends.

ISAAC CALVIN SHARP

Isaac Calvin Sharp of Knoxville, Tennessee, born December 18, 1887 passed away October 20, 1968. Survived by his wife Alberta Sharp, 4 daughters,Miss Thelma Sharp, Mrs. W. D. Ward, Mrs. Ted Maples and Mrs. Dona Akers all of Knoxville, three sons Calvin, Jr. of San Diego, California; Jack of Farmington, New Mexico and Clarence of Knoxville; 3 brothers, Asa Sharp and Ambrose Sharp of Concord and Robert of Clearwater, Florida. He joined the church at Oak Grove in Union County at an early age and was very helpful in church and finance his church.
Services at Rose, October 22, 1968. Dr. Fred Schlafer officiating. Burial Lynnhurst, grandsons pallbearers.

WILLIAM H. ROBINSON

William H. Robinson, age 79, of New Tazewell, Route 4, passed away at Claiborne County Hospital 1 p.m. Thursday. Survivors: son, Rev. Fernde Robinson, Lima, Ohio; daughters, Mrs. Gillis Carr, Mrs. Ruppert Hooper, Mrs. Dewey Collins, all of New Tazewell; 12 grandchildren; 10 great-grand-children;sister, Mrs. Jim Beeler, Knoxville, Mrs. John Jenkins, St. Peters-burg, Fla. He was a member of Oak Grove Primitive Baptist Church. Funeral, 2 p.m. Sunday at Leatherwood Baptist Church. Interment in Roselawn Cemetery in Middlesboro, Ky. Family will receive friends 7-9 p.m. Friday at Coffey Funeral Home. Body will be removed to the home of his daughter,Mrs. Dewey Collins, 10 a.m. Saturday, Coffey's Tazewell, in charge.

NATHAN ATKINS

Nathan Atkins, was born March 21, 1893, and died January 23, 1969. He was a member of Noeton Primitive Baptist Church and a veteran of World War 1. Survivors: Wife, Ida: two sons, Nathan Atkins Jr. and George H. Atkins both of Bean Station; three daughters, Mrs. Drewa Lovin of Morristown, Tenn., Mrs. Ruby Singleton, Bean Station, Tenn. and Mrs. James Rice, Parma, Ohio. Two brothers, Elder Johnny Atkins, Leslie Atkins both of Bean Station, Tenn. 17 grandchildren, 6 great-grandchildren. Funeral services were conducted 2:30 p.m. at Tock Haven Church with Rev. Hugh Jarnigin and Elder Gilbert Atkins officiating. Burial in Atkins Cemetery.

J. ALBERT CAPPS

J. Albert Capps was born April 11, 1890, and departed this life March 21, 1969, being 78 years 11 months, and 10 days old. He professed faith in Christ at an early age and joined Black Fox Primitive Baptist Church where he remained a member. He was married to Vina Davis, who preceded him in death, and to this union was born five children. Survivors: Daughters, Mrs. Cleo Long, Corryton, Mrs. Gladys Green, Washburn; sons, Roy Capps, Knoxville, Ross and Sam Capps, Corryton, several grand children and great-grand children, sisters, Mrs. Dollie Helton, Knoxville, Mrs. Lula Campbell, Morristown, Mrs. Kate Lay and Mrs. Iva Davis of Washburn, Mrs. Gertrude Greene, Corryton, brother Calvin Capps, of Maynardville, Tenn. Funeral services were held at Ailor's Chapel on March 23, 1969 with Rev. Ralph Cox and Rev. Virgil Price officiating. Interment in Cabbage cemetery. Nephews, Bennie Capps, J. H. Capps, Kermit Capps, Franklin Capps, Ralph Helton and Billy Lay served as pallbearers.

CHURCHES	DELEGATES	Restored	Received by Letter	Received by Baptism	Received by Relationship	Dismissed by Letter	Excluded	Deceased	Total Membership	Visiting Ministers	Printing of Minutes	Regular Meeting	Communion Service
Black Fox	Elder George Campbell, Bro. Dale Capps, Bro. Calvin Capps, Bro. Bennie Capps, Bro. Arthur Terry, Sis. Mary Ruth Capps, Sis. Sandra Capps, Sis. Flossie Capps, Sis. Mary Terry, and Debbie Terry.	0	0	3	0	0	2	1	97	0	$10	2nd. Sun. 1st. Sat. each mo.	Sun. after 1st. Sat. in June
Bradens Chapel	Elder J. C. Monday, Elder W. M. Sparks, Elder Noble Lee Clawson, Elder Henry Corner, Sister Winnona Monday, Sis. Leecy Sparks and Sis. Helen Clawson.	0	0	5	0	0	0	0	122	0	$10		1st. Sat. & Sun. in July
Brantleys Chapel	Elder Clifford Brantley, Bros. Von Beason, Plumer McBee, Corum Berry, Everett Brantley, Wayne Brantley, Sisters, Mamie Brantley, Barsha Brantley and Mildred Brantley.	0	1	2	0	0	0	0	85	0	$20	2nd. Sat. nite& Sun.	2nd. Sun. in July
Cedar Springs	Elder Johnnie Ayers, Bro. Bill Good, Sis. Eula Good and Sis. Vilt Munsey.	0	0	3	0	0	0	0	57	0	$10	4th Sat. Sun.	4th Sat. &Sun. in May
Davis Chapel	Elder Leonard White, Sis. Mossie White, Bro. Orice McCarty, Sis. Mollie McCarty, Bro. Hugh Hill, Sis. Ruby Hill, Bro. Onnie Parrott, Sis. Mamie Parrott, Bro. Gene Hobbs and Sis. Lassie Ellison.	0	0	1	1	0	0	3	143	$5	$10	3rd. Sat. Nite Sun. Nite Each Sun. Nite	3rd. Sun. in June

STATISTICAL TABLE

CHURCHES	DELEGATES	Restored	Received by Letter	Received by Baptism	Received by Relationship	Dismissed by Letter	Excluded	Deceased	Total Membership	Visiting Ministers	Printing of Minutes	Regular Meeting	Communion Service
Gibson Station	Bro. Harve Rhymer, Bro. Franklin Jones, Bro. Floyd Cobb, Bro. Spurgeon Thompson, Sis. Mellie Thompson and Sis. Fannie Jones.	0	0	0	0	0	0	2	90	0	$8	1st, Sat. and Sun.	Sun. after 1st. Sat. in June
Kirkwood	Elder R. H. Pettit, Elder Hugh E. Brummitt, Sis. Ruby Brummitt, Elder Walter Lyons, Sis. Callie Lyons, Bro. M. A. Norton, Sis. Lucy Norton, Bro. W. H. Taylor, Sis. Lou Emma Taylor, Bro. J. L. Sharp and Sis. Evelyn Sharp.	1	0	1	1	0	0	1	113	$5	$10	Every Sun.	Last Sun. in April
Lenoir City	Elder Charles Taylor, Sis. Agnes Taylor, Elder Alvin Graves, Bro. Hubert Spoons, Sis. Annie Spoons, Bro. Henry Chamberlain, Sis. Estie Chamberlain and Sis. Cora Hill.	0	0	1	1	0	3	3	201	0	$15	Each Sun. & Sun. nite	Sun. after 3rd. Sat. in May
Monroe, Michigan	Elder Lenvil Meyers, Bro. John Drummonds and Sis. Roxie Drummonds.	0	0	0	0	1	0	0	13	0	$5	Each Sun. nite	3rd. Sun. in July
Noeton	Bro. John Oliver, Sis. Ruth Oliver, Bro. Carroll Oliver, Sis. Mildred Oliver, Bro. Roy Oliver, Bro. Charlie Collins and Bro. Gilbert Atkins.	0	0	0	1	0	0	1	34	0	$5	3rd. Sun.	Sun. after 3rd. Sat. in May & Sept.

STATISTICAL TABLE

CHURCHES	DELEGATES	Restored	Received by Letter	Received by Baptism	Received by Relationship	Dismissed by Letter	Excluded	Deceased	Total Membership	Visiting Ministers	Printing of Minutes	Regular Meeting	Communion Service
Oak Grove	Elder George Shoffner, Elder Tony Eastridge, Sis. Francis Eastridge, Bro. Aaron Cole, Sis. Veda Cole, Sis. Genice Brantley, Bro. Mannie Shoffner, Sis. Ruth Shoffner, Bro. Alford Relford and Sis. Maggie Relford.	0	0	4	0	0	0	3	305	C	$10	1st. Sat. and Sun.	1st. Sun. in May
Pleasant Hill	Elder Albert Davis, Sis. Audra Davis, Elder J. H. Branscomb, Sis. Sarah Branscomb, Bro. Bud Branscomb, Bros. Verlin Edwards, Kubil Edwards and Ralph Edwards.	0	0	0	0	0	0	1	98	0	$13	4th. Sat. & Sun.	4th Sun. in June
Pleasant Point	Elder Claude Rosson, Sis. Doris Rosson, Bro. George Williams, Sis. Allie Williams, and Sis. Menada Keck.	0	0	2	0	0	0	0	121	0	$10	1st. Sat. nite & Sun.	Sun. after 1st. Sat. in July
Rocky Dale	Elder Joe Bush, Sis. Norma Jean Bush, Elder Everett Berry, Sis. Trula Berry, Elder Parnick Shelton, Sis. Wilma Shelton, Bro. Ralph Clapp, Sis. Wanda Clapp, Sis. Myrtle Bryant and Bro. Elmer Graves.	0	0	1	1	0	0	1	112	$5	$5	Each Sun. & Sun. nite	Sun. after 2nd. Sat. in May
Cave Creek	Elder R. B. Brantley, Sis. Amanda Brantley, Bro. Zirkle Johnson, Sis. Linda Johnson, Bro. Elmer Guetner, Sis. Hazel Guetner, Bro. J. C. Johnson, Sis. Elizabeth Johnson, Bro. Tom Johnson, Sis. Betty Johnson, Bro. Alfred Farmer, Bro. Floyd Farmer, Sis. Merrille Potter, Sis. Frankie Howard, Sis. Edra Calfee and Sis. Lorene White.	0	0	2	0	0	0	1	41	0	$17	Each Sun. Morn.	2nd. Sat. nite in May & Oct.

CHURCH	COUNTY	PASTOR	CLERK	ADDRESS
Black Fox	Grainger	Elder Parnick Shelton	Bennie Capps and Flossie Capps, Assist.	P. O. Box 91, Maynardville, Route 1, Maynardville
Bradens Chapel	Union	Elder Noble Lee Clawson, James Branscomb, Assistant	Arvil Braden	Speedwell, Tennessee
Brantleys Chapel	Blount	Elder Everett Berry, Elder Clifford Brantley, Assistant	Rina Johnson and Daniel Brantley, Assistant	Maryville, Tennessee 1201 Brown School Road Maryville, Tennessee
Cave Creek	Roane	Elder Raymond Brantley	J. C. Johnson	Loudon, Tennessee Route 3
Cedar Springs	Claiborne	Elder Claude Rosson Elder Noble Clawson, Assistant	Eula Gray Good	New Tazewell, Tennessee
Davis Chapel	Campbell	Elder Walter Lyons Elder Leonard White, Assistant	Ruth Heatherly Lassie Ellison, Assistant	LaFollette, Tenn., Route 1 LaFollette, Tenn., Route 1
Gibson Station	Lee County Virginia	Elder Leonard White Elder Everett Berry, Assistant	Roxie Cobb Lucille Freeman, Assistant	Ewing, Va. Box 140 Ewing, Virginia
Kirkwood	Knox	Elder Leonard White	Estell Petree Sharp Alice T. Powers, Assistant	1513 Jacksboro Pike, Knoxville, Tenn. 2923 Clearview, N. E. Knoxville, Tenn.
Lenoir City	Loudon	Elder Charles Taylor Elder Alvin Graves, Assistant	E. H. Scarbrough	Route 4 Lenoir City, Tennessee

1970 MINUTES OF THE

ONE HUNDRED FIFTY-FIRST ANNUAL SESSION

OF THE

POWELL VALLEY ASSOCIATION OF PRIMITIVE BAPTIST

HELD WITH THE SISTER CHURCH AT

ROCKY DALE

IN KNOX COUNTY TENNESSEE

AUGUST 14-15-16, 1970

ROCKY DALE CHURCH

The next session to be held with the Sister Church at Black Fox in Grainger County, Tenn., to begin on Friday before the 3rd Saturday in August 1971.

Elder Joe Bush will preach the introductory Sermon and Elder Tony Eastridge will be the Alternate.

OFFICERS

Elder Albert Davis . . . . Moderator
    Phone 869-3596

Elder Hugh E. Brummitt . . . . Assistant Moderator
    Knoxville, Tennessee · Phone 525-3583

Bro. W. H. Taylor . . . . Clerk
    Route 13, Knoxville, Tennessee · Phone 922-2143

Bro. O. R. Parrott . . . . Assistant Clerk
    LaFollette, Tennessee

694

FRIDAY, AUGUST 14, 1970

The One Hundred Fifty First annual session of the Powell Valley Association of Primitive Baptist was held with the sister church of Rocky Dale in Knox County, Tennessee on August the 14th, 15th and 16th, 1970.

After a good song service the Moderator read a lesson from the 12th Chapter of Ecclesiastes and called for prayer by Elder Alvin Graves of the Lenoir City Church.

After this Elder Charles Taylor of the Lenoir City church read from the 6th Chapter of Romans and the 21st verse. Then taking as a subject, Life, Death and Life Eternal. He preached one of the finest introductory sermons.

The congregation was then dismissed in prayer by Elder Tony Eastridge of Oak Grove Church, for a 15 minute intermission.

After intermission the Association reconvened at the sound of singing and followed by prayer by Elder R. H. Pettit of Kirkwood Church.

The Moderator, Elder Albert Davis, then called the Association for the businesss of the Association, pleading for Love, Peace and Unity to prevail throughout the Association.

ORDER OF BUSINESS

1. The Moderator called for the letters of the Sister Churches to be presented. Letters were received from all the churches except Cedar Springs and it was announced it would be there Saturday.
2. Motion carried to accept the letters from the Sister Churches and seat their delegates.
3. Call for any members who were not named in the letters and desire to be seated to come forward. Bro. Avril Graves, Bro. James Heatherty and Sister Heatherty came and were seated.
4. Call for any petitionary letters. None were presented.
5. Moderator called for the election of officers for the next year.
6. Motion carried that the Association re-elect Elder Albert Davis as Moderator for another year and Elder Hugh E. Brummitt as Assistant Moderator.
7. Motion carried to re-elect Bro. W. H. Taylor as Clerk for the coming year and Bro. O. R. Parrott as Assistant Clerk.
8. The Association voted to have the Moderator appoint all the Committees.
9. After being authorized by the Association the Moderator appointed the Committees to serve as follows:

COMMITTEE ON ARRANGEMENTS
Bro. Alfred Farmer
Bro. Dewey Graves
Elder Joe Bush

COMMITTEE ON PREACHING
Bro. Everett Brantley
Bro. Elmer Graves
Bro. M. A. Norton

COMMITTEE ON CORRESPONDENCE
Bro. Ditsy Russell

695

Elder Tony Eastridge
Elder Everett Berry

COMMITTEE ON REQUEST
Elder Alvin Graves
Elder R. H. Pettit
Bro. John Oliver

COMMITTEE ON FINANCE
Elder Raymond Brantley
Bro. Bennie Capps
Bro. Henry Chamberlain

10. The Committees all being completed the Association voted to adjourn until Saturday Morning when we will re-convene at 10:30 A.M.

SATURDAY, AUGUST 15, 1970

1. The Saturday service, after some good singing, was introduced by Elder Hugh E. Brummitt, the Assistant Moderator. He gave a nice welcome to all the Sister Churches and visitors and a good humble and spiritual talk. He then read a lesson from the 116th Psalm and called for prayer by Elder Claude Rosson of Cedar Springs Church.
2. The Moderator then called the Association to order for business and called for any letters from Sister Churches not received on Friday. One was received from Cedar Springs Church which was read and received and their delegation seated.
3. Called for letters of corresponding associations. One was received from the Original Hiwassee Association which was approved and their delegates seated.
4. Call for any member who was not named but desired to be seated. One came, Sister Godfrey.
5. Moderator called for the report of the Committee on Arrangements who submitted the following report, which was accepted and the Committee released.

REPORT OF COMMITTEE ON ARRANGEMENTS
1. Call for roll call of delegates
2. Call for Report of Committee on Preaching.
3. Call for Report of Committee on Correspondence.
4. Call for Report of Committee on Request.
5. Call for Report of Committee on Finance.
6. How many minutes of the Association shall we have printed? Who shall supervise the printing and distribution of same? How much shall he receive for this service? When and Where shall the next Association be held, and who shall preach the introductory sermon and who shall be the alternate?

Respectfully submitted,
Elder Joe Bush
Bro. Alfred Farmer
Bro. Dewey Graves

2

6. Call for the report of the Committee on Correspondence which was received as follows and accepted and the Committee released:

REPORT OF COMMITTEE ON CORRESPONDENCE
We the Committee on Correspondence wish to submit the following request that we keep our correspondence with the beloved Associations with which we now correspond and that we letter and delegate to each. Namely New Bethel and Original Hiwassee.

Humbly submitted,
Elder Everett Berry
Elder Tony Eastridge
Bro. Ditsy Russell

7. Call for the report of the Committee on Preaching who gave the following report which was accepted and the Committee released.

REPORT OF COMMITTEE ON PREACHING

Friday Night:	Elder Hoyt Simms
	Elder Walter Lyons
Saturday:	Elder Alvin Graves
	Elder Clifford Brantley
Saturday Night:	Elder Tony Eastridge
	Elder Everett Berry
Sunday:	Elder Leonard White
	Elder Albert Davis

Respectfully submitted,
Bro. Everett Brantley
Bro. Elmer Graves
Bro. M. A. Norton

8. Call for the Report of the Committee on Request who gave the following report which was accepted and the committee released:

REPORT OF COMMITTEE ON REQUEST
We the Committee request that we have 1,000 copies of the minutes of this Association printed and distributed to the sister churches and that we allow $50.00 for this service.
We also request that the next session of this Association be held with the good Sister Church of Black Fox in Grainger County, Tennessee, to begin on Friday before the 3rd Saturday in August, 1971 at 10:30 A.M.

Humbly submitted,
Elder R. H. Pettit
Elder Alvin Graves
Bro. John Oliver

9. Call for the Report of the Committee on Finance who gave the following

report which was accepted and the committee released:

CHURCH	PRINTING OF MINUTES	VISITING MINISTRY
Black Fox	$10.00	
Brandens Chapel	$10.00	
Brantleys Chapel	$20.00	
Cave Creek	$11.00	
Cedar Springs	$10.00	
Davis Chapel	$10.00	$5.00
Gibson Station	$4.00	$4.00
Kirkwood	$10.00	$5.00
Lenoir City	$20.00	
Monroe, Mich.	$5.00	
Norton	$5.00	
Oak Grove	$10.00	
Pleasant Hill	$15.00	
Pleasant Point	$10.00	
Rocky Dale	$5.00	$5.00
TOTALS	$155.00	$19.00

GRAND TOTAL $174.00

Respectfully submitted,
Elder R. B. Brantley
Bro. Henry Chamberlain
Bro. Bennie Capps

10.   CLERK'S FINANCIAL STATEMENT

Balance in Bank	$137.00	
Receipts	$174.00	
TOTAL	$311.00	
Expenses for 1970	220.00	
BALANCE IN BANK	$ 91.00	

11. Motion carried that the association authorize the Clerk to supervise the printing and distribution of 1,000 minutes to the sister churches and that he receive $50.00 for his service.
12. Motion carried that the next session of the Powell Valley Association be held with the Sister Church at Black Fox in Grainger County, Tenn., to begin at 10:30 A.M. on Friday before the 3rd Saturday in August, 1971 and to continue for three days.
13. Motion carried that Elder Joe Bush of the Rocky Dale Church preach the introductory sermon and Elder Tony Eastridge be the alternate.
14. Motion that we letter and delegate to the corresponding Associations, New Bethel and Original Hiwassee, and that we delegate to represent

4

us at the New Bethel Association the following: Elder James Henry Branscomb, Elder Alvin Graves, Elder Walter Lyons and Elder Henry Campbell. And to the Hiwassee: Elder Parnick Shelton, Elder Hugh Brummitt and Elder Clifford Brantley.

15. The Association authorized the Clerk to prepare a letter to be presented to each of the corresponding Associations.

16. Motion carried that we extend to the Church of Rocky Dale and the entire community our heart felt thanks for every courtesy and for the Love and Welcome while in the community.

17. After concluding one of the finest Associations, filled with Love and Spirit, in the Association's history, motion was carried that we adjourn until we meet again at Black Fox on Friday before the third Saturday in August 1971. The Association was dismissed in prayer by Elder Clifford Brantley.

Elder Albert Davis, Moderator
Elder Hugh Brummitt, Asst. Moderator
Bro. W. H. Taylor, Clerk
Bro. O. R. Parrott, Asst. Clerk

SUNDAY SERVICE

The Sunday service was introduced by Assistant Moderator, Elder Hugh Brummitt, who gave a nice welcome and humble talk then called for the opening prayer by Bro. Rina Johnson. Elder Leonard White then read for the lesson the 18th verse of the 16th Chapter of St. Matthew and preached a wonderful sermon from the text: "Upon this rock I'll build my church and the gates of hell shall not prevale against it". After a song and much rejoicing we were dismissed in prayer by Elder Parmick Shelton.

ORDAINED MINISTERS

Elder Gilbert Atkins
Route # 3
Rutledge, Tennessee

Elder Johnnie Atkins
Bean Station, Tennessee

Elder Everett Berry
Fountain City, Tennessee
Phone: 922-7004

Elder J. H. Branscomb
Speedwell, Tennessee
Phone: 869-3392

Elder Clifford Brantley
Brown School Road
Maryville, Tennessee
Phone: 982-3735

Elder Hugh E. Brummitt
1329 Brown Avenue
Knoxville, Tennessee
Phone: 525-3583

Elder George Campbell
Fritts Road
Concord, Tennessee
Phone: 966-5340

Elder Noble Lee Clawson
Route # 4
Speedwell, Tennessee

Elder Albert Davis
Speedwell, Tennessee
Phone: 869-3596

Elder Tony Eastridge
Louisville, Tennessee
Phone: 983-1068

Elder Alvin Graves
Lenoir City, Tennessee
Phone: 986-5548

Elder Joe Irwin
Gibson Station, Virginia

Elder Walter Lyons
1602 Garfield Street
Alcoa, Tennessee
Phone: 982-1183

Elder Lenvil Meyers
715 Scott Street
Monroe, Michigan

Elder J. C. Monday
Speedwell, Tennessee

Elder Roy Oliver
Bean Station, Tennessee

Elder R. H. Petitt
Jacksboro Pike
Knoxville, Tennessee
Phone: 689-5581

Elder Claude Rosson
New Tazewell, Tennessee
Phone: 626-3168

Elder Parnick Shelton
Corryton, Tennessee
Phone: 689-6183

Elder George Shoffner
Route # 2
Louisville, Tennessee

Elder W. M. Sparks
Speedwell, Tennessee
Phone: 562-7997

Elder Leonard White
La Follette, Tennessee
Phone: 562-5667

Elder Clay Widner
101 West Norris Street
Norris, Tennessee

Elder Charles Taylor
Route # 4
Lenoir City, Tennessee
Phone: 986-8172

Elder Raymond Brantley
Route # 3
Loudon, Tennessee
Phone: 1-376-7147 Kingston Exchange

Elder Joe Bush
Corryton, Tennessee

Elder Johnnie Ayers
New Tazewell, Tennessee

LICENTIATES

Bro. Odell Carpenter
Maryville, Tennessee

PREACHING RECORD

Friday, August 14, 1970

Introductory sermon by Elder Charles Taylor of Lenoir City Church reading from the 6th Chapter of Romas and the 21st verse and using the words "Life, Death and Life Eternal" preached a wonderful and spiritual sermon.

Friday Night, August 14, 1970

Elder Hoyt Simms, a visiting minister and editor of the "Banner Herald" from an Association in Georgia, preached a wonderful sermon from John 3-16 using as his theme the Doctrine of Attonment. This was followed by Elder Walter Lyons, pastor of Davis Chapel.

Saturday, August 15, 1970

After singing the Saturday service was introduced by Elder Clifford Brantley preaching a good short sermon from the 3rd Chapter of Geneses the 23rd and 24th verse. He then gave over to Elder Alvin Graves who preached a wonderful sermon.

Saturday Night, August 15, 1970

Elder Tony Eastridge preached a good sermon using for a lesson the 6th Chapter of the Book of Judges. He was followed by Elder Everett Berry who preached a very good and spiritual sermon from the 1st Chapter of Matthew and the 21st verse.

Sunday, August 16, 1970

After a good spiritual song service, the service was then introduced by Assistant Moderator, Elder Hugh E. Brummitt, who made a short talk and called for prayer by Bro. Rina Johnson. Followed by Elder Leonard White

701

7

Letter to New Bethel Association

We the Powell Valley Association of Primitive Baptist while in sessio
the sister church at Rocky Dale send greetings of Love and Fell
to your Association.

Dear Brothers and Sisters in Christ, we desire to keep our corresp
with you and we hereby delegate to sit with you our beloved Elders,
H. Branscomb, Alvin Graves, Walter Lyons and Elder George Campbel
we consider to be sound in faith to sit with you.

We missed your letter and delegates this year and hope it will be re
next year.

Remember us in prayer.

> Elder Albert Davis, Moderator
> Elder Hugh Brummitt, Asst. Moderator
> Bro. W. H. Taylor, Clerk
> Bro. O. R. Parrott, Asst. Clerk

Letter to Original Hiwassee Association

We the Powell Valley Association of Primitive Baptist, while in session
with the sister church of Rocky Dale in Knox County, Tennessee, hereby
send greetings and Love to you all.

We express our desire to continue our correspondence and relationship
with you. We enjoyed your letter and delegation with us and we are dele-
gating to sit with you in Godly conversation the following - Elder Parnick
Shelton, Elder Clifford Brantley and Elder Hugh E. Brummitt whom we think
to be sound in faith and hope you can receive them as such.

Please remember us in prayer.

> Elder Albert Davis, Moderator
> Elder Hugh Brummitt, Asst. Moderator
> Bro. W. H. Taylor, Clerk
> Bro. O. R. Parrott, Asst. Clerk

IN MEMORIAM

Elder James L. Oliver

Elder James L. Oliver, 66, passed away Nov. 14, 1969 at his home in Morristown, Tenn. He united with the Primitive Baptist Church at Norton, October 18, 1952, was baptized May 16, 1953 by his uncle Elder Mathew Oliver and ordained to the work of the Ministry in April of 1965. Survived by wife, Eunice Viola Oliver; Sister, Safronia Jarnagin; Brothers, J. L. Oliver and U. S. Oliver all of Morristown, Tenn. Services at 2 P.M. at the Norton Primitive Baptist Church with Elder Gilbert Atkins, Elder Olaf Atkins and Elder Elmer Reno officiating.

Mrs. Pearl Watson Simmons

Mrs. Pearl W. Simmons, 88, passed away April 17th, 1970, in a Knoxville Nursing Home. She was a member of Noeton Primitive Baptist Church and a long time resident of Grainger County. Survived by several nieces and nephews. Services were held at 2:30 P.M. on Saturday at the Norton Primitive Baptist Church. Interment in church cemetery.

Matilda Ausmus Lambert

Matilda Ausmus Lambert, born Dec. 5, 1879 passed away June 17, 1970, age 90 yr. 6 mo. 12 days. She was united in matrimony to Neal Lambert in Nov. 1898 and to this union were born 8 children. She is survived by eight children, twenty-eight grandchildren, forty-two great grandchildren and ten great great grandchildren, one half sister, one half brother and a host of relatives and friends. She was a charter member of the Pleasant Hill Church organized in 1907 and remained a faithful member until death. She was buried by her husband in the Ausmus cemetery.

Rachel Cordelia Collins

Rachel Cordelia Collins, 74, passed away at her home at 6:30 P.M. Feb. 24, 1970. She is survived by sisters, Mrs. Francis Rosson, Miss Eva Collins, Allie Williams and Lennie Keck all of New Tazewell. Brothers, Esco, Arlis and Dewey all of New Tazewell, eight nephews and seven nieces and a host of relatives and friends. She professed faith in Christ in early life and our loss is Heaven's gain.

W. Ernest Hamilton

W. Ernest Hamilton, 77, of 833 Louisville Pike, Alcoa, passed away 8:35 p.m. Wednesday at Blount Memorial Hospital. He was a member of Oak Grove Church in Union County. Survivors: wife, Lillius Ousley Hamilton; daughters, Mrs. Frank (Fontella) Eggers, Alcoa, Mrs. Martin (Acquila) Tallent, Rockford; grandson, Frank Eggers II, Nashville; sister, Mrs. Sally Riley, Kentucky; brother, Murphy Hamilton, Philadelphia, Tenn. Funeral 2 p.m. Friday from McCammon-Ammons Chapel. Rev. Willie Newman, Elder Leonard White officiating. Interment in Grandview Cemetery.

Joseph Lafayette Ellison, Jr.

Joseph Lafayette Ellison was born in Union County, Tenn., Aug. 24, 1874, passed away Jan 23, 1970 at Serene Manor Medical Center, Knoxville, Tenn. Age 95 yrs. 6 mo. He was the son of Joseph and Linda Ellison. United in marriage to Louisa Dossett Feb. 14, 1893 and to this union was born 12 children. He was a member and deacon of Oak Grove Primitive Baptist Church. Survived by daughters, Sarah Brantley and Ottie McBee of Maryville, Bessie McCarty and Dina Barnard of Sharps Chapel, Ester McBee of Kokomo, Indiana and Irene Bridges of Nashville, Tenn. Sons, Swan of Sharps Chapel, Jeff of Maryville and Ulysses of Walton, Indiana. Also, half sisters, Dettie Monday and Mattie Tindell, Speedwell and thirty grandchildren and fifty-six great grandchildren.

Asa R. Sharp

Asa R. Sharp, age 80 of McFee Road, Rt. # 5, Lenoir City, died 4:30 A.M. Tuesday at Fort Sanders Hospital after a lingering illness. He was a member and deacon of Kirkwood Primitive Baptist Church and a retired groceryman. Survivors: Nellie Sartain Sharp; sons, C. I. of Chattanooga, R. A. of Maryland, Kinzel of Detroit and L. E. of Knoxville. Daughter, Mrs. Margaret Atkinson of Chattanooga. Brothers Ambrose of Lenoir City, Robert of Clearwater, Fla. Sisters, Ida Lowe of Knoxville and Mrs. Alice Keck of New Tazewell. Ten grandchildren. Services at 2 P.M. Thursday at Weavers Funeral Home with Elder Charles Taylor and Rev. Gerald Myers officiating. Interment New Gray Cemetery. Pallbearers: Bill Taylor, John L. Sharp, Elder Alvin Graves, Henry Chamberlain, Tom Howard and Clarence Miller. Weavers in charge.

Willie H. Stiner

Willie H. Stiner, 79, of Sharps Chapel, Tenn., died Wednesday afternoon at Fort Sanders Presbyterian Hospital. He was a member of Oak Grove Baptist Church. Survivors: wife, Mrs. Emma Drinnon Stiner; sons, Clyde, Toledo, Ohio, Coran, Sylvania, Ohio, Carl, Monroe, Mich., Clayton, Antwerp, Ohio, Roger Maynardville; daughters, Mrs. Lillis Beeler, Maynardville, Mrs. Shirley Cannon, Alexandria, Ky.; four stepchildren, John Manis, David L. Drinnon, Mrs. Ruth Nicely, Mrs. Naomi Phillips, all of Ohio; 21 grandchildren; ten step-grandchildren; ten great-grandchildren; three step-grandchildren; sisters, Florena Stiner, Knoxville, Mrs. Hattie Simmons, Monroe, Mich. Funeral 2 p.m. Saturday at Cook Mortuary Chapel. Rev. J. M. Whitt officiating. Interment in Pleasant View Cemetery.

Rev. John Henry Comer

Rev. John Henry Comer, 70, of Route 3, Speedwell, formerly of LaFollette, Glade Springs community, passed away Tuesday night at LaFollette Community Hospital. He was a retired farmer and a Baptist minister. Survivors: wife, Mrs. Rachel Comer, Speedwell; one son, James Comer, Route 4, Lafollette; daughters, Mrs. Cordie Sutton, Mrs. Mary Walden, both of LaFollette, Mrs. Anna Mae Simms, Knoxville; stepsons, Paul and J. D. Hamlin, both of Greenville, Ohio, Carl and Dorothy Hamblin, both of Speedwell; one stepdaughter, Mrs. Cathleen Hickey, Pique, Ohio; one brother, Ben Comer, LaFollette; sisters, Mrs. Mae Richardson, Ohio, Mrs. Dora Wilderson, California. Services Friday at 2 p.m., at Glade Springs Baptist Church, Rev. Don Reynolds, Rev. Bill Sparks and Rev. J. C. Monday officiating. Burial in Glade Springs Cemetery.

A. L. (Archie) Davis

A. L. (Archie) Davis, 70 Scenic View Drive, Halls, passed away 12:05 p.m. August 28 at Blount Memorial Hospital, Maryville, Tennessee. Born in Union County, a merchant since 1921 and a retired farmer. Survivors include the widow, Maggie Acuff Davis; one son, Fred; three daughters, Jessie Messer, Knoxville, Twila Berry, Maryville, Ella Coker, Concord. Five granddaughters, one grandson, one great-grandson, and three step-grandsons. Services were held at Ailors Funeral Home with Rev. Leonard White and Rev. Everett Berry officiating. Interment in Greenwood Cemetery.

A Place Is Vacant In Our Home
A Voice We Loved Is Still
There's An Empty Place Within Our Hearts
That No One Else Can Fill.

Written by Daughter, Twila Berry

Mrs. Lissie K. Rogers

Sister Lissie Rogers, born Dec. 23, 1884, passed from this life Feb. 19, 1970. Making her stay among us 85 years, 1 month, and 24 days. She joined the Primitive Baptist Church at Lenoir City, Tenn. early in life and remained a faithful member until God called her home. She leaves to mourn her passing 7 children: Irvin Rogers, J. W. Rogers, Mrs. Bonnie Green, Miss Mallie Rogers, Mrs. Willie Nichols, Mrs. Tressie Banks, and Mrs. Jessie Brown. Two brothers, Kaney, Key. Besides these she leaves a host of friends and relatives. Services were conducted at the Lenoir City Primitive Baptist Church by Elder Charles Taylor. She was laid to rest in the Lenoir City Cemetery to await the coming of the Lord.

Mr. O. V. Anderson (Ora) Sr.

Bro. Ora Anderson, Sr., age 67, passed away suddenly at his home, 1101 Bell Avenue, on May 19, 1969. Making his stay among us 67 years. He was a member of the Primitive Baptist Church at Lenoir City for many years. He and Sister Sally were ordained to the office of deacon and deaconess and served faithfully in this capacity for many years. He will be greatly missed by the church and all who knew him. He leaves to mourn his passing his wife, Mrs. Sally (Collins) Anderson; daughter (Patsy) Mrs. Ed Lynch, Rochester, N. Y.; sons, Ray and Glen, Lenoir City; James of Louson; and O. V. Jr. of California. 11 grandchildren; 1 great-grandchild, 1 brother, Kyle Anderson. Sisters, Mrs. Dora McNabb and Mrs. Stella Brewer all of Lenoir City, Mrs. Hobert Tinnell of Knoxville. Funeral services were held at the Lenoir City Primitive Baptist Church by Elder Charles Taylor and Rev. Howard Pratt. He was laid to rest in City Cemetery with Junior QUAM officiating at graveside.

Mrs. Emma Sharp Fielden

Mrs. Emma Sharp Fielden of Knoxville, born September 23, 1892, at Sharps Chapel, Tennessee, passed away February 25, 1970. She was united in marriage on August 22, 1913 to the late Charles A. Fielden. Both were devoted members of and instrumental in establishing the Kirkwood Primitive Baptist Church.

Surviving are one son, J. H. Fielden, and two grandchildren all of Knoxville; two sisters, Mrs. Margaret Countiss of Knoxville and Mrs. Luch Martin of Chattanooga.

Funeral services were conducted at Rose Mortuary by Elder Leonard White. Interment was in Lynnhurst Cemetery.

STATISTICAL TABLE

CHURCHES	DELEGATES	RESTORED	RECEIVED BY LETTER	BY BAPTISM	RELATIONSHIP	DISMISSED	EXCLUDED	DECEASED	TOTAL MEMBERSHIP	VISITING MINISTERS	PRINTING OF MINUTES	REGULAR MEETING	COMMUNION SERVICE
Black Fox	Elder George Campbell, Bro. Dale Capps, Bro. Bennie Capps, Bro. Roy Bailey and Bro. Clayton Bailey, Sis. Mary Ruth Capps, Sis. Sandra Capps, Sis.Roma Bailey, Naomi Cabbage, Sis. Sarah Hopson.	0	0	1	0	0	2	1	95		$10.00	Second Sunday of each month	Sunday after the second Saturday in June
Bradens Chapel	Elder Wm. Sparks, Elder Noble Lee Clawson, Elder J. C. Monday, Sis. Helen Clawson, Sis. Winnona Monday, Sis. Leey Sparks and Sis. Helen Ruth Branscomb.	0	0	3	0	0	1	1	123		$10.00	First Saturday and Sunday	First Sunday in July
Brantleys Chapel	Elder Clifford Branley, Bro. Corum Berry, Bro. Jon Beason, Bro. Everett Brantley, Bro. Plummer McBee, Sis. Sarah Brantley, Sis. Barsha Brantley, and Sis. Mildred Brantley.	0	0	0	0	0	0	0	85		$20.00	Second Saturday and Sunday	Second Sunday in July
Cave Creek	Elder Raymond Brantley, Bro. J. C. Johnson, Bro. Zirkle Johnson, Bro. Elmer Guettner, Bro. Tom Johnson, Bro. Alfred Farmer, Sis. Amanda Brantley, Sis. Elizabeth Johnson, Sis. Linda Johnson, Sis. Hazel Guettner, Sis. Betty Johnson, Sis. Lorene White, Sis. Merrlie Potter, Sis. Frankie Howard, Sis.Edra Calfee, Sis. Fay Williams and Sis. Margaret Rather.	0	0	0	0	0	0	0	41		$11.00	Second Saturday Night in each month	Second Saturday night in May & October

Church	Members								Total	Amount	Amount	Schedule	Revival
Cedar Springs	Bro. Bill Good, Bro. Isom Drummonds, Bro. Clifford Robertson, Sis. Eula Good, Sis. Patricia Good, Sis. Ellen Good, Sis. Gloria Good, Sis. Velty Muncy, Sis. Ida Robertson.	0	0	0	0	0	0	0	57		$10.00		
Davis Chapel	Elder Leonard White, Bro. Orice Mc-Carty, Bro. Hugh Hill, Bro. Onie Parrott, Sis. Mollie McCarty, Sis. Ruby Hill, Sis. Mamie Parrott and Sis. Ruby Hobbs.	0	0	1	3	0	0	0	147	$5.00	$10.00	Third Saturday night and each Sunday night	Third Sunday in June
Gibson Station	Elder Joe Irwin, Bro. Spurgin Tompson, Bro. Harve Rhymer, Sis. Mollie Irwin, Sis. Mellie Tompson and Sis. Mossie Cottrell.	0	0	0	0	0	0	0	80	$4.00	$4.00	Business meeting First Saturday and Sunday In each month	First Sunday in June
Kirkwood	Elder R. H. Pettit, Elder Hugh Brummitt, Elder Walter Lyons, Bro. M. A. Norton, Bro. W. H. Taylor, Bro. J. L. Sharp, Bro. C. A. Sharp, Bro. R. O. Taylor, Sis. Lucy Norton, Callie Lyons, Sis. Ruby Brummitt, Sis. LouEmma Taylor, Sis. Evelyn Sharp, Sis. Frieda Sharp, Sis. Myrtle Taylor, and Sis. Nellie Simerly.	0	0	0	0	0	0	2	110	$5.00	$10.00	Business meeting First Sunday, Service each Sunday morning	Last Sunday in April
Lenoir City	Elder Charles Taylor, Elder Alvin Graves, Bro. Henry Chamberlain, Bro. Scott Collins, Bro. Hubert Spoon, Bro. Raymond Wilkerson, Bro. Jerry Spoon, Sis. Estie Chamberlain, Sis. Cora Hill, Sis. Agnes Taylor, Sis. Joe Collins, Sis. Annie Spoon and Janice Spoon.	0	0	0	0	0	0	2	199		$20.00	Each Sunday & Sunday Night	Sunday after the third Saturday

Church	Members								Total		Salary	Meeting Days	Meeting Days
Monroe Mich.	Elder Lenvil Meyers, Bro. John Drummonds, Bro. Ditsy Russell, Sis. Hallie Russell, Sis. Roxie Drummond.	0	0	0	0	0	0	0	14		$5.00		Third Sunday in May & September
Noeton	Elder Gilbert Atkins, Bro. John Oliver, Bro. Charley Collins, Bro. Carroll Oliver, Sis. Ruth Oliver, Sis. Doshie Collins, Sis. Mildred Oliver, Sis. Bessie Collins.	0	0	0	0	2	0	0	32		$5.00		
Oak Grove	Elder George Shoffner, Elder Tony Eastridge, Bro. Aaron Cole, Bro. Cills Shoffner, Bro. Mannie Shoffner, Bro. Alfred Relford, Sister Francis Eastridge, Sis. Veda Cole, Sis. Floy Cole, Sis. Lillie Shoffner, Sis. Ruth Shoffner and Sis. Maggie Relford.	0	3	0	0	9	3		296		$10.00	First Saturday and Sunday	Sunday after the First Saturday
Pleasant Hill	Elder Albert Davis, Elder James H. Branscomb, Bro. Verlin Edwards, Sis. Audry Davis and Sis. Cecil Edwards.	0	0	0	0	1	1		97		$15.00	Fourth Saturday and Sunday	Fourth Sunday in June
Pleasant Point	Elder Claude Rosson, Bro. George Williams, Sis. Dorris Rosson, Sis. Allie Williams, and Menada Keck.	0	0	0	0	0	0		121		$10.00	First Saturday Night and Sunday in each month	Sunday after the First Saturday in July
Rocky Dale	Elder Everett Berry, Elder Joe Bush, Elder Parnick Shelton, Bro. Elmer Graves, Bro. Dewey Graves, Bro. Ralph Clapp, Bro. Avrell Graves, Sis. Trula Berry, Sis. Norma Jean Bush and Sis. Wilma Shelton.	0	2	0	1	1	2		113	$5.00	$10.00	Sunday Night after Second Saturday Bussiness Service each Sunday and Sunday Night	Sunday after Second Saturday in May

709

CHURCH	COUNTY	PASTOR	CLERK	ADDRESS
Black Fox	Grainger	Elder Parnick Shelton	Benny Capps Flossie Capps, Assist.	Maynardville, Tenn. Box 91 Route 1, Maynardville
Bradens Chapel	Union	Elder Noble Lee Clawson Elder James Branscomb, Assist.	Arvel Braden	Speedwell, Tenn.
Brantleys Chapel	Blount	Elder Clifford Brantley Elder Everett Berry, Assist.	Rina Johnson Daniel Brantley, Assist.	Maryville, Tenn 1201 Brown School Rd. Maryville, Tenn.
Cave Creek	Roane	Elder Raymond Brantley	J. C. Johnston	Rt. 3, Loudon, Tenn.
Cedar Springs	Claiborne	Elder Claude Rosson Elder Johnny Ayers, Assist.	Eula Good Pat Good, Assist.	New Tazewell
Davis Chapel	Campbell	Elder Walter Lyons Elder Leonard White, Assist.	Ruth Haatherly Lassie Ellison, Assist.	Rt. 1, LaFollette, Tenn. Rt. 1, LaFollette, Tenn
Gibson Station	Lee County, Virginia	Elder Leonard White Elder Everett Berry, Assist.	Roxie Cobb Lucille Freeman, Assist.	Ewing, Va. Route 2 Ewing, Va. Route 2
Kirkwood	Knox	Elder Leonard White	Estelle Petree Sharp Alice Tindell Powers	5313 Jacksboro Pike Knoxville, Tenn. 2923 Clearview Ave. Knoxville, Tenn.
Lenoir City	Loudon	Elder Charles Taylor	Scott Collins	Lenoir City, Tenn.

710

CHURCH	COUNTY	PASTOR	CLERK	ADDRESS
Monroe, Mich	Monroe Co.	Elder Lenvil Meyers	Ditsy Russell	5177 Plum Creek Drive
				Monroe, Mich.
			Gertrude Swack	1825 Ipaulding Rd.
				Monroe, Mich.
Noeton	Grainger	Elder Gilbert Atkins	John Oliver	Bean Station, Tenn.
			Bessie Collins, Assist.	Morristown, Tenn.
Oak Grove	Union	Elder J. C. Monday	Maggie Relford	Sharps Chapel, Tenn.
		Elder Noble Lee Clawson, Assist.	Ruth Shoffner, Assist.	Sharps Chapel, Tenn.
Pleasant Hill	Claborne	Elder Alvin Graves	William Branscomb	Speedwell, Tenn.
		Elder Albert Davis, Assist.	Verlin Edwards, Assist.	Speedwell, Tenn.
Pleasant Point	Claiborne	Elder Walter Lyons	Elder Claude Rosson	New Tazewell, Tenn.
		Elder Claude Rosson, Assist.	Menada Keck, Assist.	
Rocky Dale	Knox	Elder Hugh E. Brummitt	Edward Collett	Luttrell, Tenn
				Rt. # 1
			Arvell Graves, Assist	Rt. # 3 Corryton, Tenn

Milton Keynes UK
Ingram Content Group UK Ltd.
UKHW031120260824
447446UK00006B/513